Historicizing "Tradition" in the Study of Religion

Religion and Society

Edited by
Gustavo Benavides and Kocku von Stuckrad

Volume 43

Walter de Gruyter · Berlin · New York

Historicizing "Tradition"
in the Study of Religion

Edited by
Steven Engler and Gregory P. Grieve

Walter de Gruyter · Berlin · New York

♾ Printed on acid-free paper which falls within
the guidelines of the ANSI to ensure permanence and durability.

ISBN-13: 978-3-11-018875-2
ISBN-10: 3-11-018875-9

Library of Congress Cataloging-in-Publication Data

Historicizing "tradition" in the study of religion / edited by Steven
Engler, Gregory P. Grieve.
  p. cm. — (Religion and society ; v. 43)
Includes bibliographical references and index.
Includes index.
ISBN-13: 978-3-11-018875-2 (15.5 × 23 cm, cloth : alk. paper)
ISBN-10: 3-11-018875-9 (15.5 × 23 cm, cloth : alk. paper)
1. Authority — Religious aspects. 2. Tradition (Theology) 3. Religious invention. I. Engler, Steven. II. Grieve, Gregory P. (Gregory Price), 1964— III. Religion and society (Hague, Netherlands) ;
43.
  BL105.H57 2005
  206—dc22
                                            2005028120

Bibliographic information published by Die Deutsche Bibliothek

Die Deutsche Bibliothek lists this publication in the Deutsche Nationalbibliografie; detailed
bibliographic data is available in the Internet at <http://dnb.ddb.de>.

Printed in Germany
Cover design: Christopher Schneider, Berlin

Contents

Tradition, Modernity, and the West

Illuminating the Half-Life of Tradition:
Legitimation, Agency, and Counter-Hegemonies

Gregory P. Grieve and Richard Weiss

There have been few attempts within the field of religious studies to articulate the particular force of tradition. 'Tradition,' for example, is absent in a recent compilation of *Critical Terms for Religious Studies*, which does not neglect to include that common foil of tradition, 'modernity' (Taylor 1998). Sociologists and historians have paid more attention to the concept of tradition, but this literature has not often been taken up in religious studies. It is a strange neglect, given that much of the field of religious studies is organized according to religious traditions. In the study of South Asian religions, for example, many scholars have rightly questioned the usefulness of Hinduism as a category, yet these reflections have not been extended to the more general notion of "tradition." Perhaps accepting and conflating the dichotomies of science/religion and modernity/tradition, scholars of religion have rarely interrogated tradition as a distinct feature of religious activity. Here we do not provide an account of this scholarly history, but rather hope to make a contribution to a better understanding of what is entailed in calling something a tradition.

Religious studies' employment of the concept of tradition arose in the great cultural explosion marked by the contact of the West with its global others. And while the scholarly and social environment has shifted, so that many of the presumptions that made it such a powerful rhetoric no longer hold, the category of tradition staggers on in the half-life of its former glory. The essays presented in this volume illuminate how the rubric of "tradition" may currently operate in the field of religious studies. Using a critical comparative framework, the goal of this volume is to suggest that tradition is a fundamental category in the historical and comparative study of religion. Key questions include "How is tradition actively constructed rather than passively received?" and "What issues are obscured by uncritical comparative/historical uses of the category?" *Historicizing Tradition* begins from the premise that religious traditions are social projects, often deliberately constructed to serve particular ideological ends.[1] The volume

---

[1] This book originated in a session held at the *American Academy of Religion* conference in Atlanta in 2003. The panel was organized by Gregory P. Grieve and Richard Weiss and included papers by Jason A. Carbine, Frederick S. Colby, Susanna Morrill, and Greg Johnson. Developed versions of the former three papers appear in this book

also presumes that scholarship about tradition itself is ideological in the sense that the academic analysis of tradition may often tell one more about scholars and scholarship than about the people it is supposedly describing. In short, to build upon Eric Hobsbawm's (1983) now foundational text, not only tradition, but traditional scholarship, is invented. Or, to place our assumptions in the rubric of this volume, to illuminate tradition's half-life, one needs not only to historicize tradition but also to problematize traditional historiography.

A Sociology of Tradition

Marx's notion of tradition is a good place to start our discussion, not only because of the influence of this particular passage but also because he articulates a prevalent notion of the force of tradition.

> Men make their own history, but they do not make it just as they please; they do not make it under circumstances chosen by themselves, but under circumstances directly found, given and transmitted from the past. The tradition of all the dead generations weighs like a nightmare on the brain of the living. And just when they seem engaged in revolutionizing themselves and things, in creating something entirely new, precisely in such epochs of revolutionary crisis they anxiously conjure up the spirits of the past to their service and borrow from them names, battle slogans and costumes in order to present the new scene of world history in this time-honoured disguise and this borrowed language. (Marx 1978, 505)

While for Marx tradition is comprised of static structures which bind subjects to inevitable action, the authors in this volume view tradition as dynamic, the "circumstances directly found, given and transmitted from the past" themselves negotiated, reformulated, abandoned, reinvented, and concealed. Even as the past constructs the present, as Marx rightly argues, the past is also remembered and configured in the present, a process over which some individuals, and some societies, have more control than others. What Marx neglects to mention is that for many, this "nightmare" of tradition is a refuge into realms of human experience over which actors can continue to exert control. Indeed, tradition, reconfigured by contemporary agendas, is precisely that realm of human practices and forms of knowledge that communities consider to be their own. It can be challenged by actors outside that community, or neglected by the youth internal to that community, or, worst of all, rejected by traitors within the specified community in favor of the traditions of an external, "foreign" community. Duty and loyalty to one's own tradition are celebrated as the recognition of the harmonious conjunction of personal essence and social forms of knowledge and practice.

---

along with a new paper by Johnson. The respondents at the session were Richard Weiss and Steven Engler.

To foreshadow and orient the following discussion, here we will briefly set out our notion of tradition, which will become more clear in its general contours in the extended discussion that follows. Formulations of traditions and community affirm a synchronic bond between actors and extend that bond into the past, into a diachronic community. Thus, traditional action involves reverence towards past action, actors, practices, and knowledge as holding a value that cannot be, or at least has not been, superseded. Traditions, however, are not only about the past but also about the present over which the past is seen to retain its relevance; thus we have *living* traditions, which also provide a model for future action. In valuing the past, a traditional orientation will tend towards conservatism rather than innovation, but it is not as static as it appears or claims to be.

Adherence to tradition is both a commitment and a duty to a community that existed in the past, exists in the present, and will continue to exist as long as its members do not abandon it. In other words, actors often consider their traditions to be *timely*, relevant in all times, and at the same time this attribute paradoxically becomes the grounds for a claim to the *timelessness* of tradition, its eternal essence. Adherence to tradition is an orientation towards an imagined timeless community, borne of the desire to submerge one's personal identity into a larger community that transcends that individual. The desire for tradition is thus also a desire for immortality.

The Duration of Tradition

Any evocation of tradition marks an attempt to forge a connection with the past. Many have therefore concluded that it is essential for a tradition to have actually been transmitted from one generation to another. Edward Shils, for example, argues that tradition must span at least three generations, and that anything passed down for less is not tradition but fashion (Shils 1981, 15). The problem with this sort of argument, we feel, is that it does not give due attention to the way traditions change, as they always do, both in their actual content and in their interpretation. Traditions are *never* static, but always changing with historical circumstances. The analysis of tradition as constant across generations would necessitate the impossibly imprecise task of *measuring* meaningful change.

Furthermore, it seems to us that Shils has missed Weber's crucial analysis of tradition as a type of *authority*. The assertion that a particular practice connects present actors to past actors, an assertion that is meant to garner authority for that practice, is more important than whether or not past actors actually engaged in that practice. The agency of tradition lies more with those who accept prior knowledge than with those who pass down knowledge, which is merely to say that the activity of making and perpetuating a tradition is more an activity of the living than of the dead.

What is required, then, is an account of tradition that considers its synchronic employment as a strategy of legitimation, where we understand synchrony as a position in complex historical contexts. Tradition gains its authority from its context, in which the important parameters are, following Bruce Lincoln's account of authority, "the conjuncture of the right speaker, the right speech and delivery, the right staging and props, the right time and place, and an audience whose historically and culturally conditioned expectations establish the parameters of what is judged 'right' in all these instances" (Lincoln 1994, 11). The synchrony implied by this sort of "conjunction" is not that of Saussure or Levi-Strauss; it is not an ahistorical "pure" synchrony which determines history, but is itself constructed through history and therefore it is in constant flux.[2]

The Consciousness of Tradition

Especially from the perspective of the Enlightenment, tradition is viewed by some as a realm of action that is followed without thought, blind imitation of the past.[3] In his typology of meaningful action, Weber describes traditional action as largely unconscious, as "determined by ingrained habituation," as "a matter of almost automatic reaction to habitual stimuli which guide behavior in a course which has been repeatedly followed" (Weber 1978, 24–25). Thus, it is hardly meaningful action at all. In fact, his equation of habit with tradition is almost complete: "The great bulk of all everyday action to which people have become habitually accustomed approaches this [traditional] type" (ibid., 25).

If Weber's primary representation of traditional action was as imitation or habit, a radically different view is presented by Eric Hobsbawm and Terence Ranger in their influential examination of "invented traditions."

> 'Invented tradition' is taken to mean a set of practices, normally governed by overtly or tacitly accepted rules and of a ritual or symbolic nature, which seek to inculcate certain values and norms of behavior by repetition, which automatically implies continuity with the past. In fact, where possible, they normally attempt to establish continuity with a suitable historic past. (Hobsbawm 1983, 1)

The language of invention, an antonym of imitation, has the advantage of registering traditions as actively and consciously engaged and constructed by historical actors. However, we feel scholars too often underestimate the conser-

---

[2]   As Marshall Sahlins points out, one must attend to the "cultural life of the elementary forms" (Sahlins 1985, xv).

[3]   See for example the "left-Hegelian" Max Stirner's idiosyncratic *Der Einzige und sein Eigenthum* (*The Ego and Its Own*—a more literal translation might be *The Individual and his Property*). For an English translation see Stirner 1995.

vative forces of history, tradition in Marx's and Weber's sense as structures formed through history that limit the range of possible action. As Alasdair MacIntyre notes, "What I am, therefore, is in key part what I inherit, a specific past that is present to some degree in my present. I find myself part of a history and that is generally to say, whether I like it or not, whether I recognize it or not, one of the bearers of a tradition" (MacIntyre 1984, 221). Tradition is never produced *ex nihilo*, but emerges precisely out of a conjunction of what is received from the past, and present aspirations of community.

Here we argue that traditional action is always meaningful, if not always conscious, because it always has the effect of unifying individuals into synchronic and diachronic configurations of community. Moreover, those aspects of tradition that are most consciously celebrated by a community are often the most "traditional." If tradition is an orientation to the past, then this orientation can hold for greater or lesser degrees of consciousness. It is primarily the consciousness of action which distinguishes tradition as imitation from tradition as invention. Here, we argue for a view of tradition that incorporates both of these extremes, insofar as both imitation and invention can be actions which entail the authority of the past in forging community. There are traditions that are unconscious, taken for granted, but that nevertheless are implicitly cognized (if not re-cognized). Such cognition, when it affirms a bond between participants that is both synchronic and diachronic, is a tradition. On the other end of the spectrum are rituals, forms of knowledge and practice, texts, or anything that symbolizes the diachrony of community, which are deliberately articulated as traditions, and which serve as central, visible representations of community. These may or may not have been performed in the past, but they are considered to forge a link between present and past manifestations of a single community.

This notion of tradition corresponds quite closely to Jean and John Comaroffs' account of hegemony and ideology, and the various forms of power associated with them, as "the ends of a continuum" (Comaroff and Comaroff 1991, 28). Where hegemony and ideology differ is in the degree to which they are articulated. Hegemony is primarily implicit, taken for granted, naturalized, habit forming, while ideology is explicit, articulated, and so more open to contestation. "Hegemony homogenizes, ideology articulates. Hegemony, at its most effective, is mute; by contrast, 'all the while, ideology babbles on'" (ibid., 24). The crucial element which links these in a continuum of power is consciousness. "For what differentiates hegemony from ideology, one face of power from the other, is not some existential essence. It is the factor of human consciousness and the modes of representation that bear it" (ibid., 28). When tradition is followed more or less unconsciously, i.e., when particular practices link actors synchronically in a community that imagines itself as a historical community in a way that this community is itself taken for granted, its power is hegemonic. When tradition is "invented," i.e. when it is consciously and expansively articulated, when its contours and content become points of contention, when arguments are made for the very criteria that qualify one's acceptance into a community, tradition becomes ideological.

We consider tradition to be a primary form of culture in the sense that the Comaroffs, following Gramsci, define it, as "the space of signifying practice, the semantic ground on which human beings seek to construct and represent themselves and others—and, hence, society and history. As this suggests, it is not merely a pot of messages, a repertoire of signs to be flashed across a neutral mental screen. It has form as well as content; is born in action as well as thought; is a product of human creativity as well as mimesis; and, above all, is empowered" (ibid., 21–22). Insofar as it is the grounds on which social identity is based, providing the content which defines communities, tradition is one of the most important cultural forms in forging communities. It differs from other modes of cultural production in that it is guided by a particular orientation to history which ascribes authority to the past.

The Ideology of Tradition

If the Comaroffs' distinction between ideology and hegemony is analytically valuable in distinguishing different poles of the modes of tradition, it also suggests historical processes and shifts. Because tradition is never "purely" ideological or hegemonic, the place that it occupies on this continuum will shift with time and place. Radical historical shifts will tend to turn hegemony into ideology, resulting from critique and engendering further critique, a process especially common with the intervention of a new force that is pursuing hegemony. Hobsbawm and Ranger likewise note that the invention of tradition is most prevalent in times of rapid social change (Hobsbawm 1983, 4). One common effect of cultural interaction, then, is often to illuminate hegemony, to enable reflection on criteria of authority. This consciousness of the underpinnings of authority is often the basis of a critique of that authority, leading to new formulations and justifications. While this might have beneficial effects, in that such conscious reflection on things previously taken for granted is one of the essential components of learning, cultural interactions are always concomitant with distinctions in power. While the "unveiling" of authority is never complete, neither is it evenly and mutually effected in the encounter of two societies.

Like Louis Althusser's treatment of ideology, the essays in this volume are concerned more with the "practico-social function" of tradition rather than with its epistemological status (Althusser 1996, 231). Traditional statements do not simply reflect or represent reality, but they also structure the way humans discern meaning. That is, traditions themselves structure consciousness, history, and memories—they provide the representations through which actors come to understand their worlds. Because explicit formulations of tradition actively construct human experience, they are more than cynical instruments (implied by "invention") with which one social group manipulates another. As Althusser holds for ideology, those who formulate the character and contents of a tradition are "caught by it, implicated by it, just when they are using it and believe themselves to be absolute masters of it" (Althusser 1996, 234). While traditions are themselves constructed and modeled, they at the same time provide the models for a variety of practices and conceptions. Traditions are, to borrow Geertz's language of "cultural patterns," models of and models for. They "give meaning, that is, objective conceptual form, to social and psychological reality both by shaping themselves to it and by shaping it to themselves" (Geertz 1973, 93). Actors perpetuate, and allow themselves to be shaped by, traditions because they perceive them to be at least partially true. Tradition is not only something constructed by prior subjects, but also contributes to the construction of subjects, insofar as it is prior to them.

Tradition and Belief

The relationship between people and tradition has been often viewed as motivated by belief. For example, Hindus are often said to worship an image at a temple because they believe that a divinity is instantiated in that image. Belief in this sense is a cognitive act, a considered judgment that something is "true" according to some relevant criterion of authority. This sort of belief is certainly a goal of all formulations of tradition—they must appear to be credible to be successful. However, there are some problems with making belief the sole, or even the primary, link between people and their traditions. Not the least of these, and perhaps the most problematic in analysis, is the difficulty in attributing belief to particular actors. How do we know whether someone really believes what they say? Belief is an internal, cognitive state, and so it is invisible to the analyst, unlike words and actions, which can be examined.

Belief itself, it seems to us, cannot be separated in clear ways from motivation and interest. When traditional medical practitioners, for example, assert that their forbearers formulated a medicine that imparted immortality, they never do so solely because they believe it, but also because such assertions confer *value* to their practice. Statements about tradition do not just represent "real" processes as our modern sense of "belief" requires, but are also meant to accomplish particular sorts of work. Wilfred Cantwell Smith, in tracing a history of the notion of belief, points out that its medieval English connotations were close to its German counterpart, *belieben*, that is, "to hold dear," "to give allegiance, to be loyal to, to value highly" (Smith 1977, 41). It is this older sense of belief that more closely describes the *intentions* of formulations of tradition—not to provide an objective representation of things, but to instill the sentiments of affiliation, loyalty, and duty in a targeted audience.

Donald Lopez distinguishes between believing something and believing *in* something (Lopez 1998, 22). To believe something is a cognitive, reflective act, a particular relationship forged between a subject and an external object. To believe *in* something is a creative, performative act, in that the statement of belief itself creates its object. To affirm that "I believe in you" confers value and confidence on the person addressed. It is this latter sense of belief that accurately describes the relationship between people and traditions. Formulations of the origin, history, and nature of traditional practices and knowledge might be phrased most accurately as "I believe in myself," as they are meant to confer *self*-confidence and *self*-respect. Formulations of tradition, then, are acts of *self*-creation in that they specify both the *value* of the self, and also the *nature* of the self.

The Essays in This Volume

Although the volume's essays cover a wide range of historical and geographic locations and have been written by a truly global representation of scholars and activists, our goal is not simply a revelation of heretofore unexamined or marginalized groups. Nor do we seek to apportion praise and blame, judging past academic approaches against the often seemingly arbitrary standards of our own time. Rather, the volume is both a moment of self-reflection on how the concept of tradition has been key in constituting the academic study of religion, and an effort in charting the future employment of the term. The volume maps the history of tradition in three interwoven strands. The first section traces how traditional authority is legitimated and legitimizing. The second section underscores how discourses of tradition are used by historical agents, especially for (re)constructing identities. The final section maps the often mutually dependant mobius interaction between tradition, modernity and the West.

Tradition, Legitimation, and Authority

The opposition between others' passive, unthinking tradition and our active, rational modernity has become such common currency that its constructed nature has been all but forgotten. Yet, where was this concept originally minted? How and why was tradition assigned such passive authority? In the volume's opening essay Michel Despland argues that the cliché of the traditional passivity begins in the battles—both historical and historiographic—between scripture-believing Protestants and the Catholic practices based in apostolic succession. The debate is focused by John Calvin (1509–1564) as "truth versus custom," and proceeds through a series of humanistic histories that attempt to deconstruct Catholic institutions by demonstrating their changing and changeable nature.

These deconstructive histories in turn engender counter-reformation arguments that demonstrate the underlying unchanging nature of Church institutions. This deadlock is finally broken in the nineteenth century with the advent of pale-ontology that completely dissolves the given world view. In reaction, tradition is reformulated in a cultural sense as an underlying organic structure that passive-ly conserves the past. Ultimately, argues Despland, in the twentieth century, the assumed passivity of tradition leads scholars to perceive religion and religious practice as innately conservative. Such conservatism can either be spun utilita-rianly as superstition, or romantically as a utopian vision.

The two essays that follow turn to how the tradition's conservative rhetoric has been used in specific historical examples to legitimate social practices. First, Frederick Colby, in "The Rhetoric of Innovative Tradition in the Festival Com-memorating the Night of Muhammad's Ascension," describes pre-modern Islam, arguing that while tradition is often posed by both scholars and participants as unchanging, it can be used to legitimate reformist agendas. For instance, as Colby shows, while the Islamic reformist Ibn al-Hajj claims to support the universal and unchanging traditional festival practices, he in fact promotes a vision of change in which the Night of the Ascension becomes celebrated in a new and radically different fashion.

In "The 'Golden Age' of Muslim Spain: Religious Identity and the Invention of a Tradition," Aaron Hughes turns to historiography. He argues that the con-cept of a "Golden Age" provides a prism through which interpreters legitimate their own ideological conception of the "essence" of Judaism. Some of these constructions hold up the Jewish experience in medieval Spain as a beacon for modern Jewish emancipation. Others, however, regarded the cultural and intel-lectual achievements of such elite Jews as inauthentic and therefore far removed from true Jewish piety. What all of these constructions share though, is the assumption that there was a "Golden Age" of Muslim Spain and that, however defined, it provided important lessons for modern Jewish existence. Ironically, then, Spain's "Golden Muslim Age" was imagined and re-imagined because it provided various scholars/reformers with a Jewish model with which to propose various changes within their own tradition.

The next two essays, those by Félix Ulombe Kaputo and Titus Hjelm, demon-strate how tradition's authority is a "gun for hire," called upon to strengthen existing conservative customs or to legitimate new religious movements. In "Central African Women: Victims between African and Christian Traditions," Ulombe Kaputo traces women's victimization since the colonial period. He argues that in Central Africa, Christian religious traditions have strategically reaffirmed traditional patriarchal practices to economically marginalize women. As early as 1900, Methodists, followed by other American and British congre-gations, started their infiltration of the continent, "redefining and re-bordering" religious and geographical frontiers. From that time, it was obvious that missionaries were not simply "Christian;" they were primarily interested in assisting colonial powers by furthering capitalist institutions. A key strategy in the spread of capitalism was the use of religion to legitimate local patriarchal customs. In the last decades, this has been further intensified through the dramatic spread of American Pentecostal Churches. Ulombe Kaputo suggests that by examining past Christian conquests and by questioning struggles over the place of tradition of Central African women can be improved in the face of the promises and threats of globalization.

Unlike Ulombe Kaputo's description of a reactionary use of tradition, in "Tradition as Legitimation in New Religious Movements," Hjelm shows how tradition can legitimate alternative religions such as the Finnish neo-pagan community. Hjelm's focus is on the sociological processes where tradition is invoked for the purpose of legitimating emergent forms of faith and religious practice. He argues that "tradition" becomes a strategy that is used in giving weight and credibility to the religion in question. For example, the Hare Krishna movement (ISKCON) has in some cases benefited from being identified with a "legitimate" Indian tradition, whereas doctrinally more controversial movements, such as Wicca, have had to recourse to more active communication of the background of beliefs in the eyes of a suspect popular image. Such external pressure brings about internal change. For instance, in Finnish Wicca this has resulted in what Hjelm terms the "new rise of tradition."

Tradition, Agency, and Identity

The volume's second section, consisting of six essays, maps the interrelationship between tradition, agency, and identity. While each essay describes a different historical case, the essays are unified in their desire to dispel the assumption that tradition is just imitation of prior practices and discourses. While varied as to methodological approach, the essays view traditions as rule-governed models that inculcate behavioral values and norms in such a way as to make those practices, values, and norms, even and especially those of relatively recent origin, appear continuous with the past. As such, the practices and discourses of tradition described are theorized as powerful instruments of communal self-positioning.

Susan Morrill's "Women and the Book of Mormon: The Creation and Negotiation of a Latter-Day Saint Tradition," asks how contextualized agents use tradition to define themselves, especially when a tradition may at first blush seem to be against their interest. How, in a religious text such as the Book of Mormon, which stresses fatherhood and patriarchal authority, does one create a positive women's identity? Morrill turns to the case study of the Church of Jesus Christ of Latter Day Saints (LDS) member Martha Cragun Cox. She argues that Mormon women such as Cox did not simply accept the patriarchal focus of the Book of Mormon; they actively interpreted this new scriptural tradition for their own circumstances. Morrill shows that religious groups are made up of multiple, shifting, and continually negotiated traditions. She suggests that "traditions" can never be fully grasped, because individuals and groups are always adapting them to fit personal, historical, and cultural circumstances. "They are the ever-shifting foundations upon which religious communities stand" (see below p. 142).

Essays by Jason Carbine and Richard Weiss explore the social and cultural purposes for which specific contextualized agents use tradition. Carbine concentrates upon the creation of continuity, while Weiss reports on rupture. In "Shwegyin *Sāsana*: Continuity, Rupture, and Traditionalism in a Buddhist Tradition," Carbine argues that contextualized agents often conceive of tradition as a dynamic tension between continuity and rupture. Regardless of history, colonialism, modernity, or socio-political agendas, tradition is seen as a means to overcome ruptures. To illustrate this position, Carbine elaborates the Shwegyin *Sāsana's* two conceptions of rupture. The first, *nirvana*, is a permanent rupture in one's successive rebirths and is considered positive. The second concerns the decay and rupture of the lineage and is perceived as negative because it terminates knowledge about the ways to reach *nirvana*. Carbine argues that the monks use such traditionalism to prevent the lineage rupture from ruling the day, and thus allow that at least a few may break through to *nirvana*.

In "The Autonomy of Tradition: Creating Space for Indian Medicine," Weiss explores the ways in which contextualized agents have sought to carve out an autonomous space for their practices by constructing boundaries that shape a unique South Asian medical tradition. He suggests that the assertion of autonomous medicine uniquely developed by and suitable for the Tamil people was developed as a strategy to counter cultural imperialism. Because their practices were under attack as unscientific or forged, these practitioners delineated a sphere of unique tradition within which they could reject the scrutiny of outsiders. As such, tradition becomes an autochthonous ground, a site over which a social self can exercise control. Weiss suggests that, because of this crucial need for self-definition, the relations between traditions often take the form of rupture, compelling discourses characterized by critique and defense.

The next three essays in this section deal more directly with theoretical approaches to the study of traditions. While varied in the theoretical models they propose, each clusters around the "insider/outsider" problem. In "Whose Tradition? Conflicting Ideologies in Medieval and Early Modern Esotericism," Kocku von Stuckrad describes the emergence of "first theology" in early modern Europe. He argues that first theology was a discursive strategy for formulating alternative genealogies of knowledge and identities that went beyond the usual scriptural ones. These debates included intense arguments between Muslims, Christians, and Jews over competing definitions of "tradition." While offered as contrasts, self-definitions of tradition in these debates were made in mutual dependency to one another. As von Stuckrad argues: "Like identities, traditions are not found but negotiated in a complex process of cultural exchange" (see below p. 223). He argues that these debates show that the notion of tradition should not be used as an *a priori* analytical category of etic historiography, but should only be employed in reference to its emic meaning and function.

Lee Rainey, in "Confucianism and Tradition," argues that the Confucian concept of tradition has been defined and shaped by the history of Western and South East Asian scholarship. In the West, tradition has been used to paint one's way out of the "is Confucianism a religion or philosophy?" corner. In contrast, in Singapore, Taiwan, and China, tradition is posited as a pure past that represents Confucian teaching, Chinese culture, and national identity. Rainey concludes that all of us interpret, translate, and understand ancient "traditions" based on our prejudices, which may be more ingrained and problematic than we previously had thought.

In the section's final essay, "Dispatches from Memory: Genealogies of Tradition," Earle Waugh argues that the academic understanding of tradition should be based upon the action of memory. He suggests that memory allows for a model for cultural retention, as well as situates tradition studies in the larger compass of human knowledge. Waugh constructs a method that consists of the dialectic relationship between *traditum*—which is bound up with the validation of local personal memory, and *traditio*—which is the social interpretation of that memory. Such a model, he suggests, is constructive for comparing religious memory across cultures and for creating a method beyond the "one-dimensional historical" view that currently dominates the discipline.

Tradition, Modernity, and the West

By confronting the notion that tradition is timeless and unchanging, one also detangles the underlying assumption that places "traditional peoples" in the sad passive position of being opposed to the dynamic change of Western modernity. This opposition does not necessarily mark the contemporary relevance of different forms of knowledge and practice, but rather it emerges from the encounter of societies with divergent notions of what qualifies as effective knowledge. Indeed, the rubric of tradition as a marker of community has become one of the most effective means through which colonized peoples have challenged the hegemonic claims of Western knowledge.

The final section of the volume untangles the Gordian knot created by the mobius interaction between tradition, modernity, and the West. In "Histories of Tradition in Bhaktapur, Nepal: Or, How to Compile A Contemporary Hindu Medieval City," Gregory Grieve maintains that most academic conceptions of tradition tend toward a romantic-historicist view that posits tradition as a passive ontological essence that will, over time, develop into "modernity." From this perspective, the people in the Nepalese city of Bhaktapur are seen to neither have tradition nor make tradition but rather, as traditional. The false dichotomy between tradition and modernity breaks down, however, when one examines tradition as it is understood emically in Bhaktapur, where people tend to use the term to describe effective everyday social practices that are compiled from past generations. Grieve glosses this second understanding of tradition as "genealogical." Unlike the romantic understanding of tradition, the genealogical model is neither the seeking of pure origins nor the plotting of an evolutionary timeline. Instead, like a "history of the present," a genealogical tradition chronicles the pragmatic use of those past social practices that are currently effective, and they are not necessarily at odds with modern practices. Traditional practices are just one choice among many.

Ira Robinson, in "Hasid and Maskil: The Hasidic Tales of an American Yiddish Journalist" argues that Samuel Rocker (1865–1936) was not simply the modernizing force within the Jewish community that he would appear at first blush. For beyond his persona of "Samuel Rocker" the American Yiddish journalist, he was also "Reb Yehoshua [Joshua] Rocker," author of a book on the Talmudic interpretation of the Bible as well as two books of Hasidic tales. Robinson maintains that Rocker served as a cultural mediator not simply between the Eastern European Jewish immigrants and their new country, but also between these Jews and their religious past. Robinson argues that Rocker attempted to use the power of the Hasidic tradition, not to oppose modernization as such, but to demonstrate that there were different paths other than a forced acculturation into the American "melting pot." By portraying the leaders of nineteenth-century Hasidism positively in the way he did, he sought to show that the Hasidic tradition had continued relevance in the here and now. For Rocker, there was something in Hasidism and its story that could speak to his contemporaries, and help them as they engaged in the vital balancing act between the Judaic tradition and Western civilization that characterized all of modern Judaism.

In "Re-Orienting Tradition: Radhakrishnan's Hinduism," Michael Hawley deals with two main areas: Sarvepalli Radhakrishnan's understanding of Hindu tradition and the tradition of orientalism. He argues that Radhakrishnan's interpretation of Hindu tradition is not only informed by, but often perpetuates and therefore further entrenches, orientalist images of India. Hawley suggests that an informed understanding of Radhakrishnan's thinking about Hindu tradition needs to be grounded in an understanding of India's colonial past and of his encounters with Western-constructed knowledge about India. Hawley maintains, that in the process of responding to his encounter with the West, Radhakrishnan appropriated and reinterpreted many of those orientalist images of India and of Hindu tradition against which he sought to argue. Because of this, Radhakrishnan's understanding of Hindu tradition is not only informed by, but in fact perpetuates and further entrenches these images of India constructed during the colonial period. This is significant, because Radhakrishnan continues to serve for many as an important source for Hindu identity and Indian pride. Hawley concludes by suggesting that Radhakrishnan's understanding of Hinduism draws our attention to the fluid and dynamic nature of tradition as a scholarly category, a category that cannot be removed from the historical and hermeneutic contexts in which it is being employed.

David W. Machacek and Adrienne Fulco, in "Rights and Values in the American Constitutional Tradition," suggest that the Constitution is more than a set of procedural rules for democratic self-government; it is also a "moral tradition" that evokes a vision of *good* government. While much constitutional theory focuses on the Constitution as a legal document, Machacek and Fulco's concern is with the Constitution as a statement and symbol of foundational principles from which a moral tradition has evolved. Their main goal is to oppose the understanding that Christian theology and American constitutional-ism are competing traditions. Machacek and Fulco argue that constitutionalism does not reject or privilege any particular viewpoints, but rather subsumes them into a larger, more complex moral debate. When one understands constitution-alism as a tradition of moral enquiry, one can see that the language of rights is not a "language of no compromise," but rather a language that makes it possible for people of conflicting viewpoints to engage in meaningful debate about the practical meaning of shared moral agreements.

In the section's final essay, "(Re)Making Tradition in an International Tibetan Buddhist Movement: A Lesson from Lama Gangchen and Lama Michel," Frank Usarski attempts to answer one of the key questions raised in this volume—*how is tradition actively constructed rather than passively received*? Usarski describes Michel Lenz Calmanowitz, a Brazilian who was identified as a reincarnated Tibetan Lama. The propagation of non-native reincarnated Lamas underscores the creative potential of Tibetan people to adjust and survive in the contempor-ary world.

Conclusion

As innovative social products, traditions have histories. Because of the obvious-ness of this statement, it seems necessary to consider the belatedness of the questions raised in this volume. Why is it for example, that an examination of the invented character of religious traditions has come only some twenty years after the publication of Hobsbawm's critique? The answer lies in the strategic use of "tradition" within the field of religious studies. While it has become common practice to historically situate key religious categories, historicizing "tradition" proves both extremely difficult and extremely important because the term has been doubly blind to history. Tradition has tended to be defined as both timeless and as the opposite of modernity.

Still while presumed dead, tradition stumbles on powered by the half-life of its former colonial rhetoric. It is within this context that the question of the past and future of the study of tradition must be posed. There is little to be gained either in embarrassingly acknowledging the orientalist and romantic past as something we do not do any more, or in waiting for a newest theory as a panacea to a diseased legacy. Simply acknowledging the past becomes an apology, and waiting for redemption by theory ignores the present. Nor is it enough to simply "get back to work"—this reproduces the positivist rhetoric of historical progress, whose mirror image is the concept of tradition we are attempting to call into question. Instead, what the essays in this volume show is that more than some pollutant, which still lingers in the very skeleton of religious studies, tradition can be analyzed as a strategic tool of cultural critique. Tradition is an important category for examination because it focuses the historical, social and political nature not only of religion, but of human society writ large. It is by the glow of tradition's half-life that these essays should be read—an illumination in which both theory and historical detail are used to invert the field of religious studies' dominant structures of knowledge and power without simply reproducing them.

References

Althusser, Louis. 1996 [1965]. *For Marx*. Translated by Ben Brewster. New York: Verso.

Comaroff, Jean, and John Comaroff. 1991. *Of Revelation and Revolution: Christianity, Colonialism, and Consciousness in South Africa*. Volume 1. Chicago: University of Chicago Press.

Geertz, Clifford. 1973. "Religion as a Cultural System." Pages 87–125 in his *The Interpretation of Cultures*. New York: Basic Books.

Henten, Jan Willem van, and Anton Houtepen (eds.). 2001. *Religious Identity and the Invention of Tradition*. Assen: Royal Van Gorcum.

Hobsbawm, Eric. 1983. "Introduction: Inventing Tradition." Pages 1–14 in *The Invention of Tradition*. Edited by Eric Hobsbawm and Terence Ranger. Cambridge: Cambridge University Press.

Lincoln, Bruce. 1994. *Authority: Construction and Corrosion*. Chicago: University of Chicago Press.

Llewellyn, John E. (ed.). 2005. *Defining Hinduism: A Reader*. New York: Routledge.

Lopez, Donald S., Jr. 1998. "Belief." Pages 21–35 in Taylor 1998.

MacIntyre, Alasdair. 1984. *After Virtue: A Study in Moral Theory*. Second edition. Notre Dame: University of Notre Dame Press.

Marx, Karl. 1978. "The Eighteenth Brumaire of Louis Bonaparte." Pages 436–525 in *The Marx-Engels Reader*. Edited by Robert C. Tucker. Second edition. New York: W. W. Norton and Company.

Stirner, Max. 1995. *The Ego and Its Own*. Cambridge: Cambridge University Press.

Sahlins, Marshall. 1985. *Islands of History*. Chicago: University of Chicago Press.

Shils, Edward. 1981. *Tradition*. London: Faber and Faber.

Smith, Wilfred Cantwell. 1977. *Belief and History*. Charlottesville: University of Virginia Press.

Taylor, Mark C. (ed.). 1998. *Critical Terms for Religious Studies*. Chicago: University of Chicago Press.

Weber, Max. 1978. *Economy and Society: An Outline of Interpretive Sociology*. Edited by Guenther Roth and Claus Wittich. Berkeley: University of California Press.

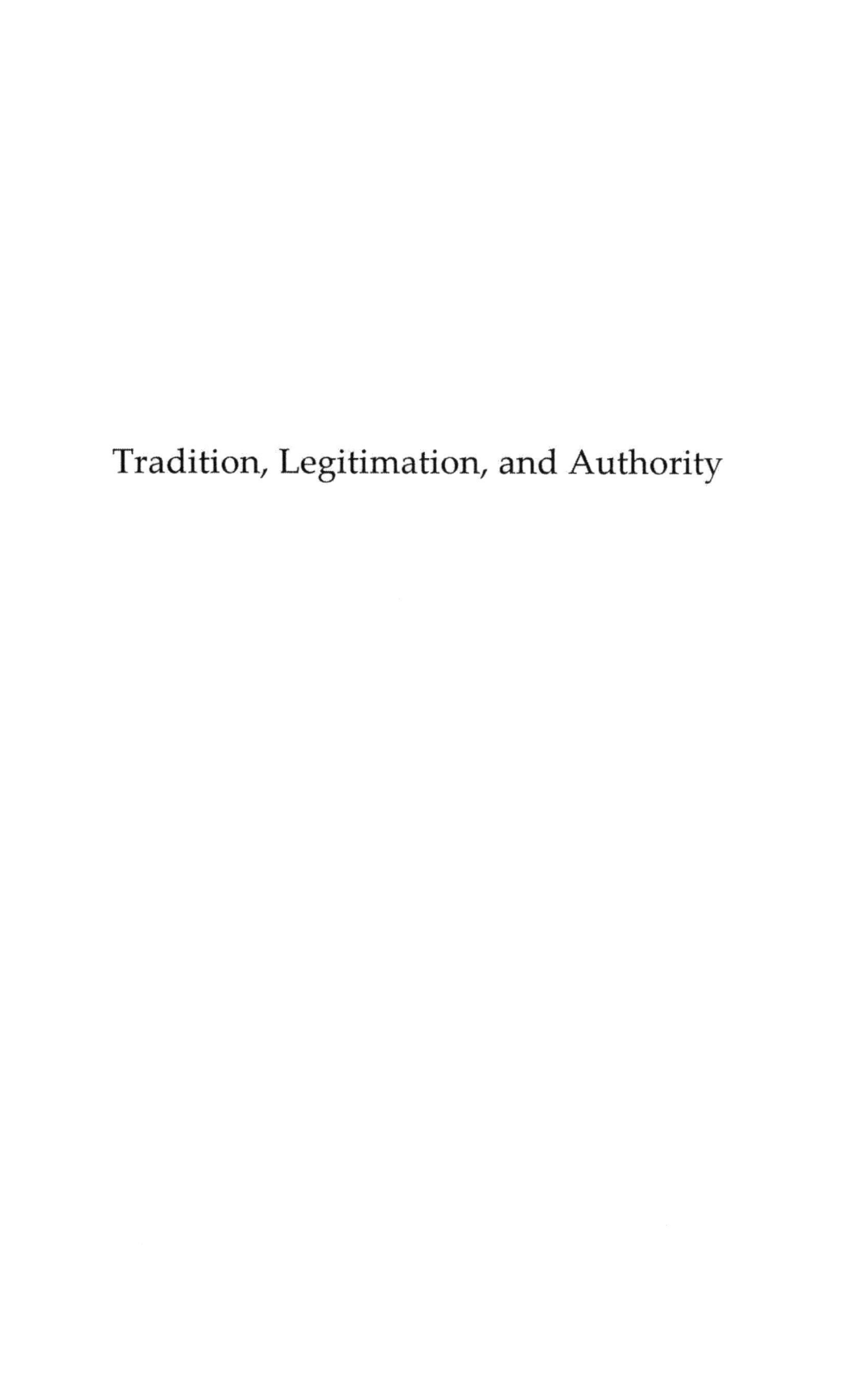

Tradition, Legitimation, and Authority

Tradition

Michel Despland

The Eastern and the Western Churches divided over the *filioque*. Protestants and Catholics split over *scriptura et traditio*. While the first disagreement was bearing upon theological matters, the second also involved epistemological issues: how do the Christian people get to know God's revelation? The term *tradition* has therefore a rich religious history and touches upon more general issues. The history was fraught with innumerable conflicts. As it becomes well-known, contemporary scholarly discussions often do not entirely shake off the semantic associations which some key words keep from their (Western) past, even when that past is declared obsolete, irrelevant or gone. The first task therefore is to establish the general context in which the matter of tradition should be explored. It is often repeated that traditions are in conflict, that traditions are being challenged. The basic intention here is to clarify the concept of tradition, to make it a usable tool in religious studies. There will also be, necessarily I think, side looks at the use of the notion in Christian history.

Tradition is part of the processes whereby humans constitute and reproduce their social bonds and identities (Ricoeur 2000, 501). What differentiates humans is that they talk (Aristotle, *Politics* 1253a). They don't just breed, they give institutions to their offspring, with language looming large among the early shapings they impose. To institute implies normativity, stresses Pierre Legendre. To survive and occupy territories, humankind has constructed institutional systems and keeps constructing them. To look into them is to explore the depths of human living, the grounds of cultural pluralism and of subjective differentiation, and, ultimately, the coping with the pain inherent in existence (Legendre 1985).

"Tradition" draws attention to the inter-generational aspect of institutional systems. For our purposes, there is one decisive difference between the living and the dead: the dead do not talk. Tradition is received as a voice of the past generations, but it is always the living who declare what the dead say. The dead leave traces. These range all the way from stones lined up in a row and cave paintings, to epic poems and last wills. Problems of interpretation of these relics vary enormously but it is always the case that, at the end of the line, the living say what they mean. One commonly sees a gap between the non-literate remains that archaeologists decipher and the inscriptions and texts that occupy the philologists. But the whole range of the cultural productions left behind by the dead comes under the common heading of objectifications.

Tradition therefore is a matter of meaning. There are things done, to be sure, but the agents see meaning in what they do. Paul Ricoeur has shown that the same hermeneutical procedures apply both to actions and to texts. "Meaningful action is an object for science only under the condition of a kind of objectification which is equivalent to the fixation of discourse by writing."[1]

Plato made it clear that the invention of writing introduced new dangers: written discourse is so to speak let loose, abandoned by its parent, and "cannot defend itself" (*Phaedrus* 274d–276a). Objectified as text, discourse falls into alien hands. Any fool can misinterpret it. Tradition then becomes seized by defenders, live voices who claim to know what the dead intended. (When locutors are there, alive and capable of defending what they said or wrote, what is happening is not interpretation of a text but dialogue between two human beings.) "The text's career escapes the finite horizon lived by its author... Discourse escapes the limits of being face to face. Henceforth the *meaning* of the action becomes detached from the *event* of the action" (Ricoeur 2000, 201, 203–204).

The significant fact is that texts remain unchanged through the centuries. They get to be read by people quite remote from the traditional processes of the society in which they were written. This is the point where history, as moderns know it, is born. Ever since Lorenzo Valla, some humans look critically at what the dead have left. The texts read, even important legal texts, are no longer taken at face value. It is not true, argued the Florentine humanist, that the Roman Emperor gave full sovereignty to the bishop of Rome. The deed known as the *Donation of Constantine* is not authentic but a later fake. And the argument for that is not the usual persuasive rhetoric but something new, namely expert historical proof, mainly, in the case of the *Donation*, the identification of technical legal terms never used in the fourth century but common later (see the discussion in Ricoeur 2000, 217–218). At this point, history becomes visible as a disciplined intellectual activity that is quite distinct from the operations of memory.

Memory is a personal possession and humans value it highly. What scientific historians offer to human minds is far less attractive. Much of what is advanced is probabilities. Witnesses remember; their testimony has weight, but witnesses tend to think their word should be authoritative and final. But in courts of law, judges and juries decide, not witnesses. By taking on the role of the jury, historians introduce a new dimension into the human and social flow of time.

Paradoxes are found in the way in which groups live their rapport to the past. Y. H. Yerushalmi wrote a whole book to explore how the Jewish people honour the injunction *zakhor* (remember!); not only do they transmit actively their memory of the past but place this duty of transmission close to the core of their identity. But never have historians been the primary depositors of this record. The first history of the Jewish people was written early in the seventeenth century by a

---

1   Ricoeur 1985, 203. Ricoeur builds his argument on Max Weber's notion of "meaningfully oriented behaviour."

French Protestant and Jews started working on their history only in the 1820s. And today, he adds, while historical facts are abundantly and competently documented, the history of collective memory of the Jews has not drawn the same attention. The very rise of professional historians of Judaism among Jews remains a historical phenomenon in need of investigation (Yerushalmi 1982).

We may add that the input of critical historians is not always welcome.

Let us take an example. In 1929 Jean Norton Cru published a big book reviewing all the publications produced by Frenchmen who wrote on the First World War and describing their "experiences" on the front. His work was thorough. He established how many days each author spent on the front, in what units, when and where. He tried to sort out "literary ornamentation" from *prima facie* credible testimony. (Many of the books were published as "war novels.") And he sorted out the books into eight categories, ranging from historically very valuable to worthless. An ensuing controversy heaped abuse on him: he was attacked as pedantic and anti-patriotic. The witnesses brought a warmth in their attacks on his historical study, not to say heat, that got more of an audience than the slow, learned weighing of evidence. In time, a few historians came to the defence of Norton Cru and openly accepted the value of his methodology. The 1993 reprinting of the book was controversial again, but this time the debate focussed more on methodological issues. What is the truth the historian has, that the witness does not have? How can historians learn the proper art of both being attentive to what the witnesses have to say and yet capable of distrusting their testimony or seeing the partiality of their point of view?[2]

This framing of the issue leads to a contrast between the direct experience of those who are seen to be at the source of the tradition and the scientific objectification and distancing of those who merely claim to study it. "Having been there" gives a certain kind of authority. Those who have not been in the Vietnam War are instinctually right when they remain silent as they meet a survivor inclined to speak about it. But this dimension of respect should not mask another issue. The witness often gives a tone of finality to his account. And properly so; how he came to terms with his experience is for him a precious possession, for him to keep, and, in this sense, he can achieve closure. But those who do not have first-hand experience should keep their distance from such closure. By definition the historian is someone who has not been there, and not being there means being able to keep some of the issues open, and to be available for fresh inquiries. Historians are not nostalgic antiquarians; they may be said to live in the past but their work preserves openness to the future. (This is what is at stake in the excessive but illustrative statement that historians cannot do their work until all the witnesses

---

2   Frédéric Rousseau (2003) reviewed the whole controversies and added a fine concluding discussion: do witnesses prevent historians from doing their work? Can historians do their work without them?

are dead.[3]) Kierkegaard differentiated ancient from modern philosophy by contrasting access to the truth by reminiscence, and awareness of what he called "repetition," namely the hoped for repossession of past experience, a repossession which to him always entailed an element of novelty, on account of the "movement of existence."[4] Modernity then seems closely wedded to the sort of practise of history illustrated by Lorenzo Valla, Y. H. Yerushalmi and Jean Norton Cru who disturbed commonly accepted views of the past and opened fresh perspectives on what was received.

We are now on frequently ploughed territory. How many times have we heard modernity contrasted with tradition? Moderns commonly claim that they have a rapport to the past that is not at all the one their parents used to have. The modern world sees itself in its difference from the pre-modern world. (Antiquity, the Middle Ages, the Ancien Régime, and the nineteenth century have each in turn been read as pre-modern.[5]) The traditionalist does not know he lives in a tradition. (This statement has been credited to Ibn Khaldun.) It is the post-traditionalist who ordinarily (and somewhat triumphantly) sees others as enmeshed in the nets of tradition. But there have been ruptures before the great one associated with the allegedly emancipating rise of the modern West.

Jacques Rancière has drawn attention to the great plebeian "secession" narrated by Livy.[6] The "people" in 494–493 BCE, dissatisfied with their rulers in the Senate, left Rome to withdraw on the Aventine Hill. This was a sort of political strike.[7] Politics as the Romans knew it, deliberation among senators of divergent opinions, broke down. The voiceless disrupted the process by their silent action. The Senators, in an unprecedented gesture (which some opposed), decided to send an ambassador to speak with them. This emissary told them the old fable of the body: the feet are less noble than the body but they are essential to the welfare of the whole. So the feet should come back and carry on their job of bearing the weight of the whole body. The plebeians returned, after obtaining some concessions, mainly the creation of the tribunate. Politics, argues Rancière, is born of the unceasing conflict between those who are *in* and those who are *out*. It is not the quiet working out of compromises between those who are in.[8] Politics is thus, by

---

3   This is one of the reasons why a young historian might prefer to cut his teeth on the Peloponnesian War rather than on Auschwitz.
4   Kierkegaard 1946, 34. The French edition translates the Danish word by *reprise*. This is what happens when a play is brought again to the stage; the text is the same, but the actors and the *mise en scène* are new. It is, properly, a new event.
5   Ricoeur 2000, 400–408. See also Benavides 1997.
6   There were three such secessions, narrated in *History of Rome* II, 31–33, III, 44–55; the third one was in Book XI, now lost.
7   Pierre-Simon Ballanche (1829) examined these pages in Livy in his attempt to find the general formula of human history. See McCalla 1998, 142–143.
8   Rancière 1995, 45–49. What Rancière calls *police* maintains order. Politics occurs when those who are not equal begin to act as if they were. See also Rancière 1998.

definition, the speechless, brutal interruption of a traditional way of doing things that was embodied in customary manners of speaking.

This political crisis was not the only time when the Roman elite had to leave its center to meet some people outside. Rémi Brague argues that the whole Roman civilization was based on an experience of de-centering.[9] These people did not work on creeds but on laws, namely on the art of dealing with contingent, unexpected circumstances. And they acknowledged that they were getting all their philosophy and poetry from the Greeks. The early Latin Church did the same as it appropriated the Hebrew Bible and admitted that its salvation came from the Jews. Henceforth civilization could be conceived by them as a closed, centred space, always capable of drawing its truth from itself.

A third example of ancient breaks from tradition may be advanced. In his discussion of the twelfth-century romances of Chrétien de Troyes, Michel Rousse (1990, 36–37) notes that these first European novels tell of adventures that are unforeseen and unforeseeable, and thus interrupt the predictable flow of time. They take for granted that humans discover themselves not by realising some predetermined destiny, but by coping with the unexpected. Fresh choices are always to be made. Knights and ladies fall in love; but this is not narrated as was presented the fatal passion between Tristan and Isolde. It is not the result of a philtre, but an accident induced internally: it originates within the individuals. Henceforth, the data of free individuality enter into social equations. From then on, one can visualise any newborn (with his unique genetic make up, we would say) as a potential source of novel disruptions of the social processes.

What the old Roman and the "modern" medieval texts point to is that there cannot be any privileged bearers of memory. We each have our own, separate, memories. It is true that there is such a thing as *mémoire collective* (Halbwachs 1992). But when one looks at it closely, one finds that some are bearers of much of this collective memory, while others appropriated only little. Some are creators of it, others consumers. But in any case it is only memory. Shakespeare's portrait of Richard III is in the common cultural baggage of many English-speaking people. What contemporary historians of the War of the Roses and of this monarch have to say is quite different. Undoubtedly more true, but less memorable. And it is Shakespeare's king that shapes contemporary moral discernment.

"Tradition" is in the hands of all. The book of Exodus states that Yahweh himself buried Moses so that his grave would be forever unknown. There is no piece of real estate on the surface of the earth that can be appropriated by some powerful person to put his throne on and thereby institutionalise a sacred legitimation of power. In the final play from the Oedipus cycle, the old king of Thebes asks to be buried by Theseus and obtains from him the promise never to reveal the location of his grave.

---

9   Brague 2002. Brague also makes a comparative point: de-centering is what makes the Latin West different from the Greek and Muslim East.

The Christian tradition has used the notion of tradition in a variety of ways. At the end of the first of the two letters addressed to him, Timothy (6:20) is exhorted to keep the "deposit of faith." The first post-apostolic generation is charged with the duty of transmitting what they have received. *Traditio* is thus linked to *depositum fidei*. *Traditio activa* is distinguished from *traditio passiva*, the act of transmission from that which is transmitted. John M. Headley finds in some of the Fathers something like substantialism: what is passed on is conceived to be as objectified and unchanging as the baton in a relay race.[10] But in the minds of most of the early Christians, the tradition is seen as a consensus of the Fathers.[11] The tradition then can be said to be a common, somewhat unconscious possession, tested over time by the rejection of heresies.

Decisive new developments occurred in the late Middle Ages when the canonists and the Curia affirmed the authority of the Supreme Pontiff to decide all contentious issues. "Consensus" becomes a juridical issue. At Leipzig (1519) the *auctoritas* of the papacy was challenged by Luther on one major point: the legal system of the Roman Church (or even the Councils) cannot settle matters relating to the interpretation of Scriptures. The Bible is clear and sufficient. In time Protestants subscribed to the circular notion of Scripture being its own interpreter.[12] It is a distinguished apologist for the Roman Church that gave durable momentum to the whole issue: in his *Assertio septem sacramentorum* (1521), Henry VIII displaced somewhat *auctoritas*, to put *traditio* at the centre of the argumentation in favour of the Roman Church (Headley 1963, 80–82).

The line of Henry's argument was followed. The fourth session of the Council of Trent (1546) affirmed that the Gospel truth and discipline is known to us through two sources: the written books of the Bible and unwritten traditions, received by the apostles, transmitted by the consensus of the Fathers, dictated by the Holy Spirit and preserved in the Catholic Church. These two sources are to be respected equally, *pari pietati ac reverentia*. This formulation framed subsequent theological debates that proved crucial in the religious history of the West. Equality could not be maintained. The Bible turned out to be not as clear as Luther thought, and proved defenceless in the hands of its readers, who became numerous in the sixteenth century and were quick to find what they wanted in it. Tradition however had an embodied voice. Live human beings could state it and had enough institutional authority to make their ruling stick. The Roman hierarchy therefore could claim to be the only authorised interpreter of Scripture.[13] It is alleged that Pius IX, who promulgated the doctrine of papal infallibility in 1870,

---

10 Headley 1963, 57. Headley links this trend to platonic views of founding legislators.

11 This view is still very much alive in Eastern Orthodoxy, where such consensus is strongly believed in but rarely verified. The same can be said of the Muslim view of the consensus (*ijma*) of the believers.

12 For a study of the impact of the scriptural principle on the West, see Kort 1996.

13 For instance, the Encyclicals *Spiritus Paraclitus* of Benedict XV (1920) and *Humani generis* of Pius XII (1950).

stated, *tradizione c'è io,* echoing the well-known formula of royal absolutism, *l'État c'est moi.*

The strength of Luther's position rests on his radically new ecclesiology. He borrowed from humanist historiography the ability to think of the history of the papacy as that of a human institution developing its power. But to him the Church existed on a different level; it is constituted by the Gospel: its source is extra-mundane, its essence located beyond itself. Following the example of Paul and of Augustine, Luther was impressed by the contrast between Cain and Abel. Cain enjoys primogeniture: his status is based on a rule which lies at the origin of all worldly ranks, but he misinterprets his standing and misuses his power. He joins the ranks of the damned, while Abel, the murdered one, belongs to the elect. The response to the Gospel reverses human rankings. The high are brought low. The Church is the arena in which these dramas occur. In the true Church, the Gospel is preached and the Christians wait. Tribulation is constant. Christians are always on the edge of the *eschaton* and there is no progress in the Church. Luther shared in the common wish to define periods in the history of believers in this world. He painted in bright colours the life of the patriarchal households: they were vegetarians, did not have the law and lived good lives; revelation was dim but faithfulness strong. Abraham was fully righteous, by faith, before the law was given at Sinai. But as soon as the law was given, apostasies began: Aaron fell. The history of the Christian Church after Pentecost is also a record of repeated falls, without a sudden break. Gregory the Great, Boniface III, and Boniface VIII are the more serious falls. The increase of the legal powers of the papacy looms large in his reading, along with the introduction of the private masses, and the eclipse of the theology of the Cross in the universities. But all this is part of visible history and is beside the main point: the true Church is the hidden one.[14]

Calvin's view, carefully focussed, is more nuanced. The *Letter to Francis 1st* (1536) defines the issue as that of conflict between custom and truth. Whatever may be the merits of custom, it cannot carry weight when confronted with truth. The debate is thus placed on anthropological grounds. Adversaries of Rome had already pointed out that the Church was entirely caught in the rut of bad, human customs, and that this meant that God had let it die. Calvin's answer is that there has been a remnant (I Kings 19:18, Romans 11:4). God always preserved his people, even when scattered and hidden—as is well shown by the history of Israel. In the final edition of the *Institutes,* the opening affirmation is theocentric: authority in the Church belongs to God alone. In the course of history the Church adopted vain traditions like those Christ denounced in his polemics with the Pharisees (e.g. Matthew 15:3). These are useless and, worse, they burden consciences, and lead conscientious people away from Christ. They were not initiated by the apostles. To speak ill of them is not to show contempt for the Church: the Church is to be praised when it offers to God the obedience of praise.

---

14   Headley 1963, 59; also chapters 3, 4, and 5.

There is no duty of obedience to pastors. True, there must be some *police* in the life of the Church. There must be some visible honesty, peace and concord. But the ensuing and serious rulings are worldly or civil matters, not issues on which salvation hangs. As they consent to them, the believers keep their freedom of conscience.[15] The difference between Lutheranism and Calvinism is that in the latter these "rulings" found more successful, somewhat democratic authorities to enforce them, and acquired much more historical weight.

A new breed of church historians undertook to write (newly documented) histories within one or the other of the confessional frameworks. As early as 1531 Sebastian Franck, a follower of Luther turned Spiritualist, produced (in German) a *Chronica* which is rich with information on the young Anabaptist groups and argues that in church matters, all externals are insignificant. (His book was burnt in Strasbourg.) Mainstream Protestants got their cues from Matthias Flacius Illyricus (1520–1575), who was armed with a humanist education and began his career with a refutation of a 1547 sermon by the bishop of Mainz. This preacher had claimed that the Latin mass had remained unchanged throughout the centuries, and was still said in the very words employed by the apostles. Flacius had no difficulty finding a long series of variant texts (Olson 2002, 89). He then published a *Catalogue of Witnesses to the Truth*; there always was a remnant of true Christians, he argued, thereby demonstrating continuity of doctrine (*successio doctrinae*) in the absence of a succession of persons (*successio personarum*). He then presided over the multi-volume, multi-authored *Magdeburg Centuries*, a major attempt, with abundant primary sources, at a comprehensive history of the Christian religion (published between 1559 and 1574 in Basel). Each volume covers a century. While the papacy claimed that no innovations had occurred and everything was coming from tradition, the *Centuries* seek to demonstrate that much was added that was false.[16] The papacy is portrayed as the instrument of the devil and full attention is given to making visible the remnants of the true Church. (Luther did not work so hard to find a historic "chain of witnesses"; Saint Bernard is Calvin's second most quoted author — after Saint Augustine — but the Reformer did not comment on the ecclesiological significance of this.) Thus began the protestant historiographic attention to the Albigenses, the Waldensians, the Franciscan spirituals, the Lollards and the Hussites.[17]

---

15 *Institutes of the Christian Religion* IV, x, 8–27.

16 *Nihil innovetur nisi quod traditum est*, or *falsum quod posterius immissum.* Quoted in Pullapilly 1975, 52.

17 Napoléon Peyrat, a nineteenth-century protestant minister, spread very Romantic views of the Albigenses making them the ancestors of everything vital in South-Eastern France. See Brenon 2000.

     Michel Jas collected interesting evidence on historical lineage. Having established a list of all people condemned or burnt as Cathars by the Inquisition between 1237 and 1329, he traced indices of confessional belonging by people with these patronyms from 1569 to 1789. There are significantly more Protestants among those than among the

Caesar Baronius marshalled the Counter-Reformation response. His *Annales,* buttressed by the wealth of documentation available to him in Italy, present the evidence on a year by year basis. The uninterrupted orthodoxy of the Church is his theme, and much attention is given to the lives of the saints. Theologically unsound documents are rejected on the grounds that they could not be authentic. Baronius sees his role as primarily didactic. Thus he does not follow the methods employed in Renaissance historiography. Historical events are the work of God; the *Annales* undertake to show how God built his Church. He therefore keeps away from all events in secular history (deemed too controversial).[18]

The terms of the confessional controversies were thus set and remained dead-locked for three centuries. The grooves of theological debate remained unaffected by the philological skills that developed and became applied to new terrain. The seventeenth century was the century of erudition. Numerous textual scholars found documents, published them and, above all, established or rejected their authenticity. The Renaissance skill at discriminating (contrasted with the medieval habit of accumulation) becomes professionalized. But, as Anthony Grafton (1991) showed, this learned wealth of assured knowledge (often in the hands of eccle-siastics, Benedictines in particular) did not much affect the didactic historians and the common culture. Forgeries pursued their careers for decades if not centuries after they were exposed. Clearly they were still meeting the needs that led to their apparition (Grafton 1990). One debate became a matter of some public concern. In France, the Jansenists admired the purity of the Early Church and made its discipline and doctrine (the first four Ecumenical Councils and Saint Augustine) their norm. (They sound very much like Anglicans, but without the Arminianism.) This led them to a criticism of the Jesuits, who, in their praise of the new "positive" theology, were defenders of legitimate innovations. The issue thus is broached among Catholics: is Christian history the record of shortcomings in the transmission of a deposit, or is it a progressive growth in understanding? (Neveu 1994, 15)

The terms of the theological debate were finally changed with the work of John Henry Cardinal Newman. *An Essay on the Development of Christian Doctrine* (1845) which led to a notion of tradition usable outside the limited realm of Christian polemics. It was however offered as a way to break the deadlock among Catholics and Anglicans. The idea of development was in the air. Palaeontology was becoming established as a science. *The Origin of Species* came out in 1859. But the discovery of history and of enormously significant changes in it was an even greater challenge (as is witnessed by debates on the idea of progress) than the discovery of evolution in nature. Just in time for the dogmatic definition of the Immaculate Conception (1854), Newman established credibility for the Jesuit view

---

general population. The demonstration cannot be pursued after the French Revolution since confessional affiliation ceased to be part of official records. Jas 1992, 61–73.

18   Pullapilly 1975, chapter 9.

on the history of dogma by providing a reasoned discussion of "development of ideas." "True development" is defined: it preserves type, shows continuity in principles, has assimilative power, anticipates the future and conserves the past. It thus enjoys "chronic vigour" and is easily differentiated from corruption. From now on, tradition, as a widely accepted concept, attributes to history an organic nature, and acquires such letters of nobility that it can claim usefulness in historiography, both for religion and for culture in general, or for literature in particular.

Another, more recent, way of breaking the deadlock is illustrated by an article from a twentieth century Dutch Calvinist theologian. (The context now is that of ecumenical discussions.) A. A. Van Ruler argues that God invites man to formulate dogma. The "deposit of faith" is not an egg laid in a human nest to hatch progressively. Dogma is the product of human activity and is thus a participation of thought and speech in the reality of revelation. Scriptures are the source, but the source is not the same as the brook. It is typical of the Spirit to use man; dogma as reaction to the *viva vox evangelii* changes in the course of the centuries. Human beings live on the edge of the unknown; there is an eschatological dimension in their lives which is not to be found in that of trees (Van Ruler 1959).

It is thus the contest between past and future that gets hammered out as our contemporaries debate tradition. Referring to Edmond Burke's great exhibition of conservative sensibility and principles, Clifford Geertz argues that in the golden assemblage of "ancient opinions and rules of life" the role of ideology is marginal. People then act largely out of "untaught feelings" (also Burke's phrase). They hardly hesitate, or remain unresolved, in moments of decision. But crises do occur, cultural strains manifest themselves, and ideological formulations come to the forefront. Then, if we believe Burke, instead of good change like in 1776, we have bad change, like in 1789. But Geertz draws a different conclusion: "the function of ideology," he writes, "is to make autonomous politics possible." Political imagination ceases to be stifled by privileges, habits, or general cultural orientation (Geertz 1973, 218–219). I should add that ideological innovations can be reactionary, as with Lamennais and the traditionalism he expounded in Restoration France, as well as egalitarian and progressive.

Many social-scientific studies stress the conservative features of "traditional religion," or of "religion" itself. (Burke and Newman still have many disciples.) Rituals stabilize societies; myths provide durable framework for thought and action, initiation ceremonies smooth over transitions rife with potential crises. But in this look at religion as a force for social control, do we really find *religion*? Robert T. Baird pointed out a long time ago that "the functional analysis of religion is in reality more an analysis of society than an analysis of religion" (Baird 1971, 65). I am not denying the value of such analyses, but merely wish to point out that they do not treat the whole topic. Pilate and Pope Leo X, to name only two, found some religious zeal clearly dysfunctional. And what is more dysfunctional than placing a soul inside a creature of clay? Than the coexistence of eternal aspiration and mortal body?

In any case, most contemporary authors promoting "tradition" pursue a sort of utopian dream; they tend to see tradition as issuing in a perfectly transparent and egalitarian community, where no one rules over any one else, since "tradition" rules. They try to save themselves the trouble of being political. They ignore the wall that exists in any group or society between those who talk with each other in good faith (more or less), and those outside, who do not participate in the deliberation, and to whom talk (more or less manipulative) is directed after those inside have made up their mind.

So I would argue for the enduring value of a point made by Wilfred Cantwell Smith: any traditional religious act (gesture or affirmation) is modified by what he called the faith, what I would call the subjectivity, or the performance, of the agent (Smith 1962, chapter 4). The act of transmission and the conditions and manner of appropriation affect what is transmitted. This awareness of the central role of subjectivity should get increasing currency with the abundance of historical and sociological work about hybrid forms of religiosity today and secret forms of religion in the past.[19]

In somewhat of a contrast, Danièle Hervieu-Léger (1993) defined religion by its links with memory. She sees clearly that tradition is not reducible to the *tradita*. Tradition uses anteriority as ground of authority, and she adds that often it is innovation that gets justified by invoking continuity. She thus concludes that believing is religious when it is grounded in a lineage of previous witnesses, even if this line is entirely imaginary (Hervieu-Léger 1993, 141). Her book concludes with a look at the fragmentation of memory in the contemporary world and an invitation to pursue research on the religious groups today that reconstitute representations of the "line of witnesses." Her focus, clearly, is of great help when it comes to the study of the more political sorts of religious movements.

In the end we might do well to return to the analysis of Kierkegaard. The young man who had fallen in love and broken the engagement, could not recapture the joy of life, the "ironic elasticity," the bounce we might say. The gentleman who observed him, talked with him and then undertook to write *Repetition. An Essay in Experimental Psychology*, made an experiment of his own. He returned to Berlin to see again a play he had greatly enjoyed. But he found no contentment; everything had changed. "Life is not given back to one" (Kierkegaard 1946, 79). Experience is fleeting. The experimental psychologist could take comfort only from the example of Job, who dared to go to law with God—who, in time, gave him everything in return (Kierkegaard 1946, 124, 132). Repetition, moving toward reality and welcoming it, comes only from transcendence (Viallaneix 1990, 16, 23). Otherwise everything is vanity.

---

19 See, for instance, the work of Nathan Wachtel (2001) on the lives (and fates) of seventeenth-century Marranos in New Spain and on the contemporary Portuguese "New Christians" in Brazil. These "Jews" strove to remember their lineage but they changed so much that many were reluctant to join mainstream Judaism when they had the opportunity to do so in the eras of religious freedom.

A similar point, but less theologically focussed, can be made by citing a page from Sir Walter Scott in *Waverley*. Family traditions, he writes, the stories grandparents tell in the evening by the fire, are "the reverse of amber." They are not a precious substance saving forever a dead insect (some of which may be entomological rarities). They "excite the imagination" and thus "perpetuate a great deal of what is rare and valuable in ancient manners."[20] In his next novel, *The Tale of Old Mortality*, Scott narrated a story from the time of the Covenanters; the author found himself promptly attacked by historians from both sides. The Whigs found him too soft on the tyrant-monarch and his troops, while the Tories blamed him for painting a favourable image of the rebels. Both kinds of professional historians agreed the novelist should not pollute the popular mind with historical fictions (Ferris 1991). But the people went on reading Scott, who released them from the deadly grip of opposing ideologies—and they erected him a national monument.

Inter-generational communication is poetic. To be historical is to narrate. We tell stories because we know we die and want to nourish the memories of those who come after us.[21] Moreover, as Hölderlin put it, only aesthetics enable us to understand life without crying. Narrating also restores to us some autonomy. Heteronomous social orders always legitimate themselves by recourse to indisputable *facts* in the past. The *source* claims superiority simply because it precedes (Gauchet 2002, 94). What place then for the past, when one is no longer prepared to give its facts authority?

Marcel Gauchet answers thus:

> Between the dictatorship of tradition, the pseudo break with it, and the simple pure and simple oblivion (in the absence of the necessary resources to bear its weight), it is required to find, on all levels, a way of assuming it, which, by procuring a more reflexive mastery of what is required, simultaneously releases us from it, thereby opening freedom of the future for the human with memory.[22]

Methodical, critical, knowledge of the past reveals to us what Roy A. Rappaport calls our operational models, the laws (or regularities) of our (past) behaviour.[23] Meanwhile we have our cognized models in our heads and bodies, and may, thanks to reflexivity, somewhat modify them. "The criterion of the adequacy for a cognized model is not its accuracy, but its adaptive effectiveness." Cognized and operational models never entirely overlap. Appropriated meanings and observed

---

20 Walter Scott, *Waverley*, chapter 4 (p. 59 Penguin edition).

21 Hentsch 2002, 228–233. See my review in *Religiologiques* 28, Fall 2003.

22 Gauchet 2002, 167–168. See the last pages on oblivion and difficult forgiveness in Ricoeur 2000, 536, 656.

23 "The *cognized model* is a description of a people's knowledge of their environment and of their beliefs concerning it." The *operational model* "describes the same ecological system (including the people and their activities) in accordance with the assumptions and methods of the objective sciences" (Rappaport 1979, 97).

laws remain for ever heterogeneous. "As law cannot do the work of meaning, neither can meaning do the work of law" (Rappaport 1979, 98, 142).

The political, we saw, is the rupture of the laws governing everyday behaviour and the formulation of new laws. This is an intrinsic part of life within any tradition. Even when they are not attacked by enemies, their ordinary ways of coping with natality and mortality are under pressures. Traditions are always under threat of de-centering, from outside (the Romans impressed by the Greeks they had conquered), or from inside (the Lutheran turned Spiritualist). The dialectic between the religious and the political is today the most visible form of de-centering. Religion tends to offer to individuals and groups a grafting onto shared memories and invites to ensuing beliefs and actions. Politics is necessary to cope with hermeneutical dissensions that give rise to grabs for power. Politics and religion then can be said to be the two legs we depend on to walk toward the future.[24] But our weight rests on each in turn. When we stand on both, we do not move.

References

Baird, Robert T. 1971. *Category Formation and the History of Religion.* The Hague: Mouton.

Ballanche, Pierre-Simon. 1829. "Formule générale de tous les peuples, appliquée à l'histoire du peuple romain. Premier Fragment." *Revue de Paris*, première série, tome 1–3 (May): 140–156.

Benavides, Gustavo. 1997. "Modernity." Pages 186–204 in *Critical Terms for Religious Studies.* Edited by Mark C. Taylor. Chicago: The University of Chicago Press.

Brague, Rémi. 2002. *A Theory of Western Civilisation.* Translation: Eccentric Culture. South Bend: St Augustine's Press (Translation of *Europe, la voie romaine.* Paris: Gallimard, 1999).

Brenon, Anne. 2000. "Les ultra-chrétiens. Les intuitions théologiques de Napoléon Peyrat en matière de catharisme." Pages 341–356 in *Les archipels cathares: Dissidence chrétienne dans l'Europe médiévale.* Cahors: Dire Éditions.

Ferris, Ina. 1991. "The Problem of Generic Propriety." Pages 137–160 in *The Achievement of Literary Authority.* Ithaca: Cornell University Press.

Gauchet, Marcel. 2002. *La démocratie contre elle-même.* Paris: Gallimard.

Geertz, Clifford. 1973. "Ideology as a Cultural System." Pages 193–233 in his *The Interpretation of Cultures.* New York: Basic Books.

Grafton, Anthony. 1990. *Forgers and Critics: Creativity and Duplicity in Western Scholarship.* Princeton: Princeton University Press.

———. 1991. *Defenders of the Text: The Traditions of Scholarship in an Age of Science, 1450–1800.* Cambridge: Harvard University Press.

Halbwachs, Maurice. 1980. *The Collective Memory.* Translated from the French by Francis J. Ditter Jr. and Vida Yazdi Ditter. New York: Harper and Row.

———. 1992. *On Collective Memory.* Edited, Translated, and with an Introduction by Lewis A. Coser. Chicago: The University of Chicago Press.

---

24 See chapter 13 on "Religion and adaptation," particularly 427–429, "Sanctity, vacuity, mystery and adaptiveness" in Rappaport 1999.

Headley, John M. 1963. *Luther's View of Church History*. New Haven: Yale University Press.

Hentsch, Thierry. 2002. *Raconter et mourir: Aux sources narratives de l'imaginaire occidental*. Montréal: Presses de l'Université de Montréal.

Hervieu-Léger, Danièle. 1993. *La religion pour mémoire*. Paris: Cerf.

Jas, Michel. 1992. *Braises cathares: Filiation secrète à l'heure de la Réforme*. Portet sur Garonne: Loubatières.

Kierkegaard, Søren. 1946. *Repetition*. Princeton: Princeton University Press.

Kort, Wesley A. 1996. *"Take, Read": Scripture, Textuality, and Cultural Practise*. The Pennsylvania State University Press.

Legendre, Pierre. 1985. *Leçons IV. L'inestimable objet de la transmission. Essai sur le principe généalogique en Occident*. Paris: Fayard.

McCalla, Arthur. 1998. *A Romantic Historiosophy. The Philosophy of History of Pierre-Simon Ballanche*. Leiden: Brill.

Neveu, Bruno. 1994. *Érudition et religion au XVIIè et XVIIIè siècles*. Paris: Albin Michel.

Olson, Oliver K. 2002. "Matthias Flacius." Pages 83–93 in *The Reformation Theologians*. Edited by Carter Lindberg. London: Blackwell.

Pullapilly, Cyriac K. 1975. *Caesar Baronius. Counter-Reformation Historian*. South Bend: University of Notre Dame Press.

Rancière, Jacques. 1995. *La Mésentente. Politique et philosophie*. Paris: Galilée.

———. 1998. *Aux bords du politique*. Paris: Gallimard.

Rappaport, Roy A. 1979. "On Cognized Models." Pages 97–144 in *Ecology, Meaning and Religion*. Berkeley: North Atlantic Books.

———. 1999. *Ritual and Religion in the Making of Humanity*. Cambridge: Cambridge University Press.

Ricoeur, Paul. 1981. "The model of the text: Meaningful action considered as text." Pages 197–221 in *Hermeneutics and the Human Sciences*. Edited and translated by John B. Thompson. Cambridge: Cambridge University Press.

———. 2000. *La mémoire, l'histoire, l'oubli*. Paris: Seuil.

Rousse, Michel. 1990. Introduction to *Le chevalier au lion*, by Chrétien de Troyes. Paris: Flammarion.

Rousseau, Frédéric. 2003. *Le procès des témoins de la Grande Guerre. L'Affaire Norton Cru*. Paris: Seuil.

Smith, Wilfred Cantwell. 1962. *The Meaning and End of Religion*. New York: Macmillan.

Van Ruler, Arnold A. 1959. "The Evolution of Dogma." Originally published as "De Evolutie Van Het Dogma" in *De Evolutieleer Na Honderd Jaar*. Haarlem, the Netherlands: De Erven F. Bohn N. V., 1959. Translated by Tjaard Hommes. http://althusius.net/theology/evolution_of_dogma.html.

Viallaneix, Nelly. 1990. Introduction to *La Reprise*, by Søren Kierkegaard. Paris: Garnier-Flammarion.

Wachtel, Nathan. 2001. *La foi du souvenir. Labyrinthes marranes*. Paris: Seuil.

Yerushalmi, Yosef H. 1982. *Zakhor: Jewish History and Jewish Memory*. Seattle: University of Washington Press.

The Rhetoric of Innovative Tradition in the Festival Commemorating the Night of Muhammad's Ascension

Frederick S. Colby[1]

In examining how premodern Muslims use the concept of tradition in their discourses, one quickly recognizes that the idea of tradition becomes closely bound to the idea of authority. Often such discourses seek to promote an idea of tradition as something unchanging and fixed, despite the fact that constructions of tradition undoubtedly vary over time. This essay focuses upon a case wherein a premodern Muslim articulates a conception of tradition as part of a rhetorical strategy that serves his reformist agenda. The discourse on the celebration of the Night of the Ascension festival constructed by the fourteenth century legist Ibn al-Hajj ʿAbdari provides the framework through which to observe certain techniques of "tradition-building" in the premodern Muslim context. While Ibn al-Hajj claims to support the universal and unchanging Muslim traditional festival practices in opposition to those practices that he considers malicious innovations (*bidaʿ*), this essay suggests that his text in fact promotes a vision of change in which the Night of the Ascension becomes celebrated in a new and different fashion. Ibn al-Hajj's discourse on this celebration illustrates how appeals to tradition are intertwined with appeals to authority. By looking at Ibn al-Hajj's discourse on the Night of the Ascension in some detail, by placing this discourse into its historical context, and by evaluating the theoretical approaches toward this type of discourse that contemporary Islamicists offer, this essay will argue that these current theoretical approaches are most valuable to the degree that they describe the role of power and authority in the construction of Muslim tradition.

I.

Since the argument that follows is partially based upon claims made by the author of a work entitled *Introduction of the Noble Law*, it is important to begin our examination of this text with a brief discussion of the life of its author,

---

1   This essay first took the form of a paper presented at the Annual Meeting of the American Academy of Religion, Atlanta, Ga., November 24, 2003. I would like to thank both Greg Johnson and Matthew Gordon for their comments on an early draft of this essay.

Ibn al-Hajj. His full name is Abu ʿAbd Allah Muhammad b. Muhammad b. Muhammad Fasi ʿAbdari (d. 1336). The name "Ibn al-Hajj" is no more than a nickname by which this Muhammad ʿAbdari became famous. As the portion of his full name "Fasi" indicates, Ibn al-Hajj's family probably came from the city of Fez, which is located in present-day Morocco. His family ancestry notwithstanding, Ibn al-Hajj seems to have been born and spent most of his life in Egypt. He became a prominent student and colleague of the famous Sufi scholar Ibn Abi Jamra (d. 1300), and he was said to have died in Cairo at the age of eighty (Brockelmann 1936, vol. 2, 95; Kahhala 1993, vol. 3, 682–683; Ibn Mulaqqin 1998, 311). Although Ibn al-Hajj could be characterized as little more than a "minor jurist" of the Maliki school of law, his work *Introduction to the Noble Law* can profitably assist the attempt to reconstruct the beliefs and practices of the Cairene populace in thirteenth–fourteenth century Egypt, so long as one keeps in mind its fundamentally polemical stance as a tract written to expose the malicious innovations (singular *bidʿa*; plural *bidaʿ*) perpetuated by that populace (Langner 1983; Fierro 1992; Berkey 1995).

Ibn al-Hajj's work against *bidʿa* or innovation seeks to change the behavior of his contemporaries in order to bring it in line with his vision and understanding of the behavior of the earliest generations of Muslims. The title of his work, *Introduction of the Noble Law [Based] Upon the Four Methods [Madkhal al-sharʿ al-sharif ʿala ʾl-madhahib al-arbaʿa]*[2] is most frequently cited as *Introduction of the Noble Law* or simply *Introduction [Madkhal]*. Some editions of the work carry a more elaborate subtitle: *Introduction to the Development of the Practitioners Through the Correction of Intentions and Cautioning Over Many Recent Innovations and Adopted Customs [al-Madkhal ila tanmiyyat al-ʿummal bi-tahsin al-niyyat waʾl-tanbih ʿala kathir min al-bidaʿ al-muhadditha waʾl-ʿawaʾid al-muntahila]* (Kahhala 1993, vol. 3, 683; cf. Berkey 1995, 42 n. 11). The present essay focuses upon a portion of Ibn al-Hajj's *Introduction* that comprises such an attempt at "correction" and "cautioning," for it concerns the chapters in which Ibn al-Hajj describes what he sees as the reprehensible innovations (*bidaʿ*) in the observance of Muslim religious festivals in Mamluk Egypt. The primary criticism that Ibn al-Hajj levels at those festival practices that he deems objectionable is that they have little or no foundation in the festival practices of the early Muslim community. For Ibn al-Hajj, the practices thus represent unfounded and reprehensible "recent innovations" (*bidaʿ muhadditha*) that he believes all proper Muslims should reject. This essay does not seek to evaluate the veracity of either Ibn al-Hajj's claims or those of his rivals, nor does it take a position on

---

2   The base text for this study is the following: Ibn al-Hajj 1929; cf. Ibn al-Hajj 1972, 288–289. Although I have consulted both editions, all references to this text refer to pages in the first edition. Translations from Arabic to English in this paper are my own. Select excerpts from the text appear in German translation in Langner 1983, a study of popular beliefs and practices in Mamluk Egypt.

the merits of the practices that Ibn al-Hajj describes. Rather, the analysis that follows seeks to scrutinize Ibn al-Hajj's use of the concept of tradition as a rhetorical strategy to promote his own authority over that of his rivals.

Let us begin our examination of Ibn al-Hajj's *Introduction* by investigating how the concept of normative tradition is constructed in the festival section of his work. One quickly notices that Ibn al-Hajj brandishes tradition as a rhetorical weapon with which to attack his opponents for deviating from what he defines as ideal traditional practice. He thus often accuses his rivals of perpetuating mere "custom" (*'ada*) that masquerades in the guise of the authentic and prophetically established path (*sunna*). The words and deeds of Muhammad, transmitted in the form of *hadith*-reports and collectively comprising the Prophet's *sunna*, are the most common way to construct an appeal to "tradition" in Muslim discourses. Given this conventional strategy, it is remarkable how infrequently Ibn al-Hajj explicitly cites *hadith*-reports to support his own positions in this festival portion of his *Introduction*.

Instead of citing *hadiths*, Ibn al-Hajj often states on his own authority that a practice is contrary to the established path (*sunna*) of the Prophet and/or the first generations of Muslims. He assumes either that his own authority in defining Muslim tradition is self-evident, or that his audience has access to the same sources as he, and that they will inevitably interpret these sources in the same fashion that he does. For instance, describing those whose practices during the "Festival of the Sacrifice" represent reprehensible innovations, Ibn al-Hajj charges these Muslims with "[departing] from the *sunna* of the Sacrifice that the [Prophet] Lawgiver (*sahib al-shar'*) established" (Ibn al-Hajj 1929, 283). Attacking in another case the practice of repeatedly reciting the same chapter of the Qur'an in a single cycle of ritual prayer, a technique of ritual petition that some Muslims practice on the first night in the holy month of Rajab, Ibn al-Hajj proclaims such a technique to be forbidden since "no one from the past did that, and all goodness springs from following [their example]" (Ibn al-Hajj 1929, 294). Authentic Muslim practice, as defined by Ibn al-Hajj, derives from following the putative teachings of the pious ancestors in general, and those of the Prophet Muhammad in particular. Ibn al-Hajj considers the mere invocation of these pious ancestors to be sufficient evidence to make his case, for he seldom directly quotes from these figures to support the assertions that he makes in their name.

When referring to the generations of the past, Ibn al-Hajj identifies the pious ancestors with the first three generations of Muslims, whom he frequently labels with the term "the forebears" (*al-salaf*). With such an approach, Ibn al-Hajj draws upon a pragmatic methodology that was well established by his time, the idea that the first generations of Muslims could be collectively considered as having been sound in their practice and in their transmission of *sunna*.[3] Ibn

---

3   In this case, Ibn al-Hajj does defend his identification of the pious early forebears with the first three generations of Muslims by citing a *hadith*-report ascribed to the Prophet:

al-Hajj suggests that the Muslim community progressively strays farther and farther from the pious model set by the Prophet: "Each year the innovations increase and the *sunna*s decrease" (Ibn al-Hajj 1929, 300). Of course the theme of the progressive degeneration or corruption of the Muslim community is well known from many different Muslim genres, including the writings of the Sufi scholars (Geoffroy 1995, 175–176). Ibn al-Hajj draws upon this trope in order to justify his effort to revive what he considers to represent the authentic traditions of the first three generations of Muslims, attempting to keep the community from straying even farther from the "straight path."

In his fight against this gradual corruption of the Muslim community, Ibn al-Hajj identifies his primary enemy as not simply the abandonment of what he takes to be authentic Muslim tradition, but also the adoption of contrary practices that are passed off as authentic Muslim tradition. He does not attack those who openly apostasize or teach contrary doctrines so much as those Muslims who surreptitiously dilute the strength of normative Muslim practices from within:

> The straight path is the Book of God [i.e. the Qur`an] and the *sunna* of his Messenger [i.e. Muhammad]. The Accursed-one makes an imitation of it out of what has no foundation in it, substituting [for the straight path] what contradicts it, until the substitution itself becomes *sunna* for them. (Ibn al-Hajj 1929, 300)

Ibn al-Hajj makes it clear that the party responsible for this surreptitious substitution is none other than the whispering voice of the satanic tempter, Iblis:

> Consider the snare of Iblis, the Accursed-one: How he follows the [prophetic] paths (*al-sunan*, plural of *sunna*) one by one, and casts veils over he who accepts his whispers, in order that he will abandon that *sunna* and practice some other thing that he presents to them as worship, but which is an absurdity, manifestly forbidden, manifestly innovative. (Ibn al-Hajj 1929, 285)

On one level, this entire section of Ibn al-Hajj's work is formulated as a struggle against the machinations of the tempter who introduces corrupting innovations into Muslim festival celebrations under the guise of the pious example of the Prophet and the earliest generation of Muslims (cf. Taylor 1999, 183). On another level, however, we shall see that Ibn al-Hajj directs his polemic not only at the devil but also at those of his contemporaries whom he characterizes as being under the influence of the satanic whisperer in the manner that they celebrate Muslim festivals.

"The best of generations is my own, then those after them, then those after them" (Ibn al-Hajj 1929, 300). For Arabic references to this *hadith*, see Wensinck 1992, vol. 5, 372.

In his *Introduction*, Ibn al-Hajj offers a threefold typology of Muslim festivals, categorized by what he takes to be the status of the festivals in terms of Islamic law or *shari'a* (Ibn al-Hajj 1929, 282–313). First are the lawful (*shar'i*) festivals, those whose observance is sanctioned under the *shari'a*; these include the Breaking of the Fast, the festival of the Sacrifice, and the holiday known as 'Ashura. The second category comprises those festivals that Ibn al-Hajj claims are ascribed to the law without enjoying any actual legal basis; these include the pious observance of the first night in the month of Rajab, the observance of the Night of the Ascension, and the observance of the night of the full moon in the middle of the month of Sha'ban. The third category comprises those festivals that Ibn al-Hajj thinks Muslims observe in imitation of the Christians; these include the Birthday of the Prophet Muhammad and the New Year's festival (cf. Fierro 1992, 124–128). All three of these categories receive Ibn al-Hajj's scrutiny in his *Introduction*, for even though he privileges those festivals that he identifies as having a basis in Islamic law, even still in those cases he describes what he considers to be the mistaken ways that his contemporaries observe these *shar'ia*-based holidays.

As mentioned above, Ibn al-Hajj assigns the Night of the Ascension (*laylat al-mi'raj*) festival to the category of those festivals (*mawasim*) that claim to have a legal basis without enjoying any such basis in actuality (Ibn al-Hajj 1929, 291–292). His classification rests upon the idea that since this festival is not explicitly mentioned in the classical Muslim sources, it thus has only a tenuous connection to the early period of Islamic history. Yet despite this lack of official legal basis, interestingly Ibn al-Hajj states that the earliest Muslims did in fact commemorate the anniversary of the Prophet's miraculous journey to and from the heavens in their own pious fashion:

> Among the innovations that they originated…in the month of Rajab is the night of the 27th of it, which is the Night of the Ascension, during which God honored this community with what he commanded them to follow through his general favor and abundant goodness. In honor of their Prophet, the forebears used to praise [this night] through their own noble custom (*'ada*) by increasing their worship on it, increasing the length of their standing in ritual prayer, abasement, crying, and other beautiful customs of theirs already known. (Ibn al-Hajj 1929, 294)

In this discussion of the festival, Ibn al-Hajj offers a mixed message regarding the degree to which he understands the observance of the Night of the Ascension festival to comprise a part of acceptable Muslim practice. On the one hand, he identifies the festival itself as an innovation (*bid'a*), and he refrains from connecting it in any way with the concept of prophetic *sunna*. On the other hand, he claims that the first generations of Muslims commemorated the Night of the Ascension with extra zeal in worship, and they did so as part of an early custom (*'ada*) that Ibn al-Hajj describes as noble and beautiful. He justifies this practice out of the thanks that Muslims owe to their Lord for the way that God generously multiplied the effect of their daily ritual prayers, the duty alluded to in the above phrase, "what he commanded them to follow" (Ibn al-Hajj 1929, 294).[4] Although Ibn al-Hajj considers the idea of commemorating the Night of the Ascension to be an innovation, he traces certain devotional customs associated with it back to the earliest period, lending its pious observance—if not its joyful celebration—a degree of legitimacy. That is, Ibn al-Hajj's discourse supports a limited observance of this holiday as representing what is authentically traditional, even though he refrains from assigning the holiday the force of law that other holidays based upon the *sunna* enjoy.

I would argue that this compromise position, which Ibn al-Hajj traces to the earliest generations of Muslims, represents an innovative way of understanding the holiday. As a Maliki jurist, Ibn al-Hajj understands the custom of the people of Medina as carrying with it the force of binding legal precedent, which could explain why he cannot reject this festival entirely. Perhaps Ibn al-Hajj's compromise could also be explained as an attempt to criticize the actions of his scholarly contemporaries while making room for a limited celebration of the festival. One might imagine that two of Ibn al-Hajj's important constituents, the select group of Mamluk political elites and the large mass of common people, both might have resisted a call to abandon the celebration entirely. By defining what he constructs as the acceptable parameters of the celebration, Ibn al-Hajj thus asserts his control over the discourse. This interpretation of why Ibn al-Hajj offers a compromise position will be further supported through a comparison with the case of Ibn Taymiyya, which will be discussed briefly below. It will become clear that Ibn al-Hajj's position on the Night of the Ascension festival is innovative in the context of fourteenth century Cairo to the degree that it breaks with the practices established by his Muslim contemporaries whom he criticizes, especially since he furnishes no real evidence to prove that the first generations of Muslims observed the festival in the fashion he describes.

If Ibn al-Hajj approves of the manner in which the forebears supposedly observed the Night of the Ascension, he nevertheless disapproves of the manner in which some of his contemporaries celebrated the festival. He asserts that his contemporaries' approach to the evening is "in opposition to how the forebears used to observe it" in a number of ways (Ibn al-Hajj 1929, 294). For instance, Ibn al-Hajj finds it offensive that some of his contemporaries take over mosques and hold all-night vigils there on the Night of the Ascension. He describes how Muslims light candles, spread out rugs, and even place copper mugs and water

---

4 Beginning with the official *hadith* collections, most typical official Sunni ascension accounts contain a reference to the fact that the daily ritual prayers were originally revealed as fifty per day and only later reduced to five after the repeated pleas from the Prophet. Instead of using this language of reduction, Ibn al-Hajj uses the language of multiplication: "[God] had made the 5 prayers worth from 50 to 700 times" (ibid.).

jugs around mosques, "as if the house of God were their [own] house." According to Ibn al-Hajj, these celebrants forget that a mosque is for worship, not for mundane activities such as "lounging, sleeping, eating, and drinking" (Ibn al-Hajj 1929, 294–295).[5] While Ibn al-Hajj sometimes attempts to portray himself as the champion of the common person, as Berkey illustrates (Berkey 1992, 88 and 183–184), here Ibn al-Hajj takes the common person to task for not acting with the proper decorum or respect while in a mosque on the Night of the Ascension.

Furthermore, Ibn al-Hajj objects to the manner in which men and women interact in the mosque during the evening of the festival. Such mixing between the sexes, according to the author, allows for too much of an opportunity for impropriety, especially since the women customarily adorn themselves with jewelry and makeup on this occasion (Ibn al-Hajj 1929, 297).[6] To make matters worse, Ibn al-Hajj describes the men as urinating in a corner of the mosque. Women who need to urinate are forced to urinate into a vessel, to carry the vessel with them in the mosque, and to pay a person to dispose of it (Ibn al-Hajj 1929, 297–298; see Berkey 1995, 56–57). To say that Ibn al-Hajj is horrified at the manner in which his contemporaries treat this sacred place of ritual prayer would be an understatement, and he uses the rhetoric of tradition to express his disapproval.

As if the manner that people treat the mosque on the Night of the Ascension were not enough, Ibn al-Hajj gives details of what appear to be Sufi gatherings in the mosque that same evening, and he characterizes these gatherings as a kind of parody of worship. Multiple devotional circles form that night, perhaps in imitation of educational circles that form around scholars in mosques (Berkey 1995, 59). Ibn al-Hajj goes on to describe the scene as follows:

---

5   At this point Ibn al-Hajj presents a *hadith* that could be cited to challenge his stated position, a *hadith* which essentially states, "The mosque is a house for each god-fearing person" (I have been unable to trace this *hadith*, but see Wensinck 1992, vol. 2, 467). To this challenge, Ibn al-Hajj replies that the *hadith* refers specifically to the "People of the Bench," who lived outside the mosque in Medina solely because of their utter destitution, and therefore does not apply to the behavior of the Muslim population in general toward their places of worship. Cf. Berkey 1995, 48, where he cites another passage in which Ibn al-Hajj registers his disapproval of "loafing" in mosques: Ibn al-Hajj 1929, vol. 2, 226. Fierro 1992, 219–221, lists a series of activities in mosques that earn the censure of the anti-*bid'a* works that she surveys.

6   Cf. Berkey 1992, 171–172, who quotes Ibn al-Hajj's opinion disapproving of men and women meeting together in the context of education in mosques and other public spaces. In Ibn Taymiyya's text translated by Memon 1976, 250–251, the author objects to men and women mixing in mosques during festival seasons. Shoshan 1993, 72, describes how similar intermingling between the sexes during overnight campouts preceding the annual *mahmil* processions led to an official ban of this practice in the year 1422 CE. Finally, Fierro 1992, 235–236, offers a survey of teachings about women in *bid'a* literature.

Each circle has an elder whom they all imitate in ritual remembrance
(*dhikr*) and recitation. If only that were [simply] ritual remembrance and
recitation! Instead they play with God's religion. For instance, for the
most part the chanter does not say, "There is no god but God (*la ilaha
illa allah*)," rather he says, "Don't follow him, let's go! (*la yalahu yal-
lah*)..." When they say, "Glory be to God" (*subhan allah*), they quicken the
pace of it so much and repeat it until you almost cannot understand. The
reciter recites the Qur'an, adding to it what is not in it, subtracting from
it what is in it, in accordance with intonations and reverberations which
resemble singing (*al-ghina'*) and scales which they adopted, the reprehensible conditions of which you already know. Then there is a great
matter. The reciter begins with the recitation of the Qur'an, and another
reciter delivers lines of poetry, or wishes to do so, so they silence the
Qur'an reciter, or pay [no] attention to him, or leave this one and his
poem and that one and his reciting on account of noticing others listening
to the musical audition (*sama'*) of poetry and those forged intonations.
These types of games with religion, were they to be held outside the
mosque, would be prohibited. How then [are they allowed] when it is
inside the mosque, moreover, on this noble night? (Ibn al-Hajj 1929, 297)

According to this description of the observance of the Night of the Ascension,
one could conclude that the festival serves as a type of carnival in which norms
of behavior are inverted or suspended. The text of sacred phrases are altered,
and the boundaries between qur'anic and non-qur'anic passages are blurred.
People recite the Qur'an in the manner of singing, and several recitations and
other performances go on simultaneously; both of these practices were specifically condemned in a series of anti-*bid'a* treatises even prior to Ibn al-Hajj's
work (Fierro 1992, 211–214). In addition to these critiques, the references to ritual
remembrance (*dhikr*) and musical audition (*sama'*) in the above quotation,
rituals typically associated with Islamic mysticism or Sufism, suggest that Ibn
al-Hajj's censure is being directed at certain forms of Sufi practices on the
Night of the Ascension.

One should not mistakenly assume that Ibn al-Hajj's discourse, being aimed
at exposing and critiquing reprehensible innovations, is necessarily directed
against Sufism as a whole. Note that in the quotation above Ibn al-Hajj does
not object to *dhikr* in a general sense, but rather he objects to the way that some
carry out this ritual on the Night of the Ascension (cf. Winter 1982, 30). In
addition, Ibn al-Hajj's critique says little about the content of the qur'anic
verses, the poetry, or the ascension narratives that his contemporaries recite.
For instance, Ibn al-Hajj does not deride his contemporaries for their mystical
interpretations of the Prophet's night journey and ascension, nor for their
claims to have had visions of ascent themselves. The latter types of writings
must have been known to Ibn al-Hajj, since the controversial and pivotal
Andalusian Sufi known as Ibn al-Arabi (d. 1240) describes his ascension vision
in several of his major works. In fact, even Ibn al-Hajj's own teacher, the Sufi-

inclined Maliki scholar Ibn Abi Jamra (d. 1300) records numerous ascension experiences among the visions that he witnessed while composing a commentary on Bukhari's foundational *hadith* collection (Katz 1992, 89–90; Ibn Abi Jamra 1997, vol. 2, 1535–1536). Sufi interpretations or mystical experiences pertaining to the Night of the Ascension festival do not appear to be the central issue concerning Ibn al-Hajj, therefore. Instead, Ibn al-Hajj takes aim at those Muslims, Sufi and non-Sufi, whose behaviors on the Night of the Ascension contradict the norms that Ibn al-Hajj believes pious Muslims should uphold.

The passage quoted above makes clear that Ibn al-Hajj focuses upon not so much what his contemporaries believe about Muhammad's night journey and ascension, but how they act on the Night of the Ascension. Recall that Ibn al-Hajj holds up the example of the first generation of Muslims, who "used to praise [this night]...by increasing their worship on it, increasing the length of their standing in ritual prayer, abasement, crying, and other beautiful customs" (Ibn al-Hajj 1929, 294). Unlike these pious forbears, some of Ibn al-Hajj's Egyptian contemporaries recite the *dhikr* phrase so quickly that it becomes incomprehensible, and they treat the Qur'an on par with poetry in competing for the attention of an audience. Moreover, Ibn al-Hajj critiques those who recite the Qur'an in a musical fashion, a criticism that appears throughout the *Introduction*. Ibn al-Hajj depicts these practices as a mockery of religion that have no foundation in what he defines as legitimate Muslim practice. His text could therefore be said to make use of the rhetoric of tradition in order to construct a model of Muslim orthopraxy.

Even though Ibn al-Hajj's text does largely focus on rigidly defining a concept of Muslim orthopraxy that one might be tempted to label conservative, it also contains a number of complexities that resist conventional labels and typologies. For instance, Ibn al-Hajj actually defends the observance of the Night of the Ascension by citing the customary practice of the first generation of Muslims, despite the fact that he recognizes that the festival has no actual basis in *shari'a* law. He therefore cannot be considered to be someone who rejects any and all new practices as heretical; some customs he portrays as malicious innovations introduced by the devil, while others are "beautiful customs" promoted by the pious forebears. Furthermore, Ibn al-Hajj refers to the Sufi practice of *dhikr* with general approval, only faulting the "innovators" for the particular manner in which their *dhikr* ritual mocks or distorts conventional Muslim norms. He thus portrays himself as a moderate Sufi, challenging those models that perpetuate a sharp break between Muslim legists and mystics. While Ibn al-Hajj sometimes cites the Qur'an and *hadith* to support his legal arguments in other passages in his *Introduction*, when it comes to the Night of the Ascension he argues mainly on the basis of his own religious authority, without regularly citing from other sources. In this manner, his discourse suggests that his reformist approach should be accepted as self-evident, and that his construction of the *doxa* of "orthodox tradition" corresponds with the general *habitus* of the historical Muslim community (Bourdieu 1977). These complexities need to be kept in mind as one examines the historical context of Ibn al-Hajj's work, and the theoretical tools that are useful in analyzing its significance to the study of the historical construction of tradition.

II.

It is difficult to know the degree to which the practices that Ibn al-Hajj depicts as taking place on the Night of the Ascension are representative of the festival practices of Muslims inside and outside Egypt, especially since Ibn al-Hajj's *Introduction* remains one of the earliest extant sources to describe such practices.[7] Ibn al-Hajj's categorization of the festival as one that falls outside the prophetic *sunna* appears to be substantiated by the fact that the vast majority of *hadith*-reports on Muhammad's night journey (*isra'*) and ascension (*mi'raj*) describe the story of the Prophet's miraculous journey away from and back to Mecca, but do not describe how the event should be commemorated by later Muslims (Colby 2002). As discussed above, however, Ibn al-Hajj maintains that the pious forbears observed the festival in a restrained fashion as part of their noble custom (*'ada*), a position which presupposes that a certain number of Muslims observed the festival from the earliest years of Islamic history. Ibn al-Hajj thus gives legitimacy to some commemoration of the festival in Mamluk Egypt on the authority of pious Muslim custom, which he portrays here as a lesser type of Muslim tradition. Despite the fact that Ibn al-Hajj's account tells one little in particular about the identity of the celebrants whom he depicts, and despite the fact that it offers no way of determining how widespread these practices may have been, his discussion suggests that by the fourteenth century at the latest Cairenes did in fact commemorate the Night of the Ascension. It furthermore suggests that Ibn al-Hajj and some of his peers sharply disagreed on the proper way to observe that festival. One may surmise that Ibn al-Hajj's account distorts or exaggerates the practices of his contemporaries in order to discredit them in the eyes of other Muslims. This being as it may, there is little doubt that Ibn al-Hajj uses the rhetoric of tradition in order to promote his reformist agenda.[8]

---

7   Gruber 2005, 85–86, offers recently discovered evidence from the work of Ibn al-Hajj's near contemporary Rashid al Din (fl. 706/1306) that suggests an annual celebration of the *mi'raj* took place in the Ilkhanid lands to the East.

8   Fierro 1992, 239–240, presents some important methodological remarks with regard to treating anti-*bid'a* tracts as descriptions of contemporary practices. Her recommendation of the need to find corroborating evidence to supplement reports in the anti-*bid'a* works is certainly justified, and although I have not been able to locate such evidence for the fourteenth century observance of the Night of the Ascension festival, I agree that such evidence would significantly strengthen the interpretation that I have offered here.

To understand Ibn al-Hajj's reformist discourse in its context, it is important briefly to discuss the intellectual environment of Cairo in the thirteenth to fourteenth centuries, and the political atmosphere of early Mamluk Egypt during the years in which Ibn al-Hajj was writing. The eighty years of Ibn al-Hajj's life roughly correspond with the first eighty years of the Bahri Mamluk rule in Egypt, during which the rulers largely concentrated upon several key concerns: "The crusader presence, the Mongol threat, the incorporation of Syria, the organization of the empire, and the protection of the trade routes..." (Northrup 1998, 251). Beginning as slave warriors of foreign and non-Muslim origin, the Mamluk rulers who controlled Egypt during this period had to work to establish their legitimacy in the eyes of the wider Muslim populace.

The Mamluk sultans recognized that that their popularity often hinged on religious issues (Irwin 1986, 95), and they had to carefully negotiate and arbitrate between the conflicting positions of diverse religious authorities. This Bahri Mamluk period witnessed the increasing support of Sufism among the Egyptian populace, and the rising influence of Sufi leaders among many of the Mamluk elites (Fernandes 1988, 96; Shoshan 1993, 11; Northrup 1998, 266). For instance, the Mamluk sultan al-Zahir Baybars I (r. 1260–1277) allegedly took the Sufi holy man Khadir Mihrani (d. 1271) as his spiritual advisor, and not only built a Sufi lodge for him but also regularly joined him in performing the *dhikr* ceremony (Fernandes 1988, 97; Irwin 1986, 54). Although the religious devotion of Baybars I may well have been exaggerated by later biographers, the Bahri Mamluks supported a Sunni and Sufi approach out of a combination of piety and political expediency (Northrup 1998, 268–269). In order to forge a consensus and unity among disparate groups of Muslims, the Bahri Mamluks increasingly intervened in religious affairs, and they promoted a movement to standardize and control religious discourse under the aegis of moderate Sunni Sufi Islam (Northrup 1998, 270–271). In this general political and religious context, Ibn al-Hajj uses his *Introduction* to expose those religious practices of his contemporaries that he found to be particularly abhorrent. The work should therefore be read on the one hand as part of this historical context, and on the other as part of a wider genre of "anti-*bid'a*" works which became popular among middle period reformist scholars (Fierro 1992, *passim*; Shoshan 1993, 67–68; Berkey 1995, 45).

Ibn al-Hajj was not alone among the Mamluk period religious scholars in formulating a discourse about Muslim tradition in order to oppose the beliefs and practices of other Muslims, for his contemporary, the famous Hanbali scholar Ibn Taymiyya (d. 1328), offers a similar reformist discourse on Muslim ritual behavior. In his *Kitab iqtida' al-sirat al-mustaqim mukhalafat ashab al-jahim* [The Necessity of the Straight Path against the People of Hell] (Memon 1976) and in other works, Ibn Taymiyya's critique of pilgrimage to and worship at graves and shrines echoes many of Ibn al-Hajj's attacks on the practices of his contemporaries (see Taylor 1999, ch. 5). Like Ibn al-Hajj, for example, Ibn

Taymiyya does not oppose the performance of the *dhikr* ritual per se, but he objects to the use of *dhikr* in ways that allegedly contradict the Prophet's *sunna*, such as during a visit to a "tree, rivulet, mountain or cave" (Memon 1976, 255). In addition, Ibn al-Hajj's critique of the way that groups of Muslims chant the Qur'an and poetic verses on the Night of the Ascension should be understood in the context of a wider controversy about the permissibility of poetic and musical chanting discussed in the anti-*bid'a* tracts in general (Fierro 1992, 211–216) and surfacing in the fourteenth century Mamluk context in particular (Geoffroy 1995, 414–416). Both Ibn al-Hajj and Ibn Taymiyya could be said to represent a scholarly trend within early Mamluk Egypt that seeks to establish a sense of Muslim tradition by formulating a critical and reformist discourse that challenges the legitimacy of competing constructions of this tradition.

Although Ibn al-Hajj and Ibn Taymiyya share similar approaches, the tension between their positions also helps to explain how appeals to tradition become intertwined with power relations. Both Ibn al-Hajj and Ibn Taymiyya seek to present themselves as "tolerant moderates," not categorically opposed to most of the practices they criticize, but seeking to reform these practices and to curb the influence of their most objectionable elements (Winter 1982, 30; Taylor 1999, 190–191). Despite this effort at appearing moderate, Ibn Taymiyya and his followers undoubtedly represented a "minority view," and they were imprisoned for advocating some unpopular positions that were opposed by those in power (Taylor 1999, 195). The politics behind these theological struggles becomes more apparent when one recognizes that the chief jurist who brought Ibn Taymiyya to trial was from the Maliki school of law, the same methodological school as that of Ibn al-Hajj, as opposed to the Hanbali school of law followed by Ibn Taymiyya and his supporters.[9] Ibn Taymiyya set aside the scholarly consensus of his contemporaries in favor of critically reinterpreting the early sources, and as such he alienated himself from the vested interests of those in power.

Unlike Ibn Taymiyya's reformist discourse, which often draws upon an interpretation of the Qur'an and *hadith* proof-texts to support its positions

---

9   Shoshan 1991, 93. According to Fierro 1992, 211, the Maliki and Shafi'i legal schools reflect one approach to the *bid'a* texts (Shafi'i authors often dependent upon the work of Malikis), and the Hanbali and Hanafi schools seem to reflect a second and independent approach (Hanafi authors often dependent upon the work of Hanbalis). The rift continues after Ibn Taymiyya and Ibn al-Hajj have died, for as Taylor 1999 discusses in his ch. 6, Ibn Taymiyya's positions and those of his student and follower Ibn Qayyim Jawziyya (d. 1350) are refuted in the fourteenth century by the Shafi'i chief *qadi*, Taqi al-Din Subki (d. 1355). The idea that this methodological and epistemological rift in the fourteenth century Mamluk context between Malikis and Shafi'is on the one hand and Hanbalis and Hanafis on the other may reflect political divisions is supported by Taylor's study, and the thesis bears further consideration.

(Taylor 1999, 171), Ibn al-Hajj's discourse on the Night of the Ascension festival bases its authority almost exclusively on two factors: first, the prestige and credentials of Ibn al-Hajj himself, and second, upon an appeal to an unspoken consensus of what constitutes legitimate Muslim tradition and custom. As for the first, we have seen how Ibn al-Hajj asks his readers to accept his portrayal of how the forebears used to observe the festival without offering any substantiating evidence, and how he often asks his readers to reject certain practices on the basis of his word that these practices contradict prophetic *sunna*. As for the second, Ibn al-Hajj's discourse claims to need little supporting evidence because it purports to be based upon the sense that Muslims have about their common tradition. He criticizes some of his Muslim contemporaries for promoting behaviors on the Night of the Ascension that he assumes would shock most of his other Muslim readers: distorting the text of the Qur'an, sullying the purity of the mosque, encouraging the licentious mixing of the sexes, and promoting the performance of music and poetry to a status on par with or superior to the Qur'an itself.[10] Ibn al-Hajj's reformist discourse draws its authority from an appeal to an ideal sense of unchanging Muslim tradition that Ibn al-Hajj contends requires no further explication or proof.

III.

Turning from this particular text and context to discuss how scholars of Islam use and apply the concept of tradition, the first thing that needs to be recognized is that the word tradition has many meanings. Until relatively recently, contemporary scholars would uncritically juxtapose tradition to modernity, so that one might discuss the struggle of traditional peoples in maintaining their identities and viability as autonomous peoples in the midst of modern global capitalism. Underlying this juxtaposition is the idea that tradition represents what is unchanging and fixed, while modernity represents what is in constant flux. Such models continue to be deployed by scholars of Islam, even in relatively recent studies (e.g. Salvatore 2001). However, this dichotomous model of static and timeworn tradition opposed to dynamic and fresh modernity is belied by the realization that conceptions and performances of tradition are constantly subject to reinterpretation and reformulation. While this idea may seem to have become relatively commonplace within academia in the past

---

10   Thus Ibn al-Hajj's discussion of the Night of the Ascension festival neatly illustrates all three of the categories of concerns that Berkey attributes to the discussion of festivals in the genre of anti-*bid'a* works as a whole: concern with the carnivalesque nature of festivals, concern with the preservation of sexual boundaries during festivals, and concern with the non-canonical nature of festivals (Berkey 1995, 56–59).

few decades, nevertheless the essays in this volume illustrate that the term tradition is subject to significant conceptual slippage, and that both scholars and those about whom they write make use of the term in a variety of ways.

In the already troubled waters in which various scholars have applied the concept of tradition differently, scholars of Islam have generally muddied the waters even further by translating one or more Arabic technical terms, such as *hadith* and/or *sunna*, with the English word "tradition." Some American and European scholars continue to refer to the prophetic body of teachings as the Muslim "Tradition" (i.e. *sunna*), which is comprised of oral "traditions" (i.e. *hadith*-reports) from the Prophet Muhammad (e.g. Coulson 1964; Schacht 1964; Juynboll 1983; Wensinck 1992; Taylor 1999).[11] The equation between the terms *hadith* and/or *sunna* with the concept of tradition often is made unreflectively, ignoring the fact that different *hadith*s could be cited to promote different constructions of tradition, and downplaying the role that power and authority play in the creation of such constructions.

Although often lagging behind scholars in other areas in terms of theoretical sophistication, in the past twenty years scholars of Islam have increasingly paid closer attention to theoretical issues surrounding the idea of tradition. For instance, in the mid-1980's Marilyn Robinson Waldman drew upon the insights of theorists such as Eric Hobsbawm (1983) to suggest that tradition should be viewed as a modality of change:

> I will use the words "tradition," "traditional," and "traditionalistic" very broadly and almost interchangeably – for anything that is accepted as authoritative primarily because of its being perceived as having been transmitted over time and inherited and from its having set a binding precedent that helps maintain a sense of continuity with some valued point in the past. I will also use these words for a modality of change that relies on this concept of authority, without, of course, ignoring the content and ideology that accompany it. (Waldman 1986, 327)

Waldman's definition is valuable in that it focuses upon legitimacy derived from perceived continuity, and upon the possibility of change through an appeal to such legitimacy. As Waldman points out, the term tradition carries with it a sense of authority based upon a perception. She suggests that the "stuff" of tradition, the content of beliefs and practices, may or may not change over time, but the way this stuff is understood by various parties is subject to change.

---

11 Berkey, who offers a more deliberate and sophisticated approach to the discussion of tradition, notes that when it comes to scholars stereotyping Muslim cultures as "traditional" cultures, "confusion arises in part from the central role that prophetic *hadith*, often called 'traditions,' play…" (Berkey 1995, 47). Here Berkey implicitly critiques the translation of the word *hadith* as tradition, but I would contend that the strong connection that Berkey draws between the term *sunna* and the ideal concept of tradition (see below) remains just as problematic.

One might further refine Waldman's observations by noting that not only do perceptions of tradition change over time (a characteristic associated with receivers of tradition), but also articulations of tradition change over time (a characteristic associated with formulators and transmitters of tradition, such as Ibn al-Hajj).

A more recent work by Islamicist Daniel Brown discusses those who articulate such a discourse on tradition, surveying textual evidence from both the premodern and modern periods. Brown asserts that modern Muslims invoke the Prophet's *sunna* in diverse ways, "using it selectively, rejecting it, or reinterpreting it." He claims that "dealing with *sunna*...is therefore essential to any effort by Muslims to adjust to changed circumstances" (Brown 1996, 138). Like Waldman, Brown shows how the rhetoric of tradition can be used to justify change. He further suggests that in contemporary religious debates, all parties defend their positions by claiming to advocate a position that is most in line with prevailing ideas of tradition (Brown 1996, 139). Brown advances the discussion of tradition among Islamicists by recognizing that tradition does not represent any definite group of texts or body of ideas and practices so much as a rhetorical label that is contested by competing parties.

Acknowledging that both perceptions and articulations of traditions change over time, Islamicist Jonathan Berkey draws directly upon the work of Eric Hobsbawm in order to juxtapose an ideal tradition (*sunna*) on the one hand and an innovative custom (*bid'a*) on the other (Hobsbawm 1983, 2–3; Berkey 1995, 47). This formulation describes the concept of tradition as representing the ideal of an unchanging body of teachings, whether or not those teachings change over time in actual practice. Berkey labels those who maintain and promote this ideal of tradition "rigorously 'traditional' in the technical sense of the term" (Berkey 1995, 42). Berkey's approach resembles that of Waldman, for both borrow from Hobsbawm the notion that tradition forms an "alleged" and "perceived" ideal of continuity. Like Hobsbawn, Berkey insists that the binary categories of "tradition" and "custom" are not reified, and he notes instances of fluidity and movement between the two (Berkey 1995, 40, 49, 55). Nevertheless, the sharp distinction between tradition and custom that he and Hobsbawm both make in the way that they define these terms gives rise to some difficulties in analyzing concrete Muslim cases. While at times Ibn al-Hajj speaks of custom as a type of degeneration and movement away from the prophetic ideal (Berkey 1995, 48), at other times Ibn al-Hajj speaks approvingly of some custom as legitimate Muslim tradition, as illustrated by his description of how the pious forbears observed the Night of the Ascension festival. Despite the rigidity in which Berkey defines the categories of tradition and custom, which leads him to define tradition and *sunna* as virtually interchangeable, Berkey's discussion of the anti-*bid'a* tracts immensely contributes to the project of understanding these reformist treatises within their historical contexts.

Berkey identifies a series of contextual factors that help to explain Ibn al-Hajj's reformist discourse. First, he notes that the Middle Periods of Islamic history witnessed massive upheaval and change within Muslim communities, with a large influx of people of different cultural backgrounds into the ranks of Muslims (e.g. the Mamluks), the spread of deadly plagues throughout the *oikoumene*, and the continued political and intellectual struggles between different religious factions (e.g. the new "Sunni-internationalism" that fought against the spread of Shiʿi doctrines). Therefore, the discourse of tradition served as a tool for promoting a sense of stability in a chaotic world (Berkey 1995, 46). Second, the discourse of tradition did not require these historical factors for its impetus, for in a culture which exalted religious and especially prophetic precedent to such a degree, the discourse of tradition became self-perpetuating and self-reinforcing (Berkey 1995, 44). Third and perhaps most importantly, Ibn al-Hajj and other scholars used the discourse of tradition to bolster their own authority vis-a-vis the military elite, the popular preachers, and/or their scholarly peers. It was used to assert the control of reformist scholars over the religious beliefs and practices of their contemporaries, especially in the face of challenges to this control presented by others (Fernandes 1988, 99; Berkey 1995, 58). Ibn al-Hajj's criticism of how his contemporaries celebrated the Night of the Ascension festival should be understood, therefore, not only as an effort to preserve the continuity and legitimacy of Muslim religious practice, but also as an effort to promote Ibn al-Hajj's authority as an interpreter of what he construes as self-evident Islamic tradition.

The description of the Night of the Ascension festival from Ibn al-Hajj's *Introduction* offers a lens through which to examine the construction of a discourse on tradition by a premodern Muslim scholar, and it offers an historical case with which to test the utility of contemporary theories of tradition formulated by scholars of Islam. By examining the discussion of a controversial Muslim festival as articulated in the text of the medieval Cairene scholar Ibn al-Hajj, this essay illustrates how the concept of tradition has been deployed as part of a rhetorical strategy in a bid for authority and power in a specific historical context. In appealing to tradition through his rhetoric, Ibn al-Hajj presents a discourse in which a notion of tradition is constructed in the service of a reformist agenda. As Berkey and Brown suggest, this same process can also be seen in contemporary Muslim appeals to the concept of tradition (Berkey 1995, 65; Brown 1996, ch. 2), and Lincoln reminds us that "all language [is] 'the historical product of discursive processes'" (Lincoln 2003, 2, quoting Talal Asad). Thus, scholars of Islam would do well to move beyond reified constructions of tradition as a certain body of teachings, examining instead the discourse of tradition as part of a rhetorical strategy that is expressed and received within particular historical contexts.

References

Berkey, Jonathan. 1998. "The Mamluks as Muslims: the military elite and the construction of Islam in medieval Egypt." Pages 163–173 in *The Mamluks in Egyptian politics and society*. Edited by Thomas Phillip and Ulrich Haarmann. Cambridge: Cambridge University Press.

———. 1995. "Tradition, Innovation and the social construction of knowledge in the medieval Islamic Near East." *Past and Present* 146: 38–65.

———. 1992. *The Transmission of Knowledge in Medieval Cairo: A Social History of Islamic Education*. Princeton: Princeton University Press.

Bourdieu, Pierre. 1977. *Outline of a Theory of Practice*. Translated by Richard Nice. Cambridge: Cambridge University Press.

Brockelmann, Carl. 1936–1942. *Geschichte der arabischen Litteratur. Supplementband.* 3 vols. Leiden: Brill.

Brown, Daniel. 1996. *Rethinking Tradition in modern Islamic thought*. Cambridge: Cambridge University Press.

Bulliet, Richard. 1994. *Islam: The View from the Edge*. New York: Columbia University Press.

Colby, Frederick. 2002. "Constructing an Islamic Ascension Narrative: The Interplay of Official and Popular Culture in Pseudo-Ibn 'Abbas." Ph.D. Dissertation, Duke University.

Coulson, Noel J. 1964. *A History of Islamic Law*. Edinburgh: Edinburgh University Press.

Fernandes, Leonor. 1988. *The Evolution of a Sufi Institution in Mamluk Egypt: The Khanqah*. Berlin: Klaus Schwarz Verlag.

Fierro, Maribel. 1992. "The Treatises against Innovations (*kutub al-bida'*)." *Der Islam* 69: 204–246.

Geoffroy, Eric. 1995. *Le Soufisme en Egypte et en Syrie*. Damascus: Institut Français de Damas.

Gruber, Christiane. 2005. "The Prophet Muhammad's Ascension (Mi'raj) in Islamic Art and Literature, ca. 1300–1600." Ph.D. Dissertation, University of Pennsylvania.

Hobsbawm, Eric. 1983. "Inventing Traditions." Pages 1–14 in *The Invention of Tradition*. Edited by Eric Hobsbawm and Terence Ranger. Cambridge: Cambridge University Press.

Ibn Abi Jamra, 1997. *Bahjat al-nufus* and *al-Mara'i al-hisan*. Vol. 2. Edited by Bakri Shaykh Amin. Beirut: Dar al-'Ilm al-Malayin.

Ibn al-Hajj, Muhammad b. al-Muhammad 'Abdari. 1929. *al-Madkhal*. Vol. 1. Edited by Muhammad Mahmud 'Abd al-Latif. Cairo: al-Matba'a al-Misriyya bi'l-Azhar.

———. 1972. *al-Madkhal*. Vol. 1. 2nd edition. Beirut: Dar al-Kitab al-'Arabi.

Ibn al-Mulaqqin, Siraj al-Din. 1998. *Tabaqat al-Awliya'*. Edited by Mustafa 'Abd al-Qadir 'Ata. Beirut: Dar al-Kutub al-'Ilmiyya.

Juynboll, Gautier H. A. 1983. *Muslim Tradition: Studies in chronology, provenance, and authorship of early hadith*. Cambridge: Cambridge University Press.

Kahhala, 'Umar Reza. 1993. *Mu'jam al-Mu'allifin*. 4 vols. Beirut: Mu'assasat al-Risala.

Katz, Jonathan G. 1992. "Visionary Experience, Autobiography, and Sainthood in North African Islam." *Princeton Papers in Near Eastern Studies* 1: 85–118.

Langner, Barbara. 1983. *Untersuchungen zur historischen Volkskunde Ägyptens nach mamlukischen Quellen*. Berlin: Klaus Schwarz Verlag.

Lincoln, Bruce. 2003. *Holy Terrors: Thinking about Religion after September 11.* Chicago: University of Chicago Press.

Memon, Muhammad Umar. 1976. *Ibn Taimiya's Struggle Against Popular Religion*. The Hague: Mouton.

50   Frederick S. Colby

Northrup, Linda. 1998. "The Bahri Mamluk sultanate, 1250–1390." Pages 242–289 in *The
     Cambridge History of Egypt*. Volume 1: *Islamic Egypt, 640–1517*. Edited by Carl F.
     Petry. Cambridge: Cambridge University Press.
Rispler-Chaim, Vardit. 1991. "Toward a New Understanding of the Term *bid'a*." *Der Islam*
     68: 320–328.
Robson, J. "Bid'a." 1960. Page 1199 in volume 1 of *Encyclopaedia of Islam*. 2nd (new) edition.
     Edited by Hamilton A. R. Gibb et al. Leiden: Brill, 1960–.
Salvatore, Armando (ed.). 2001. *Muslim Traditions and Modern Techniques of Power*. Münster,
     Germany: Lit Verlag.
Schacht, Joseph. 1964. *An Introduction to Islamic Law*. Oxford: Oxford University Press.
Shoshan, Boaz. 1991. "High Culture and Popular Culture in Medieval Islam." *Studia
     Islamica* 73: 67–109.
———. 1993. *Popular Culture in Medieval Cairo*. Cambridge: Cambridge University Press.
Taylor, Christopher. 1999. *In the Vicinity of the Righteous*. Leiden: Brill.
Ukeles, Raquel. 2004. "Comparing Religions One at a Time: Juxtaposing Jewish and
     Islamic law to Illuminate Islamic Normative Practice." Unpublished paper delivered
     at the 2004 Annual Meeting of the American Academy of Religion (San Antonio,
     Tex., November 21, 2004).
Vadet, C. J. 1971. "Ibn al-Hadjdj." Page 779 in volume 3 of *Encyclopaedia of Islam*. 2nd (new)
     edition. Edited by Hamilton A. R. Gibb et al. Leiden: Brill, 1960–.
Waldman, Marilyn Robinson. 1986. "Tradition as a Modality of Change." *History of
     Religions* 25.4 (May): 318–340.
Wensinck, Arent J. 1992. *Concordance et Indices de la Tradition Musulmane*. 2nd edition. 8
     vols. in 4. Leiden: Brill.
Winter, Michael. 1982. *Society and Religion in Early Ottoman Egypt*. New Brunswick, N.J.:
     Transaction Books.

The "Golden Age" of Muslim Spain:
Religious Identity and the Invention of a Tradition in Modern Jewish Studies

Aaron W. Hughes

Introduction

The events of 9/11 have ushered in a renewed interrogation of Islam and its relationship to other religious traditions. In an attempt to show that the "real" Islam could have nothing to do with such horrific events, certain scholars, commentators, and journalists have pointed to the "golden age" of Muslim Spain. They proclaim that this period (ca. 950–1150) provides an example of a liberal Islam that created a culture of tolerance wherein Jews, Muslims, and Christians could live together.[1] According to this reading, all three of these religious traditions engaged in a healthy and competitive relationship, in which Jews and Christians, but especially Jews, drank from the cultural and intellectual waters of Arabo-Islamic civilization and in so doing nourished their own traditions in ways hitherto impossible. Others however have pointed to the same period and have argued exactly the opposite.[2] In particular, the tolerance witnessed in Muslim Spain was, if it even existed, the result of the social uncertainty associated with various warring political factions (the so-called "party kings" or *muluk al-tawāʾif*) and had nothing whatsoever to do with any "real" Islam or official Islamic policy towards minorities. Rather than stress the developments and innovations in the cultural or intellectual spheres, this paradigm prefers to highlight the often-onerous humiliations and burdens placed on non-Muslim minorities. The emphasis is now put on the heavy taxes levied on non-Muslims, the distinctive clothing that non-Muslims had to wear, and various other prohibitions (e.g., general deference, architectural restrictions).

Although both of these hermeneutical strategies make use of the same historical data, they emphasize different aspects and not surprisingly reach radically different conclusions. For example, whereas the more optimistic of these two approaches often emphasizes "great men," such as Shlomo ibn Gabirol (1021–ca. 1058), Judah Halevi (1075–1140), and Moses Maimonides (1135–1204),

---

1   The best recent example of this is Menocal 2003; see also the collection of essays in Mann et al. 1992.
2   See, for example Ye'or 1985; R. Lewis 1977.

the other approach marginalizes such individuals and is more interested in the persecution of Jews as a nameless collectivity (e.g., the massacre of "the Jews" in Granada in 1066). The end result is that Muslim Spain is everywhere, yet nowhere; a trope meaning different things to different interpreters depending upon their previous assumptions of either what "Islam" or "Judaism" is or should be. Muslim Spain thus is a modern construction, providing a prism through which interpreters assign values that correspond to their own ideological concerns.

Like many traditions, that of Muslim Spain is an invented one and of a decidedly modern provenance. For the most part, it corresponds to the modern European intellectual encounter with Islam. Interestingly, many of the earliest constructions of the "golden age" in Muslim Spain originated in scholarship associated with the emergence of Jewish Studies (*Wissenschaft des Judentums*) as an academic discipline in nineteenth-century Germany. In what follows, I attempt to chart some of the processes involved in the various constructions of this "golden age tradition." I have no intention of either wading into the actual debate (i.e., was Muslim Spain tolerant or intolerant) or examining medieval primary sources. My goal, on the contrary, is to peruse the writings of some of the major late nineteenth- and early twentieth-century German-Jewish histor-ians in order to illumine the invention of a tradition. What follows examines the various ways that the tradition of Muslim Spain has been imagined, constructed, reimagined, and manipulated. Instead of taking the "golden age" of Muslim Spain as a historical given, I prefer to map the various social, intel-lectual, and political sites where this tradition was developed and deployed.

The "golden age" of Muslim Spain (Arabic, al-Andalus; Hebrew, ha-Sefarad) has always loomed large in the Jewish imagination. Yet even the term "golden age" is distinctly modern, coined by a non-Jewish Hebraist, Franz Delitzsch,[3] in 1836. Jewish scholars, engaged in wrestling the study of Judaism out of the hands of Christian scholars whom they accused of misrepresenting the tradi-tion for their own apologetical purposes, quickly picked up on this term and subsequently bequeathed it to later generations. These scholars however were not simply engaged in an intellectual endeavor; their struggle in developing and subsequently disseminating the tradition of a "golden age" was directed at two perceived antagonists, one internal and the other external. Internally, the "enlightened" and "cultured" Jews of medieval Spain served as a liberal and intellectual counterpoint to the traditionalism and talmudism that characterized much of nineteenth-century European Jewry. Externally, the creation of the "golden age" of Spanish Jewry was directed at the Prussian authorities and other critics of Judaism. Implicit here was that whenever Jews were historically

---

3   Delitzsch 1836, 44–45. On the place of Delitzsch in the field of Jewish poetry, see
     Davidson 1928, esp. 41–42. Delitzsch, however, had a rather complex relationship to
     Judaism, one of his ultimate goals being the conversion of Jews to Christianity. In this
     regard, see Heschel 1998, 194–198.

granted emancipation, they become active and productive members of society.[4] At this point in history, it is important to remember that Jews were only gradually being accepted into German society and were, for the most part, regarded with extreme suspicion.[5] The tradition of a "golden age" in Muslim Spain was in large part the result of a romantic and ultimately distorted reading, one that put modern assumptions about freedom and equality onto a period in which Jews were but protected minorities and who were religiously and socially subservient to Muslims. Moreover, in stressing the philosophical, literary, and scientific achievements of the "great men" of Muslim Spain, those scholars who subscribed, and indeed continue to subscribe, to this position not only marginalized important developments in fields of *halakhah* (Jewish law) in Spain but also ignored contemporaneous creativity in other Jewish cultures.[6]

In what follows I examine four different constructions of the "golden age." These constructions—chronologically by Abraham Geiger, Heinrich Graetz, Yitzhak Fritz Baer, and Shlomo Dov Goitein—represent some of the earliest conceptualizations of what comprised this "golden age." Constructions by subsequent scholars, for the most part, build upon the foundations laid by these four thinkers. For each one of these individuals offered a distinct vision of what constituted the "essence" of Judaism, what the "tradition" of Muslim Spain consisted of, and to what uses this "tradition" could be put in the present. Some of these thinkers held the Jewish experience in medieval Spain up as the beacon for modern Jewish emancipation. Others however regarded the cultural and intellectual achievements of such elite Jews as inauthentic and therefore far removed from true Jewish piety. What all of these constructions share though is the assumption that there was a "golden age tradition" of Muslim Spain and that, however defined, it provided important lessons for modern Jewish existence.

The Uses and Abuses of "Tradition": Defining Terms

Central to group identity and legitimation is the concept of "tradition." "Tradition" or "traditional" however are terms or categories that are often taken for granted in the discourse of religious studies. If tradition represents a response to the onslaught of modernity, it, paradoxically, becomes a distinctly modern creation. Or, has the traditional always existed? In which case it is amorphous, but becomes identifiable once it is put in counterpoint with something "untraditional." What both of these accounts have in common is that "tradition" is a response to some other variable (e.g., modernity, the "non-traditional") and as such is heavily weighted with ideological factors.

---

4   See the important comments in Cohen 1994, esp. ch. 1.
5   In this regard, see the studies of Meyer 1967, esp. 115–143; Sorkin 1987, 13–40.
6   Marcus 1985. In employing the term "Jewish cultures," I am influenced by Shmueli 1990, 10–42.

With its ability to ground the ambiguity of the present within various contexts imbued with the familiarity of the past, tradition has the propensity to formulate the "really real" for its practitioners. In a world perceived to be in a state of flux, tradition provides the one constant necessary to encounter the quotidian (see, in this regard, Hughes 2003). In what follows, I use "tradition" as a modern construct, something that effectively allows a particular group to inscribe themselves and their values on an earlier time or space. This temporal or spatial period is subsequently upheld as the standard by which to live in the present. Although, "tradition" is ostensibly about the past, it actually is a response to modernity and contemporaneous concerns. Likewise, my working definition of "golden age" is an era or epoch that has become so romanticized and idealized that it ceases to be a historical reality. In dealing with religion, it is a term that is as much theological as it is historical. The "golden age" thus often functions as an inverse mirror of the present.

In his classic study of tradition—its invention, use, and manipulation—Eric Hobsbawm contends that "insofar as there is such a reference to a historic past, the peculiarity of 'invented' traditions is that the continuity with it is largely factitious" (Hobsbawm 1983, 2). Within this context, tradition is never handed down from heaven *ex nihilo*; nor is it, despite appeals to the contrary, something that subsequent groups and/or practitioners passively accept and follow. Tradition, on the contrary, is the site of active construction, around which circulate a number of competing, even hostile, political, social, ideological, and cultural forces. Although they differ in their respective goals and mandates, common to all traditions is the claim to an ontology rooted in the distant and ancient past.

Traditions, despite claiming a connection to the past, are social creations embedded in the present to justify or validate a particular ideological or political claim. According to Hobsbawm, the invention of tradition occurs most frequently in times of rapid social transformation (Hobsbawm 1983, 4). Whenever old social patterns are undermined or destroyed, it becomes necessary to develop new models to ground the changing and the ambiguous.[7] This is often done by cloaking these new models, new ideas, or new actions in ways that are easily perceived or recognized to be "old" and "timeless."

Historical Introduction:
Wissenschaft and the Transformation of German Jewry

The intellectual milieu of the nineteenth-century German academy was composed of a number of complex and overlapping trajectories. These included, *inter alia*, historicism, idealism, higher Biblical criticism, and the development

---

7   This theme has been explored in a number of important studies by Jonathan Z. Smith. See, in particular, his *To Take Place: Toward Theory in Ritual* (1987).

of the *religionsgeschichtliche Schule*. All of these trajectories, not to mention the negative repercussions of anti-Semitism associated with German Romanticism, left an indelible mark on German-Jewish scholars. Indeed, one could quite easily make the case that the formation of Jewish Studies as an academic discipline was tantamount to the absorption of the aforementioned trajectories in order to understand Judaism from a non-religious perspective. In employing these various trajectories, these Jewish scholars were making a major break from the way in which Judaism had hitherto been conceived.[8] By subjecting the religion to the categories supplied by the nineteenth-century German academy, they effectively overturned Judaism's non-historical mode of thought. This was not simply an academic exercise; at stake for many of these scholars was the very survival and florescence of Judaism in the modern world.

The rise of Jewish Studies therefore was intimately connected to various ideological and political concerns, at the forefront of which was the emancipation of Jews and the development of an aesthetically pleasing construction of Judaism. Although admitted as students at German universities, Jews were ultimately prohibited, either by decree or convention, from teaching at such institutions (see Myers 1995, 21ff.). Not surprisingly, Jewish Studies and Jewish topics, with the exception of the "Old Testament," were excluded from the university curriculum. Those Jewish scholars who graduated from German universities with higher degrees (often in Oriental Studies) would push, with little success, for the development of courses in Jewish topics. The desire for integration of Jewish Studies within German universities thus became a metaphor for general Jewish emancipation and acceptance into mainstream German society.[9]

German-Jewish scholars absorbed the Protestant-inspired categories of the day, especially those dealing with the relationship between history and nation, and began to apply them to Judaism. The result was an academy within an academy since Jewish voices were completely marginalized within the German university system. There were essentially two options open to promising young Jewish intellectuals in this period: either convert or teach at a Jewish day school or rabbinic seminary.[10] Despite the fact that Jews were prohibited

---

8   There were of course important precursors to these scholars, most important are Nachman Krochmal and Moses Mendelssohn. For important studies that connect these individuals to the modern study of Judaism, see Harris 1991; Altmann 1973. Baruch Spinoza is another important individual in this regard, but his relations to Judaism were extremely complicated, culminating in his *herem* ("excommunication") on July 27, 1656. In this regard, see Nadler 1999, 116–154.

9   See, for example, the comments in Geiger 1836, 6. Moreover, Leopold Zunz petitioned the Prussian authorities three times in the 1840s to create a chair in Jewish history or literature at a German university. All three petitions were rejected.

10   Just as importantly, Jewish scholars were shut out of the German scholarly journals of the day because they were either devoted solely to Protestant or Catholic scholars. For example, *Zeitschrift für wissenschaftliche Theologie* was devoted to Catholic theology written by Catholic theologians. As such, Protestants or Jews were not allowed to

from teaching at German universities, this period ushered in a new way of thinking about Judaism as Jewish scholars engaged in a full-scale historical investigation of Jewish topics. Although they, along with their non-Jewish colleagues, claimed to be working in the objective spirit of *Wissenschaft*, their historical investigations were imbued with various ideological assumptions about the nature of history, peoplehood, and the way in which they intersected. The goal of these researches then was not simply confined to the past but was intimately connected to present and future concerns (Myers 1997, 707).

Before proceeding to the various ways in which these scholars imagined and constructed the "golden age" of the Jews in Muslim Spain, it might be worthwhile to examine briefly some of the operating assumptions of German historiography, something to which all of the scholars below were indebted. Under the guise of *Wissenschaft*, German scholars created a paradigm of the humanities (*Geisteswissenschaften*) grounded in the myth of "facts" and the objective description of them.[11] Within this context, tradition—that which was perceived to define the essence of a particular nation or group (*Volk*)—was something often taken for granted.[12] The "science" (*Wissenschaft*) of history, grounded in the "rigorous, technical and specialized" accumulation of facts (Novick 1988, 24), does not correspond exactly to modern notions of history. These facts though were not simply to be described, but to be understood as the unfolding of God's plan *qua* World Spirit (*Geist*).[13] As such, the study of history was not utilitarian but intimately caught up in the attempt to construct seminal periods of the past in order to rejuvenate a people or a "race" in the modern period.[14] History thus became the means by which a group or *Volk* could articulate its own identity by knowing and grasping its essence. Intimately connected to this was the notion of Idealism, which regarded ideas as the substance and motivator of history. Although such ideas are only visible in manifested forms, the World Spirit was perceived as unfolding most perfectly in Christianity. Subsequent attempts to depict a Christian and/or a German essence often coincided with carving out an ontological space for them in ways that were independent or untouched by other ethnic groups (especially that of the Jews).[15] Although

---

publish in them. In order to respond to attacks or criticisms by Christian scholars, Jews had to write in their own journals, which rarely had a circulation beyond a very limited audience.

11 The classic study of this is Novick 1988.

12 Such traditions were usually intertwined with the mythic. For an excellent account of the ideology of myth and its interpretation, consult Lincoln 1999, esp. ch. 3.

13 See, e.g., Hegel's introduction to his *Philosophy of History* (Hegel 1953); von Ranke 1973.

14 See, for example, Anrich 1956; Schelling 1966, esp. 34ff.

15 See Mack 2003, 1–16. The fact that Jesus was a Jew caused many of these historians a great deal of problems. Some even went so far as to suggest that Jesus' racial identity was probably Aryan and that his real goal was the destruction of Judaism. Such views, not surprisingly, became increasingly popular, culminating in the mythology of the Third Reich. See the discussion in Heschel 1998, 11–12.

Jewish historians were critical of this attempt to sever Christianity from its Jewish sources, they nevertheless absorbed many of the assumptions of this discourse and used the same categories to create a "Jewish History" (see the comments in Schorsch 1975, 2–9).

Any historical "reconstruction" is based on an intricate system of presences and absences that, more often than not, privileges one reading at the expense of others.[16] In their endeavor to re-create the Jewish past, many German-Jewish scholars attempted to make Judaism in their own ideological images. Perhaps this is best witnessed in what is generally regarded as the manifesto of *Wissenschaft des Judentums*, Leopold Zunz's "Etwas über die rabbinische Literatur."[17] For Zunz, the goal of historical research is "to recognize and distinguish among the old and the useful, the obsolete and the harmful, the new and the desirable" (Zunz 1995, 222). The subsequent historical researches of German-Jewish scholars represent a number of attempts to define the inner spirit of the Jewish nation and the various ways in which this spirit manifested itself historically. Anything that did not fit with their notion of what Judaism should be was marginalized or discarded.

One of the central components that contributed to the formation of Jewish identity in the nineteenth century was the "golden age" of Muslim Spain. Here it is important to remember that Jewish historical scholarship was, especially among the first generation of scholars, intimately connected to reforming Judaism. Such a reformation would be possible only if one could ascertain, by means of *Wissenschaft*, that (1) there existed an eternal essence of Judaism (which was variously defined), and (2) there also existed other features that were not essential and thus susceptible to change. Many of these scholars/reformers contrasted the "shtetl-like" mentality and particularism of *contemporary* Eastern European Jews (the Ashkenazim) with the cosmopolitan and universal nature of the *medieval* Jews of Spain (the Sephardim). In many ways, the interest in the Sephardim was influenced by the contemporaneous German fascination with the Orient.[18] But whereas Germans were bedazzled by the civilizations of

---

16 On this trope in writing about religion more generally, see the comments in Gold 2003.

17 Found in his *Gesammelte Schriften*, vol. 1, 1–31. An English translation of this important essay is "On Rabbinic Literature" (Zunz 1995). Quotations come from the English translation.

18 Mendes-Flohr 1991. Edward Said curiously omits any discussion of German Orientalists in his *Orientalism* (1978). His excuse is that Germany did not possess colonial holdings in the Middle East and, therefore, German scholarship did not have the same ideological overtones as that produced in France or England. However, all of the major nineteenth-century scholarship on Islam was produced by German scholars, many of whom were Jewish. Said succeeds then in effectively writing out, for his own ideological reasons, the contributions of Jews (themselves a "colonized" group within Europe) in his attempt to write a historiography of Islamic Studies. Important corrections may be found in B. Lewis 1973; also, see the important collection of essays edited by Martin Kramer (1999). See the methodological comments in Heschel 1998, 19–22.

China and India, German-Jews were captivated by medieval Spanish Jewry whose ancestors were scattered throughout North Africa and the Middle East after the expulsion of 1492. The great paradox was that these German-Jewish intellectuals were, despite being acculturated to the intellectual and aesthetic ideals of modern Germany, Ashkenazim themselves. The result was the Ashkenazic construction of the "Sephardic experience," one that glorified the philosophical, cultural, aesthetic, and theological supremacy of the Jews of Muslim Spain, while at the same time downplaying the achievements of the Jews of Central and Eastern Europe (Schorsch 1989, 71).

For these German-Jewish scholars, this romanticized and idealized fascination with Muslim Spain became the model for contemporary reform, which they thought would provide the key to acceptance and emancipation. In so doing, they constructed a dichotomy: whereas the growth of their unenlightened Eastern European Jewish compatriots was stunted by the casuistry of talmudic law, the great intellectuals of Muslim Spain engaged in philosophical, grammatical, and poetic studies.[19] The "golden age" of Spain thus held the key to a Jewish renaissance in the modern world. The Jewish experience in Muslim Spain, according to their reading, was based on decidedly modern concerns. In many ways, however, it had to be, for without a Jewish model for intellectual and political emancipation, these scholars/reformers would have been unable to challenge the non-historicist paradigm of Judaism and its ideals of Jewish life (Schorsch 1989, 78).

This myth of Sephardic supremacy was not confined to the Jewish intelligentsia of Germany. The mystique of Spain soon trickled down into all areas of life. Jewish reformers, for example, regarded the prayer books and *piyyutim* (liturgical poetry) associated with Ashkenazic practice as unedifying and artless. In their stead, they attempted to replace them with Sephardic-inspired liturgy, melodies, and pronunciation. Moreover, this period in Germany also saw the increased popularity of the Moorish style in synagogue architecture. The 1850s and 1860s, for example witnessed the construction of "Moorish" synagogues in Leipzig, Frankfurt, Cologne, Mainz, Budapest, Berlin, and Vienna (Schorsch 1989, 79).

The Jews of Muslim Spain became for the German Jewish scholars and reformers what the Greeks were to German scholars (see, for example, Butler 1958). For the latter, the Greeks represented the epitome, and thus the ideal, of human civilization. Germans would do well, according to these scholars, to emulate the Greeks.[20] Yet in their overzealous attempt to re-create the ideal of Greece in contemporary Germany, such individuals read Greek history,

---

19 This, of course, ignores the fact that the greatest achievement in rabbinic law (the *Mishneh Torah*) was created in Muslim Spain by an individual who was also regarded as the greatest Jewish philosopher, Moses ben Maimon, better known as Maimonides.

20 For an interesting case study full of ideological implications, see Lincoln 1999a.

philosophy, and literature selectively. All that fit with the ideological concerns of the German intelligentsia was allowed to remain; all that did not was conveniently expurgated. The Greeks that these German scholars idolized therefore were not real Greeks, but idealized and romanticized constructs that represented the shining goal to which German civilization should aspire (Butler 1958, 80–81). In like manner, medieval Spanish Jewry became the intellectual and cultural forbearers to these German-Jewish scholars/reformers, who were responsible for constructing a "tradition" to show both their Jewish and non-Jewish contemporaries that Judaism need not be "backwards."

The Tradition of Golden Age Spain, Take One: The Universalist Construction of Abraham Geiger

Abraham Geiger (1810–1874),[21] the intellectual founder of Reform Judaism, spent most of his life attempting to establish a place for the scientific study of Judaism within the modern German university, while holding down rabbinic positions in Breslau and later Frankfurt. Like most of his Jewish colleagues he had absorbed the *Wissenschaft* categories of German historicism and spent much of his life attempting to apply them to Judaism. Although critical of German theologians who imported religious assumptions into their "historical" researches, Geiger himself had his own assumptions of what Judaism was and should be. Whereas much of traditional Jewish self-understanding was predicated on the perceived uniqueness of the Jews, Geiger emphasized Judaism's universality (see Funkenstein 1993, 20ff.). For him, the key to understanding Western civilization resided in Judaism and Jewish values. Whereas many German theologians instead located such universality in Christianity, Geiger argued that it originally resided in Judaism from where it was eventually absorbed into Christianity during the Late Antique period. A theme that weaves throughout Geiger's diverse *oeuvre* is that both Christianity and Islam were derivative from Judaism and therefore both received their messages and central ideas from Jewish sources and practices.

Geiger quickly came to the attention of non-Jewish thinkers when as a doctoral student he submitted an essay in a competition sponsored by the faculty of philosophy at the University of Bonn. The competition was devoted to the subject: *Inquiratur in fontes Alcorani seu legis Mohammeicae eas qui ex Judaismo derivandi sunt* ("An enquiry into the sources of the Qur'ān derived from Judaism"). The young Geiger won the prize and his essay subsequently secured for him a doctorate from the University of Marburg. Enlarged and translated into

---

21 Requisite biographies may be found in L. Geiger 1910; Wiener 1981, 3–80; Lassner 1999; Heschel 1998, 23–49.

German as *Was hat Mohammed aus dem Judenthume aufgenommen?*,[22] Geiger's thesis was that Muhammad consciously looked to the Jews when he established his own religion.[23] Since Muhammad would not have had direct access to Jewish texts, the subsequent message of the Qur'ān in particular, and Islam in general, is, according to his reading, a distortion of Jewish themes that nevertheless enabled Muhammad to authenticate his message.[24]

Geiger's methodology was based on the necessity of understanding religious texts within their immediate historical, intellectual, and social contexts. He would subsequently take the method he used in his doctoral thesis and apply it to an understanding of Christianity and Judaism. His goal, motivated in large part by ideological concerns, was to demonstrate the evolutionary nature of Judaism. In particular if he could demonstrate that the aridity of the rabbinic period was but one point on the evolutionary grid of Judaism, then it could be naturally superseded in the modern world. Geiger's academic goals were thus identical to his religious goals (see Schorsch 1990), both of which were predicated on the notion that the normative sources of rabbinic Judaism could be revised because they were not an essential part of the religion (see Myers 1995, 20ff.). In order to bolster his case, he looked to the spiritual and intellectual achievements of medieval Spanish Jewry.

Muslim Spain, according to Geiger's construction, was the shining light in an otherwise dark landscape of medieval Judaism brought on by the aridity of the rabbinic tradition. Muslim Spain represented a temporary reversal in what he otherwise characterized as Judaism's general state of devolution.[25] In particular, Geiger contrasted the civilizational achievements of the Jews in Spain with what he considered to be the cultural and intellectual barrenness of the Ashkenazic Jews in Eastern and Northern Europe.[26] The grounds for contrast were manifold. Whereas the Ashkenazim were characterized by an individual-less community, the "degenerate" language of Yiddish, and a propensity for mystical speculation, the Sephardim consisted of famous individuals ("great men"), were responsible for the renaissance of Hebrew as a literary and

---

22 Bonn 1833. The German literally translates as "What did Muhammad borrow from Judaism?" The book, however, was translated into English with the more innocuous title *Judaism and Islam* (1970).

23 See the comments in Pearlman 1970; Lassner 1999, 106–118.

24 A. Geiger 1970, 17–21. Despite the fact that Geiger claimed that Muhammad was the author of the Qur'ān, his portrayal of Muhammad and Islam was positive, especially when compared with contemporaneous non-Jewish treatments. Indeed, Geiger was criticized by many for his overly positive portrayal of Muhammad and his message.

25 E.g., A. Geiger, *Das Judentum und seine Geschichte* (1871). An English translation may be found in A. Geiger, *Judaism and Its History in Two Parts* (1985), 286–288, 354–362. All citations to this work are from the English translation. Also see A. Geiger 1867, 4–14. For secondary literature, consult Meyer 1975.

26 See the citations in the previous note.

religious language, and made important innovations in philosophy, science, and poetry.[27] Geiger writes of Medieval Spain:

> Let us imagine as present, the three brilliant centuries as they passed before our eyes. What magnificent results that period offers to us! Science is not only nurtured, it is enriched in every relation. Knowledge of the Hebrew language rises into science and attains a degree which has not been passed until the last century. Interpretation and explanation of Scripture enter deep into its meaning and stimulate the greatest problems. Philosophy becomes common property, and though it is not creative, it is yet ennobling and enlightening. (A. Geiger 1985, 352)

This passage is significant for a number of reasons. Primary is that Geiger holds up Muslim Spain not so much as a period long past but as the touchstone of Jewish existence *until his own day*. Spanish Jewry, according to this construction, becomes the paradigm for modern Jewish florescence. Geiger thus creates a number of structural parallels between the Jews of Spain and those enlightened Jews of his own day. Just as the great Jewish grammarians of medieval Spain had rediscovered the beauty of the Hebrew language, so too had his own Jewish scholarly contemporaries. Geiger held the scholars of Muslim Spain in such high esteem because of their interest in the literal meaning of the Biblical text and their unwillingness to follow blindly the interpretive flights of fancy of rabbinic literature (e.g., A. Geiger 1981). The Jews of Muslim Spain were not a nameless and persecuted mass, the passive objects of history, but a strong community led by individuals who were models of emulation not only for Jews but for all of humanity. Medieval Spanish Jewry thus

> produced men who have remained bright stars at all times. On Ibn Ezra, Spinoza grew up. Maimonides was the teacher of the whole Middle Ages, and every enlightened mind that arose later, drew eagerly from him, found stimulation in him, and gladly acknowledged himself his pupil. (A. Geiger 1985, 352–353)

Geiger, like many of those associated with *Wissenschaft des Judentums*, was particularly fond of Shlomo ibn Gabirol, the famous poet and philosopher.[28] Geiger compares him—and his beautiful, consecrated, and thoughtful poetry—favorably to his own contemporaries. For example, Geiger distinguishes him from Wagner, whom he describes as "self-complacent" and "superficial" (A. Geiger 1985, 307). Similarly when ibn Gabirol is compared to Schopenhauer, Geiger argues that although both have a similar theory of will the latter "stands far below [ibn Gabirol] in moral enthusiasm and depth of investigation" (315).

---

27 Spain, however, was the birthplace of the mystical work *par excellence* in Judaism, the *Zohar*. Despite this, many of the *Wissenschaft des Judentums* scholars considered Jewish mysticism to be an aberration. See the critique in Scholem 1979.

28 Geiger devotes an entire book to ibn Gabirol: *Salomo Gabirol und seine Dichtungen* (1867).

Despite the fact that Jews of medieval Spain lived under Muslim rule, Geiger is not particularly interested in Islam. Indeed, his construction of Islam, according to Heschel (1998, 57), is as much a construction of Judaism. What made Islam hospitable to the Jews at certain times and places in its history was its universal and liberal tendencies, both of which Geiger had already argued derived from Jewish sources in the first place. When Islam is at its most tolerant, Geiger implies, it most closely resembles Judaism. In dealing with the Jews of Muslim Spain he tends to represent Islam as nothing more than the general backdrop against which Jews were able to engage in an extremely creative moment of their history. He signals out the willingness to leave Jews alone as the greatest virtue that the rulers of Muslim Spain possessed:

> Islam rendered great service to Judaism by leaving to it room; it did not go in advance of it in everything and could not offer everything to it, but it gave it room for the development of its powers. And thus we look back upon that illustrious time as a brilliant period of Judaism. (A. Geiger 1985, 352)

Implicit here of course is not only a criticism of medieval Christianity, but, more pointedly, a criticism of the German authorities of his own day. If Jews are not persecuted and are given room to develop, they will become productive members of society, producing individuals with the magnitude of Maimonides or ibn Gabirol. Geiger thus holds up the "golden age" of Muslim Spain not so much as a historical moment in Judaism that has long departed, but as a construct serving as the basis for Jewish renewal in the modern period.

The Tradition of Golden Age Spain, Take Two: The Nationalist Construction of Heinrich Graetz

In the earliest years of *Wissenschaft des Judentums*, the historical method and its radical re-reading of Judaism was predominantly used in the service of reforming Judaism—religiously, liturgically, and aesthetically (see the comments in Schorsch 1975, 25ff.). Although Heinrich Graetz (1817–1891)[29] was arguably the most important nineteenth-century Jewish historian, he was radically opposed to the program of reform-minded scholars and their philosophy of Jewish history. One of the explicit goals of Graetz's multi-volume *Geschichte der Juden* ("History of the Jews") was to provide an alternative reading of Jewish history. Just as reform-minded scholars turned to history to validate their claims, Graetz, looking at the same data, attempted to show the illegitimacy of such claims.

Whereas reform-minded scholars stressed the universal character of Judaism and defined its essence as its confessional or universal character (Schorsch

---

29 The best biography of Graetz remains Meisl 1917; also, see Schorsch 1975, 31–62.

1975, 39), Graetz declared that Judaism was comprised of a twofold essence consisting of both a political and a religious dimension (Graetz 1975, 71). This nationalist definition—stressing both the Torah and the Land of Israel—led Graetz to divide Jewish history into three distinct periods. The first period ended with the destruction of the temple in 587 BCE, the middle period ended with the destruction of the second temple in 70 CE, and the final period continues to the present. Whereas reform scholars envisaged an evolutionary schema in the unfolding of Jewish history, Graetz argued for a cyclical pattern, in which earlier phases are never completely transcended (Schorsch 1975, 44).

Graetz's desire was to compose an overarching history of the Jewish nation.[30] Within this context, he was extremely critical of Christian historians who refused to grant the Jews a history beyond the destruction of the temple in 70 CE; for them, Judaism was nothing more that the *mis en scène* of Jesus and early Christianity. Graetz on the contrary aimed to create a "story of a single people, still very much alive, whose unique historical experience spanned some three millennia" (Schorsch 1975, 51). Like the majority of his contemporary non-Jewish historians, Graetz's conception of history was not devoid of broader ideological concerns; his goal was to create a new national consciousness based on a common national identity that could be retrieved in history. This national history of the Jews however would not just be a pariah history but would be crucial for understanding the various themes of general history. Following Geiger (although the two were extremely critical of each other), he argued that Jewish sources were crucial to understanding the full development of early Christianity (Graetz 1889/90). Likewise the rise of Islam in seventh-century Arabia was incomprehensible without due attention to the Jewish tribes and Jewish sources of the area.[31]

Despite the fact that Geiger and Graetz differed radically in terms of their respective ideologies of Judaism, they did agree on the "golden age tradition" of the Jews in Muslim Spain. According to Graetz,

> Judaism ever strove towards the light while monastic Christianity remained in the darkness. Thus in the tenth century there was only one country that offered suitable soil for the development of Judaism where it could blossom and flourish—it was Mahometan Spain. (Graetz 1894, 214)

The Jewish experience in Muslim Spain, according to Graetz's idealized reading, was characterized by its inner spirituality, religious vitality, and its desire for scientific and philosophical knowledge. This was, for him as for Geiger, a bright

---

30 He was not, however, the first to do this. Isaak Marcus Jost wrote a 12-volume work entitled *Geschichte der Israeliten* between 1820 and 1847. See the comments in Meyer 1967, 170–173; Schorsch 1977.

31 Heinrich Graetz, *Geschichte der Juden von den ältesten Zeiten bis auf die Gegenwart*, 11 vols. (1853–1876). This was translated into English as *History of the Jews*, 6 vols. (1891–1898). Here Graetz 1894, 53–85. All citations come from the English translation.

spot in the otherwise bleak Middle Ages and was historically unsurpassed at least until the present (i.e., the time in which Graetz himself was writing). Graetz affirms the products of Jewish culture in Muslim Spain in the following manner:

> The first half of the twelfth century produced a vast number of clever men in Jewish circles, poets, philosophers, Talmudists, and almost all their labors bore the mark of perfection. The Jewish culture of this period resembled a garden, rich in odorous blossoms and luscious fruits, whose productions, though varied in color and taste, have their root in the same earth... The poets eulogized each other, and cordially praised the men that devoted their powers to other intellectual work. They took the greatest interest in one another's successes, consoled one another in misfortune, and regarded one another as members of one family. (Graetz 1894, 313–314)

In this passage Graetz wistfully romanticizes the spiritual and religious *unity* of Spanish Jewry. What he perceives to be the *raison d'être* for their greatness is, on a fundamental level, the exact opposite of what threatened the Jewish community of his own day, which was wracked by warring ideological factions and in danger of permanent fragmentation. Graetz holds up the Jewish community of medieval Spain as the shining example of what a united Jewish community could achieve. Once again this is not simply a historical construct, but an example that must be emulated by his contemporaries. Graetz's audience is essentially twofold. On the one hand, to his fellow Jews by warning them that fragmentation stands in the way of Jewish redemption, whether historical or messianic;[32] on the other hand, to German leaders by telling them that they have much to gain by granting Jews political emancipation.

One of the key individuals that Graetz focused on was the Jewish poet Shlomo ibn Gabirol. But whereas Geiger had emphasized the poetic and sacred components of ibn Gabirol's *oeuvre*, Graetz is more interested in his philosophical and scientific legacy. In the following passage, Graetz shows not only the debt that Western civilization owes to Gabirol (and by extension the Jews), but also how this contrasts with medieval Christendom:

> It is true that the leading ideas of ibn Gabirol's system had been expressed by earlier philosophers, but he formed into one organic whole a confused mass of scattered thoughts... A Christian emperor destroyed the temple of philosophy in Athens, and exiled its last priests. Since that time philosophy had been outlawed in Europe... The Jewish thinker, ibn Gabirol, was the first to transplant it again to Europe, and he built an altar to it in Spain, where it found a permanent habitation. (Graetz 1894, 270)

Although he spends a considerable amount of time on the history of Muslim Spain, Graetz is also not particularly interested in the Arab or Islamic component

---

32   On Graetz's messianism, see Schorsch 1975, 43ff.

of that history except in so far as it serves as the backdrop to his own drama. On the whole Graetz is generally critical of Arabs, despite the fact that Jews enjoyed comparatively more freedom under Muslim rule than they did under the Christians.[33] In many ways this is in keeping with Graetz's larger theme of persecution. He does not then hesitate to focus on Muslim persecutions of the Jews.[34] Yet despite this he argues that Muslim hostilities against the Jews were far less severe than in Christianity. For example, even though he focuses on the slaughter of the Jews in Granada in 1066, he is quick to mention that it "had no effect, however, upon the Jewish inhabitants of other parts of Spain" (Graetz 1894, 279). Indeed he is less willing to blame such persecutions on the leaders of Granada as the "fanatical Mahometans" of the rank and file (Graetz 1894, 257).

Graetz further contributes to the myth of the "golden age tradition" in Muslim Spain. This tradition provided a convenient counterpoint to the plight of Judaism in his own day. In this respect, Graetz and Geiger share, despite their personal hostilities, a common goal: to demonstrate that Jews deserve emancipation in Germany and that, if granted, they will easily integrate themselves into mainstream society. Although Graetz and Geiger have different ideas concerning the philosophy of Jewish history, both bought into and further articulated the myth of the supremacy of the Jews in medieval Spain and how, based on their readings, it could serve as the catalyst for Jewish renewal in the present.

The Tradition of Golden Age Spain, Take Three: The Negative Construction of Fritz Yitzhak Baer

Yitzhak Fritz Baer (1888–1980) was born in Germany but subsequently migrated to what was then Palestine in 1930.[35] Baer therefore was at the forefront of a generation of scholars responsible for transplanting the ideals of German *Wissenschaft* into a new environment at the emerging Hebrew University of Jerusalem (see Mosse 1996; Myers 1996). There Baer became the founder of the Department of Jewish History and a co-founder of the "Jerusalem School" of Israeli historiography.[36] Unlike Geiger and Graetz, Baer was generally uninterested in questions of religious reform within Judaism. Indeed he was generally critical of his predecessors for holding a monothetic dimension of Jewish history; rather, Baer focused on traditionally marginalized topics such as messianism and class conflict.

Moreover Baer was not interested *per se* in an overarching history of the Jewish people; his main scholarly contribution was the two-volume *A History*

---

33   See, for example, Graetz 1894, 88.
34   See, for example, Graetz 1894, 311ff.
35   For requisite biographical studies, see the essays in Beinart et al. 1983; Ettinger et al. 1980; Myers 1995, ch. 5.
36   See the extended study of this school in Myers 1995, esp. 129–150, and Myers 1994.

of the Jews in Christian Spain, first published in Hebrew in 1945 (and subsequently revised in 1959).[37] As the title demonstrates, although Baer's main focus is Spain, he is most interested in the Christian as opposed to the Muslim backdrop. Despite his criticism of earlier Jewish historians and their philosophies of history, Baer was not immune from trying to apprehend the "inner causality" of Jewish history by examining "the unique force guiding it, a force whose initial vitality is universally recognized and whose future course arouses widespread interest" (Baer 1961, 1). This, according to David Myers, created a tension as Baer, like earlier Jewish historians, tried to mediate the ambiguity between studying Jews within local contexts on the one hand, while also acknowledging the immanent features of Jewish historical development on the other (Myers 1995, 146).

One of the overriding themes of Baer's early scholarship was his emphasis on the central role of Christianity in shaping the cultural and intellectual spheres of Judaism.[38] As a result, he was generally critical of any notion of a "golden age" in Muslim Spain. For him the synergy between Jew and Muslim, especially in the realm of poetry and philosophy, was an inauthentic form of Jewish expression created by a religiously lax courtier class:

> The Hebrew poetry of this period reflects primarily the life of the upper classes, the bourgeoisie and courtiers, who enjoyed their life, tasted the pleasures of wine, women, palaces and gardens, and pursued the literary arts and the sciences. (Baer 1961, 37)

These courtier Jews, Baer goes on to explain, reflected neither the majority of Spanish Jews nor Jews in general. In keeping with his emphasis on class-consciousness, he argues that elite cultural forms cannot form the centerpiece in a proper understanding of Jewish history. For example, he claims that

> Jewish communal leadership was in the hands of a small group of men of wealth and education who were influential at court. The Jewish court official of this period, like those who served in a similar capacity in the courts of Christian monarchs later on, were the owners of large estates and even entire villages. But the Jewish masses derived their livelihood from the cultivation of fields and orchards, from manufacture and handicraft. (Baer 1961, 37)

Whereas historians like Geiger and Graetz held the scholars and poets of medieval Spain in high esteem, Baer chastizes them for their distance from the "Jewish masses." Not coincidentally it was the same "Jewish masses" who in Baer's own day were responsible for the recreation of a Jewish homeland in the

---

37 For the purposes of this study, I use the two-volume English translation by Louis Schoffman (Baer 1961).

38 I say early, because later in life Baer shifted his attentions from the Middle Ages back to the world of antiquity, where he perceived a vibrant and authentic Jewish culture divorced from any Christian influences. See the study of Yuval 1998.

land of Israel.[39] Rather than celebrate the fruits of the Jewish-Muslim encounter in Muslim Spain, Baer seems to favor the simplicity and Talmud-centrism of Eastern European Jewry:

> Jewish culture in Muslim Spain was guided by a line of thinking different from that of the authors of the Mishna and expressed itself in a way of life different from that of the pietists of German Jewry who died a martyr's death for their faith... The cultural activity fostered by the courtiers was allowed to flourish only through the neglect and the religious and moral laxity of the rulers, and not as a result of the definite policy of tolerance and individual freedom. In the south and in the north, both in Islam and in Christianity, nationalist and religious movements, primitive in character, were forming, which were due to make an end of the existing laxity. (Baer 1961, 37–38)

Baer was particularly critical of what he considered to be a tendency among cosmopolitan Spanish Jews to convert to Christianity in times of crises. He put this tendency in marked contrast with the Ashkenazic preference to embrace martyrdom.[40] Whereas Geiger and Graetz constructed the tradition of a "golden age" in medieval Spain in order to show the greatness that Jews could attain when granted civil and legal rights, Baer is highly critical of such a construction. Significantly though he looks at the same data as they do, but filters it through a completely different hermeneutic. The result however is an equally artificial construction. For Baer, the preoccupation with poetry and philosophy in medieval Spain was inauthentic and when examined historically had negative repercussions on Spanish Jewry. Rather than regard the "golden age" of Muslim Spain as the epitome of Jewish civilization, he regarded it as tantamount to the disappearance of traditional Jewish life that had sustained Jews for centuries. This was in keeping with his assumption to "reconfigure Jewish history to Zionist criteria" (Myers 1995, 148).

A major preoccupation for Baer, especially in his later years, was the negative repercussions of *galut* ("exile") on the Jewish people. Authentic Jewish existence, for Baer, could not take place amidst the dangers and persecutions of exile, but only in the land of Israel where Jews could live without such worries. Muslim Spain thus represents for Baer one more chapter in the Jewish experience of exile. This is evident in the individual that he singles out as his model in Muslim Spain. Whereas Geiger and Graetz were fond of pointing to the cultural and intellectual achievements of ibn Gabirol, Baer frequently emphasizes the life and thought of Judah Halevi (1075–1140; Baer 1970, 39–46). Halevi was an important individual who, despite being one of the best secular court poets of his generation, ultimately left the glamour of Spain in order to

---

39   On the tension between the Hebrew University and the Zionist ideal of agricultural labor at this time, see Shapira 1996.

40   Here Baer shares the assumption of David Gans in his *Zemah David* ("The Shoot of David") published in 1592.

set sail for Israel "to teach his contemporaries and all who came after him that redemption may be won only by a real and active longing for reunion with God in Palestine—that man himself must create the conditions that will lead to redemption."[41] This of course was exactly what Baer himself did in 1930.

The Tradition of Golden Age Spain, Take Four: The Symbiotic Construction of S. D. Goitein

Shlomo Dov Goitein was born in 1900 in Bavaria and in 1923 he emigrated to Palestine. In 1928 he became a lecturer in the history of Islam and Muslim peoples at the Hebrew University of Jerusalem. In 1970 he moved to the U.S. where he was appointed professor of Arabic at the University of Pennsylvania, and then later became a fellow at the Institute for Advanced Study at Princeton.[42] Although Goitein's publications touched on a number of areas, in particular the Cairo Genizah (or synagogue storeroom),[43] the major theme that runs throughout his writings is that of "the Jewish-Arab encounter on all levels and its varying impact" (Libson 1998, 171). Goitein's early work was almost solely in Islamic Studies, primarily emphasizing the Jewish milieu from which Islam emerged; his later work however focuses on Jewish society as it emerges out of the Genizah documents.

Goitein is best known for importing the term "symbiosis" from the natural sciences in order to describe Jewish-Muslim relations. His definition of the term is right out of a biological textbook: "the co-existence of two organs in such a way as to benefit from the proximity, in the sense that one party benefits while the other does not suffer."[44] Goitein argues, much like Geiger did, that what enabled this symbiosis to occur was a fundamental substrate that Judaism and Islam shared: a common language, culture, and religious worldview. Goitein, at least in his later writings, was extremely sensitive to the categories and the language that he employed to describe these relations.[45] He tended to avoid the problematics of "influence" and preferred to speak of "parallels," "dialogue," and "difference."

---

41 Baer 1947, 33. The original German version was published in 1936 when the fate of German Jews was very precarious.

42 Biographies of Goitein may be found in Ayalon 1984; Friedman 1991.

43 The fruits of his labor were published as *A Mediterranean Society* (Goitein 1967–1974).

44 S. D. Goitein, "On Jewish-Arab Symbiosis" (Hebrew), *Molad* 11 (1949): 259. Quoted in Libson 1998, 175. For a discussion that problematizes the term "symbiosis" in Jewish-Muslim relations, see Wasserstrom 1995, 3–12.

45 Although this was not always the case in his earlier writings where, for example, he once proclaimed that "Islam is nothing but Judaism in an Arabic pattern… The entire religious typification of Islam as a faith of religious law is nothing but a reflection and an extension of Judaism." See his "On the Israel-Arab Encounter" (Hebrew), *Molad* 95 (1956): 265.

Goitein located, not surprisingly, the highpoint of this symbiotic relationship in the "classical period," i.e., between the tenth and thirteenth centuries. Yet unlike the other thinkers discussed above, Goitein spent the most formative years of his academic life in Palestine. So whereas Geiger or Graetz could romantically project their own ideological concerns onto the "golden age" of Muslim Spain without ever having met an Arab, Goitein lived and worked among Arabs. In his memoir of the development of the School of Oriental Studies at the Hebrew University, Goitein recollects that in "the early and middle 1920s, Jerusalem was a small and peaceful place. The intellectuals of all races and religions met with one another frequently and amiably. The country was secure; one could go to the most remote places without fearing anything" (Goitein 1987, 168). Goitein goes on to describe these early relations between Jews and Arabs in Jerusalem as one of "symbiosis" (168). Increasingly, Goitein continues, the dream of a bi-national Jewish and Arab state disintegrated among the violence between the two sides.

For Goitein, again unlike the previous thinkers, symbiosis was not a just thing of the past but something that he also witnessed personally in his early years in Jerusalem. Moreover, although Goitein was intimately concerned with the contours of Jewish-Muslim relations, he did not spend a considerable amount of time on the "golden age" of Muslim Spain. On the contrary, he was most interested in the conditions of Jewish-Muslim relations in medieval Cairo. However much like his older contemporary Baer, Goitein was quick to emphasize that the Jewish communal organization of the Middle Ages existed independently from its immediate environment (see e.g. Goitein 1955, 125–130). Here Goitein is quick to reject the thesis that carried a certain amount of weight with his contemporaries that the origins of Israel were to be discovered in ancient Arabia (see e.g. Goitein 1955, 19–32). So although Judaism would play a formative catalyst in the emergence of Islam, Goitein quickly dismissed the idea of Israel's origin in ancient Arabia.

Goitein considered Jewish communal organization to be essentially democratic in nature.[46] Jewish society as preserved by the halakhah (divine law) thus preserved the basic freedoms of the Jewish people. Although there were certainly Islamic influences on this communal organization, the "essence" of Judaism remained untouched. According to Goitein,

> Islam…is from the very flesh and bone of Judaism. It is, to say, a recast, and enlargement of the latter, just as Arabic is closely related to Hebrew. Therefore, Judaism could draw freely and copiously from Muslim civilization and, at the same time, preserve its independence and integrity far more completely than it was able to do in the modern world or in the Hellenistic society of Alexandria. (Goitein 1955, 130)

---

46 In *Jews and Arabs* (Goitein 1955), he refers to Israel as a "primitive democracy" (see, in particular, 27ff.). Here I am following the comments in Libson 1998, 179.

Implicit here for Goitein is that the symbiosis between Judaism and Islam enabled the former to make contact with and absorb certain trajectories of the latter without any sort of compromise to its integrity. The Jews of Spain, for example, could use the prosody of Arabic to create "Hebrew poetry" as opposed to "the Arabic literature of the Jews" (Goitein 1955, 155). So although he is comfortable talking about an Arabic influence on the Jews of Spain, Goitein argues that the Jews used such influences not to create *ex nihilo* but to mine what was already in Judaism in the first place.

Although on one level Goitein's construction of Muslim Spain was to demonstrate the intimate connection between Jew and Muslim, on another level he hoped to show how the Jewish community, as a religious and national polity, continued uninterruptedly from earliest rabbinic times to the modern period. Modernity however brought an important change in Judaism. In this regard, Goitein was part of a generation of Jewish scholars living after the Shoah who became increasingly critical of many of the presuppositions of German *Wissenschaft*.[47] Increasingly from the vantage point of Israel, he perceived the modern period to be antagonistic to Jewish culture. For him, the German-Jewish scholars/reformers could at best only "justify" Judaism by making it correspond to the highest ideals of German civilization. This, he claims, is not the same as the medieval Jewish thinkers who flourished under Islam. For them, they could use the Arabic language and Arabic categories not to justify Judaism, but to show its absolute superiority (Goitein 1955, 130).

Goitein's analysis of the Jewish-Muslim encounter, including the "golden age" of Spain, is probably the most nuanced of the four paradigms discussed here. Despite this however his construction of the ideal of Jewish-Muslim symbiosis is not devoid of ideological concerns. Goitein was often criticized for taking modern concepts (e.g., "democracy," "free-enterprise") and reading them back into the textual sources of medieval Judeo-Islamic civilization. As such, much like those thinkers mentioned above, he constructs the "golden age" of Muslim Spain or Cairo in light of modern day concerns. But whereas Geiger and Graetz sought to show how this "golden age" could (1) rejuvenate modern Judaism, and (2) lead to a full-blown political emancipation for the Jews of Europe, Goitein lived in the newly-created state of Israel. If anything, his construction of Jewish-Muslim relations in medieval Spain or Cairo is a response to the worsening conditions between Jews and Arabs in the aftermath of 1948.

Conclusions

This paper has argued that the tradition of a "golden age" in Muslim Spain is of a decidedly modern provenance. It was a tradition, like so many other

---

47   For the gradual Jewish reaction against German historicism, see Myers 2003.

traditions, that was created in order to respond to modern concerns. Although it claimed to be about the historical past, this tradition was developed by a group of German-Jewish scholars who, in their attempts to reform Judaism from within, sought legitimation in the Jewish past. As a result the "golden age" of Spanish Jewry represented everything that these scholars perceived to be lacking in the Judaism of their day. Moreover, although it was directed at reforming Judaism, it was a tradition that was also meant to appeal, at least for Geiger and Graetz, to the German authorities. The message here was that if such authorities gave Jews the freedom that they so desired, the result would be another "golden age." For Baer and Goitein the situation is somewhat different. Yet, both also look to the "golden age" of Muslim Spain, one negatively and the other positively, in order to examine and evaluate present concerns.

The formation of a "golden age tradition" in Muslim Spain was a direct response to the perceived negative status of Jewry in nineteenth-century Germany. It became a useful category with which to critique those elements of contemporary Judaism that were regarded as unaesthetic or backwards. If modern Ashkenazic Jewry could emulate the model of their medieval Sephardic ancestors, it was argued, Judaism could thrive in the modern world. As such the "essence" of Judaism was imagined and re-imagined in the light of the broader intellectual and ideological currents of the German academy. The "golden age" of Spain was necessary because it provided various scholars/ reformers with a *Jewish* model to propose various changes within the tradition. Although someone like Baer would argue that such change was inauthentic (because Muslim Spain taught Jews "bad habits"), it did not stop many others from pointing to the plight of Jews in Spain as the polar opposite of their plight in modern and by extension medieval Europe. Although the scholars examined above differed in their portraits of this period, they all ultimately imagined Muslim Spain in their own images based on their own concerns.

References

Altmann, Alexander. 1973. *Moses Mendelssohn: A Biographical Study*. University, Ala.: University of Alabama Press.

Anrich, Ernst (ed.). 1956. *Die Idee der deutschen Universität: Die fünf Grundschriften aus der Zeit ihrer Neubegründung durch klassischen Idealismus und romantischen Realismus*. Darmstadt: H. Gentner.

Ayalon, David. 1984. "S. D. Goitein and His Academic Work" (Hebrew). Pages 9–13 in *A Bibliography of the Writings of Prof. Shelomo Dov Goitein*. Edited by Robert Attal. Beer Sheva: Ben Gurion University Press.

Baer, Yitzhak Fritz. 1947. *Galut*. Translated by Robert Warshow. New York: Schocken.

———. 1961. *A History of the Jews in Christian Spain*. 2 vols. English translation by Louis Schoffman. Philadelphia: The Jewish Publication Society of America.

———. 1970. "Rabbi Yehudah Halevi." Pages 39–46 in *Rabbi Yehudah Halevi: Qovets mehkarim ve-ha-arakhot*. Edited by Israel Zmora. Tel Aviv: Mahbarot le-sifrut.

Beinart, Haim, Jacob Katz, Joshua Prawer, and Samuel Ettinger. (eds.). 1983. *Le-zikhro shel Yitzhak Baer*. Jerusalem: ha-Akademiah ha-le'umit ha-yisre'elit le-mada'im.

Butler, Eliza M. 1958. *The Tyranny of Greece over Germany: A Study of the Influence Exercised by Greek Art and Poetry over the Great German Writers of the Eighteenth, Nineteenth, and Twentieth Centuries*. Boston: Beacon Press.

Cohen, Mark R. 1994. *Under Crescent and Cross: The Jews in the Middle Ages*. Princeton: Princeton University Press.

Davidson, Israel. 1928. "The Study of Mediaeval Hebrew Poetry in the Nineteenth Century." *Proceedings of the American Academy for Jewish Research* 1: 33–48.

Delitzsch, Franz. 1836. *Zur Geschichte der jüdischen Poesie*. Leipzig: Tauchnitz.

Ettinger, Samuel, Haim Beinart, and Menahem Stern (eds.). 1980. *Sefer zikharon le-yitzhak baer*. Jerusalem: ha-Hevrah ha-historit ha-yisre'elit.

Friedman, Mordechai A. 1991. "On S. D. Goitein's Contribution to Interdisciplinary Studies of Judeo-Arab Culture" (Hebrew). *Sefunot* 8: 11–20.

Funkenstein, Amos. 1993. *Perceptions of Jewish History*. Berkeley: University of California Press.

Geiger, Abraham. 1836. "Die Gründung einer jüdisch-theologischen Facultät, ein dringendes Bedürfniß unserer Zeit." *Wissenschaftliche Zeitschrift für jüdische Theologie* 2: 1–21.

———. 1867. *Salomo Gabirol und seine Dichtungen*. Leipzig: O. Leiner (reprinted New York: Arno Press, 1980).

———. 1970. *Judaism and Islam*. Translated by F. M. Young. New York: Ktav (reprint of the edition Madras: M.D.C.S.P.K Press, 1898; English Translation of *Was hat Mohammed aus dem Judenthume aufgenommen?* Bonn: F. Baaden, 1833).

———. 1981. "A General Introduction to the Science of Judaism." Pages 166–169 in Wiener 1981.

———. 1985. *Judaism and Its History in Two Parts*. Hanover, N.H.: University Press of America (English Translation of *Das Judentum und seine Geschichte*. 2 vols. 2nd ed. Breslau: Schletter, 1871).

Geiger, Ludwig. 1910. *Abraham Geiger: Leben und Lebenswerk*. Berlin: G. Reimer.

Goitein, Shlomo D. 1955. *Jews and Arabs: Their Contacts Through the Ages*. New York: Schocken.

———. 1967–1974. *A Mediterranean Society*. 5 vols. Berkeley: University of California Press.

———. 1987. "The School of Oriental Studies: A Memoir." Pages 167–173 in *Like All the Nations? The Life and Legacy of Judah L. Magnes*. Edited by William M. Brinner and Moses Rischin. Albany: State University of New York Press.

Gold, Daniel. 2003. *Aesthetics and Analysis in Writing on Religion: Modern Fascinations*. Berkeley: University of California Press.

Graetz, Heinrich. 1889/90. "The Significance of Judaism for the Present and the Future." *Jewish Quarterly Review* 1 (1889): 4–13, and 2 (1890): 257–269. Reprinted in Graetz 1975, 275–302.

———. 1894. Vol. 3 of *History of the Jews*. 6 vols. Philadelphia: Jewish Publication Society of America, 1891–1898 (English Translation of *Geschichte der Juden von den ältesten Zeiten bis auf die Gegenwart*. 11 vols. Leipzig: O. Leinier, 1853–1876).

———. 1975. *The Structure of Jewish History and Other Essays*. Translated, edited and introduced by Ismar Schorsch. New York: The Jewish Theological Seminary of America Press.

Harris, Jay M. 1991. *Nachman Krochmal: Guiding the Perplexed of the Modern Age*. New York: New York University Press.

Hegel, Georg Wilhelm Friedrich. 1953. *Philosophy of History*. Translated in *Reason in History: A General Introduction to the Philosophy of History*. Translated by Robert S. Hartman. New York: Liberal Arts Press.

Heschel, Susannah. 1998. *Abraham Geiger and the Jewish Jesus.* Chicago: University of Chicago Press.

Hobsbawm, Eric. 1983. "Introduction: Inventing Traditions." Pages 1–14 in *The Invention of Tradition.* Edited by Eric Hobsbawm and Terence Ranger. Cambridge: Cambridge University Press.

Hughes, Aaron. 2003. "Making the Past Present: the Genre of Commentary in Comparative Perspective." *Method and Theory in the Study of Religion* 15.2: 148–168.

Kramer, Martin (ed.). 1999. *The Jewish Discovery of Islam: Studies in Honor of Bernard Lewis.* Tel Aviv: Moshe Dayan Center for Middle Eastern and African Studies.

Lassner, Jacob. 1999. "Abraham Geiger: A Nineteenth-Century Jewish Reformer on the Origins of Islam." Pages 103–135 in Kramer 1999.

Lewis, Bernard. 1973. "The Pro-Islamic Jews." Pages 123–137 in Bernard Lewis, *Islam in History: Ideas, Men and Events in the Middle East.* London: Alcove Press.

Lewis, Rose. 1977. "Muslim Glamor and the Spanish Jews." *Midstream* (February): 26–37.

Libson, Gideon. 1998. "Hidden Worlds and Open Shutters: S. D. Goitein Between Judaism and Islam." Pages 163–198 in *The Jewish Past Revisited: Reflections in Modern Jewish Historians.* Edited by David N. Myers and David B. Ruderman. New Haven: Yale University Press.

Lincoln, Bruce. 1999. *Theorizing Myth: Narrative, Ideology, and Scholarship.* Chicago: University of Chicago Press.

———. 1999a. "Nietzsche's 'Blond Beast'." Pages 101–120 in Lincoln 1999.

Mack, Michael. 2003. *German Idealism and the Jew: The Inner Anti-Semitism of Philosophy and German-Jewish Responses.* Chicago: University of Chicago Press.

Mann, Vivian B., Jerrilyn D. Dodds and Thomas F. Glick (eds.). 1992. *Convivencia: Jews, Muslims, and Christians in Medieval Spain.* New York: G. Braziller.

Marcus, Ivan G. 1985. "Beyond the Sephardic Mystique." *Orim: A Jewish Journal at Yale* 1: 35–53.

Meisl, Josef. 1917. *Heinrich Graetz.* Berlin: L. Lamm.

Mendes-Flohr, Paul. 1991. "Fin de Siècle Orientalism, the *Ostjuden,* and the Aesthetics of Jewish Self-Affirmation." Pages 77–132 in *Divided Passions: Jewish Intellectuals and the Experience of Modernity.* Edited by Paul Mendes-Flohr. Detroit: Wayne State University Press.

Menocal, María Rosa. 2003. *The Ornament of the World: How Muslims, Jews, and Christians Created a Culture of Tolerance in Medieval Spain.* Boston: Little, Brown and Company.

Meyer, Michael A. 1967. *The Origins of the Modern Jew: Jewish Identity and European Culture in Germany, 1749–1824.* Detroit: Wayne State University Press.

———. 1975. "Abraham Geiger's Historical Judaism." Pages 3–16 in *New Perspectives on Abraham Geiger: An HUC-JIR Symposium.* Edited by Jakob J. Petuchowski. Cincinnati: Hebrew Union College Press.

Mosse, George L. 1996. "Central European Intellectuals in Palestine." *Judaism* 45.2: 134–141.

Myers, David N. 1994. "Was there a 'Jerusalem School'? An Inquiry into the First Generation of Historical Researches at the Hebrew University." Pages 66–92 in *Reshaping the Past: Jewish History and the Historians.* Edited by Jonathan Frankel. New York: Oxford University Press.

———. 1995. *Re-Inventing the Jewish Past: European Jewish Intellectuals and the Zionist Return to History.* New York: Oxford University Press.

———. 1996. "A New Scholarly Colony in Jerusalem: The early History of Jewish Studies at the Hebrew University." *Judaism* 45.2: 142–158.

————. 1997. "The Ideology of Wissenschaft des Judentums." Pages 706–721 in *The History of Jewish Philosophy*. Edited by Daniel H. Frank and Oliver Leaman. London: Routledge.

————. 2003. *Resisting History: Historicism and Its Discontents in German-Jewish Thought*. Princeton: Princeton University Press.

Nadler, Steven. 1999. *Spinoza: A Life*. Cambridge: Cambridge University Press.

Novick, Peter. 1988. *That Noble Dream: The "Objectivity Question" and the American Historical Profession*. Cambridge: Cambridge University Press.

Pearlman, Moshe. 1970. "Prolegomena." Pages vii–xxiv in A. Geiger 1970.

Said, Edward. 1978. *Orientalism*. New York: Vintage.

Schelling, Friedrich Wilhelm Joseph. 1966. *On University Studies*. Translated by E. S. Morgan. Athens, Oh.: Ohio University Press.

Scholem, Gershom. 1979. "Mi-tokh hirhurim ʿal hokhmat Yisraʾel." Pages 153–168 in *Hokhmat Yisraʾel: Hebetim historiyim u-filosofiyim*. Edited by Paul Mendes-Flohr. Jerusalem: Zalman Shazar Center.

Schorsch, Ismar. 1975. "Editor's Introduction: Ideology and History in the Age of Emancipation." Pages 1–62 in Graetz 1975 (reprinted on pages 266–302 in Ismar Schorsch, *From Text to Context: The Return to History in Modern Judaism*. Hanover: University Press of New England, 1994).

————. 1977. "From Wolfenbüttel to Wissenschaft: The Divergent Paths of Isaak Marcus Jost and Leopold Zunz." *Leo Baeck Institute Yearbook* 22: 109–138.

————. 1989. "The Myth of Sephardic Supremacy." Pages 71–92 in Schorsch, *From Text to Context* (see above; originally published in *Leo Baeck Institute Yearbook* 34 [1989]: 47–66).

————. 1990. "Scholarship in the Service of Reform." Pages 303–333 in his *From Text to Context* (see above; originally published in *Leo Baeck Institute Yearbook* 35 [1990]: 73–101).

Shapira, Anita. 1996. "The Zionist Labor Movement and the Hebrew University." *Judaism* 45.2: 183–198.

Shmueli, Efraim. 1990. *Seven Jewish Cultures: A Reinterpretation of Jewish History and Thought*. Translated by Gila Shmueli. Cambridge: Cambridge University Press.

Smith, Jonathan Z. 1987. *To Take Place: Toward Theory in Ritual*. Chicago: University of Chicago Press.

Sorkin, David. 1987. *The Transformation of German Jewry, 1780–1840*. New York: Oxford University Press.

von Ranke, Leopold. 1973. *The Theory and Practice of History*. Edited by George Iggers and Konrad von Moltke. Indianapolis: Bobbs-Merrill.

Wasserstrom, Steven M. 1995. *Between Muslim and Jew: The Problem of Symbiosis under Early Islam*. Princeton: Princeton University Press.

Wiener, Max. 1981. *Abraham Geiger and Liberal Judaism: The Challenge of the Nineteenth Century*. Translated by Ernst J. Schlochauer. Cincinnati: Hebrew Union College Press.

Ye'or, Bat. 1985. *The Dhimmi: Jews and Christians under Islam*. Translated from the French by David Maisel et al. Rutherford, N.J.: Farleigh Dickinson University Press.

Yuval, Israel Jacob. 1998. "Yitzhak Baer and the Search for an Authentic Judaism." Pages 77–87 in *The Jewish Past Revisited: Reflections in Modern Jewish Historians*. Edited by David N. Myers and David B. Ruderman. New Haven: Yale University Press.

Zunz, Leopold. 1995. "On Rabbinic Literature." Pages 221–230 in *The Jew in the Modern World: A Documentary History*. 2nd ed. edited by Paul Mendes-Flohr and Jehuda Reinharz. New York: Oxford University Press.

Central African Women:
Victims between African and Christian Traditions[1]

Félix Ulombe Kaputu

This paper traces women's place, and their victimization, in Central Africa since the colonial period, emphasizing the role played by African and Christian religious traditions.[2] One significant cause of this victimization is economic margin-

---

1 [This chapter is a substantially shortened and edited version of the originally submitted paper. The substantive changes made took into account a series of discussions with the author, most recently at the International Association for the History of Religions (IAHR) conference in Tokyo in March, 2005. Cuts aside, these include the consistent distinction between "custom" and "tradition" and the addition of the following footnote. Prof. Ulombe Kaputu has been unavailable for consultation since that time. He was arrested by the Congolese government upon his return from Tokyo and has been imprisoned in the Centre Pénitentiaire et de Rééducation de Kinshasa (CPRK) since that time (without charges and, according to Amnesty International, without adequate medical attention). Prof. Ulombe Kaputu was released in August though he faces ongoing legal entanglements. He has given his approval to this final form of his paper. (Steven Engler, September 9, 2005)]

2 [Drawing on discussions with the author regarding the resonances between his draft paper and the idea of invented tradition, I have made more explicit a distinction implicit throughout that paper between "custom(ary)" and "tradition(al)," and one of his central claims relates closely to this distinction. "Custom," as used here, refers to the beliefs, practices and institutions that existed in Central Africa prior to European conquest or that maintained continuity with these, whereas "tradition" refers to aspects of these as conceived of or reconstructed in part and separate from that irretrievable historical matrix. The distinction is one that offers a certain analytical purchase; clearly there is no sharp line between the two; rather they can be considered extremes of a spectrum.

On the one hand, this is to recognize that modern conceptions of pre-colonial Africa embody invented traditions. Terence Ranger, in *The Invention of Tradition*, argued that Western scholars and administrators invented African "tradition" as the other of modernity. Whereas African societies had, in fact, been characterized by "multiple identities" and "overlapping networks of association and exchange," this "pre-colonial movement of men and ideas was replaced by the colonial custom-bounded, microcosmic local society," whereas "there rarely existed in fact the closed corporate consensual system which came to be accepted as characteristic of 'traditional' Africa" (Hobsbawm and Ranger 1983, 247–248, 254). In this sense, "tradition" refers to modern (both Western and African) portrayals of custom.

On the one hand, the complexity of historical custom, over against the unitary simplicity of perceived tradition, was rooted in material, economic realities. "Customary" beliefs, practices and institutions formed a complex and varied whole in which, for example, religious beliefs, women's roles, and the conditions of economic self-sufficiency were integrally related. Seeing these beliefs, practices and institutions as

alization caused, in part, by Christian and colonial attacks on traditional practices and by strategic reaffirmations of these same traditions. Given that Central Africa currently lacks facilities that link effectively with the institutions and processes of globalization—with respect to, e.g., communications, culture, education, women's rights, and economic infrastructure—it is important to question the links between the arrival of western religions and the rise of globalization.[3] Although the Church may be said to contribute greatly to the well being of people's lives by working with NGOs, it is also evident that, for centuries, it has

---

"traditional" inevitably abstracts some part of them for positive or negative evaluation. Christian missionaries and colonial officials attacked African religious traditions as immoral or counter-productive. As discussed below, the recent resurgence of African religious traditions emphasizes their perceived practical benefits in the face of disruption and insecurity. In both these cases, the act of abstracting cuts "tradition" from its roots. More significantly, it abstracts custom from its material base, severing it from the means of economic production and subsistence. Tradition is custom dematerialized, denaturalized, fetishized. Emphasizing some limited aspect of customary ways of life in order to make a judgment, positive or negative, fails to see that customary ways of life can only be *ways of life* when their connections within a broad network of beliefs, practices and institutions remains viable. Attacking tradition, changing tradition, reclaiming tradition, inventing tradition, even respecting or preserving tradition, can undermine it. "Tradition," that is, erodes custom. To critique or attack or praise or preserve or reclaim the part while ignoring its relation to the whole is dangerous: some abstractions make sense out of context, but most are reduced to nonsense; some plant cuttings survive in new soil, but most perish.

In these terms, one of Ulombe Kaputu's central claims is that Christian traditions, with their judgmental views of central African traditions, have acted, like globalization, to destabilize and marginalize the social and economic situations of Central African women. Women's place in customary society was far from ideal. However, colonial and post-colonial changes to their place and status—changes accomplished in the name of rejecting or reaffirming "tradition"—have reduced their economic agency. The global economy is structured in a manner that leaves Central Africa at the margins, and Central African traditions (Christian and indigenous) are structured in a manner that leaves women at the margins. Ulombe Kaputu insists repeatedly that women's issues have been ignored. It is precisely this lack of attention that most sharply distinguishes custom and tradition, as these terms are used here: processes of rejection, reaffirmation, and invention of tradition all neglected those parts of customary life where women's social and economic agency was rooted. Women are marginalized by both Christian and African tradition because women's participation and contribution tend not to be taken into account in the struggle of which parts of custom are to be rejected or reclaimed. Without affirming the desirability of customary ways of life, we can affirm the necessity of a form of integration with material conditions found to some extent there but lacking in the traditions invented for strategic reasons by Christian missionaries and by modern practitioners. As the papers in this volume attest, "tradition" is a means to talk of many things. The case of women in Central Africa reminds us that we must move beyond such talk to pay attention to the material basis of people's lives. (Steven Engler)]

3   This approach considers the place of Central African women in terms of a four-stage model of social development: customary ("traditional") conditions, starting up, progress to maturity, and the communication era (Rostow 1963, 13).

built up major impediments to the progress and well being of women. Christian churches of all denominations are at the origin of women's discrimination and victimization, in contradiction to the alleged goals of their ministry, by perpetuating "traditions" that are incompatible with existing social conditions, now, for example, under globalization. Gender, religion, custom, "tradition," and poverty intermingle in a web that leaves Central African women in conditions far distant from the expectations of a globalizing economy. The world economy perpetuates market conditions that aggravate human poverty; and religion contributes to, or at best fails to ameliorate, these unacceptable conditions. Clearly, Central African women's social roles and conditions contribute to poverty: they are neglected by policy; they lack financial means; and they are not trained for economically productive activity. Religions (of all types and denominations) have never helped in any substantial way to integrate them with dignity in the social spheres that would allow for effective economic action.

This text proposes a return to the past to examine how religious agents marginalized woman's participation in development. As early as 1900, Methodists, followed by other American and British congregations, started their infiltration of the continent, "redefining and re-bordering" religious and geographical frontiers. From that time, it was obvious that American missionaries were not simply "Christian" missionaries; they were primarily capitalists and entrepreneurs, assisting colonial powers such as Belgium, France and Portugal through their cooperation. They condemned "traditional" paternalistic attitudes but backed up capitalism. The latter was supposed to produce miracles from God, through demystified Church rites, universal access to Biblical authority, the priesthood of all believers, and an extreme belief in miracles. In the last decades, this has been further intensified through the dramatic spread of American Pentecostal Churches. Throughout this history, little specific attention was paid to women (apart from such negative developments as harassment for giving birth to mulattoes without permission). The paper ends by suggesting possible ways to increase women's participation in social welfare and religious institutions. It is only by examining past Christian conquests and by questioning struggles over the place of "tradition" that the lot of Central African women can be improved in the face of the promises and threats of globalization.

Catholic Conquest

More than 400 Portuguese missionaries (including Franciscans, Jesuits, Dominicans, Carmelites, and Capuchins) accompanied the European conquest of Central Africa, arriving primarily in two waves, in 1482 and 1835 (Ndaywel 1998). Little effort was made to train a local clergy, with the exception of a King's son made a bishop, nor were issues of women's social promotion given any consideration. The late nineteenth century saw a proliferation of Catholic missionary activity:

a dramatic increase from 1865–1880, including the Belgian Missionaries of Scheut, as encouraged by King Leopold II, Trappists (1894) in Kwango, Redemptorists (1899) on the coast, Spiritans (1907) in Katanga, Capuchins (1910) in Ubangi, Benedictines of Bruges (1910) in Katanga, Salesians (1911) in the Southern Katanga, Franciscans (1920), and Sacred Heart Missionaries (1925). Brothers began to arrive from 1891, followed closely by various orders of nuns. The latter had a limited interest in women's issues: they emphasized teaching prayers to children and cooking for husbands but contributed nothing to empowering women. In the forty-year period from 1880–1920, Central Africa accumulated more than twenty missionary institutions of Fathers, more than six of Brothers, and more than fifty of Nuns. Many missions were officially charged with helping the new colonial powers to extend their presence, in part through programs of "education" that aimed at replacing traditional worship with Christian worship. There were no clear programs dealing with women's issues.

Occupation aimed at gaining cheap manpower. Lord Hailey was correct to condemn as savage, retrograde and unworthy of sacrifice this project of shaping a population in order for it to be productive in areas selected by the occupiers, without any consideration for the indigenous cultures (1945, 1207–1223). It goes without saying that some minor aspects of some people's lives were improved, e.g. by the construction of small houses and other facilities. (Women, obviously, could expect no improvement; they were to continue serving men, sometimes as their slaves.) However, we must absolutely condemn the elimination of complex economic and cultural systems that had survived through centuries without any proposal for an effective replacement. Consequently, in many ways, Central Africa as a whole is still supposed to live through the help and assistance of others, and to look at the world through their eyes. To sketch the scope of this violence against Central African values, the next section will contrast customary religious and education systems of Central Africa to those brought by the missionaries.

Customary Religious and Education Systems

To begin with, we must remind ourselves that the peoples of Central Africa were not always recognized as having "religion." Mulago (1973, 12–13) notes that anthropologists at first looked at rituals developed in many countries as objects of curiosity, considering certain practices as primitive. However, more recent scholars have paid attention to the broader context of the life of specific communities. The practices that drew the attention of these anthropologists form part of a complex system, along with beliefs and highly structured social organizations, by virtue of which human beings are seen as linked to an invisible world or to the gods. It is this web of relationships that is known as "religion" and which is characterized by the presence of different rites.

In all social groups present in Central Africa, formalized rites accompanied by given formulae foster beliefs in absolute values, framed in terms of a relationship to an invisible creator. It is this being or source, in its relation to values embodied in the community, which is called "God" or the First Force. This "Great Spirit" is far from worldly realities and not directly accessible. Consequently, there is a need for secondary divinities closer to human beings. The latter may be good or bad. They are supposedly responsible for the motion of water, trees, thunder, animals and human beings. Floods and desertification, fertility and barrenness depend on the same gods. However, a monotheistic conception of God is not found, with the exception of Benin where Mahou, the Omnipotent, is portrayed in the form of a woman. Examples of female gods are legion in many countries of Central Africa, illustrating one aspect of women's roles prior to colonization.

Thus, it makes sense to talk of customary "religion" in Central Africa. This religion was and is characterized by beliefs that divide the world in a visible part and its invisible counterpart. The two are linked and are expressed through a common representation of community, hierarchy and a particular sort of interaction. Above all, this understanding retains a belief in a Supreme Being, the Creator of everything. Scholars of comparative religion today universally acknowledge the presence of religion in the customary beliefs and practices of Central Africa.

Colonization, as a whole, wilfully denigrated or refused to recognize African spirituality and rituals. The occupying forces condemned everything as being linked to darkness, i.e., to satanic forces and to mistaken and savage understandings of the world. They considered that they were the only ones having the power and God's permission to convert the world. Though to speak of "converting" is misleading in this context; we should rather talk about the eradication of all the so labelled "primitive" systems of beliefs (Mulago 1973, 14).

The transition from colonial misapprehension to modern scholarly appreciation can be traced in the vocabulary of writing about Central African religions. The Portuguese at first coined the concept "fetishism," in reference to wooden sculptures used in various rituals, primarily by the Bassin of the Kongo. Later, the concept "paganism" was used, echoing early tensions between Roman religions and Christianity. Later, the word "animism" was used, with a strong emphasis on the African agro-pastoral life. Finally, mid-twentieth-century comparisons based on the elements prevailing in religious cults around the world find that the very elements that were condemned in Central African Countries are "religious."

However, early categorizations of Central African belief systems were inseparable from ideological agendas. In fact, Christianity, as the formal face of "religion," was a major force of conquest since it consistently adopted a conciliating tone with respect to the colonial powers and opposed all forms of traditional beliefs, practices and forms of social organization.

Condemnation of Central African religious traditions rested on three pillars of allegation: fetishism, naturalism, and animism. The first one consisted mainly of the use of small objects considered as incarnating sacred powers. (This critique was, of course, patently ridiculous given the Catholic attachment to relics, rosaries, scapulars, crosses and other sacred objects.) The second category, naturalism, was used to condemn the belief that all animate and inanimate objects partake in a vital force. (This view was based on a failure to recognize parallels from cultures around the world, including immanentist tendencies in Christianity.) The third attack, on animism, critiqued the more specific belief that all elements participate, through intermediary forces and spirits, in the forces that originate and guide the world. (Again, parallels to Christianity are obvious.) A further lesser critique focused on the concept of "ancestor" and its centrality to Central African cultures. (Here again, this may be rejected due to parallels with Christian forms of sacred mediation.)

A more important reason to reject this critique of both the Central African view that all of reality is linked through hierarchical sacred relations and of the related place of "ancestors" is because this African vision of a religious world goes hand in hand with the education of youth. The African educational system, in most areas, is collective and inseparable from religion. Ulombe Kaputu (1984) states that, from birth, individuals are inserted in a Chain of Being that links them to ancestors, and they have the duty to perpetuate this chain. One's very name determines one's presence and place in the chain, providing an identity and protection from occult forces and from other people. All education is therefore based on the effort to include individuals in their environment, including their clan, through practical training, respect for rites and customs, moral and social education, and progressive initiation to codes of behavior, including ways of regarding foreigners and providing them hospitality. This progressive integration follows clearly defined steps, with each corresponding to a kind of social as well as psychological mutation, one marking an incremental inclusion of the individual in the clan.

Customary education aimed to integrate children and youths into their local society. Mothers are responsible for the care during the first two years of childhood, providing the starting point of social life. At seven years of age, boys go out from their parents' house, usually accompanied by their father, to be initiated to the knowledge and skills of their future lives: agriculture, fishing, hunting, basketwork, pottery, or working with wood, tin and fur. These physical and technical aptitudes are later developed during the initiation period in the bush. The father or an initiated man teaches the youth incantations, so that ancestral spirits might always bless their enterprises, and magical spells, to expel bad spirits. Elderly people and parents provide guidance with specific tasks, e.g., using a hoe or machete, hunting, paddling canoes, and recognizing medicinal plants. Girls learn from their mother and aunts, including the conduct of domestic tasks, such as fetching water and dead wood, and caring for younger siblings. Girls are gathered from time to time, with their gradual integration into the clan marked by symbolic gestures. During their official initiation period, they are taught knowledge and skills related to housekeeping, marital conventions, clan relationships, and the conduct of certain rituals and ceremonies. Women are seen as conservers of custom and are generally the ones who lead rituals. Songs, tales, proverbs, plays, dances and sanctions help children's intellectual, spiritual, moral and ethical education. Young men are now allowed to share elders' food and drinks, and they learn to follow a common discipline in a variety of tasks and responsibilities. Young women are admitted to women's groups. Age groups allow children to consolidate friendly relationships, strengthened by an egalitarian status. Thus, different groups of young people have a given degree of autonomy and live following rites, traditions and developing social solidarity. This practical education gives young people an important role in the community and continues their integration into their society (Thomas 1997). It is clear that women were not men's slaves within customary clan structures. In many tribes, women were almost venerated because of their place in rituals and social organizations, and, above all, due to their place in procreation and initial education.

The core function of this customary mode of education is to integrate children with their family and clan, engendering a profound sense of social responsibility. This function was generally ignored, and often actively suppressed, by the European educational system, above all because children were often separated from their parents in order to attend missionary schools.

The colonial education system left most Central Africans economically marginalized. Both the religious world and the customary education of the past were violently rejected and replaced by western systems. As far as education is concerned, the Independent State of the Congo and Central Africa as a whole provided a very weak colonial education system (Ndaywel 1998, 353). "Proper" education was found only in Europe, and very few Africans were sent, with generally disappointing results.

Local Christian education also effectively produced colonial agents rather than members of customary society. It aimed at producing catechists and evangelists. Such persons were often exempted from paying taxes and freed from certain aspects of Colonial Law. However, their training and roles acknowledged and maintained colonial power. For example, the explicit contract that linked the Catholic Church to the Colony granted land to the Church in order to build schools for Congolese children. However, these schools were to emphasize farming, wood cutting, and handwork, in other words, a very weak education system unable to compete with others in the world, offering few benefits to girls, and maintaining a marginal role relative to the colonial economy.

In such conditions, the independence of missionaries was greatly restricted. They had to work along the lines decided upon by the government and to please the colonial authorities. The extension of missions was not simply a matter of evangelization; rather, it sought to ensure a greater presence of missionaries as representatives of colonial power. These schools did not aim at scholastic success or internationally completive training. They promoted a colonial occupation of the country's ideological and religious space, with the strategic help of missions. Girls were completely forgotten, under the official guise that parents did not want them to attend the western education. In fact missionaries delayed the development of any policy that might provide educational opportunities to women. It was only in the 1940's that some emphasis was placed on training them for employments as cooks.

The extent to which the education system aimed at furthering colonial goals at the expense of customary society is further illustrated by military recruitment. Many schools explicitly sought to produce soldiers, recruiting youths who were less integrated with customary society, especially slaves and abandoned children. Many were recruited by force and were severely punished if they tried to escape or to return to their home villages. These young soldiers were expected to fight the Arabs who came seeking slaves. Later on, during World War I and World War II, these sorts of schools provided most of the soldiers who went to fight beside European forces.

Due to the nature of the colonial system of education, at the time of independence, extremely few Central African men (not to even speak of women) were able to work in offices or to fill any other function required from a civil servant. This was especially evident at the level of post-secondary education:

> not a single Congolese lawyer, or judge was trained according to European standards before independence. It was only in 1952 that the first Congolese students to register in a University left Leopoldville to attend the University of Louvain in Belgium. In 1954, after much deliberation as to whether higher education was suitable for Congolese, Belgians opened the University of Lovanium under the auspices of the Catholic University of Louvain. (Gondola 2002, 176)

Didier Gondola clearly illustrates the Belgian failure in equitable hiring in the case of the civil service:

Rank	African	European
High ranking functionaries	0	5,900
Office managers	9	1,690
Assistant managers	24	1,976
Clerks	726	774
Low-level functionaries	10,791	0
Total	11,550	10,340

Table 1. Employees in the (Belgian) Congolese civil service by rank and race, June 1960.
(Gondola 2002, 116)

These developments ensured that, at the time of independence and since, Central African countries did not have enough high-ranking functionaries to deal with many crucial issues. Nor, of course, does Gondola's survey allude in any way to women, who were entirely absent from the visible scene. The example of the Congo reflects the situation in other countries in Central Africa as well.

Tradition as Collaboration and Resistance

In the tensions between customary and colonial social structures, women's position was eroded, in part because the customary was reframed as the traditional. That is, the most visible and effective manifestations of "traditional" society were, on the one hand, a subsidiary, alternative power structure opposed to yet integrated within colonial structures and, on the other hand, a site of resistance to centralization and integration. Those limited aspects of customary society that were emphasized by these "traditional" developments were not those that had provided economic roles for women.

From the beginning of the colonial period, westerners at first (i.e., Belgians in the present case) and, later, African leaders had to deal with a key question: whether to keep and respect customary values or to judge them as inconsistent with modern values and, hence, with progress. In general, the tendency was to stress the colonial economy, foregrounding the principle of National Consciousness and leaving little space for ethnic, geographic and religious diversity (Berger 1966, 28–29).

However, state power was quickly called into question by customary kings and chieftains who embodied religious and ethnic distinctions. Some states decided to simply ignore the chieftains' power (e.g., Guinea). The Ivory Coast and the Democratic Republic of Congo decided to integrate them as a subsidiary element of the central power structures. This revealed many contradictions between customary society and the modern state. For instance, customary laws of property hindered modern economic development, and different religious and ethnic groups within the same state raise questions regarding integration.

Not surprisingly, tensions between modern and customary worlds consistently revealed the latter's inability to offer economic solutions to problems of development. As a result, "traditional" reactions became sites of resistance, especially through rituals and ceremonies that asserted religiously sanctioned social divisions.

At the same time, those who saw themselves as freed from the constraints of customary society considered the new situation an opportunity, provided by Westerners, to recreate themselves as a new social class, avoiding the authority of customary leaders. This resulted in many conflicts that were generally resolved by the colonial power, almost invariably to the disadvantage of customary leaders. This resulted in a strategy, pursued by most African leaders who sought universal obedience and submission, of fostering conflicts in customary lands, allowing them to resolve the situations by establishing chieftains that they themselves selected. These new "traditional" leaders often did not even belong to the customary lineage of authority.

These tensions between traditional and colonial structures were associated with a mythologization of the white world, most specifically with myths explaining the origin of inequalities. In these myths, the black world is shown as linked to social degradation and malediction on the basis of biblical verses and traditional stories. Gaston Berger (1966, 17), referring to a fable from Gabon, points to a divine decision: "You Blacks, embrace your wives and fill up this world where you will always be naked. You Whites will be rich, richer than you have ever dreamt." These myths led to new (racist) views of creation, justifying colonization and inequality. Many philosophers and historians took this dangerous approach. James Ngugi wa Thiongo (1981) alludes to this in suggesting that the Black would do whatever possible to become a White for even a few minutes. In this process of mythologization, the role reserved to women is clearly stated: procreation. Unfortunately, according to Ngugi wa Thiongo, this prejudice was reinforced by Christianity, especially through the churches' role in education. Many people rejected custom for modernity, generally in pursuit of material advantages (Berger 1966).

However, this conversion to modern values was superficial. Christianity, for example, helped one achieve certain social and economic positions, but reversion to tradition was frequent. The example of President Mobutu is outstanding. He was Christian, achieving favors from the Christian, i.e., western, world. Whenever possible, however, he would stop contact with Churches, asserting what he called "authenticity," with either a return to the (invented) past or a move beyond the colonial situation to re-build a new, albeit traditional, ideal.

It is within such a context that reactionary innovations have occurred since the early thirties. New religious movements began to burst out, echoing late nineteenth-century messianic movements. These new movements yielded new interpretations of the Bible, emphasizing either the superiority of Blacks or universal equality. Other movements actively sought to suppress traditional practices of witchcraft and fetishism along with many traditional values. Unfortunately, these often-violent contradictions continued after the independence. It is within such turmoil that we have to situate the world in which the Protestant, and later Pentecostal, Churches began to have an important impact.

Throughout the period of Catholic implantation in Africa, women were relegated to the household and were denied conditions comparable to those of men. Despite (or because of) tradition's place as an element of colonial power structures and as a site of resistance to centralization and integration, women lost their important customary roles and had to accept the role of observers. The victimization of women worsened as they were ignored, falling into the cracks between Christian and African traditions.

Protestant Conquest

When speaking about Protestant churches' conquest, we have to keep in mind that in many places the survival of these churches depended on the will of colonial powers. In spite of opportunities and in spite of their own traditions, the Protestant Churches did not maximize their chances to bring any significant improvements to the lives of the African people to whom they ministered. On the contrary, they adopted a rather passive position. This section traces their presence in Central Africa up to independence. The following section will concentrate on new Churches coming from the United States during the post-independence period.

The implantation of Protestant Missions did not benefit, in most countries, from government provision of land or facilities; nor did they receive the advantages linked to any official function (e.g., education). On the contrary, they were often resisted. They also suffered from internal (inter-denominational) tensions and the confusion of public perceptions that this entailed. By 1940, there were about forty Protestant Missions present in the Congo, including the American Baptist Foreign Mission Society (ABFMS), the Garenganze Evangelical Mission (GEM), the Baptist Missionary Society (BMS), the Svenka Missions Förbundet (SMF), the American Presbyterian Congo Mission, the Africa Inland Mission (AIM), the Congo Balolo Mission (CBM), the Heart of Africa, the Free Swedish Mission, and the Congo Evangelistic Mission (Ndaywel 1998, 347).

One of the major contributions of the Protestant churches was their criticism of slavery. In their journals and reports sent home, they attacked the policies developed by the Independent State of the Congo, recognizing that labor policies were the main source of exploitation and violence. Despite this historical role, however, it is now the Catholic missionaries that have become the primary Christian voices opposing the State and standing up for the rights of citizens. Protestant missionaries are silent and do not participate in the evolution of Central African societies or play roles in leading citizens toward democratic maturation. This lack of social activism extends to their attitudes towards women: Protestant women are gathered in groups to learn of conservative readings of the Bible, which emphasize the blind acceptance of men's authority and the reality of miracles.

The collaborationist behavior that characterized Catholic Churches during the colonial period now seems to motivate Protestant Churches in their relationship with Central African governments. They cannot benefit from laws regarding land and the building of schools because Catholics have already absorbed these resources and performed these functions, but at least they can avoid problems and live in peace.

This kind of passive, non-confrontational stance lies behind another phenomenon that has led to the creation of many new Churches and to many departures from existing congregations. Faced with disappointment, many people have started slowly returning to traditional values, often with political leaders leading the way. In sum, the work of Protestant missionaries has not gone far within the African personality and has done little for women's progress. Again, as was the case with Catholicism, African tradition stood over against Christian tradition.

Pentecostal Churches' Expansion Policies

A dramatic growth in the number of Pentecostal churches, primarily of American origin, started in the decade 1990–2000, a period when Central African countries were undergoing serious crises. They grew as most of the people were suffering greatly from hunger and from violence due to war. We have to keep in mind that the drastic conditions of these crises led people to find in religious organizations a refuge and some means to face the daily problems of hunger, insecurity, and joblessness. Women especially sought solace, social support, and, above all, miracles with the Pentecostals.

The number of Protestant and Pentecostal churches is relatively large, though their physical sites and congregation sizes tend to be smaller than those of the Roman Catholic Church. For example, the city of Lubumbashi in the Democratic Republic of Congo counts 267 places of worship, of which 79% or 210 are Protestant and 5% or 14 are Catholic. These figures are representative of Central Africa as a whole. Protestant and Pentecostal churches tend to have small congregations, often not exceeding 50, though some have as many as 600, with these larger churches found usually in the periphery of the city. Catholics have large buildings inherited from the period of colonization and boast well-organized Christian communities. Protestant and Pentecostal churches tend to consist of very small buildings of clay, tents, poor shanties, even gathering places under trees. Congregants, above all women, tend to spend long hours of prayer at these sites waiting for miracles.

In terms of the arrival of these churches as missionary movements, we must keep in mind that Central African states have invested much in supporting Pentecostal churches, something they did not do in the case of previous Protestant groups. These new congregations stressed that the authority of the State comes straight from God. Recognizing this, governments began recruiting their personnel from these newly born congregations, making sure that these new civil servants would be the defenders of their authority. As such, Pentecostals have become agents of neo-colonialism from within.

These Churches develop policies that we might call American Capitalist Religious Trade. This trade manifests five characteristics: (1) social proximity; (2) an emphasis on miracles; (3) a tendency for worshippers to spend long hours at church sites in prayer; (4) lack of engagement with non-governmental organizations (NGOs) and other civil society movements; (5) and an absence of political participation and commitment.

The first element is illustrated through an exaggerated social proximity that echoes traditional forms of social affiliation. Pentecostal Churches have become a pretext that allows people to gather to try to solve together their social problems, but where dogmatic questions are not considered. Pentecostal Churches emphasize "brotherhood" and "sisterhood." These labels allow these Churches to develop a web-like environment in which privacy has little meaning and every personal problem represents a challenge to be solved by this big family. As a matter of fact, everybody can pretend to live in brotherhood with members of the group as long as they share the same Church and espouse the same interpretations of certain passages from the Bible. These social arrangements seem to recuperate a purely African understanding of community and clan, reaching back to the past and including the prominent participation of women (Kizobo 2001). Again, we find here a selective reclamation of tradition which, because of its apolitical nature and its emphasis on the miraculous rather than on effective economic agency (especially for women), fails to ground social relations in actual material conditions as did customary relations.

The second and third characteristics of these Pentecostal groups are their emphasis on miracles and a tendency to use worship spaces as sites to fasten for long periods of prayer. Most insist on Revelation and the presence of God in daily life as the means to solve all problems, effectively denying that human beings are responsible for their own destinies through work and responsible production. Pentecostal Churches of American origin are especially effective in persuading congregants that miracles can happen and solve their daily problems, effectively neglecting their own development and that of their community. The fact that women are especially prominent in the churches in prayer and the expectation of miracles reflects that fact that normal (non-miraculous) paths of economic agency are less available to them, but, at the same time, this passive anticipation of miraculous solutions diverts them from pursuing those opportunities for effective action that are available and from creating new opportunities.

The fourth characteristic of the Capitalist Religious Trade of American Pentecostals is their lack of engagement with civil society groups. They simply do not acknowledge or reflect the economic and social realities and the needs of the people. This removes the possibility of common ground with most NGOs, whose primary mandates are structured by exactly this acknowledgment. Consequently, there is almost no social activism in Protestant and Pentecostal churches, which includes, of course, a failure to recognize gender problems. Their lack of engagement with political structures and discourse is rooted in the same failure to engage with the material conditions of their congregants' lives. These congregations do nothing to raise the consciousness of their members as responsible citizens and active participants in civil and national society. They all show the weakness of a system that fails to link the religious field to its political, social and economic contexts.

Globalization, Gender, Poverty and Religion

Gender, religion, tradition, and poverty intermingle in a web that leaves Central Africa women marginalized from the economic expectations consistent with globalization.

Structural impediments to full access to globalization by Central African nations are numerous: including non-parity of buying power; limited access to global markets; national indebtedness, population growth; over-reliance on primary resource production; poor governance; a lack of fit between education and social and economic needs ; as well as war and violence, with the accompanying social, political and economic instability (Gilbert 1996, 311–342; Lafay 1997, 15; Ndaywel 1998, 739; Islam and Morrison 1996, 5–6).

Disease is a very serious threat, worsening many of these structural problems. There is almost no public health education related to prevention or fighting measles, cholera and other diseases that are important contributors to poverty. The most destructive disease, of course, is AIDS, with two thirds of the world's HIV positive population in Africa (Haddad 2003, 109). In Central Africa, the media are talking about AIDS, but there is not yet an organized campaign of information, a lack felt especially in the case of providing information to women. The question of culture imposes restrictions on such a topic, and religious visions and restrictions do not allow pastors and priests to clearly address the problem. Even the disease itself is not easily mentioned. People refer indirectly to "this disease of these times" or "a long suffering disease" or to some other specific disease that may be prominent. In many rituals of purification, especially after the death of the male spouse, women are forced to take a man chosen by the family without any regard for risks of infection. Many Christians return to traditional practices for revealing the witches believed to have caused disease and death. It is necessary to find some means of quickly spreading trustworthy and useful information to members of both sexes.

Impediments to women's participation include lack of birth control, a normative emphasis on large families, lack of education, and limits to freedom of movement and activity imposed by a patriarchal culture. For example, whereas international NGOs work in surroundings where actors are supposed to travel and participate in international conferences, only single women from Congo can travel whereas married ones cannot. When, for instance, Chokwe boys are selected for their initiation, their mothers are not informed at all. Boys are educated to look at themselves as builders of communities, whereas women have to follow them. Girls are left at home when boys are sent to school; the majority will, at most, attend primary school for a couple of years. Their education is considered as a waste since they have to get married and work as birth givers and housewives. When given a chance to continue their studies, women are often considered to be "insubordinate agitators." In many places, women who choose to live alone are considered to be prostitutes or social degenerates. Churches have perpetuated negative images, often based on readings of the narrative of Eve and Adam. Churches of all denominations have failed to participate in the building of a world where the material basis of Central African people, especially women, makes real contact with the increasingly important elements of globalization.

Women have been victimized by custom, by colonization, and by the tensions between tradition and modernity. They are most often relegated to some informal economy with the obligation of working for their household and praying for miracles to benefit their husbands (Ulombe Kaputu 2002, 1289–1290). The evangelization of semi-literate people props up interpretations of the Bible that reinforce mythical images of women's subordination. Women have not developed skills of critical assessment. Existing media channels do not serve African women's interest. It would be important to work with women's existing social networks. For example, oral forms of communication, especially working with small groups, would be an effective means of education and information. Uganda, for example, has started developing networks to link women at the local level.

To go forward and solve numerous problems, NGOs should stress particularly the importance of appropriate education. A special effort should be made to extend adapted schools from cities to villages. The city's life and values extends to only about twenty kilometres distance. In the countryside, eleven-year-old girls stop going to school and start getting ready for marriage.

Some efforts are being made to develop more effective market networks, including women at the local level. These developments recognize a crucial fact: informal markets developed by women in Africa help families to survive. In many countries, economic recession has led many companies to close, leaving workers jobless. Yet, thanks largely to informal economies developed by women, people survive. Despite this fact, however, the mythical belief persists that women can do nothing to improve Africa, a belief reinforced by Pentecostalism's emphasis limiting women's roles to praying for miracles.

Conclusion

Tensions between custom and modernity and the tug-of-war between Christian and African traditions have left women falling through the cracks. Catholic education sought to impose one religious tradition by eradicating another, separating children from their parents and elders. The colonial education system at most taught male students "traditional" manual skills appropriate for low-level participation in the colonial economy, eroding the full participation in a complex economic system that had been customary. "Tradition" as collaboration preserved something like the customary authority of chieftains, but only by integrating this authority within a colonial hierarchy, eroding its customary place at the head of a more fully integrated and economically viable society. "Tradition" as resistance to centralization and integration again offered a narrow and limited vision of customary practices, one that left women's roles and participation largely aside. The selective reaffirmation of or resistance to aspects of tradition by new religious movements was also so narrowly focused that the material conditions of women were, at best, ignored. The turn from mainline Christianity to traditional magical practices (aided by the failure of Protestant churches to address political issues) is an attempt to gain protection and power, often overlapping with the Pentecostal emphasis on prayer and miracles, and it turns its back on effective political and economic agency. In all these ways, the presence of debates over "tradition" is a sign that the broader material context is being ignored. And it is only by paying attention to this context that the place of women in Central Africa will be improved.

Many Africans are often disappointed with their prospects when faced with the supremacy of the Whites' world and its followers, as ensured through political systems organizing the global circulation of capital. They start slowly returning to customary values, often with political leaders leading the way. Central African politicians are surrounded by witchdoctors. Our informants tell us that they will not appear in public without the "authorization" of their religious guide. They carry amulets all around their bodies. They are Christians by day and juju seekers by night. Given that the highest levels of the state embody a religious ambivalence found in many citizens, this hidden progress or resurgence of African traditions is closely related to the failure of western religious, political, and economic traditions to deliver on their promises.

Similar confusions are found in many areas. In the post-independence war, many Katangan soldiers carried both amulets and rosaries; their water bottles contained fetishes; and they used their Bibles as pillows. The same mix of practices was repeated during the Alliance of Democratic Forces of Liberation (AFDL) war of liberation under President Laurent Kabila in 1997 in the Democratic Republic of Congo. During this war, customary taboos circulated with no consideration for the beliefs of Christian soldiers.

In the quickly multiplying and fragmenting Protestant and Pentecostal churches, young pastors attract people through their sermons and publicity regarding miracles. They organize long prayer sessions against evil. They seek paradise without solving any practical daily problems. They consider God a means rather than an end. The pastors, especially the American Pentecostal ministers, put their Central African congregants in a dream-like world where all solutions can be taken for granted as long as total faith is put in God. With such practices, no future can be envisioned nor project executed with regard to the development of the country. Consequently, poverty and tribalism are characteristic of their prayer places. Witchcraft and other traditional practices are quite common. Women continue to organize rites and rituals as in the past but in different contexts, the new ones ensuring absolute misery because their links to economic structures have been severed.

Globalization, though very up-to-date conceptually, is extremely ambivalent in Central Africa. It spreads throughout the world, but it does not serve all peoples and countries in the same way. Some countries see obvious improvements whereas others (e.g., in Central Africa) see their conditions worsen from day to day. Different strategies are developed here and there to catch up with time and organize markets or chains of interest and apply pressure to get a place within globalization. NGOs may theoretically work for the well being of the population. Women-centered NGOs may also contribute largely to development within a global system. However, as long as women are treated as inferior beings and are not put in conditions that may contribute to their participation in global conditions as observed in many places, poverty will continue to plague Central Africa (Gilbert 1996, 312; Soldatos 1996, 74).

The churches and NGOs have to work together to fight traditions and ideologies that cultivate poverty and make it an accepted phenomenon. NGOs should focus on education as the key to changing minds and building a better future. Jamaica and South America are among the examples to be followed. It is time for Central African women to start contributing more clearly to the economies and economic standards of their respective countries. To aid in achieving this goal, religions must avoid general policies inherited from colonization. Women can achieve many things if their powers to achieve self-reliance are fostered. This step requires a realistic evaluation of social and economic circumstances and prospects, not a struggle over the value, good or bad, of "tradition."

References

Berger, Gaston. 1966. *L'Afrique en devenir: Essai sur l'avenir de l'Afrique noire, milieu rural, population urbaine, construction nationale et stabilisation politique.* Prospective 13. Paris: Puf.

Gilbert, Guy. 1996. "Le fédéralisme financier-perspectives de microéconomie spatiale." *Revue économique* sous la direction de Pierre-Henri Derycke et Jean-Marie Huriot 47.2: 311–363.

Gondola, C. Didier. 2002. *The History of Congo.* London: Greenwood Press.

Haddad, Addan. 2003. *Pistes de réflexions sur l'implosion de l'Union Soviétique, l'émergence de l'Empire Américain, la mondialization-globalization, la première guerre du siècle.* Lubumbashi: Presses universitaires de Lubumbashi.

Hailey, William M. 1945. *An African Survey: A Study of Problems Arising in Africa South of the Sahara*. Issued by the Committee of the African Research Survey... 2nd edition. London: Oxford University Press.

Hobsbawm, Eric, and Terence Ranger (eds.). 1983. *The Invention of Tradition*. Cambridge: Cambridge University Press.

Islam, Nasir, and David R. Morrison. 1996. "Governance, Democracy and Human Rights." *Canadian Journal of Development Studies* (Special Issue): 5–18.

Kizobo, O'bweng Okwess. 2001. *Les associations socioculturelles à Lubumbashi (1990–2000): Témoignage d'une nouvelle solidarité en milieu urbain congolais*. Lubumbashi: Presses universitaires de Lubumbashi.

Lafay, Gérard. 1997. *Comprendre la mondialisation*. Paris: Economica.

Mulago, gwa Cikala Musharhamina. 1973. *La Religion Traditionnelle des Bantu et leur Vision du Monde*. Kinshasa: Presses Universitaires.

Ndaywel e Nziem, Isidore. 1998. *Histoire générale du Congo: De l'héritage ancien à la République Démocratique*. Paris: Agence de la Francophonie, De Boeck & Larcier.

Ngugi wa Thiongo, James. 1981. *Decolonising the Mind: The Politics of Language in African Literature*. Portsmouth, N.H.: Heinemann.

Rostow, Walt Whitman. 1963. *Les Etapes de la croissance économique* (English original: *The Stages of Economic Growth*). Paris: Seuil.

Soldatos, Gerasimos T. 1996. "Growth and the interaction between money and the Underground Economy." *Revue économique* 1: 73–84.

Thomas, Louis-Vincent. 1997. "L'être et le paraître: Essai sur la signification de l'initiation en Afrique noire." Pages 124–160 in *Fantasme et Formation*. Edited by René Kaës, Didier Anzieu, Louis-Vincent Thomas. Paris: Dundod.

Ulombe Kaputu, Félix. 1984. *The Evolution of the African Crisis as seen from Peter Abrahams' Mine Boy, A Wreath for Udomo and This Island Now: A Historical Approach*. Lubumbashi: Presses Universitaires de Lubumbashi.

———. 2002. "Religion and Memory: The Well-Being in Question for Half a Century in the Democratic Republic of Congo." Pages 1280–1295 in volume 3 of *The Power of Oral History, Memory, Healing and Development. XIIth International Oral History Conference, Pietermaritzburg, 24–27 June 2002*. Edited by Philippe Denis and James Worthington. Pietermaritzburg: Sinomlando Project.

Historicizing Modern Shinto:
A New Tradition of Yasukuni Shrine

Michiaki Okuyama

Koizumi Jun'ichirō and Yasukuni Shrine

The current prime minister of Japan, Koizumi Jun'ichirō, began his fifth year in office in April 2005. Since then his administration was dragged into unforeseen diplomatic conflicts with China and South Korea, complicating the already thorny issue of its relationship to North Korea.

Mass demonstrations against Japan held in several major cities in China early in April were widely reported in the Japanese media. Late in the month the Chinese government took measures to calm the situation, but then another problem flared up. A meeting between the prime minister and the Chinese vice premier Ms. Wu Yi scheduled for 23 May was cancelled abruptly and without warning. From one day to the next, on the flimsiest of official reasons, she was hustled out of the country and back to China. Only later did Japan learn what it had supposed all along, that her withdrawal was a protest against the attitude towards history of the Koizumi government. The issue is no doubt multifaceted, but the most glaring problem is the positive position the prime minister has taken towards one particular Shinto shrine, the Yasukuni Jinja.

Since the composition of his first cabinet in 2001, Koizumi has visited Yasukuni Shrine once each year and publicly bowed to honor those enshrined there with his own understanding of the Japanese tradition, a gesture that has continued to infuriate China and Korea. What *is* this Yasukuni Shrine? How is the Yasukuni Shrine related to the other Shinto shrines? Before addressing these questions, it is useful to provide a brief account of Shinto itself, Japan's "traditional religion."

What follows will not offer direct answers to all these questions but only attempts to put them in perspective by taking a brief look at recent arguments about Shinto, religious legalization in modern Japan, and the history of the Yasukuni Shrine, before turning to some final remarks on Shinto as tradition in modern Japan.

Definition of Shinto[1]

Pick up any introduction to Japanese religions and turn to the section on Shinto. It probably begins with a definition not unlike that of Michiko Yusa's recently published *Japanese Religions*:

> Native Japanese religious practices acquired the name "Shinto" ("the way of *kami*") only to distinguish them from "the way of Buddha," once Buddhism was introduced into Japan in the sixth century C.E. Until then, there had obviously been no need to label the indigenous religious practices of the Japanese people. The first appearance of the term "Shinto" is found in Book 21 ("Emperor Yomei" r. 585–587) of the *Nihongi*, or the *Chronicles of Japan*.
>
> The word "*kami*" has several meanings. It can refer to spirits of nature— mountains, rivers, trees, rocks, and ocean—all conceived to be alive and sacred. It may also refer to the deity dwelling in these natural objects, or indeed to a supernatural power, a collective ancestor spirit that protects a clan (the early Japanese social unit). The *kami* spirit may be incarnate in certain individuals—brave, unusual, or gifted—and these individuals may be deified as living *kami*. The *kami* may deliver its oracles through shamanic mediums, who were considered the "children of the spirit," or *miko*. (Yusa 2002, 19)

In a few words the author distinguishes Shinto as an indigenous religion that took shape in response to the arrival of Buddhism from abroad and points to the variety of meanings of its central notion of *kami*. This all seems straightforward enough.

But when we turn to see what the scholars of Shinto have to say, the clear-cut definition begins to fray around the edges. Consider, for example, the collection of essays entitled *Shinto in History* (2000). In their introductory essay the editors, John Breen and Mark Teeuwen, begin by calling into question the apparently self-evident place of Shinto in contemporary Japan. Some 100,000 shrines or *jinja* served by Shinto priests attest to its physical presence nationwide. In addition, one observes a basic uniformity in the presence of certain symbols and the practice of basic rituals, such as the rinsing of the mouth after passing through the *torii* (shrine gate), the clapping of hands and bowing of heads to greet the *kami* deities, the ringing of the deity-summoning bell (*suzu*), and the tossing of coins. Finally, the authors note, there are any number of annual events associated with Shinto, among them "New Year, the Dolls' festival in March (*hinamatsuri*), children's day in May (*tango no sekku*), the *tanabata* and *bon* festivals in July and the autumn harvest festival," and also rites of passage such as "the birth of a child, special (November) ceremonies in a child's third, fifth and seventh years, coming-of-age ceremonies (on 15 January), and weddings"—all of which provide the Japanese opportunities to visit a shrine (Breen and Teeuwen 2000, 1–2).

---

1   See Okuyama 2003, 2004.

After pointing out other characteristic features of Shinto, such as its relation-ships to the world of nature and to the imperial household, the authors begin to question the disparity between the image of Shinto and its reality. Official statis-tics from the *Jinja Honchō* (Association of Shinto Shrines) give the number of Shinto practitioners at approximately ninety percent of the population of Japan. Given the fact that the estimate was generated internally, such figures may not be reliable, but neither are they very surprising. The far greater surprise is Breen and Teeuwen's claim that "'Shinto'—as opposed to, say, *jinja* or *kami*—has no meaning at all for the vast majority of Japanese, regardless of generation":

> Japanese attend shrines and beseech kami at festivals and on other occasions, too, but they have no awareness that their practice constitutes something called "Shinto," or that they themselves are "Shintoist." They certainly do not, themselves, profess affiliation to the Shinto religion... These slippages suggest that there is an obvious case for deploying the term "Shinto" with very considerable caution in discussions of contem-porary Japanese religiosity... We clearly overlook this slippage, these ten-sions and contradictions, at our peril. "Shinto" is not, then, in any obvious sense, what contemporary Japanese 'do at shrines,' nor what they think before the kami, since it is not what they themselves understand that they do and think; Shinto is, rather, what the contemporary establishment and its spokesmen would have them think and do. (Breen & Teeuwen 2000, 3)

Breen and Teeuwen give principal credit for the challenge to the Shinto establish-ment's reconstruction of Shinto history to a series of seminal articles by the his-torian Kuroda Toshio (1926–1993). In contrast to the officially propagated image of Shinto as the native and indigenous religion of Japan whose tradition reaches back in an unbroken line to prehistoric times, Kuroda offers a more scholarly, and sobering, view of the matter. A brief resume of his 1981 essay on "Shinto in the History of Japanese Religion" offers a good place to begin a discussion of the changing definition of Shinto.

Kuroda Toshio on the Idea of "Shinto"

As Kuroda makes clear, the aim of his essay is to "demonstrate that before modern times Shinto did not exist as an independent religion." He does this in four steps:

> 1) It is generally held that an indigenous self-consciousness is embodied in the word Shinto. I would argue that the original meaning of the word differs from how it is understood today. 2) The ceremonies of Ise Shrine, as well as those of the imperial court and the early provincial govern-ment, are said to have been forms of "pure Shinto." I would like to show that they actually became one component of a unique system of Bud-dhism which emerged in Japan and were perceived as an extension of Buddhism. 3) It is said that Shinto played a secular role in society and existed in a completely different sphere from Buddhism. I would main-

tain that this very secularity was permeated with Buddhist concepts and was itself religious in nature. The greater part of this paper will examine this question and the preceding two in their ancient and medieval contexts. 4) Finally, I would like to trace the historical stages and the rationale whereby the term Shinto came to mean the indigenous religion or national faith of Japan and to clarify how and when Shinto came to be viewed as an independent religion. (Kuroda 1981, 3)

Regarding the first point, Kuroda criticizes Tsuda Sōkichi's use of the oldest Japanese chronicle in the eighth century, *Nihon shoki* (also called *Nihongi*, as mentioned above) to argue for the indigenousness of "Shinto." Of the several meanings that Tsuda allows for the term "Shinto," Kuroda acknowledges the validity of only one of them: "the authority, power, activity, or deeds of a *kami*, the status of *kami*, being a *kami*, or the *kami* itself" (Kuroda 1981, 5). He then goes on to consider two other possible interpretations of Shinto: (1) as a generic term for popular beliefs in east Asia; and (2) as another term for Taoism, based on the actual usage of the same term for Taoism in China, and on the Taoist influences on beliefs and ceremonies in Japan during the first several centuries in the common era (5–6). He goes on:

> Early Japanese perhaps regarded their ceremonies and beliefs as Taoist, even though they may have differed from those in China. Hence, it is possible to view these teachings, rituals, and even the concepts of imperial authority and of nation as remnants of an attempt to establish a Taoist tradition in Japan. If that is so, Japan's ancient popular beliefs were not so much an indigenous religion but merely a local brand of Taoism, and the word Shinto simply meant Taoism. (6)

In this interpretation, *"shin"* in Shinto must be taken as an adjective that means "divine," *"to"* as a noun *"dō"*(in Japanese, "tao" in Chinese) or "way," different from the interpretation of "the way of *kami*." Kuroda concludes, "none [of these three interpretations] view Japan's ancient popular beliefs as an independent religion and none use the word Shinto as a specific term for such a religion" (7).

Limitations of space oblige me to skip to the final point of Kuroda's argument, but as a summary of his second and third points on the Shinto-Buddhism amalgam, I refer again to Breen and Teeuwen:

> Before the Meiji policy that authorized the 'separation' of Shinto and Buddhism, Japanese religious culture had been to all intents and purposes defined by Buddhism. Shrines and shrine-based practices were nothing more than Buddhism's 'secular face'; kami, for their part, were understood to be "manifestations of the Buddha." (Breen and Teeuwen 2000, 4)

Regarding Tsuda's explanation of Shinto as a body of "concepts and teachings concerning *kami*" that promoted its advance to autonomy, Kuroda points out the important role played by the priests at the Ise Shrine, by fourteenth-century Shinto thinkers such as Kitabatake Chikafusa, Jihen, and Ichijō Kanera, and by the Shinto-only school (Yuiitsu or Yoshida Shinto) at the end of the fifteenth century. The treatises of these latter in particular stimulated the move towards making Shinto synonymous with the indigenous religion of Japan. With the appearance of Confucian theories of Shinto by Hayashi Razan and others in the seventeenth century, "the definition of Shinto as the indigenous religion of Japan, as opposed to Taoism, Buddhism, or Confucianism, became firmly fixed" (Kuroda 1981, 19). According to Kuroda, the Confucian understanding of the way (*dō*) influenced the word Shinto, "imbuing it with the meaning of 'the way, as a political or moral norm' (Tsuda's fifth definition of Shinto)." Kuroda continues:

> The notion of Shinto as Japan's indigenous religion finally emerged complete both in name and in fact with the rise of modern nationalism, which evolved from the National Learning school of Motoori Norinaga and the Restoration Shinto movement of the Edo period down to the establishment of State Shinto in the Meiji period. The Meiji separation of Shinto and Buddhism (*shinbutsu bunri*) and its concomitant suppression of Buddhism (*haibutsu kishaku*) were coercive and destructive "correctives" pressed forward by the hand of government. With them Shinto achieved for the first time the status of an independent religion, distorted though it was. During this period the "historical consciousness" of an indigenous religion called Shinto, existing in Japan since ancient times, clearly took shape for the first time. This has remained the basis for defining the word Shinto down to the present. Scholars have yielded to this use of the word, and the population at large has been educated in this vein. (19)

Following Kuroda's argument, we can better understand the vague awareness of Shinto among the Japanese people, who actually observe "traditional" customs without considering whether they are Shinto or not. Uncritical usage of the concept of Shinto blinds to the historical invention of this "tradition." As Kuroda argues, Shinto became independent during the Meiji period, but it remains unclear whether it became an independent "religion" or not. This question relates to Shinto's legal status in modern Japan, which we will turn to next.

Religious Legalization in Modern Japan

Since normalizing international relations around the mid-nineteenth century, and after more than two hundred years of virtual seclusion from the outer world, Japan adopted two different constitutions in accord with modern legal systems in its attempt to assimilate Western ideas: the Meiji Constitution (Constitution of the Great Empire of Japan) and the Constitution of Japan, promulgated respectively in 1889 and 1946 (each enforced the following year).

The principle underlying the Meiji Constitution is given in a Dedication preceding the Preamble. In it Emperor Meiji humbly offers the Constitution to the divine spirits of the Imperial Ancestors. The last part of the Dedication reads:

In addition to praying for the divine assistance of the Imperial Founders, Ancestors, and Fathers, I, the Emperor, swear to my subjects that I will take upon myself the responsibility of seeing that this Constitution is carried out, that neither now nor in the future will I sway from this task. I earnestly wish the divine spirits to consider this. [author's translation]

The Meiji Constitution was thus promulgated within the framework of an Imperial prayer to the divine spirits. In effect, this places both the Meiji Constitution and the governmental system that it inaugurated under a kind of sacred canopy. The religious legalization is, therefore, twofold. On the one hand, the Constitution legitimizes religious freedom within certain restrictions. On the other, the framework itself is religiously authorized. To treat the Meiji Constitution system in its totality, with the whole complex of relationship among religion, politics, the juridical structure, and education, falls beyond the modest scope of this paper. I will therefore concentrate on the guarantee of religious freedom.

The question of religion and the sacred is located in the following sections of the Constitution:[2]

Chapter 1: The Emperor
Article 3: The Emperor is sacred and inviolable.
Chapter 2: Rights and Duties of Subjects
Article 28: Japanese subjects shall, within limits not prejudicial to the peace and order, and not antagonistic to their duties as subjects, enjoy freedom of religious belief.

This guarantee of religious freedom—with the proviso against antagonism to "duties as subjects"—leaves ample room for interpretation concerning just what these "duties" might be. Thus obligatory visits to Shinto shrines, as one duty of all imperial subjects, found its way into law after Shinto was proclaimed a "basic reverence for the nation" (kokka no sōshi), rather than a religion. Leaving aside a detailed discussion of how this came about, we may single out a crucial turning point in the history of modern Shinto, namely, the year 1900 when a Shrine Office (Jinja kyoku) was established within the Home Ministry to administer shrines, detaching its authority from the Religion Office (Shūkyō kyoku) within the Ministry of Education whose task was to oversee "religions."

Characterizing Shinto as a way of reverence rather than a religion has an odd ring to our ears today, and indeed even at the time questions were raised about granting Shinto the status of a non-religion. "Is Shinto a religion or not?" Behind this question lies the deeper and more complicated problem of defining the concept of "religion" itself. The concept (the approximate Japanese equivalent being shūkyō) was by no means self-evident in Japan but had to find its way into post-Meiji Japan through contact with the outside world, especially with the West and, more specifically, in response to the newly introduced "religion" of Christianity.

---

2   For the articles of the "Meiji Constitution" and "the Constitution of Japan," see Beer and Maki 2002, 185ff.

Thus, the question of whether Shinto is a religion or not hinges on defining a term that was in itself a neologism. Without going any further into the history of the concept, it must be born in mind that when the Meiji Constitution incorporated the ideal of freedom of religion, it did so with a term whose meaning was not yet settled. (And even today, the definition of "religion" is debated.)

After the defeat of Japan in World War II and occupation by the Allied Forces, the Constitutional system of Japan underwent a radical transformation. The General Headquarters (GHQ) and the Supreme Commander for the Allied Powers (SCAP) worked to reform the country into a modern democracy, beginning with a disarmament of the military and a dismantling of what remained of its political machine. This process continued from 1945 until the formalization of a Peace Treaty between Japan and the Allied nations in 1952.

The GHQ and SCAP regarded what they called "State Shinto"[3] a perversion of Shinto into a means of militaristic and ultra-nationalistic propaganda, and accordingly issued a "Directive for the Disestablishment of State Shinto from the Supreme Commander of Allied Powers" (hereafter "Shinto Directive") on 15 December 1945. It opens with a statement of the aim of the Directive:

> In order to free the Japanese people from direct or indirect compulsion to believe or profess to believe in a religion or cult officially designated by the state, and
>
> In order to lift from the Japanese people the burden of compulsory financial support of an ideology which has contributed to their war guilt, defeat, suffering, privation, and present deplorable condition, and
>
> In order to prevent a recurrence of the perversion of Shinto theory and beliefs into militaristic and ultra-nationalistic propaganda designed to delude the Japanese people and lead them into wars of aggression, and
>
> In order to assist the Japanese people in a rededication of their national life to building a new Japan based upon ideals of perpetual peace and democracy.

This is followed by the first item of the directive:

> (1. a) The sponsorship, support, perpetuation, control, and dissemination of Shinto by the Japanese national, prefectural, and local governments, or by public officials, subordinates, and employees acting in their official capacity are prohibited and will cease immediately.[4]

A critical ingredient in the disestablishment of "State Shinto" was, of course, the redefinition of the status of the Emperor. An imperial rescript was issued on 1 January 1946 by Emperor Hirohito (posthumously, Emperor Shōwa) in which he formally denied his divinity.[5] In it he states:

---

3   The concept of "State Shinto" has also come under critical scrutiny. See Shimazono 2001a and 2001b, as well as my own essay on "Religious Nationalism" (Okuyama 2002).

4   For the text of the "Shinto Directive," see Mullins et al. 1993, 97–102.

5   For the text of this rescript, see Mullins et al. 1993, 102–103.

We stand by the people and we wish always to share with them in their moment of joys and sorrows. The ties between us and our people have always stood upon mutual trust and affection. They do not depend upon mere legends and myths. They are not predicated on the false conception that the Emperor is divine and that the Japanese people are superior to other races and fated to rule the world.

As a result, the Emperor's sacredness that had been declared in the Meiji Constitution and the alleged superiority of the Japanese race that had been advocated by the militaristic regime, were both repudiated. The Emperor system itself was transformed into a "symbolic" system under the Constitution of 1946.

The new religious system after World War II may thus be summarized in three points:

1. the survival of the Emperor System with the Emperor as a symbol, consequent on a declaration denying his divinity;
2. the denial to Shinto of the status of an institution for national reverence, demoting it to a religion on the same level as other religions; and
3. the formalized separation of politics and religion, and the declaration of the freedom of belief.

Related articles in the Constitution of Japan are as follows:

Chapter 1: The Emperor
    Article 1: The Emperor shall be the symbol of the State and of the unity of the people, deriving his position from the will of the people with whom resides sovereign power.
Chapter 3: Rights and Duties of the People
    Article 20: Freedom of religion is guaranteed to all. No religious organization shall receive any privileges from the State nor exercise any political authority.
    (2) No person shall be compelled to take part in any religious act, celebration, rite, or practice.
    (3) The State and its organs shall refrain from religious education or any other religious activity.
Chapter 7: Finance
    Article 89: No public money or other property shall be expended or appropriated for the use, benefit, or maintenance of any religious institution or association, or for any charitable, educational, or benevolent enterprises not under the control of public authority.

The issue of the "Shinto Directive" and the promulgation of the Japanese Constitution obliged persons connected with Shinto to rethink its status as a religion in order to insure its survival under the law in the new era of religious freedom. This was especially important for Yasukuni Shrine, which had official ties to Japanese militarism in that its administration had largely been in the hands of the Ministries of the Army and the Navy until 1945. We will later trace the history of Yasukuni Shrine, but before that, some of the backdrop of the establishment of Yasukuni should be reviewed.

Enshrining Human Beings

Yanagita Kunio (1875–1962), "the acknowledged father of Japanese folklore studies" (Dundes 1990, ix), researched Japanese traditions from a perspective more or less critical of the ad hoc appropriation by the nation of Shinto under the Meiji Constitution. While working as a bureaucrat chiefly specializing in agro-politics from 1900 to 1919, and then working as a reporter for the newspaper *Asahi Shimbun* from 1920 to 1930, Yanagita started visiting various rural areas in Japan, and writing books and articles based on his visits and interviews conducted there. In 1920 and 1921, he served as a delegate to the Mandates Commission of the League of the Nations (by recommendation of Nitobe Inazō, the then under-secretary-general of the League), and his stay in Geneva enabled him to learn about the developing academic disciplines of sociology and anthropology (Kawada 1997, 36).[6] In the 1930s to early 1940s, Yanagita concentrated on writing and on organizing folklorists nationwide in his research group. After World War II he established a research institute of folklore studies, where he organized group research projects to visit various remote parts of Japan.

In 1926, Yanagita wrote an article entitled "A Custom of Enshrining a Human Being as a Deity," in which he explicates this custom in the title by clarifying three prerequisite conditions: first, those who died a natural death at an old age are not enshrined; second, those who are believed to have left strong feelings of regret or revenge after their death are enshrined as venerable deities; third, these enshrined are, in his view, allotted relatively low status in the divine hierarchy and are subordinate to higher deities (Yanagita 1990, 647–648). Yanagita presented the following as examples of the deities that derived from enshrined human beings: the deities called *Hachiman* or their variants (there exist several explanations of the meaning of *Hachiman*), *Goryō* (vengeful souls), and *Reijin* (spiritual deities) or *Myōjin* (apparent deities). He also manifested doubt as to the reasons for enshrining such historic figures as Toyotomi Hideyoshi (1536–1598), because of his happy death (ibid., 651).[7]

Taking Yanagita's work as a classic, a contemporary folklorist, Miyata Noboru (1936–2000), also took up the subject of enshrining a human being as a deity in his book entitled *Cults of Living Deities* (1970). In this book, Miyata divides this custom into two types: enshrining a human being after his or her death; and enshrining a human being while he or she is still alive. Miyata states that the second type emerged in the modern period, and that they are enshrined not because of their regret or revenge, but because of their various contributions to society (Miyata 1970, 6–7).[8] His interest in the second type leads him to the study of cults of living charismatic figures such as founders of new religious move-

---

6   For Yanagita's biography, including his commitment to literature, see Morse 1990.
7   Toyotomi Hideyoshi is enshrined at Toyokuni Jinja in Kyoto. Yanagita also mentions Nikkō, where Tokugawa Ieyasu (1542–1616) is enshrined at Nikkō Tōshōgu.
8   Historical examples of enshrinement of living people were studied in Katō 1985.

ments, and also of a cult of the living Emperor of Japan. Here I would like to review Miyata's argument of the first type.

As for the first type, enshrining a human being after their death, Miyata distinguishes enshrinement of vengeful souls from enshrinement of another category. This latter refers, for example, to the cases of Toyotomi Hideyoshi and Tokugawa Ieyasu (15). Miyata classifies this category, enshrinement of a dead person, into four subtypes (chapter 1). The first subtype is enshrining local leaders because of their respected authority and virtue in their lives. The second is enshrinement of *Goryō* (vengeful souls).[9] The third is enshrining the dead person because the latter made a bequest that he or she would save the living people if they enshrine him or her. In this third subtype, Miyata explains, the dead person suffered a specific obstinate disease in life, and would relieve the same suffering of the living after being enshrined after death. The fourth subtype is enshrinement of ascetics who sacrificed themselves with the vow of saving the living from various sufferings. Miyata considers these latter to be a savior type.

Miyata's argument moves towards cults of the living Emperor and founders of new religious movements in the following chapters of his book. Here let us go back to the issue of Yasukuni Shrine with this background in mind.

The History of Yasukuni Shrine and Related Issues

Yasukuni Shrine (the name means "peaceful country") was originally built in 1869 as a Tokyo Shōkonsha (Tokyo Shrine for the Consolation of Departed Souls). It was one of a number of special shrines established after the first year of Meiji to pray for the repose of the souls of those who had sacrificed their lives fighting for the unity of the country during its process of modernization. Yasukuni Shrine was placed under government control: mainly the Ministries of the Army and the Navy and for a brief period under the Home Ministry. Consistent with its ideology of loyalty to the Emperor and the nation, Yasukuni enshrined (and has continued to do so to this day in line with the intentions of Emperor Meiji) those who had given their lives for the nation as soldiers, and excluded those who died in civil wars opposing the state as well as foreigners who died in wars waged against Japan.

The practice of enshrining the spirits of the departed belongs to a wider tradition of Kami worship in which certain guardian deities (*kami*) of a clan, a social group, or a region were venerated in a shrine. This kind of deification is a common religious custom in Japan—in Buddhism as well as in Shinto—concerning which a great deal has been written. Some of these Kami had originally been

---

9   After enshrinement, *Goryō* are said to become *Reijin* favorable to the living people (Miyata 1970, 29).

human beings but had been enshrined, as was illustrated above with Yanagita's and Miyata's arguments.[10]

After World War II, Yasukuni Shrine, along with other Shinto shrines, lost its national patronage. Immediately after the issue of the "Shinto Directive," the Religious Corporations Ordinance was issued on 28 December 1945, stipulating the legal status of religious corporations. William P. Woodard, liaison officer, until 1949, of the Civil Information and Education Section of the Allied Occupation, summarizes the features of the Religious Corporations Ordinance as follows:

> Anyone who desired to create a denomination, sect, order, shrine, temple or church was required to provide certain specified regulations governing the control of its property and register the same at the appropriate local registry office. Incorporation was effected by registration. The denominations then reported their registration to the Ministry, while local shrines, temples, and churches reported to their respective prefectural government. (Woodard 1972, 91)

As the passage makes clear, the religious administration authorized in this Ordinance begins with incorporation by registration. This led to some confusion and abuse, but rather than focus on the immediate aftermath of the Ordinance, we need to look at an amendment issued a few short weeks later on 2 February 1946. The intent of the amendment was to announce that Shinto shrines, including *Ise Jingu* (the Ise Grand Shrines) and Yasukuni Shrine which are singled out by name, are to be regarded as religious corporations, and the suggestion is made that they register, as prescribed in the Ordinance, within six months. Should they fail to do so, the amendment states, those corporations shall be regarded as disbanded. On the following day, 3 February, the vast majority of shrines nationwide — about 80,000 out of a total of 100,000 — merged to establish a new religious corporation, the *Jinja Honchō* (Association of Shinto Shrines). Yasukuni Shrine, however, opted to remain independent of the Association and established itself as a religious corporation by registering at the Tokyo local government in September 1946.

In line with the 1946 Constitution of Japan, the Religious Juridical Person's Law was enacted in 1951, replacing the Religious Corporations Ordinance that had been in effect for about five years. Helen Hardacre, a specialist on Japanese religions, reviewed the new legalization of juridical persons in these terms:

> Drafted with the cooperation of Japanese religious leaders and the Religious Affairs Section of the Ministry of Education, the law granted religious organizations tax-exempt status and specified the mechanism of incorporation. The latter were formulated specifically to prevent the government from using the fact of incorporation or nonincorporation as a litmus test for whether the organization was a religion or not. Several religious organizations actually requested some distinction between "true"

---

10 For recent scholarship on this question, see, for example, Komatsu 2001, who treats 16 shrines that honor historical figures.

and "false" religions, apparently in fear of the marked contemporary
growth of new religious movements, but these requests were denied.
(Hardacre 1989, 139)

In the period of transformation during the first few years after the war, the
Association of Shinto Shrines was obliged to negotiate with the GHQ, the
government, and the Diet to acquire the right to use the property where their
shrines were located, which officially belonged to the state, at reduced cost or
free of charge. Since they had become private juridical persons, any request for
the transferal of property to them would conflict with one of the articles of the
Constitution being drafted at the time, according to which religions would be
prohibited from disposing of or appropriating public property. Strenuous efforts
by the Association resulted in the legal approval of the transfer of state lands to
Shinto shrines in 1947. Permission for Yasukuni Shrine was delayed, however.
Scrutiny by the GHQ concerning the shrine continued for some years until the
approval was finally given in 1951, the year in which the Religious Juridical
Person's Law was enacted and the Peace Treaty with Japan was signed.

Allow me briefly to summarize the history surrounding Yasukuni Shrine
after 1952.[11] The same year in which the Peace Treaty went into effect, 1952, the
Emperor and the imperial family renewed their visits to Yasukuni (Shōwa
Emperor, now a "symbol" as prescribed by the Constitution, visited Yasukuni
seven times until 1975), one day before the Autumn Festival of Yasukuni, held
for the first time after the war. Prime Minister Yoshida Shigeru also made the first
official visit to Yasukuni since its privatization. Prime Ministers after Yoshida —
except for two, Hatoyama Ichirō and Ishibashi Tanzan — continued to visit Yasukuni during its Spring or Autumn festivals until 1974.

In 1952 the Japan League for the Welfare of the Bereaved (*Nihon Izoku Kosei
Renmei*, founded in 1947 and renamed the Bereaved Society of Japan, *Nihon
Izokukai* in 1953 as an incorporated foundation for approximately two million
bereaved families) began to solicit financial support from the state for Yasukuni
Shrine. From 1960 on, the aim of the petition shifted from financial assistance to
complete state support.

In 1952, a law authorizing support to former soldiers, civilian employees of
the military, and the bereaved was proclaimed, initiating the payment of pen-
sions (until recently, excluding those in former colonies). The law was reformed
in 1953 to include the bereaved of executed war criminals and those who had
died in prison. As a result, Yasukuni Shrine came to enshrine not only soldiers,
and civilian employees of the military, but also war criminals who were executed or died in prison, and even convicted war criminals from former colonies.

In 1955 and 1956, the status of Yasukuni Shrine was discussed again and
again on the Diet floor in the effort to secure state support for the shrine (one
possibility is to remove the religious character of the shrine, a move that is all

---

11   This summary is based in large part on Murakami 1974, and Tanaka 2002.

but certain to be opposed by those in the Shinto world). In the course of these debates it was disclosed that, in the process of enshrinement, Yasukuni had relied on cooperation from the Office of Demobilization (which had taken over from the Ministries of the Army and Navy as a new ministry in 1945, and later relinquished to the Ministry of Health and Welfare) to obtain data on those to be honored. According to an official document dating from 1956, the expenses for collecting the data had been covered by the official state budget. At the time discussions in the Diet did not consider the possibility that this might be in violation of Articles 20 and 89 of the Constitution. In any event, the debate in the legislature concerning the nationalization of Yasukuni Shrine continued until 1975.

In 1959, a national cemetery was founded in Chidorigafuchi, Tokyo, to house unidentified relics retrieved from battlefields abroad. A national ceremony for the memorial to the war dead was performed there in that year. A similar ceremony was held annually from 1963, first in Hibiya, at Yasukuni in 1964, and then at Nippon Budōkan from 1965 on. The Chidorigafuchi cemetery has been in the charge of the Ministry of Health and Welfare and is open to those of all religions or without any religious affiliation.

In 1965 a lawsuit was filed for the first time objecting to the use of public monies for the conducing of Shinto rites at a construction site. In its 1977 ruling on the case, known as the Tsu Ground Purification Case, the Supreme Court judged the use of public funds for the purification rite to be constitutional on the grounds that it was more a "custom" than a religious activity. The first lawsuit having to do with the enshrinement of the dead at Nation-Protecting Shrines (local shrines with the same function that Yasukuni Shrine has at a national level) was filed in 1973. The widow of a Self-Defense Force officer, herself a Christian, requested the withdrawal of her dead husband's enshrinement at a Nation-Protecting Shrine in Yamaguchi prefecture. (The Supreme Court dismissed the suit in 1988.) Since the 1970s a number of other cases have arisen to question the relation between Shinto and the public sector.

In 1975, Prime Minister Miki Takeo visited Yasukuni on 15 August, the day marking the end of World War II. This gave a new meaning to official Yasukuni visits, since 15 August did not otherwise have any other traditional importance for the shrine. In the ensuing years several Prime Ministers followed Miki's suit.

In 1978, Yasukuni enshrined fourteen Class A war criminals, among them seven who had been executed. On 15 August 1985, Prime Minister Nakasone Yasuhiro visited Yasukuni, publicly announcing it as an official visit. Criticism from Asian countries was immediate. Even the United States and the Soviet Union questioned the wisdom of the act. In response to international reactions, the Liberal Democratic Party tried to persuade Yasukuni to withdraw the enshrinement of the Class A war criminals, but Yasukuni refused. Nakasone had to discontinue his visits during the rest of his term as Prime Minister (1985–1987). The next visit by a Prime Minister came only eleven years later, in 1996, by Hashimoto Ryūtarō, again provoking a storm of criticism from abroad, mainly

aimed at the enshrinement of the Class A war criminals. Against this historical
backdrop, Koizumi Jun'ichiro took office in 2001.

Current Issues and Concluding Remarks

Since becoming Prime Minister, Koizumi Jun'ichiro has visited Yasukuni Shrine
four times: 13 August 2001, 21 April 2002, 14 January 2003, and 1 January 2004.
No less than seven lawsuits have been filed against these visits, in each case dismissed by district courts.

As reported by the media, Koizumi's reaction to complaints against his visits
may be summarized as follows:

1. He visits Yasukuni Shrine to renew his vow not to engage in war.
2. He visits Yasukuni Shrine to express reverence and gratitude to all the
   war dead, despite the fact that these include Class A war criminals.
3. The way one chooses to remember those who died in war is an
   internal matter not to be interfered in by foreign countries.

A brief comment on these reasons: To begin with, it is highly questionable whether
Yasukuni Shrine is a suitable place to pledge never to engage in war. Secondly, it
is one thing for an individual to make up one's own mind about visiting a shrine
that honors Class A war criminals; it is another for elected government officials
to do so. Given that the declared position of the Japanese government has been
to accept the decision of the International Military Tribunal for the Far East from
1946 to 1948, government officials need to adjust their actions in accord with the
position. But even setting aside the question of honoring war criminals, this
question of elected officials making formal visits to a private religious facility
needs to be clarified. Regarding the final point—even though a number of
people take this for granted, the Japanese people in general need to rethink the
extent and propriety of memorial activities for those who died in the war.

There are still other questions surrounding the Yasukuni issue. I would
single out three of them:

1. Yasukuni Shrine, as a private religious corporation, itself decided
   whom to enshrine and whom not.[12] What grounds are there to
   interfere in the activities of a private corporation in a country where
   freedom of religion is guaranteed?
2. All government officials, including elected politicians, share in the
   common right of religious freedom. To what extent should an official's

---

12   As we saw, the Ministry of Health and Welfare cooperated in this decision, in direct
     violation of the principle of the separation of state and religion. In addition, enshrine-
     ment is decided without any reference to the wishes of the bereaved family, and as
     such has become the subject of lawsuits brought by Christians and Koreans against
     Yasukuni.

religious activities be tolerated as a matter of individual choice, and at
what point do they endanger public impartiality towards religion?
3. Those who died in a series of modern wars are not the only Japanese
   in history to have given their lives for the country. Should the state
   perform national rites of commemoration to include others as well? In
   any case, how can such rites be justified under the principle of the
   separation of religion and state? And if justifiable, should a new
   institution other than Yasukuni Shrine be set up for the purpose?[13]

My tentative answer to the first question is that people outside of Yasukuni Shrine
cannot and should not interfere in a shrine's activities that are constitutionally
guaranteed under the rubric of the freedom of religion. If one criticizes their
enshrinement on their own private decision, this criticism should be based on
convincing reasons. If individuals pray for the rest of the dead souls, it would
likely be considered entirely acceptable. Then why is it that a private religious
corporation cannot enshrine certain dead people based on their own choices?
Those who criticize Yasukuni's enshrinement should be required to present very
detailed and delicate arguments on this matter.

As to the second question, it seems to me that, at the very least, high-ranking
officials should refrain from visits to a place like Yasukuni where Class A war
criminals are enshrined. This seems to be the solution that the Chinese government favors. But this only partially tackles the problem and additional public
discussions are called for. The same is true of the third point.

As it happens, the recent storms of protest in China and Korea oblige the
Japanese to take the whole question more seriously than before. A final solution
will not come easily, but at least the effort to come to grips with it should be
broadened beyond the confines of a diplomatic dispute to engage the population
at large in reflection on the past, the present, and the future to which they aspire.

In sum, Shinto is not a religion that originated from time immemorial. Rather,
the concept of Shinto has been constructed in history, especially in modern
history. The modern legal development of Japan also proceeded in parallel to
this process of conceptualization, containing an ambiguous treatment of Shinto.
These two processes, however, have not resolved all the issues in regard to Shinto.
Among them, a newly invented "tradition" of Yasukuni Shrine poses one of the
most difficult issues. At this sixtieth anniversary of the closure of the Japanese
sacred and militaristic regime, Japanese people are now pressed to reconsider
the history and historicity of their modern traditions, including Shinto in general
and Yasukuni Shrine in particular.

---

13 This last point was the subject of nearly a year-long discussion, beginning in December
    2001, by a committee convened by the Director of the Minister's Secretariat. The final
    report of the committee, issued in December 2002, stresses the need for a new national
    institution, areligious in character, to remember those who have fallen in battle and to
    pray for peace. One such national institution, as indicated above, already exists in the
    form of the Chidorigafuchi cemetery.

References

Beer, Lawrence W., and John M. Maki. 2002. *From Imperial Myth to Democracy: Japan's Two Constitutions, 1889–2002*. Boulder: University Press of Colorado.

Breen, John, and Mark Teeuwen. 2000. "Introduction: Shinto past and present." Pages 1–12 in *Shinto in History: Ways of the Kami*. Edited by John Breen and Mark Teeuwen. University of Hawai'i Press.

Dundes, Alan. 1990. "Editor's Preface." Pages vii–xi in Morse 1990.

Hardacre, Helen. 1989. *Shintō and the State 1868–1988*. Princeton: Princeton University Press.

Katō, Genchi. 1985. *Honpō seishi no kenkyū* [Study of shrines that enshrine the living in Japan]. Tokyo: Kokusho kankō kai [1931].

Kawada, Minoru. 1997. *Yanagita Kunio: Sono Shōgai to Shisō* [Yanagita Kunio: His life and Thought]. Tokyo: Yoshikawa Kōbunkan.

Komatsu, Kazuhiko. 2001. *Kami ni natta hitobito* [People who became deities]. Kyoto: Tankō sha.

Kuroda, Toshio. 1981. "Shinto in the History of Japanese Religion." Translated by James C. Dobbins and Suzanne Gay. *The Journal of Japanese Studies* 7.1: 1–21.

Miyata, Noboru. 1970. *Ikigami shinkō* [Cults of living deities]. Tokyo: Hanawa shobō.

Morse, Ronald A. 1990. *Yanagita Kunio and the Folklore Movement: The Search for Japan's National Character and Distinctiveness*. New York and London: Garland Publishing.

Mullins, Mark R., Shimazono Susumu, and Paul L. Swanson (eds.). 1993. *Religion and Society in Modern Japan*. Berkeley: Asian Humanities Press.

Murakami, Shigeyoshi. 1974. *Irei to shōkon: Yasukuni no shisō* [Consolation of spirits and departed souls: The idea of Yasukuni]. Tokyo: Iwanami shoten.

Okuyama, Michiaki. 2002. "Religious Nationalism in the Modernization Process: State Shinto and Nichirenism in Meiji Japan." *Bulletin of the Nanzan Institute for Religion and Culture* 26: 19–31.

———. 2003. "Redefining Shinto." *Hieron: Religionistická ročenka* (Bratislava) VI–VII: 46–51.

———. 2004. "Shinto in the Japanese Religious System and the Western Influences." *Revue Roumaine de Philosophie* 48.1–2: 183–190.

Shimazono, Susumu. 2001a. "Kokka shintō to kindai nihon no shūkyō kōzō" [State Shinto and the Structure of Religions in Modern Japan]. *Shūkyō Kenkyū* [Journal of Religious Studies] 329: 319–344.

———. 2001b. "Jūkyū seiki nihon no shūkyō kōzō no hen-yō" [The shift of religious structure in nineteenth-century Japan]. Pages 1–53 in *Iwanami kōza, Kindai nihon no bunkashi*. Volume 2: *Kosumorojī no "kinsei"* [The "early modern period" in cosmology]. Tokyo: Iwanami Shoten.

Tanaka, Nobumasa. 2002. *Yasukuni no sengoshi* [Postwar history of Yasukuni]. Tokyo: Iwanami shoten.

Woodard, William P. 1972. *The Allied Occupation of Japan 1945–1952 and Japanese Religions*. Leiden: Brill.

Yanagita, Kunio. 1990. "Hito o kami ni matsuru fūshū" [A Custom of enshrining a human being as a deity; originally published in 1926]. Pages 644–680 in volume 13 of *Yanagita kunio zenshu* [The complete works of Yanagita Kunio]. Tokyo: Chikuma shobō, Chikuma bunko.

Yusa, Michiko. 2002. *Japanese Religions*. London: Routledge.

Tradition as Legitimation in New Religious Movements

Titus Hjelm

New religious movements (NRMs) seem to offer a paradigmatic example of the constructed nature of tradition. The "newness" of the movements itself lends to an understanding of NRMs as having no tradition or having invented one. However, many of the groups classified as NRMs draw their teachings from one of the world religions (Hinduism, Buddhism, etc.) and, according to some scholars, tend to resemble their "parent group" more than each other (Melton 1996). Classification along the lines of this perceived family resemblance has also been an often-used approach in textbooks on NRMs (e.g. Melton 1992; Miller 1995; Chryssides 1999; Lewis and Petersen 2005). No consensus about the proper approach to classify tradition in NRMs has been reached, but it seems that a genealogical point of view alone cannot produce a satisfactory and an all-compassing schema regarding the significance and meaning of tradition in NRMs.

Although the concept of "tradition" itself implies a historical approach, my focus in this chapter is on the sociological processes where tradition is invoked for the purpose of legitimating alternative and emergent forms of faith and religious practice. The aim is to examine the different ways in which tradition is used as a legitimation strategy (Lewis 2003, 13) in countering tension created between NRMs and mainstream culture in different social contexts.

The focus will also be on the *outward* legitimation of new religions. It is clear that every religion has to legitimate its creed and practice to its adherents, and tradition is often used for this purpose—the dominant popular perception of NRMs thriving solely on the charismatic authority of the "cult" leader notwithstanding (Beckford 1985, 235–236; Jenkins 2000, 4; Dawson 2003b, 113). However, in the case of NRMs the outward legitimation plays an especially important role, as tension with the surrounding society can be described as one of the most important characteristics of new and alternative religions (Melton 2003, 78–79; cf. Stark 1996, 137–138). Tradition becomes a strategy used for giving weight and credibility to the religion in question. For example, the Hare Krishna movement (ISKCON) has in some cases benefited from being identified with a legitimate Indian tradition, whereas doctrinally more controversial movements, such as Wicca, have had to be more active in their public relations, demystifying and countering false claims. I will also consider the interaction between outward legitimation and inward legitimation in cases where external pressure brings about internal change in NRMs. In Finnish Wicca this has resulted in what I have termed the "new rise of tradition."

There are two disclaimers I want to make at this point. Firstly, I am by no means implying that "using" tradition as a legitimation "strategy" is always a conscious effort to construct a credible and convincing image of a religion, comparable to a marketing strategy or a military strategy (Lewis 2003, 13). In addition, while some groups do invest time in outward legitimation, there are some so-called world-rejecting NRMs (Wallis 1984, 9–39) that have little interest in outward legitimation.

Secondly, it would be quite bold of me to claim I could demonstrate how tradition is understood in all NRMs since there is not even a consensus of what constitutes the category of "new religious movements." However, approaching NRMs from the viewpoint of alternativity gives some leeway in this sense. Because the "alternative" status of a religion is always dependent on the social context, case studies shed light on the *dynamics* of the legitimation process, which in turn can be applied to different groups, situations and social settings.

I will begin by outlining a perspective on NRMs as alternative religions, after which I will take a look at the concept of legitimation and how tradition is used in legitimating NRMs. In the latter part of the chapter, I will demonstrate the dynamics of legitimation with examples from the history of Wicca and my own studies of Finnish Wiccans.

New Religious Movements as Alternative Religions

Since the early twentieth century, the English-speaking world has been occupied with the "cult problem." Alternative and fringe religions have, of course, always existed wherever religion has been institutionalized, but the word "cult" came into public prominence only during this period (Jenkins 2000, 4–8). It was soon loaded with negative connotations, as one contemporary scholarly definition reveals: "at best, the cults are a dreadful reality in modern religious life" (Binder 1933, quoted in Jenkins 2000, 11). It is easy to see that the contemporary news media and the "true crime" industry (see McCloud 2004) had even less inhibitions in describing the evil of the cults, to the effect that the term came to be used only in a disparaging sense (Dawson 2003a, 2). Being labeled as a cult meant identification with deviant sexual practices, coercion, and what would be later called brainwashing.

Academic definitions of cults gave way in the face of the pejorative use of the word. The concept of new religious movements was developed in the 1970's as a response to this pejorative use. However, from the outset the concept has been challenged for its vagueness and inconsistent use.

The temporal novelty of a religious group might be an appropriate way of categorizing religions, but it is very difficult to draw the line between new and old religions. For example, Jehovah's Witnesses and the Mormons are still treated as part of the family of new religious movements—alongside with much younger groups—while at the same time late twentieth century African Christian movements which display decidedly syncretistic features are often called "independent African churches." In this case it seems that theological considerations weigh more than the novelty of a group (Ketola 2001). However, theological definitions of new religious movements seem to rest on an equally uneven surface.

In fact, it has been proposed that an all-encompassing definition of new religious movements is impossible to find (Barker 1999, 20; Beckford 1985, 23; Wilson 1990, 204). All *substantial* definitions seem to fail in some ways (Melton 2003, 79–82).[1] However, from a *contextual* point of view, the situation is different. Therefore, in my opinion, the best way to understand NRMs is not to try to circumvent the "problem" of contextuality, but to embrace it by acknowledging that the most common feature of groups described as NRMs is their alternative status vis-à-vis the wider society. And as it is, "alternative" and "mainstream" are always defined by the social context (cf. Jenkins 2000, 16–18). This means that, depending on context, the substantial definition of NRMs changes radically. It would be somewhat anachronistic to call Mormonism a new religious movement in Utah, while at the same time it would be quite appropriate to do so in China.

The considerations presented above are by no means meant to be exhaustive and the final word in the discussion surrounding the study of new religious movements. I am also aware that many objections to my approach could be raised. Firstly, it might be argued that in a postmodern world the idea of mainstream religion and alternative religion is unconvincing (Hunt 2003, 6–9). But no matter what significance the modernization process has had for the emergence of multiculturalism and religious pluralism, I find it difficult to subscribe to a view where all religions are considered equal in all contexts. On the contrary, recent global developments seem to imply that the maintenance of strict boundaries has remained a constant feature of modern societies and religions— whether modernization as such is opposed or embraced (cf. Beyer 2003; Kniss 2003).

Secondly, my definition in essence encompasses *all* religion, including so-called world religions. In predominantly Lutheran (if quite secularized) Finland, for example, Islam fulfills the status of an alternative religion. However, when approached from the perspective of legitimation, world religions still occupy a substantially different position compared to NRMs. While the religious practices and behavior of the followers of world religions might arouse suspicion, the legitimacy of the tradition itself is very rarely questioned. Indeed, it could be said that often in the case of "alternative world religions" appeals to tradition are used for maintaining followers in a secularized and plural environment (inward legitimation), rather than as a legitimation strategy with an intent to gain popular acceptance (outward legitimation).

---

1   Eileen Barker (2003) questions this view. However, her list of common features of NRMs can be considered complementary, rather than contrary, to the approach presented here.

Melton (2003, 80) uses the following categories to describe a similar contextualized classification of NRMs:

1. Churches (e.g. dominant religious traditions in a given culture)
2. Ethnic Religions (e.g. Jews, Asian Buddhists, and Middle eastern Muslims in Western countries, for example)
3. Sects (e.g. splinter groups of dominant traditions)
4. New Religious Movements (e.g. everything else)

Thus, using Melton's categorization, the Evangelical Lutheran Church of Finland would represent the "church" in Finland, Somali Muslims the ethnic religions, Pentecostalists sects, and finally, Hare Krishna and Wicca the NRMs. Although all groups other than the Lutheran church could be defined as alternative, there are different "levels of alternativity," as noted above. The main difference between the groups is that while both sects and ethnic religions have "some recognized legitimacy in the eyes of the religious establishment, the *new religions* have yet to prove themselves" (Melton 2003, 80. Emphasis in the original). This is evidently so in Finland, and in all likelihood in other contexts, although the denominators in the model vary according to cultural characteristics.

Tradition as a Legitimation Strategy

The above quote from Melton hints at the process of legitimation that I see as one of the most important aspects of the study of NRMs. In his recent book *Legitimating New Religions*, James R. Lewis argues that "although scholars of new religions use the term [legitimation] freely, no one has published a single article, much less a book, focused on this issue—despite the fact that legitimacy is a core issue for emergent religious movements" (Lewis 2003, 11). Max Weber's (1978, 215) classic schema of legitimate authority is often mentioned in discussions of religious authority, and especially his concept of charisma is still recurrently used in studies of leadership in new religions (e.g. Robbins 1988, 116–117; Ketola 2002). Lewis employs Weber's tripartite schema of rationality—tradition—charisma in his assessment of the legitimation strategies of new and alternative religions (Lewis 2003, 13–14). He also emphasizes the point that new religious movements need to legitimate their views not only to converts and followers, but also to the wider society (Lewis 2003, 12).

Legitimation by tradition means that claims of legitimacy are based on "an established belief in the sanctity of immemorial traditions and the legitimacy of those exercising authority under them" (Weber 1978, 215). Among NRMs this doesn't necessarily mean a strictly historical interpretation, because as Barker notes, there is also the "tradition of inventing tradition" (Barker 2003, 91). That is why NRMs like ISKCON can claim descendancy from ancient Indian beliefs (legitimation by tradition) and also behold swami Prabhupada as the rightful interpreter of those beliefs (legitimation by charisma). As Lewis (2003, 14) suggests, tradition is often reinterpreted to legitimate innovation. Thus, NRMs with theologically novel ideas may call upon tradition as the legitimate source of the new creed, because existing interpretations do not catch the "essence" of the religion.

Weber's understanding of legitimation by tradition certainly applies to inward legitimation, the affirmation of beliefs and practices in the eyes of the adherents. Outward legitimation, on the other hand, is somewhat different. The legitimation of authority in Weber's sense means exercising power over other people, whereas the outward legitimacy of NRMs should be understood in the context of social acceptance and a religion's right to exist within a society (Lewis 2003, 15). However, as we will see in the case of Wicca, these two dimensions are often intertwined.

It is also fairly obvious that legitimation by tradition cannot be entirely separated from the other parts of Weber's model. Legitimation by referring to rational arguments or to the charisma of a leader of a NRM often overlaps with tradition discourse, as the previous example of the intertwining of tradition and charismatic leadership in ISKCON shows. Although the spheres overlap in this way, it is useful to separate them for analytical purposes (Lewis 2003, 13).

Because of prevailing popular representations of NRMs, studies of the legitimation strategies of NRMs often focus on the leader's charismatic abilities, marking him the most important way to salvation for the followers. Alternatively, as in the case of many so-called "client cults" (Stark and Bainbridge 1985, 28–29), studies may focus upon the rational argument in which the practice of a religion is argued to have healthy effects. However, tradition still has a role in the legitimation process of NRMs. The development of the history and mythical history of Wicca serves as a good example of this. In the next sections I will outline the development of the movement, the role of tradition in it, and the process where tradition has radically changed its meaning in Wicca.

Legitimating Wicca I: The Disputed Origins of a Religion[2]

Wicca, or modern witchcraft, is a diverse collection of beliefs and practices. What brings most of the practitioners together is the reverence for nature in all of its forms. However, while for some this reverence manifests itself in the form of complex rituals, for others it is a personal relationship that doesn't require the element of mystery religion that the more ceremonial forms represent (Harvey 1997, 35). Within this framework prevails a great variety of views on whether divinity is revered as one, many, or all-encompassing; male, female, or both, and whether magic plays a role in the beliefs. However, the

---

2   My aim here is to look at the legitimation of Wicca in its early stages and not to shed any new light on the discussion of the origins of the movement as such. Therefore, I have relied mainly on Hutton's (1999a, 1999b) presentation of the history of Wicca.

varieties of Wicca are not my main concern here. What makes Wicca interesting from the perspective of this chapter are the controversial claims of its early proponents regarding the role of tradition in the movement.

In 1954 Gerald B. Gardner, the "father" of modern Wicca, published his influential *Witchcraft Today* where he presented his version of the history of witchcraft and its contemporary manifestations. What made it different from other histories was the fact that Gardner claimed to write "from the inside," as a practicing witch. Although sworn to secrecy, he had been "permitted to write, as fiction, something that a witch believes" in his previous book *High Magic's Aid* (1996 [1949]). In *Witchcraft Today* he took on the same task, only now "in a factual way" (Gardner 1954, 18–19).

In his book, Gardner outlined a history of witchcraft that dated back from the Stone Age and survived in modern witch covens. In the title page Gardner is introduced as a "member of one of the ancient covens of the Witch Cult which still survives in England" (Gardner 1954, 1). His version of the history of (English) witchcraft was supported by a foreword by Egyptologist Margaret Murray, who earlier wrote *The Witch-Cult in Western Europe* (2003 [1921]), a very influential and widely-read book, where she espoused the view that the early modern witchcraft trials were an attempt to quench the ancient cult of a nature goddess, surviving from the pre-Christian era. Although their views diverged in some issues, Murray's support for Gardner made her somewhat of a "godmother of Wicca" (Hutton 1999a, 24–35; Hutton 1999b, 194–195, 225).

Considering that British witchcraft laws were not repealed until 1951, Gardner's insistence on the unbroken tradition of pre-Christian witches' religion can be seen as an attempt to legitimate a religion which still had plenty of negative connotations in public consciousness and discourse (Hutton 1999a, 54). Naturally Gardner's reinvention was also an attempt to homogenize the varied witchcraft beliefs, thus functioning as a tool for inward legitimation (Hutton 1999a, 55). In both cases these aims were only partially realized.

Despite Gardner's attempts to present witchcraft as an ancient benevolent tradition of nature religion, the English press repeatedly equated it with Satanism and evil. The beliefs and practices of Wicca were too far from the cognitive mainstream to rise above suspicion and hostility. Denouncements by the media led to a breach between factions of the core group of Wicca. On one side Gardner was feeding media interest while on the other a London coven led by high priestess Doreen Valiente tried to guarantee the continuity of her group by retreating from the limelight (Hutton 1999a, 50, 54; Hutton 1999b, 253–271).

Only in the 1960s and 1970s did Wicca start to receive more positive press when it was connected to the burgeoning youth counterculture. Alex and Maxine Sanders, the self-styled "King and Queen of the Witches," contributed to this development in their biographical accounts where they "told their life stories as medieval hagiographers, full of miracles and portraying the protagonists as warriors in a constant battle of good magic against bad" (Hutton 1999a, 59). In this way the image of the good witch could be reinforced. But the good witches were not a new invention either. Although Alex Sanders drew most of his teachings from Gardner, he legitimated his version with a new historiography. He claimed to come from a long line of witches and have a natural aptitude for magic, thus appealing to the image of hereditary witchcraft that had survived in the form of healers and cunning women throughout the centuries. Also, his "Alexandrian" branch of Wicca wasn't named so accidentally. While being self-referential, it was also an allusion to Alexandria, the ancient city with a history of multiplicity of religious and magical traditions (Hutton 1999a, 58–60).

The subsequent development of Wicca led to an increasing atomization of the movement. In America, witchcraft was taken as a symbol for the feminist movement, which led to the formation of the so-called goddess movement (Pearson 2002a, 36). This in turn led to a new emphasis on the figure of the goddess also in British Wicca in the 1980s. In its renewed form, the history of Wicca was now represented as a survival of a pre-Christian goddess religion, in which the reverence of "Mother Earth" was the central theme. The new historiography not only combined the elements of feminism and nature awareness, but also gave the movement a history and a tradition to look back upon. Starhawk (1999, 27), the most influential of the figures of this period, saw witchcraft as the Old Religion of the Mother Goddess, predating Christianity and other world religions. Twenty years after the original publication of *The Spiral Dance*, her most famous book, she admitted that her interpretation is a *mythic* history of witchcraft. However, at the same time she reaffirmed her belief in the correctness of this view, academic criticisms notwithstanding (Starhawk 1999, 263–264, 231–232).

Already at the time of writing of the first edition of *The Spiral Dance* (1979) the historiography that had its origins in Murray's thesis and spanned from Gardner to the more current Wiccan authors and figureheads came under attack from academic historians. Although suspicion and outright dismissal towards Murray's (and later Gardner's) views had been voiced earlier (Hutton 1999a, 33–36, 44), the definite blow was struck in the 1970s with several important studies of witchcraft and heresy dismissing it altogether (Thomas 1971, 514–519; Cohn 1993, 152–161; Russell 1980, 41–42). Tradition as a legitimation strategy was turning against Wicca as the credulity of Wiccan historiography was put under serious scrutiny.

At the onset of the 1980s the history of Wicca as presented originally by Gardner and based on the Murray thesis began to be treated in more critical terms also amongst Wiccans. Many influential Wiccan writers saw the thesis more as a foundation myth and treated the whole concept of Old Religion increasingly as a metaphor (Adler 1986, 86–87; Hutton 1999a, 65, 70). Concurrently, many of the Gardnerian and Alexandrian covens ceased to regard the alleged ancient origins of Wicca as a central facet of their faith, instead acknowledging (in varying degrees) the significance of Gardner's pioneering work as a founder of a new religion, which drew its influences from many different sources.

The 1980s also saw an increased eclecticism in Wicca, with a growing number calling themselves Wiccan, but ignoring most of the pioneers' teachings or combining them with other neopagan beliefs and practices. Consequently, it is nowadays possible to find a Wiccan who practices shamanistic drumming, prays to Norse deities, and practices divination with the tarot deck. There are even some Christian witches who call themselves "Christo-Wiccans." In this situation it is clear that the importance of tradition as a tool for legitimation is diminished or even disregarded. Some Wiccan authors, like the prolific and widely-read Scott Cunningham (e.g. Cunningham 1988), place virtually no significance on tradition in Wicca. Solitary and eclectic practitioners of Wicca have made their own "do-it-yourself religion" where a unified tradition is replaced by a sense of pragmatism: whatever works for me is good, no matter where its origins lie (Hutton 1999a, 71). However, tradition—now understood quite differently—has resurfaced as a tool for legitimation in situations where strain with the wider society exists, as the case of Finnish Wicca shows.

Legitimating Wicca II: The New Rise of Tradition[3]

The above presentation of the development of Wicca has unavoidably been brief and selective. Nevertheless, it lays the background for the examination of the meaning of tradition in contemporary Wicca, namely in the emergence of Wicca in the religious landscape of Finland.[4] In accordance with the contextual view presented above, the emergence of Finnish Wicca serves as one example of the dynamics of legitimation (and delegitimation). While the Finnish case does not exhaust the varieties of outcomes that a delegitimation-legitimation situation can possibly have, it serves as an illustrative framework for understanding the legitimation process and the role of tradition in it. I will concentrate on three main points: "conversion" as an implicit legitimation strategy, delegitimation by state authorities, and the "new rise of tradition" and the division of Finnish Wicca.

"Conversion" as an Implicit Legitimation Strategy

It has been noted that the religious group a person affiliates with conditions the depictions of the "past life" and the conversion experience itself (Beckford 1978, 251–258). This is evident especially in cases where the boundaries between the

---

3   Parts of this section have been reworked from a paper that will be published in the
    Journal of Contemporary Religion. See Hjelm (forthcoming).
4   The data for the study includes questionnaires, interviews, and notes from participant
    observation conducted at three "Wiccan Sabbats," informal gatherings of Finnish
    Wiccans of all traditions. The data is analyzed more comprehensively in Hjelm (forth-
    coming). All quotations here are from the questionnaires, unless specified otherwise.

past life and the "new life" are drawn sharply. But in the case of Wicca the matter is more complicated. Since the Wiccans don't proselytize and don't have a set pattern of "conversion" (Adler 1986, 14), it is interesting to find that the discourse used in portraying the identification (a more appropriate term in the case of Wicca) process is very similar among practitioners. For many of the respondents in my study, Wicca is a term which best describes those views that the respondents held already. Like one respondent wrote: "I found the English word Wicca, which best described my religion."[5] When asked how she became acquainted with Wicca, she went on to specify:

> Through literature and the Internet mostly, but the logic here is upside down, because my religiosity, which has existed since my childhood, "happened to be" Wicca. I did not adapt my religion to Wicca nor did I learn anything dictated by anybody. I *recognized* Wicca and the fact that I wasn't a lonely, strange creature in the world. (Woman, 39; original emphasis)

The idea that becoming a Wiccan or calling oneself a Wicca as a logical end point to one's worldview is a recurrent theme.

> It was something I had always been. Some sort of homecoming. (Woman, 19)
>
> I grouped together everything I had been vaguely aware of so far. I was surprised to notice that there were others like me. (Woman, 20)
>
> My world of ideas has always been "Wicca"... I heard about Wicca about 1997–1998. I found a name for my religion. (Man, 34)
>
> I had already formed my own worldview after an atheistic period. I felt that Wicca grouped my beliefs under one name. (Woman, 23)

Finding a name for one's pre-existing religion or a "home" are not expressions unique to Wicca (e.g. Lewis 2003, 117). However, the "logic of conversion" in Wicca seems to be the opposite compared to, for example, evangelical Christianity. Whereas the evangelical Christian is "born again" and sees her previous life behind her, with a sharp line between it and her current status, the Wiccan finds her past life in front of her: the past is defined as something which now has a name (see Pearson 2002b, 140).

What is significant is that few of the respondents offered any substantial reasons for identification with Wicca at this point (see Harvey 1997, 192–193). Some mentioned the reverence for nature and goddess worship as important factors, and these are most likely meaningful also for those who did not mention them when asked about their "conversion." However, from the perspective of legitimation, it is important to note that in this case the rhetoric of conversion downplays the importance of the content of the beliefs. The respondents identify with Wicca, while at the same time distancing themselves from it by stating

---

5   Adler (1986, 14) describes the discourse of American Wiccans in exactly the same terms.

that whatever you would call it, this would be my religion anyway. Although the beliefs remain the same, this strategy is used—although often implicitly—to avoid the negative labeling often resulting from the use of the terms "witch" or "Wiccan" (cf. Harvey 1997, 35).

The individualism of the conversion accounts relegates tradition to a less important or even an unimportant position. Adding this to the eclecticism of beliefs the respondents expressed in the survey, it seems that few of them felt that they were "converting" to an established tradition—at least in the sense of the Murray thesis. Substantial beliefs and the role of tradition were over-shadowed by functional interests like female empowerment and disappoint-ment with the prevailing religious institutions.

Thus, it could be said that the Finnish Wiccan community has been built more on a shared sense of alternativity and hostility or trivialization on the part of the wider society than a shared sense of tradition. The need for outward legitimation has overridden the need for inward legitimation. This in turn has created an inclusive community where the meaning of "Wicca" has been con-structed largely by self-definition. In the Q&A section of the annual "Witches' Sabbat," an informal gathering of Wiccans of all persuasions, the answer to the question "who is welcome to the sabbat?" was: "Wiccans are welcome. We use self-identification as the definition of Wicca: you are welcome if you consider yourself a Wiccan" (http://www.wicca.fi/wiccasapatti/ukk.html; July 8th, 2005). However, the attempt to legally and officially legitimate and register Wicca as a religious community has brought this inclusiveness under considerable strain.

Delegitimation by State Authorities

Legitimation strategies aiming at securing a place among registered religions in Finland for Wicca rang to dead ears when the The Finnish Free Wicca Associ-ation (SVWY ry.) applied for a status of a registered religious community in the beginning of 2001. Practicing religion in Finland does not require registration but it brings with it some benefits, notably the right to levy taxes on members for religious purposes (Seppo 1998). However, in the case of Wicca the aim was rather to gain public recognition as a serious religion (Hjelm 2005, 96).

With respect to tradition, the application submitted by SVWY ry. tried to be as inclusive as possible. In fact, it can be read almost like a popularized academic introduction to Wicca. Awareness of the academic refutations of the Murray thesis, for example, can be seen throughout the document. Instead of repeating the controversial claims concerning the ancient origins of the movement, the application positions tradition in the different forms of Wicca that have developed since Gardner's time. Thus, it included under the name "Wicca" a diverse array of different beliefs and practices, including some that many inside the neopagan movement do not consider "Wicca." This turned out to be the stumbling block for the registration attempt.

In late 2001 the department responsible for the registration at the Ministry of Education denied the application on the grounds that Wicca did not fulfill the requirements of a religious community as defined in the former Freedom of Religion Act.[6] As justification the ministry wrote:

> The community has been established for the practice of a neopagan movement called Wicca. The movement is not based on a creed, texts considered sacred, or other specified and established foundations considered sacred, but every person or group involved in the movement defines his/her/its view and ritual practice mainly by him/her/itself by combining influences from different sources. The movement's views and ritual practices are heterogeneous and fluctuating. Under these circumstances the community is not to be considered a religious community whose purpose is the public practice of religion, as defined in the 2nd clause of the Freedom of Religion Act. (Ministry of Education, 18 December 2001, Dnro1/901/2001)

The Finnish Free Wicca Association made a complaint about the decision to the Finnish Supreme Administrative Court, but their appeal was rejected. Consequently, all Wiccan groups in Finland operate under the register of associations. From the Wiccans' point of view the negative or trivializing public image of Wicca was legitimated by the authorities' decisions.

The "New Rise of Tradition"

The shortcomings of the application have been noted in academic studies (Sjöblom 2005). The major problem was that the Finnish Free Wicca Association tried to include all different branches of Wicca in their application (Hjelm 2005). This would be analogous to trying to register "Christianity" or "Lutheranism," whereas the registration applies only to clearly defined groups like the Finnish Methodist Church or the Jewish Congregation of Helsinki. Even if the Finnish authorities' definition of religion could be justly considered to have a Judeo-Christian bias, the application could not have worked the way it was drafted. The eclectic and inclusive nature of Wicca in Finland turned against itself when confronted by the authorities.

Soon after the initial disappointment for the failure of the registration process, the Wiccan community also recognized the problems with the application. Although the inclusive atmosphere of the community had never been shared by everyone (the reclusive Gardnerians being a prime example), this setback put new strains on the unity of the movement. Especially important is the growing worry about the motivations of new recruits and the loss of credi-

---

6 The Freedom of Religion Act of 1922, which was in effect at the time of the Wiccans' application, was amended in 2003 but the provisions regarding the definition of a religious community remained unchanged.

bility such "Wiclettes"[7] may bring (cf. Pearson 2002a, 41–44). For some (who conveniently identified themselves as "traditionalists")[8] a turn to what I have termed the "new rise of tradition"[9] has served as the best legitimation strategy.

In an interview one traditionalist stated clearly what was the difference between herself and the "wannabees": "I don't think everybody can call themselves Wiccan. We have a tradition. We have a doctrine. Read Gerald Gardner. He founded it all. Reading one 'fluffy' [a term she used in English] book doesn't make you a Wiccan." Her remark echoes the sentiment felt more broadly among the traditionalists and summarizes the position that to be a legitimate Wicca, one should know the basic writings of the "classics" (although there was some variation on which were defined as the definitive works). Some also indicated that being part of a coven is necessary. In the eyes of the modern traditionalists Gerald Gardner's teachings have supplanted the Murray thesis (endorsed by Gardner himself) as the legitimate source of tradition. Interestingly enough, these claims conform very well to the complaints made by the Ministry of Education quoted earlier. One cannot avoid the impression that, for some, turning to tradition is a response to the authorities' denial of the religion status.

This exclusivity expressed by the traditionalists is in stark contrast to the professed openness of the Finnish Wicca community and undoubtedly a response to the pressure created by the public reception of Wicca. While all the respondents of my study seem to share the concern for Wicca as a true, genuine religion, it remains to be seen which will be defined as the proper ways to practice that true religion. That is, will orthodoxy be introduced into the hitherto eclectic and open community? This marks the change of the role of tradition as a primarily outward legitimation strategy to an inward one. It also unavoidably creates tension within the movement, since the growing popularity of Wicca makes the traditionalists define the boundaries of "real Wicca" even sharper and at the same time relegates them further to the margins of the movement (Pearson 2002a, 42–43).

Conclusion

In the first part of this chapter I proposed alternativity as the main characteristic of new religious movements. Although in different contexts even so-called world

---

7   By this term the older members referred to young girls interested in Wicca through popular culture witches.

8   In Finnish Wiccan terminology "traditionalist" usually refers to Gardnerian and Alexandrian Wicca, whereas "eclectic" refers to solitary Wiccans, different goddess spiritualities, and a variety of other branches of modern witchcraft (cf. Harvey 1997, 35).

9   If the claims of the first-generation Wiccans (discussed in the previous section) are regarded as the original tradition, i.e. ancient goddess-worship, the "new tradition" holds Gerald Gardner and his immediate contemporaries as the true source of tradition.

religions can be considered alternative, it is usually the groups labeled new religions that have to legitimate their existence most actively. Tension with the wider society—whether real or imagined—is apt to create implicit and explicit legitimations of varying types among new religious movements. In this process tradition becomes an important legitimation strategy, as I have shown in the case of Wicca.

However, because of the necessarily contextual nature of defining "alternative," one representative case is bound to be insufficient to cover the whole field of new religious movements. Although legitimation as such can be described as a more or less universal feature in the positioning of new religious movements vis-à-vis the wider society, the role that tradition plays in legitimation depends on each religion and each social context where the process takes place. What the alternative status and the novelty ascribed to new religious movements in general implies is that tradition is actively constructed and that its importance for any given group is situational: each social and cultural context generates different uses for tradition as a legitimation strategy. As the case of Wicca shows, in some circumstances this has implications for both outward legitimation and inward legitimation, as tradition can become a unifying or a divisive factor.

References

Adler, Margot. 1986. *Drawing Down the Moon: Witches, Druids, Goddess-Worshippers, and other Pagans in America Today*. Revised and Expanded Edition. New York: Penguin.

Barker, Eileen. 1999. "New Religious Movements: Their Incidence and Significance." Pages 15–31 in *New Religious Movements: Challenge and Response*. Edited by Bryan Wilson and Jamie Cresswell. London: Routledge.

———. 2003. "Perspective: What Are We Studying? A Sociological case for Keeping the 'Nova'." *Nova Religio* 8: 88–102.

Beckford, James A. 1985. *Cult Controversies: The Societal Response to the New Religious Movements*. London and New York: Tavistock.

Beyer, Peter. 2003. "Social Forms of Religion and Religions in Contemporary Global Society." Pages 45–60 in *Handbook of the Sociology of Religion*. Edited by Michele Dillon. Cambridge: Cambridge University Press.

Chryssides, George D. 1999. *Exploring New Religions*. London and New York: Cassell.

Cohn, Norman. 1993. *Europe's Inner Demons: The Demonization of Christians in Medieval Christendom*. Revised Edition. London: Pimlico [1975].

Cunningham, Scott. 1988. *Wicca: A Guide for the Solitary Practitioner*. St. Paul, Minn.: Llewellyn Publications.

Dawson, Lorne L. 2003a. "Introduction: The Book and the Subject." Pages 1–4 in *Cults and New Religious Movements: A Reader*. Edited by Lorne L. Dawson. Oxford: Blackwell.

———. 2003b. "Joining New Religious Movements." Pages 113–115 in ibid.

Gardner, Gerald B. 1954. *Witchcraft Today*. London: Rider & Company.

———. 1996. *High Magic's Aid*. Hinton, Indiana: Godolphin House [1949].

Harvey, Graham. 1997. *Contemporary Paganism: Listening People, Speaking Earth*. New York: New York University Press.

Hjelm, Titus. 2005. "Wicca kohtaa valtion." Pages 95–132 in *Mitä wicca on?* Edited by Titus Hjelm. Helsinki: Like.

———. "Between Satan and Harry Potter: Legitimating Wicca in Finland." *Journal of Contemporary Religion*, forthcoming.

Hunt, Stephen J. 2003. *Alternative religions: A Sociological Introduction*. Aldershot: Ashgate.

Hutton, Ronald. 1999a. "Modern Pagan Witchcraft." Pages 3–79 in Willem de Blecourt, Ronald Hutton, and Jean La Fontaine, *Witchcraft and Magic in Europe: The Twentieth Century*. London: Athlone.

———. 1999b. *The Triumph of the Moon: A History of Modern Pagan Witchcraft*. Oxford: Oxford University Press.

Jenkins, Philip. 2000. *Mystics and Messiahs: Cults and New Religions in American History*. Oxford: Oxford University Press.

Ketola, Kimmo. 2001. "Uudet uskonnolliset liikkeet. Katsaus käsitteisiin, luokituksiin, teorioihin ja tilastoihin." Pages 10–38 in *Vanhat jumalat, uudet tulkinnat. Näköaloja uusiin uskontoihin Suomessa*. Edited by Jussi Niemelä. Comparative Religion 6. Helsinki: Department of Comparative Religion, University of Helsinki.

———. 2002. An Indian Guru and His Western Disciples: Representation and Communication of Charisma in the Hare Krishna Movement. Ph.D. diss., University of Helsinki, 2002. Available at <http://ethesis.helsinki.fi/julkaisut/hum/uskon/vk/ketola/>

Kniss, Fred. 2003. "Mapping the Moral Order: Depicting the Terrain of Religious Conflict and Change." Pages 331–347 in *Handbook of the Sociology of Religion*. Edited by Michele Dillon. Cambridge: Cambridge University Press.

Lewis, James R. 2003. *Legitimating New Religions*. New Brunswick: Rutgers University Press.

———, and Jesper Aagaard Petersen (eds.). 2005. *Controversial New Religions*. Oxford and New York: Oxford University Press.

McCloud, Sean. 2004. *Making the American Religious Fringe: Exotics, Subversives, & Journalists, 1955–1993*. Chapel Hill: The University of North Carolina Press.

Melton, J. Gordon. 1992. *Encyclopedic Handbook of Cults in America*. Revised and Updated Edition. New York: Garland.

———. 1996. *Encyclopedia of American Religions*. 5th edition. Detroit: Gale Research.

———. 2003. "Perspective: Toward a Definition of 'New 'Religion'." *Nova Religio* 8: 73–87.

Miller, Timothy (ed.). 1995. *America's Alternative Religions*. Albany: State University of New York Press.

Murray, Margaret. 2003. *The Witch-Cult in Western Europe*. Whitefish, Montana: Kessinger Publishing [1921].

Pearson, Joanne. 2002a. "The History and Development of Wicca and Paganism." Pages 15–54 in *Belief Beyond Boundaries: Wicca, Celtic Spirituality, and the New Age*. Edited by Joanne Pearson. Aldershot: Ashgate.

———. 2002b. "Witches and Wicca." Pages 133–172 in ibid.

Robbins, Thomas. 1988. *Cults, Converts, and Charisma: The Sociology of New Religious Movements*. London: Sage.

Russell, Jeffrey B. 1980. *A History of Witchcraft: Sorcerers, Heretics and Pagans*. London: Thames and Hudson.

Seppo, Juha. 1998. "The Freedom of Religion and Conscience in Finland." *Journal of Church and State* 40: 847–872.

Sjöblom, Tom. 2005. "Uskontona olemisen taidosta—keskustelua wiccan virallistamisesta uskonnoksi." Pages 133–149 in *Mitä wicca on?* Edited by Titus Hjelm. Helsinki: Like.

Starhawk. 1999 [1979]. *The Spiral Dance: A Rebirth of the Ancient Religion of the Great Goddess*. New York: Harper.

Stark, Rodney. 1996. "Why Religious Movements Succeed or Fail: A Revised General Model." *Journal of Contemporary Religion* 11: 133–146.

———, and William Sims Bainbridge. 1985. *The Future of Religion: Secularization, Revival, and Cult Formation*. Berkeley: University of California Press.

Thomas, Keith. 1999. *Religion and the Decline of Magic*. London: Penguin [1971].

Wallis, Roy. 1984. *The Elementary Forms of the New Religious Life*. London: Routledge & Kegan Paul.

Weber, Max. 1978. *Economy and Society: An Outline of Interpretive Sociology*. Edited by Guenther Roth and Claus Wittich. Translated by Ephraim Fischoff et al. Berkeley: University of California Press.

Wilson, Bryan R. 1990. *The Social Dimensions of Sectarianism: Sects and New Religious Movements in Contemporary Society*. Oxford: Clarendon Press.

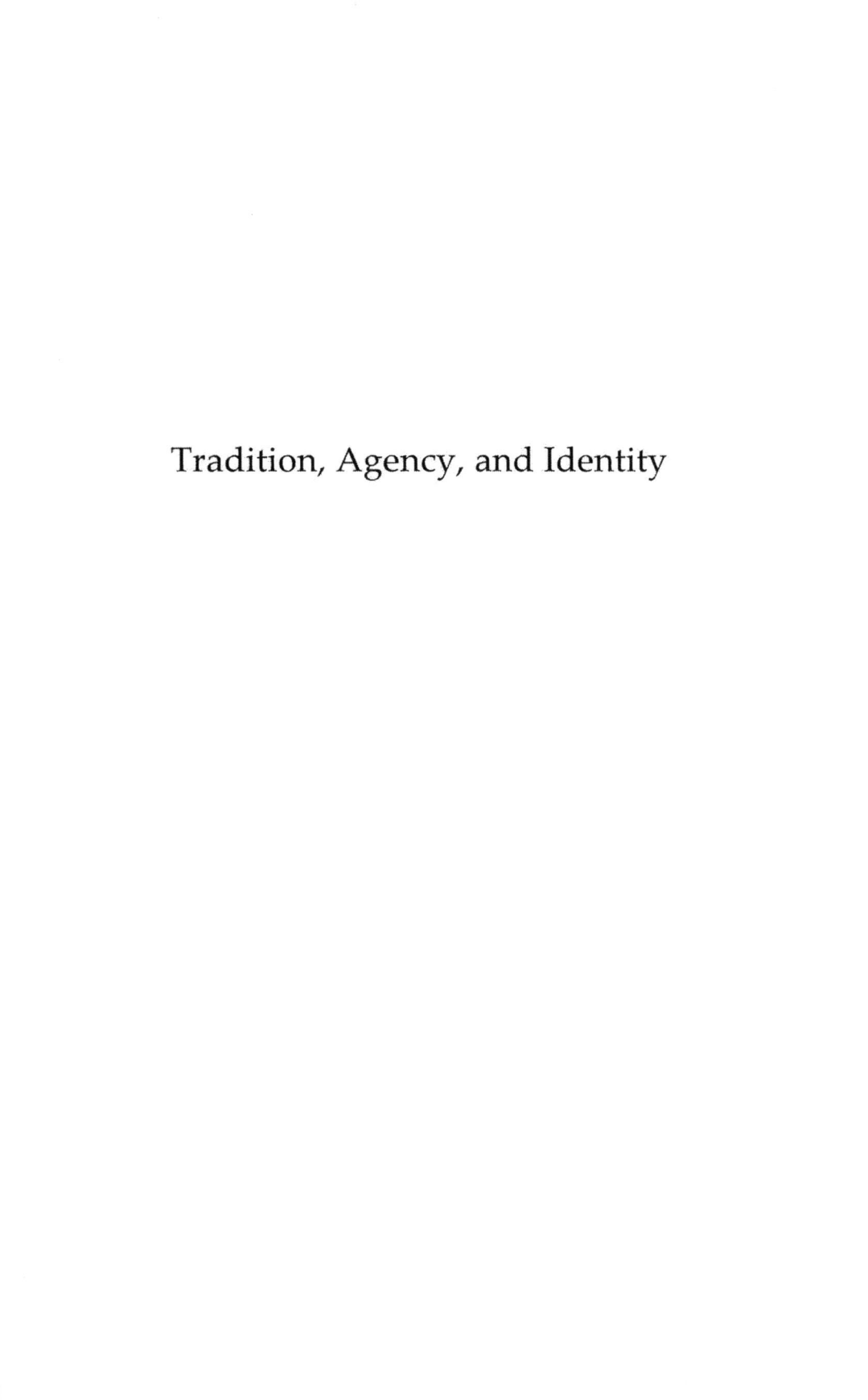

Tradition, Agency, and Identity

Women and the Book of Mormon: The Creation and Negotiation of a Latter-Day Saint Tradition

Susanna Morrill

At the turn of the nineteenth century, when Mormon schoolteacher Martha Cragun Cox took a trip through Arizona to New Mexico, she visited an ancient Native American dwelling. In her autobiography, she describes this dwelling as a "Nephite mansion." To her mind, this archaeological treasure was the construction of one of the Israelite tribes that the Book of Mormon records as living in the ancient Americas.[1] The Book of Mormon shaped such simple, everyday perceptions, even as it drove the most profoundly religious actions of Latter-day Saint members. Martha Cragun Cox also tells the story of an eccentric missionary to Native Americans who was directed on his missionary work by the Three Nephites, three American followers of Jesus who, according to the Book of Mormon, had been left behind to roam the earth and provide spiritual help to the faithful until the Second Coming (Cox 1928–1930, 222).

Looking at these very personal stories, we can see that, as the founding scriptures of the Church of Jesus Christ of Latter-day Saints (the LDS Church), the Book of Mormon and related texts have had a pervasive influence on the history and worldview of the Mormon community. Yet Mormon women such as Cox did not simply exist unconsciously within the Book of Mormon worldview, they also actively helped create this worldview. They had a vital hand in building the traditions within which they lived and understood the world. Cox's straightforward, Book of Mormon-oriented descriptions reveal only a small, passive part of how women interacted with this scripture.

When LDS women and men accepted the Book of Mormon, they rejected both the Catholic reliance on a line of temporally continuous apostolic power, and the Protestant faith focused on localized leadership and individual interpretation of the Bible. The Book of Mormon introduced a new, American scriptural narrative and, just as importantly, it described a lay apostolic and revelatory power that originated from nineteenth-century visitations by various biblical and extra-biblical characters. This presumably unadulterated divine power cut through what Mormons viewed as centuries of corrupted, Christian belief and practice.

---

1 Similarly, she ruefully recounted her visit to Phoenix, a city originally settled and then given up by Mormon pioneers. She was disturbed that a city fed by—in her words—an ancient Nephite canal had been abandoned to non-Mormon by these latter-day successors of the Nephites (Cox 1928–1930, 222).

Well into the twentieth century, viewed as dissenting radicals by the mainstream American religious establishment, LDS faithful lived in a religious culture that scripturally re-centered Judeo-Christian religious history within the American context.

Marcel Sarot has argued that the Book of Mormon is an example of Eric Hobsbawm's concept of an "invented tradition"—but a specifically religious case of this phenomenon (Sarot 2001). Sarot uses Karl Popper's discussion of tradition as an expansive wedge to make Hobsbawm's concept more flexible and more relevant to the historical study of religion. Perhaps most usefully, Sarot widens Hobsbawm's concept to include not just rituals and symbols, but most aspects of religious life, including narrative and scriptural elements. Sarot explains this concept of tradition:

> A tradition is a set of practices, normally governed by overtly or tacitly accepted rules, which presuppose a factual context. Traditions may help us 1. to discern order in a *prima facie* chaotic world, 2. to know how to act within this world, 3. to participate in groups and communities, 4. to claim an identity for ourselves, 5. to let other people know what we expect of them, and 6. to change the contexts within which we live. These rules seek to inculcate certain values and norms of behaviour by repetition, which automatically implies continuity with the past. Traditions need not be invariable, but they do need to exhibit a certain degree of continuity over time. (Sarot 2001, 27)

For Sarot, traditions are the structuring, but flexible guidelines, assumptions, practices, and expectations that members of a religious community live within and, when necessary, modify.

Sarot is not entirely clear on whether he considers Mormonism as a whole a new tradition and the Book of Mormon simply one aspect of that tradition, or whether he considers the Book of Mormon itself a tradition along with other traditions that make up Mormonism as a religious community—temple rituals, weekly worship, tithing, patriarchal blessings. His interpretation seems to assume the latter, and, as I hope the following discussion demonstrates, the idea that a religious community is made up of numerous, sometimes externally and internally contradictory and changing traditions represents most accurately and usefully how this and other religious groups actually exist and operate. Refining this Sarot-Hobsbawm model, in this case study, women writers were agents of tradition-making—one group among many similar agents within their religious community. They looked to the Book of Mormon tradition for guidance, but also provided conflicting, woman-centered guidance on how this tradition was shaped in concert with the other traditions, elements, and membership segments of the Mormon community. Traditions within religious groups are many, and many, even seemingly incompatible individuals, influences, and points of view combine to create them.

As a key tradition within the LDS re-positioning of Judeo-Christian culture—from the Mormon point of view, a re-awakening—the Book of Mormon created a religious narrative that emphasized the importance of fatherhood and patriarchal authority. Thus, the Book of Mormon tells of a series of prophet-patriarchs who either led their families and communities along the true, godly path, or towards religious destruction. Lawrence Foster has noted this recurring theme of family disorder and structuring in the Book of Mormon: "Indeed, the restoration of family ties was implicit in the commission Joseph Smith said had been given in his vision of September 21, 1823—when, according to his account, the angel Moroni told him that he would bring forth the Book of Mormon" (Foster 1984, 132). The Book of Mormon was to be a definitive model for ideal patriarchal family, gender, and divine interactions.

Founder Joseph Smith sought to redress what he felt was the corrupting imbalance of authority between the genders. For him, the original church had declined because the role of the father within the family and the church had corroded. Smith reacted against a nineteenth-century mainstream American culture that promoted or simply assumed mothers to be the central moral anchor of the family. The nineteenth century was the heyday of what has been termed the "cult of domesticity" and, particularly, the cult of motherhood. By way of describing this ethos, Ann Douglas notes:

> The cult of motherhood was nearly as sacred in mid-nineteenth-century America as the belief in some version of democracy. Books on mothers of famous men, especially Mary Washington, mother of George Washington, poured from the presses in the 1840s–1850s; their message was that men achieved greatness because of the instruction and inspiration they received from their mothers. (Douglas 1988, 74)

In the popular and religious press, motherhood was adulated and described in glowing and idealized terms as the foundation of families and societies. Religion and the family were "feminized," to use Douglas' term. Women became domestic and spiritual centers who, through their sacrifice and selflessness, controlled the behavior and characters of their husbands and children.

Smith, and then his successor, Brigham Young, sought to reorder this perceived disorganization by instituting a church based on ascending levels of lay patriarchal, priesthood power, and also establishing the practice of polygamy. Their scriptural, patriarchal focus was reflected transparently in the familial and institutional structures of the LDS Church. They made the father-patriarch the pivot point around which the family and the church rotated. Elizabeth Kane, a sympathetic non-Mormon who visited the LDS community in the 1870s was forcibly struck with the patriarchal focus of the society, likening it to the biblical model in which Smith and Young self-consciously found inspiration: "During my whole stay in Utah, I have found the poetry of the Bible running in my mind. I have felt myself to be living in that old Syrian work amid a people whose ways are like those of the ancient pastoral folk to whom Isaiah spoke" (Kane 1995, 129).

In the Hobsbawm-Sarot model, the Book of Mormon was a tradition that claimed to leap-frog back and activate and reinterpret part of the biblical, Christian narrative in order to provide explanation and continuity for a community undergoing a radical shift in familial and social structure. The Book of Mormon authoritatively explained how and why the patriarch was the driving social, religious, and familial force within the Mormon community. This was how God ordained society in the beginning, and it was how God's chosen people had to live in order to take part in a reactivated and authentic relationship with God. According to the Book of Mormon, the patriarch was the prophetic figure through whom the community authoritatively received God's will and God's words. These patriarch/prophets were the religious light towards which the ancient (and modern) Mormon communities turned for direction. Within the scripture, these patriarchs provided a cohesive narrative that ordered the LDS world, showed members how to act and participate within this world, gave religious models for behavioral expectations, and, thus, actively changed the religious world in which members lived (Sarot 2001, 27).

This male-centered scriptural, institutional, and social focus did not deter women from joining the LDS Church and embracing the Book of Mormon as a meaningful religious document. However, LDS women did not simply accept the patriarchal focus of the Book of Mormon, they actively interpreted this new scriptural tradition for their own circumstances. At around the time Martha Cragun Cox was making her way across Arizona, as a group, women of the church were undergoing their own time of transition as they moved from limited access to prophetic, revelatory authority and actions, and toward the modern LDS Church where female institutional and prophetic presence is, generally speaking, more circumscribed and controlled.[2] At this crucial time of religious standardization and rationalization (1880–1920), LDS women writers played an important role in how the Book of Mormon was integrated into the modern church. These writers helped to negotiate what parts of the Book of Mormon were interpreted, and participated in creating and validating the process of tradition-making. They sought to make the scripture effective and meaningful for their own lives and priorities.

To do this, Mormon women writers selectively focused on two Book of Mormon episodes: the story of the stripling warriors, and the LDS reinterpretation of the Fall and Eve. Publishing in the *Woman's Exponent*, the semi-official publication of the Mormon women's auxiliary, the Relief Society, LDS women explored and discussed these stories and, thereby, adapted them to voice female concerns and to support a definable women's culture and authority within the Mormon community. Balancing the Book of Mormon focus on prophet-patriarchs, these women writers emphasized the importance of motherhood within

---

2   For a full discussion of this pivotal time period and its institutional changes, see Alexander 1986.

the plan of salvation. By interpreting these stories in conjunction with the Old and New Testaments, as well as through a filter of long-standing Victorian gender norms, women writers shared in and shaped the theological discourses of their community.

Further, by presenting these stories within the context of religious, but popular literature, women writers participated in an extended, continuing, and often subtextual discussion about what tradition was and how it should be comprehended and enacted. They played a part in negotiating the theological contents of their religion, but they also helped to structure how their religious community internally understood scriptural tradition, history, and interpretation. At this transitional time, for women writers, the Book of Mormon tradition became a combination of scriptural and authoritative institutional revelation combined with more communal public and literary discussions that were fueled by individual prophetic encounters with the divine. Though ostensibly based in obedience to LDS scripture and institutional, patriarchal prophecy, in this case study, in practice, this Mormon tradition became a kind of contained, textual conversation generated by women.

Sarot has developed the term, "counterfactuals," in order to better grasp the dynamic of how traditions are generated within religious communities. For Sarot, counterfactuals are events or facts that, from the point of view of scholars or outsiders, are open to question, but, from the point of view of members of a religious community, are major generators of meaning and symbolism. They are events, facts, or concepts that serve as a focus of a new tradition—and that must be believed as fact in order to serve as this focus of the community. He writes: "Thus, though the truth of the counterfactual cannot be ascertained, its untruth should not be established either" (Sarot 2001, 33). Sarot argues that the Book of Mormon is an exception to the rule because members continue to believe in the scripture, though it has been proven that Smith was the author of the scripture and borrowed many points from Ethan Smith's *View of the Hebrews* (33). Putting aside the controversy about the origin of the Book of Mormon, about which there are countless scholarly views both within and without the LDS community, perhaps we should not single out the Book of Mormon and Mormonism as an exception to the rule. Most religious groups contain elements of tradition that outsiders and scholars believe are not factually true, but members accept on some level as truth. Humans are able to hold simultaneously starkly contradictory beliefs—oftentimes without much difficulty, and even with a perceptive self-consciousness. More important to understanding any religious group or tradition within a group is to more fully understand how and why traditions develop and become meaningful and authoritative within a community.

As this case study will show, traditions are not simply generated from above and accepted *in toto* from the members below. The Book of Mormon as, from Sarot's point of view, a crucial "counterfactual," was accepted as divinely generated scripture by most members of the early Mormon community. Yet it had to be adapted and interpreted in order to function effectively within the community; it had to be integrated into existing and emerging social, cultural, and religious structures and traditions. In this instance, LDS women writers who also lived within a larger American culture that espoused rather different gender values from their chosen faith community, selected certain, relevant episodes within the narrative. Then, utilizing other traditions within the Mormon community including direct, individual access to God, they spun out further interpretive possibilities for a seemingly inflexible and unchangeable scriptural tradition. As they negotiated and tested the elements of their religious community, LDS women writers and readers created their own scriptural, interpretive sub-tradition that inevitably influenced the more general Mormon scriptural tradition. Here, a tradition was so effective because it claimed to hark back to older days, but also because it was made relevant to the present day by those who had to deal with these present-day realities.

Necessary Preconditions to Negotiation: Literary and Revelatory Opportunities

Women were able to participate in the shaping of their community and their scriptural tradition because they had access to authoritative literary means — and they had issues on which they could speak authoritatively. These developments are essential to understand as a prelude to setting up how and why LDS women writers participated in scriptural discussions.

The years 1880–1920 saw a renaissance in Mormon women's literature. The *Woman's Exponent* was the most important forum in which women of the LDS Church stretched their literary wings — it was a key part of this female literary efflorescence. The *Exponent* was founded in 1872 with the permission and encouragement of then church prophet, Brigham Young. However, its status within the Mormon community was ambiguous because of its somewhat fuzzy relationship with the Relief Society.

The Relief Society was the women's auxiliary of the LDS Church that was begun in 1842 on impetus of women of the church, but with the blessing of then prophet, Joseph Smith. The organization was disbanded shortly after this when women members, including Smith's wife, Emma Smith, openly opposed the practice of polygamy that Smith was advocating at this time. The organization was gradually and locally, and, finally, formally re-organized in Utah under the leadership of Eliza R. Snow, a plural wife of Smith and then Young, and a woman who was considered to be a prophetess because of her poetic talents and her ties to the first church prophets.

In its early Utah incarnation, the Relief Society was somewhere between a woman's parallel to the priesthood and a church auxiliary for women. Like the priesthood, it was organized from the ward (parish) to general level and had similar, repeating levels of triadic and committee leadership. However, key leaders at all levels were selected and installed by male leaders of the church. Though members of the Relief Society did perform semi-formal blessings on women before childbirth confinement, or on women who had reproductive or health problems, for the most part, members of the Relief Society looked after the less fortunate women and children of their communities, and also assisted families at times of childbirth, sickness, and death. The Relief Society had a distinctly practical, charitable mission. Nonetheless, the organization had a fairly wide range of autonomy within the church. Relief Society members collected and maintained their own funds with which they supported the needy, built their own Relief Society meeting places, and ran the basic programs of the auxiliary.[3]

The *Woman's Exponent* had a similar, parallel existence. The tabloid-formatted periodical was financed with subscriptions, and edited by women. Emmeline B. Wells was the editor for the lion's share of the periodical's existence, beginning her term in 1877 and stepping down only when the *Exponent* ended its run in 1914. The periodical was often described as the "organ" of the Relief Society.[4] Though the Relief Society did not directly fund the *Exponent*, at least one president of the Relief Society urged that local Relief Societies appoint women to collect subscriptions among local members ("The Jubilee Celebration" 1892, 132). The *Exponent* reported and vigorously supported the Relief Society, extensively describing the work and meetings of the organization from the local to the general level. In turn, members of the Relief Society actively drummed up support for the *Exponent*. However, legally and officially, the two organizations remained separate. In many ways, this is a representative snapshot of how the LDS Church as a whole operated at this time; a certain decentralization and informality linked together members and their various church-related projects.

Throughout her tenure, Wells vigorously solicited subscriptions to keep the periodical on its feet, and she also strongly encouraged Mormon women to contribute their work for publication.[5] The *Exponent* carried a wide range of genres including poetry, essays, reports, stories, sermons, obituaries, and epigrams—

---

3   For details on the history and work of the Relief Society, see Derr et al. 1992.

4   "Brigham Young and Eliza R. Snow started the Woman's Exponent, over forty years ago...made it the organ of the Relief Society of the Church" ("Second Literary Child" 1915, 38).

5   Wells frequently inserted notices within the *Exponent* that encouraged women to support the paper with subscriptions ("Notice to Agents" 1891, 4). However, just as frequently she encouraged her readers to send in submissions for publication. In one instance, she exhorted her readers: "Sisters, if you have ideas that will benefit others put them upon paper and send them to the press, they will reach a larger number of people in that way, and by that means you may be sowing some good seed that will eventually bear fruit" ("Editorial Notes" 1891, 69).

women could contribute just about any kind of literary work on just about any subject. This was a women's periodical dedicated to issues of interest to women, but it was also a religiously-focused publication dedicated to spreading information and news about the LDS Church to members and non-members alike.

Though Wells continually and often unsuccessfully attempted to increase the flow of submissions, she was especially effective in inspiring those she knew personally to write for the *Exponent*. In addition to her editorship, Wells was a highly placed woman within the Relief Society central leadership, and a plural wife to Daniel Wells, a counselor in the church presidency of Brigham Young. Wells' close friends were often women who were similarly highly placed in the Relief Society leadership, or with close ties to the central male leadership circle of the church. The women who wrote for the *Exponent*, therefore, often were well respected by both men and women members of the LDS community.

As mentioned above, one of these women, Relief Society President Eliza R. Snow was believed to communicate prophetic thoughts by means of her poetry. She converted her poem, "Oh, My Father," into a hymn that became widely popular within the church throughout the nineteenth and into the twentieth centuries. In many ways, Snow was the model for women to follow in combining literary and spiritual work in order to speak convincingly, theologically, and non-confrontationally. She started a Mormon tradition of (often elite) women using poetic and literary means to speak with authoritative voices — voices that communicated by means of the *Exponent*, and had strong and deep resonance in the institutional church.

One of the reasons that Snow and her literary successors were able to speak theologically and authoritatively was that Mormonism held within it another, more general, formal tradition of individual revelation and access to the divine by every individual. Joseph Smith established this crucial LDS tradition when he described receiving visitations from God, Jesus, and angels while still a teenager. Even more relevant, according to Mormon history, Smith translated the Book of Mormon while still in his early twenties. Members of the LDS Church felt that the communication and connection with the divine had been re-opened in the latter days, and while they looked to prophetic leaders such as Smith and Young for guidance, they also felt compelled by these weighty examples to find their own truths and answers from the ultimate, divine source.

We see this understanding and practice throughout the women's sources of this time period. In the July 15, 1884 edition of the *Exponent*, an author identified only as M., wrote approvingly about the increasing number of women writers in Utah, arguing forcefully that they were simply and by divine necessity expressing their connection and inspiration from God.

> ...[B]ut why should not the women of Utah be able to write, and to write glorious sentiments, too? Are they not living under the voice and influence of inspiration? Have they not the Spirit of God within them to guide their thoughts and expression? And why should they not be per-

mitted to write? The time has come when the Lord is not only willing that their voices shall be heard in the land, but His Spirit calls upon them to speak, and they feel that they must do it. The testimony of the truth which they have often borne to each other is burning within them and they feel they must give it to the world (M. 1884, 31–32).

The author goes on to argue that though rough and difficult missionary work was not open to women, writing was the appropriate form for women to contribute to the community's internal and external missionary work. The *Exponent* communicated the personal religious testimonies and revelations of Mormon women to each other, and to the wider reading audience.

As the twentieth century progressed, public expression of personal revelation declined as the leadership of the LDS Church sought to standardize institutional structures and practices.[6] The Relief Society also lost much of its limited autonomy and existence as this standardization process moved through all parts of the church. But, for the years we are examining, women writers, especially women of the elite inner circle of leadership, had access to a literary vehicle of expression designed purposefully to showcase and encourage their theological, revelatory expressions. Their literary voices were extensions of the wider, Mormon tradition of individual revelation, and, following the example of Eliza Snow, also deepened a Mormon sub-tradition of women speaking authoritatively through textual and literary means. It was from within this LDS female literary tradition that women contributed to the wider, scriptural Book of Mormon tradition.

Women in the Book of Mormon: A Tradition in Negotiation

The Book of Mormon introduced very few new women characters into Mormon theological discussions.[7] Only three Book of Mormon women characters are mentioned by name—Sariah, Abish, and Isabel—and even these three are only minor players in the overarching narrative of the scriptures.[8] For the most part, in the Book of Mormon, women are mentioned in the collective and usually in reference to family connections as mothers, wives, and daughters.

---

6   Thomas G. Alexander has written extensively on this process of centralization and standardization that began in the late nineteenth century and accelerated as the twentieth century progressed (Alexander 1986).

7   An article in the *Woman's Exponent* noted: "It is somewhat noticeable how little prominence is given to womankind in the historical narrative of the Book of Mormon, and unfortunately when mention is made of her it too frequently grows out of man's sins and her misfortunes" (G. 1880, 7–8).

8   Sariah has the greatest part to play. As the wife of Lehi, the first prophet of the Book of Mormon who leads his family from Jerusalem to the Americas, she even appears in dialogue with her husband and family. She appears in the dialogue of 1 Nephi 5:1–8 at first berating her husband for his prophesying and then praising God for leading and inspiring her family.

Therefore, it should not be surprising that a collective female character is one of the most mentioned and most meaningful Book of Mormon figure within LDS women's literature. The mothers of the stripling warriors appear in the book of Alma in a description of one of the continuing conflicts between factions of the Nephites and Lamanites. The Nephites were the descendants of the first Book of Mormon patriarch Lehi's godly son, Nephi, and the Lamanites were the descendants of Lehi's rebellious son, Laman. In this particular episode, a group of Lamanites had gone over to the side of the Nephites and had pledged not to shed any more blood so that, in the ensuing armed conflicts, they were not able to help their Nephite allies. Their culturally Nephite sons had not taken this pledge and, so, two thousand of them gathered under the command of the Nephite leader, Helaman.[9] They were very young and had never fought in a war. Nevertheless, before their first conflict with the Lamanites, they were not afraid because "they had been taught by their mothers, that if they did not doubt, that God would deliver them" (Alma 56:47). And, indeed, they not only successfully routed the Lamanites, all two thousand survived the battle because "they had fought as if with the strength of God; yea, never were men known to have fought with such miraculous strength" (Alma 56:56). After this first conflict, sixty more young boys joined the group and they once again proved themselves and their mothers' faith as they defended a Nephite city from the Lamanites without a single death, even as their allies in the Nephite army fell by the hundreds (Alma 57:18–27).

These unnamed, yet aggressively influential mothers spoke most meaningfully to Mormon women living in the late nineteenth century. As noted, when Joseph Smith instituted polygamous families modeled on his interpretation of the Old Testament patriarchal families, he attempted to reverse the Victorian trend that put women at the spiritual center of the home. Yet Victorian gender norms lingered and even prospered harmoniously in the LDS community. An 1880 editorial in the *Woman's Exponent* stated: "It is conceded that woman's nature is more susceptible to spiritual impressions and the growth and culture of these finer faculties than that of man, that women possess a greater degree of the elements of character that tend heavenward that lead to the worship of a Supreme Being" ("Lack of Spirituality" 1880, 92). Following this common understanding, LDS women writers selected and focused on the silently influential mothers of the stripling warriors as among the most relevant female role models in the Book of Mormon. For an era that elevated to truism the saying "the hand that rocks the cradle, rules the world," these unnamed, but powerfully influential mothers stood out. These mothers took precedence in women's literary discussions about the Book of Mormon.

The June 1880 issue of the *Exponent* offered on its first page an article entitled "The Influence of the Home" that extols the far-reaching influence of the mother

---

9   The stripling warriors and their fathers are first mentioned in Alma 53:10–22.

and home.[10] This same issue carried an article titled "Woman amongst the Nephites." The article mentions very briefly the three named women of the Book of Mormon and then goes on to speak in generalities about the relatively elevated position of Israelite and Nephite women (G. 1880). Unintentionally picking up themes from the first article on the influence of the home, the author, however, devotes a long paragraph to the story of the mothers of the stripling warriors, noting:

> Their mothers' teachings and their mothers' prayers were weapons of destruction to their foes and shields of defence to themselves. They went forth conquering and to conquer, and the All-seeing One only knows how much the teachings of those saintly women effected towards the preservation of the Nephite commonwealth from imminent destruction (G. 1880, 7–8).

The anonymity of the mothers of the stripling warriors confirmed their prophetic authenticity. Balancing the Book of Mormon focus on patriarchal prophets, this author combined contemporary gender norms with authoritative scriptural narrative to re-emphasize the spiritual importance, even precedence of the mother. Unnamed and unknown, these mothers saved their community with their faith literally and militarily embodied in their soldier sons.

Throughout Mormon women's literature of the late nineteenth and early twentieth centuries, LDS women writers were very engaged with another scriptural mother—the mother of all humanity—Eve. Eve is one of the few women characters who crosses over from the Bible and appears in the Mormon scriptures. In their work, LDS women writers pulled together different strands of the Mormon and biblical scriptural narratives in order to fully renovate and elevate the figure of Eve and, more generally, mothers. In these textual conversations, we see even more clearly how women writers argued for the theological vitality of women in LDS history, past and present.

The most important part of this renovation lies in the Mormon reinterpretation of the Fall. The Fall became a necessary step within the overarching movement towards progressive salvation. In a deathbed sermon, the first Book of Mormon patriarch, Lehi, reveals to his sons this new view of the Fall. Lehi initially appears to be rehearsing a fairly standard version of the traditional biblical story of the Fall: the devil as a serpent tempts Eve with the forbidden fruit, Adam and Eve eat and are cast out of garden with the various curses laid upon them. However, the story here takes a different turn as Lehi explains that this seeming transgression actually is an absolutely integral part of God's plan for humanity's spiritual progress. He says:

---

10   "All our great men and women who have obtained notoriety for their works, say that to home, and most of all to their mothers, is due the credit for fame they have gained" (World 1880, 1).

> And now, behold, if Adam had not transgressed, he would not have
> fallen; but he would have remained in the garden of Eden. And all
> things which were created, must have remained in the same state which
> they were, after they were created; and they must have remained for
> ever, and had no end.
>
> And they would have had no children; wherefore, they would have
> remained in a state of innocence, having no joy, for they knew no
> misery; doing no good, for they knew no sin. (2 Nephi 2:22–23)

At this time, the Mormon plan of salvation promised that humans could become
divinized and participate in the process of the creation and divinization of
other worlds.[11] However, a key part of this divinization was that humans
required the knowledge of good and evil and the will to freely choose the right
path over the wrong way.[12] Human beings were literal spirit children of God
and his female divine partner. Originally born into a preexistent state, they
had to be born into human bodies in order to be tested in the mortal existence.
Utilizing their knowledge and their free will, ideally, they proved themselves
as they suffered and found their way past the stumbling blocks of mortality to
the final destination of ultimate divinization.

The LDS scriptures revise the story of the Fall, but, significantly, they do
not positively re-fashion the image of Eve. In the above story and in a different
retelling of the Fall in another part of the Mormon scriptures, the Pearl of
Great Price, Eve is described as unwittingly falling for blandishments of the
serpent devil, even though the ultimate outcome of the scenario is necessary
and good (Moses 4–5). God the Father controls the situation and steers it to his
own liking. When Lehi describes the fall as necessary, it is Adam who does the
falling, not Eve, even though just a few paragraphs before it is clearly Eve who
gives in to the serpent. In the Mormon scriptural stories, therefore, though the
Fall is reinterpreted, there is little that directly acquits Eve for her role as the
one who initiates the necessary series of events—or that valorizes her for her
world-changing choice.[13]

When we examine Mormon women's literature of this period, we see an
extended and lively conversation about Eve. Negative interpretations of Eve
persist in some form throughout the literature. This is not surprising given
that, at this period, a large number of church members were first generation

---

11 The most famous explication of this concept is "The King Follett Discourse," a funeral
    sermon delivered by Joseph Smith upon the death of a man named King Follett. For a
    full text of the sermon, see Larson 1976.

12 A few lines down, Lehi states: "And they are free to choose liberty and eternal life,
    through the great mediation of all men, or to choose captivity and death, according to
    the captivity and power of the devil; for he seeketh that all men might be miserable
    like unto himself" (2 Nephi 2:27).

13 As one example of a more positive evaluation of Eve, in another part of the scriptures,
    the Doctrines and Covenants, Joseph Smith has a vision of heaven that includes "our
    glorious Mother Eve" (Doctrines and Covenants 138:39).

converts still carrying with them beliefs from the religions of their upbringings. In one case, assuming that Eve's act was rebelliousness against God and needed punishment, the unnamed writer of an article on polygamy claims that the marriage practice serves as compensatory and intensive suffering that will eventually lead to the lifting of Eve's curse.[14] Similarly, the pseudonymous Hehmita uses the serpent in the garden as an example of how women needed to be especially careful to guard against spiritual fraud and deception: "...this very monster appeared before Mother Eve in the Garden of Eden; 'imitating' all the affability he recollected having seen in the Mansions of Glory; for if possible, to elude aversion, and fascinate Eve, so she should not be able to discern the fraud" (Hehmita 1881, 121). In these two examples, the writers fit the negative interpretation of Eve into characteristically LDS discussions about polygamy and the best way to lead a virtuous life. An unwitting Eve is deceived, though presumably according to God's plan. The mission for modern women was to avoid or make up for their ancestor's mistakes.

More commonly, however, within Mormon women's literature of the time, Eve is a wise and knowing woman who—somehow already in possession of free will—safely guides the course of human salvation on the right path. God gives her the choice and she makes the right decision. Eve becomes a savior figure on par with her descendant, Jesus Christ: she introduces necessary mortality and suffering, just as he will end it upon the Second Coming.

Sometimes women writers simply assume a renovated Eve in their descriptions. Hannah T. King wrote a series of articles for the *Exponent* about women of the scriptures. She begins the series with Eve: "Eve, the sovereign mother of all living. She stands in close proximity to God the Father, for she is the life giving spirit of the innumerable hosts that have figured upon this earth, the one grand, stupendous act of her life is all that is told of her in the Bible and it is enough" (King 1903, 41–42). In another instance, an article describes how Brigham Young walked into a woman's meeting and, in awe at the powerful female spiritual presence he felt, he exclaimed: "What do I see before me? A congregation of Eves" ("Utah County Silk Association" 1880, 56).

Sometimes women writers are much more self-conscious that they are arguing against the grain. An unnamed author, using Lehi's speech about the Fall, wrote into the *Cincinnati Enquirer* arguing forcefully that the blame must be lifted from Eve. The article was reprinted in the *Exponent*. Noting that blame for the Fall was usually assigned fully to Eve, the article suggests that, from the point of view of the Mormon understanding of salvation, Adam appears as the

---

14 "The effect of their [plural wives'] examples upon the rising generation will be of immense value, and as the generations roll by nobler types of womanhood will be developed, until the penalty laid upon woman in the beginning, that 'thy desire shall be to thy husband and he shall rule over thee,' will be repealed, and she will stand side by side with man, full of that queenly dignity and self-control which will make her his suitable companion rather than his inferior" ("Topics of the Times" 1884, 157).

potential threat: "We could with as much propriety accuse him of being less ambitious and enterprising than the woman; 'if he could do only as he was told,' as the writer says, 'he would be no higher in the scale of moral being than the beasts, who indeed know neither virtue nor vice'" ("Answer to Woman and Sin" 1884, 145). For this author, it is Eve who took the risk of divine wrath to bequeath to humanity potential divinity. She is the unsung and unfairly maligned hero of the story.

Perhaps the most eloquent advocate for the reinterpreted Eve was S. W. Richards, a male church leader who often contributed to the *Exponent*. In an 1894 essay, he very clearly spells out the eternal consequences of Eve's actions. "When in the garden, woman was master of the situation; for a time she held the destiny of the world in her hands, and not until man yielded to her persuasive power did she commit that destiny to the keeping of her lord" (S. W. Richards 1894, 81). According to Richards, Eve pleaded with Adam to join her: "to share with her the conditions by which, and by which alone, they could become as Gods, knowing both good and evil, and thereby inherit those attributes without which there is no God" (81). In these views, a fully cognizant Eve must argue with her mate—not to deceive him, but to persuade him to join in the unpleasant task of initiating the slog through mortality so that humans have the opportunity to reach a final salvation, a final divinization. A Victorian-styled Eve stands at the spiritual center of the first family and quietly uses her influence for the good, then fades into the background, only re-appearing to sacrificially take unfair blame.

Somewhere in between the negative and positive interpretations of this female scriptural figure, Eve becomes a polemical, even humorous vehicle for discussion about the respective roles of men and women. In a lecture before a local Utah W.S.A. (Women's Suffrage Association), Amelia B. Sidwell dismisses the blame attached to Eve, noting that she was forced to wander alone for ages in a garden, deprived of her female companions that she knew in the preexistence. Her only company was Adam, who, Sidwell argues: "...if I am allowed to judge Adam by most men of my acquaintance, he was probably very indifferent company, as men's conversational brilliance is seldom exerted to any considerable extent for the benefit or entertainment of a wife" (Sidwell 1890, 136). Taking a slightly different tack, L. L. Greene Richards poetically and enviously imagines Eve's idyllic existence in the garden where she had nothing to do but enjoy the beautiful nature:

> No dishes to wash after breakfast,
> No planning of what to have next,
> For luncheons or dinner or supper,
> No man disappointed and vexed" (L. L. G. Richards 1899, 28).

LDS women writers utilized a now unfairly maligned Eve as a kind of literary catharsis to release frustration about their own, seemingly mundane troubles and injustices. The woman who set humans on the path to divinization through humanization offered a model of how to think about the complicated religious question of free will and the purpose of mortal life. She also served as a literary safety valve for women to express their frustrations about the daily grind of dishes, meals, and family obligations. She gave women writers an opportunity to directly, though non-confrontationally critique the patriarchal family structure so emphasized in the Book of Mormon. For these writers, she was a creative, female model in an otherwise overwhelmingly male scriptural line-up.

Interestingly and tellingly, today, within official talks and pronouncements, the dominant interpretation of Eve is overwhelmingly positive.[15] Eve (often in conjunction with Adam) is shown to have consciously made the right choice for her descendants and, thus, to have been a crucial player in the Mormon plan of salvation. Women's early literary work helped to create this scriptural interpretation, and the tradition of non-centralized Mormon scriptural, prophetic discussions that continue within both formal and informal church talks, testimonies, periodicals, and books—despite the more controlled and standardized twenty-first century church. Even today lively intra- and extra-church interchanges continue about how to interpret the Book of Mormon. In the March 2004 issue of *Sunstone*, a Mormon magazine not affiliated with the church, four LDS members of varying professions and backgrounds wrestle with how to reconcile the Book of Mormon claims of an Israelite descent for Native Americans with the DNA evidence that Native Americans are genetically related to Asian populations (*Sunstone* 2004). As a vital religious tradition, the Book of Mormon continues to be interpreted and adapted in order to fit the changing social, cultural, and, in this case, scientific context within which Mormon members live.

Conclusion

Added to the existing biblical tradition, the Book of Mormon shaped the beliefs and practices of the Mormon community. As with many millennialist groups of the early to mid-nineteenth century United States, within the early LDS community, religious traditions—especially as these were manifested in established clergy or institutional authority—were examined with deep skepticism and suspicion. For LDS members, this new scripture upended American

---

15   One of the Twelve Apostles, Apostle Dallin Oaks noted in a General Conference talk: "It was Eve who first transgressed the limits of Eden in order to initiate the conditions of mortality. Her act, whatever its nature, was formally a transgression but eternally a glorious necessity to open the doorway toward eternal life. Adam showed his wisdom by doing the same. And thus Eve and 'Adam fell that men might be' (2 Ne. 2:25)" (Oaks 1993).

Christianity, and the understanding of tradition as an abstract concept. With the opening of direct communication with God, members looked to fresh prophecy and scripture for guidance. When Joseph Smith described his first, teenaged vision, he offered a new and different alternative to the established religious institutions of the day.

However, LDS members inevitably adapted these "new" scriptural and prophetic traditions to fit times and circumstances. In the religious, popular women's literature of the *Exponent*, we see part of the process of how women writers communally sculpted the scriptural tradition. We see the give-and-take about the role of women within the Mormon theological and scriptural tradition. We see also how, in practice, the women writers of the community negotiated their LDS revelatory understanding of authority; how they moved between newly established scripture, current social norms, and the personal revelatory aspect of Mormonism that was to them so important a part of the latter-day communication between God and the church. Christian history was stood on its head with a new set of scriptures, at the same time that the concept of scriptural tradition was redefined. Mormon women writers helped to create another conception of this tradition in which individual, in this case mostly female voices, participated in a negotiating, theological discussion in order to adapt the Book of Mormon to their nineteenth-century women's lives. For a time, women writers created theological discourse and, thereby, helped to establish the parameters of theological, scriptural tradition for their religious community.

With this case study, we see that religious groups are made up of multiple traditions as described in the Hobsbawm-Sarot model. Further, these traditions provide meaning, structure, and stability to members of religious groups. But, we also see that traditions are not simply imposed from above. The successful tradition is one that passes through many different interpretive hands. Finally, when we look very closely, we witness that even within religious traditions, there are multiple and contradictory interpretations and voices. Traditions are continually negotiated, and shifting. They can never be fully grasped, because individuals and groups are always adapting them to fit personal, historical, and cultural circumstances. They are the ever-shifting foundations upon which religious communities stand.

References

Alexander, Thomas G. 1986. *Mormonism in Transition: A History of the Latter-day Saints, 1890–1930*. Urbana: University of Illinois Press.

"Answer to Woman and Sin. In the *Cincinnati Enquirer*." 1884. *Woman's Exponent* 19, no. 12 (March 1): 145.

The Book of Mormon. 1888. Salt Lake City, Juvenile Instructor Office.

The Book of Mormon: 1981. *Another Testament of Jesus Christ; The Doctrine and Covenants of The Church of Jesus Christ of Latter-day Saints; The Pearl of Great Price.* Salt Lake City: The Church of Jesus Christ of Latter-day Saints.

Cox, Martha Cragun. 1928–1930. "Biographical Records of Martha Cox." Archives and Manuscripts Division of the Historical Department, The Church of Jesus Christ of Latter-day Saints.

Derr, Jill, Janath Russell Cannon, and Maureen Ursenbach Beecher. 1992. *Women of the Covenant: The Story of Relief Society.* Salt Lake City: Deseret Book Company.

Douglas, Ann. 1988. *The Feminization of American Culture.* New York: Anchor Books.

"Editorial Notes." 1891. *Woman's Exponent* 20, no. 9 (November 1): 69.

Foster, Lawrence. 1984. *Religion and Sexuality: The Shakers, the Mormons, and the Oneida Community.* Chicago: University of Illinois Press.

G. "Woman Amongst the Nephites." 1880. *Woman's Exponent* 8, no. 25 (June 1): 7–8.

Hehmita. 1881. "Familiarity Breed Contempt." *Woman's Exponent* 9/16 (January 15): 121.

"The Jubilee Celebration: The Need of Press Representation." 1892. *Woman's Exponent* 20, no. 18 (March 15): 132–133.

Kane, Elizabeth. 1995. *A Gentile Account of Life in Utah's Dixie, 1872–1873: Elizabeth Kane's St. George Journal.* Salt Lake City: Tanner Trust Fund, University of Utah Library.

King, Hannah T. 1903. "Women of the Scripture." *Woman's Exponent* 32, no. 6 (November): 41–42.

"Lack of Spirituality." 1880. *Woman's Exponent* 9, no. 12 (November 15): 92.

Larson, Stan. 1976. "The King Follett Discourse: A Newly Amalgamated Text." *BYU Studies* 15 (Summer): 193–208.

M. 1884. "Literary Women of Utah. Thoughts on 'Homespun Talk.'" *Woman's Exponent* 13, no. 4 (July 15): 31–32.

"Notice to Agents." 1891. *Woman's Exponent* 20, no. 1 (July 1): 4.

Oaks, Dallin. 1993. "The Great Plan of Happiness." General Conference talk, October 3, 1993 <http://tinyurl.com/3ka87> (June 19, 2004).

Richards, L. L. Greene. 1899. "Charity and Labor." *Woman's Exponent* 28, no. 4 (July 15): 28.

Richards, S. W. 1894. "Woman's Exponent." *Woman's Exponent* 22, no. 11 (January 15): 81–82.

Sarot, Marcel. 2001. "Counterfactuals and the Invention of Religious Tradition." Pages 21–40 in *Religious Identity and the Invention of Tradition.* Edited by Jan Willem Van Henten and Anton Houtepen. Vol. 3 of *Studies in Theology and Religion*, edited by Jan Willem Van Henten. Assen, The Netherlands: Royal Van Gorcum.

"Second Literary Child of the Relief Society." 1915. *Relief Society Magazine* 2, no. 1 (January): 38.

Sidwell, Amelia B. Cox. 1890. "Women of the Bible." *Woman's Exponent* 18, no. 17 (February 1): 136–137.

Sunstone 131 (March 2004).

"Topics of the Times." 1884. *Woman's Exponent* 12, no. 20 (March 15): 156–157.

"Utah County Silk Association." 1880. *Woman's Exponent* 9, no. 7 (September 1): 56.

World, Nannie. 1880. "The Influence of the Home." *Woman's Exponent* 9, no. 1 (June 1): 1.

Shwegyin *Sāsana*: Continuity, Rupture, and Traditionalism in a Buddhist Tradition

Jason A. Carbine

I. Shwegyin *Sāsana*

In 1981, Edward Shils drew attention to the notion of "substantive" tradition as a way to think through the ways in which people value past accomplishments and wisdom, as well as desire the continuing role of such accomplishments and wisdom in the present and future (Shils 1981, e.g. 21). In 1983, Eric Hobsbawm elaborated on the notion of "invented" tradition as a way to examine the construction and deployment of rule governed practices intended to inculcate behavioral values and norms in such a way as to make those practices, values, and norms, even and especially those of relatively recent origin, appear continuous with the past (Hobsbawm 1983, 1). This essay takes a point of departure from the treatments of tradition by Shils and Hobsbawm; it addresses a substantive Buddhist tradition, a Buddhist monastic tradition, but recognizes that that tradition is as "invented" and "re-invented" as any other tradition. The specific tradition is the Shwegyin, which was founded in 1860 in Burma. In terms of general communal ethos, Shwegyin pride themselves on rigorous scholarly study of the *Sāsana*, the corpus of teachings attributed, ultimately, to the Buddha (P. Enlightened One) who lived and preached in Northeastern India some 2,500 years ago. Additionally, Shwegyin also pride themselves on strict disciplinary adherence to the Basket of Monastic Law (P. *Vinaya Piṭaka*), one of the Three Baskets (P. *Tipiṭaka*) that comprise the *Sāsana*. The Shwegyin are one among nine monastic sects (P. *nikāya* and sometimes B. *guiṇ'''*) or groups (B. *guiṇ'''*) officially recognized by the current Burmese military government.[1]

The Shwegyin and other monastic Burmese sects/groups are part of a much larger Buddhist tradition, nowadays commonly referred to as the Theravāda (P. Way of the Elders). A composite historical narrative of Theravāda Buddhism runs as follows. "Theravāda" took on many of its foundational institutional, doctrinal, and liturgical features over two millennia ago in Sri Lanka. In the early to mid centuries of the second millennium CE, a reconstituted Theravāda tradition, encompassing a variety of emphases both "orthodox" and otherwise,

---

1   Pali and Burmese words are marked with a P. or B., respectively. On Pali, see below.

became a dominant form of Buddhism in Sri Lanka and mainland Southeast Asia. And, in contemporary times, various versions—e.g. Sri Lankan, Burmese, Thai—of Theravāda tradition continue to thrive, albeit having been challenged by colonialism, modernity, globalization, etc. In this essay, I am not concerned with debating this kind of narrative history of "Theravāda" Buddhism. However, one observation is central to the direction I take in this paper.

Of late, there has been a move among scholars of South and Southeast Asian Buddhism to question both the accuracy and utility of the term "Theravāda." As put by Peter Skilling, research into various Buddhist sources, across South and Southeast Asian regions and languages, "suggests that 'Theravāda Buddhism' is a colonial or globalized construction, one of the 'religions' or 'faiths' defined to satisfy census needs, to contrast with Christianity" (2004, 2). As Skilling also points out, the term Theravāda becomes especially problematic when one considers, for example, that it "is an *extremely* rare term in Pāli [the canonical language of the "Theravāda"], and that for nine hundred years it was scarcely *if ever* used in the Pāli or vernacular inscriptions, chronicles, and other texts of Southeast Asia" (1; brackets mine). If, as Skilling suggests, using the term Theravāda can lend itself to creating "artificial and ahistorical entities," what then are we to replace it with? In our studies of Buddhism in South and Southeast Asia, should we jettison the term Theravāda?

Since it is clear that the term "Theravāda" is an important referent for many Buddhists in South and Southeast Asia, and elsewhere, it is unreasonable and undesirable to jettison it entirely. The International Theravāda Buddhist Missionary University in Yangon (the capital of Burma) is a case in point. Yet, it is also clear that further attention can and should be placed on the local categories of tradition-making through which Buddhist knowledge and practice are and have been constructed (Hallisey 1995). A paradigm shift is needed, as a way to open up new and potentially more accurate discussions and investigations into the kinds of phenomena that have been grouped under the rubric of Theravāda. Skilling himself suggests turning to various issues involved in the constitution of monastic lineages. Here I pursue this line of inquiry, by examining how Shwegyin monks, as a lineage, attempt to embody and transmit the *Sāsana*. For Shwegyin monks, and for many of their Burmese co-religionists, the *Sāsana* and *Sāsana*-related terms such as "building the *Sāsana*" (B. *Sāsana pru*), "lineage of the *Sāsana*" (e.g. P. *Sāsana vaṃsa*, B. *Sāsanā to' e* anvay' achak'*), and "Shwegyin-*Sāsana*" (B. *Rhvekyaṅ' Sāsanā*) are central to their self-identification as what I call a tradition.

In this essay, the term "tradition" is used as an interpretive category to refer to particular thoughts, practices, and people which have coalesced around particular visions of social, historical, and/or religious continuity and rupture. Shwegyin monks, with their emphasis on being, for example, a "lineage of the *Sāsana*," comprise one such tradition. In terms of Shwegyin monks, I ask and answer this question: What are the specific ways in which they conceive of continuity and rupture, in the past, present, and future, and what are the ways in which their conceptions of continuity and rupture relate to their specific efforts, whether through discourse or practice, to make themselves into a tradition? Shwegyin conceptions of continuity and rupture are hardly normative for all Buddhists, monastic or otherwise, in South and Southeast Asia; yet their conceptions are representative of certain positions regarding continuity and rupture that have had a rather illustrious history in the life of the *Sāsana* in South and Southeast Asia.

To understand Shwegyin conceptions of continuity, it is first necessary to understand something about their conceptions of two kinds of rupture. The first kind of rupture, and a kind of rupture that is considered to be good but extremely difficult to achieve, is a permanent rupture in one's successive rebirths (P. *paṭisandhi*) in Saṃsāra (P. the cycle of rebirth). In achieving that rupture, one makes the breakthrough to the peaceful-bliss (P. *santi-sukha*) of *Nirvana*. In *Sāsana* parlance, *Nirvana* is the "unconditioned" and "non-compounded," whereas the existents (P. *dhammā*) that make up Saṃsāra are "conditioned" and "com-pounded." In contrast to *Nirvana*, Saṃsāra is composed of many conditioned existents that are ultimately reducible to three classes: consciousness or aware-ness of objects (P. *citta*), which is neither good nor bad; mental concomitants or mental factors (P. *cetasika*), which play particular roles in the various processes of cognition; and matter (P. *rūpa*), which comprises the material phenomena in cognitive and other acts. These three classes of conditioned existents combine, decay, and recombine in such a way as to make up the rebirth of beings in Saṃsāra. According to Shwegyin and similar *Sāsana* traditions, the *Sāsana*, when and if properly transmitted, illuminates the Path (P. *Magga*) of thought and practice that allows beings, both individually and collectively, to cause a permanent rupture in their conditioned flow in Saṃsāra, thereby making the breakthrough to the peaceful-bliss of *Nirvana*.

Exactly what *Nirvana* is has been debated both in and outside of Burma. As put in a short account by a very famous Shwegyin monk, Ashin[2] Janakā-bhivaṃsa (1900–1977):

> People talk differently about Nibbana [here, Nibbana is an alternate spelling of *Nirvana*]. Some say that Nibbana is a special kind of mind and matter [here and in the following quote, mind refers to both consciousness and mental factors]. Others say that in mind and matter there is an eternal quality like the perpetual core; when mind and matter come to cessation, that eternal quality or perpetual core remains and continues to exist; Nibbana is just existing as that eternal core. Still others say, "How can Nibbana be said to be blissful if you do not get to enjoy [it] since there are no mind and matter in Nibbana?" (Janakā-bhivaṃsa 1997, 296–297, brackets mine)

---

2   "Ashin" is a term of respect for a monk. Sometimes, it is shortened to "shin."

However, Janakābhivaṃsa then goes on to explain his "orthodox" position on *Nirvana*, even quoting a source, the *Dhammasaṅganī* (P. Enumeration of Phenomena), from the Pali canon to support his point:

> Nibbana is one ultimate truth distinct from other ultimate truths, namely, consciousness, mental factors, and matter. Since it has nothing to do with mind and matter, it cannot be a special kind of mind or matter. Neither is it some kind of element that exists inside the body as an eternal core, because, among internal and external states, it is included in the external states as evidenced [in the *Dhammasaṅganī*]. Unlike persons or beings, it is not something that experiences or enjoys...nor is it something that is experienced or enjoyed like the desirable sense objects... Therefore, it is true that there is no enjoyment-feeling [a kind of enjoyment associated with mind and matter] but only the 'peaceful-bliss' in Nibbana... The nature of 'peaceful-bliss' which is not contaminated with such [enjoyment-feeling] is peacefulness due to the cessation of mind and matter, the conditioned states. (297, brackets mine)

According to Janakābhivaṃsa, and according to many others who think like him, attaining the peaceful-bliss of *Nirvana* rests on cutting off one's flow in *Saṃsāra*. It deserves emphasis that some Buddhist traditions are famous for collapsing the distinction between *Saṃsāra* and *Nirvana*, and for (re)articulating the path of the Buddha and Bodhisattva (a being on the path to enlightenment) in light of a unity of rather than rupture between *Saṃsāra* and *Nirvana*. But Shwegyin and other monks who think like Janakābhivaṃsa have not made this move. In fact, for them, a goal has often been, at times explicit and at times implicit, to prohibit or inhibit the misuse or misapplication of metaphysical doctrine that could, in their view, not only undermine metaphysical correctness, but also chip away at the health and vitality of the *Sāsana* itself.

The second kind of rupture, and a kind of rupture that should be held in check, then, concerns the decay and rupture of the *Sāsana* itself, in both textual and communal ways. The Shwegyin tradition presupposes that the *Sāsana*, as a textual body and as an embodied community, like all compounded and conditioned things, is actually in a process of decay and will eventually disappear, thereby suffering its own kind of rupture. There are numerous Buddhist narratives that illustrate this point (Nattier 1991; Blackburn 2001). Some of the narratives refer to the decline and discontinuity of the three kinds of *Sāsana*: the *pariyatti Sāsana*, or *Sāsana* as it is studied; the *paṭipatti Sāsana* or *Sāsana* as it is put into daily practices; and, the *paṭivedha Sāsana* or *Sāsana* as it is experienced as a fruit of study and practice. Additionally, some of the narratives refer to a five-fold process of decline: first, a loss in an ability to achieve certain spiritual attainments related to the Path to *Nirvana*; second, a loss in an ability to uphold certain dimensions of practice; third, a loss in the study of the *Sāsana*; fourth, a loss in an ability to maintain the signs or marks of monasticism, such as the robes; and finally, a loss of the Buddha's relics themselves. Whether pitched in terms of a three-fold or five-fold decline, the narratives of decline of the *Sāsana* emphasize a point that is intrinsic to notions of *Sāsana*-continuity: the definitive "other" against which the Shwegyin tradition, and other *Sāsana*-traditions, have been and continue to be constructed is not a person or group, but the truth of impermanence (P. *anicca*) and the decline and rupture of the *Sāsana* itself, in terms of the texts in which it is preserved and in terms of the communities who strive to embody it.

A key link between the two kinds of rupture (one metaphysical, desirable and possible though difficult to attain; the other textual, communal, undesirable, and inevitable), is lineage (e.g. P. *vaṃsa*, B. *anvay', anvay' achak', anvay' acañ'*). A "lineage of the *Sāsana*" constitutes the communal expression of the metaphysical and narrative *Sāsana* worldview described above. That is, based on the evidence explored in this essay, any monastic lineage comprised of "sons of the Buddha" (e.g. B. *Mrat' cvā bhurā" sā" to'*) must see to the transmission of the *Sāsana* which illumines the Path to *Nirvana*, for that is its lineage duty. This is precisely why lineage and lineage-related themes, centered on the *Sāsana*, figure so prominently in Shwegyin and other *Sāsana*-oriented Buddhist imagery of socio-religious continuity and rupture. By militating against one kind of rupture (of the *Sāsana*), they promote the possibility of another kind of rupture (of beings out of *Saṃsāra*).

To help reflect on continuity and rupture in and among Shwegyin monks, it is useful to draw attention to one more category, "traditionalism," as discussed by Rosalind Morris in regard to contemporary developments in Thailand.

> ...traditionalism needs to be understood as a discourse, which has been elaborated around the fear of tradition's loss. 'Traditionalism' does not mean a mode of practice characterized by historical repetition, nor actual continuity. It is, rather, a paradoxical concept encompassing various kinds of practices, one whose definitive but abstract characteristic is pastness and whose theoretical *raison d'etre* is the healing over, or sublimation of, radical discontinuity. Clearly, there were practices whose value accrued partly from the perception of their antiquity in pre-modern times, but these are better understood as individual practices with singular histories than as part of a generic conceptual category. And, insofar, as such a contrast is possible, it seems likely that the value of such pre-modern pastness assumed continuity with antiquity rather than a rupture. 'Traditionalism' on the other hand, is the inherently belated effect of modernity, not its displaced antecedent. (Morris 2002, 71)

Morris' emphasis on "traditionalism" as discourse captures very well some of the aspects of the dynamic quality to tradition-making this essay, in keeping with Shils, Hobsbawm, and others, seeks to portray. Moreover, her focus on "traditionalism" as a form of discourse specifically oriented around the fear of a tradition's loss is also helpful; as pointed out above, there is much in Shwegyin traditionalism regarding this very point. Yet, in light of the Shwegyin material, it is possible to suggest a different way of looking at traditionalism than Morris proposes.

The material addressed in this essay suggests that the kind of traditionalism represented by Shwegyin discourses and practices is not most appropriately described in terms of a "healing over, or sublimation of, radical discontinuity." Rather, Shwegyin traditionalism focuses on slowing an inevitable movement towards an inevitable form of radical discontinuity; the discontinuity of the *Sāsana* is always in progress in the present. It cannot be healed over or sublimated; only slowed or temporarily put in check. The narratives of decline of the *Sāsana* aptly summarize these points, but so do specific images used by Shwegyin monks and others (both monks and lay people) to refer to particular components of the *Sāsana*. For instance, in *Sāsana* thought and practice, the Basket of Monastic Law is commonly referred to as the "life" (P. *āyu*) of the *Sāsana*; thus, when that Basket stands, so too does the *Sāsana*. Similarly, many Buddhists in contemporary Burma/Myanmar itself have given a distinctive interpretation to the *Paṭṭhāna* (P. Conditional Relations), widely recognized as a most difficult treatment of metaphysics in the Basket of Fundamental Law (P. *Abhidhamma Piṭaka*). The *Paṭṭhāna* is identified as the *Sāsana's* "front-line fortress." When the *Paṭṭhāna* falls (through corrupt doctrines and improper transmission, for example), the territory of the *Sāsana* can be invaded and destroyed.

If we are to reject the idea that Shwegyin traditionalism constitutes a healing over or sublimation of radical discontinuity, we must also reject the idea that it is a "belated effect of modernity." Indeed, the traditionalism of slowing *Sāsana* rupture has been a recurrent theme throughout the history of the *Sāsana*. The "pre-modern pastness" of *Sāsana* traditions may have striven for continuity with antiquity (e.g. the life and activities of the Buddha and early Buddhist community), but it assumed that the rupture of the *Sāsana* was in progress as well. The same point is true for what can be called the "contemporary pastness" of *Sāsana* traditions such as the Shwegyin. So far as the historical evidence suggests, the traditionalism of trying to slow *Sāsana* rupture has never been displaced, in either the "pre-modern" or "modern" periods. The modern world may have ushered in more speedy forms of *Sāsana*-decline, but it did not usher in anything distinctively new, at least in terms of that decline itself.

Following but departing from Morris, traditionalism can be understood as a tactic for constructing tradition and thus for negotiating the dynamics of continuity and rupture, however they are understood within particular traditions. Shwegyin traditionalism emphasizes both the embodiment and textualization of the *Sāsana*, as a way to prevent the rupture of the *Sāsana* while increasing the chances that at least some, not necessarily in the present life, may make the rupture into *Nirvana*. For Shwegyin monks, and for many other monks like them, the human body is, clearly, an important repository of memories concerning the Buddha, other monastic exemplars, and the *Sāsana*-based lifestyle for which they advocated. (On social memory, see, for example, Connerton 1989;

Stoller 1995; Tanabe and Keyes 2002.) In wearing the robes, in shaving their heads, in holding monastic rituals, in adhering to the laws of monastic life, in teaching about the Fundamental Law, and in doing many other monastic things, monks in their minds and on their bodies sustain memories of the Buddha, other exemplars, and the *Sāsana* itself. As such, monastic life is intended to be a collective embodiment of the kind of world depicted above all in the various Baskets and related texts of the *pariyatti Sāsana* or *Sāsana* as it is studied.

Nevertheless, over and against any kind of embodiment of the *Sāsana*, it is essential to recognize the significance of the continual (re)textualization of the *Sāsana*, as another component of Shwegyin traditionalism. From a perspective of the continuity of the *Sāsana*, the (re)production of a non-embodied, textual corpus is crucial. (Here, I have in mind a broad notion of *Sāsana*-texts, written and oral, Pali and vernacular, and thus including materials not only from the canon, but also materials like contemporary histories and biographies, monastic administrative records, and sermons that have been recorded, transcribed and published.) Even if Shwegyin and other monks and lay supporters fail to embody the *Sāsana* in their daily actions, they can still assist in the process of retaining in the world textual repositories of what the Buddha and others have taught, *vis-à-vis* the transmission of the various texts of the *Sāsana* itself. That is, to draw on Collins' discussion of the imaginative world associated with *Nirvana*, they sustain the *Sāsana* as a kind of "cultural system," in which the integration and consistency of *Sāsana*-texts at the level of logic, narrative, and imagery are marks of a faithful reproduction of the Buddha's own words and attitudes and, as the case often is, of the words and attitudes of other revered monks (Collins 1998, 79–81).

As the narratives of *Sāsana* decline and rupture suggest, when and if the teachings of a Buddha become both thoroughly disembodied (i.e. no human beings—or any beings anywhere for that matter—are capable of embodying any part of the *Sāsana*), as well as thoroughly detextualized (i.e. the [re]production of all *Sāsana*-texts stops), a *Sāsana* has run its course, and it vanishes. Thus, through their collective efforts, many monks and lay people try to facilitate, in the day-to-day contexts of communal interaction, the back and forth movement of embodying and textualizing the *Sāsana*. That back and forth movement, which takes as its culminating point the breakthrough to *Nirvana*, constitutes the heart of Shwegyin traditionalism.

In connection to the viewpoints offered by Shils, Hobsbawm, and Morris, it is important to point out that this essay is also inspired by and seeks to steer clear of structuralist/functionalist studies that address continuity in terms of different kinds of stasis and repetition that take place on sociological and other levels (e.g. Durkheim 1915; Radcliffe-Brown 1952; Eliade 1958; Levi-Strauss 1962; Jay 1992). For example, for Shwegyin and other monks, there are certain structures of law (both Monastic Law and Fundamental Law) which condition their lives. As such, any analysis of continuity among these monks should consider these kinds of structures. Yet, notions of structure and function, and of stasis and repetition, do not capture the overall kind of dynamics explored here. Indeed, as exemplified by the Shwegyin tradition, there is an inherent difficulty in the maintenance of any and all patterns of socio-religious continuity, regardless of how static, repetitive, and automatic such patterns may seem. For members of the Shwegyin tradition, there is nothing automatic about their continuity; they believe that they must invest an immense amount of substantive labor to offset an ongoing process of socio-religious rupture—a process in which knowledge of and practices associated with how to make the rupture out of *Saṃsāra* and into *Nirvana* are increasingly lost.

II. A Genre of Traditionalism: *Sāsana* Histories and Monastic Biographies

The remainder of this essay focuses on two dominant themes in *Sāsana*-oriented discourses and practices of socio-religious continuity—"lineage" and "sons of the Buddha." By focusing on the themes of lineage and son-ship, the essay pursues a broad consideration of the discourses and practices which are believed to maintain the health of the *Sāsana* and to allow people to make the breakthrough to *Nirvana*. To develop this point, the discussion draws from representative *Sāsana* histories (e.g. P. *Sāsana vaṃsa*, B. *Sāsana vaṅ`*) and biographies of elder monks (e.g. P. *theruppatti*); such histories and biographies constitute a literary domain intrinsic to Shwegyin traditionalism.

Shwegyin monks may explicitly or implicitly claim that they have more purity (P. *parisuddhi*) than other monks, both inside and outside of Burma/ Myanmar. Their attitude towards their purity is summed up well in one of the ecclesiastical titles of the Shwegyin *Sāsana* Proprietor (the highest Shwegyin leader), which runs as follows: "Shwegyin Sect Supreme Presiding Authority and General of the Law." However, Shwegyin monks, as participants in a larger *Sāsana*-oriented culture, do not see themselves as unique: they share common cause with their co-religionists in transmitting the *Sāsana*. My purpose is, then, to provide insight into how Shwegyin monks consider themselves, in historical and biographical ways, as carriers of the *Sāsana*. The purpose is also to show how, as a genre of traditionalism, *Sāsana* histories and biographies about exemplary monks testify to and participate in the work that lineages and sons of the Buddha, and the communities which they comprise, are expected to do.

When Shwegyin and similar monks want to stress the continuity of the thoughts and activities of their community with the Buddha through an unbroken succession of monks (especially in terms of both Monastic Law and ritual of Higher Ordination), they will often use the notion of lineage (e.g. Ferguson 1975; Mendelson 1975; Huxley 2000; Skilling 2004). Sometimes, Shwegyin and others will explicitly identify themselves as a "lineage of the

Sāsana" — an identification which stresses the importance of both *Sāsana* embodiment and textualization. Importantly, in Burmese cultural understanding, monastic lineages are like trees that branch out as given Preceptors (P. *Upajjhāya*), such as Ashin Jāgara (the founder of the Shwegyin sect) working in tandem with other monks, ordain and train more novices and monks, more monastic sons of the Buddha. The Preceptor is a "trunk," while those who descend out from him are his "branches."

The notion of being a son of the Buddha adds a distinctive dimension to the discourse and practice of lineage: when Shwegyin or other monks want to stress their affection for and obedience to their father (B. *apha*) the Buddha, or when they want to stress the affectionate, protective, and parental role of the Buddha, they will often use some notion of being a son of the Buddha. Consider this passage:

> While taking ordination as a monk in an ordination hall, a new monk has to accept the Buddha's admonishments; as for what the Buddha admonished: "Dear son (B. *khyac' sā"*), now you are a monk; you can't make a living any longer by, for instance, trading and farming like lay people. Live just by food that you get while wandering around, also known as what you get by going from house to house. Do strive to make a living in this way. I am fond of this kind of food; I praise it greatly. It is very suitable and appropriate for monks who are my sons (B. *sā" to'*)." (Pho Kyā 1925, 55–56)

Where notions of lineage emphasize historical connection to the Buddha *vis-à-vis* ordination-based succession, notions of being a son of the Buddha emphasize the affective, familial dynamics of a benevolent father-son relation. In this social relation, affection and obedience take center stage, as one human being (the Buddha) helps another human being (the monk who is the Buddha's son) to live in and thus build further the *Sāsana*.

Sāsana histories and monastic biographies are some of the most important loci for the dissemination of themes of lineage and monastic son-ship. However, before dwelling in detail on this point, attention should be given to the fact that many if not most *Sāsana* histories and monastic biographies highlight an affinity between monks and non-monks (e.g. lay people) with respect to transmitting the *Sāsana*. This affinity is driven by several kinds of cultural and socio-political emphases. One emphasis consists of efforts made by monks and their supporters (or by lay people and their monastic supporters) to educate potential readers (monks and non-monks) about the orientations of Buddhist monks and the ways in which they carry the *Sāsana*. Another emphasis consists of an effort to show how monks are linked with specific lay families or lineages, i.e. how "this" monk came from "that" family, how "this" monk (e.g. Ashin Jāgara) was supported by "that" king (e.g. King Mindon), and so forth. A third kind of emphasis consists of an attempt to attract lay support for a given monastic lineage, as well as to give special prominence to the laity who support that monastic lineage. In other words the affinity between monks and non-monks is driven in great part by an attempt to create an aura of exemplary practice among them as they mutually work for the continuity of the *Sāsana* and thus the dynamic preservation of the Path to *Nirvana*.

III. *Sāsana* Histories, Monastic Biographies, and the Ethics of Traditionalism

Following the work of Charles Hallisey and Anne Hansen, it can be argued that some Buddhist histories and biographies as part of their "worklike" qualities possess a key "sub-ethical" foundation that has the capacity to enlarge "an agent's moral horizon," to "expose the opaqueness of moral intention," and to foster emotional healing and transformation (1996, 308; see also Harpham 1992). Much of this work occurs through helping people to leave aside their own social location and cultivate a critical self-detachment and an other-oriented empathy. Here, I am not interested in trying to elaborate further upon the intricacies of the sub-ethical dimensions of particular Buddhist histories and biographies. Nonetheless, Hallisey and Hansen's arguments help my effort to explain the vital connection between the constitution of monastic lineages and/ or monastic sons of the Buddha on the one hand and Shwegyin traditionalism on the other.

Two points are relevant here. First, as seen in Shwegyin and Burmese historical and biographical materials, monks (and others) are supposed to be grounded in the self-detachment and other-oriented empathy Hallisey and Hansen find in the cultural uses of the Buddhist narratives they study. Shwegyin and Burmese histories and biographies suggest that the transmitting of the *Sāsana* is most effective when monks (and others) possess such dispositions. If they are detached to themselves, and if they are empathetic towards others, they can be free from the constraints (e.g. worldly passion) which could cloud their efforts to focus on the transmission of higher things (i.e. the *Sāsana*). In other words, in the histories and biographies, there is, especially in terms of monastic life, at least one type of ideal moral, traditionalist agent: the monk who properly embodies the *Sāsana* as a lineage carrier, and/or as a pure son (B. *sā" to' cac'*) of the Buddha.

Second, in my approach to the worklike qualities of Shwegyin histories and biographies, I focus on how they are used to create important links between the mythic past on the one hand and the contemporary life of Buddhism on the other. I show how they are used to illustrate the continuing developments of the *Sāsana* in the present day by describing the activities of monks (and non-monks) as they carry on its message and practice. In doing so,

I illustrate how they are employed to instruct their readers in the following topics: the history and development of the *Sāsana*; the components of monastic training; the *sīla* (P. moral conduct) of religiously exemplary people; the effort to purge the mind of *kilesa* (P. defilement) that keep people embedded in *Saṃsāra*; the authority of the Buddha; the states of mental well being and joy that come with exposure to the *Sāsana*; and, the dispositions (such as self-detachment, generosity, friendship, lack of fear, other-regard, and care for the *Sāsana*) that are supposed to form the bedrock of monastic life. Thus, I discuss how, as practice-oriented handbooks for textualization and embodiment of the *Sāsana*, certain histories and biographies are geared towards the continual reproduction of lineages and sons of the Buddha by illuminating the modes of communal life which allow them to thrive. To draw on a work by Bourdieu and Passeron (1977), they are one of the genres through which the monastic "class" reproduces itself through certain kinds of educational materials and strategies; the histories and biographies are meant to testify to and participate in the work that lineages and sons of the Buddha, and the communities which they comprise, are expected to do, as *Sāsana* carriers.

The approach taken here to Buddhist histories and biographies as a genre of traditionalism *vis-à-vis* lineage and monastic son-ship may be briefly compared with an approach taken by S. J. Tambiah to Thai Buddhist biographies as a locus of negotiating socio-political crisis *vis-à-vis* ideas and ideals of sainthood (Tambiah 1984). Both of our studies are concerned with the paradigmatic significance of the life and actions of the Buddha, if not structurally then thematically. Both of our studies are concerned with processes of localization which ground Buddhist ideas and images within specific socio-cultural contexts. However, for Tambiah the crucial question concerns social and political crisis and the various roles played by Buddhist monks and others in creating and responding to that crisis. His investigation of the intersection between biography and lineage speaks to this issue. A biography of a given saint, when done in a "masterful" way, unites two features. First, it provides a written record of the development of the saint's "charisma" ("sedimentation of power")—a charisma mediated especially by lineages of forest monks associated with the saint and/or with the kind of lifestyle the saint embodies. Second, it speaks to the collective socio-political crisis at hand, articulating in the process certain "societal ideals such that the protagonist is acclaimed a hero or saint" (128). Ultimately, Tambiah encompasses his discussion of these two issues within a socio-political analysis oriented around the circulation and contestation of religious and political power.

Tambiah's analysis could potentially be applied in an illuminating way to the Burmese case, especially given the political circumstances that have faced and still face Burma/Myanmar. However, for my purposes, I want to keep the focus on the imagery and activities of lineage and son-ship in as much as they relate to the continuity of the *Sāsana* and thus also to the breakthrough to

Nirvana. The crucial question for this analysis is how Shwegyin histories and biographies reflect some general dynamics that keep the fabric of monastic life, and thus of the *Sāsana*, intact.

The approach taken here can also be placed against the backdrop of John Ferguson's *The Symbolic Dimensions of the Burmese Sangha*, which also addresses the Burmese historical and biographical genre, as well as notions of monastic lineage. In Ferguson's view, the most important "symbolic" dimension of the monastic community in Burma is its sense of continuity with the Buddhist past, preserved especially in the notion of lineage (Ferguson 1975, 4–5). In his analysis, lineage is itself the focus of a larger set of "bonded symbolic dimensions," which are a limited number of paired, symbolic extremes through which the flexibility of—and tension within—the monastic community in Burma has been negotiated and maintained. These bonded dimensions include forest and town monks; meditation and education; Lower Burma and Upper Burma; and Sinhalese and Burmese (5–12, 253–259). In terms of these bonded dimensions themselves, Ferguson remarks,

> The symbolic system of the Sangha is such that its bonded dimensions keep it in a state of constant change in the sense of being in a kind of multiple oscillation, but these very changes give it the resiliency to preserve itself when faced with outside pressures. Its survival and viability today I attribute to its remarkable dynamic potential for symbolic adjustment, not necessarily to preserve any monarch or type of government but to preserve itself and the religion it teaches. (271)

Ferguson quite effectively distills a consistent set of concepts in the Burmese literature dealing with lineage concerns. However, in my view, the continuity of Shwegyin monks, of other monks, and of the *Sāsana* as such, does not rest on a process of sociological flexibility ensured by a "potential for symbolic adjustment." Rather, the continuity of Shwegyin monks, the *Sāsana*, and other things Buddhist, is the product of human labor, rooted in a traditionalist drive to carry the *Sāsana*.

IV. Buddhist Histories and Biographies in and beyond Burma/Myanmar

Buddhist histories and biographies are ubiquitous in contemporary Burma/ Myanmar. They can be purchased at roadside bookstalls and bookshops, at monasteries, at Buddhist universities, and at meditation centers. They are available in many different styles and formats: historical treatments of the *Sāsana*; full length biographical treatments; compilations of biographical sketches; historical and biographical summaries in monastic commemoration volumes; historical and biographical notes in discussions that link the lives of particular monks with particular Buddhist monuments; and, biographical stories about

Buddhist saints. (Readers interested in a bibliographic list may consult Carbine 2004.) Some materials in the historical and biographical genre, such as the autobiography of Ashin Janakābhivaṃsa, have been reprinted several times and have become very popular, particularly among Burmese lay people. And, some include both handwritten and printed remarks about lay donors, moneys spent to help defray publication costs, dates on which a particular biography was given to a specific monk, as well as devotional remarks from the people who have read them. Such details are only suggestive of how the histories and biographies circulate among monks and lay people, and of the kinds of meaning that such materials have for the monks or lay people who read or exchange them. Even so, the details help highlight the vibrant role that Buddhist histories and biographies play in the "affairs related to the life of the *Sāsana*" (B. *Sāsanā re"*) in contemporary Burma/Myanmar.

Buddhist histories and biographies in and beyond Burma can be disting-uished from another genre of Buddhist traditionalism: commentarial materials concerning the *Tipiṭaka* (P. Three Baskets). Both genres of traditionalism play important roles in the dissemination of *Sāsana* knowledge and practice. Both genres are involved in local processes of legitimation, pedagogy, discipline, legal practice, and moral training. Both genres are often written or oral, and composed in Pali, in vernaculars, or in combinations of both. However, the *Tipiṭaka*-commentarial genre consists of components of the Pali canonical tradi-tion, including commentaries, handbooks, and related materials. In contrast, the historical and biographical genre includes narrative materials (e.g. P. *vaṃsa*, P. *theruppatti*) that chronicle the foundation and spread of the Buddha's *Sāsana* within specific geo-cultural contexts, often tracing in the process the relations between monks and non-monks. Materials in the historical and biographical genre may draw upon ideas, themes, issues, and interpretive strategies em-bedded in the materials from the *Tipiṭaka*-commentarial genre, and vice-versa. However, historical and biographical materials generally depart from materials in the *Tipiṭaka*-commentarial genre because they are not primarily concerned with a commentarial-style approach, i.e. a word-by-word exposition and analysis of facets of the canonical tradition.[3]

Many Burmese Buddhist histories and biographies exhibit many common features regarding the dynamics of sustaining the transmission of the *Sāsana*. These features consist of instruction in topics like the authority of the Buddha as a father-figure, the ritualized aspects of monastic daily life, and the processes of monastic education. The features also include an effort to incorporate Pali ideas into monastic life, as well as an attempt to show the dynamics of practice through which monks bring themselves together as socially and historically

---

3   Clearly, there are some kinds of material that stand outside of or bridge the two-fold typology proposed here. For instance, some data, like the Kalyāṇī Inscriptions in lower Burma/Myanmar, represents an intertwining of the two types.

continuous lineages. Most importantly, the histories and biographies involve a didactic quality that makes reading them a mode of *Sāsana* education. Ultimately, they affirm and describe the conduct of particular monks, thereby providing idealized patterns for individuals to think about, support, and, potentially, personally embody.

1. Case-Study 1: The *Abridged History* and Aspects of Lineage

The *Abridged History of the Shwegyin Sect* (1988) compiled by the Shwegyin monk Ashin Paṇḍita, is a revised and edited version of the much longer *History of the Shwegyin Sect*, which Paṇḍita completed in time for the "10th All Shwegyin Meeting Concerning the *Sāsana*" in 1963. (These All Shwegyin Meetings are like "business meetings" in which Shwegyin "executives" assemble to discuss the future of their sect and its transmission of the *Sāsana*.) Like the longer *History*, the *Abridged History* covers the lives of many monks, as well as the developments of the *Sāsana* over a large social and historical scale, including developments in India, the area where the *Sāsana* originated. However, the text discusses not so much the Buddha's *Sāsana*—e.g. the nature of *pariyatti*, *paṭipatti*, and *paṭivedha* as portrayed in the Pali canon and related literatures— but rather the activities of a specific lineage of monks who, in comprising a specific sect, have been active participants in the embodied life of the *Sāsana*.

The *Abridged History* divides into two thematic parts. For the first part Paṇḍita begins with a summary of the transmission of the *Sāsana* in Majjhimadesa (a Pali name used by Burmese and other Buddhists for India). Paṇḍita then goes on to discuss certain disciples of the Buddha such as Upāli, the master of Monastic Law. He also discusses the first three Buddhist Councils (P. *Saṅgāyanā*) and the monks who played a role in them. Paṇḍita then brings the first section to a conclusion with accounts of the activities of particular monks prior to the rise of the Shwegyin sect itself.

The second and larger part of the *Abridged History* portrays the monastic trajectories of the First Shwegyin Sayadaw, Ashin Jāgara, and his successors, such as the Mahāvisuddhārāma Sayadaw[4] (Shwegyin *Sāsana* Proprietor, 1894–1916) and the Myaung Mya Sayadaw (Shwegyin *Sāsana* Proprietor, 1972–1975). It also focuses on other leaders in various places in Upper and Lower Burma/Myanmar, such as the Kyauntawya Sayadaw (1843–1925), a famous disciple of Ashin Jāgara. Thus, in its second and main part the *Abridged History* provides a pedagogically oriented overview of the leading monks who have been the "branches and twigs" (B. *atak' alak'*) that have embodied and extended the vitality of the Shwegyin lineage and the *Sāsana* for which it carries responsibility (B. *tā wan'*) (Paṇḍita 1988, 4). To assess the way in which lineage notions

---

4   Here, "Sayadaw" is a term of respect for a revered monastic leader.

inform and are deployed in the *Abridged History*, attention can be directed towards some of the front matter contained in the *Abridged History*. This front matter distills lineage themes that occur, explicitly and implicitly, throughout the *Abridged History*.

1.1. Sīlānandābhivaṃsa's "Introduction": Bearing a Lineage

The *Abridged History* opens with an introduction written by the monk Sīlānandābhivaṃsa, who frames his discussion with a passage, translated into Burmese, from a Pali source, the *Milindapañha* (Questions of King Milinda). The *Milindapañha* uses conversations between the King Milinda and the monk Nāgasena to clarify different Buddhist teachings. The passage from the *Milindapañha* focuses on the reverence that a lay donor (P. *dāyaka*) who has "entered the stream" (P. *sotāpanna*) should give to ordinary monks (B. *puthujañ' rahan'*), i.e. monks of no special spiritual advancement. On this topic, Nāgasena tells King Milinda,

> King, take, for example: a prince takes his education, the duties of a king, in the presence of a court brahmin. At a later time, after that prince has been consecrated as king, he thinks of the brahmin with the thoughts, "this brahmin taught me," and reveres and welcomes him.
>
> King, just in the same way, a layman who has entered the stream, is fit to revere and welcome an ordinary monk, thinking of him with the words, "an ordinary monk undertakes the twenty modes of monastic practice, and the two physical characteristics that enable him to be a monk; he carries a lineage." (Paṇḍita 1988, i)

Sīlānandābhivaṃsa tells his readers that the passage under consideration deals with a disjunction between two Buddhist positions: one, that the *Dhamma* is the highest thing in the present life and in lives yet to come; and two, that a lay person who has entered the stream should revere and welcome ordinary monks. The conundrum is this: Which has precedence, the *Dhamma*, or an ordinary monk? Or, why should a spiritually advanced lay person revere an ordinary monk? According to Sīlānandābhivaṃsa, the reason has to do with following the modes of monastic practice, and "carrying a lineage of the *Sāsana*" (B. *Sāsana to' e* anvay' achak' chon'*) (i–ii).

A footnote in the *Abridged History* tells readers to look in *Milindapañha* itself for the twenty kinds of monastic conduct and the two physical characteristics that enable an individual to be a monk. The twenty modes of monastic conduct include many activities, such as delighting in *sīla*, and undertaking the codes of monastic practice. The two physical characteristics consist of wearing the monastic robes and being shaven bald. According to Sīlānandābhivaṃsa, though an ordinary monk does not possess the high degree of insight that would allow him, for instance, to "enter the stream" (one of the states of religious advancement on the Path of breakthrough to *Nirvana*), he still follows the forms of monastic practice that enable him to be a monk. And, furthermore, the ordinary monk can instruct men so that they too will become monks and follow the monastic Path as indicated in the "twenty" and the "two." Sīlānandābhivaṃsa thus re-emphasizes that the lay person who is a stream-enterer should revere the ordinary monk, because the monk is a lineage-bearer (P. *vaṃsa dhara*), a person who carries, without severing it, a lineage of the *Sāsana* (ii).

Furthermore, Sīlānandābhivaṃsa comments that in reading Nāgasena's explanation to King Milinda, people can see just how much individuals who support or keep guard over a lineage (given in his text as both P. *vaṃsa dhara puggala* and B. *anvay' achak' coṅ' sū*) should be revered. And, they can see just how much importance is placed on the continuing existence of an un-destroyed lineage (B. *anvay' achak' ma pyak' ma cī"*). He then comments:

> Therefore every member of the lineage has the responsibility to protect his own lineage. (ii)

However, Sīlānandābhivaṃsa suggests that there is a potential problem: a monk may be unable to carry out his duty to protect his lineage if he does not know how the lineage itself has come to exist. To that end, Sīlānandābhivaṃsa suggests the following kind of literary-based pedagogy, drawing specific attention to the kind of phenomena I group under the rubric of traditionalism:

> Therefore, this second edition Shwegyin history is, for those individuals who are members of the Shwegyin group (B. *guiṅ'"*), a text that they should always depend upon while striving to know their own lineage. This text will make the bearers of the Shwegyin lineage, who will without fail protect and restrain the lineage of the Shwegyin group, come out, and it gives a light, just like a blazing flame, to them. (In doing so,) it will serve, in a way that substantially contributes to communal understanding, the responsibility of the Shwegyin *Sāsana*. (vii–viii)

These comments are directed above all to monastic readers who are to envision themselves as bearers of a Shwegyin lineage deriving from the Buddha. Being a bearer of a monastic lineage means knowing how it has come to exist and its standards of practice based in Monastic Law. Bearing a lineage also means knowing the various kinds of *Sāsana* interpretations and emphases members of the lineage have maintained, including and extending well beyond the concerns of Monastic Law. In order to learn in this way, monks can read the historical and biographical material in the *Abridged History* (as well as in other sources) in order to help bring into their own everyday world certain visions of the communal work of transmitting the *Sāsana*. The *Abridged History* is thus a type of practice-oriented handbook especially for monks as they try to know how they should carry themselves and the *Sāsana*, so that they as a communal embodiment of the *Sāsana* do not suffer rupture.

1.2. Paṇḍita's Verse and Commentary: Types of Lineage

The front matter to the *Abridged History* also includes a Pali passage and Burmese commentary in which Ashin Paṇḍita pays reverence to the Buddha, *Dhamma*, and *Saṃgha*, as well as to the leading elders of the Shwegyin sect. This is the verse:

> *savaṃsadesakaṃ buddhaṃ dhammaṃ saṃghañca samsuddhaṃ vaṃsānupālake there Shwegyin-nikāyabhūsane paṇāmaṃ sādaraṃ katvā Shwegyin-nikāya-vaṃsakaṃ saṃkhepaṃ dīpakaṃ kassaṃ suddhavākyena saṃyuttaṃ.*

Paṇḍita's full word-by-word commentary is this:

> *ahaṃ* (the implided subject): I
> *savaṃsadesakaṃ:* who had the ability to clarify and preach about the line-age of Buddhas, (which was) his own lineage
> *buddhaṃ ca:* and the Buddha
> *samsuddhaṃ:* which is good and pure
> *dhammañca:* and the *Dhamma* (P. Teaching)
> *samsuddhaṃ:* which is free from and purged of the *kilesa* (P. mental defilements), etc.
> *samghañca:* and the *Saṃgha* (P. Monastic Community)
> *vaṃsānupālake:* who have the ability to safeguard, so that the thread isn't snapped (B. *amhyaṅ' ma prat'*), the lineage of Shwegyin monks
> *Shwegyin-nikāyabhūsane:* who are the very high quality ornaments of the Shwegyin group
> *there:* (and) the noble great elders, who are each endowed with the qualities beginning with *sila* (ethical conduct), etc.
> *sādaraṃ:* along with respect
> *paṇāmaṃ katvā:* respectfully bowing before, adoring, and honoring
> *suddhavākyena saṃyuttaṃ:* using words free from anger and wrong
> *saṃkhepaṃ:* in summary form
> *Shwegyin-nikāyavaṃsakaṃ:* the unbroken lineage of the senior elders of Shwegyin monks
> *dīpakaṃ:* a treatise that demonstrates
> *kassaṃ:* having collectively covered things in a summary way, will write for readers in a way that is different from before. (xix)

Put into more conventional English prose, Paṇḍita's commentary gives:

> I will write a book, in summary form, and in a way different than before, for many different readers using words free from anger and wrong, demonstrating the unbroken lineage of the senior elders of the Shweg-yin monks. I do this after respectfully bowing before and adoring and honoring: the Buddha, who had the ability to preach about the lineage of Buddhas, (which was) his own lineage; the *Dhamma*, which is good and pure; the *Saṃgha*, which is free from and purged of the *kilesa*, etc.; and the respected elders, who are each endowed with the qualities beginning with *sila*, etc., who are the very high quality ornaments of the Shwegyin group, and who have the ability to safeguard, so that the thread isn't snapped, the lineage of Shwegyin monks.

In the course of his Pali verse and Burmese commentary, Paṇḍita uses a Pali word which is particularly relevant to the analysis at hand: *vaṃsa*. Paṇḍita uses the term *vaṃsa* in three compounds: *savaṃsadesakaṃ*, *vaṃsānupālake*, and *Shwegyin-nikāyavaṃsakaṃ*. When he explains each of these compounds, Paṇḍita in each case uses Burmese words that mean lineage (using the word B. *anvay'*, "creeper," in combination with an additional word meaning "continuity" or "succession"). Paṇḍita glosses *savaṃsadesakaṃ* as an adjective of the Buddha, explaining in Burmese that the phrase means he "who had the ability to clarify and preach about the lineage of the Buddhas, (which was) his own lineage." The unexpressed implication of this statement is that the Shwegyin lineage is an offshoot of the lineage of Buddhas; Shwegyin monks may trace their lineage to the Buddha, but even the Buddha has his own lineage—he, like the First Shwegyin Sayadaw, Ashin Jāgara, is a branch as well as a trunk.

Paṇḍita glosses the phrase *vaṃsānupālake* as an adjective of the Pali term "monastic elders" (P. *there*): *vaṃsānupālake* refers to the elders "who have the ability to safeguard, so that the thread isn't snapped, the lineage of Shwegyin monks." The force of Paṇḍita's metaphor is hard to overlook: the Shwegyin lineage as a whole has persisted through time and place as an enduring lineage that has not suffered a permanent rupture because of the efforts on the part of leading monks to ensure the integrity of the Shwegyin lineage.

Finally, Paṇḍita glosses *Shwegyin-nikāyavaṃsakaṃ* as "the unbroken lineage of the senior elders of the Shwegyin monks." Paṇḍita takes it as his task in the *Abridged History* to write a book concerning these elder monks and their efforts on behalf of the Shwegyin lineage. He wants to show the roles these monks have played in keeping the Shwegyin lineage (and sect of which it is a part) dynamically persistent.

Given his Pali verse, and given his Burmese commentary on the verse, Paṇḍita expresses lineage in three ways: a lineage of the Buddhas, which is the Gotama Buddha's own lineage; a lineage of the Shwegyin sect as a whole, which is considered to be an offshoot from the lineage of the Buddhas; and, a lineage of Shwegyin leading elders who take on the particular activities of safeguarding the lineage of Shwegyin monks. It is crucial to recognize that all three lineages—Buddhas, Shwegyin leaders, Shwegyin monks as a whole—are part of the same lineage. However, distinctions can and should be made among them in terms of the manner in which they have contributed to the construction of the *Sāsana*. For example, for Shwegyin as well as many other South and Southeast Asian monastic communities, the Buddha is the exemplary *Sāsana*-constructor. However, the Buddha's importance does not obviate the significance of those leaders who continue to uphold the Shwegyin line so that the "thread doesn't snap." And, lastly, the contributions to the Shwegyin lineage of those monks who are everyday monks should also not be overlooked; everyday monks are a vital part of the Shwegyin lineage, as it continues to branch out and carry the *Sāsana*.

1.3. Paṇḍita's Verse and Commentary: Dynamics of *Kilesa* and *Sīla*

In participating in a lineage deriving from the Buddha, monks are supposed to engage in an important and basic task: they are to strive hard to free themselves from the *kilesa* (P. mental defilements) that prevent them from breaking out of *Saṃsāra* and attaining the peaceful-bliss of *Nirvana*. Paṇḍita touches on this point in an implicit but significant way; he gives reverence to the *Saṃgha* "which is free from and purged of the *kilesa*, etc." Here, the *Saṃgha* is not the *Saṃgha* as it is comprised of ordinary monks; such ordinary monks are, like other people, still in the grips of *kilesa*. Rather the *Saṃgha* in this sense is the *Saṃgha* as it is constituted by spiritually advanced individuals. Being free from and purged of *kilesa* is a necessary condition for, and a common reference to, attaining to *Arahant*-ship (P. *Arahant* is a spiritually and morally perfected being who makes the breakthrough to *Nirvana*; the Gotama Buddha is a quintessential *Arahant*).

There is a widely recognized Pali list of ten basic *kilesa*: greed, anger, delusion, doubt, wrong view, shamelessness, not being afraid of vice, sloth, pride, and over-agitated mental activity. The first three of these *kilesa*—i.e. greed, anger, delusion—are also known as the three kinds of bad roots (P. *akusala hetu*) that, from the perspective of Fundamental Law, fuel the "Samsāric" operations of mind (P. *nāma*) and matter (P. *rūpa*), and thus the flow of beings, in often quite negative ways. In commentarial literature, the *kilesa* are expanded to 1500; the destruction of the "1500 *kilesa*" is part of the process of attaining the omniscience (P. *sabbaññutanāna*) of a fully enlightened Buddha (e.g. Pranke 2004, 38). The *kilesa* clutter the mind and make it dingy, dull, and difficult to move ahead on the Path towards wisdom. Hence, Paṇḍita's Burmese gloss on *kilesa*: filth or excrement (B. *annac' akre"*). In ideal terms, monastic lineages (and the sect or group of which they are a part) consist of those people who are trying in various ways to curb *kilesa*, so that they can be part of the *Saṃgha* which is free of *kilesa*, etc.

One of the primary ways in which people can curb *kilesa* is through the cultivation of *sīla*. (Two other primary ways are through meditation and the cultivation of wisdom.) Again, Paṇḍita touches on this point in an implicit but important way: he also pays reverence to the "noble great elders, who are each endowed with the qualities beginning with *sīla*, etc." *Sīla* has a very large semantic range, parts of which apply to monks and/or parts of which apply to non-monks. With respect to monks, nuns, and lay people, *sīla* is a term that in its most general sense refers to good forms of speech and other activity that stem from and/or help produce good states of mind or volition. For instance, in the Noble Eightfold Path, a basic distillation of Buddhist conduct referred to by both monks and non-monks, *sīla* consists of "right speech," "right action," and "right livelihood."

When used with respect to monks themselves, the notion of *sīla* expands to include many more levels of conduct which do not typically apply to lay people. For monks, *sīla* involves conformity especially to the wishes of the Buddha as laid out in the specific rules and guidelines in the Basket of Monastic Law. Therefore, when Paṇḍita suggests in his commentary that he also reveres the elders of the Shwegyin group/lineage who are "endowed with *sīla*, etc.," he situates those elders within a well-defined repertoire of Pali-related terms and practices concerning proper behavior for monks, such as "restraint with regard to the monastic disciplinary code" (P. *pāṭimokkha saṃvara sīla*). Additionally, like other monks, Shwegyin monks are often instructed to observe very strictly four kinds of *sīla*, which consist of refraining from sexual activity, from taking human life, from stealing, and from telling lies, particularly in regard to the achievement of meditative states or of stages of the Path. In other words, monks are not to be guided in their actions by the *kilesa* (e.g. greed or desire, anger, delusion) which would drive them to such acts.

Such lists of *sīla* could be detailed in different ways; we will do so on a limited basis with the biography of the Kyauntawya Sayadaw below. However, for the moment, it is necessary to emphasize a fundamental point: the various forms of *sīla* stand in opposition to—and can help people overcome—the *kilesa* which prevent beings from breaking through to *Nirvana*. In terms of supporting the *Sāsana* while living inside it as a member and carrier of a monastic lineage, an individual really should not be guided in his actions by the *kilesa* of greed, anger, delusion, etc. If he is guided by these kinds of mental defilements or "bad roots," then he may be compelled to act in ways unbecoming to a lineage member. In the worst case scenarios, he may cause great harm to himself and others, through, for example, desire- and anger-driven acts of violence, and may thus be expelled from the community for doing so. In such a case, a monk is considered "really unfit to proceed further along the path to *araha*nship because he lacks the disciplined volition necessary for its perfection" (Holt 1981, 123), and, put in terms of the perspective taken in this essay, because he lacks the "disciplined volition" necessary for the continued health and prosperity of the *Sāsana* itself.

2. Case Study 2: The *Kyauntawya Sayadaw* and Being a Son of the Buddha

Like the *Abridged History*, the *Kyauntawya Sayadaw* provides an excellent place to investigate the thoughts and activities associated with traditionalism among Shwegyin and other monks. Said to have based his account on the works of two monks, Pho Kyā, the author, portrays the Kyauntawya Sayadaw as an exemplary son of the Buddha. Indeed, in the course of the biography Pho Kyā explicitly identifies the Sayadaw as "a pure son of the Buddha" (B. *Bhurā sā" to˙ cac˙*), because of his lineage and his *sīla* (Pho Kyā 1925, 23). As depicted in the biography, the Kyauntawya Sayadaw's disciple-ship to the Buddha is not exhausted by his lineage and *sīla*, but these qualities do make him a monk who really embodies what it means to be a disciple-son.

Kyauntawya is the name of the monastery in Yangon (the capital of Burma) where the Sayadaw eventually became abbot. Taking Ashin Jāgara as his Preceptor, the Kyauntawya Sayadaw received a Higher Ordination in 1863, thus being formally incorporated into the Shwegyin lineage as a full monk. Initially known by his ecclesiastical name Ashin *Sāsana* (literally: Worthy Dispensation), the Kyauntawya Sayadaw spent sixty-three years of his life as a fully ordained Shwegyin monk. As a Preceptor himself, he ordained many monks, including the monk who eventually became the twelfth Shwegyin *Sāsana* Proprietor, the Shwehinthā Sayadaw (1893–1995; *Sāsana* Proprietor, 1989–1995). And, as a teacher, he instructed a large number of monks, and is even credited with teaching one who played a role in establishing a Shwegyin branch in Sri Lanka. Like many Shwegyin Sayadaws, the Kyauntawya Sayadaw has been remembered for his strict discipline relative to the Basket of Monastic Law, a strong sense of duty to the Shwegyin *Sāsana*, as well as a desire to strive on the solitary Path to *Nirvana* by meditating.

In recounting the Sayadaw's life, Pho Kyā divides the *Kyauntawya Sayadaw* into five parts. The first part of the biography covers the life of the Sayadaw from the time of his conception up to his ordination as a full monk. The second part spans the life of the Sayadaw as a monk until his arrival at the Kyauntawya monastery. The third part deals with the Sayadaw's activities as the abbot of the Kyauntawya monastery until his death. The fourth part focuses on the virtues of the Sayadaw. The fifth and last part summarizes the life of the Sayadaw and praises his life. While being attentive to the structural parts of the biography, I do not attempt to use them as a framework from which to investigate the Kyauntawya Sayadaw's life. Rather, I use a thematic approach, oriented around the fact that the Sayadaw is considered to be an exemplary son of the Buddha. This kind of approach will help to convey in a more effective way the relevant insights that a study of the biography can yield, in terms of carrying the *Sāsana*.

2.1. Dreams: Signs of a Good Disciple-Son

The *Kyauntawya Sayadaw* begins by pointing out that when and after meritorious people take up life in an embryo, other people have various sorts of auspicious dreams about them. Several such dreams occur in the biography. For instance, the Sayadaw's mother, upon his conception, dreams of a radiant and sublime looking monk who comes to her house not to gather alms but to live. And prior to his birth, she dreams that she sees a palace, situated between two Badauk trees (trees associated with tranquility), and, while there, gives birth to a son-gem (B. *sā" kon'" ratanā*) (7). Even the First Shwegyin Sayadaw, the Kyauntawya Sayadaw's Preceptor, dreams about him. He dreams of a cultivated field, completely filled with fruits and grains, which belongs to his student, the Kyauntawya Sayadaw (48).

With these visions of physical well being—a sound and beautiful body (radiance and sublime-ness), tranquility (Badauk trees), prosperity (a palace, a gem), and abundance (a fertile field)—the dreams situate the Kyauntawya Sayadaw within a culturally defined semantic field related in specific ways to the Buddha and other meritorious people. There is in the *Sāsana* traditions of Southeast Asia and Sri Lanka a basic conception that good conduct in past lives correlates with physical and mental well being in a person's/being's present life, especially when it comes to people who will be good monks, like the Buddha himself. The dreams reflect this understanding, and thereby suggest the *Sāsana* environment that the Sayadaw will help foster, as an exemplary disciple of the Buddha.

2.2. A Son's Lineage: The Role of Monastic Law and the Higher Ordination

Part one of the *Kyauntawya Sayadaw* concludes by providing a list of the Sayadaw's lineage. The list covers about twenty-four hundred years of purported *Sāsana* history. It spans most if not all of what many Burmese and non-Burmese Buddhist historians have thought of (and constructed) as the major periods in the development and spread of the *Sāsana* to and in Burma/Myanmar. These periods cover the beginnings of the *Sāsana* in India; the rule of the great Indian emperor Asoka (ca. 270–230 BCE), who sent out emissaries to various parts of the South and Southeast Asian world; the growth of the *Sāsana* as part of the culture of Thaton; the life of the *Sāsana* as part of the efflorescence of the culture of Pagan (in upper Burma); and the roles of the *Sāsana* in post-Pagan Burma.

As presented in the *Kyauntawya Sayadaw*, the list is introduced by a heading—"The Succession of Teachers"—as well as by a brief note stating that the ensuing list presents the lineage of the Kyauntawya Shwegyin Sayadaw that descends from the Buddha. Here, I include only the parts of the list directly relevant to the analysis.

Elders in Majjhimadesa (India)
1. Shin Upāli, the disciple-son of the Buddha recognized to be pre-eminent in the Monastic Law. ...
5. Shin Moggaliputtatissathera: this venerable one is the disciple of Shin Siggava and Shin Candavajjī. He led the Third Council, and sent Shin Soṇa and Shin Uttara to Thaton to build the *Sāsana*.

Elders in Suvannabhumi, Thaton
6. Shin Soṇa and Shin Uttara, who built the *Sāsana* (in) Thaton. ...
14. Shin Byānadassī, also known as Pyāṇadassī. This venerable one, having attained the meditative states and supernatural knowledges, went, early every morning, to the Mahābodhi tree[5] in Uruveḷa village, in

---

5   This is the tree under which the Buddha was enlightened.

the Magadharāja region. After he swept the area around the Mahābodhi
tree, he always returned to go on his alms rounds in Thaton. Because
merchants, traveling from Thaton to Magadharāja and trading in
Uruvela, personally witnessed that matter and then told it to natives of
Thaton, many people were able to know that the monk attained the
meditative states and supernatural knowledges. ...

Elders of the Pagan Region
17. Shin Dhammadassī, also called Shin Arahan. Starting from the arrival
of this venerable one in Upper Myanmar during the reign of Pagan
Anawyatha, the *Sāsana* flourished. ...
21. Shin Uttarajīva, who went to Sri Lanka. ...
33. Shwegyin Sayadaw.
34. Kyauntawya Shwegyin Sayadaw. (Pho Kyā 1925, 20–22)

By including the lineage list, Pho Kyā tries to show that the Kyauntawya Sayadaw is traceably legitimate as a monastic disciple-son of the Buddha. Indeed,
he is an heir to such purported *Sāsana*-notables as Moggaliputtatissathera, who
convened the Third Council; Soṇa and Uttara, who brought the *Sāsana* to
Thaton; Byānadassī, an adept at meditative attainments and supernatural
knowledges; Arahan, who is commonly believed to have played a prominent
role in the flourishing of the *Sāsana* at Pagan;[6] Uttarajīva, a famous teacher who
went to Sri Lanka for the purpose of worshipping Buddhist shrines; and the
Shwegyin Sayadaw himself.

In terms of the lineage list, two issues should be emphasized. One issue is
the importance of adherence to the rules and codes of monastic conduct outlined in the Basket of Monastic Law. The importance of the Monastic Law to
Shwegyin notions of lineage is explicit from the outset of the list, where Upāli
sits in the no. 1 position. As implicated at various points in this study, Upāli is
allegedly the foremost specialist on the Monastic Law at the First Council,
which followed the Buddha's death.

The second issue, in keeping with the first, is the significance of the Higher
Ordination (P. *Upasampadā*, B. *Mraṅ' mrat' so rahan'''*), which is arguably the
most important legal ritual codified in the Basket of Monastic Law. From the
perspective of the Basket of Monastic Law, the development of the Higher
Ordination into a rather complex legal ritual represented an early stage in a
communal perception of decline in the institutional and spiritual qualities of
the monastic community, as well as an early stage in the history of the *Sāsana*
that sought to control those kinds of decline through the careful use of a legal
ritual. In keeping with this point, the lineage list provided in the *Kyauntawya
Sayadaw* doubles as a list of Preceptors, the monks who have taken a leading

---

6   Arahan is credited with urging King Anawyatha to acquire a complete set of the Pali
    canon as well as relics of the Buddha from the Mon kingdom of Thaton. According to
    Burmese narratives, for which we lack any historical evidence, Anawyatha invaded
    Thaton to achieve the goal.

role in the Higher Ordination of new monks. For example, Uttarajīva, the teacher
in slot no. 21, traveled to Sri Lanka, and conferred there a Higher Ordination
on his student Chapada. He did so in union with Sinhalese monks who
preserved a pure ordination line deriving from Mahāmahinda (the Buddhist
emissary sent to Sri Lanka at the same time that Soṇa and Uttara were sent to
Thaton). Thus, the list makes an implied but nevertheless important claim
about purity of the Kyauntawya Sayadaw's ordination line as it derives from
and relates to famous monks in India, Burma/Myanmar, and Sri Lanka. In
terms of an ordination-based interpretation of the lineage list, the Kyauntawya
Sayadaw is really pure, from a regional *Sāsana* perspective.

2.3. A Son and his Practice

As a son of the Buddha, a monk is to exhibit certain types of devotional and
ritual relationships to the Buddha. For the Kyauntawya Sayadaw, these relationships are concisely depicted in the fourth part of his biography. In that part,
the reader learns more about the Sayadaw's activities as a young boy, as a
young apprentice, as a novice, and as a monk. For example, as a young boy,
the Sayadaw was restrained in his sense faculties (P. *sikkhā indriya*). He played
at being a monk and collecting alms. He didn't speak obscenely, wasn't in the
habit of speaking trivially or flippantly, and didn't attend village festivities (49).

As a young apprentice, he practiced insight meditation (P. *vipassanā*),
observed *sīla*, and performed two austere ascetic practices (P. *dhutaṅga*), e.g.
eating in a single sitting and eating with only one bowl. Additionally, every
day he swept the monastery and carried seven buckets of water, offering them
to the Buddha and *Saṃgha*. He paid obeisance to the Buddha three times,
offered four lamps to the Buddha, and offered five trays of flowers to the
Buddha. And, he recited his beads (49–50).

As a novice (P. *sāmaṇera*), he observed the ten *sīlas* and the seventy-five
training codes (P. *sekhiya*). He practiced eight more austere practices, including
the wearing of discarded robes and not omitting any house while on alms. He
swept the monastic grounds once a day, he carried fifteen buckets of water,
offering them to the Buddha and *Saṃgha*. He paid obeisance to the Buddha four
times a day, offered four lamps and five trays of flowers to the Buddha every
day, and recited his rosary prayers every day. And, he devoted his remaining
time to his studies (50–53).

As a fully ordained monk, he (and his students) adhered to the monastic
disciplinary code (P. *pāṭimokkha saṃvara sīla*) and controlled sense faculties
(P. *indriya saṃvara sīla*). He lived in pure ways (P. *ājīva pārisuddhi sīla*) and sub-
sisted on the four kinds of requisites (food, robes, shelter, and medicine) for
monastic practice (P. *paccaya sannissita sīla*). He collected alms, wore robes, lived,
and used medicine in accordance with the wishes of the Buddha. He swept

once a day and carried twenty-five buckets of water a day, offering five to the Buddha and twenty to the *Saṃgha*. He paid obeisance to the Buddha five times a day, offered ten lamps to the Buddha a day, and offered twenty trays of flowers to the Buddha a day. He fed the animals around the monastery daily. He continually gave his students both day and night lessons. He slept from twelve midnight until three a.m., and meditated twice a day, from ten p.m. until twelve midnight, and from three until four in the morning. And, he made offerings to the Shwedagon pagoda (a very important religious site in Yangon, the capital of Burma) (54–63).

Of particular interest in these details of the Sayadaw's life and regimen is how the biography portrays the high degree of ritualization involved in the patterns of *sīla* and other forms of practice that course through his life. The focus of his ritualized regimen is the Buddha, who provides a locus for the daily organization of the Sayadaw's movements and reflections. Virtually every moment of the Sayadaw's activity becomes a moment for reflection on the Buddha, orientations of his body around representations of the Buddha, and/or transmissions of the *Dhamma* (P. Teachings) believed to be taught by the Buddha in his *Sāsana*. The ritual relationship between the Sayadaw and the Buddha governs even the basic dimensions of the Sayadaw's activity on a very general level; he eats, dresses, lives, and uses medicine following the Buddha's wishes.

Encompassed within the ritualized relationship to the Buddha is of course the Sayadaw's relationship(s) to his own students. Following the Buddha's example, he teaches his students to safeguard the restraints (P. *saṃvara*) associated with monastic life. He instructs them in both day and night lessons. And, he models by personal example the modes of livelihood appropriate to monastic pursuits. The repetitive passages about the Sayadaw's virtues appear to be rooted in an effort to instill in the reader a sense of the care he has for the general trajectories of Shwegyin practice, for the training of his students, and for the Buddha's *Sāsana* in its communal activity and ritualistic diversity. Above all, through his various kinds of work, he cares for, preserves, and carries on the *Sāsana* that can save beings from *Saṃsāra*.

2.4. Sons of the Buddha: A Classic Conflict and a Shwegyin Solution

Becoming a disciple-son of the Buddha may involve a considerable amount of personal struggle between what counts as good for oneself and what counts as good for the wider context—social or otherwise—in which one is involved. Thus, the personal struggles associated with renunciation may work in tandem with a great deal of social tension as well. This point lurks just beneath the surface of the biography as it relates the Kyauntawya Sayadaw to Prince Vessanta-ra, a quintessential figure of self-detachment and generosity. Vessantara, a birth precursor to the Gotama Buddha, perfected his capacity to give and, as stories about him go, tensions mount as he plunges his kingdom into ruin and his family into despair. In cultivating his "Perfection of Generosity," he gives away the kingdom's riches as well as his wife and children. His so-called self-detachment and compassion, which bring about well being for some people (including himself), actually bring about great suffering for others (e.g. his wife and children).

Stories about Vessantara insist "on conflicts of value." Indeed, Vessantara's

> fulfillment of the Perfection of Generosity weaves its way through two conflicts: socially, between the ascetic values of renunciation and the mundane need for prudential government; and psychologically, between the aspiration to mental detachment, to a love universalized and depersonalized, and the immediate joys and ties of particular affection, filial, marital and paternal. (Collins 1998, 500)

Becoming a monastic disciple-son of the Buddha, or better, becoming a *buddha*, one who ultimately has complete awareness, and attains to *Nirvana*, may very well involve at certain and crucial stages of religious advancement apparent disregard for some kinds of suffering that one brings upon other people. These kinds of disregard and conflict indicate a new level of spiritual advancement, as well as a detachment that must occur from worldly things if *Nirvana* is to be attained.

The highly problematic moral explorations raised by the Vessantara story concerning individual versus collective goods do not enter into the biography of the Kyauntawya Sayadaw in an immediately apparent way. Indeed, after noting that the Sayadaw has the same astrological signs as Prince Vessantara, signs that indicate the Sayadaw's own disposition towards generosity, the biography follows with short accounts about how he (the Sayadaw) was generous (Pho Kyā 1925, 64–66). The biography even goes so far as to announce that the level of giving that the Sayadaw undertakes could not be carried out by ordinary people; the Sayadaw is able to give so much because of the good result of his *sīla* and the perfection of his acquired merit (66).

The biography does occasionally render apparent the tension between personal and collective goods as understood within and in relation to the *Sāsana*. For instance, the second section of the biography is structured by the struggle the Sayadaw often made between his desire to meditate in solitude on the one hand and the needs of the monastic community with respect to his ability to teach and administrate on the other. For instance, the biography records that the Sayadaw made several trips to secluded monastic settings, so that he could meditate without interruption, before becoming the abbot at the Kyauntawya monastery.

One passage in particular recounts the efforts made by the Kyauntawya Sayadaw's own teacher to call him back from his meditative endeavors to help teach. The passage is compelling in how it resolves the conflict between the Kyauntawya Sayadaw's individual soteriological interests and the needs of his monastic community. As shown below, the passage resolves the tension by an appeal to the figure of the Buddha himself, an appeal particularly attentive to the collective needs of the monastic community. Ultimately, the appeal prioritizes the importance of collective life in the *Sāsana* over the importance of personal advancement on the religious Path.

> In 1234 [1872], in his tenth year as a monk, when he had meditated for about two years at Dhūtintauṅ tawya, the Shwegyin Sayadaw (Ashin Jāgara) sent him a letter calling him back. The gist of the letter was: My chief student, it's extremely good that you've meditated while living at (Dhūtintauṅ) tawya. I approve. However, right now I need a great deal of help with teaching, etc. Among the three aspects of the *Sāsana*—*pariyatti, paṭipatti*, and *paṭiveda*—the *pariyatti Sāsana*, the teaching of texts, is the foundation of the other two. You are not responsible for yourself alone. I wish you to take responsibility for the *Sāsana* too. Although our father (B. *apha*), the (Gotama) Buddha, could have attained *Nirvana* at the feet of Dīpaṅkarā Buddha, he made tiring efforts to become a *buddha* both for his own benefit and for the benefit of others because he was sympathetic towards (all) beings drowning and drifting (in *Saṃsāra*). In accordance with that, my chief disciple, return to the monastery; I want you to complete here the *gantādhura* and *vipassānadhura*, respectively, the teaching of texts and meditation. He called him back by writing that in the letter. When he was called back and shown his teacher's wishes concerning the *Dhamma*, he certainly wanted to stay and meditate where he was. But it wasn't opportune. He graciously accepted the authority (B. *āṇā*) of his teacher. He returned to Hmainlontaik, one of the five Shwegyin establishments…and strove after both *pariyatti* and *paṭipatti*. (24–25)

If there was any great struggle within the Sayadaw about the appropriateness of pursuing his individual religious aspirations for *Nirvana* and fulfilling a larger obligation to the monastic community, it is resolved, at least on the level of practical action, by an appeal to two types of interlocking spiritual authority, which sit at the heart of Shwegyin traditionalism. Neither type, interestingly, hinges on the figure of Vessantara, who is too morally problematic to deploy in some contexts. (An appeal to the figure of Vessantara might actually justify the Kyauntawya Sayadaw's efforts to continue his meditative pursuits at the expense of taking his part in the communal life of the Shwegyin community.) One type of authority is that of one's teacher, who one is obligated to follow, because he is his teacher's disciple-son. The other type of authority is that of the quintessential Shwegyin father himself, the Gotama Buddha. The Kyauntawya Sayadaw's teacher draws on one of the former lives of their father (B. *apha*) the Buddha, in order to emphasize the importance of *pariyatti*. Like his ultimate father before him, the Kyauntawya Sayadaw is not to try to obtain *Nirvana* quickly, but to pursue a slower track, working tirelessly for personal as well as communal benefit. In effect, there are two fathers with whom the Sayadaw must contend, his teacher and the Buddha, who are both presented as individuals who have a sense of great responsibility for *Sāsana*-continuity. Thus, following their lead, the Sayadaw must return and help to continue the collective work of both embodying and textualizing the *Sāsana*, even if it means pursuing a slower track to *Nirvana*.

V. Shwegyin Traditionalism and Beyond

As locally produced pedagogical texts, Shwegyin histories and biographies testify to and embody the work that lineages and sons of the Buddha are expected to do. Without question, the histories and biographies idealize some of the lineages and monks of whom they speak; Shwegyin histories and biographies are no exception in this regard. However, such idealizations have an important function; they help illustrate the dynamics of tradition-making, e.g. from the perspective of the Shwegyin *Sāsana*. But Shwegyin histories and biographies, like many other Buddhist histories and biographies, do more than just illustrate the dynamics of constructing the *Sāsana*; they themselves are yet one more component in the process of that construction. In them, people continue to have imaginative access to the visions that have driven certain exemplary monks to structure their lives around particular kinds of exemplary practice. In them, people continue to have paradigmatic access to an understanding of the ways in which monks, as part of a lineage claiming descent from the Buddha, have tried to maintain the patterns of communal responsibility attributed to the Buddha himself. In the histories and biographies, people have an opportunity to learn about exemplary disciple-sons and their efforts. Ultimately, Shwegyin monks themselves can learn about the possible courses of action that they should undertake to ensure that they uphold their social and historical connections to one another as a lineage, as sons of the Buddha, as carriers of the *Sāsana*.

Based on the Shwegyin material discussed in this essay — and based on scholarly writing across several disciplines on "traditions" and the various media and means through which they are constructed and deployed — I take it that traditions are pretty much what they have always been, and what they will always be: patterns of thought and feeling, in some way relating to visions of continuity and rupture in the past, present, and future, created by multiple agents who develop multiple forms of meaning and engage in multiple forms of discourse and practice. This observation may strike some readers as common sense. Or, it may strike other readers as far too broad to be of much interpretive use. However, I believe it is crucial for a methodologically and theoretically balanced consideration of the dynamics involved in any tradition. For example, the observation presupposes that while some aspects of a given tradition can be highly socio-political in nature, other aspects may not. Certainly, Shwegyin assertions of their purity *vis-à-vis* the *Sāsana* have been, depending on context, explicitly and implicitly concerned with religio-political messages directed towards, for instance, other monks and lay people. However, the Shwegyin drive to carry the *Sāsana* is first and foremost based on certain metaphysical and narrative claims which appear to transcend any notion of politics: the possibility though difficulty of attaining *Nirvana*, and the eventual rupture of the *Sāsana*. As with all conditioned things, the *Sāsana* will die, and in that death the knowledge of the Path to *Nirvana* will be lost.

But perhaps most important, the observation suggests a productive way for addressing the dynamics within and across traditions. The productive way hinges on recognizing that traditions, in as much as they consist of complex patterns of thought and feeling created by multiple agents, are often conceived of, by those who participate in the traditions themselves, in terms of a dynamic tension between continuity and rupture, mediated through the efforts of what can be called a locally constituted traditionalism. Regardless of whether they are of historically distant or more recent origin, regardless of whether they have been impacted by or emerged from the forces of colonialism and modernity, and regardless of whether their content and focus is socio-political in nature, a tradition's traditionalism comprises a domain of a struggle for the kind of socio-historical, or as the case may be socio-religious, continuity that can either stave off or foster different kinds of rupture. In regard to monastic lineages comprised of sons of the Buddha, such as the Shwegyin, traditionalism prevents *Sāsana*-rupture from ruling the day. In regard to the conditioned flow of beings in *Saṃsāra*, traditionalism, ideally, raises the chances that at least some may, if not now then in future lives, be able to follow the Buddha in making the radical breakthrough to the mystery of *Nirvana*.

References

Blackburn, Anne. 2001. *Buddhist Learning and Textual Practice in Eighteenth-Century Lankan Monastic Culture*. Princeton: Princeton University Press.

Bourdieu, Pierre, and Jean-Claude Passeron. 1977. *Reproduction in Education, Society, and Culture*. Translated by Richard Nice. London: Sage Publications.

Carbine, Jason. 2004. *An Ethic of Continuity: Shwegyin Monks and the Sāsana in Contemporary Burma/Myanmar*. Ph.D. Dissertation, University of Chicago.

Collins, Steven. 1998. *Nirvana and Other Buddhist Felicities: Utopias of the Pali Imaginaire*. Cambridge: Cambridge University Press.

Connerton, Paul. 1989. *How Societies Remember*. Cambridge: Cambridge University Press.

Crosby, Kate. 2004. "Theravada." Pages 836–841 in *Encyclopedia of Buddhism*. Editor in Chief, Robert E. Buswell. New York: Macmillan Reference USA.

Durkheim, Emile. 1915. *The Elementary Forms of the Religious Life*. Translated from the French by Joseph Ward Swain. London: Allen and Unwin.

Eliade, Mircea. 1958. *Patterns in Comparative Religion*. New York: Sheed & Ward.

Ferguson, John P. 1975. *The Symbolic Dimensions of the Burmese Sangha*. Ph.D. Dissertation, Cornell University.

174   Jason A. Carbine

Hallisey, Charles. 1995. "Roads Taken and Not Taken in the Study of Theravāda Bud-
    dhism." Pages 31–62 in *Curators of the Buddha: The Study of Buddhism Under
    Colonialism*. Edited by Donald S. Lopez, Jr. Chicago: University of Chicago Press.
———, and Anne Hansen. 1996. "Narrative, Sub-ethics, and the Moral Life: Some
    Evidence from Theravada Buddhism." *Journal of Religious Ethics* 24: 305–327.
Harpham, Geoffrey. 1992. *Getting it Right: Language, Literature, and Ethics*. Chicago: Univer-
    sity of Chicago Press.
Hobsbawm, Eric. 1983. "Introduction: Inventing Tradition." Pages 1–14 in *The Invention of
    Tradition*. Edited by Eric Hobsbawm and Terence Ranger. Cambridge: Cambridge
    University Press.
Holt, John Clifford. 1981. *Discipline: The Canonical Buddhism of the Vinayapitaka*. Delhi:
    Motilal Banarsidass.
Huxley, Andrew. 2000. "Rules, Buddhist (Vinaya): Lineage." Pages 1091–1093 in *Encyclo-
    pedia of Monasticism*. Edited by William M. Johnston. Chicago: Fitzroy Dearborn.
Janakābhivamsa, Ashin. 1997. *Abhidhamma in Daily Life*. Translated and edited by U Ko
    Lay. Yangon: International Theravada Buddhist Missionary University.
Jay, Nancy. 1992. *Throughout Your Generations Forever*. Chicago: The University of Chicago
    Press.
Levi-Strauss, Claude. 1962. *Totemism*. Translated by Rodney Needham. Harmondsworth:
    Penguin.
Mendelson, Edward Michael. 1975. *Sangha and State in Burma: A Study of Monastic
    Sectarianism and Leadership*. Ithaca: Cornell University Press.
Morris, Rosalind. 2002. "Crises of the Modern in Northern Thailand: Ritual, Tradition, and
    the New Value of Pastness." Pages 68–94 in Tanabe and Keyes 2002.
Nattier, Jan. 1991. *Once Upon a Future Time: Studies in a Buddhist Prophecy of Decline*. Berke-
    ley: Asian Humanities Press.
Pandita, Ashin. 1988. *Abridged History of the Shwegyin Sect* (Paṇḍita, Arhan´. Rhvekyan´
    nikāya sāsanāvan´ akyañ´". Ran´kun´: Ū " Thin´ Wan´").
Pho Kyā. 1925. *Kyauntawya Sayadaw* (Phui" Kyā. Kyon´"to´rā rhvekyan´ charāto" bhurā" krī".
    Ran´kun´: [?]).
Pranke, Patrick Arthur. 2004. *The 'Treatise on the Lineage of Elders' (Vamsadipani): Monastic
    Reform and the Writing of Buddhist History in Eighteenth-Century Burma*. Ph.D.
    Dissertation, University of Michigan.
Radcliffe-Brown, Alfred R. 1952. *Structure and Function in Primitive Society: Essays and
    Addresses*. London: Cohen & West.
Shils, Edward. 1981. *Tradition*. Chicago: University of Chicago Press.
Skilling, Peter. 2004. "Ubiquitous and Elusive: In Quest of Theravāda." Unpublished paper
    delivered at the conference Exploring Theravāda Studies: Intellectual Trends and
    the Future of a Field of Study. August 2004.
Stoller, Paul. 1995. *Embodying Colonial Memories: Spirit Possession, Power, and the Hauka in
    West Africa*. New York: Routledge.
Tambiah, Stanley J. 1984. *The Buddhist Saints of the Forest and the Cult of Amulets: A Study in
    Charisma, Hagiography, Sectarianism, and Millennial Buddhism*. Cambridge: Cambridge
    University Press.
Tanabe, Shigeharu, and Charles F. Keyes (eds.). 2002. *Cultural Crisis and Social Memory:
    Modernity and Identity in Thailand and Laos*. Honolulu: University of Hawaii Press.

The Autonomy of Tradition:
Creating Space for Indian Medicine

Richard Weiss

The history of the globalization of biomedicine is as much a history of imperialism as it is one of the spread of rationality (Arnold 1988, 1993; Comaroff and Comaroff 1992; A. Kumar 1998). In the last century, practitioners of Indian medicine, like other specialists of non-Western medicine throughout the world, have seen the legitimacy of their knowledge seriously challenged by biomedicine. The debate over medical efficacy has been part of larger discussions of the future viability of non-Western cultural practices, especially those that impinge on disciplines that are classified as "sciences." *Vaidyas*, practitioners of Sanskrit *ayurveda* and Tamil *siddha* medicines, and *hakims*, practitioners of the Islamic *unani* medical system, have responded to these attempts to undermine their authority in a variety of ways. One of the most effective has been to argue for the unique efficacy of Indian medicine, to assert that its features are distinct from those of Western medicine, and that its practices cannot be assimilated into any other medical system. In this essay, I will explore the ways in which these *vaidyas* and *hakims* have sought to carve out an autonomous space for their practices by constructing boundaries that shape an Indian medical tradition.

While the rhetoric of tradition is that of duration, continuity, and eternal essence, traditions are sites of innovation. This is to say that traditions have histories. In nineteenth and twentieth century India, "tradition" emerged as a realm of Indian knowledge and practice that was opposed to Western science— indeed, the dichotomy of science and tradition is an historical one. While much has been made of the way colonial authorities employed this dichotomy to relegate the knowledge of their imperial subjects to the past, less attention has been given to how this notion of tradition has also served as an autonomous space over which Indians could exert control (Chatterjee 1990). The use to which *vaidyas* have employed this distinction in the last two centuries suggests not that they appropriated an imperial category and used it against their colonial masters, but that the dichotomy itself emerged from a cultural encounter that those on each side of the conflict used to their advantage. In interrogating contemporary assertions of a unique and bounded traditional medical system, I will suggest ways of understanding how one society, confronted with domination, has developed strategies in its struggle to counter cultural imperialism.

1. Western Science and the Critique of Indigenous Medicine

Since the early decades of the nineteenth century, one of the major issues concerning indigenous medical knowledge in India has been whether it should be treated as unique and self-sufficient, or whether it should be supplemented by, or integrated into, biomedical learning. Biomedical doctors have argued for a singular medical efficacy, dismissing the possibility of an enduring medical landscape whose contours are constituted by theories and practices of both bio-medicine and indigenous medicine. These doctors have faith in a self-regulating notion of efficacy, assuming that the rationality of their own medicine is indisputable and therefore will, in accordance with a historical teleology of progress defined by the absorption of the traditional other, gradually effect the desiccation and ultimate demise of indigenous medicine.[1]

Some indigenous medical practitioners have called for the synthesis of Western and indigenous knowledge into a singular and universal medicine. The College of Integrated Medicine was founded in Madras in 1947, the year of Indian independence, with this goal of integrating biomedical and indigenous medical knowledge. Others have argued that given the disparities of power inherent in colonial and post-colonial processes, traditional knowledge suffers neglect in the hands of the modern state and so is in peril of disintegration. These latter practitioners commonly delineate a realm of traditional activity with the defining feature of autonomy, in which they feel free to formulate their own rules and insist on the relativity of truth vis-à-vis external critiques.[2] In arguing that the purity of their traditions must be recaptured and pre-served, cultural revivalists take on the unenviable task of sealing the porous boundaries of tradition, boundaries which are themselves variously conceived.

These promoters of pure tradition, who today segregate themselves along linguistic lines—Tamil (*siddha*), Sanskrit (*ayurveda*), and Arabic and Urdu (*unani*)—have been unified in their opposition to the universalizing goals of biomedicine. It was not without reason that they have felt the need to circum-scribe and withdraw into an autonomous realm over which they might assume control. The history of their interaction with "allopathy," a word used in India to denote medical practices and theories introduced by the British, reflects the power differential of the colonial encounter. The first Western-style school to teach a course in indigenous medicine was the Native Medical Institution,

---

1   Of course, the challenges that biomedicine has posed to traditional techniques did not disappear with Indian independence, but have increased over the last half century. The independent Indian state continues to heavily subsidize biomedicine, and ever-expanding education in rural schools brings Western sciences to new areas.

2   This is not to say that these practitioners did not make the further move of insisting on the universality of their knowledge. Like a one-way mirror, they affirmed their impunity from the external gaze while celebrating the transparency of the errors of biomedicine.

founded in Calcutta in June, 1822. The purpose of the new school was to better train Indians to contribute to the medical needs of the East India Company, most commonly as assistants in military battalions. The school was run with much controversy for just over a decade, teaching *ayurveda* and clinical medicine side by side. The institution was finally dissolved in 1835 on the recommendation of a government committee report which asserted that theories of science were incompatible with the principles of Ayurveda (*Report* 1958; A. Kumar 1998; Gupta 1998).

When the school was closed, formal teaching in *ayurveda* was also discontinued. Subsequently, the Calcutta Medical College was founded to continue the education of native doctors, this time without the traditional medical component. Training would be carried out in English and would be exclusively dedicated to clinical medicine, as students would "learn the principles and practice of medical science in strict accordance with the mode adopted in Europe" (*Report* 1958, 53). The dissolution of the Native Medical Institution is seen by many to have been a watershed in the victory of "Anglicists" over "Orientalists" in the debate over the proper relationship of Western and South Asian practices (Arnold 1993, 13; Gupta 1998, 370; D. Kumar 1997, 48). The decision to discontinue colonial support of ayurvedic education reflects the prevalent, dismissive attitude of both the British and Indians trained in allopathic medicine towards indigenous practices and theories, exemplified by James Mill in his 1824 objection to the Native Medical Institution. "With respect to sciences it was worse than a waste of time to employ persons to teach and learn them in the state in which they were found in the Oriental books. Our great aim should be not to teach Hindu learning, but sound learning" (A. Kumar 1998, 20).

After the close of the Calcutta Native Medical Institution in 1835, the teaching of traditional medicine in classrooms, and official government research into indigenous practices, were to wait eight decades before being taken up again. On November 26, 1915, A. S. Krishna Rao proposed a resolution in the Legislative Council of the Madras Presidency, that the Madras government "direct a research and investigation of the Ayurvedic system of medicine, with a view to improve and encourage that system" (Hausman 1996, 116). The resolution was passed in 1917, though in a much revised form: "to direct a research and investigation of the pharmacological action of Indian drugs." From its initial goal of encouragement of Ayurvedic medicine, the final resolution was to undertake an investigation of indigenous drugs in order to supplement and improve the *biomedical* system. The colonial medical leaders thereby expressed faith in the physical material of India but not in the knowledge produced and recorded in, as surgeon general G. G. Giffard put it, the "unintelligible" Sanskrit writings, a language of "priestly mysticism" and so clearly unsuited for scientific truths (Hausman 1996, 165). When Dr. M. C. Koman was appointed chairman of this committee and began to carry out the investigation, the nature of this inquiry was not lost on the local vernacular press. The *Andhra-patrika*, a Telegu paper, observed that "the appointment of Dr. Koman to make a research regarding these systems was not made with the object of improving them but for incorporating in the English pharmacopoeia the efficacious drugs which are used therein" (Hausman 1996, 155). The colonial plundering of native material wealth with a rejection of indigenous forms of knowledge was manifested in many realms of activity, and medicine was no exception.

2. The Defense of Indigenous Theory

Dr. Koman submitted three reports to the government of the Madras Presidency from 1918 to 1920. In these reports, he considered a range of ingredients used for indigenous medicines and tested their effects on patients according to the standards of Western science. What I want to focus on here, however, is not the Koman Report itself, but the response to this report by The Dravida Vaidya Mandal and the Madras Ayurveda Society. The Dravida Vaidya Mandal represented primarily Tamil *vaidyas* of South India, and the Ayurveda Society represented Sanskrit *vaidyas*.

Their *Reply to the Report on the Investigation into the Indigenous Drugs* was published in 1921. A response of this sort was necessary, these practitioners argued, because the "learned doctor, appointed by the Government, had thoroughly failed to understand the indigenous systems and had grievously erred on many vital points" (2–3). Noting that Koman judged the effect of some indigenous medicines as "beneficial," the *vaidyas* continue that their protest "is not against what is declared as 'beneficial' etc., but against the mortal wound inflicted on the vital parts" (7–8). These "vital parts" are indigenous theories of the body and health, the areas of Indian medical knowledge that colonial health administrators rejected as medieval. Indeed, the dismissal of indigenous medical theories was part of the rationale for the particular focus of Dr. Koman's investigation on the possible benefits of indigenous drugs, not theories.

In his report, Dr. Koman asserts that "From what I have seen the science of Hindu medicine is still sunk in a state of empirical obscurity" (20). The *vaidyas* interpret this rightly, I think: "To them [Koman, biomedical doctors, colonial authorities] the use of drugs in Ayurveda is a matter of accidence [sic] which the learned doctor was kind enough to say as 'empirical'" (95). Koman suggests that while there may be some useful medicines in the indigenous pharmacopoeia, these were chanced upon by practitioners, not systematically hypothesized through the application of theory. The *vaidyas* admonish Dr. Koman and the project in general for only being concerned with the properties of indigenous drugs while failing "to grasp the intricate principles of the indigenous systems" (4). For example, in his examination of the ayurvedic medicine for syphilis

called "Poornachandrodayam,"[3] Dr. Koman remarks that "the action of Poornachandrodayam is very slow and does not compare favourably with that of
Salvarsan" (72). The *vaidyas* argue that Dr. Koman is influenced here by his
biomedical background, which values quick, temporary benefits over slower
but permanent results. They counter that the report

> carefully omits to mention that the treatment by Salvarsan does not
> thoroughly eradicate the disease from the body. Numerous cases of
> syphilis given up as hopeless by the allopathic physicians have been
> tried by the *vaidyas* with good and satisfactory results. The learned
> doctor has yet to learn why the action of Poornachandrodaya, though
> slow, is yet permanent while that of Salvarsan is transitory. (79–80)

The *vaidyas* assert that the proper use of their medicines can only be understood in relation to indigenous theory. Medicines cannot be extracted from the
context of local knowledge and integrated into a foreign system of knowledge
without radically changing the nature of the medical applications. In broader
terms, they claim the unalienable coherence of their tradition—a piecemeal
plundering of this tradition will not be successful.

The *vaidyas* argue that there is no objective understanding of the properties
of medicines outside of particular traditions: what appears to be "slow" from
the point of view of British medicine is considered "effective" from the Indian
standpoint. Dr. Koman has dismissed the effectiveness of Poornachandrodayam
because he has failed to understand the traditional preparation of mercury,
which effects a transformation that can only be understood through ayurvedic
theory.

> Ayurveda has recognized that there are seven important poisonous
> sheaths covering mercury which are highly injurious to the body and to
> remove them it has prescribed seven processes of purification as
> Sodhana, Jarana, Utthapana etc. By these processes mercury is made
> absolutely harmless. The British Pharmacopoea is quite a stranger to
> these methods... (80)

When Koman asserts that there is little for "us" to learn from the *vaidyas* and
hakims, his frame of reference is that of Western medicine. The *vaidyas* counter
that Koman's lack of understanding of indigenous medical theories prevents
him from successfully completing even the more circumscribed task of testing
the effectiveness of indigenous drugs.

Just as most doctors of Western medicine denied that South Asian languages were capable of representing Western science, likewise the *vaidyas* trace

---

3   T. V. Sambasivam Pillai defines the Tamilized *pūranacantirōdayam* as "an infallible
    Ayurvedic medicine capable of curing many ailments and promoting secretion of
    semen. It is a Siddha Medicine, too. It contains gold, sulphur and mercury" (Pillai
    1931, vol. 5, 550).

Koman's misunderstanding to his use of translations and the fact that he "ridiculed" indigenous terminology, terminology which would have "greatly helped him to understand why one medicine acts either slowly or quickly or in a particular way in a disease" (9–10). They take Koman to task for his misunderstanding of the application of the preparation called "Vasaka" in Sanskrit. While Koman tested Vasaka on patients with pulmonary tuberculosis, the *vaidyas* assert that it is specifically meant to remedy haemorrhage. To support their case, they quote a canonical Ayurvedic text by Vagbhata: "*Vṛṣo jayatyasrapittam sa hyasya paramauṣadham,*" or "Vrisha (Vasaka) conquers haemorrhage for it is an excellent specific for it" (12). They insert the Devanagari script into a polemic in English to mark the disjunction between different languages and so, as synecdoche, the disjunction between different worlds of understanding. This abrupt change of script highlights that those without a deep understanding of South Asian scripts, languages, and texts cannot understand South Asian traditions well enough to offer an informed critique.

While for Western doctors the impossibility of translation was an indication of the poverty of indigenous language and tradition, for these *vaidyas* the boundary of communication is a rampart against the attacks of an arrogant foe.[4] "So long as the properties of drugs are not known, to the practitioners of the Western system, in the terminology of Ayurveda also, so long will it have to be reckoned that all have not been 'already known' and that much is left which has to be known" (*Report* 1921, 27–28). Indigenous medicine can only be understood, and therefore can only be critically scrutinized, by those with a knowledge of South Asian languages and theories. In countering biomedical attacks, these *vaidyas* invoke a relativity of language and theory, making critique across traditions impossible.

3. Creating Traditional Space: Indian Orientalism

We have seen one case in which indigenous practitioners defend the slow action of their drugs in response to Koman's critiques. They make this point often, for example with reference to a medicine called "Salmali" in Sanskrit or "Mullila-vamaram" in Tamil: "this slow action of the indigenous drugs with permanent

---

4   In 1833, a group of administrators led by Alexander Duff, the head of the Scottish Free Church Institution, questioned the capability of South Asian languages to represent scientific notions and so also dismissed the utility of the Native Medical Institution. Instead, they advocated "a knowledge of the English language which we consider as a *sine qua non*, because that language contains within itself the circle of all the sciences and incalculable wealth of printed works and illustrations, circumstances which give it obvious advantage over oriental languages in which are only to be found the crudest elements of science or the most irrational substitutes for it" (A. Kumar 1998, 22).

results is highly to be preferred to the quick action of the drugs of the British pharmacopoea with fleeting results" (*Report* 1921, 9). This claim that British medicine brings quick but only temporary relief, while the indigenous systems bring slower but permanent cures, is common throughout *siddha* and ayurvedic literature. These generalizations are best understood in the context of a prevalent attitude of Indian medical practitioners, which echo Orientalist scholarship, according to which the primary successes of the West are in the superficial material realm, whereas the mystical East can claim a more secure understanding of the deeper, metaphysical essences of things (Inden 1992). While for Europeans this schema provided a justification for imperial intervention, for *vaidyas* it offers a way to define a unique space for traditional knowledge.

For some, the juxtaposition of a materialistic Western science and traditional knowledge of the intangible person offers the possibility for peaceful coexistence or integration of medical systems.[5] For others this difference provides a space apart from the dominance of biomedicine. This is not to say that South Asian medical notions of the influence of non-physical forces on health only emerged in colonial times. *Vaidyas* have long posited both physical and non-physical matter and processes in the cosmos, both of which are relevant to illness and healing. The *siddhars*, the *yogis* who are said to have founded *siddha* medicine, "had divided everything in the cosmos [*aṇṭam*] and the body [*piṇṭam*] into two classes: those physical objects that are composed of the five elements [*aimpūtaṅkaḷ*] and those subtle objects" (*Tamiḷ [Citta] Maruttuvak Kōṭpāṭu*, 8). Likewise, drawing from yogic views of the body, *siddha* scholars and practitioners distinguish a gross, physical body from an invisible, subtle body.

> There are two kinds of structures in humans—one is the external structure of the body, and the other is the internal form. The former is conventionally known as the corporeal body (*ittūla uṭampu*) [Sanskrit "sthūla"—bulky, corpulent] and the other is called the subtle body (*cūkkuma uṭampu*) [Sanskrit "sūkṣma"—minute, subtle]. Therefore, if we know the structure of the internal body, then we will easily know, by means of the root substance (*mūlavastu*), human diseases and their remedies. (Pillai 1931, 2110)

Insight into this subtle side of things requires something which the technologies of modern science cannot provide: a "mental eye," "wisdom eye," or "inner eye" (Kastūri 1970, 31; Velan 1963, 38). "A physician or physiologist is concerned with the gross physical body. He is not aware of the subtle life force

---

5   For example, in 1957, S. Nijalangappa, the Chief Minister of Mysore, wrote: "I think it is time that men of medical science should cast off prejudice or bias towards one system of medicine or the other and with an open mind learn from all systems and above all endeavour to know more of man—his heredity, his mental, spiritual and mystical potentialities—apart from what little of him is revealed by the application of the several branches of science such as physiology, pathology, psychology, etc." (Nijalangappa 1957).

of the gross physical body which is not visible to his external sense organs. One who has developed his inner vision knows the subtle life force in him" (Velan 1963, 38).

The contrast of this inner eye and its intuitive powers to the instruments and knowledge available to Western medicine is common in *siddha* medical discourse. The development of this inner eye is accomplished through South Asian religious practices of *yoga* and asceticism. As such, indigenous medical practitioners argue, it is an ancient and unique possession of South Asian traditions.

> According to modern medicine, if one wants to see what is inside a body, one needs to dissect a corpse. Siddha practitioners, thousands of years ago, had clear knowledge about the body, and knew of all the body's internal organs with the mental eye... Therefore, if one dissects and observes [a body] in this [modern] way, one cannot see the true structure [of the body]. With the method of new medicine, it is not possible to discover the empty space in our bodies. (Kastūri 1970, 31)

Biomedical doctors insist on the visibility (via two eyes) of knowledge and so they overlook the metaphysical composition of our bodies. They misunderstand both the body and disease as being wholly physical, and so their remedies do not address the essence of disease rooted in the subtle body. It is this "empty space" of the body that is only perceptible by means of traditional Indian methods, a bodily space that is likewise an epistemological space, an aspect of truth over which Indian tradition claims a monopoly of expertise.

This critique of biomedicine is at the same time a critique of the Western scientific method, which demands a link between visibility and knowledge. "The ancient philosophers of Siddha School knew more about the powers that move the world and of communications of thought at a distance without the employment of any visible means which is thought current. Modern Western Medicine knows only the dead body of man and not the living image in him presented by Nature...and so, modern science knows more about the superficiality of things..." (Pillai 1931, 2106). Modern science, and therefore biomedical knowledge and medicines, are necessarily limited to the material realm, rendering their effects superficial and temporary, as they are incapable of penetrating the non-visible essence of things. When indigenous practitioners oppose the speedy but superficial remedies of biomedicine to their own methods, which bring slower but permanent results, it is this view of the body that they have in mind. In asserting that Western and Indian knowledge are radically different in their essential nature, *vaidyas* argue for an incommensurable distance between medical traditions that critique cannot traverse. The space that traditional practitioners carve out for themselves therefore lies *apart* from that claimed by Western medicine (metaphysical vs. physical knowledge), a space which can be mastered through meditation and self-denial, not through the mechanical apparati of the sort that the British so impressively possessed. More importantly, this space lies *below* that of biomedicine, not in a hierarchical sense of being inferior, but rather in indicating that traditional knowledge describes the *root* of things.

4. An Organic Correspondence: Indian People and Indian Medicine

Another way that traditional practitioners have argued for their medical priority to heal Indians has been to assert a link between the Indian climate, culture and language, on the one hand, and the bodily constitution of the Indian people on the other. A "Committee convened under the direction of the President of the Eastern Medical Association of Southern India, Madras," a guild of *unani* practitioners, invoking natural law rather than divine design, argue that local environments have all the material necessary to remedy diseases that prevail in a particular region. "It is one of the laws of nature that wherever we find a disease, in its very neighbourhood we do find cure for the same disease; that is to say, for the diseases prevailing on India, we need not go beyond India to procure medicines to efficiently cure the disease, for there is in India itself plenty of medicines to counteract the prevailing diseases" (*Report* 1923, 234). Medical products of the land from which a people emerged are uniquely suited to cure the ailments of that people, an argument against the importation of foreign medicines.

This environmental correspondence is not limited to local medicines and local diseases, but extends to local people as well. These *unani hakims* assert: "The 'Ayurvedic' and 'Unani' systems of medicine are unquestionably and beyond a shadow of doubt more useful for this country than the so-called 'Allopathic' or the 'Western' principles of medical treatment, as they are operated on Indians by Indians through the media of Indian productions of herbs and drugs, on the efficacy of which climatic influences have not a little to partake of" (*Report* 1923, 232). In his opening address of the 1935 "Exhibition of Indian Medicines," the *siddha* practitioner A. J. Pandian declares that the founders of Indian medical knowledge, the "Saints, Rishis or Angels," developed "the subtle treatment that has been prescribed for the very many diseases of our land, particularly suited to the physical and mental constitution of our people..." (Pandian 1935, 32). This conjunction of Indian bodies and Indian medicine is described as neither accidental nor conventional, but historical and, even more importantly, essential, as the essences of each have a single origin and evolved in a symbiotic relationship.

The linking of environment, disease, medicines, and bodies evokes a material logic which asserts that the local community is autochthonous. *Vaidyas* extend these organic links to inorganic processes such as "culture" and "civilization."

Thus, the Qaumi Report [on Unani Medicine], released on April 4, 1917, characterizes "indigenous medical practice whether Unani (Grecian) or Ayurvedic"
as "an essential part of our civilization" (Hausman 1996, 126). Four years later,
the *siddha* practitioner Ponnuswami Pillai writes from Kumbakonam:

> Just as each country naturally has a particular type of civilization,
> education, and religious practices, likewise medicine is appropriate for
> each country's natural environment, climate, and culture. India's own
> medical procedures, research and experience have been followed from
> the beginning of time by generations of great medical people. This medi-
> cal system is structured such that it adheres to the culture of the people,
> it employs plants and metals that are found in the climates throughout
> the country, and it can be practiced without special expensive materials
> without compromising its perfection (*Report* 1923, Part 2, 356).

This organic idiom calls for the exclusive and exhaustive conjunction of a
particular people and a particular practice, both circumscribed within strict
historical and geographic boundaries. This conjunction is most effective when
these boundaries are hermetic, keeping foreign elements (whether bodies or
ideas) out and preventing the escape of any traitors of tradition. The penetration
of a foreign culture will upset this natural relationship, intervening between a
pure culture and a pure people. In the nostalgic rhetoric of tradition, Indian
medicine emerged with the beginning of the Indian race and so its effectiveness on Indian individuals is undeniable and unsurpassable. As Roland Barthes
points out for mythologies, practitioners of Indian medicine envisage history
as eternal nature, an eternal essence which has historical effects (Barthes 1972)

Indigenous medical practitioners declare these organic boundaries in order
to provide a space for tradition against the universal claims of biomedical
doctors. The sort of "space" the *vaidyas* create is geographic, in the sense that
they assert the importance of the unique locale of Indian medicine in their
history. It is also an organic space, in that practitioners distinguish Indian
bodies from European bodies and propose an inalienable, material connection
between disease, medicines, climate, and an autochthonous people. Allopathic
medicines, they say, do not have the proper organic material to effectively heal
Indian bodies. Finally, this geographic and organic uniqueness is the basis for
assertions of a unique *cultural* space, a site for indigenous medical theories and
practices as a whole, since the cultural products of a local tradition are
celebrated as best suited for the local people.

5. Historical Teleologies and the "Stagnation" of Indigenous Medicine

A cornerstone for British claims to a superior rationality was a view of history
as progression towards greater (if no longer final) rationality, a race that the

British saw themselves as leading. Contrary to this view, both Tamil revivalists and Indian nationalists tended to regard history as a process of decay from an original perfection, a perfection that might be reestablished with the restoration of cultural and racial purity. This notion of history as decay in South Asia is not limited to colonial times but has a precedent in the idea, first described in Sanskrit texts, that history proceeds in cycles. History is a succession of four epics (*yugas*), the first being the best, and devolving to the present degenerate age, the Kali Yuga. History, however, does not just devolve but is circular, as the Kali Yuga ends in a great conflagration, followed by a time of regenerative sleep, and awakening again into the first, glorious, age. Likewise, formulations of Indian nationalism and Indian medicine, while narrating a history of decay, affirm the potential of a future in which medical glory can be recaptured in an independent India.

Biomedical doctors seized upon Orientalist scholarship that told of the degeneration of Indian civilization from its ancient, Aryan roots, asserting that indigenous practitioners had much to learn from British doctors.[6] In August, 1918, A. G. Cardew, Minister for Medicine, objected to the dedication of government funds to a school of indigenous medicine. Ayurveda, he argued, is only of "antiquarian interest" to the colonial government. "It is interesting as an old survival, just as the dodo was an interesting survival in the island of Mauritius when that bird was still alive. As an archaic system it is of interest… But unfortunately it has stopped still at that stage and the enormous progress which science has made in the last century has been a closed book to it…" (Hausman 1996, 163). These indigenous techniques are "lore," of literary and historical, but not scientific, interest. Understanding medical difference through an evolutionary hierarchy of knowledge, colonial ministers and allopathic doctors assumed a natural progression of history, a prognostic view according to which the eclipse of indigenous medicine by allopathy was assured. Like the dodo bird, which was not up to the demands of the new imperial world, indigenous medical knowledge lacks the strength to resist the force of truth, embodied in biomedical reason. Its time is past, and so it must, as all survivals, "succumb before long."

In their *Reply to the Report on the Investigation into the Indigenous Drugs*, *vaidyas* respond to Cardew's views.

> Long ago Ayurveda developed a system of its own and reached a point beyond which it had become practically impossible to proceed. And that is why it is even now accused of having become stagnant long ago.

---

6   This notion that traditional medical practice was in a state of decay by colonial times has been accepted not only by biomedical doctors, traditional doctors, and colonial authorities, but also by scholars and historians of medicine in India. Historical data for this degeneration, however, is absent from these accounts. For a recent example, see Jaggi 2000, 311.

Sir Alexander Cardew, late of the Madras Executive Council, bore testimony to this fact in a debate in one of the Legislative Council meetings.
The practitioners of Ayurveda simply rely on those ancient theories and
are even now doing their profession by administering the ancient
medicines without even caring to introduce innovations. It is really
therefore the western system of medicine that is still in the experimental
stage or empirical... Day after day we learn both from the medical papers
and news papers [sic] that numerous experiments of various drugs and
of vaccines invented by faddists who pose as scientific men, are being
made on the lower and helpless animals and results pronounced with
but dubious or trifling virtues only to be refuted and hooted down by
other faddists. (*Report* 1921, 21–22)

For these *vaidyas*, the innovators that propel the historical development of
allopathic theories and techniques are erratic "faddists," while the knowledge
of tradition is beyond history, contained in "immortal treatises" and authored
by a "noble galaxy" of "great souls" who were "illustrious, virile, and learned."
Innovation itself is in this view not a sign of progress towards a greater rationality but an indication of imperfection, as the notion that a practice that was once
"'within the date' mysteriously becomes 'out of date'" is absurd (*Report* 1921).

Innovation and the fickle ideas of individuals are contrasted to the wisdom
of countless generations. The authors of the response quote "a well-known
English authority on medicine," Dr. Clifford Albutt. "Prevalent opinions though
not formal truths, contain truths and this the practical physician does not fail
to perceive, nor does he forget that the observations of any person however
profound, being the observations of an individual of brief life and limited
faculties need some tampering by traditional lore by the embodied opinions of
a vast number of observers over a long period of time" (*Report* 1921, 24). Rather
than bold, impetuous innovations by individuals, the idiom of tradition, its
strength, is that of cautious measure, a sifting of all information by large
numbers of people over vast stretches of history. In another Orientalist idiom,
indigenous practitioners oppose the careful and measured accumulation of
knowledge afforded by a coherent community, to the haphazard knowledge
created by individualistic Western societies.[7] The argument that there is no
need to improve indigenous medicine serves to shield it from critique: a
perfect medicine needs to import nothing, as medical value is measured by
traditional purity.[8] While the British seized on the notion of the stagnation of

---

7   This notion of a sifting and sorting of knowledge, discarding some and keeping the
     best, contradicts the view of an original perfection of knowledge and subsequent
     corruption. Both views are commonly held with respect to Indian medical traditions.
     Of course, the indigenous practitioners here parody the Western sciences, in which
     knowledge evolves subject to the review by peers, i.e., others in a scientific *community*,
     and accumulates in "traditional" ways.
8   It is important to note, however, that the freedom to innovate is valued by many
     indigenous practitioners. This has probably been true for centuries, as palm-leaf

Indian medicine to justify its replacement by biomedicine, *vaidyas* drew on stagnation and decay to assert the essential perfection of their system and its need for preservation.

Both *siddha* and *ayurveda vaidyas* trace their past perfection to the extraordinary insight of the founders of their knowledge, insight which modern people no longer possess.

> The fundamentals on which the Ayurvedic system of medicine is based are so essentially true for all ages that they would have yielded to no changes... The originators of the Ayurvedic system of medicine have not based their theories on any experiments. They were seers... As their vision is far beyond the human reach and their knowledge all comprehensive, they could give a system which is far beyond approach. (Narayanaswami 1957, 79)

Indeed, it is time itself which testifies to the enduring truth of unchanging tradition. "Time which antiquates antiquity and hath an art to make dust of all things finds and shall find the Ayurveda unsurpassed and inexpugnable" (*Report* 1923, Part 2, 249). While the technique of an empirical science admits to current inaccuracies, the purportedly unchanging nature of traditional science is invoked as testimony to its perfection.[9] The orientation that *vaidyas* work to impress upon their audience, that of devotion to tradition, is this sort of orientation, a commitment to conserve knowledge in order to sustain the link to past community.

While biomedical doctors admit that their current state of medical knowledge is imperfect, they argue that the value of their method lies in its constant goal to innovate. From their point of view, medical knowledge can never be perfect, and any claim to an infallible lexicon of medical knowledge must be

---

manuscripts speak of knowledge gained through one's own experience (*kaipākam*). The call for purity has been hotly debated in the twentieth century. The leadership of the Government College of Indigenous Medicine in Columbo, Sri Lanka in the late 1950's and early 1960's was strongly divided between ayurvedic purists and those who wanted to develop Ayurveda along the lines introduced by biomedicine. The conflict was so hotly debated that the Minister of Health and a faculty member of the College were arrested in connection with the assassination of Prime Minister Bandaranaike in 1959, who had sympathy with the innovators and was killed by a purist (Leslie 1993).

9   This notion of the perfection of texts and tradition has precedence in the consideration of the Sanskrit Vedas as "sruti," i.e., as heard from an original, divine source. The knowledge contained in the Vedas is of cosmic, not human origin, and therefore it is perfect knowledge. Classical Sanskrit medical treatises display this veneration of ancient tradition. Suśruta, for example, wrote on medicinal plants: "No need to examine them, no need to reflect on them, they will make themselves known, the remedies that the clear-sighted must prescribe in accordance with tradition... Were there a thousand reasons to do so, the ambaṣṭā group will never set itself to purging! The wise must therefore adhere to tradition, without arguing" (Suśruta, sūtra XL, 19–21; Zimmermann 1987, 158).

discounted. However, innovation on the lines of biomedicine requires an expensive technological infrastructure on a scale that Indian medical systems cannot support. I believe that arguments for the potential perfection of traditional medicine are in part motivated by a recognition of the technological and economic disparity between indigenous medicine and biomedicine. With both the colonial government and the independent Indian state giving nearly all of their medical resources to biomedicine, traditional practitioners suggest that perfect knowledge is to be found in the teachings of the past, not in the discoveries of the future.

6. The Danger of Mixing Culture

Perhaps the majority of Indians today use both biomedicine and indigenous medicine, either simultaneously to cover their bets, or else successively after unsuccessful attempts by the other to heal the illness.[10] Many indigenous practitioners integrate biomedicine into their healing repertoires, especially those who have studied in an indigenous medical college, as the curriculum would include some courses in the sciences and application of biomedicine. Charles Leslie notes that ayurvedic *vaidyas* in Bombay had incorporated "English medicines" into their practice as early as 1839 (Leslie 1998b, 362–363). This sort of concurrent practice of biomedicine and traditional medicine was institutionalized in 1947, the year of India's independence, in the College of Integrated Medicine in Madras.

It is notable, then, that rhetoric among many practitioners is often sceptical of the benefit or even the possibility of the coexistence or synthesis of biomedical and traditional knowledge and practice. The Koman report was designed to investigate indigenous medicines and to incorporate these medicines into the British pharmacopoeia. Indigenous practitioners feared that at the end of such a process of incorporation, the colonial government, satisfied that it had extracted everything of value in traditional knowledge, "will be able to declare clearly that since indigenous drugs and medicines are used in our Government Hospitals no special expenditure need be incurred in helping Ayurvedic dispensaries and hospitals or the Ayurveda itself in any other way." The result is that "soon will then Ayurveda dwindle into oblivion" (*Report* 1921, 96).

The danger is even worse than it might seem. It is not just that the benefits of Ayurveda would only endure in the context of biomedicine. The *vaidyas* propose a grim fantasy in which "Western chemists" analyze and lay bare the qualities of indigenous drugs "for their industrial enterprise." Discovering the

---

10   A vast ethnographic literature attests to this. For two South Indian examples, see Djur-
     feldt and Lindberg 1975; Beals 1998.

value of these preparations, they will proceed to export Indian medicines in vast quantities, making them unavailable for use in India (*Report* 1921, 96). The fear is not simply that tradition will be corrupted, transformed, or obliterated, but that it will be stolen and enjoyed by those who are other, depriving its rightful owners of their medical heritage.

Nor did independence bring the enthusiastic acceptance of indigenous medicine that practitioners had expected. In line with the Indian Congress's emphasis on the scientific, technological and industrial progress of the Indian nation, the first prime minister of India, Jawaharlal Nehru, set the agenda for the scientific scrutiny of indigenous sciences. Speaking about the Government College of Integrated Medicine in Madras, he writes:

> The so-called conflict between Ayurvedic and modern medicine has to be studied and resolved. The only right approach has to be one of science, that is, of experiment, trial and error. In whatever type of medicine we may deal with, we cannot profit by its study unless we apply the methods of science. In this there should not be many conflicting methods but various aspects of one scientific approach. (Nehru 1957)

This nationalist confidence in the potential of science derives in part from an awareness of the global diffusion of scientific knowledge. Thus, Dr. Srinivasalu Naidu, M.D., argues, "India should evolve a system of medicine consistent with world opinion. India cannot be secluded in matters of medicine and cannot be content with what patriotism and emotion would stimulate people to adopt" (Naidu 1957, 41). For those Indians with biomedical training, patronage to a system of medicine that looks at ancient texts for perfect knowledge is motivated by patriotism, not by the objective, rational truth of science. Such patriotism, they argue, will lead to an isolated India, while the development of biomedicine will preserve for India a place among the great nations of the world. The high status for India on the world stage will be won at the expense of its native forms of medical practice, a price worth paying for these educated, biomedical doctors.

For many indigenous practitioners, however, the integration of medical systems would be tantamount to admitting the inferiority of their own practices. Indeed, many defenders of cultural purity asserted that the decay of traditional medicine has been a direct consequence of the introduction of foreign medicine into India.

> As a result of the spread of foreign civilization in India from the West, and because of the recent lust [for that civilization] that has unfortunately taken hold of the Indian people, some perverse beliefs have taken root in their minds, changing many of their habits and customs (*palakkavalakkankal*). The people's belief in and appreciation of ancient principles and texts have decreased. These are the primary causes of the decay of our native (*cutēca*) medicine. (*Report* 1923, Part 2, 363)

Far from benefiting from the importation of Western scientific techniques, such a mixing of traditions will lead to the deterioration of Indian medicine and its abandonment by the Indian people. The only way to stem this decay, in the logic of cultural purity, is to maintain its distance from ideas deemed to be foreign.

According to many *siddha* practitioners, the weakness of Tamil society in resisting this medical imperialism is due to the lack of unity among Tamils. Captivated by the materialistic promises of the West, many Tamils have abandoned the components of their tradition and therefore have created dissension in the community.

> The Tamil people, who prospered since the time of creation, who justly and benevolently ruled many nations, who were the first to develop knowledge for medical texts, who knew events happening in many different places through their yogic practice (like radios), with the change of times, they forget their greatness, and with the changes of times they suffer without government support. A few among the Tamil people have learned English, deride their mother tongue, flaunt their ignorance of their mother tongue, and ridicule the Tamil people and Tamil doctors. The obstacles for native medicine have multiplied. (Cuppiramaṇiyam 1940, 50)

For these promoters of tradition, traditional action is not habitual imitation of one's forbearers, but allegiance to one's community and recognition of one's true identity. Imitative action consists in aping foreign culture and abandoning one's tradition. The notorious report on the efficacy of indigenous medicines was flawed not only because Dr. Koman had misunderstood traditional theory, but also because he had become a "slave to the western so-called scientific superstitions" (*Report* 1921, 27). The *vaidyas* connect the "degeneracy" of indigenous medicine to this "tendency to imitate the vanity of the West, that is now slowly devouring the indigenous *vaidya*," leading to the "maya [illusion] of bitter prejudice" and "prejudice against the ancient system" (*Report* 1921, 27). The patronage of Western medicine at the expense of indigenous medicine is seen as part of a larger trend towards Westernization, and is symptomatic of processes that will lead to the division of the community and subsequently the destruction of all traditional practices. "We must realize that blindly following western ways will, in the course of time, result in the decline of siddha medicine and will result in grave danger to the country" (Meykaṇtar 1968, 48).

Biomedical doctors and traditional practitioners are united in narrating a decay of traditional medicine, from its position as an "ancient system [that] possessed an imposing treasure of empirical knowledge and technical achieve-ment" to a "decadent condition of the present day" (*Report* 1923, Part 1, 2). The language of decay was convenient for both colonial authorities and *vaidyas*. For biomedical doctors, degeneration was an excuse for intervention, as Indians left to themselves stagnate and need external intervention. *Vaidyas*, as we have seen, locate the source of decay in foreign intervention that culminated with British colonialism. What is required for medical revival, according to these *vaidyas*, is not further synthesis of foreign culture and medical practice but a purification of Indian medicine of all its alien elements. The language of decay highlights the need to come to the defense of traditional medicine, calling on patriotic Indians to support and "revive" their beleaguered tradition.

If it was foreign political and cultural imperialism that led to the degeneration of Indian medicine, many practitioners likewise link any hope for its revival in the unification of the community of tradition.

> Modern medicine (allopathy), connected with Westerners, came just yesterday and showed its head. But Siddha medicine, which emerged, grew, and lives with excellence in the Tamil land, today is in a state of decay. It is the duty of every siddha practitioner—indeed, of every Tamil person—to dispel this degraded state and to restore siddha medicine to its eminent position. (Perumāḷ 1968, 72)

As if the effectiveness of *siddha* were not self-evident, *siddha* practitioners often assert the *responsibility* of all Tamils to patronize this "Tamil" system, duty thereby bridging gaps in confidence in *siddha's* healing potential. For those who hold on to the utopian ideal of a society following a pure tradition, the conjunction of duty and essence provides a powerful rationale to promote Indian medicine as the exclusive medicine of the Indian people. The coherence of tradition is an essential precondition for the recovery of the greatness of Indian medical traditions. The boundaries of tradition, then, are not only to keep foreign elements out, but also to keep the members of the community of tradition in.

7. Conclusion

The assertion of *siddha* medicine as a medical system uniquely developed by and suitable for the Tamil people constructs the boundaries of a system of knowledge that separates it from other systems. As T. M. Luhrmann notes with secret knowledge, this has the effect of not only reifying a relation of possession between a people and particular knowledges and practices, but it also protects this knowledge from external critique. "The differentiation between insider and outsider separates the magical from the mundane; this not only makes the magician feel special, but also shields his magic from conflict with scepticism" (Luhrmann 1989, 139). What is true for magicians in contemporary England is also true for *siddha* practitioners in modern Tamil Nadu—their practices under attack as unscientific or forged, they delineate a sphere of unique tradition within which they reject the scrutiny of outsiders.

The autonomy of tradition shares much with the language that Levinas uses to describe the site of self-identification. It is a ground of possibility, an "'at home' which we inhabit" (Levinas 1969, 33). The act of self-identification is forged not in isolation but begins with a relationship between an "I" and an external world that is radically other.

> In a world which is from the first other the I is nonetheless autochthonous... It finds in the world a site and a home. Dwelling is the very mode of *maintaining oneself*, not as the famous serpent grasping itself by biting onto its tail, but as the body that, on the earth exterior to it, holds *itself* up and *can*. The 'at home' is not a container but a site where I *can*... The site, a medium, affords means. Everything is here, everything belongs to me... (Levinas 1969, 37–38)

Tradition is such an autochthonous ground, a site over which a social self can exercise control. It serves as the grounds for self, not a self that is prior to tradition, but a self which is forged in the very creation of tradition. To paraphrase Levinas, this home, this residence and ground of the self, is not the end or goal of human activity but its condition, and so its commencement.

The delineation of a distinct community is at the same time a claim for the uniqueness of that community. If the character of a community is not sufficiently unique, then that community faces the danger of assimilation into other, often larger, more powerful communities. At the same time that the boundaries of tradition shield the community from external criticism, then, they are also asserted in attempts to preserve the purity and coherence of tradition, even as these borders themselves define the criteria for what is pure and what is foreign. Alien languages, ideas, and people must be prevented from entering and diluting the glory of tradition. These boundaries also delineate the contours of *duty*, of devotion to tradition, that might instill adherence and commitment to tradition in order to counter the centripetal influences of external traditions. These boundaries only inaccurately reflect the nature of cultural interaction, which is never pure. Rather, they are ideal constructions and hopeful aspirations, meant to establish models for social cohesion and exclusion.

References

Arnold, David (ed.). 1988. *Imperial Medicine and Indigenous Societies*. New York: St. Martin's Press.

———. 1993. *Colonizing the Body: State Medicine and Epidemic Disease in Nineteenth-Century India*. Berkeley, Calif.: University of California Press.

Barthes, Roland. 1972. *Mythologies*. Selected and Translated from the French by Annette Lavers. New York: Hill and Wang.

Beals, Alan R. 1998. "Curers in South India." Pages 184–200 in Leslie 1998a.

Chatterjee, Partha. 1990. "The Nationalist Resolution of the Women's Question." Pages 232–253 in *Recasting Women: Essays in Indian Colonial History*. Edited by Kumkum Sangari and Sudesh Vaid. New Brunswick, N.J.: Rutgers University Press.

Comaroff, Jean, and John Comaroff. 1992. "Medicine, Colonialism and the Black Body." Pages 215–233 in their *Ethnography and the Historical Imagination*. Boulder, Colo.: Westview Press.

Cuppiramaṇiyam, Eṉ. 1940. *Cittavaittiyattiṉ Muṉ ṉeṟṟam*. [The Development of Siddha Medicine]. Taramapuram, Tamiḻ Nāṭu: Ka-ikāparamēsvari Press.

Djurfeldt, Göran, and Staffan Lindberg. 1975. *Pills Against Poverty: A Study of the Introduction of Western Medicine in a Tamil Village*. Scandinavian Institute of Asian Studies. New Delhi: Macmillan.

The Government College of Integrated Medicine Decennial Souvenir. Chennai, 1957.

Gupta, Brahmananda. 1998. "Indigenous Medicine in Nineteenth and Twentieth Century Bengal." Pages 368–378 in Leslie 1998a.

Hausman, Gary J. 1996. "Siddhars, Alchemy and the Abyss of Tradition: 'Traditional' Tamil Medical Knowledge in 'Modern' Practice." Ph.D. dissertation, University of Michigan.

Inden, Ronald. 1990. *Imagining India*. Cambridge, Mass.: Blackwell.

Iraṇṭām Ulakattamiḻ Mānāṭu Citta Maruttuva Karuttaraṉku Ciṟappu Malar [Second World Tamil Conference, Siddha Medicine Seminar Special Souvenir]. Chennai, 1968.

Jaggi, Om Prakash. 2000. *History of Science, Philosophy, and Culture in Indian Civilization*. Volume IX, Part 1: *Medicine in India: Modern Period*. Delhi: Oxford University Press.

Kastūri, Irā. 1970. "Citta Maruttuvam" [Siddha Medicine]. In *Tiruvaḷḷuvar Īrāyiramāṉṭu* (see below; unpaginated).

Kumar, Anil. 1998. *Medicine and the Raj: British Medical Policy in India, 1835–1911*. New Delhi: Sage Publications.

Kumar, Deepak. 1997. *Science and the Raj, 1857–1905*. Delhi: Oxford University Press.

Leslie, Charles. 1993. "Interpretations of Illness: Syncretism in Modern Ayurveda." Pages 177–208 in *Paths to Asian Medical Knowledge*. Edited by Charles Leslie and Allan Young. New Delhi: Munshiram Manoharlal Publishers.

———. (ed.). 1998a. *Asian Medical Systems: A Comparative Study*. Delhi: Motilal Banarsidass.

———. 1998b. "The Ambiguities of Medical Revivalism in Modern India." Pages 356–367 in Leslie 1998a.

Levinas, Emmanuel. 1969. *Totality and Infinity: An Essay on Exteriority*. Translated by Alphonso Lingis. Philosophical Series 24. Pittsburgh: Duquesne University Press.

Luhrmann, Tanya M. 1989. "The Magic of Secrecy." *Ethos* 17.2 (June): 131–166.

Meykaṇtar, C. 1968. "Citta Vaityattiṉ Tevai" [The Needs of Siddha Medicine]. Pages 44–48 in *Iraṇṭām Ulakattamiḻ* (see above).

Naidu, A. Srinivasalu. 1957. "Medical Education and Medical Relief." Pages 41–48 in *The Government College of Integrated Medicine Decennial Souvenir*. Chennai.

Narayanaswami, V. 1957. "Systematic Development of Ayurveda: A Short Survey." Pages 79–84 in *The Government College of Integrated Medicine Decennial Souvenir*. Chennai.

Nehru, Jawaharlal. 1957. "Preface." In *The Government College of Integrated Medicine Decennial Souvenir* (unpaginated). Chennai.

Nijalangappa, S. 1957. "Preface." In *The Government College of Integrated Medicine Decennial Souvenir* (unpaginated). Chennai.

Pandian, A. J. 1935. "Exhibition of Indian Medicines: Opening Address." *The Journal of Indian Medicine* 1.1 (April): 32–33.

Perumāl, V. 1968. "Citta Maruttuvattin Māṇpu" [The Dignity of Siddha Medicine]. Pages 69–73 in *Iraṇṭām Ullakattamil* (see above).

Pillai, T. V. Sambasivam. 1931. *Tamil-English dictionary of Medicine, Chemistry, Botany, and Allied Sciences*. In 5 Volumes. Madras: The Research Institute of Siddhar's Science.

The Report of the Committee on the Indigenous Systems of Medicine. Madras, 1923.

Report of the Committee to Assess and Evaluate the Present Status of Ayurvedic System of Medicine. Delhi: Government of India, Ministry of Health, 1958.

Report of the Special Committee Appointed by the Joint Board of the Dravida Vaidya Mandal and The Madras Ayurveda Sabha in Reply to The Report on the Investigation into the Indigenous Drugs. Srirangam, South India: Sri Vani Vilas Press, 1921.

Tamil (Citta) Maruttuvak Kōṭpāṭu [Tamil (Siddha) Medical Theory]. Chennai: Tamil Nadu Government, Department of Indian and Homeopathic Medicine, no date.

Tiruvaḷḷuvar Īrāyiramāṇṭu Niṟaivu Viḷā Malar [Commemorative Volume of the Celebration of Two Thousand Years of Tiruvalluvar]. Kōvai, Tamil Nāṭu: Pāvēntar pāratitāca-Maṉram, 1970.

Velan, A. Shanmuga. 1963. *Siddhar's Science of Longevity and Kalpa Medicine of India*. Madras: Shakti Nilayam.

Zimmermann, Francis. 1987. *The Jungle and the Aroma of Meats: An Ecological Theme in Hindu Medicine*. Berkeley: University of California Press.

Incarcerated Tradition: Native Hawaiian Identities and Religious Practice in Prison Contexts

Greg Johnson

> They followed a leader for chanting and prayers in the Hawaiian language, welcoming the day and pleading for wisdom and forgiveness. They processed in the yard. Some dressed as their Hawaiian ancestors had, in togalike wraps tucked under bare arms. Others wore blue prison uniforms...
>
> Sunday's ceremony came about after a two-year struggle. The Corrections Corporation of America, which runs Diamondback, had resisted giving the inmates permission to meet and conduct liturgies, in deference to state officials in Hawaii who had expressed doubts that the Hawaiian religion still existed. (Downes 2005, 18)

This essay seeks to contribute to the project of theorizing tradition, starting with an abstract consideration of tradition and then moving to an analysis of a contemporary context wherein the meanings and practice of tradition are in play and at stake, namely the role of tradition for Native Hawaiians incarcerated in mainland prisons. As we will see, in this context struggles over tradition concern and intersect with rights claims, sovereignty debates, and the general sphere of identity articulations.

Much of the theoretical inspiration for this piece comes from anthropological literature that is now nearly twenty years old but which is salient in numerous ways to this volume and to any attempt to theorize tradition in relationship to the politicization of culture. The literature to which I am referring is now known as the kastom (pidgin for custom) debates (e.g., Keesing and Tonkinson 1982; Babadzan 1988), which emerged in the mid-1980s and which shared much which larger "invention of tradition" discussions (e.g., Hobsbawm and Ranger 1983; Handler 1985). While pertaining initially to objectifications of traditions in Melanesia, the relevance of the kastom debates soon broadened to Oceania generally (Jolly and Thomas 1992; Hanson 1989; Sahlins 1988, 1992; Wassmann 1998). Central issues of these debates concerned the status of various forms of tradition, specifically those forms that appeared to be self-conscious and politically strategic. As might be expected, little unanimity emerged from these debates. However, considerable theoretical refinement of conceptions of tradition resulted from these discussions, as did a still growing corpus of case studies (see, e.g., Akin 2004). With its riches of contemporary cultural expressions, Hawai'i became one site of these debates (Keesing 1989; Linnekin 1991; Trask 1991; Friedman 1994). While the kastom debates have slowed in anthropology, "traditional" activities in Hawai'i have not. So it is that this essay seeks to pick up the conversation.

I. Tradition

All traditions are historically and socially constituted. I take this to be the baseline proposition explored in this volume. In my view, this is not a radical proposition, as I understand all traditions to be human, only human, and fully human. If all traditions are human and therefore historical, they should be approached by way of analytical tools that are suited to these facts. Here, then, I will sketch some of the propositions and predilections that inform my approach to "tradition."

As a point of departure for a consistent and theoretically productive engagement with the category of tradition, we should observe the obvious: tradition serves a marking function—its advocates set it apart for special attention, consideration, and reverence. In the discursive economy of tradition, this taxonomic function is also a normative function insofar as putative temporal priority and orthodox status confer the appearance of moral superiority. For those who champion it, tradition is pure; any derivative cultural form is impure and potentially dangerous. First and foremost, claims to tradition mark group boundaries, specifically in ways that reach across time and occasionally, when religious, in ways that reach beyond time. Further, relationships to traditions map and mark out social spaces within groups. Traditional boundaries, whether internal or external, are always subject to reformulation, which may include expansion, retraction, inversion, erosion, or other forms of revaluation. Given these basic points of orientation, we should ask of all traditions the following questions: By whom are they espoused and embraced? Have these changed over time? Against what external and internal rivals or threats are they articulated? With what ramifications for the socio-political order? In what relation to preceding or competing traditions? With what degree of self-consciousness on the part of its adherents?

Such beginnings move us away from questions about whether tradition is invented or not, genuine or not, orthodox or not. These debates are always about "authenticity," which is a concern that drives investigation away from what it should be concerned with: history, social processes, and cultural meanings. Authenticity is an unsuitable analytical category. More than unsuitable, it is positively debilitating. At a minimum, concerns with authenticity lead to an inordinate privileging of some articulations of traditions over others. Worse, those forms of tradition deemed authentic are almost always given positive normative values, while variants are correspondingly held in low esteem. From an academic point of view, to participate in the discourse of authenticity is to fail twice with regard to one's analytical duties: first, one has failed to discern that all claims to authenticity are ideological; second, by subscribing to a given ideology (i.e., that which is taken to be authentic), one has traded in analytical credibility and possibility in the process of becoming a voice box for tradition (cf. Lincoln 1996). If we abandon the quest for authenticity, we are led back to the quotidian domain of human lives, interests, aspirations, and machinations. Fortunately, we have productive tools for getting at these realities, though our findings will be, by definition, mundane: of this world and about this world.

Applying pressure to my argument against "authenticity" is a sense many readers may share that some traditions are simply more stable and enduring than others. I prefer to think of such traditions as entrenched cultural products. One feature entrenched traditions enjoy is relative ease of reproduction over time—in a case of the rich getting richer, the past (putative, imagined, and never simply simple) of such traditions is leveraged as a form of legitimacy in the present. Tradition in this modality can be understood as a remarkable form of locomotion: energy apparently devoted to the reproduction of the past becomes fuel for production of the present—backward looking momentum results in forward motion. On the other side of the spectrum from entrenched traditions one finds emergent traditions.[1] These enjoy far less cultural capital and must create and sustain energy by way of promoting novel interpretations of and claims upon the resources of entrenched traditions. In this process, they may seek capital by asserting that they are reclaimed traditions or formerly secret traditions, relying on perceptions of scarcity and esotericism to create value. As different as some of their techniques and technologies may be, emergent and entrenched traditions share the aspiration to be self-reproducing. Further, these modalities of tradition share the fact that they are discursive constructions. To follow up on my argument concerning "authenticity," we must keep this point in view so that cultural hegemony—synonymous with entrenched tradition—does not in our hands confer analytical hegemony.

Another way to advance the point I'm trying to make is to suggest that historicizing traditions entails as a first move that we reframe our study of tradition as the study of *representations* of traditions. It is analytically productive to approach traditions as rhetorical expressions, which, like all forms of rhetoric, seek to be persuasive (cf. Burke 1961). When we cast our efforts in this direction, comparative insights begin to emerge. Namely, it becomes readily apparent that form, not content, is crucial to the viability of tradition. Were this not so, we would

---

1   This discussion borrows from Raymond Williams (1977), James C. Scott (1985), and Antonio Gramsci (1996), among others, who argue that hegemony—in this case, tradition—is never total or totalizing, leaving room for counter-hegemonic and otherwise alternatively hegemonic manifestations.

not recognize tradition as an analytical category in the first place. The question is, then, what are the formal qualities of tradition? I have suggested above that these pertain chiefly to boundary marking functions. The salient feature of tradition in this respect is the construction of supra-historical status from manifestly historical materials and the manufacturing of the present in the name of reproducing the past. But the dynamics of tradition can be hard to perceive precisely because, like all forms of ideology, tradition is invested in the erasure of its operations.

Traditions, like religions, enjoy tremendous, even bottomless, semantic ranges. This makes understanding any tradition or religion in the abstract or "pure" form a preposterous task. However, this same condition renders possible the *historical* study of tradition and religion, as analysts can potentially track each change in doctrine, practice, and ethos of any tradition in context. Context, in this way, is responsible for the content of traditions and religions, as all points of content emerge in relief and are contrastive in character, thus structuralist theory. The formal qualities of tradition that allow for this dynamic are (a) that most traditions—and all religious ones—make truth claims that are empirically non-verifiable and, more importantly from a discursive perspective, non-falsifiable and (b) any truth claim can, in principle, be announced from this centerless center by way of metaphorical or metonymical extension (or retraction) of the prevailing perceptions of the content of a given tradition. In the end, then, content does matter, but it is only through formal understanding of the mechanisms and properties of tradition that we can grasp the meaning and function of content. To sum up thus far, I propose the following basic working definition of tradition: Tradition is a discourse of identity that relies upon representations of past practices, and claims of continuity with these, to legitimate the position and actions of the self or group in the present.

II. Incarcerated Tradition

Here we begin to move towards the topic of traditional identities and practices of Native Hawaiian prisoners who are incarcerated in mainland facilities. The link from the abstract to the concrete is that identities are doors to rights, political autonomy, sovereignty, and alternative modes of legal reckoning—doors that may be open or closed depending on the identity in question and the society within which it is articulated. The core of the issue is here: in various contexts, and particularly in the context of non-dominant indigenous groups in multicultural democracies, tradition is increasingly appealed to as a form of evidence of a person or group's identity (Gutman 2003; Taylor 2004). Since "race" is increasingly off the table as a legal means by which to signal difference from the dominant society (as made clear by various court rulings against affirmative action programs in recent years), tradition is often called upon to make the difference of stating difference. In this capacity, tradition is appealed to as a non-biological but nevertheless descent-based proxy for race. Here the non-falsifiable and plastic (metaphorical and metonymic) qualities of tradition are important: these are simultaneously the source of strength and weakness for such claims to identity. Traditional claims allow for emergent and adaptable articulations of identity. However, critics of such claims can and do challenge the empirical status of traditions. Such challenges can have serious legal and social ramifications. Furthermore, because traditional claims admit of no absolute defense, they are not thereby secure from internal abuse. Whether abused or not—and how one defines abuse is itself a difficult issue—traditional claims to identity in rights contexts are susceptible to dynamics we noted above concerning the redrawing of group boundaries. Thus, identity-based rights claims reliant on traditional evidence may be cast broadly and serve to construct or support solidarities, or they can be advanced in the course of micro-differentiation, wherein one group seeks to secure rights while limiting them from others who might assert them. Critics of tradition-based rights claims use this dynamic as evidence against the reliability and integrity of such claims.

Traditional Native Hawaiian identity is in question and at stake in a number of ways at the current moment, particularly in legal and political contexts.[2] As I write (August of 2005), Congress is debating the merits of the *Native Hawaiian Government Reorganization Act* (also known as the Akaka bill), which would provide for Native Hawaiians to self-govern and manage various assets and programs on the model of the relationship of the federal government to Indian tribes. This legislation, though far from unanimously supported by Native Hawaiians, is considered urgent by some, as a litany of recent court rulings have undercut various Native Hawaiian entitlements, including decisions against native-only policies of the Office of Hawaiian Affairs and the Kamehameha Schools (e.g., *Rice v. Cayetano; Doe v. Kamehameha*). Other issues wherein Native Hawaiian identity is at the fore include land disputes, particularly with reference to Kaho'olawe, an island long used by the United States for military training and bombing (Blackford 2004), contestations over the performance and meaning of hula dancing (Buck 1993), and repatriation battles between Native Hawaiian groups and various museums and other organizations (Nihipali 2002; Johnson 2003, 2004). These and other arenas of contemporary contention hinge on the issue of "what" and "who" is traditional Native Hawaiian. Further, these contests rest, in ways, on appeals to the category of tradition. The remainder of this essay

---

2   Alternative names for Native Hawaiians include Kanaka Maoli (original people) and Kanaka O'iwi (people of the bone). All three of these designations are, of course, politicized, particularly in contexts of local micro-differentiation of stances regarding contemporary sovereignty disputes. For the sake of consistency, I will use Native Hawaiian throughout. "Native Hawaiian" is not an unproblematic category. It shares the full burden of complexities found with all such designations that lump and elide racial, cultural, and ethnic distinctions and yet are invoked as putatively self-evident and stable categories in legal and political arenas.

takes up the question of tradition in contemporary Hawai'i through considering the role of Native Hawaiian identity expressions in mainland prisons. My goal is less to provide a definition of Hawaiian tradition than it is to illustrate and analyze some aspects of the dynamics of tradition, to explore in more concrete terms the ideas sketched above concerning the functions of tradition as a category.

Boundary Technologies

> From being an art of unbearable sensations punishment has become an economy of suspended rights... In the first instance, discipline proceeds from the distribution of individuals in space. (Foucault 1979, 11, 141)

If in the modern West prisons are the disciplinary site par excellence, and their function of policing bodies has ramifications for the larger body politic, it is no surprise that this function—or effect—should reach to the colonial context. In his own way, Kafka showed us this. Here we look to an historical example of the intersection of the prison and the colony. Since the mid-1980s, Hawaiian prisoners have routinely been incarcerated on the mainland in various facilities. In recent years, the State of Hawai'i has contracted with Correctional Corporation of America, consolidating its relocated prisoners in private facilities in Arizona, Oklahoma, and Minnesota. Of these, the one I am familiar with is the Diamondback facility in Watonga, Oklahoma. Currently the facility houses almost four hundred Hawaiian inmates, amounting to 1/4 of the population. Many of these inmates are Native Hawaiians. In such a context, Native Hawaiians are thrust into a foreign setting where they constitute a large minority and have been subjected to and involved in numerous violent episodes.[3] Needless to say, they are also displaced from their homeland at such a distance that visits from family and friends are rare or non-existent. One inmate recently told me that nobody in his social group has received a visit in the past year. Compounding this, telephone rates from the prison are exorbitant and highly regulated, with the result that few inmates are able to call Hawai'i at regular intervals. Beyond these realities, inmates speak about the bodily alienation of their incarceration in Oklahoma— noting most of all the climate differences. Taking these various factors into consideration, many Native Hawaiians speak of their diasporic incarceration as a form of exile (Kamau'u 2004). A brief excursus into the legal history behind this form of exile—an importantly religious trope—is in order here.

The initial case challenging Hawaiian incarceration on the mainland came about in 1983. At this time, incarceration on the mainland was a relatively rare phenomenon. In the case at hand (*Olim v. Wakinekona*), Delbert Kaahanui Wakine-

---

3   For example, on August 17, 1999 a riot erupted at Diamondback that involved 20–25 inmates and left five guards injured. According to a news article, the primary rioters were Hawaiian. The article also noted several other occasions of violence involving Hawaiians (Kakesako 1999).

kona was moved from a Hawaiian prison to one in California. He challenged the action, claiming his civil liberties had been violated in the process. His case made it all the way to the Supreme Court, which ruled that prisoners may be removed "from time to time" to meet the needs of prison safety and administration. Here special note was made of Wakinekona's violent crime as a legitimate reason to move him from the Hawaiian prison to a high security one on the mainland. The Court also ruled that Wakinekona could not challenge the move on constitutional grounds.

This last point is what concerns us most here. The question the Court faced was: Did interstate transfer create a substantive liberty interest protected by the Due Process Clause of the Fourteenth Amendment? Wakinekona argued that his removal violated special rules of the State of Hawai'i "which require a hearing prior to a prison transfer involving 'a grievous loss to the inmate,' which the Rules define 'generally' as 'a serious loss to a reasonable man'" (461 U.S. 238, 3). In the majority opinion, delivered by Justice Blackmun, the Court held that "An interstate prison transfer does not deprive an inmate of any liberty interest protected by the Due Process Clause in and of itself" (461 U.S. 238, 1). Citing precedent cases to argue that prison transfers do not trigger Due Process considerations, the Court quoted *Meachum* (427 U.S. 224): "The conviction has sufficiently extinguished the defendant's liberty interest to empower the State to confine him in any of its prisons" (461 U.S. 238, 4). Blackmun wrote that, while the Court has observed that "prisoners retain a residuum of liberty, a holding that any substantial deprivation imposed by prison authorities triggers the procedural protections of the Due Process Clause would subject to judicial review a wide spectrum of discretionary actions that traditionally have been the business of prison administrators rather than of the federal courts" (461 U.S. 238, 5). Blackmun then noted that in *Vitek* the Court ruled that moving a prisoner to a mental hospital did trigger due process, as this move was deemed to entail a "qualitative" change in the prisoner's conditions. Wakinekona's claim hinged on the analogy with this case. The Court rejected the analogy, stating, "Just as an inmate has no justifiable expectation that he will be incarcerated in any particular prison within a State, he has no justifiable expectation that he will be incarcerated in any particular State. Often, confinement in the inmate's home State will not be possible..." (461 U.S. 238, 5). Here the Court agreed with the argument of the State of Hawai'i that the Hawaiian prison wasn't sufficient to the violent threat Wakinekona posed. Emphasizing that such a move would not trigger constitutional protection, the Court added, "The difference between such a transfer and an intrastate or interstate transfer of shorter distance is a matter of degree, not kind" (461 U.S. 238, 5). Then, in a sentence right out of Kafka, the Court declared: "Hawai'i's prison regulations place no substantive limitations on official discretion and thus create no liberty interest entitled to protection under the Due Process Clause...the prison Administrator's discretion to transfer an inmate is completely unfettered. No standards govern or restrict the Administrator's determination" (461 U.S. 238, 6). Concluding, the Court spelled out the seamless technology of constitutional hermeticism: "Due Process is not an end in itself. Its constitutional purpose is to protect a substantive interest to which the individual has a legitimate claim of entitlement. If officials may transfer a prisoner 'for whatever reason or no reason at all' *Meachum*, 427 U.S., at 228, there is no such interest to protect" (461 U.S. 238, 6).

Enter the dissenting opinion, written by Justice Marshall and signed by Justices Brennan and, in part, Stevens. Justice Marshall wrote, "In my view the transfer of respondent Delbert Kaahanui Wakinekona from a prison in Hawai'i to a prison in California implicated an interest in liberty protected by the Due Process Clause of the Fourteenth Amendment" (461 U.S. 238, 8). Specifically, Brennan looked to the analogy drawn from *Vitek*, arguing "there can be little doubt that the transfer of Wakinekona from a Hawai'i prison to a prison in California represents a substantial qualitative change in the conditions of confinement. In addition to being incarcerated, which is the ordinary consequence of criminal conviction and sentence, Wakinekona has in effect been banished from his home, a punishment historically considered to be among the severest" (461 U.S. 238, 9). Attacking the apparent circularity of the majority's opinion, Brennan wrote that "an inmate's liberty interest is not limited to whatever a State chooses to bestow upon him. An inmate retains a significant residuum of constitutionally protected liberty… There is no iron curtain drawn between the Constitution and the prisons of this country" (461 U.S. 238, 8). Brennan turned to the State's prison regulations, arguing that the majority misconstrued these as well. Rather than providing for unfettered discretion, Brennan quoted the State's rules to argue that the "standard for classifying inmates is their 'optimum placement within the Corrections Division' in light of 'the best interests of the individual, the State, and the community'" (461 U.S. 238, 10). Brennan rounded out his criticism by taking us back to the penal colony, as it were, to assert that prisoners must retain a liberty interest "solely because there remains the possibility that an official will act in an arbitrary manner at the end of the process" (461 U.S. 238, 10).

Ethnic Islands, Big and Small

However Kafka-esque the legal history may seem, the reality is that Native Hawaiians are incarcerated on the mainland on a regular basis. Our question is: What happens to tradition in this context? To begin to answer this question, we turn to a quotation from Allen Feldman's remarkable study of prison life in Northern Ireland:

> … [T]he prison system of Northern Ireland has become a domain of action, discourse, and symbolization that has time after time escalated communal violence and precipitated new waves of politicization among the imprisoned and their respective communities. (Feldman 1991, 147)

While not as extreme as the situation of Northern Ireland, the dynamic Feldman points to has relevance to the Hawaiian context. It is well known that many prison communities are deeply factionalized along a number of lines. Whether by way of class, race, or other markers, prisoners tend to aggregate as social collectives vis-à-vis other similarly constructed groups. Sometimes groups are primarily defensive in aim; other times they can be aggressive in intent. Whatever the case, the signal observation here is that these groups are far from stable. As in the world at large, affiliations retract and expand according to context in response to perceived threats and possibilities.[4] That said, at the Diamondback facility it appears to be the case that the most stable lines of factionalization are structured by broad ethnic categories, expressed primarily through racial, geographical, and linguistic markers.

So it is that upon arrival in Oklahoma, Native Hawaiians find themselves marked and self-marked as a group vis-à-vis other substantial prison collectives. Ethnic markers become the condition of possibility of social life in the prison. Seeking familiarity and solidarity, prisoners tend to find their social niche rather quickly, and in doing so become engulfed by reified ethnic categories, practices, and language.[5] In this way, as informants have described, Hawaiianness has become a greater value for them in prison than it ever was on the "outside." This seems partially due to nostalgia for home. In other words, prisoners identify with Hawaiianness precisely as a means to cope with their absence from it, to create, as it were, an ethnic island in a land-locked oceanic prison. But more is going on here. We must look to other prisoners' perceptions to fill out the picture, for if Hawaiians create an island in prison, they do so in the context of an ethnic archipelago. Said another way, Hawaiianness is a marker that will be imposed by others, so it is best embraced as a value rather than experienced as a liability.[6]

The aforementioned cases of Hawaiians acting together vis-à-vis other groups in episodes of prison violence offer evidence that broad ethnic solidarities function in a classic manner. In a more positive way, I have been told several anecdotes by prisoners concerning their newfound sense of Hawaiianness. The following example gives a glimpse of the palpable character of incarcerated traditions. According to one source, an older inmate spends his leisure time crafting exquisite miniature voyaging canoes from rolled newspapers and shoe polish. He gives and sells these to the younger inmates, saying that they are meant as a symbol of hope and persistence. Adding to this, some inmates then send these canoes to friends and families, metaphorically sending themselves across the seas to the homeland in a recapitulation of the ancient settlement of Hawai'i. Without wanting to go too far, I would suggest that such an anecdote illuminates how radical

---

4   On the mechanics of ethnic formations, I rely especially upon Evans-Pritchard 1940, Barth 1969, and Lincoln 1989.

5   On the rich but delicate topic of the relationship between identities and reification in the political realm, see Herzfeld 1997.

6   For illuminating discussions of this aspect of ethnicity in other contexts, see Govers and Vermeulen 1997.

relocation from Hawai'i—and the sentiments this experience gives rise to—has fostered a kind of Hawaiian ethnic renaissance. I will return to this theme below.

I wish my story ended here. For if the *Olim* decision resulted in a form of banishment, Native Hawaiian prisoners have demonstrated the power of the human spirit to mount a profound symbolic resistance to this condition. Rather than being absorbed into the mainland and mainstream, Native Hawaiians have become, in Marshall Sahlins' memorable phrase, "more like themselves." But becoming "more like themselves" entails a grim side as well. Namely, I am referring to intra-group tension. If Hawaiian prisoners constitute a group vis-à-vis other prison populations, they are themselves constituted by a number of factions that differentiate themselves according to putative markers of race, religion, and, finally, geo-piety.

If maps shift, which seems well established by now, at times so do the territories to which they refer. Or, more precisely, we might say that forms of geo-piety can go mobile, can be re-placed, and, in doing so, give rise to the fullest sense of "turf war." If "authenticity"—whether as an emic or etic distinction—is related to people and place both, the point here is that neither of these can be taken as given. Rather, both variables should be viewed as discursive resources available to members of groups who can use them to fortify external boundaries or mark off internal ones. In the case at hand, the consequences are chilling enough. Informants have reported that some of the most intense violence they have experienced has been between Hawaiians. In heated moments when Hawaiians turn upon themselves, their terms of antagonism reproduce the structure of ethnic divisions simmering "back home."[7] That is, when internal disputes arise, sub-groups claim Hawaiianness for themselves. In this way Native Hawaiians are pitted against Chinese, Japanese, and Samoan Hawaiians, among others. At the moment, the various groups of Hawaiians at Diamondback are kept separate because of recent violence between them. In a vertiginous way, these prison disputes resuscitate tensions from earlier epochs of immigration, demonstrating that migrations and relocations are true human constants, as are the legal and religious stories that seek to fix them in place.

Culture of Communication, God of Peace

I would like to conclude by letting the pendulum swing back to a consideration of tradition as a form and mechanism of solidarity. In the wake of the displacement and violence at institutions such as Diamondback, prison officials, prisoners, and cultural experts have struggled to address these problems. Violence, in this case, turns out to be the mother of invention. That is, violence motivated these parties to seek cultural remedies. In the process two traditional Hawaiian practices have been appealed to as a means to foster communication and reduce tensions. One is a form of alternative dispute resolution known as *ho'oponopono*.

---

7   Regarding issues of identity and ethnicity in contemporary Hawai'i, see Linnekin 1990.

The other is the classic Makahiki ceremony, made famous in academic circles by the acrimonious dispute between Marshall Sahlins (1985) and Gananath Obeyesekere (1992) concerning the fate of Captain Cook at Kealakekua Bay. Engagement with these traditions has been re-invented in prison settings.

By re-invention I do not mean to suggest that these traditions have been wholly fabricated *de novo* or that they stand in a spurious relationship to "real" tradition. In the sense I invoke it here, "invention" is meant to signal on-going processes of cultural evaluation and construction, by which the past is valued and indeed constructed in the terms and according to the needs of the present. Indeed, I would follow Jocelyn Linnekin (1992) here in suggesting that scholars emphasize terms like "construction," over "invention," even when we mean the latter in Roy Wagner's sense of everyday symbolic practices (1981).[8] Public perceptions of scholarly uses of terms like "invention" have consequences in ways we cannot control but which are frequently a hindrance to various parties; in a twist of fate, scholarly discourse designed to disable the analytical space of "authenticity" may end up restoring it along with the specter of its implied opposite, inauthentic or fake tradition. This is one of the principal reasons to avoid and undermine the category of "authenticity": its champions utilize its naturalized status as a means to discredit variant cultural expressions. In the Hawaiian case this has been true in a number of contexts, particularly as invoked by those who argue in court and in law journals that Hawaiian religious traditions do not exist in the present because representatives of the Hawaiian royalty renounced the *kapu* system and the temple religion founded on it in 1819 (e.g., Sullivan 1998). Such an argument is predicated on the reification of one interpretation of tradition at the cost of all others.

Incarcerated Native Hawaiians provide a different window on tradition. They manage it as a resource, articulate it as speech, embody it as practice. *Ho'oponopono*, for example, is a Hawaiian concept that means "to make right" or to restore order (Pukui and Elbert 1986, 342; Pukui, Haertig, and Lee 1972, 60–70). Historically, *ho'oponopono* was utilized to mediate and restore relationships with ancestral *'aumakua* (deities or spirits) and the *ohana* (extended family, social group); today it is being used in prison settings with the dual purpose of "setting inmates right" with the justice system and with other inmates. While the context of *ho'oponopono* has shifted, its basic mechanisms have not: it operates through dialogue aimed at mutual understanding and forgiveness. In a non-threatening, non-hierarchical manner, the practice of *ho'oponopono* seeks to emphasize bonds of allegiance, commitment, and reciprocity (Aitken 2001). The content of the tradition, then, is but a vehicle of its form—to define the community to itself, to assert its integrity, and to restore its capacity to function as an entity. The work of tradition here, as elsewhere, is counter-posed to those forces perceived to threaten it, whether these

---

8   As another alternative to "invention," I would add "articulation," following Stuart Hall's usage (1985, 1986). For a more sustained discussion of this point, see Johnson 2005.

are angry spirits or unjust wardens. *Ho'oponopono* is meeting with success in a variety of prison contexts at this time; what remains to be seen is if the state and federal governments will be persuaded by Hawaiian cultural experts to consider sending convicts to *ho'oponopono* centers instead of to prisons (see McGhee 2000).

More dramatic than the relatively uncontroversial practice of *ho'oponopono* has been recent celebration of Makahiki in prisons on the mainland and in Hawai'i. Unlike *ho'oponopono*, which is similar to some forms of Western "talking therapies," Makahiki is emphatically non-Western—it is a tradition clearly marked by its practitioners as well as by observers as "other." Added to this, it is emphatically religious. Its practice, therefore, may be accorded special legal protection— if institutions and courts deem it religious in the first place. This is currently at issue. In the face of a lawsuit advanced by the Native Hawaiian Legal Corporation, several prisons are currently allowing for the Makahiki to be practiced, with several limiting stipulations (Vorsino 2005; Kamau'u 2004). However, the legal right to practice Makahiki has not been granted in court, though cases are in the pipeline. When these cases are heard, tradition will be at issue in a number of ways. First, native practitioners will need to present a compelling narrative that represents Makahiki as central and essential to Native Hawaiian religious life. Second, those wishing to participate in the Makahiki will need to persuade the courts that they are Native Hawaiian and that Native Hawaiian religion is important to their wellbeing. Courts will likely desire empirical evidence concerning the historical continuity of the tradition in attempting to rule on this matter. Based on the model of tradition I have been arguing for, another kind of evidence seems more relevant—at least as far as analytical purposes go. Semantic evidence, found in meanings and membranes (often thin and permeable), not in factoids or functionaries, provides a path more in line with the human, cultural condition.

Let us explore the relationship of historical celebrations of Makahiki to its contemporary incarcerated form in these terms. Here we find a metaphorical relationship—the latter stands for the former, though in a selective, modified, refocused way. Undoubtedly, Makahiki took many forms in Hawai'i in pre-European times. With the advent of Europeans, it took notable new forms, including the fateful celebration of 1779 with Cook unwittingly at the helm (Sahlins 1981). However, with the end of the *kapu* system and temple religion in 1819, Makahiki fell out of celebration, at least in public view. In recent years it has made a comeback, with prison celebrations being one iteration of the resurgent ritual.

Before continuing, I want to be clear that in sketching the metaphorical relationship between past and present forms of Makahiki I am not positing a "pure" form of the pre-European ritual. Nor am I suggesting that it was not ideological— surely it was, and I think one can suspect with good reason that much of the "celebration" was mystificatory of the sometimes brutal and frequently uneven power relationships that characterized Hawaiian society. These recognitions, however, do not immobilize our current task, which is to chart the metaphorical ways the tropes of Makahiki are being expressed in the present.

The historical Makahiki was the Hawaiian New Year celebration. Unlike our single night of revelry, Makahiki lasted for about four months, beginning with the rise of Pleiades in the late fall and ending in the early spring. It can be argued that Makahiki was emblematic of Hawaiian religion as a whole—in Ortner's terms (1973), it was a key symbol. The ritual centered on and made clear the relationship between the two dominant *akua* (deities) of the Hawaiian cosmos, Kū and Lono. The year was ritually marked and socially organized by the antagonistic but complementary relationship between these *akua*. Kū, the god of war, fishing and sacrifice, among other things, was held to be ascendant during the non-Makahiki months, which were characterized by warfare and labor. Lono, the god of peace and reproduction, among other things, was celebrated in various forms during the Makahiki season, which was characterized by play, sexuality, and prohibitions on war and sacrifice. Upon the transition into Makahiki various rituals were performed that dramatized the renewal emphasis of the season and its rites of passage characteristics in particular. As Valerio Valeri has shown, these include themes of cleansing, purification, rebirth, and social leveling (1985, 203–206). Themes of renewal and rebirth were framed with reference to the cosmos writ large (Makahiki has a strong cosmogonic component), the *aina*, society, and individuals. In this context Lono was held to serve a fatherly and nurturing role, as can be deduced from his various ritual appellations (ibid., 205).

In the present, Makahiki is appealed to in a most "traditional" sense: as a symbol of Hawaiian culture, religion, and identity. Makahiki has been temporally compressed and symbolically condensed to meet the conditions of its new contexts (a closing and opening ceremony of several hours duration as opposed to a four month cycle). But it has not thereby been semantically impoverished: Makahiki continues to signify Hawaiianness in clear ways. Now this task takes on a contrastive function vis-à-vis the non-Hawaiian world. Makahiki as a symbol is well-suited to this, as it is predicated on a reinstatement of the Hawaiian *akua*, a redefinition of the calendar, an implicit recognition of specifically Hawaiian forms of social legitimacy and rule, and a liminal emphasis upon collective identities over individual ones. Furthermore, Makahiki carries into the present its cosmogonic component, though here at the level of aspirations and hopes—it provides inmates with a rebirth into their Hawaiian identities and a creation of Hawaiian time out of time and place out of place. Themes of renewal, cleansing, and healing figure prominently in inmates' accounts of Makahiki celebrations. Kalehai Kamau'u, a pivotal figure in bringing Makahiki to prison settings, said, "It is a recovery effort, spiritual healing... This whole thing just fills me with life" (Vorsino 2005, 2). Elaborating, Kamau'u declared: "Coming to know my culture helps me out to know who I am... Maybe it will help me to keep staying on track in my life" (ibid.; see also Adamski 2005). Describing his experience of Makahiki and other Native Hawaiian cultural events in prison, Howard Kealohapau'ole Kekakuna foregrounds the relationship between these activities and his sense of identity: "My culture helped me get my life together... I hope I got a chance to come home.

But it don't matter if I never go free again because I am at peace with myself and I have an identity today... I'm Kanaka Maoli, Polynesian forever" (Sodetani 2004). Just as significantly, Makahiki today serves an internally critical function, with particular reference to its prohibition against violence. Furthermore the ritual demands of participants that they "step up to" their identities, that they become Hawaiian enough, comported enough to celebrate Makahiki with integrity.

The transition and transformation of Makahiki that we have briefly considered here can be characterized as a form of cultural recalibration. "Traditional" boundaries and categories have been recalibrated: now the year is not marked by a time of war and a time of peace; now space is marked that way—prisoners live in the space war and must construct spaces of peace. Relationships to the *aina* have also been recalibrated: now the literal landscape is not reconstituted; rather, the spirit of the land is re-placed as an organizing trope for the relationship of the person to the cosmos. Human productivity is recalibrated as well: no warden will subscribe to the idea of inmates abandoning labor in favor of play for four months, but the inmates certainly cherish the symbol of playful exuberance and release that Makahiki implies. In these ways, Makahiki is helping to construct community-building sentiments in the present on the basis of the imagined and paradigmatic past. When successful, however fleetingly, the incarceration of tradition is simultaneously its liberation. Prisoners are in that moment a community of Native Hawaiians being and becoming "more like themselves."

While hardly a rectification of the banishment imposed by *Olim*, the practice of Makahiki, *ho'oponopono*, and other Native Hawaiian traditions restores a bit of *aloha* and *ohana* to the community. Here we are reminded that tradition is best viewed as process rather than as a thing. However objectified—by practitioners or observers—tradition feeds back into the subjective lives of communities and individuals: it is lived, informing ethics, values, and everyday life (see Akin 2004). Historicizing tradition, therefore, demands that scholars seek out the social lives of traditions as opposed to their essences. It is surely more analytically instructive to track elusive and supple realities than it is to chase after, to twist the meaning of Kierkegaard's phrase, the certainty of objective absurdity.

References

Court Cases: *Doe v. Kamehameha Schools*, 04–15044 (9th Cir. 2005). – *Meachum v. Fano*, 427 U.S. 215 (1976) . – *Olim v. Wakinekona*, 461 U.S. 238 (1983) . – *Rice v. Cayetano* (98–818) 528 U.S. 495 (2000) . – *Vitek v. Jones*, 445 U.S. 480 (1980).

Adamski, Mary. 2005. "Makahiki Allowed for Hawai'i Inmates on Mainland." *Honolulu Star-Bulletin*, February 8, 2005 (starbulletin.com/2005/02/08/news/story3.html; 13 July 2005).

Aitken, Robert. 2001. "Restorative Justice Polynesian Style" (flew.com/~aitken/writings/justice.html; 10 April 2002).

Akin, David. 2004. "Ancestral Vigilance and the Corrective Conscience: Kastom as Culture in a Melanesian Society." *Anthropological Theory* 4: 299–324.

Babadzan, Alain. 1988. "Kastom and Nation Building in the South Pacific." Pages 199–228 in *Ethnicities and Nations*. Edited by Remo Guidieri, Francesco Pellizzi, and Stanley J. Tambiah. Houston: Rothko Chapel and University of Texas Press.

Barth, Fredrik (ed.). 1969. *Ethnic Groups and Boundaries: The Social Organization of Cultural Difference*. Boston: Little, Brown.

Blackford, Mansel. 2004. "Environmental Justice, Native Rights, Tourism, and Opposition to Military Control: The Case of Kaho'olawe." *The Journal of American History* 91: 544–571.

Buck, Elizabeth. 1993. *Paradise Remade: The Politics of Culture and History in Hawai'i*. Philadelphia: Temple University Press.

Burke, Kenneth. 1961. *The Rhetoric of Religion: Studies in Logology*. Berkeley, Los Angeles, and London: University of California Press.

Downes, Lawrence. 2005. "The Blessing of Lono: A Vision of Paradise in an Oklahoma Prison." *New York Times*, February 15, 2005. Late edition. Section A, page 18, column 1.

Evans-Pritchard, Edward E. 1940. *The Nuer*. New York: Oxford University Press.

Feldman, Allen. 1991. *Formations of Violence: The Narrative of the Body and Political Terror in Northern Ireland*. Chicago: University of Chicago Press.

Foucault, Michel. 1979. *Discipline and Punish: The Birth of the Prison*. Translated by Alan Sheridan. New York: Vintage Books.

Friedman, Jonathan. 1994. *Cultural Identity and Global Process*. London: Sage Publications.

Govers, Cora, and Hans Vermeulen (eds.). 1997. *The Politics of Ethnic Consciousness*. New York: St. Martin's Press.

Gramsci, Antonio. 1996. *Prison Letters*. Translated by Hamish Henderson. London and Chicago: Pluto Press.

Gutman, Amy. 2003. *Identity in Democracy*. Princeton and Oxford: Princeton University Press.

Hall, Stuart. 1985. "Religious Ideologies and Social Movements in Jamaica." Pages 269–296 in *Religion and Ideology*. Edited by Robert Bocock and Kenneth Thompson. Manchester: Manchester University Press.

———. 1986. "Gramsci's Relevance for the Study of Race and Ethnicity." *Journal of Communication Inquiry* 10: 5–27.

Handler, Richard. 1985. "On Having a Culture: Nationalism and the Preservation of Quebec's Patrimoine." Pages 192–217 in *Objects and Others: Essays on Museums and Material Culture*. Edited by George Stocking. Madison: The University of Wisconsin Press.

Hanson, Allan. 1989. "The Making of the Maori: Cultural Invention and Its Logic." *American Anthropologist* 91: 890–902.

Herzfeld, Michael. 1997. *Cultural Intimacy: Social Poetics in the Nation-State*. New York: Routledge.

Hobsbawm, Eric, and Terence Ranger (eds.). 1983. *The Invention of Tradition*. Cambridge: Cambridge University Press.

Johnson, Greg. 2003. "Ancestors Before Us: Manifestations of Tradition in a Hawaiian Dispute." *Journal of the American Academy of Religion* 71: 327–346.

———. 2004. "Naturally There: Discourses of Permanence in the Repatriation Context." *History of Religions* 44: 36–55.

———. 2005. "Narrative Remains: Articulating Indian Identities in the Repatriation Context." *Comparative Studies in Society and History* 47: 480–506.

Jolly, Margaret, and Nicolas Thomas (eds.). 1992. *The Politics of Tradition in the Pacific*. Special issue of *Oceania* 62/4.

Kakesako, Gregg. 1999. "Prison Blames 2 Isle Inmates in Riot, Looting." *Honolulu Star-Bulletin*, August 17, 1999. Available at starbulletin.com/1999/08/17/news/story14html (9 September 2002).

Kamau'u Kaleihau. 2004. "Kanaka Maoli Prisoners Struggle for Religious Freedom." *Office of Hawaiian Affairs Newsletter*, May 2004. Available at www.OHA.org/pdf/kwo05/0504/15.pdf (13 July 2005).

Keesing, Roger. 1989. "Creating the Past: Custom and Identity in the Contemporary Pacific." *The Contemporary Pacific* 1: 19–42.

———, and Robert Tonkinson (eds.). 1982. "Reinventing Traditional Culture: The Politics of Kastom in Island Melanesia." *Mankind* 13: 297–374.

Lincoln, Bruce. 1989. *Discourse and the Construction of Society: Comparative Studies of Myth, Ritual and Classification.* New York: Oxford University Press.

———. 1996. "Theses on Method." *Method and Theory in the Study of Religion* 8: 225–227.

Linnekin, Jocelyn (ed.). 1990. *Cultural Identity and Ethnicity in the Pacific.* Honolulu: University of Hawai'i Press.

———. 1991. "Text Bites and the R-Word: The Politics of Representing Scholarship." *The Contemporary Pacific* (Spring): 172–177.

———. 1992. "On the Theory and Politics of Cultural Construction in the Pacific." *Oceania* 62: 249–263.

McGhee, Gheeza. 2000. "True Rehabilitation Emphasizes Healing, Not Punishment." *Honolulu Advertiser,* February 13, 2000. Available at honoluluadvertiser.com/2000/Feb/13/opinion9.html (4 October 2002).

Native Hawaiian Government Reorganization Act of 2005. 109th Congress. S. 147.

Nihipali, Kunani. 2002. "Stone by Stone, Bone by Bone: Rebuilding the Hawaiian Nation in the Illusion of Reality." *Arizona State Law Journal* 34: 27–46.

Obeyesekere, Gananath. 1992. *The Apotheosis of Captain Cook. European Mythmaking in the Pacific.* Princeton: Princeton University Press.

Ortner, Sherry. 1973. "On Key Symbols." *American Anthropologist* 75: 1338–1346.

Pukui, Mary Kawena, and Samuel H. Elbert. 1986. *Hawaiian Dictionary.* Honolulu: University of Hawai'i Press.

Pukui, Mary Kawena, E. W. Haertig and Catherine A. Lee. 1972. *Nana I Ke Kumu (Look to the Source): Volume I.* Honolulu: Hui Hanai.

Sahlins, Marshall. 1981. *Historical Metaphors and Mythical Realities: Structure and History in the Early Kingdom of the Sandwich Islands Kingdom.* Ann Arbor: The University of Michigan Press.

———. 1985. *Islands of History.* Chicago and London: The University of Chicago Press.

———. 1988. "Cosmologies of Capitalism: The Trans-Pacific Sector of 'The World System'." *Proceedings of the British Academy* 74: 1–51.

———. 1992. "The Economics of Develop-Man in the South Pacific." *Res* 21: 12–25.

Scott, James C. 1985. *Weapons of the Weak: Everyday Forms of Peasant Resistance.* New Haven: Yale University Press.

Sodetani, Naomi. 2004. "Culture Behind Bars: A Nation Within: Hawaiian Inmates Struggle to Practice Traditions." *Hawai'i Island Journal,* June 16–30, 2004. Available at www.Hawaiiislandjournal.com/stories2/06b04b.html (6 August 2005).

Sullivan, Paul. 1998. "Customary Revolutions: The Law of Custom and the Conflict of Traditions in Hawai'i." *University of Hawai'i Law Review* 20: 99–163.

Taylor, Charles. 2004. *Modern Social Imaginaries.* Durham and London: Duke University Press.

Trask, Huanani-Kay. 1991. "Natives and Anthropologists: The Colonial Struggle." *The Contemporary Pacific* (Spring): 159–167.

Valeri, Valerio. 1985. *Kingship and Sacrifice: Ritual and Society in Ancient Hawaii.* Translated by Paula Wissig. Chicago and London: The University of Chicago Press.

Vorsino, Mary. 2005. "Makahiki Observance in Prisons Spreads to Oahu." *Honolulu Star-Bulletin,* February 14, 2005. Available at starbulletin.com/2005/02/14/news/story3.html (13 July 2005).

Wagner, Roy. 1981. *The Invention of Culture.* Chicago and London: University of Chicago Press.

Wassmann, Jürg (ed.). 1998. *Pacific Answers to Western Hegemony: Cultural Practices of Identity Construction.* Oxford and New York: Berg.

Williams, Raymond. 1977. *Marxism and Literature.* Oxford: Oxford University Press.

Whose Tradition?
Conflicting Ideologies in Medieval and Early Modern Esotericism

Kocku von Stuckrad

The idea of a coherent line of philosophical and religious tradition that comprised doctrines that were not part of the scriptural religions has been present in European culture from late antiquity onwards. Having played an important role particularly in Islamic circles in medieval times, the concept of *prisca theologia* ("'first' or 'ancient theology'") or *philosophia perennis* ('eternal philosophy') influenced European discourses in the fourteenth century.[1] Beginning with the provocative paganism of Georgios Gemistos Plethon, the notion of *prisca theologia* and the narrative of a superior tradition shaped identities that formulated genealogies of knowledge which transgress the revelation of Jewish or Christian tradition. Usually connected to authorities (presumably) older than Moses—Hermes Trismegistus, Zoroaster, Pythagoras, Orpheus, Plato, etc.—this 'invented tradition' played a crucial role in the inter-religious and intra-religious debates of subsequent centuries.

This article describes the emergence of *prisca theologia* in early modern Europe as a discursive strategy to formulate alternative genealogies of knowledge and identities that go beyond the usual revelation of scriptural traditions. In addition, it compares the concept of *prisca theologia* to kabbalistic constructions of tradition that emerged at the same time. This is interesting not only because *qabbalah* is the Hebrew equivalent of "tradition/reception" and because Jewish authors presented their tradition as a singular line of Jewish authorities—thus partaking in an inter-religious debate about the superiority of tradition—but also because Jewish circles developed an idea of authority through authorship, which focused on the *way of transmission* as indication of truth rather than on the *commensurable content* of tradition.

As to the methodological consequences, I will argue that the notion of 'tradition' should not be taken as an analytical category of historiography. By contrast, scholars should apply it only with reference to its emic meaning and function.

---

1 Among the many important studies devoted to this issue—albeit mainly focusing on the Christian context—are Walker 1972, Schmitt 1966, Trinkaus 1970, Hankins 1990, Klutstein 1987, and Tambrun 1999.

1. The Construction of *Prisca Theologia*

The formation of alternative religious and philosophical identities that referred to a superior and often hidden 'tradition' was a decisive element of esoteric discourses between the tenth and the fifteenth century.[2] Being part of a reception of hermetic literature and the revival of a Neoplatonic philosophy, this claim of 'tradition' influenced Muslim, Jewish, and Christian debates during that time—both internally and in interreligious rhetoric. Far from being isolated social groups, the scriptural religions interacted on several levels in a pluralistic religious world (see Meyerson and English 2000; Brann 2002). Interestingly, the twelfth century not only saw the emergence of Neoplatonic mystical doctrines in Islam but also the growing interest of Jewish theologians in interpretations that came to be known as Kabbalah. Christians, for their part, were openly receptive to these doctrines—albeit often in a negative way—and certain mystical trends in Christianity influenced the formation of kabbalistic thinking. Hence, it is worthwhile to compare the different constructions of identities in this highly pluralistic situation and to follow the development of claims to 'tradition' into the seventeenth century.

Suhrawardī: Hermes as Father of Philosophy

The Islamic world was from the outset characterized by a plurality of theological and philosophical currents. Besides the dominant Aristotelianism of Avicenna (Ibn Sina, c. 980–1037) there always existed Neoplatonic schools that were more open to esoteric and hermetic doctrines, especially in the milieu of Shiite and Sufi communities.[3] One of the most interesting representatives of this thinking is the Iranian philosopher Shihāb al-Dīn Suhrawardī. The theosophical school of this mystic, who was sentenced to death in Aleppo in 1191 (aged 37), had a similar impact on Eastern Islam as Avicenna had on the West. While many scholars used to interpret Suhrawardī's doctrines in the light of some Old Iranian 'national' tradition, new studies indicate that in fact we are dealing here with the reception of Platonic philosophy in a Persian context (see Walbridge 2000, 3–11; 2001). Suhrawardī's philosophy integrates Zoroastrian, hermetic, Pythagorean, Platonic, and other ancient teachings. He describes his doctrines

---

2   On my understanding of 'esotericism' as a claim of superior knowledge see von Stuckrad 2005a and 2005b. On the esoteric notion of 'tradition' see also the overview in Hanegraaff 2005.

3   This does not mean that such doctrines were limited to the Shiite milieus. Particularly the theme of initiation into a superior knowledge was transmitted from late ancient contexts to the Ismāʿīlī and Sunni Islam and to Judaism. On the notion of *bāṭin* (inner dimension; the observance of secrets) and *ʿahd* (oath of allegiance) as esoteric element of Muslim and Jewish currents in Medieval times see Hughes 2004, 25–30. I will come back to the Jewish way of dealing with the initiation into 'hidden knowledge' later.

as 'intuitive philosophy,' i.e. a philosophy of mystical experience that supplements the speculative philosophy of the Aristotelians. The subsequent *Ishrāqī* school is therefore known as 'School of Illuminism.' In his main work, the *Philosophy of Illuminism*, Suhrawardī explains that his doctrine and its spiritual praxis will lead to an ultimate understanding of the world. The illumined masters of a philosophical chain of tradition serve as examples of the mystical vision of higher knowledge:

> In all that I have said about the science of lights and that which is and is not based upon it, I have been assisted by those who have traveled the path of God. This science is the very intuition of the inspired and illumined Plato, the guide and master of philosophy, and of those who came before him from the time of Hermes, "the father of philosophers," up to Plato's time, including such mighty pillars of philosophy as Empedocles, Pythagoras, and others. The words of the Ancients are symbolic and not open to refutation. The criticisms made of the literal sense of their words fail to address their real intentions, for a symbol cannot be refuted. This is also the basis of the Eastern doctrine of light and darkness, which was the teaching of Persian philosophers such as Jamasp, Frashostar, Bozorgmehr, and others before them. It is not the doctrine of the infidel Magi, nor the heresy of Mani, nor that which leads to associating other gods with God—be He exalted above any such anthropomorphism!
>
> Do not imagine that philosophy has existed only in these recent times. The world has never been without philosophy or without a person possessing proofs and clear evidences to champion it. He is God's vicegerent on earth. Thus shall it be so long as the heavens and the earth endure. The ancient and modern philosophers differ only in their use of language and their divergent habits of openness and allusiveness. All speak of three worlds, agreeing on the unity of God. [...] Among them are the messengers (*ahl al-sifāra*) and lawgivers (*al-shāri'ūn*) such as Agathadaemon, Hermes, Asclepius, and others. (*Ḥikmat al-Ishrāq*, para. 4, quoted from Walbridge 2001, 14)

For Suhrawardī, hence, history of philosophy begins with Hermes, the "father of philosophy." The genealogy of wisdom that Suhrawardī adheres to is handed down to Pythagoras, Socrates, Plato, and Aristotle (after Aristotle no Greek philosophers are mentioned). Interestingly enough, neither Zoroaster nor Muhammad or Jesus are mentioned, which marks a significant difference to those lines of tradition that usually are constructed in Sunnite and other Shiite contexts. In addition, the notion of pure tradition serves as an identity marker against conflicting claims of 'Magi' or 'Manichaeans.'

Suhrawardī established an influential current of theosophical Shia in the East that almost matched the importance of Ibn Arabi (d. 1240) in Spain. The thesis of concordance between Greek and Iranian philosophy was in the thirteenth century picked up by Qutb al-Dīn al Shīrazī (1237–1311). In addition, Jews embraced major parts of his doctrine, particularly in those circles that Steven M. Wasserstrom (2000) describes as "interconfessional circles," of Muslim and Jewish thinkers that were "interconfessional despite themselves."[4] Among the fifteenth- and sixteenth-century Safawides it was the famous 'School of Isfahan' that further developed Suhrawardī's doctrines. Although the links between the School of Isfahan and the 'Platonic Academy' of Florence are apparent, the influence of Muslim ideology on Christian Platonism has as yet not found the scholarly attention it deserves.[5]

Prisci Theologi in Italian Perspective

With the revival of Neoplatonism in fourteenth-century Christian contexts the construction of a chain of 'enlightened philosophers' gained further momentum. It was Georgios Gemistos (1355/1360–1454), calling himself "Plethon" after the Ferrara council of 1439, who had a decisive influence on this debate.[6] Plethon was extremely interested in the late antique *Chaldaean Oracles* and was the first to claim Zoroaster's authorship of the *Oracles*, thus setting the stage for an enthusiastic reception in Europe of Zoroaster as belonging to the *prisci theologi*.[7] By describing the Platonic doctrines as common to the Zoroastrians, the Pythagoreans, and many others, Plethon founded another line of alternative tradition that was claimed to be older than—and utterly superior to—Christian revelation. The result was a full-blown polytheistic model of religion that Plethon wanted to introduce. Presumably due to his admiration of the *Chaldaean Oracles*, Plethon did not refer to Hermes Trismegistus and the Graeco-Egyptian writings attributed to him, nor to the Jewish Kabbalah that had already taken shape (see Woodhouse 1986, 59–61).

The combination of Neoplatonism, Hermetism, and *prisca theologia* that became so influential in Renaissance esotericism was a result of the reintroduction

---

4 See Wasserstrom 2000. Since the term "interconfessional" seems to be anachronistic for the middle ages, we could also talk of "interreligious circles." In my view this characterization of exchange or—as I use to call it—'discursive transfers' is not limited to Jews and Muslims but can be found in relation to Christian milieus, as well. For fascinating examples of concrete confrontation see the contributions in Fine 2001: From an "Egyptian woman who seeks to rescue her husband from a Sufi monastery" and "visionary experiences among Spanish Crypto-Jewish women" to "Jewish devotional rites in a Sufi mode." See also Wasserstrom's contribution "Jewish Sectarianism in the Near East: a Muslim's Account" (in Fine 2001, 229–236).

5 The attitude to tackle the 'Islamic world' as something totally different than and detached from the 'Christian world' is beginning to make room for a more complex understanding of the mutual dependency of both. A good example of this changing attitude is Goffman 2002.

6 On Plethon's life and work see Woodhouse 1986.

7 As Michael Stausberg notes in his seminal study: "Plethon [hat] der europäischen Zoroaster-Rezeptionsgeschichte die entscheidenden Impulse gegeben" (Stausberg 1998, 43). And on p. 61 he concludes that "die Zoroaster-Rezeption wird somit auch zu einem autoidentifikatorischen Akt," an act of self-identification that was followed by many Christian authors.

of the *Corpus Hermeticum* into Western European culture (see von Stuckrad 2005a, ch. 4). Marsilio Ficino (1433–1499) interrupted his translation of the Platonic writings when Cosimo de' Medici asked him to translate the manuscripts of the *Corpus Hermeticum* that were discovered in 1463 and brought to Cosimo. This was only logical insofar as scholars agreed that Hermes Trismegistus was older than Plato and even older than Moses, thus making accessible the ancient ultimate knowledge of mankind.[8] Ficino's translation was printed in 1471 under the title *Book of the Power and Wisdom of God* (*Liber de potestate et sapientia Dei*) and became known as *Pimander*, referring to the corpus' first tractate. Thanks to the printing press this translation was published 25 times until 1641. Renaissance Europe thus discovered the *philosophia perennis*, the 'eternal philosophy,' as common denominator of Egyptian, Greek, Jewish, and Christian religion.

2. Genealogies of Wisdom

Due to the fact that scholars and philosophers in the fifteenth century gained access to texts that—presumably—were older than those of Jewish and Christian tradition the question arose how these alternative pieces of revelation are related to the revelations of the monotheistic religions. The answers to this question, diverse as they were, lead us right into the interreligious tensions of the time because it makes a big difference whether one's own tradition can claim a higher age and hence a closer relation to the 'original truth,' or not.

Particularly interesting is the comparison between Christian and Jewish claims of tradition, as will be demonstrated later. At this point, reference must be made to the different solutions Christian authors found for the theological problem of the existence of conflicting ways of revelation, or, in the apt terms of Moshe Idel, for the *unilinear* and *multilinear* theories of *prisca theologia* (Idel 2002a). While the unilinear model rejects the assumption that ultimate knowledge can flow from different sources (i.e. from 'pagan' authorities), the multilinear model reckons with the possibility of several sources of revelation that have to be incorporated in a Christian framework. Principally, Renaissance Christians applied two different solutions to integrate non-Christian sources: "the first contends that they agree with Christian theology because they were influenced by a primeval tradition which included or at least adumbrated the tenets of Christianity; the alternative argues that the affinity between these two bodies of thought has no historical explanation but is the result of a revelation or a series of revelations imparted separately to both pagan and monotheistic spiritual leaders" (Idel 2002a, 138–139). The unilinear model that was dominant in Christian circles before the fifteenth century and remained so in Jewish circles

---

8   On the humanist debate about the age of the hermetic writings see Mulsow 2002.

until the seventeenth century (see below) was more and more challenged. Some followed the line of Suhrawardī, Plethon, and others, and argued that there was an independent line of tradition that was even superior to scriptural revelation. But most Christian scholars were reluctant to present the *prisca theologia* in such a radical way. Marsilio Ficino in particular struggled with the implications of multilinear historiographical models and tried to combine this with the Christian tradition. The *one* truth could, after all, be revealed in quite different ways. Inspired by Plethon, Ficino nevertheless presents a line of authorities in which Mosaic sources do not occur: Zoroaster, Hermes Trismegistus, Orpheus, Aglaophamus, Pythagoras, Plato. In his *Philebus Commentary* Ficino explains:

> [T]he ancient theologians [*prisci theologi*] [...], since they brought themselves as near as possible to God's ray by releasing their souls, and since they examined by the light of that ray all things by uniting and dividing through the one and the many, they too were made to participate in the truth [*veritatis compotes effecti sunt*]. (Ficino 1975, 246)

This explanation refers to the Neoplatonic-Theurgic traditions of late antiquity that were formulated in the *Chaldaean Oracles*. The wise men of antiquity — and in their succession the wise men of Ficino's time — can get in touch with the divine sphere through an ascent of their soul. In addition, those who want "to reach the truth [...] must prepare themselves especially by purity of soul for the flowing in of the divine splendour [*ad divini splendoris influxum*]" (ibid., 246 and 248). Both the Neoplatonic Sefirot symbolism[9] and the 'Gnostic' self-empowerment of the understanding individual is an obvious characteristic of this line of interpretation. In his *Theologia Platonica* Ficino clearly attests to this 'pagan' chain of revelation. In other writings, however, Ficino offers a different explanation: In his apology of Christian religion, *De Christiana religione*, he acknowledges the influence of certain biblical figures on the *prisca theologia*. Because *Theologia Platonica* and *De Christiana religione* were written in the same period of Ficino's career, the discrepancy between those two interpretations seem to convey his opinion that the pagan theology is not necessarily superior to Christian theology but independent of it.

Giovanni Pico della Mirandola (1463–1494) shared this opinion (see Trinkaus 1970, 759–760; Farmer 1998, 61–62). In his oration usually referred to as "On the Dignity of Man" (*Oratio de dignitate hominis*) he names Orpheus as the first source of philosophical-theological wisdom, which was carried on to Pythagoras and the later *prisci theologi*. Although kabbalistic doctrines are generally in agreement with these teachings, it was Orpheus who first formulated them independently. Piero Crinito gives a slightly different account of Pico:

---

9   Note that *splendor* is the Latin name of *Zohar*.

That divine philosophy of Pythagoras, which they called Magic, belonged
to a great extent to the Mosaic tradition; since Pythagoras had managed
to reach the Jews and their doctrines in Egypt, and knowledge of many
of their sacred mysteries. For even the learning of Plato (as is established)
comes quite near to Hebrew truth; hence many called him a genuine
Moses, but speaking Greek. Zoroaster, the son of Oromasius, in practicing magic, took that to be the cult of God and study of divinity; while
engaged in this in Persia he most successfully investigated every virtue
and power of nature, in order to know those sacred and sublime secrets
of the divine intellect; which subject many people called Theurgy, others
Cabala or magic [*ut sacra illa et sublimia divini intellectus arcana cognosceret:
quam partum vel theurgiam multi, vel cabbalam alii, vel magicem etiam dixe-
runt*]. (Crinito, *De Honesta Disciplina Libri XXV*, Basle 1532, p. 81; quoted
from Walker 1972, 50)

Here, Pythagoras and even Moses are pictured as dependent from the Mosaic
theology, while Zoroaster's doctrines agree with Kabbalah but were developed
independently.

These differences in detail do not change the general impression that the
multilinear conception of esoteric tradition was a major challenge for Christian
authors of the fifteenth and sixteenth centuries. That esoteric authors began to
construct genealogies beyond the Christian revelation unmistakably influenced
the scientific discourse of later generations. By referring to an 'invented tradition' of *prisca theologia* scientific research emancipated from Christian truth-
claims.

3. Jewish Perspectives

The multilinear conception of religious historiography marked an important
break in Christian discourses, as it was an element of differentiation in Islamic
discourses of which Suhrawardī is a good example. *Claiming tradition* was
always, even if implicitly, directed *against* conflicting claims of other religions
or other groups within one's own religious heritage. If we apply to this pluralistic situation the analytical instrument of the rational choice theory of religion,
it will come with no surprise that pluralistic discourses foster religious commitments. It is the existence of alternatives that promotes the formation of strong
identities.[10] In the period between the eleventh and the sixteenth centuries,
their was no scarcity of alternatives, indeed! Therefore, let us now turn to the
Jewish construction of 'tradition' and contextualize it in this highly pluralistic
situation.

---

10 The state of the art in rational choice theory represent Stark and Finke 2000; cf. the
    discussion and further literature in Kippenberg and von Stuckrad 2003, 129–131, and
    the notion of 'plural fields' on p. 132.

Kabbalah and 'Tradition'

In order to understand the emergence of an esoteric Jewish current that was soon to be known as Kabbalah, we have to look at the specific social and religious situation of twelfth-century Sefard.[11] Although esoteric interpretations were present in late ancient and medieval Judaism, both within and outside of rabbinic milieus, these took on new characteristics as Jews were confronted with internal and external readings of their own religious heritage. The earliest documentary evidence of Kabbalah is found in the *Sefer ha-Bahir* on the one hand—circulated around 1180—and in the writings of Rabbi Isaac the Blind (d. ca. 1235) and his circle, on the other. Usually, scholars agree that the doctrines expressed in these writings where not entirely new; instead, the authors seemed to feel the need of spreading these ideas to a wider public. It is a general characteristic of these and subsequent kabbalistic authors—in particular of the circle that was responsible for the formation of the *Zohar* around 1300—that they belonged to an extremely conservative current in Jewish theological speculation. Therefore, they saw themselves as guardians of the true Jewish heritage. In fact, the Hebrew term *qabbalah* means 'reception,' 'heritage,' or 'tradition,' i.e. a tradition which was handed down from the beginning of history as a secret knowledge of the Jewish people.[12] Making use of the rabbinic doctrine of oral Torah,[13] kabbalists claimed to belong to a superior line of hidden wisdom. The main figure behind the *Zohar*, Moses de Leon (d. 1305), clearly exemplifies this:

> This is what is called "Kabbalah" [reception], owing to the fact that it is a reception [traceable back] to Moses from Mount Sinai. Moses transmitted it to Joshua, and Joshua transmitted it to the elders, and the elders transmitted it to the prophets, and the prophets transmitted it to the men of the Great Assembly, according to the same process as the reception of the Torah. They transmitted this wisdom one to the next. In fact, this path of wisdom was given to the first man at the moment of his entrance into the garden of Eden. The secret of this wisdom was given to him, and it was with him until he sinned, and was expelled from the garden of Eden. After that, when the first man died, his son Seth inherited this wisdom. After that, this wisdom made its way to Noah the righteous, and he transmitted it to his son Shem, [and this continued] until Abraham our

11   For reasons of convenience, I leave out here the Rhineland Hasidism of the twelfth century. But the picture of a pluralistic situation applies just as well to Ashkenaz, where Judaism was heavily threatened. Furthermore, there definitely were links between the Hasidei Ashkenaz and the early Kabbalah of the Provence.

12   There are several other names that were used by kabbalists to describe their teachings. Calling Kabbalah the *torat ha-sod* ('secret teaching') or *hokhmat ha-nistar* ('concealed wisdom') clearly indicates the esoteric character of Kabbalah. Rather than applying the Christian theological category of 'mysticism' to these currents, we should talk of 'esotericism,' as Elliot R. Wolfson noted (1999 and his introduction to that volume); see also Wolfson 2000a, 9–38; Fishbane 2004, 62–63; von Stuckrad 2005a, ch. 3.

13   The *locus classicus* for the rabbinic chain of tradition is *Mishnah Avot* 1:1.

father inherited it, and with this wisdom he worshipped his Creator. He transmitted it to Isaac, and Isaac to Jacob, and Jacob to his sons, [and this continued all the way] to the moment when the later generations stood at Mount Sinai and it was transmitted to Moses our master. From there it was transmitted and received orally, person to person ("*qibblu 'ish mi-pi 'ish*"), through all the subsequent generations. But in the exile this wisdom was forgotten, except for among the very few, and they reawakened this wisdom in each and every generation. For this reason, this wisdom is called "Kabbalah" (reception), transmitted orally from person to person. The entire Torah, the written Torah and the oral Torah, is grounded in this wisdom. (De Leon 1996, 17–18)

Moses de Leon's is a strong example of a monolinear construction of tradition. Furthermore, as Eitan P. Fishbane points out, it is not so much the *content* of this heritage that serves as 'identity marker' in kabbalistic discourse but the *reliability of reception*.

> For this kabbalist—who may indeed be viewed as paradigmatic—the very definition of Kabbalah is tied to a historical and cultural process. The matters that he sets out to discuss are "Kabbalah" precisely because of the line of *unbroken* historical transmission that he, as a reliable master, is able to posit and assert. His legitimacy and authority to transmit esoteric ideas and practices are entirely dependent on his ability to establish such a firm foundation for reception.[14]

By focusing on the oral transmission of esoteric doctrine, kabbalists such as Naḥmanides or Isaac of Acre (fourteenth century) not only claimed that they followed the ultimate *derekh ha-'emet* ("Way of the Truth," see Wolfson 1989) but also opened the door to pluralistic understandings of the *content* of 'tradition.' Finding 'tradition' becomes a creative process that allows for the inclusion of quite different interpretations.[15]

On a more general level of analysis it can be argued that *every* notion of a "secret tradition" is a *contradictio in adjecto* because either it is secret—then there cannot be a tradition—or it is a tradition—then there cannot be a secret. Calling this the "double bind" problem of secrecy, Hugh B. Urban concludes:

---

14   Fishbane 2004, 67. He concludes that "reliable reception [...] makes for legitimate transmission."

15   Fishbane 2004, 72, speaks of a *pluralistic hermeneutic*; see also pp. 73 and 77 with his discussion of Isaac of Acre's *Me'irat 'Einayim* and his conclusion that "we encounter a construction of pluralistic meaning that is even more extreme than the model of harmonization. Here Isaac's implication goes a step further: truth does not adhere to a single predetermined meaning, insofar as two interpretations may both be true and nevertheless be completely contradictory and incompatible." In a comparable way, Moshe Idel describes this change—although related to Abulafia and his circle—as a "shift from conceptual to technical transmission [that] caused an important change in the very nature of the kabbalist's relation to Scripture." Technical transmission "was much freer in its handling of the text" (Idel 2000, 154; see also Idel 2002b, 390–409).

> Secrecy [...] is better understood, not in terms of its content or substance—which is ultimately unknowable, if there even is one—but rather in terms of its *forms* or *strategies*—the tactics by which social agents conceal or reveal, hoard or exchange, certain valued information. In this sense, secrecy is a discursive strategy that transforms a given piece of knowledge into a scarce and precious resource, a valuable commodity, the possession of which in turn bestows status, prestige, or symbolic capital on its owner. (Urban 1998, 210)

With his application of Pierre Bourdieu's idea of "symbolic capital" Urban hits the right key: As scholars we have to focus less on the content of secret knowledge but on the very fact that this knowledge is claimed.[16]

Tradition and Identity

Now it may be asked why this rhetoric of tradition was so attractive for kabbalists during that time. Given a framework of tense pluralism in twelfth- and thirteenth-century Provence and Andalusia, Jews formulated their interpretation of tradition as an answer to both internal and external challenges. To begin with the internal conflicts, the philosophical controversies that related to Moses Maimonides (1135–1204) and his Aristotelian rationalistic interpretation of Jewish law were of crucial importance. For many Jews, his *Guide of the Perplexed* was the most authoritative work of the time, for others, however, Maimonides seemed to give up any superior, esoteric reading of Scripture, abandoned speculation about the qualities of the godhead as mere anthropomorphism, and made too much use of non-Jewish philosophers, thus watering down the uniqueness of Jewish tradition (see Green 2004, XL–XLII). These kabbalistic critics—among them Naḥmanides, Rabbi Jonah Gerondi, Rabbi Ezra ben Solomon, and Rabbi Azriel—tried to combat the implications of Maimonidean rationalism by embracing Neoplatonic concepts that were particularly suitable for sefirotic Kabbalah. It was a discourse of identity that encouraged early kabbalists to publish their teachings.

But there were external factors, as well. In the Castile, in Andalusia, and elsewhere, Jews were confronted with Muslim and Christian conflicts that had significant impact on their self-definition as well as the way the Jews were imagined from outside. The pluralistic situation created a cornucopia of clichés[17] that can only be analyzed when all parts of this discourse, i.e. the dynamic 'othering' between the scriptural religions, are taken into account.[18] As Arthur

---

16 This does not mean, of course, that the content is not interesting for historical analysis. It only means that the content is beyond scholarly verification and accessible to analysis only as *narrative*.

17 That this pejorative imagery and 'othering' is itself also a visual phenomenon is shown in Strickland 2003.

18 On the importance of this approach to esoteric studies in general see von Stuckrad 2005b. Cf. also Anidjar 2002.

Green puts it: "In this context, the *Zohar* may be viewed as a grand defense of Judaism, a poetic demonstration of the truth and superiority of Jewish faith" (Green 2004, LIX). The kabbalistic authors were well acquainted with Muslim and Christian theology and philosophy. With their claim of tradition, they not only tried to establish a self-conscious attitude in a conflicting situation but also incorporated certain Muslim and Christian doctrines into their own system.[19] "Much that is to be found in the *Zohar* was intended to serve as a counterweight to the potential attractiveness of Christianity to Jews, perhaps even to the kabbalists themselves" (Green 2004, LX).

Refusing Multilinear Narratives

As a result of this Jewish ideology, multilinear constructions of religious historiography, so crucial for the challenging Christian notion of *prisca theologia*, was generally refused by Jewish authors. Even if kabbalists allowed for a pluralistic reading of Scripture—either through the Abulafian notion of personal experience or the focus on reliable (oral) transmission rather than on content—this plurality took place in a monolinear framework. The notion of an oral tradition of revelation, taken over from rabbinic narratives into kabbalistic concepts, led to the assumption that non-Jewish authorities had learned their wisdom from Jewish spiritual teachers. This rhetoric was already widely applied in antiquity, as the works of Artapanus, Alexander Polyhistor, Flavius Josephus, and others reveal.[20] It is interesting to see that this master-narrative of 'tradition' was still defended after the hermetic writings had entered the stage. Now, Hermes could be seen as identical with the biblical Enoch. Yohanan Alemanno, who was a contemporary of Ficino and a companion of Pico in Florence, even used Platonic philosophy to show the superiority of Jewish tradition. In his commentary on the *Song of Songs* he differentiates two philosophical schools. The first is

> the sect of the ancient ones, from venerable antiquity up to the generation when prophecy disappeared. They and their sons and disciples thirstily drank their [the prophets'] words up to Plato who was in their [the prophets'] days and in their times. The second sect commenced when prophecy ceased and the days of evil came, from the time of Aristotle and later, up to our days.[21]

---

19 Besides a Neoplatonic framework that was central to esoteric discourse in general, concrete teachings that were attractive to the kabbalists included, among others, the trinity (i.e. a unity in diversity) or Mary as a quasi-divine female figure. On the relation between Marian theology and the Bahiric concept of the Shekhinah see Schäfer 2002, esp. 169–172.

20 On the motif "Abraham teaches the gentiles astrology" see von Stuckrad 2000, 239, 306–307, 351, 360–361, 451–452, 457 (Moses as astrological teacher), 809.

21 Oxford, Bodleian Library, MS Or. 1535, fol. 162, quoted from Idel 2002a, 140. See also the other examples Idel presents (especially R. Joseph Shelomo Delmedigo and R. Elijah Hayyim ben Benjamin of Genazzano).

Idel correctly remarks that here "Platonic lore is described as being the result of the influence of the Hebrew prophets. In fact, valid philosophy is considered to be contemporary with ancient Israelite prophecy and as having ceased together with it" (Idel 2002a, 140).

The assimilation of non-Jewish authorities into monolinear Jewish tradition is also a marked characteristic of Isaac Abarbanel's writings. During the decades around 1492, a bunch of Italo-Jewish scholars absorbed the Neoplatonic and hermetic discussions and attempted to find a solution to those challenges that match both the new humanist methods and the stance of a unique Jewish 'tradition.' Abarbanel, a leading Jewish scholar at the turn of the sixteenth century, was in contact with Yohanan Alemanno and the Averroist Aristotelian Elija del Medigo.[22] This is also true for Isaac Abarbanel's son Judah who would later become known as Leone Ebreo. Like Pico, Alemanno and Abarbanel sought to overcome the rivalry between philosophy and Kabbalah, albeit not, as Pico, by claiming the universal Christian truth to be found in Kabbalah but by insisting on the superiority of Jewish tradition. Even this kind of modest synthesis, however, raised suspicion among fellow kabbalists. Isaac da Pisa, Isaac Mar Ḥayyim, Judah Ḥayyat, Elijah Ḥayyim of Genazzano, and others criticized this approach and "sought to demonstrate rational philosophy's limitations and its ultimate inability to penetrate the superior insights of theurgic Kabbalah" (Lawee 2001, 46). Taken together, these conflicts clearly reveal the problematic implications of conflicting narratives of 'tradition' for religious identities in a pluralistic situation.

With their rejection of multilinear models of *prisca theologia*, Jewish kabbalists were protesting against what they felt to be a deliberate misreading of their tradition by (missionizing) Christian authors.[23] It was not until the late sixteenth and early seventeenth centuries that Jewish authors attributed at least some authority to non-Jewish *prisci theologi* and adopted elements of a multilinear historiography. Examples are Gedalyah ibn Yehiya, Abraham Yagel, Asaria de'

---

22   Abarbanel's link to the Florentine intellectual circles was indirect. Having begun his Italian sojourn in Aragonese Naples, were he was involved at court and had access to the Neapolitan royal library, he soon got into contact with Yohanan Alemanno and Elija del Medigo. As Alemanno, del Medigo, too, had personal contact with Pico della Mirandola. He was introduced to Abarbanel by Saul Hakohen as a "wise and discerning man, perfect in philosophic investigation" (see Lawee 2001, 45). Alemanno was the scholar-in-residence of the da Pisa family during the 1480s and early 1490s, which held close contact with the Abarbanel family. Another link, of course, was Leone Ebreo. His *Dialoghi d'amore* (written around 1502) ranks among the most important Platonic treatises of the Renaissance. As Lawee points out, hermetic elements are already present in the Italian writings of Judah's father. "Indeed, characteristic Alemanno adaptations of Renaissance ideas regarding magic, music, and King Solomon as the ideal Renaissance sage appear in Abarbanel's commentary on Kings, completed only a year after his arrival in Italy" (Lawee 2001, 45).

23   In so doing, they followed the example of the rabbinic critique of Christian 'misreadings'; see Idel 2003, 49.

Rossi, or Menasseh ben Israel.[24] This slight shift might be attributed to an increasing influence of Pico's and Ficino's writings on Jewish circles during that time, to be followed by Christian Kabbalah in the wake of Reuchlin's works.[25] But even where Jews adopted a seemingly 'neutral' Neoplatonic attitude the ideological background is evident, as can be seen in Leone Ebreo's *Dialoghi d'amore*. Leone Ebreo's philosophy was unmistakably colored by Jewish Kabbalah[26] and followed a synthesizing program that again led into a multilinear narrative.

4. Conclusion

The debates between Muslims, Christians, and Jews about the competing lines of 'tradition' are an example of discursive transfers between different circles that belong to different religious systems. Claims of 'tradition' are made in mutual dependence upon one another, in constructing *alternatives* in a religiously 'productive' framework of pluralism.[27] That traditions—related with, but quite different from 'history'[28]—are *claimed* in a situation of competition implies that we have to scrutinize these claims with regard to identity formation.[29] Like identities, traditions are not found but negotiated in a complex process of cultural exchange. When Eric J. Hobsbawm and Terence Ranger argue that "[i]nventing traditions [...] is essentially a process of formalization and ritualization, characterized by reference to the past, if only by imposing repetition,"[30] the

---

24 See the examples presented in Idel 2002a, 155–156.

25 In Idel's words: "It seems reasonable to assume that the Jewish Kabbalist became more open to the idea of an exoteric Kabbalah, a Jewish version of the *prisca theologia*, as the result of their contacts with the Christian contemporaries but at the same time they printed their original texts *inter alia* also in order to counteract the Christological interpretations of the Jewish lore" (Idel 2003, 58).

26 Although we should not forget that—as in the messianic writings of his father—Leone Ebreo was reluctant to substantiate his argumentation explicitly with kabbalistic doctrines (see Idel 1998, 138–140), a close reading of the *Dialoghi d'amore* reveals formulations and ideas that are only explicable against a kabbalistic background.

27 Wasserstrom's notion of "interreligious circles" (see note 4 above) is a similar approach.

28 On the problem of arriving at a notion of 'history' that is reflective of its constructivist character, see von Stuckrad 2003b.

29 The 'invention of tradition' and its relation to identity and pluralism has been the issue of a cornucopia of studies, mostly related to the modern age. See, for instance, Friedman 1994; Gephart and Waldenfels 1999. That identity and tradition are bound to discursive processes of power is argued in Bond and Gilliam 1994. On the construction of 'tradition' in modern esotericism see Faivre 1999 and Hammer 2001, 85–200 ("The Appeal to Tradition"). There is no reason to assume that—from a methodological point of view—these strategies differ widely from processes in earlier periods that are characterized by a pluralistic competition. On the fact that identity is tied to 'territoriality' see Lavie and Swedenburg 1996; Kippenberg and von Stuckrad 2003, 114–126.

30 "Introduction: Inventing Traditions" to Hobsbawm and Ranger 1983, 4.

category 'identity' provides the particular reasons why people tend to construct conflicting lines of tradition. And the categories 'pluralism' and 'competition' help identifying contexts that foster these claims to tradition.

> [W]e should expect it [the invention of tradition] to occur more fre-
> quently when a rapid transformation of society weakens or destroys the
> social patterns for which "old" traditions had been designed, producing
> new ones to which they were not applicable, or when such old tradi-
> tions and their institutional carriers and promulgators no longer prove
> sufficiently adaptable and flexible, or are otherwise eliminated: in short,
> when there are sufficiently large and rapid changes on the demand or
> the supply side. (Hobsbawm and Ranger 1983, 4–5)

To be sure, the last two centuries of European history provide an excellent example of these processes, as Hobsbawm and Ranger argue. But the debates presented in this article show that the triad of tradition, identity formation, and pluralism is a crucial element of earlier times, as well.

From a methodological point of view, it is not sufficient—or, to put it stronger: not possible—to neutrally describe 'traditions.' As the formulation of conflicting traditions within and beyond the scriptural religions' framework in medieval and early modern esotericism reveals, 'tradition' is an emic term that can be applied scholarly in a discursive way only,[31] describing its varying uses, functions, and contexts. It is not a candidate for an etic term in religious studies. Although there are identifiable continuities in the history of religions, these continuities do not necessarily constitute 'tradition.' Instead, 'tradition' is the *evocation* and *application*, if not the invention, of a set of continuities for certain identifiable purposes.

References

Anidjar, Gil. 2002. *"Our Place in al-Andalus": Kabbalah, Philosophy, Literature in Arab Jewish Letters.* Stanford: Stanford University Press.

Bond, George C., and Angela Gilliam (eds.). 1994. *Social Constructions of the Past: Representation as Power.* New York and London: Routledge.

Brann, Ross. 2002. *Power in the Portrayal: Representations of Jews and Muslims in Eleventh- and Twelfth-Century Islamic Spain.* Princeton and Oxford: Princeton University Press.

Elman, Yaakov, and Israel Gershoni (eds.). 2000. *Transmitting Jewish Traditions: Orality, Textuality, and Cultural Diffusion.* New Haven and London: Yale University Press.

Faivre, Antoine. 1999. "Histoire de la notion moderne de Tradition dans ses rapports avec les courants ésotériques (XVème–XXème siècles)." Pages 7–48 in *Symboles et Mythes dans les mouvements initiatiques et ésotériques (XVIIème–XXème siècles): Filiations et emprunts.* Paris: La Table d'Émeraude.

Farmer, Steve A. 1998. *Syncretism in the West: Pico's 900 Theses (1486). The Evolution of Traditional Religious and Philosophical Systems.* Tempe: Medieval & Renaissance Texts & Studies.

---

31 On my understanding of a discursive study of religion see von Stuckrad 2003a.

Ficino, Marsilio. 1975. *The* Philebus *Commentary. A Critical Edition and Translation by* Michael J. B. Allen. Berkeley and Los Angeles: University of California Press.

Fine, Lawrence (ed.). 2001. *Judaism in Practice: From the Middle Ages through the Early Modern Period.* Princeton and London: Princeton University Press.

Fishbane, Eitan P. 2004. "Authority, Tradition, and the Creation of Meaning in Medieval Kabbalah: Isaac of Acre's *Illumination of the Eyes.*" *Journal of the American Academy of Religion* 72: 59–95.

Friedman, Jonathan. 1994. *Cultural Identity and Global Process.* London: Sage.

Gephart, Werner, and Hans Waldenfels (eds.). 1999. *Religion und Identität: Im Horizont des Pluralismus.* Frankfurt a. M.: Suhrkamp.

Goffman, Daniel. 2002. *The Ottoman Empire and Early Modern Europe.* Cambridge: Cambridge University Press.

Green, Arthur. 2004. "Introduction." Pages XXXI–LXXXI in *The Zohar: Pritzker Edition.* Translation and Commentary by Daniel C. Matt, vol. 1. Stanford: Stanford University Press.

Hammer, Olav. 2001. *Claiming Knowledge: Strategies of Epistemology from Theosophy to the New Age.* Leiden etc.: Brill.

Hanegraaff, Wouter J. 2005. "Tradition." Pages 1125–1135 in *Dictionary of Gnosis and Western Esotericism.* Ed. by Wouter J. Hanegraaff et al. Leiden: Brill.

Hankins, James. 1990. *Plato in the Italian Renaissance.* 2 vols. Leiden etc.: Brill.

Hobsbawm, Eric J., and Terence Ranger (eds.). 1983. *The Invention of Tradition.* Cambridge: Cambridge University Press.

Hughes, Aaron W. 2004. *The Texture of the Divine: Imagination in Medieval Islamic and Jewish Thought.* Bloomington: Indiana University Press.

Idel, Moshe. *Messianic Mystics.* 1998. New Haven and London: Yale University Press.

————. 2000. "Transmission in Thirteenth-Century Kabbalah." Pages 139–165 in Elman and Gershoni 2000.

————. 2002a. "Prisca Theologia in Marsilio Ficino and in Some Jewish Treatments." Pages 137–158 in *Marsilio Ficino: His Theology, His Philosophy, His Legacy.* Edited by Michael J. B. Allen and Valery Rees (with Martin Davies). Leiden etc.: Brill.

————. 2002b. *Absorbing Perfections: Kabbalah and Interpretation.* New Haven and London: Yale University Press.

————. 2003. "Jewish Thinkers versus Christian Kabbalah." Pages 49–65 in *Christliche Kabbalah.* Edited by Wilhelm Schmidt-Biggemann. Ostfildern: Jan Thorbecke.

Kippenberg, Hans G., and Kocku von Stuckrad. 2003. *Einführung in die Religionswissenschaft: Gegenstände und Begriffe.* Munich: C. H. Beck.

Klutstein, Ilana. 1987. *Marsilio Ficino et la théologie ancienne: Oracles chaldaïques, Hymnes orphiques, Hymnes de Proclus.* Florence: Olschki.

Lavie, Smadar, and Ted Swedenburg (eds.). 1996. *Displacement, Diaspora, and Geographies of Identity.* Durham etc.: Duke University Press.

Lawee, Eric. 2001. *Isaac Abarbanel's Stance Toward Tradition: Defense, Dissent, and Dialogue.* Albany: State University of New York Press.

Leon, Moses de. 1996. *Sefer Sheqel ha-Qodesh of R. Moses de Leon.* Edited by Charles Mopsik. Los Angeles: Cherub Press.

Meyerson, Mark D., and Edward D. English (eds.). 2000. *Christians, Muslims, and Jews in Medieval and Early Modern Spain: Interaction and Cultural Change.* Notre Dame: University of Notre Dame Press.

Monfasani, John. 1995. *Byzantine Scholars in Renaissance Italy: Cardinal Bessarion and Other Emigrés.* Aldershot: Variorum.

Mulsow, Martin (ed.). 2002. *Das Ende des Hermetismus: Historische Kritik und neue Naturphilosophie in der Spätrenaissance. Dokumentation und Analyse der Debatte um die Datierung der hermetischen Schriften von Genebrard bis Casaubon (1567–1614).* Tübingen: Mohr-Siebeck.

Schäfer, Peter. 2002. *Mirror of His Beauty: Feminine Images of God from the Bible to the Early Kabbalah*. Princeton and Oxford: Princeton University Press.

Schmidt-Biggemann, Wilhelm. 1998. *Philosophia perennis: Historische Umrisse abendländischer Spiritualität in Antike, Mittelalter und Früher Neuzeit*. Frankfurt a. M.: Suhrkamp.

Schmitt, Charles. 1966. "Perennial Philosophy from Agostino Steuco to Leibniz." *Journal of the History of Ideas* 27: 505–532.

Stark, Rodney, and Roger Finke. 2000. *Acts of Faith: Explaining the Human Side of Religion*. Berkeley: University of California Press.

Stausberg, Michael. 1998. *Faszination Zarathushtra: Zoroaster und die Europäische Religionsgeschichte der Frühen Neuzeit*. 2 vols. Berlin and New York: Walter de Gruyter.

Strickland, Debra Higgs. 2003. *Saracens, Demons, and Jews: Making Monsters in Medieval Art*. Princeton and London: Princeton University Press.

Stuckrad, Kocku von. 2000. *Das Ringen um die Astrologie: Jüdische und christliche Beiträge zum antiken Zeitverständnis*. Berlin and New York: Walter de Gruyter.

———. 2003a. "Discursive Study of Religion: From States of the Mind to Communication and Action." *Method & Theory in the Study of Religion* 15: 255–271.

———. 2003b. "Relative, Contingent, Determined: The Category 'History' and Its Methodological Dilemma." *Journal of the American Academy of Religion* 71: 905–912.

———. 2005a. *Western Esotericism: A Brief History of Secret Knowledge*. London: Equinox.

———. 2005b. "Western Esotericism: Towards an Integrative Model of Interpretation." *Religion* 35.2: 78–97.

Tambrun, Brigitte. 1999. "Marsile Ficin et le *Commentaire* de Pléthon sur les *Oracles chaldaïques*." *Accademia. Revue de la Societé Marsile Ficin* 1: 9–48.

Trepp, Anne-Charlott, and Hartmut Lehmann (eds.). 2001. *Antike Weisheit und kulturelle Praxis: Hermetismus in der Frühen Neuzeit*. Göttingen: Vandenhoeck & Ruprecht.

Trinkaus, Charles. 1970. *In Our Image and Likeness: Humanity and Divinity in Italian Humanist Thought*. 2 vols. Chicago and London: University of Chicago Press.

Urban, Hugh B. 1998. "The Torment of Secrecy: Ethical and Epistemological Problems in the Study of Esoteric Traditions." *History of Religions* 37: 209–248.

Walbridge, John. 2000. *The Leaven of the Ancients: Suhrawardī and the Heritage of the Greeks*. Albany: State University of New York Press.

———. 2001. *The Wisdom of the Mystic East: Suhrawardī and Platonic Orientalism*. Albany: State University of New York Press.

Walker, Daniel P. 1972. *The Ancient Theology: Studies in Christian Platonism from the Fifteenth to the Eighteenth Century*. Ithaca: Cornell University Press.

Wasserstrom, Steven M. 2000. "Jewish-Muslim Relations in the Context of Andalusian Emigration." Pages 69–87 in Meyerson and English 2000.

Wolfson, Elliot R. 1989. "By Way of Truth: Aspects of Nahmanides' Kabbalistic Hermeneutic." *Association for Jewish Studies Review* 14: 103–178.

———. 1999. "Occultation of the Feminine and the Body of Secrecy in Medieval Kabbalah." Pages 113–154 in *Rending the Veil: Concealment and Secrecy in the History of Religions*. Edited by Elliot R. Wolfson. New York: Seven Bridges Press.

———. 2000a. *Abraham Abulafia—Kabbalist and Prophet: Hermeneutics, Theosophy, and Theurgy*. Los Angeles: Cherub Press.

———. 2000b. "Beyond the Spoken Word: Oral Tradition and Written Transmission in Medieval Jewish Mysticism." Pages 166–224 in Elman and Gershoni 2000.

Woodhouse, Christopher M. 1986. *George Gemistos Plethon: The Last of the Hellenes*. Oxford: Clarendon Press.

Confucianism and Tradition

Lee Rainey

Both terms "Confucianism" and "tradition" have been defined and shaped by history in Western and Chinese scholarship. In order to see some of the major issues involved, I propose to begin this survey by discussing the history of Western scholarship, then Chinese scholarship, and finally modern Chinese politics and culture.

Kongzi and the Ru

Before beginning any discussion about the role of "tradition" in Western approaches to Confucianism, one must begin by looking at what we mean by "Confucianism" as the term itself is shaped by history and loaded with assumptions. "Confucianism" is based on "Kong Fuzi," a rare version of the name "Kongzi," Master Kong (551–479 BCE).[1] In the 1600's, Jesuits took the name Kong Fuzi, Latinized it, and labelled the school "Confucianism," based on the Christian assumption that religions are named according to their leader or founder. On the other hand, the Chinese terms used to describe Kong Zi's followers, are Ru or *Ruzhe* and make no reference to a founder. The term "Ru" has a difficult etymology and the early dictionaries do not agree about the word's origin.[2]

By the end of the Spring and Autumn period, (770–476 BCE) a *jia*, family or school, began to develop around a teacher whose students would have included both casual and closer followers. *Jia*, or schools, were independent of clan affiliation and loyalty centred on the teacher. This lineage of teacher and student continued on throughout the Warring States period (476–221 BCE). What in English we call "Confucianism" is, in Chinese, *Rujia*, the Ru family or school, *Rujiao*, Ru teachings or *Ruxue*, Ru learning.

---

1   The title "Fu" is hardly ever attached to Kongzi, Master Kong. It is not found in classical texts nor in imperial rituals honouring Kongzi. Lionel Jensen (1997, 81–86) argues that it may be that the Jesuits wished to distinguish Kongzi from all the other Masters such as Laozi, Zhuangzi, Xunzi, and so on, and thus used the extra honorific "Fu."

2   Some scholars argue that *Ru* is related to *rou*, "pliable" and represented the resigned attitude of the Shang people who had been conquered by the Zhou. This argument is based on the definition in the ancient dictionary, *Shuo Wen Jie Zi*, that says, "*Ru rou ye*," "*Ru* means weak." However, other scholars disagree.

An opponent of the Ru, Mozi (ca. 480 BCE), was the first to identify people as Ru. Mozi describes the Ru as a group with certain shared occupations and views: the Ru were associated with funeral rituals and believed in the power of fate. He says they promoted elaborate rituals and music and that they held that a gentleman must wear the clothes of the past and speak with the speech of the past in order to be considered a proper gentleman. He complains that the rituals they practised were so minute and complicated that one could spend a lifetime studying them and never know all of them; as well, one could have a fortune and still not be able to pay for their music.[3] In later texts throughout the classical period, the Ru continued to be identified by their antique clothing and speech; while divided into sub-groups, they shared teachers, basic ideas, and an allegiance to certain ancient texts. Both the Ru and their enemies understood the Ru as a *jia*, a school and their ideas as a *jiao*, a teaching.

In the Han dynasty (202 BCE–220 CE), Ru historians classified the thinkers of the Warring States periods, dividing them into *jia*, schools, with the Rujia leading the way. The classical Ru idea of Ru scholars in government was institutionalised in a government sponsored examination system that operated, in one way or another, from the Han dynasty to 1905. Men were examined in the classics associated with the Ru and in the commentaries; one would pass from level to level of examination until finally graduating as a civil servant. Wealthy families always had an edge because they could afford the tutors, texts, and to have young men unemployed for long periods of time. Before the twentieth century, education in China was mostly aimed at passing these examinations and producing the scholar-bureaucrat, a privileged elite. This meant that the elite who governed China for almost two thousand years were educated in the Ru texts.

It was this elite that was responsible for defining Ru teaching. They did this through strict government censorship and control of which Ru texts were to be considered canonical and which commentaries were to be accepted. So, for example, the great "Neo-Confucian" thinker, Zhu Xi (1130–1200), redefined the canon and the Ru teaching itself to follow the interpretation of Mengzi (Mencius). From 1315 to 1905, this understanding of what the Ru teachings were, the canon, and Zhu Xi's commentaries, were standard governmental examination fare, dictated by government officials as the new orthodoxy. Throughout dynastic China, the elite, trained in Ru classics, saw themselves as preserving and transmitting a *daotong*, the transmission of the Ru Dao, the Way. Ru teaching and orthodoxy was decided in the name of many emperors, most dramatically, Emperors Yongzheng (1723–1736) and Qianlong (1736–1796) who instituted severe censorship, banning and destroying books that were thought to counter Zhu Xi's orthodoxy.

In addition to sponsoring examinations and defining the Ru teaching, dynastic Chinese governments also built and maintained temples to Kongzi and the Ru worthies. Major towns and cities all had one of these temples that had no priest,

---

3   *The Mozi* "Fei Ru (Against the Ru)."

no congregation, and whose rituals were carried out by government officials. Throughout dynastic China, Ru teachings retained a privileged position in Chinese culture and what constituted the proper interpretation of Ru teachings was defined by government and the scholar-officials who staffed that government.

Early Western Scholarship

Matteo Ricci (1582–1610) the greatest of all the Jesuit missionaries in China, decided that joining the ranks of the *literati*, the scholar-bureaucrat elite was the way to further his Christian mission. Ricci studied the same classics as the examination candidates and claimed to find within the classic Ru texts a common ground with Christianity. Ricci and his fellow missionaries interpreted what they found in the classics as evidence of monotheism and natural revelation. In Ricci's opinion, the original teaching of the Ru contained a universally held ethics and an embryonic theology that spoke both of a creator God and an afterlife in a way that was not radically different from Christianity.

Lionel Jensen (1997, 49–53) argues that the Jesuit missionaries in the sixteenth century virtually "invent" what is called "Confucianism" in the West. At the time of the Jesuits arrival in China, Kongzi was a multi-faceted symbol. First, Kongzi was seen as a *shengren*, a sage, the object of an imperial cult that built temples for Kongzi, performed rituals there, and performed other imperial rituals such as the *feng* and *shan* sacrifices. Second, Kongzi was the great teacher of an ancient teaching and the symbol of a fraternity of scholars, many of whom were the bureaucrats who staffed government offices. This is the Kongzi also known to examination candidates, members of private academies, scholar-officials of the local, provincial, national governments, local sodalities of scholarship, meditation, worship, and the gentry, including unsuccessful examination candidates and merchants. Third, the Kongzi discussed and extolled in ancestral veneration and other rites in ritual handbooks, was known to the general public.

This Kongzi became for the Jesuits, a holy man, a saint, (*santo*) and Confucianism was understood as representing genuine, ancient, and continuous Chinese culture. Other candidates for this honour, such as religious Daoism, for example, were ignored. This was because, Jensen argues, the Jesuits found in the Ru *literati* of the time a devotion to texts, an elevation of intellect, an organisation of scholars, and emphasis on education, in short, a mirror image of themselves. "Confucius— as the Jesuits constructed him—offered testimony through his writings of the natural theology of the Chinese and the prospect of its union with the Jesuits' own revealed theology… Confucius was their Christian other."[4]

In Ricci's view, the Ru of his day had fallen away from ancient Confucianism and become merely secular atheists. Ancient Confucianism, the Confucianism of

---

4   See Jensen 1997, 49, 93. Both groups were, as well, all male fraternities.

the classics and Confucius was, on the other hand, monotheist, and contained a natural revelation that led naturally to Christian doctrine. Given this, Ricci and the Jesuits decided that ancestor rites were, as he described them, "perhaps free of superstition" and might be regarded as memorials. Chinese converts, then, might freely participate in them.

The Rites Controversy

Other missionary groups, the Franciscans and Dominicans, based their interpretations on the religious ceremonies as they found them practised and argued that people seemed to believe that the ancestor's spirit did reside in the ancestral tablet. These ancestral spirits partook of the essence of the gifts offered by the descendants and were able to assist and to punish their descendants. These orders claimed that, when one looks at the classics, it is easy to see that Confucius was an atheist because he did not speak of God or an afterlife. The common people, on the other hand, worship their ancestors as spirits. The Franciscans and Dominicans have an interpretation in complete opposition to Ricci, who found religion in the classics and only a memorial service in the ancestral rites. There were, as well, political problems between the Jesuits on the one side and the Franciscans, Dominicans, and the *Société des Missions étrangères* on the other. These were disputes over influence and power. These political problems were added to the theological disputes about the status of Chinese ancestral rites to form the Rites Controversy.

What can make a description of these early interpreters so confusing is that early missionaries often applied one interpretation to one group and another interpretation to another group. So, for example, Ricci tells us that the *literati* of his day are atheists, but that the original classics speak of a natural religion. The anti-Jesuit position argues that the classics show signs of atheism, while the practice of the ancestral rites is superstitious.

By 1704 Ricci's teachings were condemned by the Pope and a Chinese convert's attendance at the rites honouring Confucius and at the rites honouring the ancestral dead were forbidden. Protestants followed suit, classifying Confucianism as a religion and, like all Chinese religions, characterising Confucianism as idolatrous.

By the 1930's, some Protestant and Catholic missionaries began to argue that the ancestral rites and rites honouring Confucius must be allowed for the missions to succeed and both were to be seen as civil rites. Other missionaries were questioning the "Westernisation" of Christian converts and many began to voice a new respect for Confucianism. Ironically, this was happening at the same time that many Chinese intellectuals were attacking Confucianism as backward and superstitious.

The discussion of the Rites Controversy was not limited to missionaries in China. The Jesuits published translations of some of the Confucian classics and this provided Europeans with their first exposure to Confucianism. Many European philosophers, aware only of the constructed and idealised picture that the Jesuits had presented, became Sinophiles: Voltaire, Leibniz, Wolff, Quesnay, Spinoza, and the Deist, Matthew Tindal. Of them, G. W. Leibniz (1646–1716), was most interested in the Jesuit descriptions of Neo-Confucian philosophy. Leibniz' work, *A Discourse on the Natural Theology of the Chinese* was written in 1716 and was greatly influenced by the Jesuits' search for a natural religion in China. In *Discourse* 48, Leibniz discusses the question of whether or not Confucius is an atheist. He argues that, as long as one does not deny the existence of spirits and acts virtuously to please the spirits as Confucius taught in regard to the rites, then one is not an atheist. Leibniz also interprets the word *Tian*, Heaven, as a reference to a supreme deity. In *Discourse* 66 Leibniz discusses the ancestor rituals that he saw as an expression of gratitude and as proof that the dead have access to the deity, and that the soul survives death. This, he claims, can be seen in the Confucian classics. Those Confucians who argue that theirs is a philosophy are, therefore, not in accord with their own classical literature. He agrees with Ricci that, while contemporary Confucians are atheists, the ancient Chinese were not and they followed a natural religion that believed in the survival of the soul and in a single God.[5] Leibniz, like the Jesuits, assumed that the Chinese were incapable of reporting their own teachings accurately nor were they able to understand them clearly. Thus Confucianism, when properly understood by Westerners, is actually a religion.

In general, European philosophers used their knowledge of Confucian philosophy, such as it was, to argue for their own ideas. They differ in interpretations, as we saw with the religious orders, depending on whether they accept information from the *literati*, depend on popular practices, or their translations of Confucian classics. Because of these differences, Enlightenment philosophers categorise Confucianism as atheist, agnostic, pantheist, and monotheist and find grounds for arguing that Confucianism both does and does not believe in the survival of the soul after death and in a creator god. These categories and approaches will continue on in the Western discussion.

Early discussions of Confucianism hinge primarily on whether or not one finds a belief in an afterlife, and thus the presence of the ancestors in ancestral rites and as well on whether Confucianism believes in a supreme deity. All the other components of Ru teachings: filial piety, moral behaviour, the moral dimension of ritual, the rectification of names, the concepts of gentleman and sage, the idea that government is for the benefit of the people, and so on are all ignored in these discussions. Confucianism is manipulated both in terms of its name and in terms of what is seen as crucial to it.

---

5   Leibniz 1977, 147. Others disagreed: Nicholas Malebranche (1638–1715) criticised Confucian philosophy for its atheism.

A broader understanding of Confucianism, access to Chinese scholarship, access to the original texts, and a better understanding of the history of the times has led to a greater Western understanding of Confucianism. I have divided Western and Chinese scholars here, but this is an artificial division in the twentieth and twenty-first centuries. More and more, Western and Chinese scholars read each other's works, attend the same conferences, and study together. The artificial division I am imposing here is simply for ease of description.

The debate about whether or not Confucianism is a religion continued on through the twentieth century and, in some circles, continues today. There have been, and are still, those scholars who have understood Confucianism as a religion; others have argued that Confucianism is not a religion but something else, often, a philosophy.

Confucianism Is A Religion

One approach to Confucianism can be found in Marcel Granet, and also seen in the work of Sarah Allan and Maurice Freedman. Here Confucianism is something not radically separate from the popular religious tradition. Granet argues that, while Confucians constitute an elite group in terms of rank and education, they share common religious assumptions with the rest of Chinese society.

H. G. Creel, a great scholar of the mid-twentieth century, is often credited with keeping Western interest in Confucianism alive during the 1950's and 60's. Creel understands Confucianism much as Leibniz did, although Creel's view is considerably more well-informed. Creel argues that the idea that we have of the scepticism in Confucianism has arisen from the interpretation of the Confucian classics by later Confucians. For Creel, Confucius believed in the power of Heaven and regarded it as a deity. Creel concludes that, for Confucius, "his whole life was inseparable from a cosmic and religious background."

Among those who argue about Confucianism's status as a religion, there are those who describe Confucianism as a "state cult" or "civil religion."

D. H. Smith who argues that Confucianism is a religion for three reasons: first because it is an ethical system that is grounded in religion; second, because Confucianism respects the cultic practices in which ancestors and spirits are worshipped; and third, because the dominant concept in Confucianism is the way of heaven with heaven understood as a supreme deity, regulating life and relationships. Smith says, "…if religion is concerned with the ultimate meaning of human life and destiny, then Confucianism should be classed as a religion and not simply as an ethico-political philosophy" (Smith 1968, 32–34). Confucianism, then, despite its lack of many of the things that are commonly found in religions, still contains within it some notion of the "ultimate meaning" of life and on this ground it may be classed as a religion.

Rodney Taylor also understands Confucianism in this way. Taylor argues that throughout Confucian thought, from Confucius to Neo-Confucianism there runs a central thread: this common idea is that there is a unity between human beings and heaven, between the public and private life and between the way of heaven and the way of human beings. Taylor argues that this idea is not generally found in Western thought except among mystics (Taylor 1986, 5–6). One can find much the same approach in the much studied 1987 text by David Hall and Roger Ames, *Thinking Through Confucius*.

Confucianism Is Not A Religion

Other thinkers, like Arthur Wolf, and Robert Weller argue that in Chinese culture there is a division between the common people, who maintain that there is an afterlife, and the elite, who, for example, ignore or deny the possibility of an afterlife. Here we see the argument that the elite Confucian tradition was always a sceptical tradition and that Confucians regarded the reality of the existence of the ancestors or the spirits as something that is useful only in supporting society.

There are variants on this argument: one describes Confucianism as manipulating the ancestral rites. It is Etienne Balazs' view that the Confucians used ancestor veneration as a way of regulating social relations and reinforcing a strong hierarchical system (Balazs 1964, 155). This, too, is the argument one finds in Marxist circles. Confucius is said to have emphasised funeral rites and ancestral rites in order to control society (Yang Jung-kuo 1974, 36–37).

Others classify Confucianism strictly as a state cult and argue that it encouraged ancestor worship only in order to strengthen the family and the state. Confucianism is described as a "civil religion" because Confucianism discouraged "asceticism, mysticism, and theological speculation" (Latourette 1928, 11). Confucianism supported the rituals of commoner and emperor alike only in order to stabilise society. Henri Maspero argues for the idea that Confucianism can be defined as a religion only if it is called a "civil religion" and that, as a civil religion, Confucianism is not actually interested in the supernatural or an afterlife. In sum, says Maspero, the Confucian state religion is interested only in the state and uses religious forms to ensure the state's stability (Maspero 1981, 53–75).

Among those who argue that Confucianism is not a religion, they are many scholars who describe Confucianism as sceptical. The Confucianism that developed in the later Zhou is often seen as sceptical and rational. Max Weber contrasts the "magic garden" of Daoism and the "rational disenchanted" world of Confucianism. This rationalism leaves no room for unproven beliefs such as existence after death. Joel Kupperman concedes that Confucianism has a "family resemblance" to religion, but argues that it is religious only in the sense that the full range of Confucian ethics permeates all of life.

Some thinkers argue that this kind of rationalism and emphasis on morality that can be found in Confucianism should be described as humanism. For example, Wing-tsit Chan says, "If one word could characterize the entire history of Chinese philosophy, that word would be humanism--not the humanism that denies or slights a Supreme Power, but one that professes the unity of man and Heaven" (Chan 1973, 3). He argues that humanism grew as superstition was replaced by technology: prayers for rain were replaced by irrigation. The changes from the Shang and the early Chou allowed a Confucianism to develop that was humanist and which, if not explicitly denying the survival of the soul, at least had little interest in the question (Chan 1967, 290). Confucian intellectuals, Chan says, almost entirely abandoned the idea of any kind of personal survival after death.

Benjamin Schwartz refines this description of humanist as it applies to Confucianism by arguing that, while Confucius was a humanist, he was not interested in all human things, such as the nature of man and myths. Confucianism, he says, is not humanist in the Western sense of man-centred in a valueless or hostile universe, but humanist in sense that human beings and their concerns are primary (Schwartz 1985, 120).

In general, those who do not see Confucianism as a religion emphasise its rationality and the moral approach in Confucianism. They argue that any religious overtones that are found in Confucianism come either from the ancient sources of Confucianism or from using religious terminology as a way to talk about ethics. Some do argue that Confucianism had a place as a state religion, but this was only a way in which Confucianism upheld the state and was not taken seriously by the Confucians.

Modern discussions follow the lines of earlier Western interpretations in that two definite positions are taken in understanding Confucianism. The first finds grounds for classifying Confucianism as a religion and a religion that has beliefs not solely grounded in a materialist rationality; the second line of discussion classifies Confucianism primarily as an ethical and philosophical system. Much of the same material is appealed to in both early and modern interpretations, however, one important assumption has changed: Western religious thinking is not generally taken to be the norm. In the early interpretations there is a common assumption that religion in China must be like religion in the West and that the religious norms of the West are universal norms. Early thinkers assumed that, if Western ideas and assumptions are missing, it is because the Chinese have fallen away from a true understanding. Modern scholars, for the most part, recognize differences between east and west, although they handle these differences in particular ways.

There have been a number of strategies to try to deal with the issues raised in the Western study of the Ru. One possibility is to scrap the use of the word "Confucianism." Jensen argues that the use of the term "Confucianism" continues to mislead and it "buttresses the illusion that 'Confucianism' actually represents, rather than constructs, a native Chinese reality" (Jensen 1997, 143). Jensen, and others, argue that the term itself is so problematic that one cannot see past it to evaluate the Ru or the Confucians in any serious way.

Among scholars in the field the tide has turned. The most popular term for Confucianism in the last five years has been to call it a "philosophy." Others have tried to find something else, rather than "religion" or "philosophy" to use to describe Confucianism. Some have defined as an "ideology," a "religious-moral ideology," others as a "social ethic," others as a "moral order." But, for those familiar with the "religion vs. philosophy" debate, these terms seem to imply connection with one side or the other.

No matter how often the term "philosophy" is used to describe the Ru teachings, in universities across North America, Confucianism is generally taught in Religious Studies departments or in East Asian Studies departments. World religions textbooks continue to include Confucianism. In the West, it is very rarely taught in Philosophy departments. In fact, in most Philosophy departments, a reading of the course descriptions will show that philosophy is an enterprise reserved for Caucasian males. Three hundred year old Western assumptions continue to operate in our time.

So it has been that slowly and with little fanfare or discussion, the term "tradition" has come to be used more and more to describe Confucianism. There has been virtually no discussion about the use of the term, it simply appeared and its popularity spread. "Tradition" can be a useful term for Confucianism or the Ru in a number of ways. First, it is neutral in terms of the "religion vs. philosophy" debate. Second, it evokes the long history of Ru teaching and connects Ru teaching to Chinese culture throughout the dynastic period. Third, and I think this is a more unconscious or at least unreflective motive, it tends to place Ru teaching in the past. This is a tendency, not a strict rule and one can find recent texts using the term "tradition" when referring to the Ru teachings as they are understood and practised.[6]

In the Western study of Ru teachings, the term "tradition" is not used to refer to a more ancient, higher, and more pure religious truth. Rather it is coming to be used to help to deal with the racist and culturally imperialist approaches of the past.

Chinese Scholarship in the Twentieth Century

We are often told that the very idea of "religion" is a relatively new one in Chinese culture: the word *zongjiao*, religion, came to exist only in the late 1800's as Western writings were translated into Chinese and that the term was borrowed

---

6   For "tradition," see, for example, Berthrong 1998; for "literati tradition" see Paper 1998; for "tradition" as the past, see Suleski 2002; for Ru teaching of all sorts and all times as "philosophy" see Ivanhoe and Van Norden 2001; for "humanistic social philosophy" see Koller and Koller 1998.

from the Japanese. Similarly, one reads that the term "tradition" — in Chinese, *chuantong*, is relatively new, having come from the Japanese *dento* only about a hundred years ago (e.g. Schwartz 1973, 76). Not only is there no etymological evidence advanced for these claims, which may or may not be true, but they are misleading. Organised religion was known and understood as a concept through-out dynastic China, with many dynasties included in their governments a Ministry of Cults or Religions. The idea of "tradition" is less clear, particularly if by "tradition" we mean something different from "history." Certainly Ru teachings from the beginning idealised a past and the Ru maintained that they transmitted the teachings through the *daotong*. In sum, one needs to be careful about the implicit claims in the etymologies of *zongjiao* and *chuantong* that we are often given.

In the nineteenth century, China was invaded by Westerners and Western culture. Politically, the Qing dynasty government was completely unable to cope with the military and political problems. The government's helplessness in the face of Western imperialism showed most Chinese that Western technology, particularly military technology, was far superior to China's. Many found them-selves socially, politically, and philosophically disoriented as the myth of Chinese cultural superiority dissolved. Chinese intellectuals began to look for the reasons that this had happened. Why had China, for centuries the most technologically advanced nation in the world, fallen so far behind the West? What made the West successful and China a failure?

For many Chinese the response to these questions was to reject Ru teachings, as the Ru were identified with the shortcomings of the past. The basis for this violent rejection was the belief that the Chinese culture of the past held within it fatal flaws that stopped technological and industrial development. As both the high culture and government were the preserve of the scholar-bureaucratic elite, trained in Ru teachings, it seemed clear to many that these teachings were the basis for China's failure. Ru teachings had structured a tradition that was inequitable, backward, and that had failed.

With this began the re-evaluation of Ru teaching that still goes on today. What is called *"Xin Ruxue"* (New Confucianism) is an attempt to define Ru teaching in the light of the events of the nineteenth and twentieth centuries and to deal with the impact and challenges that modernity brings. New interpretations began as early as Kang Youwei (1858–1927) and considerable scholarship is now devoted to it.

Umberto Bresciani divides the Ru reinterpretative movement into three groups. The earliest group began by trying to meld Western and Chinese learning, saying that one should use "Chinese Learning as Substance (the spiritual base); Western Learning as Function (practical, materialist, use)." In this way, the older Chinese culture could be maintained while the technology, rather than the culture, of the West could be applied. This position was adamantly rejected by the May 4th move-ment of the 1920's and 1930's. The May 4th movement wanted to discard all of the past and argued that the path to the future lay solely in the Western ideals of science and democracy. The past was clearly identified with Ru teachings. Tradition was defined as the male dominance of women; the dominance of old over young; the dominance of one class over all others; the rejection of change and glorification of the past; state and self-censorship that ended scientific and technological enquiry; and, in general, the fossilisation of Chinese culture. For the May 4th movement, all of these things were associated with a tradition that was defined and based in Ru teaching — a tradition that was entirely the responsibility of the Ru. As a result, the May 4th slogan was *"Pohuai Kongjia dian"* (smash the Confucian family shop). One May 4th writer, Wu Zhihui, advocated throwing all Ru texts down the toilet; another, Lu Xun, claimed to find the order, "eat people" in the Ru texts.

The "second generation" of Ru reinterpreters began after World War II. These were scholars who had seen the communist takeover of China and who had fled to Hong Kong, Taiwan, or the West. These scholars were faced with the loss of their country and so we find that they hold tight to Chinese culture. Their emotions and patriotism become to be heavily invested in Ru teachings. As well, much of their confidence had returned and many of them took the position that China had a long and unique culture that the West did not understand.

The third generation of scholars, from about 1980 on, have lived through the economic rise of Japan, Hong Kong, Taiwan, Korea, Singapore, and so on. All of these societies are seen as based in Ru teachings. This economic progress has given scholars a new confidence. Western commentators, like Max Weber, and a large number of Asian commentators as well, had argued that Ru teachings and capitalism were antithetical. This was one of the reasons that Ru teachings were incompatible with modernity. However, it has become evident that this is not the case, or at least, so the new argument goes.

The third generation see new political and economic situations. They also benefit from the textual and analytical work done by earlier generations of scholars. They have become more open to Western issues and methods using hermeneutics and post-modern thought. But, the great difference between the third generation and earlier ones is that since the 1980's, New Confucianism has spread to mainland China. New Confucian scholars have lectured and taught in mainland China and their work is available there. Ru teachings have reappeared in China's schools, in many cases organised by the third generation of scholars. What all of this means is that one can see that Ru teachings are going to survive and move into the future.

These modern scholars, part of the *Xin Ruxue*, New Confucianism, differ in a number of respects, but tend to have a similar position on some very basic issues.

First, much of their discussions continue to respond to the criticisms of the May 4th movement. So, for example, they argue that Ru teachings, properly understood, encourage science and democracy. Second, they tend to define some part of Ru teaching as "authentic" and to differentiate that from Ru teaching that has been misunderstood, manipulated, or is completely incorrect. Thus, they say, despotic regimes and societies are not "real" Ru teachings: dynastic China manipulated Ru teachings so as to strangle its aims. Left to its own devices, Ru teaching would have led to democracy and modernity. Third, the New Confucians are an all male fraternity, with some rare, and recent, women's voices; male New Confucians rarely, if ever, discuss the status of women in the past nor how their understanding of New Confucianism would affect the status of women in the future.

Bresciani lists other common characteristics: ascribing a leading role to Ru teachings in Chinese culture; a sense of mission and belief in the *daotong*; a belief in the moral self; an opposition to scienticism and a stress on the spiritual side of human life; and a dialogue with Western culture.[7]

In terms of approach, the New Confucians say that China's culture has always developed as a unified, spiritual, whole; Ru teachings then are not to be studied as dead history. It is only through respect and affection that one can truly reach the core of Confucian teaching (Bresciani 2001, 459). One must practice the teaching in order to understand it. If this sounds more like religious practice than philosophical analysis, it is. The New Confucians are often anti-rationalist and stress intuition over analytic knowledge. Quantitative knowledge does not give one the knowledge that a morally trained mind does, in its psychological and moral knowledge of the universe. As a result they tend to like Western philosophers like Bergson because he, "belittles science," "praises intuition" and uses the negative way.

Of all the texts associated with the Ru, the New Confucians focus on the *Yi Jing*, *The Book of Changes* as expressing the main Ru view of life that the world is great flow of changing things. As well, many New Confucians are affiliated in one way or another with Buddhism (see Bresciani 2001, 464–465). All of this means that New Confucians tend to stress the religious dimension of Ru teachings and to define those teachings as a religion. They argue that it has always played that role, or part of that role in the life of Chinese intellectuals.[8] There is a long history of mystical experience in Ru teachings that proves that this is a religion, according to many New Confucians. Not all scholars agree, Tu Wei-ming, on the other hand, argues that Confucianism is both a philosophy and religion: not an exclusively analytical philosophy, nor a religion that talks about faith and souls (Bresciani 2001, 466).

Xin Ruxue maintains that Ru teaching, properly understood, centers on the values of family and group where individuals treat each other with mutual respect. In any conflict or problem, individuals must look inward and examine

---

7 Bresciani 2001, 456–457. Interestingly, in his summation chapter, Bresciani does not notice the all male list of scholars he has compiled and does not include gender in his list of similarities.

8 Tang Junyi and Mou Zongsan, two figures central to New Confucianism openly declare Confucianism a religion. Liu Shuxian says, "... [it is a misunderstanding when] they consider Confucianism as just a set of moral rules. They utterly ignore the whole network of doctrines concerning the meaning and destiny of human beings and concerning the communion between human beings and Heaven. We New Confucians continuously stress these religious dimensions." See Bresciani 2001, 466.

themselves for moral failings; this practice builds a moral self-discipline that is expressed by the person into the social and political system. All of this is different from the moral decay of the West and superior to Western values.

Filial piety, respect for one's parents is the beginning of building a moral person: love and respect for one parent's broadens into respect for others, for teachers, and for elders. It builds a sense of loyalty to the family, to the group, to the country.

Ren, humanity or benevolence, is putting oneself in the other person's place. This means that one feels compassion for the misfortunes or weakness of others and evokes both helpful behaviour and warmth to any group or society.

Education allows one to find a good job and support one's parents and society. It gives one a broader perspective and so, as one's educational level increases so too does one's social responsibility. Hard work, both in business and education is part of one's responsibilities.

All of this comes together as the basis of Ru teaching, the basis of Chinese culture, and the lives of Chinese people. Ru teaching has provided Chinese people with a moral compass and, simultaneously, economic success.

These are the things that are truly Ru. The past, with its despotic governments, cruel family system, backwardness, and so on, should not be seen as Ru. While the past may have called itself Ru, people in dynastic China did not really understand what the Ru teachings were. Neither history nor tradition is Ru. Chinese culture, however, is Ru and this is why it has been so successful.

Xin Ruxue has not been without its critics. Marxist-Leninist-Mao Zedong thought says this is nothing but idealism. *Xin Ruxue* is merely a reworking of the past that has nothing to offer; the modern "socialism with Chinese characteristics" is fundamentally opposed to the capitalism of the New Confucians. Others charge that New Confucianism is too theoretical, too bookish, and it does not address life's real problems.

Other critics have difficulty with what is being defined as the "real" Ru of the *Xin Ruxue*. Classical Ru texts discuss the ultimate importance of social order and of the proper position that each person must take, depending on their relationships as the way to preserve social order. In the capitalist system, on the other hand, relationships are defined by money and that is how people relate to the world. However, one hears little about this important part of the Ru texts.

Similarly, classical Ru discussions focussed on governments, how they should be run and who should run them. The Ru notion of government for the benefit of the people has been used to describe Ru teaching as democratic. This description ignores the hundreds of textual references to the people as incapable of governing themselves and requiring leadership from the elite in order to live secure lives. The *junzi*, the Ru gentleman, trained in ritual and history, who as a member of the elite took his place in government and led by example, is another aspect of classical Ru teaching that is often missing from modern discussions. *Xin Ruxue* has defined Ru teachings in ways that omit or downplay important classical ideas.

Finally, the way in which New Confucianism cuts itself off from the past and denies any real connection to a "tradition" that claimed to reflect Ru ideas and values, is extraordinarily problematic.

First, what are we to make of all of the generations of people who for 2,000 years identified themselves as Ru, memorised and studied Ru texts for much of their lives, and believed that their society and government were sure reflections of Ru thought? The New Confucians argue that from the Han dynasty (202 BCE–220 CE), Ru thought was misinterpreted by scholars and manipulated by governments. Once this misinterpretation began, it continued to push Ru teachings further and further away from their true meaning. Here the New Confucians encounter the same problem that people have in a number of areas: if the past, which claimed to be authentic, believed and did things that we now find repugnant, how do we now relate to it? Buddhists, for example, in the past argued that women, as women, could not be enlightened. It is easy enough to change one's attitudes so that Buddhists, for example, can say the past was wrong, women can be enlightened. However, what are we to do with the past? Is it not really Buddhist or Ru? On what grounds can we decide that people in other times were just wrong? This is a problem the New Confucians face, but, as in other "traditions," not one that they much discuss.

A second problem, which relates to the first, has to do with examining the past. If Ru teachings in the past were misinterpreted, how did that happen? Are there parts of classical Ru teaching, such as the devaluation of women, that could lead to this kind of misinterpretation? If so, what are they and should they be considered to be authentic Ru? By not admitting to any connection to the problems of the past, New Confucians also do not address serious problems in the Ru texts. By defining "authentic" and "real" Ru teachings without any acknowledgement of the past, New Confucians continue to present merely a version of Ru teachings. New Confucians reject a connection with a past and thus with a "tradition," but this position is a difficult one.

Governmental Versions of Ru Teachings

There are a number of East Asian countries that have identified themselves as based in Ru teachings. The economic success of Chinese people in Hong Kong, Taiwan, and Singapore is said to be due to a Ru based culture. We are told that economic success in these places is due to the ancient Chinese tradition which has emphasised family values, the importance of education, and obedience to authority.

Government officials in mainland China also seem to believe that Ru teachings are crucial to economic development. Annotated versions of the Ru classics have been reprinted and there are a large number of lectures, seminars where invited scholars discuss a wide range of philosophy and history. In 1994, a major conference was held in Beijing to celebrate the 2,425th anniversary of the birth of Confucius.

Because of economic success, these same governments now face what they identify as a crisis: the growth of greed, consumerism, selfishness, as moral behaviour and respect is lost. China's government has defined the corruption that capitalism brings as the worship of money, selfishness, the search for pleasure, a corrupt bureaucracy, gambling, drug use, and pornography (Tamney and Chiang 2002, 75). Curiously, what is encouraged in a capitalist society are often the very things that run against the kind of society these governments want to preserve. In mainland China, as in Singapore and Taiwan, Ru teachings are seen as useful first to counter the bad results of the spirit of capitalism; second, to support a work ethic; and third, to support authority.

As we shall see, this means that Ru teachings are set up in schools, but it also means that legislatively, one finds an approach that is different from the Western one. In China, Taiwan, and Singapore there are laws that say that parents who are unable to support themselves must be supported by any children who have come of age; any adult child not fulfilling this support can be charged. Governments contend that this is based in filial piety. In 1996, Singapore brought in this legislation. A government official said that this was simply a moral obligation and it would be unfair to expect "the majority of Singaporeans, who are filial to their parents, to support the parents of people who had abandoned their parents" (Tamney and Chiang 2002, 72). Others argue that these kinds of laws are to replace pension or welfare systems and to get the government off a financial hook. While saving on social spending, governments, it is charged, promote conservative values.

Taiwan has defined itself as the preserver of Chinese culture and Ru teachings as opposed to their destruction in mainland China. In Taiwan, moral education is considered a part of public education. Ru teachings are found in public and high school classes and the school textbooks emphasise patriotism, filial piety, and the group over the individual. In the early 1980's, Singapore began offering Confucian ethics as a secondary school subject. Two very well known New Confucians, Yu Ying-shih of Yale and Tu Wei-ming of Harvard, set up the material for the course. When looking at the textbooks, one can see the idea that there is a core to Ru teachings that is not the same as Ru teachings were practised in the past. The textbook tells students that the study of Ru ethics will build strong character and contribute to the economic, social, and political development of Singapore.[9] It also says:

> ... The Confucian principle of 'treating others with due respect' is very useful to follow at all levels of human relationships, especially in the superior-subordinate relationship. Each level has its duties and obligations. For example, it is the duty of those in managerial positions to lead by moral example. Subordinates, on the other hand, have a duty to be responsible and loyal to the organisation...The Confucians' deep respect for learning, personal development, discipline, and diligence all work towards the fostering of good work attitudes. (Tamney and Chiang 2002, 66)

---

9   For a for description of the curriculum, see Tamney 1988.

Students learn that loyalty and hierarchy are Ru teachings and that social groups, families, organisations, and governments work best as a kind of "benevolent form of authoritarianism" (Tamney and Chiang 2002, 79).

East Asian governments understand and teach what Tamney calls "the stripped-down version of Confucianism" (ibid., 74 and passim). Here Ru teaching is filial piety, loyalty, hierarchy, hard work, education, respect for authority, and traditional "family values." The term "family values" is not so much used, rather we find "Asian-ness." If one loses one's "Asian-ness," one betrays Chinese culture. Thus women who run counter to the governmental or societal version of Ru teaching are acting like Westerners and rejecting Chinese tradition and culture.

The governmental version of Ru teachings presents these teachings as ethics, but only as a version of ethics that will fit with a paternalist society. Thus loyalty is emphasised over the moral courage discussed by Confucius in the *Lun Yu*. This too suits government bureaucrats, political conservatives, and New Confucians. All of them agree that the state's role is to protect people from themselves.

The governmental definition of Ru teaching is slightly narrower than that of the New Confucians, but both work with many of the same assumptions. Governments, however, unlike New Confucians, believe "tradition" is identical to the Ru teachings they promote and they believe the Ru tradition to be a good thing.

Both government and New Confucian versions of Ru teaching and the role of tradition stumble badly when challenged by the women's movement. Whether implicit or explicit, Ru teachings and the governments' version of Ru tradition focus on family roles based in patriarchy, filial piety, and loyalty. Governments and scholars have attempted to deal with this by telling women that they must remain in these roles in order to preserve Chinese culture. Despite this, women's roles are changing and, however grudgingly, governments have had to initiate laws allowing for divorced women to sue for custody of their children and so on. The New Confucians have rarely addressed these issues nor have they called publicly for changes in women's roles or improvement in women's lives.

In sum, the term "tradition" is used quite differently in the study of "Confucianism." Modern Western scholars use "tradition" as a way out of the "is Confucianism a religion or philosophy" debate. While this is a workable strategy, it does not address other issues such as the term "Confucianism" itself nor the continuing, and old fashioned, assumption that Confucianism is a religion.

Xin Ruxue, New Confucianism, has virtually conceded that the May 4th movement was right: Chinese tradition was entirely bad and shaped by Ru teaching. However, the New Confucians argue that the Ru teaching found in 2,000 years of Chinese tradition was mostly incorrect. "Real" Ru teaching, as taught in the classical period, was lost in the past, the mistaken tradition. "Real" Ru teaching was preserved only by a few scholars who passed on the *daotong*. As we have seen, this leads to problems that, for the most part, the New Confucians have yet to address.

Finally, the way in which various East Asian governments have understood "tradition" is somewhat more familiar. In Singapore, Taiwan, and China, "tradition" is a pure past that represents Ru teaching, Chinese culture, and national identity. This is, of course, only a version of Ru teaching.

All of us interpret, translate, and understand ancient "traditions" based on our prejudices. What we can see from this brief survey is that these prejudices may be more ingrained and problematic than we had thought.

References

Balazs, Etienne. 1964. *Chinese Civilization and Bureaucracy*. New Haven: Yale University Press.

Berthrong, John. 1998. *Transformations of the Confucian Way*. Boulder, Colo.: Westview Press.

Bresciani, Umberto. 2001. *Reinventing Confucianism: the New Confucian Movement*. Taipei: Taipei Ricci Institute for Chinese Studies.

Chan, Wing-tsit. 1967. "The Individual in Chinese Religion." Pages 286–297 in *The Chinese Mind*. Edited by Charles Moore. Honolulu: University of Hawaii.

———. 1973. *A Sourcebook in Chinese Philosophy*. Princeton: Princeton University Press.

Hall, David L., and Roger T. Ames. 1987. *Thinking Through Confucius*. Albany: State University of new York Press.

Ivanhoe, Philip J., and Bryan W. Van Norden. 2001. *Readings in Classical Chinese Philosophy*. New York: Seven Bridges Press.

Jensen, Lionel. 1997. *Manufacturing Confucianism: Chinese Traditions and Universal Civilization*. Durham: Duke University Press.

Jung-kuo, Yang. 1974. *Confucius, "Sage" of the Reactionary Classes*. Peking: Foreign Languages Press.

Koller, John and Patricia. 1998. *Asian Philosophies*. Upper Saddle River, N. J.: Prentice Hall.

Latourette, Kenneth. 1928. *A History of Christian Missions in China*. London: Society for Promoting Christian Knowledge.

Leibniz, Gottfried Wilhelm. 1977. *Discourse on the Natural History of the Chinese*. Translated by Henry Rosemont Jr. and Daniel J. Cook. Hawaii: University of Hawaii Press.

Maspero, Henri. 1981. *Taoism and Chinese Religion*. Translated by F.A. Kiernan. Amherst: University of Massachusetts Press.

Paper, Jordan. 1998. *The Chinese Way in Religion*. Belmont, Calif.: Wadsworth Publ.

Schwartz, Benjamin. 1973. "The Limits of 'Tradition Versus Modernity' as Categories of Explanation: the Case of Chinese Intellectuals." Pages 69–81 in *Intellectuals and Tradition*. Edited by Shmuel N. Eisenstadt and Stephen R. Graubard. New York: Humanities Press.

———. 1985. *The World of Thought in Ancient China*. Cambridge: Belknap Press.

Smith, D. Howard. 1968. *Chinese Religions*. London: Weidenfeld and Nicholson.

Suleski, Ronald. 2002. *Civil Government in Warlord China: Tradition, Modernization, and Manchuria*. New York etc.: Lang.

Tamney, Joseph B. 1988. "Religion and the State in Singapore." *Journal of Church and State* 30: 109–128.

———, and Linda Hsueh-Ling Chiang. 2002. *Modernization, Globalization, and Confucianism in Chinese Societies*. Westport, Conn.: Praeger.

Taylor, Rodney L. 1986. *The Way of Heaven: An Introduction to Confucian Religious Life*. Leiden: Brill.

Dispatches from Memory: Genealogies of Tradition

Earle H. Waugh

1. Fore-thoughts

1.1. The Academy and Religious Tradition

The academic study of tradition has had to deal with the historical vicissitudes of the word many of which, especially in the contemporary situation, turn out to be negative. These vicissitudes grew out of situating its meanings relative to social and cultural trends, trends that arose not out of tradition itself, but out of the milieu in which traditions sat. Thus, for example, the academy was concerned to understand tradition within the evolutionary model widely accepted after the Enlightenment. That conception seemed to imply that tradition was buried in the past, and was unchanging, whereas what was relevant was change as modernity became the ground against which much cultural analysis was made. Such a move placed tradition in the unhappy position of representing the stable and abiding values of a people, while being relegated to a past that was stolid and unavailable for development. This conception particularly affected the anthropological dimensions of the study of religion, but it lived on in the view that the least developed of the religions were archaic or primitive.

In *Religionswissenschaft* or the History of Religions/Comparative Religions, this contrast had other specific repercussions. For one thing, it meant that 'traditional' societies had no 'real' history, that though they were living today they were not dynamic like the Western culture, even though it was acknowledged that there were living 'traditions,' such as Hinduism and Buddhism. Max Müller, the father of the discipline, used tradition as a means of distinguishing the entire panoply of elements of one religion from another, while at the same time restricting the use of the term to religious items that were continuous with the past or at least were clearly not generated by modernity. The assumption was clear: modern society could not be traditional, and traditional society could not be modern—scholarship became entangled in the language of contraries and opposites.

At the same time, various religions unhampered by the evolutionary framework of scholarship, continued to use the word to define important aspects of their own religious systems. Christian scholars, whether Catholic or Protestant, constructed edifices upon tradition and eliminated each other from the building on the same ground. Another twist in the academy occurred with the Parliament of Religions in Chicago in 1893, which shifted the focus away from traditional peoples to those who had viable 'traditions' in the modern world. Traditional people continued to be used in reference to various 'primitive' societies, whereas tradition was rehabilitated to represent the continuing identity of major religions, a usage much more in keeping with Christian theological usage.

1.2. The Academy and Consequences of Traditionalism

Following the Second World War, when the academic study of religion moved to North America, some of the anomalies of this situation became more apparent. Not far from many of these new departments were enclaves of Aboriginal peoples, many with rich cultural and religious traditions, which the denizens thereof refused to call traditions but customs. There was no way to treat these customs as legitimate religions under the evolutionary model. Theoretically, the religions and customs of these peoples were given place through a vague kind of *traditionalism*, i.e. they continued to represent values of a distant religious system not clearly articulated by the peoples today. This is also the name of a movement of rather nebulous character, as so identified by the first to write of it, Mark Sedgwick (2004). As he sees it, scholars like Ananda Coomaraswamy, Huston Smith, Mircea Eliade, and Seyyed Hossein Nasr developed an intellectual tradition within America that arose out of the post-war disillusionment in Europe—the loss of faith in Christian spirituality and ethical authority, along with a rejection of the modern as the direction for the future. It cultivated a shift to Eastern religions, and it valorized the notion of a secret Perennial Philosophy held to be expressed more or less in all religious traditions. The Perennial Philosophy was based roughly on ideas developed by the French writer René Guenon (1886–1931), the Sufi convert who moved to Cairo and established his own order. This interpretation of traditionalism will need critical analysis quite beyond our intent at the moment, but some aspects of the theory are relevant for our discussion.

Sedgwick weaves together a complex history of leading individuals and a mixture of critical ideas, including primordialism. It is this later idea that interests us in this essay, for through primordialization, religion and thought of the so-called primitives were incorporated into Religious Studies. A range of ideas and terms were introduced into religious studies analyses by this notion, but it was particularly obvious in the use of terms like 'archaic religion,' that had a certain aura of antiquity and grandeur about it, or 'primitive religion,' which really could not be applied to the people down the road because they did not seem to fit and it would not be proper to refer to them as primitives—after all they were living alongside other modern religions without apparent difficulty. So, too, the term 'traditional.' This word seemed to account for the religions that did not fit the evolutionary pattern. At the same time, tradition itself seemed anything but unchanging among these peoples—that made the meaning of the term even more suspect, even false. However, one might note that with the vague notions of primordialism, traditionalism, etc., Religious Studies theory moved away from the main problems of evolution, maintaining tradition as a concept whose 'real' meaning arose only in a religious context.

Thus, whereas anthropology was caught in the overthrow of evolution, Religious Studies opted for a 'soft' traditionalism and primordialism to explain the religions of traditional peoples. In this way it escaped the most baleful implications of reducing traditional peoples to primitives. Sedgwick's study, especially of some of the important figures of traditionalism will need more critical evaluation than can be given here, but it must be noted that what such a use of traditionalism does is to argue for a sense of tradition that transcends any one tradition. In fact we find holistic notions like this quite apart from believers in this so-called movement that might indicate that traditionalism is both larger than and restricted by Sedgwick's historical model—in Chinese philosophy for one, as Harvard's Tu Weiming notes:

> Religion flows, religion is not something static. It interacts, it transforms itself. The dynamism is precisely its ability to deal with human situations, conditions, in a long-term perspective. But religion is not just personal. It is inter-personal, it is also between us as human beings and the cosmos as a whole—the animals, the plants, the trees, all these things are relevant to our religious consciousness. I don't think there's any other tradition, no matter how broadly defined—scientistic, rational, humanistic—that would be able to encompass that broader arena.[1]

1.3. Tradition Studies and the Aftermath of Colonialism

At the same time, the construction of Religious Studies departments was influenced by another movement, which espoused an enlarged meaning of tradition. Emboldened by Christian scholars (Congar, MacIntyre, Charlesworth, et al.) and, in a strange symmetry, replicated in the Muslim world (Shari'ati, Assad, Fazlur Rahman, al-Shakani, Mawdudi, et al.), insistence on a revised sense of tradition developed, now with attention to the cultural context of any flowering 'tradition.' The old focus on the details of the tradition could no longer be determined by the texts themselves, but required the whole mass of choices available at the time the element defined as tradition arose. Issues of authority

---

1   Fernandez-Armesto, raconteur of a debate on tradition on the BBC notes: "Tu Weiming sees religion as hyper-scientific; indeed, better-equipped to comprehend and manage our relations with the world and each other than science, logic, humanities or any system based on secular knowledge. If he's right, religion must have some extra in-gredient—some special power that alternative systems haven't got. This may explain why so many secular movements cannibalise religious myths, copy religious rituals." *The Mysterious Opiate: Transcript of a Recorded Documentary.* Presenter: Felipe Fernández-Armesto, Producer: Simon Coates, Editor: Nicola Meyrick. Broadcast Date: 06.04.00. Tape Number: TLN012/00VT1014.

and inclusion, constructions of future and past became ingredients for tradition. Tradition once again became a viable, and considerably expanded, paradigm.

This project had the benefit of leaving the word tradition intact for the professionals of all stripe in the universities, but it only delayed the day when the impact of evolutionary ideology would come home to roost. Once the decolonization project began in non-Western countries, then the Religious Studies academy saw that their analyses had not just been tainted by imperialist assumptions, but that their own work was the basis for governmental and church discrimination against 'traditional' peoples. Reductionisms of many sorts were found in religious scholarship. The religious academicians had to face the fact that their implicit commitments had contributed to a trajectory of dire religious consequence.

While evolutionary ideology in Religious Studies was problematic, it took on more embarrassing connotations in other disciplines. When Hobsbawm and Ranger (1983) from history and anthropology showed that those prized elements that everyone thought were quite 'traditional' were really recent inventions, it no longer became possible to use the term with any sense of security. The religious academy wondered aloud that, if traditions were invented, how could they also be the basis of a solid system of cultural values which religious scholarship so stressed? How convincing was any 'tradition'? If the tradition held by a particular religion was, in reality not 'old,' what happens to the venerated past that is so much part of most religions? What continued? If there were no continuations from a timeless past, how valid was the theological system that rested on this authoritative moment in many religions? With the potential for such knotty problems, the academy generally became very restrained in its use, or used it in only clearly defined ways; the Religious Studies academy reacted by opting for a method based on formal history to insure that facts could be distinguished from invention. The problem was that formal histories were themselves constructions, usually put together by experts, with an eye to their peers, related to formal histories rooted in the West. No non-western religious system would accept those histories as authoritative. And they certainly couldn't claim scientific objectivity, at least from the perspective of a community outside the Western orb.

1.4. Religious Tradition and the 'Scientific' Model

Religious Tradition. For us, it is always more comforting to begin with the historical, since that seems to ground the truth of what we are doing most essentially. A quick glance will show this is what the above section does. It may be false confidence, but it is our practice. The procedure has a familiar ring to it, since, as we all now know, Socrates launched us into reflection on tradition by his philosophical discussion of the issue—a discussion that puts religion on the defensive immediately. He thought you had to break through the 'sacredness' of tradition to find 'truth,' a procedure that relied on intellect and not on revelation. For anyone in the religious academy, this severing of religion from truth was a feature that did not and does not bode well for any kind of viable analysis of 'tradition'—how much of it is 'myth' and how much 'truth'? Most particularly, given the open-faced critique of religious tradition, Western religion, specifically Christianity, had to deal with an academy that divorced truth from religious tradition, despite the extreme confidence it had in the mind to construct a legitimate theology.

Greek thought having set the pattern, the religious studies academy seemed to be dealing with a topic that was divorced from intellect. Religion and tradition lay outside the realm of the mind and Western culture continued to resist any analysis that incorporated religious tradition into the centre of western development. Until our own time. What changed?

With a welter of options, let's chose Derrida: "Today once again, today finally, today otherwise, the great question would still be religion and what some hastily call its 'return'" (Derrida 1998). If Socrates had abandoned religious tradition to its own devices, and thereby set up the two parallel streams in Western consciousness, faith and reason, it follows that the religious scientist, with only a nose for truth, should follow strictly the reason track. With that argument Wiebe would heartily agree that "the objective, scientific model for the study of religion presented by Jastrow is the only appropriate model for the study of religion in the public university" (Wiebe 1999, 87, n. 5). Except that Derrida holds that (post 9/11, *today* itself demonstrates the view's falsity. In fact, then, Socrates had been in error, and with him countless scholars like Wiebe. Not only is religion back, not only is the concept of God back (Derrida speaks as if they are equivalent), but the *experience* of God is back at the same time (following Manoussakis 2005).

Today experiencing God matters in the public square, and it can be violent. *And that means that all the problems of tradition are back too, only more so.* As Watson rightly points out, "Science itself, as Popper, for example, realized, was not only inseparable from both myth and tradition, but was in fact part of a critical tradition to be traced from Socrates himself (and onward to Derrida), and similarly was inseparable from attempts to grapple with (and to circumscribe) the sacred" (Watson 2001, 43). So the point is *only more so* because we not only have built into our religious discourse the Socratic way of orienting ourselves, but now we have the full force of many religions that refuse to accept a so-called science of religion that does not appear to accept the distortion of its own memory. Most religions do not feel comfortable with *our* familiar pattern of looking at reality (i.e. *there is one official history*, cf. Hamilton 2003) and they disagree with an imperialist academy that acts like its own memory is *the* memory for all.

A case in point is Vine Deloria, Jr.'s, latest book, *Evolution, Creationism, and Other Modern Myths.* In it he attacks the scientific notion of slow 'natural' evolution, arguing rather for a third way of thinking that "examines the rich verbal traditions handed down from non-Western culture over thousands of years, which speak of worlds prior to the one we now inhabit" (Deloria 2003). He insists on the validity of the earth as formed by a series of catastrophes, a notion he finds expressed in a number of non-Western traditions, including Hindu, Tibetan and Chinese. He argues that Western scholars cannot have a clear notion of genuine tradition, because such a view already should include the notion of religion; religion cannot be separate from science or anything else. Thus he argues that our academic disciplines have invented separate categories of analysis, which have then been accepted as 'facts' by traditions within each discipline. Contrast this with Aboriginal thinkers who begin with "an ensemble vision of the world around them and seek to find our species a harmonious place in it" (Moore 2003). This view he regards as completely empirical, while the West has really taken the opposite perspective and built upon a series of segregated fields constructed from dogmas and abstract ideas.

Deloria's argument is couched in theoretical terms; it does not explicitly address the hegemonic repercussions implicit in Western scientism for religious studies. However, what seems even worse to Aboriginal thinkers and others of my acquaintance is the contemporary religion academy's apparently obliviousness to ethical realities, viz., the academy now has no moral ground upon which to apply its analytic tools willy-nilly, for it has been dealing, not with truth, but with flawed perspectives—look what it did with 'traditional' people—relegating them to the 'primitive.' Even if it does recognize distinctive Aboriginal religion's own ideas as legitimate, why would practitioners now trust the academy with their religious traditions?

1.5. Toward a Grounding of Tradition

What follows spells out another start to the tradition question. I shall argue that tradition is grounded upon memory, not a 'factual' memory in the old 'scientific' notion of an objective datum, but in terms of an experiential memory that validates a religious process of going back. Of course, that resulting past is 'constructed' but it is not manufactured, as if one could go to the assembly line and identify the objects as they are introduced. Rather tradition is comprised of a corporate past that is validated by personal experience or modified according to interaction with a variety of personal, cultural and social incursions—but the memory does not come across as forced or phoney—it is *the real past*. It is based upon the fact that all we have to build upon is our memory, so we must return to how memory operates constructively and convincingly in our lives. This is the underpinning of intellectual knowing through memory. In this sketch, some of the bases for confronting the larger issues of the study of tradition from a potential memory model are laid out, including the primacy of formative experience, the role of memory in retaining significant data and the evidence from my contemporary study of memory's operation in religion in Morocco.

2. Memory and the Underpinning of Tradition

Can we recover an innocence sense of tradition? At what moment in childhood do we become aware of religious tradition? What remnant of memory delivers 'tradition'? Of all the myriad of experiences in a child's life, why is something remembered and accorded the word tradition? We can do little more than hint at the details here. Once we begin to rummage in the past, we rarely find a consistent image arising, just a series of acts and meanings that seem to be pointers to how one first engaged what was 'important' to one's family. Here's one from my memory bank: the take-off point was the constancy of Bible-reading and prayers before bed that set us aside from my friends. Instinctively, I didn't talk about it to my friends, it was just my family who shared this "treasure"; furthermore it seemed more important than other things that we did that they didn't. This was reinforced in my case by the articulation, "We don't live like that because this is what we do" that served to define our 'tradition.' There was a line-in-the-sand, untouchable quality to it. Nobody said it was 'sacred'; I gathered it was. (That's how I knew what sacred was when priests, philosophers and Religious Studies types later talked about it, but we never used the term at home.)

Beyond that, somewhere in my impressionable mind I was also convinced that a strange occurrence on my life was 'powerful,' even beyond this world. At about five years of age, I had discovered a hidden realm within a circle of tightly interwoven trees; there I created my 'fort.' One day a strange hush fell over my domain, not a leaf seemed to move, not a twig dropped. Within that hush came another kind of sound, a still silence of something that I immediately regarded as beyond the natural. It was a sound from a transcendent realm, a spirit world if you will, although I knew little to nothing about the spirit world. The whole fort seemed transformed by this moment. Stunned, I hurried to my mother's side, and she sought to ease my perturbed mind with, "It was only a bird." I didn't believe her. (Lesson learned—parents pass on the family's tradition, but a child's does not count in defining the tradition.) Somehow, this experience had coded something important for me, and in the future this experience became more and more an element of a tradition about transcendence in nature for me. This became another line in the sand of my memory.

This reference to youth and early development suggests that formative moments serve to provide the basis for tradition—in effect a kind of validation and a consistency to meaning passed on at some moment of one's coming-to-consciousness about what matters most, and it was (is) ours (or mine), and not everybody's! At the same time, the traditions I became aware of involved also the meaning and interpretation of those memories: they had a cultural context (the prayers, the trees), and a history (my growing awareness of meaning, my mother's denial of my experience's legitimacy). Yet, at bottom, *it is an* experience *that is brought out of a context and made conscious as an authoritative memory. The experience is not invented, but rather the process of it becoming a tradition reflects the 'religifying' capabilities of one's psychology and culture. It also signifies the import-*

ance of the formative for us, since that formation is the apparent grounds for further interpretation. And that points unmistakably to memory as the foundation of tradition.

Yet we all say that memory cannot be trusted—we all forget. Surely memory cannot be the basis for how we discern reality. Well, the plain fact is we do remember, and we remember in certain ways, and we stand upon that memory. The real question is why do we do this if memory is so inconsequential? In the reading here, it is evident that there is a naïve reading back in all tradition. The point is not that this should define tradition but that it makes the point of grounding tradition in *a process of intuitive going back*, and even though we may later reject some of the results, *the reference points for tradition have been set in an experience remembered.* Such a statement has the added authority of Hegel, for he had the idea that "all thought may well (both by intuition and coherence) begin in remembrance (*Erinnerungen*)" as Watson (2001, 7) noted.

Furthermore, there is solid empirical evidence that tradition is rooted in the epistemology of memory, from whence it is writ large by the social nature of the 'we.' This point rides upon the common valuing of words and meanings in the foundation of Western tradition. Tradition, despite my 'fort' experience, is not solitary (I have not passed this experience on to my children by setting up enclosed forts for them, but it certainly has played a role in my understanding of transcendence). The meaning really goes back to the Latin origins of the word tradition, which is *tradere*, a word that reflects a composite of a prefix '*trans*' and a verb '*dare.*' The resulting meaning brought together 'across' and 'to give/ hand over' thus implying that our word tradition has *delivery, surrender,* and even *betrayal* as cognate references. All contain with them the notion of things being handed over (Rudebusch 1988). It also suggests that handing over makes claims, as the meaning of betrayal signifies. As with most words, accretions have been added with time, so that a vast range of ideas, things, solutions and processes now are said to be "a tradition," like a local brewery in business for a few years claiming a brewing tradition. Yet the processes of memory provide the same foundation, and assign a normative meaning to it. From our very first encounter, then, tradition appears to be a complex and dynamic web of relationships and norms,[2] distinguishing us from "them," and empowering identity by an authoritative pattern. It would appear that, in dispatching tradition, memory utilizes emotional, intuitive and ethical sensitivities.

In my study on the Moroccan chanters (Waugh 2005) I have found a similar model—a definitive experience that takes on a normative role in religious life, and it is directly related to the position that memory plays in Moroccan life. The finding there was that the chanter reached back through memory to a moment of encounter with spiritual verities, and tried to recast his chanting to return there during the rituals of remembrance (*dhikr*). The result is that the power of the original experience functions as a benchmark to which the chanter goes in

---

2   For one statement of the dynamic nature of tradition, see Slater 1978.

order to imbue his current chanting with that same kind of religious power. In effect, the past moment of power is imported into the current situation through memory, where it serves as the tool to bring the sacred presence to the mass of people who are participating in the ritual. For the chanter, memory is religion's means to deliver God's power to the believers. Based on this study, one could conclude that the specific process of returning to a validating experience and the tools that provide the content on any particular occasion will be religion-specific. What appears to be in place is a particular process of "experiencing tradition," a particular kind of genealogy of memory, if you will.

This suggests that, in effect, each religion has genealogies of memory, reaching across a wide range of cultural and religious elements to form distinctive paradigms of the religious tradition. Yet all claim to be within the tradition. In what follows, we will explore a few issues in the genealogy of memories. I have identified these elements as *dispatches,* implying thereby their quick and obviously incomplete configuration, but by my reading each of these elements demonstrates a distinctive genealogy—both within the religions involved, as well as the problematic of Religious Studies in understanding these genealogies. All demonstrate important assumptions about the way memory should be coded and understood religiously.

In the first dispatch, we will present two stories concerning the genealogies of religious memory, showing how memory shapes their uses: (a) shamanism within Aboriginal religion, by which the issue of who 'owns' or has authoritative claims on a definite religious experience is the key issue, and (b) *hadith,* or 'tradition' within contemporary Islam, by which the standards drawn from the Prophet's life are codified and assembled as a model for true Muslim life. Both of these demonstrate how memory is put together in various ways within religions (including, perhaps, in irrational ways)—with the implication that the contemporary reconstruction of tradition cannot rely upon a particular analytic model, (i.e. history or theology), to decode that religious tradition. In the second dispatch, we will deal with how tradition studies/religious studies relies upon its own coding structure to delineate the parameters of tradition, focusing particularly on three ideological concerns that continue to play a role in how the academy broaches the issue of tradition.

2. The First Dispatch: Stories about Genealogies of Memory

2.1. The Ownership of Shamanism

There appears to be several ways of looking at the interpretation of tradition across religious frontiers, and one of these demonstrates the problematic of applying the word, within a tradition, while allowing outsiders to apply it to a new but related tradition. Here we refer to the interpretation of shamanism for consideration. In the debate the central issue has been what the nature of this religious experience really is; furthermore and related is the issue of whether a religious tradition has to live within a particular religious context in order to be considered legitimate. For example, if shamanism is to bear the weight of one of the defining arenas of the human comprehension of the sacred, as Eliade argued, or even of its significant ritual formulations (as contemporary 'modes of consciousness' analysts suggest), can we 'know' shamanism through extracting it from its cultural and religious context? What is shamanism if it is not defined by the practices of people who developed it? Here it will be helpful to examine the Cree use of the word to see whether it delivers the meanings placed upon it by Religious Studies analysts.

One central issue in this area is 'Who...?' Who has the authority to authenticate shamanic ideology—who is remembering the 'true tradition'? Described at some length by Eliade in his *Shamanism: Archaic Techniques of Ecstasy*, the rendition he gave of shamanism foregrounds the techniques the shaman uses to relate to the spirit world. His structure emphasizes the importance of ascent to the spirit world, the mystical journey, encounter with the denizens of the otherworld, his struggle with the spirits and finally his return to this world armed with the results of his interview with the mistress of animals or the equivalent. For Eliade, the shaman was a practitioner of these techniques of interaction, at the root of which was his manipulation of the spirit world for human benefit. What Eliade is implying is that the experience of the shaman reflects the fundamental roots of religious understanding, for this experience cites interaction with the other world as the locus of all traditional religious systems. This was an archaic religious experience.

If this rendition were accurate, then one would expect it to be carried on in contemporary traditional practices, that is, among people who practice shamanism. The only other option is to argue for some kind of theory of decay, but why would a fundamental way of being religious experience ever 'decay'? What would that say about notions of fundamentals? So let us take a case of the shaman in contemporary practice.

Because of the complex situation of such practices, the shaman is not necessarily the zenith of health or medicine power in Aboriginal communities. This is demonstrated in the Cree community. In fact, there are several different specialists among the Cree, which I know best, that indicates that healing is not the primary area of the shaman at all, who, in many cases, is not a healer but a spiritual authority whose abilities in communicating with the spirit world evolved into a kind of 'guardian angel' for the social unit to which he was connected. It is true that part of this spiritual power could be expressed in prophetic form or even as advisory knowledge of the future. Still the central feature among the Cree people I know sees the shaman as handling a reality that is quite beyond the normal, and his area of jurisdiction fundamentally deals with the larger arena of the social well-being of the group itself. This is made clear by a close look at the 'healing' structure of the Cree people. This structure is much wider and deeper than our notion of healing or medicine; good medicine can encompass good food, even activities that brighten the day. In what follows I will sketch the wide range of words from the *Alberta Elders Cree Dictionary* (LeClaire & Cardinal 1998); in this collection on which our team laboured for over 27 years, the writers had to deal with many difficult constellation of terms.

Health and healing can be classified as one of those difficult areas. For example, shamanism is translated by *mamāhtāwisit*, that is, *the result of spirit power*. Yet the term can only be understood from the context of spirit world giftedness, not of unbridled power—that is, the spirit world sees fit to gift certain individuals for the benefit of the people, and the shaman is one of those gifted people. This is clear by examining other related terms: *mamāhtāweyimew*— *S/he thinks her/him to be spiritually gifted*, or *mamāhtāwihikowin*—*the spiritual power given*. The initial segment of the word, *mamāhtā* relates to exalted, or glorious as in "he holds an exalted place in the whole community." But it can also refer to something like "spiritual relationship beyond this world" or even what we would call "spiritual authority," implying a dimension of spirit encounter involved in the shaman's definition. However it is understood, there is clearly a community dimension to its understanding.

It follows that one can lose one's exalted place if it is found that one uses power improperly, because the spirit gift need not be considered permanent. This means, then, that shamanism is subject to some community restraints and conventions; what is proper in Cree tradition is that the community agrees upon a legitimate area of behaviour for a shaman, and his/her power is limited to that. It is also subject to community affirmation to begin with. Every individual has his own spiritual path to trod, and within a small community, those who deal with spiritual things are a select and small group. Their activity is closely monitored, their spiritual power minutely discussed. Note, too, that nowhere does this definition specifically dictate how that spirit power will be expressed—i.e. as a journey to the world of the spirits or as a mediator between the world of the spirits and the ordinary world of humans. Nor does it say anything about ecstasy. It certainly is known that someone with *mamāhtā* may be subject to ecstasy, but the word does not necessarily mean that that will be the case all the time. So, in Cree, the pattern of spiritual expression may differ with individuals. This view is quite in keeping with the view that the person is a composite of forces unique to each. The ideology of individual independence is quite strong among the Cree people, and this applies to the experiences of a spiritual sort (see Mann 2005 for a preliminary notion of this feature).

Properly, in Plains and Woods Cree, there are different words for "a healer"—in Woods Cree, *āstehowew*, in Plains Cree, *otiyinikahiwew*. The Woods term belongs to a set of words that mean to heal, to recuperate, to make one feel better, while the Plains word also implies stopping or placing a barrier, suggesting an inhibitional intent, along with the notion of intervention. It seems evident, then, that the *mamāhtā*-person, deals with something quite different than healing, whose propensities are related more to these other terms. The shaman, then, has a community dimension, reflecting a giftedness deemed related to the spiritual power in the community, not to the specific issue of healing or even community health *per se*.

On the other hand, medicine man is *maskihkiwiskwew*, a term that carries several meanings, one of which sometimes is translated by our term shaman. Here the emphasis is on one who treats illnesses. The term 'shaman' can be used for the medicine person if s/he uses the good spirit to offset evil spirits, in effect, utilizes contact with the good spirits to overthrow the influence of the bad spirits in the health of a person. In that case, the term best used is *nanāta-wihiwewiyinow*, whose initial segment refers to being grateful, and the later segment implies variety and diversity, suggesting that the medicine person maintains a submissive or grateful relationship with the good spirits and is rewarded with a variety of ways to assist his people.

The notion behind this is the Cree belief in two contending realities in the universe, one that may be defined as good, while the other is said to be evil—a rather unfortunate set of words from the Cree perspective. Perhaps positive and negative would be better. These realities are not beings but can be understood as perspectives within the universe that certainly do have human implications. One way of addressing these perspectives is to note that two people may look at the same sunset and one see terrible foreboding, while another see absolute beauty. These diverse options for 'seeing' are not necessarily personally gener-ated, i.e. because one is in a good mood the other not, but are part of the way the universe expresses itself to humans. These are not 'inventions,' but part of the cosmos' way of comporting itself to human observers. Thus the shaman has to 'see' correctly, because the healing of the person depends upon his ability.

Furthermore we must be aware that the *mamāhtā*-idea reflects something of the spirit power in the universe, rooted right here in the human community, in a larger sense than just for healing. George Cardinal, Cree elder who worked on the Dictionary indicated that the *mamāhtā*-idea reflects Cree notions of having a community shaman powerful enough to offset an equivalent in another com-munity who might want to bring evil upon the local people for some reason—in effect, that person is a spiritual guardian who is powerful enough and gifted enough to ward off any unsavoury influence from a shaman in a neighbouring group who, through his power, might intend evil against the community. The shaman is the community bulwark and spirit-gifted person who can be the focus of appreciation, while, at the same time, a person whom one might fear.

What all this suggests is that the use of the term 'shaman' as a kind of 'one definition fits all' paradigm cannot be sustained. Cree tradition alone indicates that our word shaman only partially addresses the complexity of healing con-ceptions in this local case, implying that other cultures might well define the whole healing tradition in another manner. We are left to conclude that there is a powerful 'shaman tradition' among the Cree, but it is much more diversified than Eliade and others had imagined. This raises basic questions about the project of extracting such a paradigm from existing data, and suggests that the tradition of shamanism might be better understood within each group that utilizes the religious practice, with much more modest results coming from that analysis than weighing it with being an archaic experience of religious humanity.

Enter Michael Harner. Harner is an anthropologist who worked among the South American Jivaro people. After considerable work among them, he came to understand shamanism as a potentially universal way of organizing human understanding of the world and of course, the spirits in it. His successful career in anthropology convinced him of the validity of the approach and he formed an independent organization to promote this 'archaic' way of knowing. He developed training sessions to awaken New Agers and others to the potential for well-being in shamanism, and continues to train seekers to this day.

He wants to argue that the shamanic experience is open to whomever the spirit picks. Harner contends that the shamanic experience is a very archaic structure in human consciousness, with the potential to revolutionize our way of looking at health and well-being. The result is that he trains many whites to be shamans, a procedure condemned by medicine people from Aboriginal traditions all over the world, including medicine people among my Cree associates.

Theoretically, von Stuckrad and others have argued that the term shaman should be expanded to include the activities of modern-day practitioners like Harner and his followers, since there is no real structural difference in what they are proposing. Aboriginal thinkers, however, argue that this is just one more example of 'white' culture appropriating the intellectual capital of Aboriginal people without proper deference to the real authorities, and without acknowledgement as to who 'owns' the tradition. They contend that people like Harner have no right to this appropriation—it was not passed on by ritual formula, according to the rules of suffering, fasting, etc. that characterized the original tradition. Moreover the entire restraint system of the community is lacking.

We are left with the query: Who has ownership of any religious memory? Furthermore, what right does an academic have to study such phenomena and then develop his/her own model of valid religious experience based upon them? If tradition is rooted in one religious and cultural context, then ethically and probably theoretically the answer appears to be 'none.' It is difficult to skirt the conclusion that tradition must be left in the hands of the practitioners, and that scholarship has no right to lift it from those roots for its own purposes, even to develop a new religion. It would appear that this conclusion denies the right of the academy to utilize the concept "tradition" unless it is willing to accept that it has its own model, drawn from its own memory, deriving from its own concerns, *which then differs from tradition born within a religious community.*

2.2. Wrestling with Tradition in Islam

Remembering the Prophet, his contribution to Islam and his normative behaviour has always constituted a fundamental element of Islamic life. In the story here, we look specifically at Sunni developments, for in Shi'ism recent debates have been stirred by Shari'ati, who has tried to update the authoritative role of the Imam in that religious worldview (Shari'ati 1979). Throughout the development of Sunni Islam (see Rahman 1966, 43–73; Burton 1995), determining and understanding tradition has always been a contested issue. The word translated as 'tradition' encompasses both the *sunna* of the Prophet and the *hadith*. The *sunna* are practices of the Prophet, i.e normative acts and activities associated with him that were subsequently reported upon and deemed to set standards for Muslims. At the same time his statements about matters relative to Muslim faith and practice were recorded and passed on in the *hadith*. Both the *sunna* and the *hadith* are held to be valuable for determining Muslim tradition. In many ways, Muslim tradition is much like MacIntyre's on Catholic tradition: "A living tradition…is an historically extended, socially embodied argument, an argument precisely in part about the goods which constitute that tradition" (MacIntyre 1981, 207). The details of the *hadith* were passed on via reports. These reports were then collected and rules of authentication were established by the collectors of the *hadith* in the years following the death of the Prophet. This material became the basis for the court system; *shari'a* or law was the chief institutional requiring this data.

Unlike Catholicism, there is no final authority for authenticating the tradition. In classical Sunni Islam, that is, from about the end of the eighth century through to the tenth, a scholarly 'guild,' the *'ulama* was fostered whose principal task it was to interpret Islam for its followers. They also were required to give guidance on matters of law. Much of their role revolved around the interpretation of tradition. These individuals, drawn from the educated classes of Islamic society, became the determiners of 'normative' Sunnism, in that their interpretations of *hadith* established the rules and behaviours of Muslim life.

Enter the modern era. Countries fell under the colonial administrations of various European powers, none of which used Islamic law as it had been utilized in classical times. In most cases, various forms of European law became the basis for the legal system, with Islamic law accorded provisional status for such things as marriage and divorce and other direct social issues (e.g. estate law).

When the colonial period ended in these countries, the issue became how much of the classical system would be re-instated. Under the impact of Western criticism, some argued for the abandonment of most forms of Islamic law, a reform of modernization designed to bring Islamic law up to date. However, there were a number of issues that had to be decided, including whether the traditions handed on from the classical scholars was really rigorous enough to meet contemporary standards. Who was to determine this? Of course the *'ulama* wanted to reserve the right to adjudicate all *hadith*—they did not want to lose powers they had accumulated over the centuries—but they were challenged by modern scholars trained in other disciplines, who wanted to bring a new perspective to the law. In this way, who should determine the tradition, how it was to be determined, the role of rationality in the process, and what role the Qur'an and secular views should be taken into consideration—all these became contested arenas.

Tradition, then, has been handed on, and the very process of that handing on is subject to debate. Of the many issues that deserve examination, we can only summarize the issue of rationality here. We have selected this because it closely relates to the debate in the West over the use of rational thought in articulating tradition; however it must be acknowledged that this issue has played a much less significant role than others in the Muslim case, for the simple reason that Islam has reserved only a limited place for theological reasoning in its development. Much more pertinent is on what occasion the Prophet may have said or done something, and what his intention was. Thus, in an effort to determine whether his act was meant to be a norm in a legal sense or whether the meaning of the act was imposed on it by later Muslim community requirements of a later period became a matter of logical debate. The handing on process required a winnowing 'rationality' regarding the ingredients of what was passed on and how it was to be understood. In the Muslim case, the issue of reason arises in the first place in the context of interpretation.

The significant Muslim question is: If *hadith* have been passed on that are contrary to reason, are they still normative? As Brown indicates in his important study, *Rethinking Tradition in Modern Islamic Thought* the context for rational thinking was set in classical times by al-'Ashari, who argued that rationality should not mediate disputes within Islamic life (d. 935). Whether these views should be continued became an arena of contention, with traditional *'ulama* standing against those who wanted to revive *shari'a* (this group is now usually referred to as fundamentalists), against those who thought the *hadith* were too suspect for directing contemporary Muslims (deniers of *hadith* and Western scholars, orientalists), and against those advocates of a return to an Islam of an earlier era (*salafis*):

> Conservative critics of revivalist approaches to sunna have been quick to label their opponents rationalists and to point out the affinity of the ideas of writers such as Mawdudi and Ghazali to the ideas of the deniers of hadith and orientalists. Salafi claims that Shibli, Islahi and Mawdudi, while not denying hadith altogether, have done irreparable damage to the cause of hadith by encouraging unrestrained personal opinion in the criticism of hadith. (Brown 1996, 130)

'Rationality' was then used as a brush to tar those who wanted significant change to the tradition even if they were not using rationalist arguments themselves. Even someone like Muhammad 'Abduh of Egypt (d. 1905), who wants to revive *hadith*, is loath to be seen as applying anything like Western logic or science (Brown 1996, 130). Hence, even reform can be taken as a code word for rationalism. Still, even Salafis will argue that some kind of rational argument is necessary, for such beloved *hadith* as the Prophet's ascent to heaven (the *mi'raj*) can be denied by them because his only miracle, sanctioned by the Qur'an is the Qur'an itself. This means that theological reason is acceptable even by those who would deny other kinds of reason.

The problems that are tinged by rationality are then not easy to articulate because they may be hidden in debate using language and perspectives rooted in the classical collections. Unlike Plato, with reason a direct option instead of revelation, Sunni Muslims are debating how much of Muslim intellectual considerations are acceptable today, how one reaches an authentic tradition, how much of today's standards of 'acceptability' should be incorporated into the *hadith,* and how open scholarship should be to alternative voices. This means that there is no doubt that Islam preserves itself through its memory, but the content of that memory and whose memory will be accepted by the majority view is at the centre of contention. As Robertson notes, we have today the self-conscious conflict between alternative memories—traditions that collide at several levels—"the issue of *competing collective memories* has also become a prominent feature of global life" (Robertson and Chirico 1985, 219).

In sum, the Muslim case demonstrates that the issue is not as simple as parallel paths of reason and faith, as Plato bequeathed to us, nor is it really the attempt to fit a traditional religion into today's world, but to what extent rationality can be utilized to construct any tradition at all. Furthermore, it indicates that the 'rational' itself becomes contentious, just because it is allied with Western philosophic and scientific hegemony. How could the Western model of that rationality deign itself to design what will or will not be the norm for the use of the rational across all religious traditions, without encountering resistance? What this means for tradition studies is then, that one cannot apply 'rational' in the same way across all religions—Muslims obviously used some kind of rational discourse in applying the Prophet's actions to everyday life, and the growth of law shows its own kind of legal reasoning. Yet it is hardly legitimate to impose a Western notion of the 'rational' on Islam or indeed, any religion, expecting that the result will be accepted ecumenically.

That the academy might wish to do so suggests that the study of religion must have its own genealogies of memory.

3. The Second Dispatch: The Genealogies of Memory in the Academy

Once we examine the problematic of tradition this way, we immediately become aware that the academy has fixed upon certain ways of reading the data, and utilized those ways to evaluate a wide range of religious tradition. The tradition of applying the universal posited in Western science has thus delivered certain ways of remembering tradition, and these ways have dominated analysis. We end our dispatches by examining a few of these.

3.1. Foregrounding Modernity

The West has been relentless in its application of time structures to reality. Indeed, it would seem that for us memory itself implies time. All the genealogies we have examined factor time into the equation in one way or another. It would appear, then, that the notion of tradition can only function if we become time-conscious, in order to prioritize the past and allow it to set the standard for the present and the future. Not all people accept time and history as normative ways of relating to reality, or at least, not all people conceive time in the spatial-sequential sense predominant in Western science and history. Why should we imbue some pattern with that kind of significance? It doesn't appear that we experience life itself this way, for example, we are aware of choices and these result in one kind of outcome, and time does not necessarily factor into the decision-making practice. That we do regard time as so important reflects a very modern way of understanding reality. We note then that modernity makes possible the significance of tradition in ways that some religions of yesteryear may not have done. It follows that the consciousness of being historically conditioned both provides the possibility of tradition, and introduces us to our role as historical actors, a fundamental plank in Western academic 'tradition'—eliciting some scepticism about the very placing of tradition itself.

That we are not even conscious that we designate time as the mediator of understanding shows how modern we are, for not all peoples mediate valued patterns by time—many of the Tribal and Aboriginal peoples of the world do not evaluate reality through time. Swain's study on the Australian Aboriginal people concluded that for the Warlpiri people "the cosmic and social orders have no temporal or historical dimension but are centred on space and place and 'country'" (Charlesworth 1997, 77). While it is true that all peoples recognize time, obviously not all think it is the defining way to know reality. 'Modern' people apparently hold that time functions in an essential manner in the knowing of the world. In that sense Islamic traditions have always been 'modern,' and similarly Western studies of tradition may not be capable of dealing with tradition that is not modern.

Perhaps we were not always so—some have argued that this way of thinking is entirely modern, and that there was another way of thinking previous to this. At some point modernity shifted the way we think about what we know and who we are, placing us in the hands of a time concept that shaped our awareness of the world we live in. We were 'thrown into time' as Nietzsche and the Existentialists suggested. Some hold that we created our own 'reality of time.' It does not seem to matter which is the real story. Once time came to dominate the way we thought, we were subject to the problems that arose from that way of thinking, and were (and are) non-escapable.

3.2. The 'Tradition' of the Academy and its Critique

Determining cultural difference is a marker of modern life, and how it is done, and who has the authority to do it, introduces an important player within tradition—the academy. Whether we are speaking of Islam or Shamanism, the 'Who' of the argument is crucial; who has the authority to speak for and determine 'the tradition' is contentious even within the scholarship of the religion. Problems of who 'belongs' to the tradition, and how legitimate they are in speaking, are a subtext of the debate.

A further species of this argument is instantiated within the Religious Studies academy, especially in the United States and Europe. Studying and analyzing distinctive traditions has been an essential part of inter-group relations, and a part of the whole colonial and postcolonial worldview. The discipline of Religious Studies, arguing for a space in an independent academy, wants to lay claim to a religion component in the modern secular university. Likewise the interpretation of cultural difference has been removed from the hands of the practitioners of traditions and placed in those of professional interpreters, bringing about a new class of persons, experts, those who 'know' and interpret the traditions. These experts mediate traditions for students, media and cultural studies.

Despite the claims of objectivity, the rise and development of professional interpreters has not guaranteed either accuracy or inter-cultural peace. A key problematic that the academic study of religion currently faces derives from the increasing awareness of the fragility of our analytic activities; these activities apparently attend any intelligent encounter with religious verities. The issue may be brought into focus by the controversy surrounding the work of historian of religion Wendy Doniger. As professor at one of America's great schools (The University of Chicago), and inheritor of the mantle of Joseph Kitagawa and especially Mircea Eliade, she has applied a wide range of analytic tools to her depiction of Hinduism, including psychological analyses of cherished Hindu texts and conceptions of sexuality within Hindu phenomena explicated with not-so-subtle reference to Freudian categories. A storm of criticism has arisen from members of Hinduism who see her description of the tradition as flawed. Rajiv Malhotra, in a wide-ranging critique (see Malhotra 2002) and expression of outrage has condemned Doniger's vigorous use of sexual imagery and her penchant for Freudian psychology as *the* interpretive *modus operandi* when interpreting Hindu religion. Malhotra cites Kazanas' critique of her *Women, Androgynes and Other Mythical Beasts*; Kazanas disagrees with Doniger's tendency to stress one meaning, the erotic, at the expense of any other interpretive model:

> [Doniger-]O'Flaherty seems to see only one function, the third one of fertility and sexuality, copulation, defloration, castration and the like: even bhakti 'devotion' is described in stark erotic terms including incest and homosexuality (1980: 87–99: 125–129). Surely, erotic terms could be metaphors for spiritual or mystical experiences as is evidence in so much literature?

Malhotra then continues:

> The different levels of Hindu contexts should be used to interpret narra-
> tives, lingam, Kali, tantra, symbols, and various ceremonies and rituals.
> For instance, when seen from the middle chakras, the head represents
> the ego, and 'cutting the head' symbolically means getting rid of the
> ego. But Wendy's children see the head as phallus, and cutting it as a
> message of castration, because they are stuck in the anal-genital perspec-
> tive. It would be less problematic if they were to acknowledge that theirs
> in [sic] not a comprehensive view, and that it might not even be the
> most desirable or relevant view for the students. Collapsing Hindu
> texts, practices, and symbolism to one Eurocentric low level is a great
> violence to the tradition. *This* is the problem with these scholars, not
> that they choose to interpret sexual symbolism. (Malhotra 2002)

It is not enough that one has a certain distance from the tradition in order to
recognize it—traditions imply distance. Aboriginal authorities tell me they
refuse to work with anthropologists or ethnologists any more, or, indeed with
anyone who represents the attitude of the academy towards their traditions,
precisely because the scholars take what they want of the tradition and use it
to say what fits their own agendas. They suggest that the very distance that
scholars talk about is a justification to say what they like or to use whatever
analytic system they wish—they are not bound by the honesty of belonging to
the tradition. This means that the academy's prized 'distance' is itself a falsifica-
tion. Indeed, with postmodernism has come the whole problematic of 'distance.'
In a particularly telling analysis, Jameson argues out of global economics that
analytic tools can no longer distinguish tradition—it simply is drowned in its
own inter-subjectivity:

> What the burden of our preceding demonstration suggests, however, is
> that distance in general (including "critical distance" in particular) has
> very precisely been abolished in the new space of postmodernism. We
> have…filled and suffused volumes to the point where our now post-
> modern bodies are bereft of spatial coordinates and practically (let alone
> theoretically) incapable of distantiation; meanwhile, it has already been
> observed how the prodigious new expansion of multinational capital
> ends up penetrating and colonising those very pre-capitalist enclaves
> (Nature and the Unconscious) which offered extraterritorial and Archi-
> medean footholds for critical effectivity. (Jameson 1991)

The result is that inventing tradition is not the issue—it is that we no longer
have an orientation that sees memory as shaped in a particular way, with
certain universal guidelines for understanding its development. There is no
one formal story, no one history.

Once we abandon a tradition's general story, we are left to accept whatever
our analytic categories dictate. Cut loose from the traditions this way, there is
no longer an authoritative version with which to deal. At the end of such an

occurrence, the local traditions affirm their control and reject the memory imposed by the global academy. They legitimately define themselves. Indeed, they may become much more powerful and even grow in an age of academic globalization. The academy, and particularly the religious academy, would seem to be heir to a major critique of its operating principles, that is, those local traditions call into question the academy's authority in applying whatever analysis it sees justified in doing. At the very least, then, Religious Studies has its own set of memories that is now subject to effective critique from the very religions it has used to construct its categories.

3.3. Tradition Both Within and Without the *Traditum*

The academy has taken some steps in uncovering its own traditions. Tradition can have several genealogies, even under one umbrella—Hannerz proposes a basic intellectual model for tradition: "Accumulating and organizing experience, the perspective goes on to generalize it in responding to new experiences and new demands for action; it becomes a personal paradigm, fosters certain habits of mind" (Hannerz 1992, 67). If we graft this perspective onto religious analysis, something like a workable model of memory and tradition emerges. Michael Fishbane (1985) points out in his study of Ancient Israel, that there was a received *traditum*, a group of texts and interpretations that provided the basis for ongoing interpretation; there was also exegetical *traditio* that is, various ways of interpreting the texts which themselves became ongoing forces in expressing the 'true' identity of the chosen peoples' religion and culture. Even the *traditum* was under pressure to be changed according to a powerful *traditio*.

Applying this model indicates a dynamic process ongoing within social memory. Indeed, what this suggests is that the academy has its own *traditum*, its own dynamic tradition. Yet it cannot then claim that that model should define how tradition is to be understood in religions, for it reflects the prerogatives of its own concerns—who is to know if my experience of tradition is what I would remember now were I not in the business of dealing every day with religious tradition? In the same manner, the academy needs a self-critique imposed by the *traditio* of each religion it hopes to analyze, as well as one arising out of the revised place the academy finds itself in today's post-colonial world.

4. Concluding Remarks

This paper has argued that the study of tradition, from the viewpoint of the academic study of religion, has waxed and waned—leaving it in a rather tenuous situation. We have held that a new and different direction can be taken by examining the formation of a tradition as it is based upon the action of memory. The contemporary study and evaluation of memory is, of course, in its infancy, but all traditions would appear to rest upon it. Memory allows us to fix upon both the processes of memory, and to determine how culture conceives and shapes memory retention. Furthermore, memory allows us to root tradition studies in the larger compass of the human family—for all religious traditions rest upon such continuities as memory. Religious memory is also a complex activity that resides in the first instance in youthful encounter with local or family's traditions, validated by personal engagements that provide access to the community's investments (ethics, identity, etc.) and opens the door for addressing the central features of tradition in an ongoing and profitable manner, without insisting upon one model for that activity.

Part of memory's process provides us with differentiation—some memories that are given the meaning of a 'religious' tradition, and some that are not; religiously, memory provides a solid sense of a general *traditum*, but it does not designate the *traditio* of its meaning—just as I rejected my mother's interpretation of the bird as the 'cause' of my fort experience, while accepting that what I heard was related to 'religion.' Thus a working hypothesis might be: One who knows tradition, knows two aspects of the process—*traditum*, which is bound up with the validation of local memory, and *traditio*, which is the interpretation of that memory. Further, a dialectic is established between the two both personally and socially that builds upon the creative use of memory.

Traditum may be said to set the parameters for those both within and without who engage with its meaning. Still that *traditum* must always be held to be known concretely and diversely by those who accept its truths claims—its meaning cannot be genuinely adduced by the import of a different *traditio*. There seems no other way to preserve the local vitality of tradition with its own quite 'personal' encounter with social memory, and this seems to imply limitations to interpretive devices imported from outside. This fact has immense implication for scholars of comparative religions, or indeed any student of religions outside his or her own purvey.

Thus the academy, and in particular the Religious Studies academy, has now to work with and be perceptive about its own *traditum*. The consequence of such endeavours could lead on the one hand to studies on the processes of religious memory across religious cultures and, on the other, to a revised awareness of the inherent religious viewpoints operating in its own categories. One would hope that the result will be a much more sensitive set of categories, as well as a much greater awareness of the processes expressed in local traditions. In the long run, the very shape of traditions study may well be transformed, with new ways of comprehending those who embrace neither modernity nor time as the West does. This would appear to provide a dramatically different genealogy of memory for the academy, and open up the potential for other ways of comprehending tradition and its placing in religious understanding than the one-dimensional 'historical' view that currently dominates the discipline.

References

Assad, Talal (ed.). 1973. *Anthropology and the Colonial Encounter*. London: Ithaca Press.
Brown, Daniel. 1996. *Rethinking Tradition in Modern Islamic Thought*. Cambridge: Cambridge University Press.
Burton, John. 1995. *An Introduction to the Hadith*. New York: Columbia University Press.
Charlesworth, Max. 1997. *Religious Inventions: Four Essays*. Cambridge: Cambridge University Press.
Deloria, Jr., Vine. 2003. *Evolution, Creationism, and Other Modern Myths*. New York: Fulcrum Books.
Eliade, Mircea. 1964. *Shamanism: Archaic Techniques of Ecstasy*. Translated by Willard R. Trask. New York: Bollingen Foundation.
Fishbane, Michael. 1985. *Biblical Interpretation in Ancient Israel*. Oxford: Clarendon Press.
Hamilton, Paul. 2003. *Historicism*. Second edition. London and New York: Routledge.
Hannerz, Ulf. 1992. *Cultural complexity: Studies in the Social Organization of Meaning*. New York: Columbia University Press.
Hobsbawm, Eric, and Terence Ranger (eds.). 1983. *The Invention of Tradition*. Cambridge: Cambridge University Press.
Jameson, Frederic. 1991. *Postmodernism, or, The Cultural Logic of Late Capitalism*. Post-Contemporary Interventions. Durham, North Carolina: Duke University Press.
Kazanas, Nicholas. 2001. "Indo-European Deities and the Rgveda." *Journal of Indo-European Studies* 29.3–4 (Fall & Winter): 257–293.
LeClaire, Nancy, and George Cardinal (eds.). 1998. *Alberta Elders Cree Dictionary*. Edmonton: University of Alberta Press.
MacIntyre, Alastair. 1981. *After Virtue*. Notre Dame, Ind.: University of Notre Dame Press.
Malhotra, Rahjiv. 2002. "RISA Lila – 1: Wendy's Child Syndrome." www.sulekha.com/ expressions/column.asp?cid=239156. Published September 6, 2002.
Mann, Charles C. 2005. "The Founding Sachems." *The New York Times*, July 4.
Manoussakis, John P. 2005. "The Revelation According to Jacques Derrida." Pages 309–323 in *Derrida and Religion. Other Testaments*. Edited by Yvonne Sherwood and Kevin Hart. London and New York: Routledge.
Moore, MariJo. 2003. "A conversation with Vine Deloria, Jr. about evolution, creationism, and other modern myths: a critical inquiry." http://www.findarticles.com/NewLife Journal/Oct.–Nov. 2003.
Rahman, Fazlur. 1968. *Islam*. New York: Doubleday & Co.
Robertson, Roland, and JoAnn Chirico. 1985. "Humanity, Globalization, and World-wide Religious Resurgence. A Theoretical Explanation." *Sociological Analysis* 40.3: 219–242.
Rudebusch, George. 1988. "Plato on Knowing a tradition." *Philosophy East and West* 38.3: 324–333.
Sedgwick, Mark. 2004. *Against the Modern World: Traditionalism and the Secret Intellectual History of the Twentieth Century*. Oxford: Oxford University Press.
Shari'ati, Ali. 1979. *On the Sociology of Islam*. Translated by Hamid Algar. Berkeley: Mizan Press.
Slater, Peter. 1978. *The Dynamics of Religion: Meaning and Change in Religious Traditions*. San Francisco: Harper and Row Publishers.
Swain, Tony. 1993. *A Place for Strangers: Towards a History of Australian Aboriginal Being*. Cambridge: Cambridge University Press.
Von Stuckrad, Kocku. 2003. "Le chamanisme occidental moderne et la dialectique de la science rationelle." Pages 281–301 in *Chamanismes (Revue Diogène)*. Edited by Roberte N. Hamayon. Paris: Presses Universitaires de France.
Watson, Stephen H. 2001. *Tradition(s) II*. Bloomington: Indiana University Press.
Waugh, Earle. 2005. *Memory, Music, Religion: Morocco's Mystical Chanters*. Columbia, South Carolina: University of South Carolina Press.
Wiebe, Donald. 1999. *The Politics of Religious Studies*. New York: St. Martin's Press.

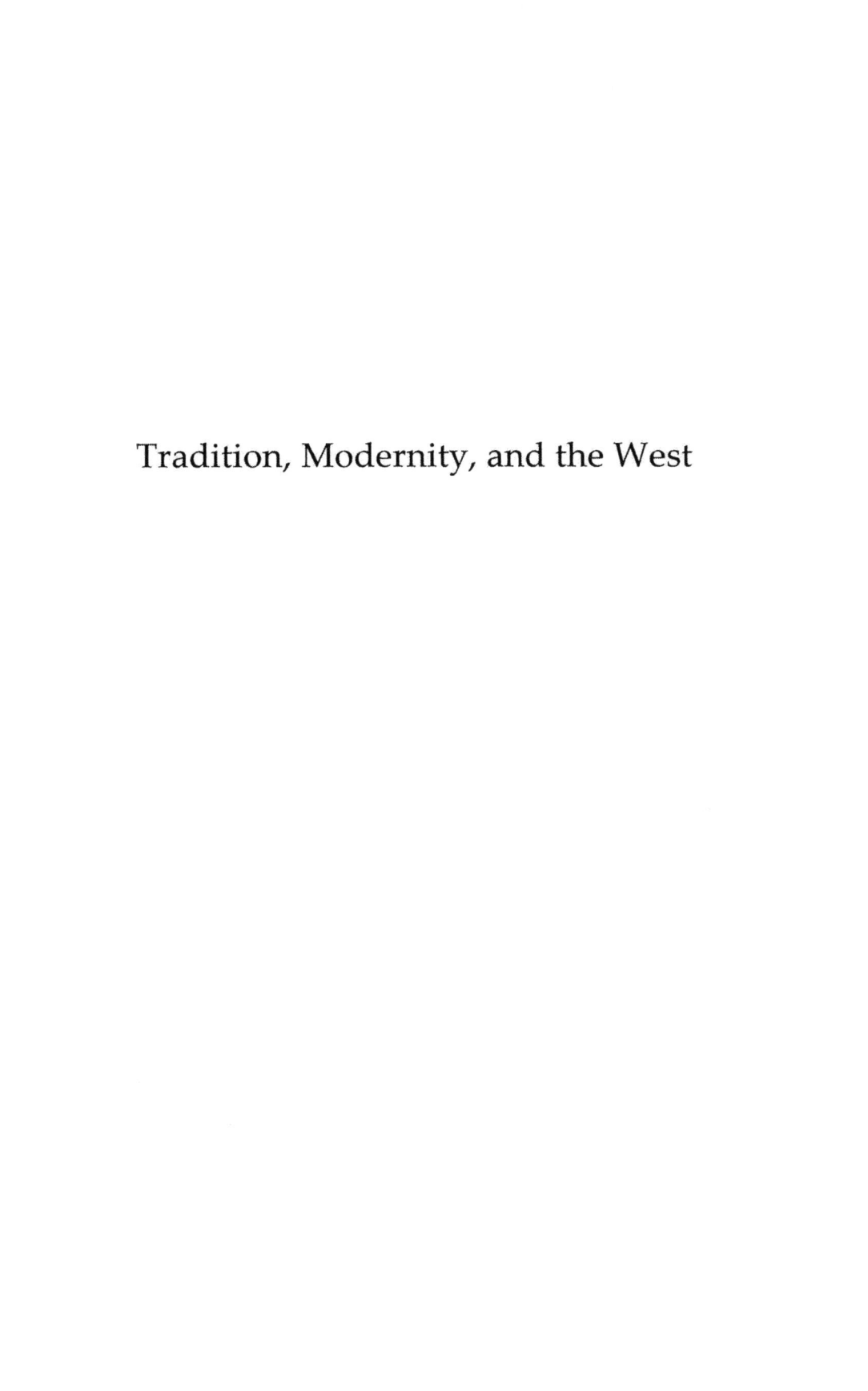

Tradition, Modernity, and the West

Histories of Tradition in Bhaktapur, Nepal: Or, How to Compile a Contemporary Hindu Medieval City

Gregory P. Grieve

> The model town and its model occupants were to be pre-
> served... He said tourists would come from everywhere to see
> the model town. We would be famous. Our businesses would
> flourish. There would be work for guides and interpreters
> and caretakers and taxi drivers and people selling soft drinks
> and ice creams.
>
> "American Dreams" (Carey 1993, 153)

Introduction: The Difference Between "Traditions"

Bhaktapur, a city of 80,000 inhabitants, lies seven miles east of Kathmandu and is one of the three "royal" centers of the Kathmandu Valley that attained prominence during the Malla dynasty (1482–1769 AD).[1] Bhaktapur is known both domestically and internationally as a traditional "Hindu medieval city," and is often posed in scholarly literature, government documentation, and tourist discourse as an ancient fossil, a cultural relic from an earlier age (cf. Grieve 2002). Standing in Bhaktapur's narrow mist-enveloped streets, with the sound of temple bells and the smell of incense wafting on the wind, it is easy to be taken in by the myth that it is a timeless ancient place. As numerous tourists voiced to me, it is easy to believe one is seeing a model of how Nepal was before the "intrusion" of the modern world. However, once one begins to scratch at the surface, there are three chief problems with the interpretation of Bhaktapur as a cultural fossil (cf. Grieve 2002). First, between 1974–1986, the Bhaktapur Development Project (BDP), a German-run historic conservation pro-gram, renovated over 187 pieces of religious structures at a cost of an estimated

---

1   The Kathmandu Valley is a multilingual landscape, with the Newar language (Nepal Bhasa), Nepali, English, and a multitude of other tongues intermingling. For instance, the city itself is referred to under three main names: in Sanskrit (hereafter np.) "Bhakta-pur," in Newar (Nepal Bhasa [hereafter nb.]) "Khwopa," and in Nepali "Bhadgāo(n)." For a balance between ease of utilization and accuracy to the material depicted, at first usage I will print the word in its np. form, followed by the nb. word in parentheses. Words in general circulation, and some proper nouns, are written in their anglicized form without diacritics. For instance, for *nepāl* I write Nepal.

DM 30 million. Many of the structures which at first appear to be "timeless," have in reality stood in their present form only a mere thirty years or less. Second, Bhaktapur receives over 100,000 Western tourists a year. Not only do tourists now play a major role in Bhaktapur's economy, starting in 1995, the municipality has charged tourists to enter the city and they are now the major source of municipal revenue. Third, under the leadership of Nārāyan Man Bijukchhe (Comrade Rohit), Bhaktapur is the center for one of Nepal's major radical political parties, the Nepal Worker and Peasant Party (NWPP).

What these three modern social forces indicate is that rather than a survival from an earlier era, it is Bhaktapur's current form of tradition that has been used to transform it into a "Hindu medieval city." In order to articulate Bhaktapur's contemporary form of tradition, we need to distance ourselves from the romantic assumption that tradition is a dichotomy with modernity. If one clears away this false dichotomy, one finds that, in Bhaktapur, modernity and tradition are co-mingled, pragmatic, world-constructing logics.

The notion that modernity and tradition are two cultural logics for the construction of lived worlds stems from a discussion I had, on February 6, 1999, with the Bhaktapur intellectual Yogesh Raj.[2] Sitting before a glass of tea, he stated that, "modernity is slowly polluting the city's tradition."[3] I asked him what the difference between tradition and modernity was. He answered:

> The idea that modernity is a break with tradition is a misconception… Some people might think that tradition and modernity are opposites. So that they welcome modernity destroying tradition. But it doesn't work that way. You can have tradition and modernity at the same time. I'm in fact a little of both (personal communication, 6 February 1999).

Puzzled, I asked Mr. Raj, "If one can be both modern and traditional, how is 'modernity slowly polluting tradition?'" He paused for a moment and then answered, 'There is a difference between ›tradition‹ (English in original) and tradition (Nepali [paramparā] in original). There is no exact translation. Paramparā is that which is still alive, paramparā is not the past, it is the present in

---

2   Obviously what is presented here is not the unmediated voice of my discussants. Their words here are as I tape-recorded them, and as I have transformed them through the act of writing. Whether to have the voices remain anonymous or to name the speakers was one of the hardest decisions I had to make. On one hand, I desired to give full credit to those who gave so much to me. On the other hand, I was worried that the information may incriminate people, especially with the change in Nepal's political climate. My strategy is a mixed one. Bhaktapur is a tightly knit community, and where the people spoken of would be recognized anyway, I've kept the authentic name. In other situations, I've either used appropriate pseudonyms, or have not used any name at all. Unless otherwise noted, the interviews were in Nepali, with a mix of Newar. Translations are the author's. For notions of transcriptions see Grieve 2002.

3   On the notion of "cultural pollution" as the hybrid mixing of religious notions of purity and environmental notions of industrial contamination see Grieve 2002.

continuity from the past'" (personal communication, 6 February 1999). In effect, what Mr. Raj was suggesting is that the "English," or romantic conception of tradition is destroying "Nepali" tradition (*paramparā*). Following the example of Dipesh Chakrabarty's work on forms of historiography (2000), I label the "English" understanding "tradition[1]," and the "Nepali" understanding "tradition[2]."

In this paper I maintain that tradition[1] (the "English" version) tends to be a romantic-historicist view that posits tradition as a passive ontological essence that will, over time, develop into "modernity." From this perspective, Bhaktapurians neither have tradition, nor make tradition, but *are traditional*. The goal of such accounts is to winnow authentic tradition from the chaff of modernity. The false dichotomy between tradition and modernity breaks down, however, when one examines tradition[2] (*paramparā*), which tends to be used to describe effective everyday social practices that are compiled from past generations. I gloss tradition[2]'s practices as "genealogical."[4] Unlike the tradition[1], tradition[2] is neither the seeking of pure origins, nor the plotting of an evolutionary timeline. Instead, like a "history of the present," a genealogical tradition chronicles the pragmatic use of those past social practices that are currently effective. Unlike tradition[1], tradition[2] is not necessarily at odds with modern practices. It just happens to be one choice among many.[5]

To articulate the difference between tradition[1] and tradition[2] this chapter describes two strands of historiography that currently circulate in Bhaktapur. First is the practice of monumental conservation that operates with a tradition-al[1] understanding. This approach can be evidenced in two texts, *Aktuelles Bauen im Historischen Kontext: Bhakapur, Nepal* (Scheibler 1982) and *Bhaktapur—A Town Changing* (Haaland 1982). Second are chronicles of the city that operate under the rubric of tradition[2]. This genealogical strand of historiography can be seen in two texts: the *Gopālarājavaṃśāvalī* (Vajācārya and Malla 1985), and *Nepālko Prajātāntrik Āndolanma Bhaktapurko Bhūmikā* (Cālise 1994).

Tradition[1]: "American" Dreams

To express the "English" understanding of tradition (tradition[1]) Mr. Raj described the short story "American Dreams" from Peter Carey's collection *The*

---

4   My use of the word "genealogy" glosses both a translation of *paramparā,* and also Foucault's historical understanding of the term (Foucault 1984). The romanization of words follows conventions of Devanāgari script. Following Levy (1990, 623), the mark "(n)" is used to avoid having to place two diacritical marks over vowels to show nasalization of that vowel.

5   There are other important notions of "tradition," such as the Nepali nationalistic use of the term. However, at the present time in Bhaktapur, the romantic historicist and genealogy-tradition (*paramparā*) notions are not only the most significant ones, but are often used to resist the "Nepali" understanding.

Fat Man in History (1993, 147–157). Carey's story describes the creation of a scale model that exactly duplicates the buildings and inhabitants of a rural village. At first the town-folk are elated, because "[t]he Americans would come… They would visit our town in buses and cars and on the train. They would take photographs and bring wallets bulging with dollars. American dollars" (Carey 1993, 155). Yet soon the town folk grew "sick of the game," because "[the American tourists] prefer the model… They spend their time being disappointed and I spend my time feeling guilty that I have somehow let them down by growing older and sadder" (1993, 57). Carey's story takes on even more resonance for Bhaktapur if one realizes that for many in the city, the words "American" and "tourist" signified the same group—all those rich people from "modern" industrial countries around the globe. As the souvenir stall owner Krisnamaya Koju explained, "Tourists are known as Americans, but really they are French, Spanish, Italian, and German. There are all sorts of tourists" (personal interview, 15 July 1999).

In Bhaktapur, "modernity" (*ādhunika*) are those American dreams that are associated with the emergence of global market capitalism. In other words, "modernity" is used to gloss the processes that have shaped the globe in the post-war period: Third World industrialization, urbanization, the rise of mass communication, the increasing commodification of cultural life, new forms of imperialism, the creation of a global economy, and the worldwide dissemination of mass culture. As Keshab Hada stated, "Tall houses and other things are not only the sign of being modern, it has to do with communication facilities, roads, and other such things. It is also about changing people's consciousness" (personal interview, 5 May 1999). Less educated people and laborers tended to see modernization as a change in forms of technology. When I asked the 67-year-old sweeper Bāsulā Dyolā what changes modernity brought to Bhaktapur, she said, "We have Hondas…television" (personal interview, 20 July 1999). Duru Kaji Suwāl, a farmer and mason, stated, "When the tractor came, it did the work of fifty men. In the past, all things were done by people, but now machines do much of the work" (personal interview, 8 July 1999). New forms of entertainment and communication were also seen as a main sign of development. As Krishna Pradhana(n)ga said, "The main source of change is television. But that is only eight or nine years ago. Before that the thresher was the sign of modernization" (personal interview, 6 June 1999). Finally, as the store-owner Ramesh Joshi stated, "A modern place should have somewhere for entertainment " (personal interview, 18 June 1999). Yet, in Bhaktapur the chief marker is, as Bijayashree Kamācharyā responded to my question, "money" (personal interview, 11 May 1999). For instance, in the locally produced film *Nhisutu*, the protagonist Dash Kumar wants to become modern by selling his family land so that he can have money to purchase consumer goods.

For almost all Bhaktapurians I spoke with, the main contact with "modernity" comes from tourists. Like the inhabitants in Carey's story, for most in Bhaktapur, tourism is seen both as advantageous and disadvantageous. Most see tourism as positive because it brings in business, helps renovate the temples, and is thereby a way to develop the city. For instance, in a speech on March 22, 1994, Comrade Rohit (Nārāyan Man Bijukchhe) argued, "Art and culture is our legend of glory and pride. Because of that reason, tourism has fostered in our country. The tourism industry comes in second or third position in badly needed hard currency." And, as a sweeper, Durukaji Suwāl put it more straightforwardly, "Tourists are Americans, from their visits we are becoming developed. When [tourists] come to Bhaktapur and buy something they leave money. It is good because we don't have much money" (personal interview, 8 July 1999).

Yet, the smokeless industry of tourism is not without its problems. Many Bhaktapurians felt that tourism leaves "›cultural pollution‹." This is a term usually uttered in English and is compiled from notions of industrial and ritual pollution. The greatest effects of cultural pollution were seen on religious practice and young people. For instance, Ram Lochā Jhā felt that tourism's pure business motive was destroying the city's religious structure.

> Tourism has changed the city because tourism is based on the Business motive. Just about earning money… It is not good to break [religious] rules (*dharma*) for money. All the rules are being broken for money, people are leaving the kind of work they should do, they are not doing their own religion, and they are not doing their rites of passage. This has caused harm to the city (personal interview, 9 May 1999).

Others, like the chief of the National Museum located in Bhaktapur, Damodar Gautam—not a native of the city but a Parbatiya Bahun—saw the worst effect of tourism as changing young peoples' attitudes:

> If people have regular interaction with tourists, they learn [bad habits] from them. Like wearing skirts. Tourists wear ›transparent‹ clothes. Isn't that true? And our women are not allowed to wear that kind of thing. And men grow long hair and wear earrings. And the most important thing is that tourists take drugs and smoke (personal interview, 21 June 1999).

Yet, it was Yogesh Raj who seemed to have given the negative aspects the most thought. After talking with him about tourism, I asked him how it was harming Bhaktapur. He answered at length:

> [It is harmful] because it increases self-consciousness about our culture, about everything. We used not to know who we were. What kind of us, what kind of we. It took outsiders to tell us that we are antiques and we have lots of culture. When we found this out, something went wrong. When we realized this we became ›alienated‹ from ourselves. In my grandfather's time they didn't care about outsiders. They didn't know about the history and they were happy (personal interview, 6 February 1999).

As indicated by Mr. Raj's words, and as seen in "American Dreams," one of the main distortions of tradition[1] is that, because it calcifies local practices, it transforms the difference between "traditional" (the town folk) and "modernity" ("American Tourists") into an essentialized dichotomy. That is, even though inhabitants of such "traditional" places as Bhaktapur are coeval with "us," tradition[1] condemns them to a quaint dustbin of history. This not only silences locals, but justifies and even promotes their poverty. Accordingly, while tradition[1] is usually spoken of in terms of chronology, it has an implied orientalist geographic element. The "West" is modern, while the rest are traditional. Beyond this geographic implication is an economic one. While the West is modern and rich, the rest are "under developed" and poor (Ferguson 1994). In any case, traditional practices are anachronisms that must be scrapped in the face of modernity.

Still, the tradition[1] does not completely condemn old fashioned practices — as in Carey's piece, the "American" tourists want to come and see the model traditional town. In other words, the driving force of tradition[1] is a "positive orientalism" (Sadik 2000; Said 1978, 2000). What is implied is that in the West's scramble for material possessions and worldly success "we developed 'American' moderns" lost our spiritual center. And just as the "folk" offered a solution to the nineteenth-century bourgeoisie, traditional places are seen to offer solace to alienated moderns. Yet, as for the inhabitants in "American Dreams," tradition[1], while seemingly a positive attribute, places Bhaktapurians in a paradoxical situation. On the one hand, they can actively scuttle their tradition and become rich, modern, and American. Or, on the other, they can remain passively spiritual, but poor and underdeveloped — the epitome of the noble savage. In either case local voices are silenced.

(Post)-Colonizing Histories

In Bhaktapur, the consequences of tradition[1] can be seen in the Bhaktapur Development Project's (BDP) historical conservation. Between 1974 and 1986, the BDP — or "German Project" as it is generally called locally — renovated over 187 pieces of the city's religious architecture. The BDP was a cooperative effort between the West German development agency, *Gesellschaft für Technische Zusammenarbeit* (GTZ), and His Majesty's Government of Nepal (HMG). While appreciated by many in Bhaktapur, the BDP also met much resistance because it did not take local concerns into consideration. In short, the BDP, which explicitly aimed to "improve the living conditions of the city's inhabitants," was plagued by a widespread hostility among Bhaktapurians — those whom it was supposedly helping (cf. Grieve 2002, 73–122). Most of the hostility stemmed from the fact that the BDP neither consulted the local people in the project's decision making process, nor had respect for the city.

For instance, in March of 1997, I spoke with a high-caste and well-educated male professional who said, "[The BDP] were always the ›expert‹ [original in English] and they knew how to do every thing…that was the bad thing." I asked him how this caused harm. His example, like that of many respondents, centered on water and sewage problems. He pointed to the faucet in front of his home and said, "[because of the BDP] it is no longer a faucet, but a kind of pond. They restored it, [he pointed to the water which filled in the sunken steps] but they did it wrong." He also gave the example of the paving bricks in front of his home. "When they dug there they found stone pavement. Big nice slabs. And what they did is that they didn't take them out, they just put the bricks over the top. They had no feeling at all for the stones." Perhaps the most telling evidence of people's widespread distrust of the BDP can be found in the fact that many people felt that the BDP had stolen local god-images. As a middle-aged store-owner said to me in April of 1997:

> It is ›alleged‹ [word in English] [that many god-images were stolen]. You can see all around the city the pieces that were there before the BDP came in. God knows where they went during the period of the BDP. For example, there used to be a deity in the Pugari Math…you know, in the upper part of the city…that should not be seen by any one but the priest. That room is empty now, there is nothing but some fresco art on the walls. There is nothing left. Who is responsible for this kind of thing?

Much of the hostility arose because people felt that the German government operated as if it owned Bhaktapur. As a member of the municipality said to me in April of 1997, "Another thing, many of the Germans regard the city as theirs." I asked him to give an example, and he answered, "Just recently a local civic group tried to put some trashcans at key city sites. Those trashcans were contributed by the Solti Group [an international hotel chain; GPG] and an Australian municipality. All those dustbins had Australian flags and the Solti Group logo. The German Embassy called on the then-mayor, and objected to those trashcans." I asked him why. He replied, "Because they had the Australian flag and the Solti Group Logo…[they] have contributed a lot in the things around here, but it doesn't mean that we are a ›colony‹ [word in English] of Germany."

Under the rubric of tradition[1], the BDP legitimated its "ownership" of Bhaktapur by producing romantic historicist accounts of the city. Take for instance, Anne Haaland's *Bhaktapur—a Town Changing: Process influenced by [the] Bhaktapur Development Project* (1982) and Giovanni Scheibler's *Aktuelles Bauen im Historischen Kontext: Bhaktapur, Nepal* (1982).

Published in 1982, Haaland's text was a promotional piece produced by the BDP. Exclusive of the first chapter, whose data was collected by the anthropologist Todd Lewis, the text swings from romantic portraits of Bhaktapur life to propagandist justification of the BDP's role in Bhaktapur. To give an example of the romantic depictions, Haaland writes, "[t]he mist lies like a heavy blanket over the winter morning, obscuring the characteristic skyline… This ghost town disappears, though, as one moves into narrow streets, where life has been busy since the first streaks of light made the roosters announce the new day" (1982, 6). Such depictions of picturesque poverty are counterpoised with the nuts and bolts of development discourse. Haaland writes, "There are still difficulties with the LDCs [local development committee], but these are, slowly but surely, being weeded out as both sides gain more experience working with each other" (1982, 89). The romantic and development discourses come together in the photographs taken by Anne Haaland which display that picturesque poverty—images of traditional craft, agriculture, and religious worship—that mark Bhaktapur as traditional and an ideal location for development.

Scheibler's work, also published in 1982, was presented as his doctoral thesis for the Swiss Federal Institute of Technology, Zurich. A study of historical conservation in Bhaktapur, the work uses architectural history to argue for the need for current/effective (*Aktuelle*) technology in Bhaktapur's development. Pragmatizing the conceptual work of other scholars, Scheibler posits Bhaktapurians as traditional people who have not yet been spoiled by colonialism or industrialization (Gutschow 1980; Gutschow and Klover 1975). His work traces out the steps by which such romantic historicist visions can be implemented. Scheibler concretizes a romantic understanding of the city.

> First and foremost, the ritual acts bind the open space in a creative context which cannot be understood functionally. They establish a spiritual infrastructure[,] which is employed daily by the inhabitants. One is no longer able to differentiate the ritualistic from the day-to-day activities, for transcendental and real world are understood as one entity, and every action of the inhabitant is orientated towards the hereafter. (Scheibler 1982, 47 [translation by author])

Layered on the romantic descriptions is a discourse of technical jargon used to justify concrete suggestions for developing local building techniques: "In order to establish decision-making principles for finding fuel substitutes, research must be done into the local market situation with respect to cost comparisons and delivery capacities of fuels" (1982, 192).

While very different in purpose and audience, both Haaland's and Scheibler's historiographies share a romantic historicist approach to Bhaktapur. By stripping people of voices and being blind to politics, such romantic historiography works as an ideology to justify and legitimate the BDP. Accordingly, as an economic actuality the BDP *could* engage in one-sided development approaches because of the asymmetrical relations between the "developed" and "underdeveloped" nations (Escobar 1995). At the level of "myth," the BDP believed that it *should* engage in such an approach because it imagined Bhaktapur's religious architecture through a romantic conservationist notion of history. The "mythic" nature of such romantic historiographies is apparent because they are not really historical. As Michel Foucault writes in "Nietzsche, Genealogy, History," histories of origin are "an attempt to capture the exact, and pure and [transhistorical] essence of things" (Foucault 1984, 78). In an oxymoronic fashion, a history of origins assumes a level of meaning preexisting the world of accident. That is, it assumes a metaphysic which predates history, and is thus magically both pre-historical and outside of history altogether.

Tradition[2]: The Difference Between Toilet Paper and Napkins

Early in the morning of 4 March 1999, I arrived at the artist Madhu Krishna Chitrakar's house to finish priming a canvas. Mr. Chitrakar lives with his wife, son, and three daughters near Bhaktapur's main Bhairava temple. The upper stories of their home are a mix of workshops and living space; the ground floor is a small tourist store. After the morning tea, Mr. Chitrakar entered and I showed the canvas to him. He nodded that it was fine and said: "the underlying canvas must be perfect so that the image is effective (*śakti*). It is like tradition[2] (*paramparā*). If we don't follow tradition[2] the painting will not have effectiveness." We then talked about what image to use. Mr. Chitrakar sketched out a rough design on a piece of scratch paper. This would become the model underlying the grid for the *paubhā* painting I would work on over the next nine months.

Mr. Chitrakar wanted to show me some other designs, so he pulled out an old cloth book that he'd put together. The book was his copybook, or *hākusaphu*. "*Hākusaphu*" literally means "black book." Mr. Chitrakar informed me that the name indicated the book's black lining, "the most important part." Other craftsmen told me that the name referred to the color of the pages, the cover, or that the book held tantric knowledge. In it he had compiled symbols, colors, and deities: block prints, photocopies, the odd picture cut out from a magazine, cards taped in the book, and drawings that he as well as his father had done. Most other artisans I met also had such model books, as well as folders and printed books that they used as templates for their work. The oldest surviving Nepali copybook is from the fifteenth century, with the majority of such books dating from the early seventeenth to the twenty-first century (Blom 1989). *Hākusaphu*s are employed by all kinds of artisans in the Kathmandu valley, including painters, woodcarvers, sculptors, goldsmiths, and architects.

Later that morning, Mr. Chitrakar's oldest daughter served a mid-morning tiffin. As we warmed our hands on the teacups, I asked Mr. Chitrakar if he had any news. He said that he did; he'd gone to a wedding feast and it had been an "*āmerican partī.*"[6] He didn't like it; he felt shy and liked the traditional Nepali

---

6   A *partī* is a type of buffet, which is perceived to be "American." It consists of folding chairs, rather than the traditional way of serving food seated in rows on the floor, and, rather than Newar food, a hybrid mix of Indian curry and European-style finger foods.

version better. The "clincher" for him was when, after eating meat, having gotten his hands sticky, he saw some toilet paper hanging from a pole (this is how it is normally done)—and he asked for toilet paper, and people laughed at him, saying, "no that's not toilet paper, that's napkins." He countered, "Well, it sure looks like toilet paper to me." Mr. Chitrakar's main point was that he mistrusts modern "myths" that have magically transformed toilet paper into napkins.

His skepticism about the myth of napkins stems from the fact that while in many ways modernity has been good for Bhaktapur, it has taken much of the effectiveness out of tradition[2]. By effective tradition, both in the concreteness of "napkins" and as the perfect preparation of a canvas, Mr. Chitrakar is indicating the successful practices by which everyday life is constructed. In Bhaktapur, such everyday practices tend to be glossed by the term *"parampara"* —a word that is usually translated as "tradition" but might better be translated as "active genealogy." Like the images in Mr. Chitrakar's model book, *parampara* means to use as your model what your father and grandfather did. As I came to learn from many people, Bhaktapurians tended to see tradition[2] (*parampara*) as an active choice among a set of possible options. You could choose to either use the "napkin" or not.

Chronicling a Traditional City

Like the compiling logic of Mr. Chitrakar's *hākusaphu*, the effectiveness of tradition[2] can be seen in two chronicles that frame the history of Bhaktapur. The first is the *Gopālarājavaṃśāvalī*, or *Chronicle of the Gopāla Kings* (Vajācārya and Malla 1985). The manuscript was "discovered" by Cecil Benal in Nepal's Bṭr Library in 1889–99, and is currently housed in Nepal's National Archive. The chronicle's earliest date is AD 1057, and the latest AD 1389. Because King Jayasthitirājamalla is eulogized as the incarnation of Rāma, Buddha, and the eight lokapālas, the chronicle was most likely complied during his reign (AD 1382–1395). Because most of the place names come from Bhaktapur, the text was most likely written there.[7] The second chronicle, Cālise Pushparāja's *Nepālko*

---

7   I worked with a facsimile copy of the manuscript compiled, with commentaries, by
     Vajrācārya and Malla (1985). The manuscript is a palm-leaf document, measuring
     twenty-eight by five centimeters, and consisting of 48 folios. The script is fly-headed
     (*bhuji[n] mola*), and was copied by a single hand (except for folio 46b). A few pages are
     moth-eaten or faded from age. The chronicle, by matter of convention, has been divided
     by scholars into three sections (V₁, V₂, and V₃). V₁ and V₂ are loosely related. Starting
     with the end of the Kali Yuga and the emergence in the Valley of Paśupatinath's fiery
     phallus, and ending with the Muslim invasions and Jayasthitirājamallas reign, V₂ and
     V₃ are basically the same narrative but were separated because of a slight break where
     a double *daṇḍa* occurs, bringing the events up to the reign of Jayasthitirājamalla.

Prajātāntrik Āndolanma Bhaktapurko Bhūmikā (1997–2047) 1994 [2051], is arguably not a chronicle at all. The book presents itself as notes to a brief political outline of Bhaktapur's democratic movement and lists political events in Bhaktapur between 1936 and 1989. It covers the initial attempts toward democracy (1936–1950), the first steps toward democracy (1950–1960), and ends with Bhaktapur's involvement in the end of the Panchāyat system and the democratic movement (1960–1989).

As evidenced in these chronicles, tradition[2] constructs Bhaktapur's lived world in four chief ways. First, both of the chronicles concentrate on Bhaktapur's locality. For instance, Vajrācārya and Malla write that the *Gopālarāja-vaṃśāvalī* has a "Bhaktapur-centric outlook" (Vajrācārya and Malla 1985, xiv), and *Nepālko Prajātāntrik Āndolanma Bhaktapurko Bhūmikā* outlines Nepal's democratic movement as it pertains particularly to Bhaktapur. In both chronicles, the local history is done to create a particular social reality. For example, the *Gopālarājavaṃśāvalī* consists of a mix of terse genealogical lists and the myth and historical narrative of *itihāsa-purāṇa*. Romila Thapar argues that the genealogical section of the *Gopālarājavaṃśāvalī* is telescoped, with only a bare bones of names and relationships, which are regarded by the chronicler "as the most significant to social needs" (Thapar 1978, 280). For instance, as Vajrācārya and Malla indicate, the miraculous origin of Paśupati (folio 17a) is brief, whereas the eulogization of Jayasthitirājamalla takes up many folios. Similarly, Cālise's main point in his history is that political action is a form of praxis. He builds a platform upon which to articulate how Bhaktapur was inflamed by the People's Movement of 1989, including the role of the Nepal Workers and Peasant Party (NWPP), especially the chairman of the central committee, Mr. Nārāyanmān Bijukche(n) ("Comrade Rohit"). This can be seen in the fact that, when Cālise chronicles the events of 1989 and the demonstrations for democracy, he slows down to a day by day, even hour by hour, account.

Second, the main subject matter of both chronicles is historically situated political intrigue. For instance, as Vajrācārya and Malla write in a commentary to the *Gopālarājavaṃśāvalī*, "most of the time, the royalty and the nobility were busy in campaigns of mutual extermination... The most frequently mentioned place of action in the chronicle is the fort, and understandably so" (1985, xvii–xviii). Similarly, Cālise's aim is to outline the interaction between different political forces in Bhaktapur. He writes: "Throughout this period [1950–1960], in Bhaktapur, as well as the rest of the country, reactionary forces were using terrorist actions *(khukuridal)* against their rivals. It was more intensified at night; and in Bhaktapur people started taking turns guarding every tole" (Cālise 1994, 32).

Third, the chronicles trace events of a socio-cultural nature. Besides forts, in the *Gopālarājavaṃśāvalī*, other important places are temples. For instance, on folios 29b–30a, the chronicler gives a list spanning six centuries of gifts that were given to the Paśupatinath temple. Similarly, in Cālise's work, temples also are an important local stage: "In 1949…for the first time the flag of the Nepal Communist party was flown on Nyā(n)ṭapola temple" (Cālise 1994, 32). Dramas also play an important part in the *Gopālarājavaṃśāvalī*; folios 60b, 61a and 62a detail the rehearsals and performances of the Bhairavānanda. The importance of cultural events is also outlined in Cālise's work. He mentions that "such [dramatic] practices included singing a religious song from the Nepal National League: 'Now it is time to open the eyes, time for darkness to leave your heart and let the bright air in.' Nārāyanmān Bijukche(n), father of Bhaktapur's Nepal Majdur Kisan Party, said this was an inspiration for him in his youth" (Cālise 1994, 27).

Finally, the chronicles focus on the economic and social importance of the monsoon. In the *Gopālarājavaṃśāvalī*, the Laṃkha-yata (rain begging festival), and the construction of aqueducts are just two of the many instances when irrigation plays an important role. In addition, kings are remembered not just for their military conquest or their construction of temples, but also for water works. For instance, on folio 31, King Śivadeva is remembered not only because he was the incarnation of Bhairava of Kāmarupa, but also because "he beautified the country by constructing water-conduits and wells in several places." Similarly, Cālise chronicles that, in 1957, the Nepal communist party established the Young Communist League, much of whose earliest work promoted public health through the cleaning of the city's ponds.

Conclusion: Compiling Tradition[3]

A traditional city is not determined by the static purity of its "ancientness," but rather by how its "ancientness" is imagined and used. But because people not only make history, they make history differently, in order to articulate how "ancientness" is imagined, one needs to look not only at history, but at historiography. As mirrored by Mr. Chitrakar's *hākusaphu*, Bhaktapur's local historiography tends to follow tradition[2], and thereby can be modeled on chronicles (*vaṃśāvalī*), which "compile the past." Compiling historiography is a form of praxis, not representation. It understands tradition genealogically, and aims to create a particular social world by compiling what is at hand. Contrarily, romantic historicist historiography follows tradition[1], a form of historiography that searches for the pure origins of the city. The problem is not simply that tradition[1] attempts to sift authentic tradition from modern pollutants. More significant, like the characters in Carey's short story "American Dreams," by placing tradition on a developmental timeline, historicist accounts posit tradition as "pre-political" and thus pave over "local" voices by museumizing local practices.

Taking into account Bhaktapur's "local" histories creates both theoretical and pragmatic benefits. Theoretically, by comparing romantic and chronicle forms of history, one can understand how tradition is configured and contested. Moreover, local historiography illustrates how people in Bhaktapur construct notions of development vis-à-vis those of tradition. Reciprocally, romantic histories reveal a European vernacular view of tradition—for instance, the assumption that modernity is a globalizing process led by the technological, economic, and political superiority of the West. On a more pragmatic level, many development schemes such as the BDP have failed because their instigators have designed them according to their own personal views of tradition, never taking into account (except as objects of their actions) the people for whom the project is ostensibly run. For instance, instead of opening a dialogue, according not only to many residents of Bhaktapur, but also to many of the expatriates who worked on the project, the BDP was run with little or no involvement from the Nepali side. As Götz Hagmüller, a German expatriate who was director of the project for five years, told me, "during the [BDP] there was no emphasis on learning the languages, either Nepali or Newar. Basically, the unwritten policy was that, except for labor, there should be no participation of the local people" (personal communication, 15 April 1997).

Yet, articulating Bhaktapur's different histories of tradition does not answer this chapter's driving question: *What kind of tradition has been used in Bhaktapur to compile a contemporary "Hindu Medieval City?"* Bhaktapur's current everyday practice of tradition cannot be reduced to either tradition[1] or tradition[2]. Instead, Bhaktapur's contemporary everyday use is a third form which has been compiled from both forms of tradition[(1+2)] and can be labeled as tradition[3]. Tradition[3] has been created through an appropriation of the "English" romantic traditional[1] discourse by the pragmatic effectiveness of a local genealogical "Nepali" tradition[2]. In the present global economy, "tradition" is a valuable commodity that can be used not only to gain distinction, but also monetary capital. Or to put it bluntly, through the social forces of politics and tourism what has occurred is the "cashing in" of the romantic myth for pragmatic local ends.

It is Bhaktapur's contemporary compiled tradition[3] that answers the question of how Bhaktapur can be both a "medieval city" and also house the NWPP, one of Nepal's most progressive political parties. The worth of the traditional city comes not because it is a remnant of an earlier era, but because it is valuable in Nepal's contemporary vernacular modernity. While having family resemblances to ancient practices, Bhaktapur's contemporary tradition[3] has been developed in the context of oppositional politics and tourism, and the catalyst was the discourse of historical conservation spurred on by the development ideology of the BDP. Yet, what recent histories of Bhaktapur show is that there is nothing inherently sinister about compiling this post-modern hybrid form. Instead, like any myth or ideology, it is, as Wendy Doniger (1998, 81) writes, "a gun for hire, a mercenary soldier: it can be made to fight for anyone." Using the flotsam and jetsam that history and the global economy have given them, the residents of Bhaktapur have used both forms of tradition[1+2] to construct an effective and often profitable new form of tradition[3].

References

Blom, Margaret Lyde Brechta. 1989. *Getekende Goden: Modelboeken van Nepali Schilders.* Utrecht: University of Utrecht.

Cālise, Pushparāja. 1994. *Nepālko Prajātāntrik Āndolanma Bhaktapurko Bhūmikā* (1997–2047 VS). Kathmandu: Ke. Ela. "Udaya": Pramukha Vitaraka Ratna Pustaka Bhandāra.

Carey, Peter. 1993. *The Fat Man in History.* New York: Vintage.

Chakrabarty, Dipesh. 2000. *Provincializing Europe: Postcolonial Thought and Historical Difference.* Princeton: Princeton University Press.

Doniger, Wendy. 1998. *The Implied Spider: Politics and Theology in Myth.* New York: Columbia University Press.

Escobar, Arturo. 1995. *Encountering Development: The Making and Unmaking of the Third World.* Princeton: Princeton University Press.

Ferguson, James. 1994. *The Anti-Politics Machine.* Minneapolis: University of Minnesota Press.

Foucault, Michel. 1984. "Nietzsche, Genealogy, History." Pages 76–100 in *The Foucault Reader.* New York: Pantheon Books.

Grieve, Gregory. 2002. *The Practice of Everyday Religion in Bhaktapur, Nepal.* Ann Arbor, Mich.: UMI Dissertation Services.

Gutschow, Niels. 1980. *Stadtraum und Ritual der Newarischen Städte im Kathamandu-Tal: Eine architekturanthropologische Untersuchung.* Stuttgart: Verlag W. Kohlhammer.

Gutschow, Niels, and Bernard Klover. 1975. *Ordered Space Concepts and Functions In a Town of Nepal: Bhaktapur.* Baden: Kommissionsverlag Franz Steiner.

Haaland, Anne. 1982. *Bhaktapur—a Town Changing: Process Influenced by [the] Bhaktapur Development Project.* Bangkok: Craftsman Press.

Levy, Robert. 1990. *Mesocosm: Hinduism and the Organization of a Traditional Newar City in Nepal.* Berkeley: University of California Press.

Reichenbach, Ernst. 1999. "Commercialization of Architectural Heritage—a Sacrilege or a Necessity?" World Bank Symposium, Washington D.C., May 3–7.

Sadik, Jalal al-'Azm. 2000. "Orientalism and Orientalism in Reverse." Pages 217–238 in *Orientalism: A Reader.* Edinburgh: Edinburgh University Press.

Said, Edward. 1978. *Orientalism.* New York: Vintage Books.

———. 2000. "My Thesis, and Latent and Manifest Orientalism." Pages 104–107 and 111–114 in *Orientalism: A Reader.* Edinburgh: Edinburgh University Press.

Scheibler, Giovanni. 1982. *Aktuelles Bauen im Historischen Kontext: Bhaktapur, Nepal.* Zurich: Swiss Federal Institute of Technology.

Thapar, Romila. 1978. *Ancient Indian Social History: Some Interpretations.* New Delhi: Orient Longman.

Vajācārya, Danavarja, and Kamal P. Malla. 1985. *The Gopālarājavaṃśāvalī.* Kathmandu: Tribuvan University Press.

Hasid and Maskil:
The Hasidic Tales of an American Yiddish Journalist

Ira Robinson

> If a Hasid says, "I have seen [it] with my eyes," maybe he has
> heard [the story]. And when he says he heard [it], it certainly
> never happened. (Rabbi Hayyim Halberstam of Sanz, cited in
> Moshkovits 1962, 6)

When Samuel Rocker died in 1936 at the age of 71,[1] he was the publisher of a
Yiddish-language daily newspaper in Cleveland, Ohio, entitled *Di 'Idishe Velt*
(Jewish World). As such, he was a person who possessed great power and influ-
ence with the members of the Eastern European immigrant Jewish community of
Cleveland, who were his readers. For those interested in gaining influence within
that community, including the leaders of the establishment of the Cleveland
Jewish community, as well as for Ohio politicians who sought the *'Idishe Velt*'s
electoral support, Rocker was a man to be reckoned with.[2]

If that were all we knew about Rocker, we would most probably characterize
him simply as a modernizing force within the Jewish community. For it is commonplace for observers of the North American Yiddish press of the early twentieth
century to view it as an "Americanizing Agency." It was thus an important link in
a process of acculturation whereby Eastern European Jews acclimatised themselves
to America and its way of life while retaining important linguistic and cultural ties to
their past.[3] Rocker, as publisher of *Di 'Idishe Velt*, certainly fulfilled this expectation.
However the writing of editorials and essays, which caused him to be remembered
as a "Yiddish Walter Lipmann" (Gartner 1978, 214), was only part of his contribution
to the acculturation process of Eastern European Jewish immigrants. For beyond
his persona of "Samuel Rocker" the American Yiddish journalist, he was also "Reb
Yehoshua [Joshua] Rocker,"[4] author of a book on the Talmudic interpretation of

---

1 On Rocker, see *Encyclopaedia Judaica*, vol. 14 (Ramat Gan: Keter Publishing House, 1970), col.
   213, and an obituary in the *New York Times*, March 19, 1936, p. 25. Cf. Shapira 1972, 123–133.
2 Gartner 1978, 214–215, 225–226. Cf. Zuckerman 1962, I, 155.
3 Soltes 1924–1925. Cf. Rischin 1972, chapter 7, and Stein et al. 1969; Sanders 1969; Metzker
   1971. There is relatively little on the "provincial" North American Yiddish press of that
   era. Cf. Anctil 2001 and Rome 1989. On *Di 'Idishe Velt* itself, see Shapira 1972, 123–128.
4 Yehoshua [Joshua] was apparently Rocker's original name. Samuel/Joshua Rocker was
   far from the only Jew in North America to adopt a personal name different from his name

the Bible[5] as well as two books of Hasidic tales.[6] This means that Rocker served as a cultural mediator not simply between the Eastern European Jewish immigrants and their new country, but also between these Jews and their religious past. This past included the study of the Talmud as a highly valued religious and cultural activity (Katz 1971, chapter 18) as well as the religious traditions embodied in the stories which he told about the great masters of the Hasidic movement. It is his presentation of the Hasidic tradition which will mostly concern us in this article.

It is important for us, at the outset, to clearly understand that the Hasidic tradition evoked in Rocker's books, concerns a movement in Judaism which emerged in the eighteenth century in Eastern Europe and played an important, if sometimes paradoxical, role in the process of the modernization of Eastern European Judaism (cf. esp. Hundert 2004, chapter 9). It is equally important for us to understand that the presentation of the Hasidic tradition in the form of collections of Hasidic stories concerning the movement's great spiritual leaders was largely a function of the late nineteenth and early twentieth centuries, the product of the clash between Hasidic Judaism and various competitive ideologies in that period (Robinson 1998; cf. Lewis 2002). It thus constitutes an example of Eric Hobsbawm's thesis that the period 1870–1914 witnessed not merely the overthrow of many premodern lifestyles, but also the "invention" of a number of national and ethnic "traditions" (Hobsbawm 1983). Finally, it is worth noting that, in a number of cases, collections of Hasidic stories were edited and published by people who were not themselves committed Hasidic Jews in the full sense and whose relationship to Hasidic Judaism could sometimes be described as ambivalent (see especially Dan 1991). Rocker himself is such an ambivalent presenter of Hasidic tales, as we shall soon see.

He was born in 1864 or 1865 in Gorlice, southern Poland, then part of the Austro-Hungarian Empire. His father, usually referred to as Reb Ephraim Fishel Gorlitser, was a fervent Hassid and Talmudic scholar, who held the position of *dayyan* (judge of the rabbinical court) attached to the retinue of Rabbi Hayyim Halberstam (1793–1876), the Hasidic leader of Sanz (Nowy Sącz).[7] Growing up in a strongly Hasidic environment, Joshua Rocker was able to personally visit several

---

of origin. Shneur Zalman Schechter, President of the Jewish Theological Seminary of America, thus changed his given name to Solomon when he arrived in the western world. Cf. Bentwich 1948. A North American immigrant rabbi of the same era, Rabbi Yeshaiah (Isaiah) Glazer used Simon as his given name. On Glazer, see Robinson [forthcoming]. Possibly Samuel was chosen because it somewhat corresponded to the Galician/Ukrainian/Hungarian pronunciation of Yehoshua = "Shia."

5   *Sefer Divrei Hakhamim* (Rocker 1919). The book was first printed in 1903, according to the title page, but a search of a number of library catalogues has not yielded an extant copy of the first edition so far. The 1919 edition is available at the website www.hebrewbooks.org.

6   The first of these books is: *Der Sanzer Zaddik* (Rocker 1926/27). This book is also available at www.hebrewbooks.org. The second book is *Toldot Anshei Shem* (Rocker 1939). Kaufteil was Rocker's brother-in-law (cf. ibid., 5).

7   He is described in a Sanzer source as "a great sage (*talmid hakham*)" (Moshkovits 1962, 57). Cf. Rocker 1926/27, 15, 52, 101.

Hasidic courts in Galicia and Hungary (Rocker 1926/27, 51, 149, 159; 1939, 147, 161, 209), and was educated in the Hasidic tradition both formally and informally. As he matured, however, while he remained an observant Orthodox Jew,[8] he drew away somewhat from his initial strong attachment to Hasidism, as did many of his contemporaries, through his exposure to the writings of the nineteenth century Jewish movement for Europeanization, the *haskala*.[9] Thus he recounted how, even as a young man in Europe, when he celebrated the Sabbath in the same town as the son and successor of Rabbi Hayyim Halberstam, Rabbi Yehezkele of Siniewa, he did not go to visit him, as a normal Hassid would, "because," he related, "my Hasidism was even then worn out (*oysgevefte*)."[10]

Rocker emigrated to the United States in 1891, and established the first Jewish print shop in Cleveland in 1898. He simultaneously began a career in Yiddish journalism in Cleveland which culminated in his becoming editor, and, eventually, sole owner of *Di 'Idishe Velt*.[11] As editor and publisher of an American daily Yiddish newspaper outside New York, Rocker could not afford the luxury of catering too exclusively one or another political or religious faction within the immigrant Jewish community, as was possible in New York. He had to be respectful to the religious and the secularist Jew alike; be sympathetic to unions while not completely disdainful of management.[12] But he also maintained his own point of view, which reflected his education and predilections. This point of view emerged even in his general articles and editorials, in which he would "draw…liberally on Jewish literature and folklore for illustration and proof."[13] It came out strongest in the three books he published.

The first of them, as previously mentioned, was his *Sefer Divrei Hakhamim*. Its subject was the Babylonian Talmud's interpretation of the Bible, and it was first published in 1903, near the beginning of his journalistic career. In this book, Rocker anthologized the aggadic comments scattered throughout the Babylonian Talmud on Genesis in the order of the verses, adding a commentary of his own based largely upon classic rabbinic expositions on the subject. While this book amply demonstrates the expertise in rabbinic literature Rocker acquired in his Hungarian yeshiva education, that was not the major purpose of the book. The book rather emerged from

---

8   Thus Rabbi Max Wohlgelernter in a letter dated March 24, 1936, described Rocker at the time of his death as a person "who both in his personal life as well as in his communal and journalistic activities was a true exponent and staunch defender of Orthodoxy" (Samuel Rocker Papers, Western Reserve Historical Society, Cleveland, Ohio).

9   Shapira 1972, 124. On the *haskala* movement, cf. Stanislawski 1988; Mahler 1961.

10   Rocker 1926/27, 66. On R. Yechezkele, cf. Bromberg 1986, 214–300.

11   Samuel Rocker Papers, 1910–1984 (1913–1947). The *Encyclopaedia Judaica* indicates that he began his Yiddish journalistic career in Cleveland as early as 1896.

12   He was, however, far from spineless and supported the workers in the 1911 Cloakmakers' strike even though the manufacturers threatened to withdraw their advertising. Shapira 1972, 126.

13   Gartner 1978, 214; Shapira 1972, 127. David Eidelsberg recalls that Rocker "sat over an editorial like over a page of Talmud, rocking back and forth" (Eidelsberg 1936).

his concern that Talmudic study, the backbone of Eastern European Jewish education, was being forgotten in the New World.[14] In his introduction, he began by speaking of the crucial importance of Talmud study in Jewish history. Then he stated:

> However now the times have changed…a new land and new heavens are revealed before us, and the conditions of life have changed completely. While we were dwelling on the soil of Europe, even though we were occupied the entire day with making a living…we nonetheless devoted time to the Talmud. Instead [here] we have abandoned it completely and forgotten it… What has become of us here that Talmud study has become the possession of a few individuals while the nation as a whole has no part in it? I will not exaggerate if I were to say that it is habit alone…which is to blame in this matter… It is within our power, even here, even now, to establish for ourselves at least a small period of time to study the words of the Talmud… For if this present situation will continue for the period of two or three generations, then, God forbid, the teaching of the Talmud will be forgotten among us, and even more so among our descendants in our country.[15]

It is apparent that this book was not addressed to the younger, American-born generation, but rather to Rocker's contemporaries who had studied Talmud in Europe and had then abandoned it. Reading his book, Rocker hoped, would "arouse in them the memory to remember what they studied in their youth, which would arouse in them the desire…to establish times for Torah [study]."[16] From nostalgia for fading memories of a youthful Talmudic education, then, an improvement in the situation of American Judaism might well emerge.

The reader who peruses this book will quickly understand that Rocker was a genuine master of rabbinic literature as a whole. He will also sense that the author was definitely not interested in going much beyond traditional sources.[17] While Rocker occasionally demonstrates hesitation at accepting literally some Talmudic statements which seem contrary to scientific observation or common sense (Rocker 1919, 4, 17, 104), he tends to absolve the Talmudic sages of any blame in any such misrepresentation. Thus in commenting on the Talmud's statement "Israel has no *mazal* [predestined fate]" (Tractate *Shabbat* 156a), Rocker comments:

---

14 Thus the Talmud Torah, the major expression of Jewish education in North America in that era, had little room in its curriculum for Talmud (M. Ginzberg in *Keneder Adler* [Montreal], November 19, 1950; Rabbi Simon Glazer, "The Talmud: Fundamental Principles," in *Jewish Times* [Montreal], October 23, 1903). Cf. Farber 2003.

15 Rocker 1919, Introduction, unpaginated [v].

16 Rocker 1919, unpaginated [vi]. Rocker himself was described as having established times for personal Torah study.

17 On only two cases does he cite figures who were themselves traditionalist, but not entirely within the boundaries set by contemporary yeshivot: a citation from Moses Mendelssohn, found in the Hebrew encyclopedia *Otsar Yisrael* (Rocker 1919, 38), and one from "the sage [Alexander] Kohut" (ibid., 67). On Rocker's traditionalism and attitude toward "critical" literature, see Shapira 1972, 128–129.

Though in several places in the Talmud we find a belief in *mazal*...the sages concluded that this belief was so rooted in the heart of the masses of Israel that they were unable to uproot it completely. Truly this belief is opposed to the religion of Israel, for if we believe in *mazal*, man has no free will, God exercises no personal providence and there is no place for reward and punishment. (Rocker 1919, 52)

Rocker's *Divrei Hakhamim* was an experiment which apparently did not generate much enthusiasm. In his introduction, he expressed the hope that the completion of his work on Genesis would soon be followed by similar anthologies for the other books of the Pentateuch (Rocker 1919, unpaginated [viii]). No other book in this series was published, however. In the 1920s and 1930s, Rocker would try another way of influencing his readers to preserve the Jewish tradition—by writing about the great masters of the Hasidic tradition.

In order to understand the novelty of what Rocker was attempting in his Hasidic works in the North American context of the early twentieth century, we have to understand the sort of "press" that Hasidism was receiving at the moment he was writing. The most authoritative reference book on Judaism at the time was the *Jewish Encyclopedia*. Searching that work for the term "hasidism" would yield the following in the entry on "Cabala":

> While the doctrines of the ḤaBaD have shown that the Lurianic Cabala is something more than a senseless playing with letters, other forms of Ḥasidism, also derived from the Cabala, represent the acme of systematized cant and irrational talk. (Kohler and Ginzberg 1902, 470)

The entry on Hasidism itself, written by Simon Dubnow, would inform the reader that at the beginning of the twentieth century, though the movement's "vitality cannot be doubted," it was being nourished "by its stored-up reserves of spiritual power," and that "the period of stagnation which it has lately passed through must...result in its gradual stagnation" (Dubnow 1904; cf. Schwartz 1991, 121). Many reports in the Jewish press, both English and Yiddish, treated the first manifestations of Hasidic life in North America in the late nineteenth and early twentieth centuries as if Hasidism were a disease which it were best to quarantine so as not to infect American Jewry.[18] Rocker was, therefore, going to have to counter a great deal of negativity if he was determined to present Hasidism in anything resembling a positive light.

Both his Hasidic books began as series of articles for *Di 'Idishe Velt*, which were afterwards published in book form.[19] The ostensible occasion for the first of his series of articles on Hasidism was the fiftieth anniversary of the death of Rabbi Hayyim Halberstam of Sanz in 1926 (Rocker 1926/27, 224). Not only was Rabbi

---

18 Robinson 1992, 501–515; 1995, 331–332. Cf. Rome 1996, 33–37.
19 Numerous books in that era originated as a series of newspaper articles. An example of a series of articles, published originally in Montreal's Yiddish daily *Der Keneder Adler*, and subsequently appearing in book form is Kruger 1933.

Halberstam well-known to Rocker through his personal experience, and through his father's stories,[20] but, as we will see, Rabbi Halberstam's interpretation of Hasidim, which de-emphasized kabbala and miracles and stressed halakhic observance and Talmud study, was particularly congenial to Rocker.

There was, however, another reason why Rocker may have wanted to write about Rabbi Halberstam. In 1916, Yitzhak Even (1861–1925) had published a series of articles in the Hebrew language periodical, ha-'Ivri on the lengthy and bitter conflict between the Hasidism of Sanz and those of Sadigoreh in the 1860s and 1870s which rocked the Jewish world.[21] Even promised, in his preface, that his account of the conflict would be "evenhanded" favoring neither side and presenting only historical facts. In doing so, however, he also undertook to demonstrate that "all the accusations of "new sect" (kat hadasha) or "wicked sect" (kat ha-resha'a) which the Hasidim of Sanz called the Hasidim of Sadegureh had no substance to them" (Even 1916, 5). In an "evenhanded" way, in other words, Even tried to place the onus for the quarrel on the Sanzer side (Even 1916, 19–21). Though he was no longer a Sanzer Hassid in the strictest sense of the terms, Rocker retained much of his youthful loyalty to Sanz. He thus felt that he could do a better job, one fairer to the Sanzer side than Even's account.[22] Whether that is the case or not, it is certain that Rocker had Even's work on the conflict, as well as his other book on the Hasidic dynasty of Rabbi Israel of Rizhin in front of him (Even 1922), and learned from it, not least, that there was an historical importance to the Hasidism of the previous generation.[23]

From the perspective of Hasidic history, Rocker was also dissatisfied with attempts on the part of the Sanzer Hasidim themselves to tell their leader's story. He thus noted in his introduction to his account of the Sanzer that:

> The history of the Sanzer Zaddik, Rabbi Hayyim Halberstam, has not yet been written, neither in Yiddish or in the Holy Language [Hebrew]... Several small books (bikhlekh) in the Hebrew language have indeed been written about him. They are, however, no more than a gathering together of short stories, quotations, and Torah thoughts which have no historical value.[24]

His work, by contrast, was oriented toward illuminating "a chapter of the highest importance in Jewish history."[25]

The result was largely a retelling of Hasidic tales of zaddikim. Rocker often prefaced these tales with some indication of the nature of the source. Thus a tale might

---

20 Rocker 1926/27, introduction, unpaginated. Cf. also p. 15.
21 Even 1916. It is interesting, and possibly significant, that the Artscroll account of the Sanzer dynasty chooses to dismiss this conflict in less than one page (Bromberg 1986, 128).
22 Shapira (1972, 129) notes Rocker's attempt to be fair while yet demonstrating a certain affinity for the Sanzer side of the dispute.
23 Rocker 1926/27, introduction, unpaginated.
24 Ibid. Rocker is probably referring to Raphael ha-Levi Zimetboim's Darkhei Hayyim (Cracow, 1923), reprinted in Moshkovitsh 1962.
25 Rocker 1926/27, introduction, unpaginated.

begin "Hasidim relate," "old Hasidim relate," "Sigeter Hasidim relate," "a Hasidic legend (*aggada*) relates," or "Hasidic books state."[26] These tales were supplemented with written sources when available, as will be seen, but Rocker was characterized by Shapira as "not delving deeply into [Hasidism's] original sources. Rather he himself was a 'source' for the phenomenon of Hasidism" (Shapira 1972, 128).

Rocker was thus by no means a "scientific" historian of Hasidism either by the standards of the *Wissenschaft des Judentums*, exemplified by Simon Dubnow, or of the Eastern European *haskala*, as exemplified by the work of Samuel A. Horodetzsky.[27] He was, however, well aware that there were a number of contemporary Orthodox authors who had begun to attempt to tell the Hasidic story as history and theology, and not merely to accumulate a collection of "stories, quotations and Torah thoughts." Yitzhak Even's work, previously referred to, was one example of an author consciously writing what he thought of as Hasidic history. Another example familiar to Rocker was that of Rabbi Mattityahu Yehezkel Gutman of Husi, Romania, whose 1922 book on Rabbi Israel Ba'al Shem Tov was subtitled, in the best academic style, "His Life, His Works and His Teaching."[28] In that book, Gutman (1922, 32) uses terms like "the Hasidic legend" (*ha-'agada ha-hasidit*) and clearly has in mind a reader who is not necessarily steeped in Hasidic life, but for whom the story of the Ba'al Shem Tov may be relevant in other ways (ibid., 2).

Rocker gives us some further clues to his attitude toward Hasidism in his last book, published posthumously, entitled *Toldot Anshei Shem* (Rocker 1939). This book consists of a collection of Rocker's work on Rabbi Shneur Zalman of Liadi,[29] founder of Habad Hasidism, and the Hungarian *zaddikim* Isaac of Kalev, Moshe Teitelbaum, Yekutiel Yehuda Teitelbaum, Lipele Teitelbaum, and Yeshaiale Kristirer, also published in the *'Idishe Velt*, apparently after his work on the *Sanzer Zaddik*.[30] In his introductory remarks to his work on Rabbi Shneur Zalman, he makes the following programmatic statement:

> Hasidic literature, stories and customs of "Good Jews"[31] which recently have become an important part of Hebrew and Yiddish literature, have been of great use to Jewry. They have opened the curtain on a portion of the Jewish people (Hasidim), which has been portrayed by the *Mitnagdim* on the one

---

26 Rocker 1926/27, 7, 13, 19, 26, 32; 1939, 82, 137, 151.
27 Rocker (1926/27, 127) refers to Horodetzsky's work on Hasidism, *ha-Hasidut veha-Hasidim* (Berlin: Dvir, 1922).
28 *Rabi Yisra'el Ba'al Shem Tov: Hayyav, Pe'ulotav ve-Torato* (Gutman 1922). Cited in Rocker 1926/27, 45, 159. The work also boasted a title page in German. Cf. Rapoport-Albert 1988. Rapoport-Albert in this article deals almost exclusively with Habad hagiography.
29 This series is noteworthy in that Rabbi Shneur Zalman is the only Hasidic leader portrayed who lived other than in Galicia or Hungary. It also did not tell the entire story, stopping with Rabbi Shneur Zalman's release from imprisonment on the nineteenth of Kislev.
30 Rocker 1939, 8. His series on R. Moshe Teitelbaum apparently appeared in 1928 (ibid., 79), and his essays on R. Lipele Teitelbaum in 1930 (ibid., 212).
31 An alternative name for *zaddik* or rebbe, particularly in Galicia.

hand, and the *Maskilim* on the other as dark and superstitious. Both the *Mitnagdim* and the *Maskilim* have noticed their mistake. Both have noticed that in that camp (of the Hasidim) there is no darkness, but rather light and life; no superstition but rather a world in which a great portion of the Jewish people found comfort and consolation, life and holiness. Whether we agree with the Hasidic way or not, we must admit that where Hasidism lived and spread its wings, Judaism remained whole, and with a soul. (Rocker 1939, 7)

Rocker clearly wanted his own writings on the Hasidim to be part of this new branch of Jewish literature and history. What was he trying to accomplish?

First and foremost, he was trying to move discourse on Hasidism within the Jewish community into the mainstream. His strategy was twofold. First of all, he utterly denied the accusation that the Ba'al Shem Tov, and Hasidism as a whole, did not sufficiently respect Talmudic scholarship (Rocker 1926/27, 47). On the contrary, the Ba'al Shem Tov is portrayed by Rocker as a great Talmudic scholar, though he admits that not all of his successors were outstanding scholars (*geonim*) (Rocker 1939, 148). He was also prepared to admit that many later Hasidim fell short of this ideal:

> [Talmudic] learning became secondary (*tafel*) and Hasidism became the essential. A saying of the Rebbe became more [important] than studying a page of Talmud with Tosafot, and a "grandchild" [of the Rebbe] in swaddling clothes took on more importance than the greatest Torah scholar (*gaon*). Drinking "*tikkun*," relating stories, conversing about "Good Jews" began playing the most important role in Hasidic life. (Rocker 1926/27, 47)

It is noteworthy, however, that if, indeed, Hasidim themselves fell short of the ideal, in Rocker's view, their leaders were hardly ever to blame. Thus in the great controversy between the Sanzer and Sadegorer Hasidim, Rocker carefully tried to minimize the active part taken by both the Sanzer and the Sadegorer leadership. In particular, Rocker took pains to distance the Sadegorer leadership from provocative acts on the Sadegoreh side such as placing the Sanzer Zaddik in excommunication in a ceremony held at the Western Wall in Jerusalem (Rocker 1926/27, 195). Similarly, the persecution of Rabbi Elazar Nisan Teitelbaum by the Hasidim of Rabbi Mendele of Kassov in Sighet was described by Rocker as not emanating from Rabbi Mendele himself (Rocker 1939, 126, 128). The Hasidic leaders, then, were almost invariably portrayed as great and benevolent Torah scholars, who stood above the fray which often pitted one Hasidic group against another.

Beyond that, Rocker put forward in his books a vision of an ideal Hasidism. It was, perhaps not surprisingly for one who so closely identified with the Sanzer Zaddik, one which emphasized traditional Talmudic learning, and de-emphasized mysticism and claims of miracle-working (Rocker 1926/27, 79). The embodiment of this ideal, of course, was Rabbi Hayyim Halberstam of Sanz. Not only does Rocker portray Rabbi Halberstam as a world-class Torah scholar (*velts gaon*) in both Talmud (*nigleh*) and kabbala (*nistar*), thus harmoniously combining "the way of the Vilna Gaon with the way of the Ba'al Shem" (ibid., 42) but he also emphasizes the primacy of Talmud study for Rabbi Halberstam (ibid., 47).[32] Similarly, he approves the fact that Rabbi Halberstam and others, like Rabbi Hershele Lisker discouraged tales of miracles and wonders relating to themselves (Rocker 1939, 200). Rocker was characteristically ambivalent concerning the issuing of amulets (*kameot*), which he considered a gentile custom which was adopted by Jews during the Babylonian exile. Rocker asserted that "many great Jewish scholars (*gedolei yisrael*) in nearly every generation were against the issuance of amulets, and that those rabbis who gave them, like Rabbi Jonathan Eybeschutz, were persecuted for it. Therefore even Hasidic rabbes, for the most part dispensed amulets in secret (Rocker 1939, 109–110).

The world that Rocker portrayed in his Hasidic books was one in which modern Jews, who had abandoned the Hasidic tradition, yet derived many positive things. Thus, for example, "modern" cantors came to Hasidic singers for inspiration, and Rabbi Isaac Kalever's songs were sung by even the "enlightened" among Hungarian Jewry.[33] At least some nonobservant Jews came to Hasidic rabbis for their blessing (Rocker 1939, 182–183). In a word, the Hasidism he portrayed was one in which those elements which would appear most foreign to modern civilization were either suppressed or else de-emphasized. One of the most important aspects of this is the fact that in his lengthy portrait of Rabbi Hayyim Halberstam and his teachings, he barely refers to his rulings which forbade Jews, especially women, from adopting western modes of dress,[34] and Rocker's reference, which he could have hardly avoided, has to do with the notorious accusation that the women of the Sadegoreh dynasty had adopted western dress and manners, which he could not entirely avoid in dealing with the dispute.[35]

A second factor to note is Rocker's treatment of *maskilim*. They were, as mentioned earlier, depicted as mistaken opponents of Hasidism, like the *mitnagdim*. They are generally portrayed in Rocker's books entirely from a Hasidic perspective. Thus a *maskil* of Chernovits, Dr. Yehuda Leib Reitman, who figured in the affair of Rabbi Dov [Berenyu] of Leova which touched off the Sanz-Sadegoreh conflict, is described as follows: "He was an early *maskil* and a student of Joseph Perl, the author of *Megale Tmirin*. [He was] a terrible devourer of Hasidim (*Hasidim fresser*) and a known nonbeliever ('*apikoros*)" (Rocker 1926/27, 158). There is nothing in his books that overtly lets the reader in on the fact that Rocker was in fact greatly influenced by the works of Galician *maskilim* such as Joseph Perl, Nahman Krochmal and Shlomo Yehuda Rapoport (Shapira 1972, 124).

What, then, was Rocker trying to do by writing his Hasidic books in Yiddish in Cleveland, Ohio? Perhaps the best answer is to compare Rocker's works with

---

32 Cf. Hayyim Halberstam, *She'elot u-Teshuvot Divrei Hayyim*, part 2, number 47, p. 33.
33 Rocker 1926/27, 35–36, 39. Rocker notes that Rabbi Halberstam would not let the "modern" cantors perform for him.
34 Hayyim Halberstam, *Divrei Hayyim* (see above n. 32), part 1, number 30, pp. 54–55.
35 Rocker 1926/27, 140, 154. It is instructive to contrast this treatment with Even's emphasis on this importance of this charge (Even 1916, 8, 13).

a book written at the same period by the editor of Montreal's Yiddish daily, *Der Keneder Adler*, Hirsch Wolofsky.[36] Its title was *Oyf Eybigen Kvall: Gedanken un batrachtungen fun dem hayntigen idishen leben un shtreben, in likht fun unzer alter un eybig-nayer tora, eingeteylt loyt di parshiyos fun der vokh* (Wolofsky 1930). As with Rocker's books, Wolofsky had first published his book as a series of articles in his newspaper in 1928–1929. He was attempting to create nothing less than a contemporary commentary or homily (*drush*) on the Pentateuch. The form the book took, commentary, as well as its division according to the weekly synagogue Torah readings, both reflected a respect for the Judaic tradition. It also appropriated that tradition so as to shed new light on the dynamics of the contemporary Jewish community, whose life and aspirations Wolofsky wished to reflect. In his introduction Wolofsky began by consciously placing his work in the tradition of the ancient midrashic and later homiletic (*drush*) literature of Judaism. These premodern works, he asserted, sought to explain contemporary problems in terms of the Torah, utilizing the literary means of allegory, fantasy and imagination. These elements were added to the true story of Torah[37] in order to affect the hearts of the audience. This process was precisely what Wolofsky wished to follow, only in the twentieth century and "according to the American version (*nusakh*)."[38] In a North American Jewish cultural atmosphere, *drush* also had to become different. There was no twentieth-century audience for a homily lasting hours on end. Jews who were willing to listen at all to words of Torah wanted the speaker to come to the point in fifteen to twenty minutes without either elaborate introductions or difficult questions. Having this situation in mind, Wolofsky was not about to create a "serious" commentary on the Torah in the old style (Wolofsky 1930, 6). Wolofsky, in writing this work, thought of his enterprise in the context of the age-old Jewish custom of reviewing the weekly Torah portion (*ma'avir sedra zayn*) with the original biblical text read twice and the translation/interpretation (*targum*) once. At present, however, Wolofsky asserted that the original "text" of Jewish life has largely been forgotten and that therefore contemporary Jews are living their lives at a remove from the original (*targum-lebn*) in a world where practically nothing is "original" and all is *targum*. For Jews living in such a world, Wolofsky proposed to present a series of homilies which might, indeed, be more "*targum*" than original, but which were conceived by him to be in the spirit of the original (Wolofsky 1930, 7).

I would say that Rocker, like Wolofsky, understood that the Jews who constituted his audience had detached themselves from an immediate connection with

---

36 On Wolofsky, see his autobiography *Mayn Lebens Rayze* (Wolofsky 1946). This memoir was translated into English as *The Journey of My Life* (Wolofsky 1945), and into French as *Mayn Lebens Rayze: un demi-siècle de vie yiddish à Montréal 1946* (Wolofsky 2000). Cf. also Robinson [forthcoming], chapter 8.

37 It is clear from a careful reading of *Eybigen Kvall* that Wolofsky believed in the essential historicity of the narratives of the Torah.

38 Wolofsky 1930, 2, 5. It is worth noting that, for the most part, Wolofsky speaks of "America," and does not seem to be looking at a Canadian specificity in the situations he depicts.

the Jewish tradition of yesteryear, but might yet be reached through innovative literature emanating from that tradition. Wolofsky found himself in the mainstream of a cohort of contemporaries in Montreal, who, through their teaching and publication, attempted to utilize the hallowed resources of the Jewish past, including Midrash, and Mishna, to recreate a thriving and culturally innovative Jewish community through the medium of Yiddish. As David Roskies described these people, they took for granted that the old, Judaic culture of Eastern Europe had to be reinvented. If the original had become inaccessible to the average Jew in the street, then a compelling Jewish life in *targum* had to be established both intellectually and institutionally (Roskies 1990).

Rocker himself had a group of intellectual companions in Cleveland. They included pioneering Hebrew educator H. A. Friedlander (Rocker 1939, 5). More importantly, however, they included a pair of Orthodox rabbis who originated in Galicia and Hungary, and who themselves were authors of books about Hasidism which were both departures from traditional Hasidic literature and yet which retained a respect for Hasidism itself and for Orthodox Judaism. One was Menachem Mendel Eckstein, rabbi of Congregation Bnai Jacob Anshei Marmorosh of Cleveland, author of *Tena'e ha-nefesh le-hasagat ha-Hasidut* (1920/21).[39] The other was Rabbi Yekutiel Greenwald (1889–1955) of Columbus, Ohio, whose monumental oeuvre includes books on the Jews of Hungary,[40] and several biographies of great rabbis.[41] Rabbis Eckstein and Greenwald are credited by Rocker with lending him books and sharing their knowledge of Hasidism (Rocker 1939, 160, 215). An intensive study of their works would doubtless yield more insight into Rocker's intellectual world.

When Samuel Rocker died in 1936, his funeral service, as reported by the *New York Times* was conducted by rabbis of the three branches of American Judaism — Reform, Conservative, and Orthodox.[42] It is nonetheless clear that characterizing Rocker on the standard Orthodox-Conservative-Reform continuum of twentieth century American Jewry does a disservice to the complexity of his personality. A better basis of understanding was presented by three of his contemporaries who wrote about him in the language in which he wrote — Yiddish. Baruch Zuckerman, an important leader of the Poalei Zion movement in the first half of the twentieth century, compared Rocker in his memoirs to Hillel Zeitlin (1871–1942), the Warsaw journalist and mystic who, in the words of Arthur Green, "tried to create chasidism for those who lived outside the chasidic world."[43]

---

39 This book was later reprinted in Israel under the title *Mavo' le-Torat ha-Hasidut* (Tel-Aviv: Nezah, 1960).

40 *Ha-Yehudim be-Ungaria* (Vac, 1912); *le-Pelagot Yisrael be-Ungaria* (Devo, Romania, 1929); *Toizend Yohr 'Idish Leben in Ungarn* (New York, 1945).

41 *Ha-Rav R. Yehonatan Eybeshits* (New York: Hadar Linotyping, 1954).

42 *New York Times*, March 19, 1936, p. 25.

43 Cited in Shapira 1972, 133. Cf. John Dorfman, "Radical Theology: Arthur Green Translates a Chasidic classic," in *Forward*, December 4, 1998.

The Yiddish journalist David Eidelsberg wrote an obituary for Rocker in the
Jewish Morning Journal (*Morgen Journal*) of New York on March 24, 1936 under the
title "Hasid and Maskil" (*Hasid un Maskil*). Rocker, in his opinion:

> ...embodied the infrequent combination of Hasid and Maskil—first of all
> Hasid, and then Maskil... In his youth, like many Torah students of that
> era, he was satiated with the rationalistic teachings (*torah*) of the Haskala,
> but his Hasidic soul was not touched. So to speak, he ate the fruit and threw
> away the peel. In his best maskilic convictions, he remained a Hasid...
> Rocker used to say that great maskilim like [Joseph] Perl, [Judah] Levin-
> sohn, [Isaac] Erter and [Nahman] Krochmal persecuted Hasidism to the
> end because they were completely Jews of mind, while a deeper [maskilic]
> thinker like Eliezer Zweifel[44] looked on Jewry also with the eyes of the
> heart. And thus, as a maskil he was able to evaluate the great importance
> of the Hasidic movement for Jewish history. Rocker did not only write well
> about Hasidism, but he practised its high morality and life.

Yosef Shapira, who had worked closely with Rocker for several years on the staff
of *Di 'Idishe Velt*, and had subsequently moved to Palestine, also wrote of Rocker's
paradoxical mixture of Hasid and Maskil:

> Reb Joshua Rocker, the Torah scholar (*talmid hokhom*) with the clear mind,
> was educated in a Hasidic environment and was well versed (*baki*) in its
> teaching...when he distanced himself from it, like Rabbi Meir, he ate the
> content and threw away the husk... Often I felt as if I were sitting in front
> of one of the most faithful heirs of...the generation of true *maskilim*: an heir
> in knowledge, humor, love of Israel, and also an heir in the struggle against
> those who sought to bring foreign culture into Jewish life... The struggle
> of Joshua Rocker against assimilation in all its forms was conducted with
> enthusiasm, and the entire fervor of his Jewish soul. (Shapira 1936)

In this struggle, Joshua Rocker attempted to use the power of the Hasidic tradition,
not to oppose modernization as such, but to show his readers that there were different paths available to them as Jews other than a lockstep acculturation into an
American "melting pot." By portraying the leaders of nineteenth century Hasidism
positively in the way he did, he sought to convince his readers that the ideas and
ideals of the Hasidic tradition had continued relevance in the here and now, and
had not simply been left behind in the forward march of civilization (Robinson
1998, 409). For Joshua Rocker, there was something in Hasidism and its story that
could speak to his contemporaries, and help them as they engaged in the vital
balancing act between the Judaic tradition and western civilization that characterized all of modern Judaism.

---

44 Cf. vol. 16 of *Encyclopaedia Judaica* (Ramat Gan: Keter Publishing House, 1971), cols. 1245–
1246.

References

Anctil, Pierre. 2001. *Through the eyes of the eagle: The early Montreal Yiddish Press (1907–1916)*. Translated by David Rome. Edited and introduced by Pierre Anctil. Montréal: Véhicule Press.

Bentwich, Norman. 1948. *Solomon Schechter: A Biography*. Philadelphia: Jewish Publication Society.

Bromberg, Avraham Y. 1986. *The Sanzer Rav and His Dynasty*. Translated by Shlomo Fox-Ashrei. Brooklyn: Mesorah Publications.

Dan, Joseph. 1991. "A Bow to Frumkinian Hasidism." *Modern Judaism* 11: 175–193.

Dubnow, Simon. 1904. "Hasidim." Pages 255–256 in vol. 6 of *Jewish Encyclopedia*. New York: Funk and Wagnall. Online at www.jewishencyclopedia.com.

Eidelsberg, David. 1936. "Hasid un Maskil." *Jewish Morning Journal* (March 24, 1936).

Even, Yitzhak. 1916. "Mahloket Sanz ve-Sadigore: kol korot ha-pulmus mi-tehilato 'ad sofo, 'al pi mekorim ne'emanim uve-ruah bikoret ne'emana." *Ha-'Ivri* (New York).

———. 1922. *Fun'm rebin's hoyf zikhroynes un mayses gezehn, gehert un nokhdertsehlt*. Brooklyn: self-published.

Farber, Seth. 2003. *An American Orthodox Dreamer: Rabbi Joseph B. Soloveitchik and Boston's Maimonides School*. Hanover: University Press of New England.

Gartner, Lloyd. 1978. *History of the Jews of Cleveland*. Cleveland: Western Reserve Historical Society.

Gutman, Mattityahu Yehezkel. 1922. *Rabi Yisra'el Ba'al Shem Tov: Hayyav, Pe'ulotav ve-Torato*. Jassy: self-published.

Hobsbawm, Eric. 1983. "Mass-Producing Traditions: Europe, 1870–1914." Pages 263–307 in *The Invention of Tradition*. Edited by Eric Hobsbawm and Terence Ranger. Cambridge: Cambridge University Press.

Hundert, Gershon David. 2004. *Jews in Poland-Lithuania in the Eighteenth Century: A Genealogy of Modernity*. Berkeley: University of California Press.

Katz, Jacob. 1971. *Tradition and crisis: Jewish society at the end of the Middle Ages*. New York: Schocken.

Kohler, Kaufmann, and Louis Ginzberg. 1902. "Cabala." Pages 456–479 in vol. 3 of *Jewish Encyclopedia*. New York: Funk and Wagnall. Online at www.jewishencyclopedia.com.

Kruger, Hayyim. 1933. *Der Rambam: Zayn leben un Shafn*. Montreal: Keneder Adler.

Leon Stein, Abraham Conan, and Lynn Davison (trans.). 1969. *The Education of Abraham Cahan*. Philadelphia: Jewish Publication Society of America.

Lewis, Justin Jaron. 2002. "Imagining Holiness: A source-Critical, Historical and Thematic Study of Collections of Hasidic Tales with particular focus on the works of Isaac Berger and Abraham Hayim Simhah Bunem Michelson." Doctoral dissertation, University of Toronto.

Mahler, Raphael. 1985. *Hasidism and Haskalah in Galicia and the Congress Kingdom of Poland, in the first half of the nineteenth century*. Translated into English by Eugene Orenstein, Aaron Kelin, and Jenny Machlowitz Klein. Philadelphia: Jewish Publication Society (Hebrew original, Merhavia, Israel: Sifriat Poalim, 1961).

Metzker, Isaac (ed.). 1971. *A Bintel Brief: Sixty Years of Letters from the Lower East Side to the Jewish Daily Forward*. Garden City: Doubleday.

Moshkovits, Zvi. 1962. *Kol ha-Katuv le-Hayyim*. Jerusalem: self-published.

Rapoport-Albert, Ada. 1988. "Hagiography With Footnotes: Edifying Tales and the Writing of History in Hasidism." Pages 119–159 in *Essays in Jewish Historiography: In Memoriam Arnaldo Dante Momigliano*. Edited by Ada Rapoport-Albert. Atlanta: Scholars Press.

Rischin, Moses. 1972. *The Promised City: New York Jews, 1870–1914*. Cambridge, Mass.: Harvard University Press.

Robinson, Ira. 1992. "The First Hasidic Rabbis in North America." *American Jewish Archives* 44: 501–515.
———. 1995. "An Identification and a Correction." *American Jewish Archives* 47: 331–332.
———. 1998. "Hasidic Hagiography and Jewish Modernity." Pages 405–412 in *Jewish History and Jewish Memory: Essays in Honor of Yosef Haim Yerushalmi*. Edited by Elisheva Carlebach, John M. Efron and David N. Myers. Hanover: University Press of New England.
———. *Rabbis and Their Community: Studies in the Immigrant Orthodox Rabbinate of Montreal, 1896–1930* [forthcoming].
Rocker, Samuel. 1919. *Sefer Divrei Hakhamim: Derashot Hazal mi-Talmud Bavli, milukatim mi-kol ha-mekomot asher hema mifuzarim, u-mesudarin be-seder nakhon 'al mikraot ha-tora. Mizuraf le-zeh sefer avnei hefez: devarim yekarim ve-nehmadim, mi-sefarim rishonim ve-aharonim le-varer u-lelaben ma'amarim temohim ve-amukim*. Cleveland: Rocker Printing Company.
———. 1926/27. *Der Sanzer Zaddik: R. Hayyim Halberstam, zts"l/ di vunderbare lebens-geshikhte fun dem sanzer zaddik, velkher iz aroys fun a mitnagdishe svive, zu veren eyner fun di greste gute iden in zayn dor/ zayn leben. zayn virken. zayne taten, zayn tetigkeit in hasidus. zayn geonus in nigleh un nistar biz/ di moradige mahlokes Sanz un Sadagure/dertseylt zum ersten mol in a reyn idishe shprakh.* Vienna: Union Buchdruckerei for Hayyim Zvi Heshe Kauftel [New York], 5687 [1926/27]. Reprint Bnei Brak, Israel, 5730 [1969/70].
———. 1939. *Toldot Anshei Shem/ di lebens geshikhte fun dem gaon u-mekubal R. Shneur Zalman Ladier, di ungarishe geonim R. Moshe Teitlboym, R. Yekutiel Yehuda Teitlboym, un andere zaddikim; zeyr leben, zeyr virken, zayere taten, zayr tetigkeit in hasidus, zayr geonus in nigle un nistar/ Dertseylt zum ershten mol in a reyn 'idisher shprakh.* Cleveland: Progressive Printing Company, 5699 [1939]).
Rome, David. 1989. *Men of the Yiddish Press*. Canadian Jewish Archives n.s. 42. Montreal: Canadian Jewish Congress.
———. 1996. *The Canadian Story of Reuben Brainin, Part 2*. Canadian Jewish Archives n.s. 48. Montreal: Canadian Jewish Congress.
Roskies, David. 1990. "Yiddish in Montreal: The Utopian Experiment." Pages 22–38 in *An Everyday Miracle: Yiddish Culture in Montreal*. Edited by Ira Robinson et al. Montreal: Véhicule Press.
"Samuel Rocker papers, 1910–1984 (1913–1947)." Western Reserve Historical Society, Cleveland, Ohio. www.wrhs.org.
Sanders, Ronald. 1969. *The Downtown Jews: Portrait of an Immigrant Generation*. New York: Harper and Row.
Schwartz, Shuly Rubin. 1991. *The emergence of Jewish scholarship in America: The publication of the Jewish Encyclopedia*. Cincinnati: Hebrew Union College Press.
Shapira, Yosef. 1936. "Reb Yehoshua Rocker." *Di 'Idishe Velt* (Cleveland), May 4, 1936.
———. 1972. *Morai u-Mehankhai: Zikhronot, Reshamim, Havayot*. Tel-Aviv: Netiv.
Soltes, Mordecai. 1924–1925. "Yiddish Press: An Americanizing Agency." *American Jewish Year Book* (1924–1925): 165–372.
Stanislawski, Michael. 1988. *For whom do I toil? Judah Leib Gordon and the crisis of Russian Jewry*. New York: Oxford University Press.
Wolofsky, Hirsch. 1930. *Oyf Eybigen Kvall: Gedanken un batrachtungen fun dem hayntigen idishen leben un shtreben, in likht fun unzer alter un eybig-nayer tora, eingeteylt loyt di parshiyos fun der vokh* [From the Eternal Source: Thoughts and Observations from Contemporary Jewish Life and Aspirations in the Light of Our Old and Eternally New Torah, Organized According to the Weekly (Torah) Portions]. Montreal: Eagle Publishing Company.
———. 1945. *The Journey of My Life*. Montreal: Eagle Publishing Company.
———. 1946. *Mayn Lebens Rayze*. Montreal: Eagle Publishing Company.
———. 2000. *Mayn Lebens Rayze: un demi-siècle de vie yiddish à Montréal 1946*. Translated by Pierre Anctil. Sillery: Septentrion.
Zuckerman, Baruch. 1962. *Zikhronos*. New York: Farlag 'Idisher Kempfer.

Re-Orienting Tradition: Radhakrishnan's Hinduism

Michael Hawley

> Tradition is not always just what it seems, but has constantly been undergoing reinterpretation to accommodate new understandings and changed circumstances. Innovation is not the enemy of tradition but that by which it maintains its relevance. Hinduism does not reject the old in favour of the new but blends the two, expressing new dilemmas in traditional language and accommodating fresh insights to established viewpoints. (Brockington 1981, 209)

> Indian society and culture are not "traditional" in the sense of the nineteenth-century stereotype that is dominated by unchanging traditions and immemorial customs, not even in the sense that many characteristic institutions, culture patterns, values, and beliefs have persisted in spite of numerous changes that have occurred. The traditionalism of the Indian civilization lies elsewhere – in its capacity to incorporate innovations into an expanding and changing structure of culture and society. This capacity is reflected in a series of adaptive mechanisms and processes for dealing with the novel, the foreign, and the strange. The operation of the adaptive mechanisms makes possible a kind of "cultural metabolism" that ingests foreign cultural bodies, segregates them, breaks them down into usable forms, and eventually builds them into indigenous "cultural protoplasm." (Singer 1972, 385)

This essay deals with two main areas: Sarvepalli Radhakrishnan's understanding of Hindu tradition and the tradition of orientalism. My view is that Radhakrishnan's interpretation of Hindu tradition is not only informed by, but often perpetuates and therefore further entrenches, orientalist images of India constructed during the colonial period. As an historian of religion, I am suggesting that an informed understanding of Radhakrishnan's thinking about Hindu tradition needs to be grounded in an understanding of India's colonial past and of his encounters with Western-constructed knowledge about India.

In the Indian context, as a philosopher, academic and statesman, Sarvepalli Radhakrishnan (1888–1975) is perhaps the most prominent exponent of Hindu tradition. Radhakrishnan's concern for defining and defending his religious tradition and his extensive knowledge of the Western philosophical and literary traditions has earned him the reputation of being a bridge-builder between India and the West. He often appears to feel at home in the Indian as well as the Western philosophical contexts, and draws from both Western and Indian sources throughout his writing. Because of this Radhakrishnan has been held up in academic circles as a representative of Hinduism to the West. Moreover, his

lengthy writing career and his many published works have been, and continue
to be, influential in shaping the West's understanding of Hinduism, India, and
the East. Radhakrishnan's apologetic appears to be indicative of how India's
encounter with the West has influenced many Hindu thinkers' understanding
about religion in India. Radhakrishnan's apologetic skill, his knowledge of the
Western philosophical and literary traditions, his ability to speak across cultural
boundaries, and the colonial context in which he worked make his thought a
valuable subject for the present volume.

In what follows, I want to highlight several notable instances in which one
specific historical agent (i.e. Radhakrishnan) has understood his tradition in
order to demonstrate what he believed to be the superiority of his religious
tradition. Specifically, I want to show how Radhakrishnan interprets his religious tradition in a way that reflects, incorporates and perpetuates orientalist
ways of thinking. This discussion is divided into two sections. The first clarifies
the theoretical framework of orientalism as it relates to the present discussion.
The second examines the relationship between a selection of orientalist categories and Radhakrishnan's understanding of Hindu tradition.

I. Orientalism

A critical reference point for this discussion is Edward Said's 1978 book,
Orientalism. Said employs the term "orientalism" in order to question Western
representations of the Islamic world and of the Middle East. These Western
representations of the "Orient" are in Said's words "a system of ideological
fictions, whose purpose is to reinforce and justify Western power over the
Orient" (Said 1985, 155). While Said has in mind the Islamic world, and in particular the Middle East, the category "orientalism" has since been extended to
include South, South-East and East Asia. Following this trend, I will appropriate
"orientalism" as a category for understanding the West's representations of
India and of Hinduism.

Undoubtedly, since its publication Said's *Orientalism* has been a theoretical
reference point for a growing body of scholarship. However, Said's views have
not gone unchallenged, and here I join several of Said's critics. First, I reject
Said's characterization of orientalism as a singular, homogenous, dominant
narrative. Said's use of orientalism is informed by Michel Foucault's notion of
a "master narrative" in which power and knowledge are inextricably linked.
Following Foucault, Said agues that orientalism is a device by which the West
could imagine, control and subjugate an Eastern Other. The recent work by
scholars such as Carol Breckenridge, Peter van der Veer, Ronald Inden, Richard
King, John J. Clarke and the like criticizes Said's assumption that orientalism is
a "single discourse, undifferentiated in space and time and across social,
political and intellectual identities" (Breckenridge and van der Veer 1993, 215).

I think this rightly highlights Said's tendency in *Orientalism* to essentialize and idealize both Occident and Orient. In this light, it is appropriate to view Radhakrishnan's account of Hinduism as *one* "Indian story" among many which sought to respond to a diverse collection of Western categories, attitudes and approaches concerning India.

As a technical, but important corollary to this, I must be clear that I do not wish to make a case for either an authentic India or authentic Europe. Richard King rightly notes Said's ambiguous position(s) concerning the authenticity of the Orient. King observes that at times Said "appears to endorse an anti-representational view, akin to Foucault's own position, whereby there is no authentic Orient, only representations of it." At other times, Said seems to suggest there is an authentic Orient which is being "actively misrepresented" (Said 1985, 5; King 1999, 83). I will, therefore, leave aside the question of authenticity, and instead focus on how Radhakrishnan engages these oriental-ist constructions of and colonial strategies concerning India.

My reference to colonial strategies points to a further issue in need of clari-fication. In *Orientalism*, Said argues for a bond between orientalist knowledge and colonial power. However, Said seems to neglect those orientalist traditions that are not directly tied to the politics of colonialism. Conspicuously missing in Said's *Orientalism* is the contribution of nineteenth century German scholar-ship on India.[1] To be sure, Radhakrishnan took seriously India's loss of political autonomy under British colonialism. But he also sought to confront those under-standings of India and of Hinduism put forth by such scholars as Paul Deussen and G. W. F. Hegel. While such thinkers are removed from the colonial context of British India, their work has nonetheless been used to support a view of Western intellectual and cultural superiority over and against an Indian Other. While I recognize that orientalism is *often* bound up with colonial agendas, I wish to construe orientalism in such a way as to accommodate those Western categories, attitudes and approaches to India which are removed from the immediate domain of colonialism.

Finally, I want to add my voice to those who have challenged Said's often implicit denial of the agency of the Oriental Other. Indeed, this issue is at the heart of the present volume. In *Orientalism*, Said seems to characterize the people of the Orient as passive recipients of Western knowledge and the accepting subjects of colonial power. Said "does not really discuss, nor even allow for, the ways in which indigenous peoples of the East have used, manipulated and con-structed their own positive responses to colonialism using Orientalist conceptions" (King 1999, 86). King rightly remarks that "Orientalist presuppositions about the 'spirituality' of India, were used by reformers such as Rammohun Roy, Dayanan-da Saraswati, Swami Vivekananda, and Mohandas K. Gandhi" (King 1999, 86).

---

1   This is also noted by King 1999, 85.

This no doubt reflects not only the level of permeation of Orientalist ideas amongst the native (and colonially educated) intelligentsia of India, but also the fact that such discourses do not proceed in an orderly and straightforward fashion, being in fact adapted and applied in ways unforeseen by those who initiated them. (King 1999, 86)

Following J. J. Clarke, I take the category "orientalism" to refer to the vast and often diverse constellation of categories, attitudes and approaches by which Europeans sought to construct and affirm identities for both themselves as well as for an Eastern, and specifically an Indian, Other.[2] Informed by orientalist traditions, Europeans created their own knowledge about and images of India to which many Indians found it necessary to respond. In the process of responding to their encounter with the West, Indians, arguably out of effectiveness if not necessity, often found themselves adopting and reinterpreting many of those European images of India and of Hindu tradition against which they sought to argue. This process is strikingly evident in the case of Radhakrishnan.

II. Radhakrishnan, Orientalism and Hindu Tradition

1. Vedānta as Hinduism

The orientalist search for India worked from the assumption that there was "a coherent religious system possessing such established markers as sacred texts and priests" (Metcalf 1995, 10). The idea that the structure of Hindu tradition could be founded on "texts and priests" is not coincidental, for it is precisely these categories which lay in the background of European religious consciousness, a consciousness informed by Christian institutional structures and canonical (i.e. biblical) authority. This assumption led many of the early orientalists to seek out the assistance of those they saw as the dominant religious authorities in Hindu India, namely the *brahmins*. It is not surprising that the texts to which these scholars were directed were precisely those that served to reinforce the status and authority of their *brahmin* assistants. Among the authoritative texts identified were the Vedas (in which the *Puruṣasūkta* appears), the *Laws of Manu*, the *Bhagavad Gītā*, and the Upaniṣads along with selections from their classical commentators. Of the latter, the writings of the eighth century *advaitin* thinker, Śaṅkara, captured the imagination of the orientalists. It was, therefore, Vedānta and its *brahmin* purveyors that were taken to be the authoritative markers of Hindu tradition and Indian culture. For the orientalists, Vedānta was the religion of India, and it was Vedānta that was most widely presented to Europe as the essence of Hindu religion and wisdom.

---

2   Clarke 1999, 7. Clarke uses orientalism to "refer to the range of attitudes that have been evinced by the West towards the traditional religious and philosophical ideas and systems of South and East Asia." I take this characterization of "orientalism" as functional as understood by Baird 1971, 5 and 15–16.

In Europe, Vedānta functioned as the dominant representation of Hinduism. More importantly, it was Śaṅkara's Advaita Vedānta with which many Christian missionaries in India were most familiar. This is not insignificant for it plays a decisive role in Radhakrishnan's definition and defense of Hindu tradition. In his 1908 Master's thesis, a work entitled *The Ethics of the Vedānta and Its Metaphysical Presuppositions*, Radhakrishnan offers an explanation for his acceptance of Vedānta. After a cursory discussion of the views of Madhva, Rāmānuja, and Śaṅkara in turn, Radhakrishnan writes:

> Of these interpretations of which we have given the logical (but not the historical) development we have to confine our attention to one of them to prevent confusion and voluminousness. The first may be safely dismissed from discussion without further examination. Thus the field of choice lies between Ramanuja and Sankara. Ramanuja's system has found favour with the million while *Sankara's is admired by philosophers and learned disputants of every country*. The choice at once and necessarily falls on Sankara, for his system, as stated above, forms the logical conclusion of Ramanuja's theory. Beside intrinsic reasons render it in the highest degree probable that his expositions agree in all essential points with the beliefs of the authors of the original Vedanta texts. The grandeur of spiritual oneness which very few thinkers can appreciate is brought out most sublimely. (Radhakrishnan 1908, 21–22; emphasis mine)

It is not insignificant that the first reason Radhakrishnan gives us for his choice of Vedānta points us in the direction of orientalist scholarship. Knowledge of Vedānta in Europe is a direct result of the orientalist enterprise, and many of the western scholars and missionaries with whom Radhakrishnan associated during his early education drew from it.

A reference to A. G. Hogg is appropriate here. As a missionary and Radhakrishnan's M.A. supervisor at Madras Christian College, Hogg knew little of Hinduism before he arrived in India. Hogg did not "read Sanskrit or speak any Indian language. [However, his] early writings indicate that one of his chief sources for a knowledge of…Hinduism was *Das System des Vedanta* written by the German scholar, Paul Deussen" (Cox 1977, 10n38). Deussen, himself a student of Schopenhauer, benefited greatly from the new wave of oriental literature making its way to Europe. Informed by Deussen's exposition of Vedānta, Hogg undertook his influential apologetic work *Karma and Redemption*. In short, Hogg concluded in *Karma and Redemption* that Hinduism, and in particular Advaita Vedānta, lacked a viable ethic and was philosophically incoherent. It was Hogg's book which prompted Radhakrishnan to embark on his initial definition and defense of Hinduism.

Radhakrishnan and Hogg agree on the "fact" of Vedānta being the high water mark of Hinduism, a "fact" constructed and legitimized by the orientalist scholarship from which they both drew.[3] Undeniably the two come to different

---

3   Here I follow Ronald Inden's sense of orientalist constructed "facts." Inden uses "facts" in the sense that they "have been produced by an 'episteme' (a way of knowing that

conclusions about the philosophical and ethical coherence and viability of
Vedānta. However, neither Radhakrishnan nor Hogg contest the essentialized
and idealized place of Vedānta in Hindu tradition, nor do they question its
assumed acceptance by "scholars" generally. To this extent, Radhakrishnan
accepts Vedānta as the essence and fullest expression of Hindu tradition, an
acceptance which is based on and thus serves to validate and perpetuate the
orientalist view that Vedānta is the essence of, and indeed synonymous with,
Hinduism.

2. "Mystic" and "Spiritual" India

The orientalist search for Hinduism constructed and employed an essentialized collection of ideological markers to distinguish Europe from India. These
categories served to entrench in Western consciousness a diverse constellation
of dichotomies relating to the public and private spheres. In his *Orientalism and
Religion*, Richard King outlines a short inventory of these dichotomies and
observes a pattern in post-enlightenment Western thinking (King 1999, 13). In
King's view, the public/private bifurcation carries with it the parallel oppositions
of society/individual, science/religion, institutional religion/personal religion
or mysticism, secular/sacred, rational/irrational or non-rational, male/female. If
these dichotomies provided a model for European (i.e. "Western") identity and
affirmation, they were also readily appropriated for constructing, representing
and understanding India and Hindu tradition. Europe, King observes, understood itself in the terms and categories associated with the public sphere. Europe
saw itself as socially oriented and scientifically minded. It was secular and
rational. By contrast, India was conceived of in terms of the mystical and
spiritual, the irrational, and the other-worldly.

Radhakrishnan accepts the image of an India preoccupied, and indeed
saturated with, mysticism and spirituality. Radhakrishnan explicitly affirms
that not only is India a land covered with shrines and religious sanctuaries
(Radhakrishnan 1927b, 33), but its philosophical tradition "is essentially spiritual" (24). He promotes an image of India whose "dominant character of…mind
…is the spiritual tendency. Spiritual experience is the foundation of India's
rich cultural history. It is mysticism…leading to a realization of the spiritual"
(Radhakrishnan 1923, 41). At the same time, Radhakrishnan argues that India's

---

implies a particular view of existence)" which "presupposes a representational view
of knowledge. It assumes that true knowledge merely represents or mirrors a separate
reality which the knower somehow transcends. Adherence to this position has
allowed the scholar to claim that his (rarely her) knowledge is natural and objective
and not a matter for political debate. It has also operated to produce a hierarchic
relationship between knower and known, privileging the knowledge of the scientists
and other experts and leaders who make up the former while subjugating the knowledges of the people who compromise the latter" (Inden 1986, 401–402).

inherent mystical and spiritual prerogative illustrates India's philosophical comprehensiveness and superiority. It supplements the rational and the logical with the mystical, spiritual, and intuitive. In Radhakrishnan's mind, India's concern for things mystical and spiritual lays bare the deficiencies of a Europe whose concern for things empirical and rational has compromised its philosophical potential.

So, while "mysticism" and "the spiritual" were categories constructed to subordinate India to Europe, they become in Radhakrishnan's hands exactly the characteristics which give India its superior disposition. But, while Radhakrishnan's apologetic reverses the power relations the philosophy-mysticism dichotomy was designed to promote, the orientalist structure on which it rests remains unchallenged. In other words, the "India versus Europe" paradigm for understanding is further crystallized.

3. "Science" and "Progress"

The translation of Indian texts that emerged in the late eighteenth and early nineteenth centuries challenged the previously held notion of an inherent difference between India and Britain. It quickly became clear that India possessed a long-standing, well-developed legal code as well as well-established literary traditions. Confronted with this, the eighteenth-century British claim that India was a despot in the strongest sense could no longer be held. In order to justify their continued rule of India, new ideologies of difference needed to be articulated. The view that India and Europe were fundamentally different gave way to a way of thinking that saw India and Britain distinguished by degrees of difference (Metcalf 1995, 6).

At the end of the eighteenth century, orientalist scholars began to theorize about what they saw as the ancient wisdom of India. H. T. Colebrooke for one, working under the auspices of the Royal Asiatic Society of Bengal, began to speak of India's Golden Age. Having identified a link between Sanskrit and European languages, Colebrooke "romanticized the virtues of the Aryan inhabitants of North India, describing their worship as non-idolatrous monotheistic faith, free from fertility goddesses, rites and rituals of contemporary Hinduism" (Rambachan 1994, 14). For Colebrooke, this was India's Golden Age. Colebrooke argued that not only did an Indian civilization flourish, but India was indeed the origin of civilization, both Indian and European. In fact, he suggested that "the West owed a debt of gratitude to the East for its contribution to the arts and sciences" (14).

The liberalism of the early nineteenth century in Britain found expression in the publication of James Mill's *History of British India*. In his book, Mill sought to determine the state of India's civilization. Mill worked from the assumption that the degree of civilization of any society could be studied, analyzed, measured, and then compared to other societies. Appealing to the liberalism of

nineteenth century Britain which affirmed that society was shaped by the work-
ings of law, education and a free economy, Mill studied India's arts, literature,
religion and laws, and assessed these areas on the basis of a utilitarian model.
In Mill's view, a hierarchy of civilizations could be derived from careful observation and "scientific" analysis.

Mill determined that India "did not possess, and had never possessed, a
high state of civilization" (Metcalf 1995, 30). He concluded that Indians had
made "but a few of the earliest steps in the progress to civilization" which had
left it in nothing short of "a hideous state of society" (30). For Mill, Hindus were
bound to "a system of priestcraft, built upon the most enormous and tormenting
superstition that ever harassed and degraded any portion of mankind" (30). In
the final analysis, it was clear to Mill that Hindus were the most "enslaved
portion of the human race" (30). Mill's assessment of India provided an ideological foundation upon which Thomas Macaulay would dismiss the "entire
native literature of India" as not up to snuff with "a single shelf of a good
European library" (34).

James Mill rejected Colebrooke's suggestion of a Golden Age in India.
However, Colebrooke's view would ultimately lend itself to Mill's assessment
of India, for Colebrooke went on to argue that while civilization, which had its
origin in Asia, was now in a state of decline in India, whereas the West was
steadily progressing (Rambachan 1994, 14). So, while pleading his case for
India's Golden Age, Colebrooke is "harsh in his judgement and evaluation of
all post-Vedic developments" (14). This was all James Mill needed to boldly
declare that "in beholding the Hindus of the present, we are beholding the
Hindus of many ages past; and are carried back, as it were, into the deepest
recesses of antiquity" (Metcalf 1995, 30).

Radhakrishnan adopts the empirical and "scientific" methodology upon
which Mill claims his analysis and ranking of Indian society is based. However, Radhakrishnan does not share Mill's concern for assessing civilization.
Instead, Radhakrishnan appropriates Mill's method and model to the areas of
philosophical and spiritual progress. For Radhakrishnan, philosophy and its
related discursive disciplines are not simply fields of study but sciences, the
development of which culminates in what Radhakrishnan variously identifies
as Vedānta, Hinduism, religion and integral experience.

Hindu tradition as Radhakrishnan understands it possesses an experimental
and scientific basis. "If philosophy of religion is to become scientific, it must become empirical and found itself on religious experience" (Radhakrishnan 1929,
184). True religion, argues Radhakrishnan, remains open to experience and encourages an experimental attitude with regard to its experiential data. Hinduism
more than any other tradition exemplifies this scientific attitude. "The Hindu
philosophy of religion starts from and returns to an experimental basis" (Radhakrishnan 1927b, 19). Unlike other religions which set limits on the types of
spiritual experience, the "Hindu thinker readily admits of other points of view

than his own and considers them to be just as worthy of attention" (19). What sets Hinduism apart from other religions, according to Radhakrishnan, is its unlimited appeal to and appreciation for all forms of experience. Experience and experimentation are the origin and end of Hinduism as Radhakrishnan understands it.

Radhakrishnan argues that a scientific attitude has been the hallmark of Hindu tradition throughout its history. In a revealing passage, Radhakrishnan explains:

> The truths of the ṛṣis are not evolved as the result of logical reasoning or systematic philosophy but are the products of spiritual intuition, dṛṣti or vision. The ṛṣis are not so much the authors of the truths recorded in the Vedas as the seers who were able to discern the eternal truths by raising their life-spirit to the plane of universal spirit. They are the pioneer researchers in the realm of the spirit who saw more in the world than their followers. Their utterances are not based on transitory vision but on a continuous experience of resident life and power. When the Vedas are regarded as the highest authority, all that is meant is that the most exacting of all authorities is the authority of facts. (Radhakrishnan 1929, 89–90)

If the ancient seers are, as Radhakrishnan suggests, "pioneer researchers," the Upaniṣads are the records of their experiments.

> The chief sacred scriptures of the Hindus, the Vedas register the intuitions of the perfected souls. They are not so much dogmatic dicta as transcripts from life. They record the spiritual experiences of souls strongly endowed with the sense of reality. They are held to be authoritative on the ground that they express the experiences of the experts in the field of religion. (Radhakrishnan 1927b, 17)

Radhakrishnan's understanding of scripture as the scientific transcripts of spiritual insights holds not only for Hinduism, but for all religious creeds. Correctly understood, the various scriptures found in the religions of the world are not infallible revelations, but scientific hypotheses. "The creeds of religion correspond to theories of science" (Radhakrishnan 1929, 86). Radhakrishnan thus recommends that "intuitions of the human soul…should be studied by the methods which are adopted with such great success in the region of positive science" (85). The records of religious experience that are the world's scriptures constitute the "facts" of the religious endeavor. So, "just as there can be no geometry without the perception of space, even so there cannot be philosophy of religion without the facts of religion" (84).[4]

---

4 "What [scriptures] say is not scientifically true; but what they mean is a different matter… If God works in an office, employing charwomen and smoking cigars, it is only a metaphor, rather crude perhaps, as much as glassy seas or many mansions" (Radhakrishnan 1929, 98).

Religious claims, in Radhakrishnan's mind, are there for the testing. They ought not be taken as authoritative in and of themselves. "It is for philosophy of religion to find out whether the convictions of the religious seers fit in with the tested laws and principles of the universe" (85). "When the prophets reveal in symbols the truths they have discovered, we try to rediscover them for ourselves slowly and patiently" (202). The scientific temperament demanded by Hinduism lends itself to Radhakrishnan's affirmation of the advaitic Absolute. The plurality of competing religious claims among the world's religions ought to be taken as "tentative and provisional, not because there is no absolute, but because there is one. The intellectual accounts become barriers to further insights if they get hardened into articles of faith and forget that they are constructed theories of experience" (199).

For Radhakrishnan, the marginalization of mysticism and intuition, and thus the abandonment of the experimental attitude in matters of religion, has led Christianity to dogmatic stasis. "It is an unfortunate legacy of the course which Christian theology has followed in Europe that faith has come to connote a mechanical adherence to authority. If we take faith in the proper sense of truth or spiritual conviction, religion is faith or intuition" (Radhakrishnan 1927b, 16). The religious *cul de sac* in which Europe and Christian theology find themselves testifies to their reluctance to embrace the Hindu maxim that "theory, speculations, [and] dogma change from time to time as the facts become better understood" (Radhakrishnan 1929, 90). For Radhakrishnan, the value of religious "facts" can only be assessed "from their adequacy to experience" (90). Just as the intellect has dominated Western philosophy to the detriment of intuition, so too has Christianity followed suit in its search for a theological touchstone in scripture.

Hindu tradition, Radhakrishnan claims, insists on a graduated scale of religious knowledge and spiritual progress:

> The worshippers of the Absolute are the highest in rank; second to them are the worshippers of the personal God; then come the worshippers of the incarnations like Rāma, Kṛṣṇa, Buddha; below them are those who worship the ancestors, deities and sages, and the lowest of all are the worshippers of the petty forces and spirits. (Radhakrishnan 1927b, 32)

One could hardly ask for a clearer exposition. That Radhakrishnan ranks with "scientific" precision the world's religions speaks volumes as to his appropriation of Mill's method to the sphere of religion. Thus, what was originally a socio-cultural model appropriated to justify the British colonial agenda in India has been transformed into a religious model functioning to invert the existing hegemonic-subaltern relationship between Christianity and Radhakrishnan's Hindu tradition.

Both James Mill's theory of degrees of civilization and Colebrooke's appeal to the Golden Age represent denials of Indian history. While Britain found its lofty place at the apex of Mill's hierarchy, India had made but little progress; and Colebrooke negated all religious development since the time of the Vedas. Radhakrishnan accepts the notion of India's Golden Age, and, not surprisingly, locates it in the Upaniṣadic era. Radhakrishnan takes full advantage of the possibility that India and Europe share a common wisdom, a wisdom which has its roots in Indian soil. Radhakrishnan appropriates Colebrooke's suggestion of a Golden Age, not for the purpose of denying India's history, but as a device to account for what he sees as its historical accretions. Radhakrishnan does not deny the orientalist "fact" of the Golden Age, but characterizes it in such a way as to account for India's present situation and to affirm what he sees as the philosophical and spiritual impulse of Hinduism. Moreover, Radhakrishnan sees in India's Golden Age the "scientific" and experimental basis of Hindu tradition, a methodology he ascribes the to the ancient ṛsis.

4. Hindu Tolerance

In order to justify their political presence in India, the British made use of several ideological devices that served to distance India from, and subordinate India to, Britain. One of these ideological tools was the notion of Oriental despotism. From the British perspective, India was a land suited to despotism. This implied that India had no laws, no concept of property rights, and that Indians willingly submitted to political absolutism (Metcalf 1995, 6). This image of India was reinforced time and again by references to India's climate. In what Thomas Macaulay called "a constant vapour bath" of heat and humidity produced in Indians "languor," tranquillity, ease, a natural passivity and tolerance (Metcalf 1995, 8). These traits, according to the British, contributed to Indians' unquestioning acceptance of arbitrary authority (6). Moreover, the very nature of India's climate produced in Indians a poor work ethic and an unsurpassed unreliability. By virtue of their inherent disposition to passivity and acceptance, Indians required, if not deserved, to be ruled (6).

For Radhakrishnan, Hinduism is an inherently receptive and tolerant tradition. The receptivity and tolerant disposition of Hinduism Radhakrishnan believes is implied by its adherence to intuition and its scientific faithfulness to the provisional nature of religious claims. "With the openness of mind characteristic of the philosophical temper, the Hindus believe in the relativity of the creeds to the general character of the people who profess them" (Radhakrishnan 1922, 7). For Radhakrishnan, the heart of Hinduism recognizes that however "inadequate the symbols may be as expressions of the real, they are tolerated so long as they help the human spirit in its effort after the Divine" (11–12).[5]

---

5   See also Radhakrishnan 1929, 119: "The different traditions are like so many languages in which the simple facts of religion are expressed. Speech may vary but the spirit is the same. There is significance in all forms of worship, however crude and foolish they may seem."

To Radhakrishnan's thinking, tolerance is at the heart of Hinduism's syn-thetic impulse. Radhakrishnan's hierarchy of religions is not only demonstra-tive of Hinduism's scientific temper, but is indicative of its inherent hospitality and synthetic capacity.[6] Unlike Christian theology, which Radhakrishnan sees as preoccupied with maintaining dogmatic, orthodox views and is thus exclu-sive in its orientation, "Hinduism" correctly understood embraces in thought and in practice a scientifically grounded inclusivism. For Radhakrishnan, Hinduism's resistance to conform to orthodoxy has allowed it to remain free from Christian theology's "dualistic philosophy that encourages the spirit of exclusiveness" (Radhakrishnan 1929, 119).

Radhakrishnan repeatedly affirms the tolerance of the Hindu mind. And his affirmation reflects the well-entrenched, though often implicit, colonial ideology of Oriental despotism. As early as his Master's thesis, Radhakrishnan saw a tolerant disposition in the Upaniṣadic ṛṣis:

> Living as they [the ancient Indians] did in a environment where the struggle for physical existence was easy, untroubled as they were by the pressure and excitement that men ordinarily experience, they in the limitless silence of the desert, meditated upon the deeper problems of life, 'things which are more excellent' which are often forgotten and obscured amid the surface froth and business of a commercial nation. (Radhakrishnan 1908, 2)

This climatic theme is reaffirmed in his writings in the 1920s. "Once again it is the natural conditions of India that account for the contemplative turn of the Indian who had the leisure to enjoy the beautiful things of the world..." (Radhakrishnan 1923, 31). And Radhakrishnan further concedes that "'the brooding East', frequently employed as a term of ridicule, is not altogether without its truth" (31). The tolerance of the Hindu mind is further underscored with Radhakrishnan's insistence on the necessity for "intellectual passivity" in the acquisition of intuitive, religious insight (Radhakrishnan 1929, 180). More-over, for Radhakrishnan, tolerance is the mark of ethical behavior and courage. Radhakrishnan denies the implication that Indian tolerance is indicative of weakness and cowardice, traits the British often associated with what they saw as the effeminate Indian, particularly Bengalis. Rather, Radhakrishnan sees the tolerance and "gentleness" of India's mystics "is born of courage and strength and not by fear and cowardice" (114).

Radhakrishnan accepts the orienalist images of the tolerant, accepting, passive Hindu. At the same time he inverts the claims of Western superiority

---

6   Three years after setting out his ranking of religions, Radhakrishnan explained: "The Hindu thinkers admit the ineffability of the [intuitive] experience but permit them-selves a graduated scale of interpretations from the most 'impersonal' to the most 'personal.' The freedom of interpretation is responsible for what may be called the hospitality of the Hindu mind. The Hindu tradition by its very breadth seems to be capable of accommodating varied religious conceptions" (Radhakrishnan 1929, 100).

for which these images were constructed. While the "fact" of Hindu tolerance remains uncontested by Radhakrishnan, he puts a positive spin on it. What was originally a device to differentiate and to subordinate India to Britain is for Radhakrishnan a powerful apologetic tool. It is precisely the ease of the Hindu mind which makes Hindus "superior" to those who lack a genuine spiritual inclination. And it is the Indian environment to which Radhakrishnan attributes the Hindu propensity for philosophical ferment, ethical courage and spiritual mastery.

5. "Secular"

As an academic and statesman, Radhakrishnan is concerned with both education and politics. Education and politics are for Radhakrishnan separate but related issues. He sees Hindu tradition as promoting both secular education and secular nationalism. It is therefore necessary to deal with each of these issues in turn before showing the relationship between them. I begin with Radhakrishnan's vision of secular education as it relates to his understanding of Hindu tradition.

The distinction between the religious and the secular did not hold in the early Victorian educational context. In England, all education was religiously oriented as "intellectual training was not conceived of as existing apart from the moral training of Christianity" (Metcalf 1995, 39–40). Likewise, missionary schools in India were implemented along these lines. The British government in India, however, resisted the introduction of Christian morality and doctrine into government sponsored schools, anxious as it was to minimize conflict between itself and Indians" (40). At the same time the British authorities were equally anxious to remedy what it saw as the ethically degenerate practices it associated with India and with Hinduism. This administrative dilemma was resolved by the introduction of Western literature. Echoing Gauri Viswananthan, Thomas Metcalf observes:

> Although education in India was to be secular, moral training was to be supplied by study of the great works of England's historic literature. No such schools existed in England, nor was English literature seen there as a substitute for Christian training. The guiding ideal was that of "godliness and good learning", enunciated by the educator Thomas Arnold. (Metcalf 1995, 40)

For the British Raj, the intimate bond between education and Christian ethics in England was reformulated in terms of "secular" education under the auspices of "moral training," the sources for which were to be found in the great literary achievements of England and of the West. The Raj did not support Christian education *per se*, but made morality and religious neutrality, like "secularism," a liberal virtue of its own (Metcalf 1995, 40).

Radhakrishnan critiques what he sees as the lack of creativity in modern education, taking on the accusation that Indian education is non-intellectual.

Radhakrishnan argues that modern education in India has become overly intellectual, making it excessively conservative and cautious. Indian education has abandoned its loyalty to first-hand experience, trusting instead the scientific and academic achievements of others. Intellectual freedom, Radhakrishnan counsels, is possible only when the chains of scholasticism are broken.

> If we are to be credited with intellectual power, we cannot afford to say, "let others make the experiments, we will benefit by their experience". The assumption that we are metaphysically minded and are not interested in the pursuit of science is not quite true. ...however, there has been a decline in scientific activity owning to the cramping effects of scholasticism. (Radhakrishnan 1936a, 15)

For Radhakrishnan, the "modern mind" and it accompanying scholasticism breeds intellectual stasis. The "tragedy" is modernism's "excessive intellectuality" (Radhakrishnan 1933, 15) which stifles the creative impulse, for it is "only from those of deep thought and large experience that we can get a breadth and depth of understanding, a hold on essentials too often absent from the works of a mere intellectual" (8). Radhakrishnan does not see modernism simply as overly intellectual, but as an evil. "Lucifer," Radhakrishnan quips, is "the prince of intellectuals" (15).

In Radhakrishnan's view, to "redeem the universities from the charge of commonplaceness we require among their leaders a few creative personalities, a few priests of learning and prophets of spirit" (Radhakrishnan 1944, 88). Only then will university education and the creative and ethical individuals they produce be capable of affirming and promoting the "psychological oneness" of India (88). For Radhakrishnan, education correctly understood is a spiritual investment in the future which ought not to be compromised by the trappings of the "modern mind" and the intellectualized education it breeds, marginalizing as it does the creative and spiritual side of personal development.

Radhakrishnan is not arguing against the necessity of intellectual rigor in education. Rather, intellectual concerns ought not to dominate university life to the detriment of cultivating creative individuals who are capable of challenging, synthesizing and raising the intellectual achievements of the past. Radhakrishnan calls for an educational shift, a reappraisal of educational ideals.

> Not that in India we neglected the logical. We also insist on the intellectual approach to the central problems of life. At a time like this, when teachers are setting themselves up in all parts of the country and requiring of their disciples complete surrender of the intellect; it is well to be reminded of the Indian tradition that the intellect is to be satisfied and not surrendered. Freedom and not slavery of the mind is the prerequisite of spiritual life. But intellectual fruition is in intuition, vidyā ends in anubhava. (Radhakrishnan 1944, 183)

Radhakrishnan has in mind an integral system of education which affirms the importance of all experiences and spheres of life. Such a system facilitates the intellectual, artistic and ethical development of its students by remaining aloof from the cautious conservatism and scholasticism Radhakrishnan identifies with the modern mind.

Radhakrishnan's call for a revitalized education is accompanied by an appeal to the Indian past. That Radhakrishnan locates the spirit of true education in the Indian past does not imply that he is advocating a return to what he understands as narrow sectarian religious instruction. In fact, Radhakrishnan sees contemporary traditional religious teachers as having abandoned the experimental methods of their predecessors. Today's religious leaders, according to Radhakrishnan, are unable to assume the roles of true teachers. They are self-interested and dogmatic. They demand conformity and suppress the experiential hallmark of Radhakrishnan's Hinduism (Radhakrishnan 1936a, 2–3). For Radhakrishnan, that traditional leaders demand conformity is tantamount to religious despotism (3).

Instead, Radhakrishnan recommends the reclamation of the "scientific" methods of the ancient seers. Just as Radhakrishnan claimed to find in the Upaniṣads the basis for his experimental religion, a religion which he believed advocated the scientific method, the creative potency of mystical intuition, and tolerance, so too does Radhakrishnan look to the perennial methods of these same sages for a corrective to India's educational woes.

> India of the ages is not dead; nor has she spoken her last creative word. The time has come for a new religious expression, a new language for the old everlasting emotions in terms of modern knowledge, a religious form that should contradict no fact and check no inquiry. The everlasting spirit of love and righteousness which has inspired the religions of the past must now quicken and inform the new learning. (Radhakrishnan 1933, 16)

Radhakrishnan locates his educational curriculum in what he sees as "traditional" education. The aim of traditional education in India, Radhakrishnan claims, "is *brahmacarya*, initiation into a disciplined life of spirit, the development of the chastity of mind and body. [It] is to help free the growth of the soul" (Radhakrishnan 1944, 78ff.). Traditional education, according to Radhakrishnan, has never attempted to deal piecemeal with the various dimensions of human life. Nor has it been simply a means to worldly ends. Rather, traditional education in India "is an initiation into the life of spirit, a training of human souls in the pursuit of truth and the practice of virtue. It is a second birth, *dvitiyam janma*" (*Report of the University Education Commission* 1949, 43).[7]

---

7   Radhakrishnan was appointed by Jawaharlal Nehru to head up the University Education Commission. This section of the Report (as well as the others cited in this paper) was authored by Radhakrishnan. See also his discussion of *dharma* and *mokṣa* in education in Radhakrishnan 1944, 105.

For Radhakrishnan the Upaniṣadic ṛṣis were not only pioneer researchers in the realm of experience, nor were they simply spiritual teachers, but the watershed of university culture. "The ancients," Radhakrishnan argues, "symbolized culture which is acquired in a college," a cultural "torch that is passed from hand to hand down the generations" (Radhakrishnan 1936a, 65). For Radhakrishnan, the "cultural torch" which he believes has been passed down from the sages of old symbolizes the spirit of revolution in all spheres of life. "If we are afraid of the upturnings of the soil, of the social, economic and political upheavals consequent on the spread of this fire, we should not go near a University. We may as well shut it down" (65–66). Just as the ancients had refused to accept second-hand religious formula as authoritative, so too did they call for experimentation in the realm of education and politics.

The programme of the ancients, so Radhakrishnan claims, supports his vision for a university residential system.

> In ancient times the teacher and the pupil shared a common life. They shared the same simple food and life and in the process was established a close relationship between the teacher and the pupils. Education was regarded as a co-operative enterprise. [For] the teacher not only imparts instruction but transmits the power of the spirit. (*Report of the University Education Commission* 1949, 54)

Likewise, an active community life in modern India should also involve teachers: "Members of the teaching staff may participate in them actively, not to dictate or supervise but to advise and help, to make available to youth their wide knowledge and mature experience" (54).

Robert Minor has argued persuasively for the notion of "secularism" as a religious category in Radhakrishnan's thought (Minor 1987, 92–93, 120–121). Secularism as Radhakrishnan understands it is not hostile to religious belief and practice, but is the promotion and refinement of all religious views. For Radhakrishnan, the universal values of fellowship and unity are affirmed by all religions as well as by creatively inspired works of literature. In this light, Radhakrishnan's educational vision is as "spiritual" as it is "secular," affirming as it does that intellectual training cannot exist apart from moral training.

Radhakrishnan emphasizes the value of moral training in education. Moral training, as Radhakrishnan envisions it, is not associated with one or another of the various religions, identified as they are in Radhakrishnan's mind with unscientific dogmatism and a resistance to personal experience. Instead, the literary achievements of both India and the West possess the potential for moral development, informed as they are by the universal creative spirit. Clearly, Radhakrishnan and the colonial strategists disagree as to what constitutes "great literature." Neither do the two agree as to what constitutes "godliness and good learning." But the proposition that moral individuals could be raised in an atmosphere of "religious neutrality" is preserved. A contagion of moral spirit through education is the end which both Radhakrishnan and the educational administrators of the British Raj strove to realize.

At the same time, secularism becomes in Radhakrishnan's hands an apologetic tool whereby he is able to affirm as superior the experiential basis and experimental methods of Hindu tradition. As he understands it, a secular education is one in which all religious views are accepted, and subsequently raised, in accordance with their genuine experiential roots. But, Radhakrishnan holds that the authentic core of all religions is integral experience, an experience he identifies with Hindu (i.e. Vedānta) tradition. Thus, the affirmation of all religious traditions under the auspices of "secular education" is, for Radhakrishnan, not only a vehicle for creating ethically responsible individuals but a testament to the superiority of Hinduism. In other words, Radhakrishnan does not simply appropriate the category of secularism, but inverts the colonial strategy for secular education in India so as to strengthen his apologetic programme. What was originally a strategy implemented by the British to promote (Christian) "godliness and good learning" is effectively transformed by Radhakrishnan into a category for Hindu self-affirmation and Indian superiority.

6. "Nation"

In the early years of the Raj, the British attempted to legitimate their presence in India on the grounds that India lacked national coherence. India was, for them, a fragmented assemblage of competing groups and interests which could only be administered by a (benevolent) despot. Ironically, the lack of national coherence the British saw in India was reinforced with the formation of nationalist organizations, several of which were organized along religious lines.

In the early 1930s, Muhammad Iqbal's vision for a Muslim political identity, Muhammad Jinnah's subsequent call for an independent Pakistan, and the recognition by the British government at the Round Table Conferences of "non-Hindu" interests, an India of "no nations" had become an India of "two nations." British colonial ideologies introduced nationalist discourse into the subcontinent while at the same time resisting Indian claims of national affirmation, and often contributed to the construction of communal identity and the perpetuation of national discord.

The category "nation" figures prominently in Radhakrishnan's thinking.[8] For Radhakrishnan, Hindu tradition is antithetical to a narrowly conceived political nationalism. Political nationalism and its ideology of the nation state is not only myopic, but is irrational and irreligious. It acts as a barrier to the goals of democracy, justice, equality and fraternity, and encourages self-interest and zealous patriotism. It is nationalism in this negative sense that Radhakrishnan associates with the West and with the colonial programme. Radhakrishnan deplores this narrowness of national vision when he says:

---

8   Paul Hacker has suggested that a "nationalist impulse" is the chief marker of Neo-Vedānta apologetics. See Hacker 1978.

> Nationalism is not a "natural" instinct. It is an acquired artificial emotion. Love of one's native soil, loyalty to regional traditions, do not mean violent hostility to one's neighbours. If today the feeling of national pride is intense, it only shows the prodigious capacity of human nature for self-deception. Self-interest, material greed and lust for domination are the operative ideals. Patriotism has killed piety, and passion logic. (Radhakrishnan 1947, 16)

Such an ideology, Radhakrishnan argues, lies not only at the foundations of the colonial enterprise, but is part and parcel of Christianity's uncompromising religious sensibilities. Having cut itself off from experience and having crystallized its theological positions, Christian dogmatism has been used to justify an oppressive political arrangement in India.[9]

For Radhakrishnan, colonial rule has resulted not only in India's political domination, but has compromised what he sees as the true nature of nationalism. In what Radhakrishnan describes as a political obsession, a misconstrued nationalism has obscured the cultural ideals of a spiritually united India:

> The living continuity of Indian life is to be seen not in her political history, but in her cultural and social life. Political obsession has captured India since the battle of Plassey. To-day politics have absorbed life. The State is invading society, and the India of "no nations", as Rabindranath puts it, is struggling to become a "nation" in the Western sense of the term, with all its defects and merits. (Radhakrishnan 1922, 15)

Radhakrishnan believes that British rule has made positive contributions to India in the realm of security and economics. But these accomplishments Radhakrishnan argues have neglected the creative spirit of the Indian nation as he understands it.

> British rule has given India peace and security, but they are not ends in themselves. If we are to put first things first, then we must admit that economic stability and political security are only means, however valuable and necessary, to spiritual freedom. A bureaucratic despotism which forgets the spiritual ends, for all its integrity and enlightenment, cannot invigorate the people beneath her sway, and cannot therefore invoke any living response from them. (Radhakrishnan 1927a, 772)

Not only has India been sequestered from its spiritual heritage under British colonialism and Western nationalism, but the capacity of Hindu tradition for integration and its promotion of what Radhakrishnan sees as its social ideals of equality, justice and fraternity have become ineffective. For him, India's loss of political autonomy resulted in political conservatism, religious exclusivity and social exploitation. In short, India has lost sight of its capacity for creative unity which Radhakrishnan sees as the hallmark of Hindu tradition.

---

9   For a brief summary of Radhakrishnan's views on religion and politics in the West, see for example Radhakrishnan 1929, 46.

While Radhakrishnan affirms that colonialism is an obstacle to India's impulse toward creative unity, Indians who embrace and promote national stasis are culpable in India's continuing subjugation. Radhakrishnan accuses India's leaders who have abandoned Hinduism's experiential and experimental methods of being colonial brokers of intellectual mediocrity:

> If the leaders of recent generations have been content to be mere echoes of the past and not independent voices, if they have been intellectual middlemen and not original thinkers, this sterility is to no small extent due to the shock of the Western spirit and the shame of subjection. (Radhakrishnan 1927a, 772)

Radhakrishnan does not advocate a national renewal in which India rejects wholesale all things Western, but pleads for a national catharsis, a purging of political conservatism to affirm India's creative and experiential authenticity. A national cleansing would provide a long term creative vision for India's future and would inoculate India against the divisive effects of communal interests. Indians, Radhakrishnan counsels, must

> shake off the oppressive traditions of the past and to equip themselves to face the future, a future in which they will be called upon to play their part as leaders, statesmen, and administrators in the national life of a Self-governing India. (Radhakrishnan 1936a, iv)

For Radhakrishnan, India's political freedom is contingent on the spiritual and intellectual freedom of the individual. Radhakrishnan advises that the creative development of the inner spirit is necessary for national reconstruction (Radhakrishnan 1936a, 14). Indians must learn to revolt, not only against what Radhakrishnan sees as oppressive, dogmatic socio-political domination (British or otherwise), but more importantly against the bondage of the soul.

Radhakrishnan speaks of a national freedom and self-determination as a "resurrection into unity," a "restoration into some kind of wholeness or some kind of integral life" (Radhakrishnan 1936b, 234). But such a national resurrection must remain open to the creative impulse which he understands as the essence of Hindu tradition. Without it politics will remain antisocial and antiscientific, and society exploitive and unjust (Radhakrishnan 1929, 46). For Radhakrishnan, experience and experimentation have the power to counter religious communalism and narrow political agendas.

Radhakrishnan finds support for his understanding of nationalism in the language and ideals of the Upaniṣads and later *smṛti* literature. Radhakrishnan understands *ānanda* in terms of freedom: "The three note-worthy features of spiritual experience are reality [*sat*], awareness [*cit*] and freedom [*ānanda*]."[10] He readily appropriates his identification of *ānanda* as freedom to the national

---

10   See for example, Radhakrishnan 1929, 102.

and political spheres. For when we experience the subordination of self to something greater, Radhakrishnan tells us, whether it be "family or nation... we have faint glimpses of mystic moods" (Radhakrishnan 1929, 93).

According to Radhakrishnan, the Hindu Epics affirm his programme for national consolidation in which communal self-interest is subordinated to greater national ideals, as well as his paradigm for cross-cultural integration. The "acceptance of new tribes and their gods" of which the *Rāmāyaṇa* speaks, Radhakrishnan argues, were affirmed though subordinated as aspects of the one supreme reality. "The polytheism was organized in a monistic way. Only it was not a rigid monotheism enjoining on its adherents the most complete intolerance for those holding a different view" (Radhakrishnan 1927b, 40).[11] For Radhakrishnan, nationalism whose impulse it is to foster an integrated and creative union of long-standing Indian spiritual values is antithetical to intolerance, communalism and political domination.

For Radhakrishnan, moral exemplars are also national heroes:

> These sanyasis [sic] do not cut themselves off from the world and let it go to rack and ruin. The greatest of their class, Buddha and Sankara, Ramanuja and Ramananda, and scores of others, have entered into the life-blood of the nation and laid the foundations of its religion. Their names to-day are part of the national heritage. (Radhakrishnan 1922, 16)

For Radhakrishnan, national heroes are "political *saññyāsins.*"[12] They are dispassionate ascetics who remain above the ever-shifting sands of public opinion and to whom the populace may look for ethical and national guidance.[13] For Radhakrishnan, political *samnyāsins* are made in universities. For it is only in a university setting, Radhakrishnan believes, that one is "protected from the State" (Radhakrishnan 1936a, 58). Universities are political, intellectual and ethical

---

11 See pp. 38–43 in this work for Radhakrishnan's full argument.
12 Radhakrishnan 1944, 1. The spelling and diacriticals are Radhakrishnan's.
13 Richard King has observed Gandhi's successful inversion of colonial discourse surrounding what British had construed as the "effeminate," "other-worldly" and "passive" *samnyāsin* (King 1999, 134). Just as King observes in the case of Gandhi, Radhakrishnan reapplies these "cultural symbols" in an organized, experientially informed social and political protest. Radhakrishnan's "experiential religion" is compatible not only with a highly moralized social activism, but with disciplined political involvement. And in what King describes as an "inability of the British to control the implications and direction of their own colonial discourses," Radhakrishnan calls for a new order of political *samnyāsins* who would direct a revitalized Indian consciousness, a national awareness based on a common heritage faithful to the experiential fruits of reconciliation and tolerance. At the same time, Radhakrishnan reinvents the traditional *samnyāsin* ideal. Far from staging his own social death, Radhakrishnan's *samnyāsin* is a political actor and national architect. For Radhakrishnan, a political *samnyāsin* is a dispassionate visionary who has renounced not society but partisan politics. A political leader of this calibre expedites the realization of what Radhakrishnan sees as the age old values of Hindu tradition: democracy and equality, justice and fraternity.

greenhouses. They offer a retreat from the world and nurture in the student the simplicity of life and the restraint necessary for leadership.

Radhakrishnan readily assimilates Western nationalist discourse into his affirmation of Hindu tradition. But Radhakrishnan's conception of the Indian nation is defined not merely in terms of a political arrangement or geographical boundaries, but by its intellectual heritage. For Radhakrishnan, the nation is India's philosophical inheritance, a long-standing religious heritage which he identifies with the experiential and experimental methods he finds in the Upaniṣads.

The political difficulties Radhakrishnan sought to address were to be remedied by affirming India's historic creative ingenuity through which India's national pride would be restored. A national restoration of this sort would not only curb what Radhakrishnan saw as the irreligious and misguided zealous patriotism of the West, but would lay the groundwork for realizing India's spiritual potential. In education, the modern mind acquiesces to second-hand experience and to a curriculum which defers to the intellectual rehearsal facts and theories at the expense of the spiritual betterment of the whole person. Modern thinking breeds intellectual complacency. It is unscientific scholasticism which inhibits the creative development of the individual. On the national level, a modern mentality represents a "failure of nerve" and "loss of self respect" under which the *status quo* goes unchallenged, a temperament which Radhakrishnan believes has left India in not only political, but national bondage.

Thus, what was originally a discourse by which the Raj could implement and maintain its administrative efficiency in India becomes in Radhakrishnan's hands the keynote of India's past, an interiorized and idealized device for not only practical political consolidation but for intellectual restoration and spiritual fulfillment.

Concluding Remarks

In the process of responding to his encounter with the West, Radhakrishnan appropriated and reinterpreted many of those orientalist images of India and of Hindu tradition against which he sought to argue. Because of this, his understanding of Hindu tradition is not only informed by, but in fact perpetuates and further entrenches these images of India constructed during the colonial period. Undoubtedly, Radhakrishnan had, and continues to have, his critics. But his apologetic continues to serve for many as an important source for Hindu identity and Indian pride. Radhakrishnan's understanding of Hinduism draws our attention to the fluid and dynamic nature of "tradition" as a scholarly category, a category that cannot be removed from the historical and hermeneutic contexts in which it is being employed. "Tradition" is not static. Rather, it is a category that is continually being (re)imagined and (re)created to serve particular ideological ends.

References

Baird, Robert D. 1971. *Category Formation and the History of Religion*. Second Edition 1991. New York: Mouton de Gruyter.

Breckenridge, Carol A., and Peter van der Veer. 1993. *Orientalism and the Post-Colonial Predicament: Perspectives on South Asia*. Philadelphia: University of Pennsylvania Press.

Brockington, John L. 1981. *The Sacred Thread: Hinduism in Its Continuity and Diversity*. Edinburgh: University of Edinburgh Press.

Clarke, John J. 1999. *Oriental Enlightenment: The Encounter Between Asian and Western Thought*. London: Routledge.

Cox, James L. 1977. *The Development of A. G. Hogg's Theology in Relation to Non-Christian Faith: Its Significance for the Tambaram Meeting of the International Missionary Council, 1938*. Unpublished Ph.D. dissertation, University of Aberdeen.

Hacker, Paul. 1978. "Aspects of Neo-Hinduism As Contrasted With Surviving Traditional Hinduism." Pages 580–608 in his *Kleine Schriften*. Wiesbaden: Franz Steiner Verlag.

Inden, Ronald. 1986. "Orientalist Constructions of India." *Modern Asian Studies* 20.3: 401–446.

King, Richard. 1999. *Orientalism and Religion: Postcolonial Theory, India and "The Mystic East."* London: Routledge.

Metcalf, Thomas. 1995. *Ideologies of the Raj*. New Delhi: Cambridge University Press.

Minor, Robert N. 1987. *Radhakrishnan: A Religious Biography*. Albany: State University of New York Press.

Radhakrishnan, Sarvepalli. 1908. *The Ethics of the Vedānta and Its Metaphysical Presuppositions*. Madras: The Guardian Press.

———. 1922. "The Heart of Hinduism." *The Hibbert Journal* XXI.1: 5–19.

———. 1923. *Indian Philosophy*. Volume 1. London: George Allen & Unwin, Ltd.

———. 1927a. *Indian Philosophy*. Volume 2. London: George Allen & Unwin, Ltd.

———. 1927b. *The Hindu View of Life*. London: George Allen & Unwin, Ltd.

———. 1929. *An Idealist View of Life*. London: George Allen & Unwin, Ltd.

———. 1933. "Intellect and Intuition in Sankara's Philosophy." *Triveni* VI.1: 8–16.

———. 1936a. *Freedom and Culture*. Madras: G. A. Natesan & Co.

———. 1936b. "Spiritual Freedom and the New Education." *New Era in Home and School* XVII: 233–235.

———. 1944. *Education, Politics and War*. Poona: The International Book Service.

———. 1947. *Religion and Society*. London: George Allen & Unwin, Ltd.

Rambachan, Anantanand. 1994. *The Limits of Scripture: Vivekananda's Reinterpretation of the Vedas*. Honolulu: University of Hawaii Press.

The Report of the University Education Commission. 1949. New Delhi: Ministry of Education.

Said, Edward. 1985. *Orientalism*. Harmondsworth: Penguin Publishers.

Singer, Milton. 1972. *When a Great Tradition Modernizes: An Anthropological Approach to Indian Civilization*. New York: Praeger Publishers.

Rights and Values in the American Constitutional Tradition

David W. Machacek and Adrienne Fulco

It must be acknowledged that the Constitution of the United States is, and was always, much more than a written plan of government. From the beginning Americans regarded the Constitution with a reverence ill befitting a mere blueprint for organizing and limiting governmental power. James Madison, the "philosopher of the Constitution," was clear that in a system of popular government, the Constitution would be effective only if the people internalized its fundamental values. This is particularly evident in his ambivalence about a bill of rights—a bill of rights, "parchment barriers" to the abuse of power, would offer little protection if its requirements ran counter to popular opinion in a government where the real power lay with voters. The spirit of the Constitution was, to Madison at least, as important as the Constitution itself. That is to say, the Constitution is more than a set of procedural rules for democratic self-government; it is also a symbol that evokes a vision of *good* government.

It is in this sense that some have described American constitutionalism as a "religion" (Bellah 1967, 1975), a "faith" (Levinson 1988), or a "moral tradition" (Powell 1993). While much constitutional theory focuses on the Constitution as a legal document (the province of courts) or as instituting a framework for political debate and action (the province of legislature), our concern is with the third dimension, the Constitution as a statement and symbol of foundational principles from which a moral tradition has evolved.

Constitutionalism as a Tradition of Moral Enquiry

In his book, *The Moral Tradition of American Constitutionalism* (1993), H. Jefferson Powell makes a compelling case for looking at American constitutionalism as a tradition in the MacIntyrean sense, and we follow Powell's lead in this chapter by employing Alasdair MacIntyre's definition of "tradition." That is, a tradition is a socially embodied "argument extended through time in which certain fundamental agreements are defined and redefined in terms of two kinds of conflict: those with critics and enemies external to the tradition who reject all or at least key parts of those fundamental agreements, and those internal, interpretive debates through which the meaning and rationale of the fundamental agreements come to be expressed and by whose progress a tradition is constituted" (MacIntyre 1988, 12).

MacIntyre's definition of tradition, of course, is presented in the context of a critique of liberalism and contemporary liberal social orders, which he argues by rejecting tradition reduced public moral discourse to the mere assertion of individual wants and preferences without reference to any basis on which moral conflicts might be rationally debated and resolved. He writes:

> One of the most striking facts about modern political orders is that they lack institutionalized forums within which these fundamental disagreements can be systematically explored and charted, let alone there being any attempt made to resolve them... We thus inhabit a culture in which an inability to arrive at agreed rationally justifiable conclusions on the nature of justice and practical rationality coexists with appeals by contending social groups to sets of rival and conflicting convictions unsupported by rational justification... Disputed questions concerning justice and practical rationality are thus treated in the public realm, not as a matter of rational enquiry, but rather for the assertion and counter-assertion of alternative and incompatible sets of premises. (1988, 2, 5–6)

Meaningful public moral discourse is possible only in reference to certain fundamental agreements and only in an institutional context characterized by rules of "practical rationality" by which disputes can be resolved; meaningful moral discourse, in short, is "tradition-constituted" and "tradition-constitutive."

Whether or not it was what the Founders intended, it is clear to even a casual observer that American constitutionalism has become a tradition of moral enquiry in the MacIntyrean sense. More and more the moral questions that vex the public, legislators, and courts, from displays of the Ten Commandments in courthouses to end-of-life decisions, are framed in terms of Constitutional values. The language of rights has become the dominant language of American public moral discourse, and the political and legal process established by the Constitution provides the institutional context for the systematic exploration and resolution of public moral disputes, which themselves can be seen as disputes about the practical meaning of certain fundamental moral agreements.

The Moral Foundation of American Constitutionalism

Whether the moral foundation of American constitutionalism was derived from secular liberalism or Protestant Christian sources is a matter of much dispute. It is probably safe to say that the foundational agreements at the core of the tradition are the product of the encounter of English Common Law, Enlightenment liberalism, and Protestant Christianity in the context of colonial America.[1]

---

1   See McGraw (2003), Jacoby (2004), Pole (1978), and Katz (1988), among others on this point.

The American constitutional tradition developed out of the real experiences of the first immigrants who made their way to the colonies and were required to establish structures and institutions by which to govern their inhabitants. Different approaches to governing were adopted in the various colonies, and when the time came to write first the Articles of Confederation and then the Constitution, the central task for the authors of those documents was to facilitate compromises that would weave the distinctive strands of constitutionalism together. The federalist solution, of course, allowed just this kind of diversity in unity. While it is certainly true that by the time of the writing of the Constitution in 1787 there was substantial agreement on particular fundamental principles, the different emphasis delegates from various states placed on one principle over another gave rise to the compromises that made ratification possible. The diverse experiences of the Framers with colonial governing became the basis for specific elements of American constitutionalism, including the kinds of protections and guarantees that appear in the Bill of Rights.

As Leonard Levy has noted, "[T]he American colonial experience, climaxed by the controversy with England leading to the Revolution, honed American sensitivity to the need for written constitutions that protected rights in the 'immutable laws of nature' as well as in the British constitution and colonial charters" (Levy 1999, 8). But Levy also emphasizes that Americans "had a novel concept of *constitution*. The word signified to them a supreme law creating government, limiting it, unalterable by it, and paramount to it" (1999, 8). And, as Jack Rakove has observed, Americans believed that "their rights would be secure only when they were explicitly incorporated into the texts of their newly written constitutions" (Rakove 1998, 3). It should be noted that the way in which rights were understood and defined evolved during the 1760s and 1770s. As Daniel Rodgers has pointed out in his nuanced discussion of rights in colonial America, the subject was deeply contested, and "[t]alk of Natural Rights was a tool, sharp with subversive possibilities, and always controversial" (Rodgers 1987, 47).[2] Moreover, the process of naming and identifying rights became part of an American political tradition that had already taken root in the explicit guarantees of state constitutions, which then served as models for the Framers who gathered in Philadelphia in 1787.

---

2   For an illuminating discussion of the evolution of natural rights in the Revolutionary era, see Chapter 2 in Rodgers' *Contested Truths: Key Words in American Politics Since Independence* (1987). For example, Rodgers argues: "Had the Americans merely discovered the rights of human beings once and contented themselves with periodic declarations of what they had found, their enumeration of rights would quickly have hardened into settled, stabilizing forms... But out of the slogan makers' compounding of the words "right" and "nature" emerged a way of talking about politics far less predictable than that. Set the words together in the manner forged in the heat of the Revolutionary agitation of the 1760s and 1770s, and they invited inquiry, not simply into the rights which human beings possessed, but into those rights, which, given their nature, they ought to possess" (46).

Although prior to the Revolution Americans became increasingly critical of British rule, they remained essentially loyal to the British constitutional tradition, framing their arguments in terms of the rights of Englishmen that ought to be guaranteed and respected. This is evident in an episode involving writs of assistance. In order to enforce tariffs on goods imported to the American colonies, the courts issued writs of assistance allowing customs officers to enter warehouses, stores, and private homes in search of illicit goods. When George II died in 1760, writs issued in his name became void after six months and would have to be reissued. When courts in England issued a series of rulings refusing to issue new writs on common law grounds, American merchants claimed that, because the colonists were English citizens, such writs were also illegal in the colonies. But in 1767, Parliament passed the Townshend Act, imposing new tariffs on imports to the colonies and formally legalizing writs of assistance in America. English citizens in America, from the Parliament's perspective, did not enjoy the same rights as English citizens in England.

Fortified by the compelling case for independence, rather than for mere reform, that Thomas Paine made in *Common Sense*, Americans begin "to think about constitutions in an entirely different sense" (Rakove 1998, 3). According to Rakove, Americans came to understand that "a constitution was a document adopted at a known moment of historical time and an expression of supreme law that would henceforth regulate what government could and could not do" (3).

The relationship between the Declaration of Independence and the emerging American constitutionalism is noteworthy. The Declaration of Independence delineated the causes of the colonial rebellion and provided the rationale for terminating fealty to the Crown and the British constitution. But in the Declaration Jefferson prosecuted the case against George III in terms of a theory of justice based on three foundational and interrelated propositions, which the colonists took to be "self-evident." These are, of course, the equality of all "men," the existence of "certain unalienable Rights," and that the legitimacy of government is determined by "consent of the governed." And the evolution of American constitutionalism can be seen as an "historically extended argument" about the meaning of these "fundamental agreements." Thus, the decision to abandon the British constitutional model, which had developed incrementally and found expression in multiple documents and practices, allowed Americans to elaborate the new theory of justice articulated in the Declaration by means of a novel kind of constitutional experiment.

Equality

Gordon Wood, the distinguished professor of early American history, has remarked that equality is "the most powerful idea in all of American history" (2003, 100). As early as 1831, when Tocqueville began his nine-month tour of America, equality stood out as the most important influence on American social and political development, a "fundamental fact" that conditioned thought and behavior. Kenneth Karst, a contemporary legal scholar who has written extensively on the meaning of equality, reaffirms Tocqueville's central insight: "[t]he ideal of equality is one of the great themes in the culture of American public life. From the Declaration of Independence to the Pledge of Allegiance, the rhetoric of equality permeates our symbols of nationhood" (Karst 1983).[3]

The ideal of equality, however, has always stood opposed to the reality of various inequalities in American society, creating a dynamic tension that has propelled a lively debate about what equality means in practice—Who is equal? And in what sense? As a result, the practical meaning of "equality" in the American constitutional tradition has changed dramatically over time.

The authors of the Constitution were painfully aware of the inconsistency between the principle of equality and the reality of slavery, but it was also clear to them that the public moral debate over slavery was, at that time, sufficiently removed from a general resolution that to make provisions to end slavery would doom the cause of the Constitution. Madison's records of the convention indicate that debates about slavery were intense. As Eric Foner explains, the delegates to the Convention labored to meet the demands of both proponents and opponents of slavery, a word that never appears in the Constitution itself. The constitutional compromises they finally crafted "prohibited Congress from abolishing the African slave trade for two decades; required states to return to their owners fugitives from bondage; and provided that three-fifths of the slave population be counted in determining each state's representation in the House of Representatives and its electoral votes for President" (Foner 1998, 35). A crucial and highly divisive issue was left unresolved, guaranteeing that the question of slavery would continue to fuel constitutional battles for decades to come. Indeed, some have argued that it was the desire to avoid the divisive issue of slavery that explains the absence from the 1798 Constitution of any direct mention of "equality."

But it would be mistaken to think that no notion of equality made it into the Constitution that the Framers sent to the States for ratification. Article I, section 9 provides that "No Title of Nobility shall be granted by the United States: And no Person holding any Office of Profit or Trust under them, shall, without the Consent of the Congress, accept of any present, Emolument, Office, or Title, of any kind whatever, from any King, Prince, or foreign State." For the most part, the Framers' understanding of equality was opposed to European aristocracies. Equality in this sense meant that there would be no classes of persons entitled to legal privileges by virtue of birth. It is in this anti-aristocratic sense that the Declaration's assertion that all men are "created equal" must be understood—that is, as an assertion that privileged classes are

---

3 For an insightful and comprehensive treatment of the meaning of equality in America, see Pole 1993.

not a natural or God-given condition, but a human creation. Equality was thus foundational to American constitutionalism, even though it was not yet equality in the modern, twentieth century sense.

It was, furthermore, this kind of equality that so impressed the French aristocrat Alexis de Tocqueville during his nine-month tour of America in the 1830s. Tocqueville opened his survey of democracy in America by announcing that "no novelty in the United States struck me more vividly during my stay there than the equality of conditions" (1969, 9) a theme that he would carry throughout the book. Writing to his fellow Frenchmen, Tocqueville juxtaposed equality in America with the French aristocracy:

> I should like for a moment to consider the state of France seven hundred years ago; at that time it was divided up between a few families who owned the land and rule the inhabitants. At that time the right to give orders descended, like real property, from generation to generation. (9)

What Tocqueville meant by "equality of condition" in America was that there was apparently no "value of birth." In the northern states, Tocqueville remarked, "even the seeds of aristocracy were never planted. There only intellectual power could command influence, and the people came to respect certain names as symbols of enlightenment and virtue" (1969, 50). In the South, to be sure, one found a system with rich landowners, but even there "their influence was not exactly aristocratic, in the sense in which that word is used in Europe, for they had no privileges, and the use of slaves meant that they had no tenants and consequently no patronage" (1969, 51).

Tocqueville understood, nonetheless, that the equality of condition that he found so remarkable did not extend to America's non-European inhabitants. Of the "Negroes" and "Indians" he observed:

> These two unlucky races have neither birth, physique, language, nor mores in common; only their misfortunes are alike. Both occupy an equally inferior position in the land where they dwell; both suffer the effects of tyranny, and, though their afflictions are different, they have the same people to blame for them. (1969, 317)

Despite the manifest inequalities in American society, however, the *idea* of equality had been firmly planted in the American mind, and this, Tocqueville saw, would profoundly influence all manner of social relationships. The second volume of *Democracy in America* is devoted more or less exclusively to the effect of equality on American civil society. As is often the case, his words on the subject now seem prophetic:

> When castes disappear and classes are brought together, when men are jumbled together and habits, customs, and laws are changing, when new facts impinge and new truths are discovered, when old conceptions vanish and new ones take their place, then the human mind imagines the possibility of an ideal but always fugitive perfection. (1969, 453)

Although the Americans had not achieved perfect equality, Tocqueville observed, the experience of equality, limited though it might be, inspired in Americans a passionate love of equality, which "is daily acquiring a greater hold over the human heart" (1969, 503). Limited equality had oriented the Americans to an ideal, if always fugitive perfection.

The struggle to expand an originally narrow view of equality and thus to bring more Americans under the umbrella of equality has shaped some of the most important moments in the evolution of the American constitutional tradition. Westward expansion, the extension of the franchise, and questions concerning the status of slaves in the new territories ensured that the moral and political debate about equality would only intensify.

Two related and often-overlapping political movements—abolitionism and the women's suffrage—dominated political debate about the meaning of equality in the nineteenth century, a term that changed significantly over the course of the century. The language of these debates was moral; it is only in the aftermath of the Civil War, with passage of the Reconstruction Amendments, that the moral claims to equality were transformed into legal rights.

While they referenced the Declaration of Independence, the arguments made by abolitionists in favor of the emancipation of slaves stressed the Biblical origins of their claims. Angelina Grimké, an early abolitionist author and activist, appealed to "Christian women of the South":

> Search the Scriptures daily, whether the things I have told you are true. Other books and papers might be a great help to you in this investigation, but they are not necessary... The Bible then is the book I want you to read in the spirit of inquiry, and the spirit of prayer. Even the enemies of Abolitionists, acknowledge that their doctrines are drawn from it. (A. Grimké 1988, 297)

Other abolitionists delivered similar moral appeals, expressing their conviction that if all human beings—slaves included—were equal before God, they should also be equal before the law. By melding Christian theology with the principles stated in the Declaration of Independence, "abolitionists...invented the concept of equality before the law regardless of race, one all but unknown before the Civil War" (Foner 1998, 87).

Although both the abolitionists and their opponents used biblical language to make their arguments, efforts to resolve the dispute over slavery ultimately required legal solutions. The Missouri Compromise and the *Dred Scott* decision nationalized the question of slavery, which in turn ignited a general debate in America about the legal meaning of equality that persisted throughout the nineteenth century—well beyond the end of the Civil War.

At the same time, advocates for women's equality, many of whom served in the abolitionist cause, came to see that the moral arguments in favor of emancipation and equality for slaves applied with equal force to women.

Sarah Grimké, the older sister of Angelina, appealed to the Bible in her letters to the Boston Female Anti-Slavery Society (1837). In "The Original Equality of Woman," she concluded:

> God created us equal; – he created us free agents; – he is our Lawgiver, our King, and our Judge, and to him alone is woman bound to be in subjection, and to him alone is she accountable for the use of those talents with which her Heavenly Father has entrusted her. (Grimké 1837, Letter I)

Neither nature nor God had made women unequal to men; inequality of the sexes was a product of human laws and therefore demanded a legal resolution:

> There are few things which present greater obstacles to the improvement and elevation of woman to her appropriate sphere of usefulness and duty, than the laws which have been enacted to destroy her independence, and crush her individuality; laws which, although they are framed for her government, she has had no voice in establishing, and which rob her of some of her *essential rights*. (1837, Letter XII; emphasis in original).

One of the most striking aspects of Grimké's statement is the assertion that the legal inferiority of women denied them their "essential rights," a claim that advocates of women's suffrage would make in even stronger terms after the Civil War. Sarah Grimké and other defenders of equality for slaves and women transformed a moral dilemma into a high stakes political battle over the meaning of equality. Now understood as a matter of essential rights, they set the terms of a constitutional debate that continued well into the twentieth century.

This understanding of equality—equality before the law—was not yet firmly established in the constitutional tradition, however. The Fourteenth Amendment, ratified in 1868, guaranteed "equal protection" of the law, but not equal standing before it. Whether or not equal standing was intended by the Amendment's "privileges and immunities" clause—"No State shall make or enforce any law which shall abridge the privileges or immunities of citizens of the United States"—for the remainder of the nineteenth century and most of the twentieth, black Americans were routinely denied access to the political process through a variety of legal (poll taxes and literacy tests) and illegal means (outright intimidation). Indeed, given the appalling behavior of many public officials toward black Americans, one would rightly question whether the Amendment's affirmative guarantee of equal protection amounted to anything more than nice words.

Without effective access to the political process, political solutions to persistent problems of legal inequality seemed not only remote but were also in fact exceedingly dangerous. The legal policies of the Jim Crow South excluded Blacks from political and social participation, and, increasingly, relied on violent means to enforce segregation. And when the courts addressed questions challenging the legality of segregation, as in *Plessy v. Ferguson* (1896), they failed to find a constitutional violation. By the middle of the twentieth century, activists who saw no hope of legislative action to end segregation either at the state or federal level instead turned to public opinion. Popular protest movements advocating equal rights for black Americans, migrant farm workers, women, and homosexuals defined the latter half of the twentieth century. Although the Nineteenth Amendment finally established a woman's right to vote and the passage of New Deal legislation created new economic benefits premised on the idea of equality, the public moral discourse about equality was transformed by the struggles of the civil rights movement.

In 1938, Justice Harlan Stone wrote a famous footnote in the *Carolene Products* case[4] that set the terms of the debate. The footnote addressed three circumstances in which the Court might legitimately overrule democratically enacted legislation: 1) when the legislation falls within a specific prohibition in the Constitution; 2) when legislation interferes with the democratic process itself; and 3) when "prejudice against discrete and insular minorities...tends seriously to curtail the operation of those political processes ordinarily to be relied upon to protect minorities." Two went directly to the issues raised by the civil rights movement. Public moral debate about the practical meaning of equality would henceforth be squarely located within the constitutional tradition.

Perhaps the best evidence, as Wald notes, is the "civil rights rhetoric of Martin Luther King Jr. Although steeped in Christianity, based in the church, and a master of using religious metaphors to mobilize his flock, King's public appeal for equality tapped into core American values—what Thomas Jefferson called self-evident truths—that were familiar to all Americans, religious or not" (Wald 2003, 317). Machacek and Hammond explain further: "To be sure, Civil Rights leaders invoked the language of Protestant Christianity, but their appeal was effective precisely because one did not have to share the religious viewpoint of black Baptists—or Methodists or Muslims—in order to perceive the justice of their cause." Because he framed his moral argument in terms of the constitutional tradition, "one could disagree with Martin Luther King, Jr.'s exegesis of Exodus and still recognize the legitimacy of the moral claim he was making" (Machacek and Hammond [forthcoming]).

It was on the basis of concern for preserving access to the political process that the Court in 1954 ruled school segregation unconstitutional in *Brown v. Board of Education*. The evil of school segregation stems from the fact that the democratic process depends on an educated citizenry. Unequal education undermined the democratic process and, significantly, contradicted a moral commitment on which the legitimacy of American democracy rests—consent of the governed. When citizens are deprived of access to the political process, they can hardly be said to have given their consent to the laws. The principle of equal

---

4   Footnote 4 in this case is often referred to as the "most famous footnote in the history of constitutional law" (Choper, Fallon, et al. 2001, 62).

access became quickly ensconced, as evidenced by the ratification of the Twenty-fourth Amendment, outlawing poll taxes (one of the insidious devices used to prevent black and poor white Americans from voting), only ten years later.

But it was the persistent problem of discrimination that most captured the public's moral imagination. The idea that legislation that targeted particular racial groups required a higher level of scrutiny by courts than say legislation regulating the fat content of milk (the issue in the *Carolene Products* case) became the basis for the Court's discrimination jurisprudence. The Court developed a general test for evaluation of cases involving alleged discrimination, determining that legal classifications based on race are "suspect" on their face and require "strict scrutiny" by the Court. In other words, the states may treat persons differently under the law—for example, by setting the driving age at 16 or providing tax advantages to homeowners—but the classifications cannot be "invidious, arbitrary, or irrational" (Walker 1992, 848). Furthermore, according to the Court, the only way in which the state may substantiate legislation based on suspect classifications is to demonstrate "a compelling state interest," a hurdle that is very difficult to overcome.

The Court's jurisprudence in this area placed the problem of discrimination in the center of a national moral debate. Whereas racial discrimination was once simply a part of daily life, by 1964 Congress had passed the Civil Rights Act, which outlawed discrimination based on race and other invidious classifications in public accommodations and employment (Title II and Title VII respectively). Before long other groups—namely women, the disabled, and gays and lesbians—began to litigate in court, arguing that they too had suffered unconstitutional discrimination. In a remarkably short period of time, new legislation was passed at many levels of government that aimed to prevent discrimination and to penalize those in both the private and public sector who continued to deny equality to groups that had been victims of discrimination in the past. The language of public discourse about equality was now constitutional and rights-based.

Public support for anti-discrimination measures and for Supreme Court decisions enforcing them was strongest when groups and individuals could clearly demonstrate a history of past discrimination. Once, however, the question turned to cases involving competing equality rights claims, especially in the area of affirmative action, court decisions and policy mandates became far more controversial. Although Americans strongly supported the principle of equal treatment, critics argued that the Constitution must be "color-blind." According to this view, the Constitution requires only equality of opportunity, but not equality of result or outcome. The Supreme Court's decision in *Regents of University of California v. Bakke* (1978), which found the use of racial quotas in a state-funded medical school admissions plan unconstitutional but upheld programs that used race as a "plus factor" in student selection, set off a national debate that continues to the present.

Rights

One of the more unusual features of the Declaration of Independence lies in the understanding of rights implied by the assertion that some rights are "unalienable." As noted above, prior to 1776, when Americans claimed their rights were being violated, they were generally referring to their rights as English citizens and guaranteed by Magna Charta, English common law, or the colonial charters. That is, in contemporary terms, Americans were operating under a "constructionist" view of rights—rights are *created* by their inclusion in a written constitution.

By 1776, as is evident in the Declaration, Americans were claiming that certain rights are not concessions of government, but are inherent in what it means to be human. And they claimed that respect for these fundamental rights is a measure of the justice of government. Rights in this view are not created by constitutions; they must be *discovered*. The existence of inalienable or natural rights thus became one of the agreements that lay at the foundation of American constitutionalism. And the purpose of the Constitution was not only to establish a government committed to protecting those rights but also an institutional context for debate about rights and the nature of justice. Ultimately, we come to an understanding of what rights are through an ongoing public debate *about* rights, which is to say that the American conception of "rights" is tradition-constituted and tradition-constitutive.

As Hammond, Machacek, and Mazur (2004) point out, this accounts for the Founders' apparent concern to preserve the freedom of conscience and a public realm in which conscience might be freely expressed. They argue that the First, Ninth and Tenth Amendments can be read "as an invitation to continue the conversation about rights" that gave rise to the revolution and to demands for a bill of rights in the Constitution:

> What limited understanding of rights anyone in the early Republic had, what limited understanding they had of how to form a "more perfect Union, establish Justice, ...and secure the Blessings of Liberty" was a product of the lively public debate over rights that characterized the era; one that took place, notably, in the institutions of religion, voluntary political and fraternal associations, and the press, as well as through review of claims of right by the judiciary... The Bill of Rights, in brief, begins—in the First Amendment—by singling out for protection a realm in which matters of conscience, rights, and freedom could be publicly discussed and debated; it ends—in the Ninth and Tenth Amendments— by asserting that the debate is not over just because the Constitution now had a Bill of Rights. (2004, 14–15)

The debate over fundamental rights, of course, *has* continued, and the language of rights has moved beyond a purely legal application and has become the preferred language of a much broader public moral debate.

This has not always been as evident as it is today. We described above how in the nineteenth century the moral authority of the Bible was brought to bear on the cause of abolition and women's suffrage. Machacek and Hammond (forthcoming) note that although legally disestablished in the nineteenth century, Protestant Christianity was so prevalent in the population that it "remained sovereign in public life, defining the language and values by which public issues were discussed and debated. The mainline churches, in particular, could be seen—and were seen by both social scientists and most Americans—as custodians of the public culture". Indeed, until late in the twentieth century, the courts themselves practiced a "jurisprudence of deference" to majority opinion on moral issues, with the effect being that moral codes based on Protestant religion were codified into law (Machacek and Fulco 2004). Both popular and legal discourse, in other words, employed Protestant religious language and categories for understanding and discussing public moral issues.

A number of factors contributed to a reduction of Protestant hegemony in public moral discourse. Not the least of these was growing religious diversity in the United States, including growing fragmentation within Protestantism over Biblical interpretation, the natural and social sciences, and modernity generally. That is to say, in MacIntyrean terms, the Protestant tradition was unable to resolve its own internal debates over how to live faithfully in the modern world—giving rise to at least two Protestant traditions, liberal and fundamentalist, external to and in conflict with each other. Much less was Protestantism able to answer non-Protestants, external to the tradition, increasingly in evidence in the American population. For these reasons, Protestantism simply became *unable* to function as the basis of public moral discourse. The Grimké sisters' Biblical-moral arguments simply would not carry the weight in public moral discourse today as they did in the nineteenth century.

At the same time, the American experience in World War II led to a much greater national commitment to the notion of fundamental human rights. Franklin D. Roosevelt's "Four Freedoms" speech had called Americans to join the conflict abroad, citing freedom of speech and freedom of religion, as well as freedom from want and freedom from fear as the fundamental values for which Americans were fighting. After the war, Americans joined the Allies in prosecuting war criminals for "crimes against humanity"—violations of rights inherent in what it means to be human—at Nuremberg and Tokyo, and Eleanor Roosevelt led the commission to write the International Declaration of Human Rights.

In that context, it is entirely unsurprising that Americans began to turn a critical lens on themselves, and one result, facilitated by Roosevelt's progressive Supreme Court appointments, was a renewed emphasis on and conflict over rights in the United States. After World War II, Americans increasingly framed their opinions about public moral issues in terms of constitutional rights and increasingly turned to a newly receptive Supreme Court to resolve disputes over the meaning of those rights. In the twentieth century the language of rights and the authority of the Constitution have come to define the public moral questions themselves.

The number of cases involving the First Amendment's religion clauses that came before the Court after 1940 dramatically illustrates the pattern. "From 1845 to 1940," Hammond, Machacek, and Mazur note, "the Court heard fewer than a dozen cases raising constitutional questions related to religion... For the next three decades (from 1940 to 1970), it averaged about a case a year. However, since Warren Burger became Chief Justice in 1969 to the present, the Court has averaged slightly more than two church-state cases per year" (2004, 85).

As Hammond has shown, one result has been that the meaning of religious freedom has undergone a significant change, with each resolution giving rise to new conflicts. Thus, for instance, when the Court decided in 1940 that the Free Exercise Clause protects religiously motivated behavior from arbitrary legal restraint, it forced the questions: 1) under what circumstances might religiously motivated actions legitimately be restrained? And 2) what is religious? (Hammond 1998, chapter 3). Through a series of cases the Court eventually arrived at what is known as the Sherbert test, named for the case in which it was most clearly articulated, *Sherbert v. Verner* (1963), for deciding when the law might legitimately restrain the free exercise of religion. When a law burdens the free exercise of religion, according the test, the state must demonstrate that it has a legitimate and compelling interest in upholding the law and that there is no less burdensome means of accomplishing the law's purpose. Moreover, in order to avoid getting mired in the problem of distinguishing between "true" and "false" religions, the Court eventually recognized that it is individual *conscience* that the Free Exercise Clause protects.

As the Court was expanding the possibilities for individual religious expression and action, it was narrowing the possibilities of state-sponsored religious expression and action under the Establishment Clause. If the free exercises cases involved the question of what kinds of behavior can and cannot be legally *prohibited*, the Establishment Clause cases asked about what can and cannot be legally *required*. The most famous and controversial of these were the decisions involving prayer and Bible reading in public schools. More recently controversies over the Pledge of Allegiance and public displays of the Ten Commandments have joined them. Court cases involving the religion clauses of the First Amendment, in brief, reveal a vital debate about the meaning of religious freedom as a fundamental constitutional value.

A second line of cases is equally vital and informative, in large part because it so dramatically illustrates the shift on the Supreme Court from a jurisprudence of deference to majority opinion to an "activist" jurisprudence of enquiry into individual rights and the profound effect this has had on the way Americans discuss and debate public moral issues. These are the cases involving individual "liberty rights."

The religion cases just discussed were made possible by an interpretation of the Fourteenth Amendment known as "substantive due process" that began its ascendance in property rights cases in the nineteenth century.[5] The Due Process Clause of the Fourteenth Amendment provides that no state shall "deprive any person of life, liberty, or property, without due process of law." If rights to life, liberty, and property form the substantive concerns of the Due Process Clause, Machacek and Hammond (forthcoming) point out, the Court had to be able to say what "liberty" was.

At the very least, the Court said, liberty referred to those rights enumerated in the Bill of Rights, but might it also mean more? The Ninth Amendment— "The enumeration in the Constitution, of certain rights, shall not be construed to deny or disparage others retained by the people"—implied the existence of rights not yet discovered (or fully acknowledged) that were eligible for Constitutional protection. It fell to the Court to sort out legitimate claims of right from mere assertions of self-interest, but in order to do this effectively the Court had to find some way to legitimate its decisions in cases where the Constitution is not explicit in order to convince the public that they were not simply imposing their own private moral judgments or engaged in an arbitrary use of judicial power but acting faithfully to the constitutional tradition. Cases involving the right to privacy illustrate the challenge.

In *Griswold v. Connecticut* (1965), the Court announced that implicit in the concept of liberty is the right to be free of unwarranted government interference in private life. Although the right to privacy is not explicitly guaranteed in the Constitution, Justice Douglas, delivering the opinion of the Court, argued that when taken together the rights guaranteed by the Bill of Rights create "penumbras" sufficient to protect the right of privacy. Moreover, this unenumerated right to privacy was declared to be fundamental and worthy of full constitutional protection.

One aspect of a right to privacy, for instance, had evolved out of prior property rights cases. Thus, Justice Douglas noted that the Court had previously protected the "sanctity of a man's home." In other cases, the Court related privacy to the "right to educate one's child as one chooses" and "the freedom to associate and to privacy in one's associations," which the Court had also recognized as worthy of protection. In *Griswold*, privacy was conceived as an aspect of a relationship—marriage—worthy of constitutional protection against arbitrary governmental intrusion. Each of these aspects of privacy refers both to a particular amendment in the Bill of Rights and to specific practical applications that the Court had established in prior cases.

Justice Goldberg, in his concurring opinion, went even further, asserting that "the concept of liberty protects those personal rights that are fundamental, and is not confined to the specific terms of the Bill of Rights." In Goldberg's view, the ability of individuals to make certain moral decisions as to the

---

5 Ironically, the *Dred Scott* decision was among the first applications of the substantive due process doctrine. The Missouri Compromise, which prohibited slavery in U.S. territories, was ruled unconstitutional because it deprived John Sanford, Scott's owner, of his property without due process of law.

marital relationship is rooted in a right that is so fundamental as to be prior to rights specifically guaranteed in the Bill of Rights.

In a later contraceptives case, the Court expanded its understanding of privacy, in the direction suggested by Goldberg, to include personal moral decision-making (*Eisenstadt v. Baird*, 1972). Privacy came to be conceived as an aspect of personality, an unalienable right as opposed to a right that one gained upon acquisition of property (the home) or entering a private relationship (marriage). It was on the basis of this understanding of privacy that the Court in *Roe v. Wade* (1973) ruled anti-abortion laws unconstitutional.

The Court's privacy decisions were controversial from the beginning, and even more so once the right of privacy became closely identified with the legalization of abortion. William Rehnquist, then an associate justice, staked out the terms of the argument in his dissenting opinion in *Roe*, asserting that the right to privacy lacked constitutional grounding. In the immediate aftermath of *Roe*, the Court continued to uphold the privacy right in its abortion jurisprudence despite efforts by states and Congress to severely restrict access to abortion services.[6] By 1983, however, Republican presidents had appointed several conservative justices to the Court, and the right to privacy was under attack.

Only ten years after *Roe*, the Court began to uphold restrictions on abortion. More importantly, Sandra Day O'Connor, the first female justice on the Supreme Court, joined Rehnquist's conclusion that the right of privacy lacked sufficient constitutional credentials. The Court's jurisprudence now took a different turn, and in a string of cases, the majority upheld restrictions and directly challenged the right to privacy.[7] Finally, in 1992, Justice O'Connor wrote the plurality opinion in *Planned Parenthood of Southeastern Pennsylvania v. Casey*, which sustained "the central holding of Roe"—the right to choose—but anchored it this time not in the right to privacy but rather in a broad liberty interest.

O'Connor was clearly aware of and concerned about the difficulties of legitimating a decision based on unenumerated rights. On this point her opinion is worth quoting at length:

> It is tempting, as a means of curbing the discretion of federal judges, to suppose that liberty encompasses no more than those rights already guaranteed to the individual against federal interference by the express provisions of the first eight amendments to the Constitution. But of course this Court has never accepted that view.
>
> It is also tempting, for the same reason, to suppose that the Due Process Clause protects only those practices, defined at the most specific level, that were protected against government interference by other

---

6   *Planned Parenthood v. Danforth* (1976) (spousal and parental consent restrictions); *Bellotti v. Baird* (1979) (parental or judicial consent restrictions).

7   A variety of restrictions were upheld in the following cases: *Akron v. Akron Center for Reproductive Health* (1983); *Thornburgh v. American College of Obstetricians and Gynecologists* (1986); *Webster v. Reproductive Health Services* (1989).

rules of law when the Fourteenth Amendment was ratified. But such a view would be inconsistent with our law. It is a promise of the Constitution that there is a realm of personal liberty which the government may not enter. We have vindicated this principle before.

Neither the Bill of Rights nor the specific practices of States at the time of the adoption of the Fourteenth Amendment marks the outer limits of the substantive sphere of liberty which the Fourteenth Amendment protects.

... The inescapable fact is that adjudication of substantive due process claims may call upon the Court in interpreting the Constitution to exercise that same capacity which, by tradition, courts always have exercised: reasoned judgment. Its boundaries are not susceptible of expression as a simple rule. That does not mean we are free to invalidate state policy choices with which we disagree; yet neither does it permit us to shrink from the duties of our office.

She was also clearly aware that the Court's opinion would not only have to satisfy her fellow justices, but also the general public:

Men and women of good conscience can disagree, and we suppose some always shall disagree, about the profound moral and spiritual implications of terminating a pregnancy, even in its earliest stage. Some of us as individuals find abortion offensive to our most basic principles of morality, but that cannot control our decision. Our obligation is to define the liberty of all, not to mandate our own moral code. The underlying constitutional issue is whether the State can resolve these philosophic questions in such a definitive way that a woman lacks all choice in the matter.

Finally, citing prior cases in which the Court had extended protection to "personal decisions relating to marriage, procreation, contraception, family relationships, child rearing, and education," the right of individuals "married or single, to be free from unwarranted governmental intrusion into matters so fundamentally affecting a person as the decision whether to bear or beget a child," and "the private realm of family life which the state cannot enter," she provided the following rationale for the Court's decision in case at hand:

These matters, involving the most intimate and personal choices a person may make in a lifetime, choices central to personal dignity and autonomy, are central to the liberty protected by the Fourteenth Amendment. At the heart of liberty is the right to define one's own concept of existence, of meaning, of the universe, and of the mystery of human life. Beliefs about these matters could not define the attributes of personhood were they formed under compulsion of the State.

The Court extended the reasoning of *Casey* in *Lawrence v. Texas* (2003), another controversial decision concerning moral choices, when it overturned the Texas sodomy statutes and all others like them across the country. The right to decide moral questions that involve deeply personal matters was now firmly embedded in the liberty interest explicitly mentioned in the Fifth and Fourteenth Amendments to the Constitution.

Those decisions had a profound impact on the way Americans understand and debate morally contentious issues such as abortion and homosexuality as we demonstrated in our study of public response to the Massachusetts state supreme court decision legalizing same-sex marriage (Machacek and Fulco 2004). Most of those who expressed opinions, for and against the decision, on the *Boston Globe* website framed their opinion of the decision in terms of constitutional rights. That most of those who did so favored the court's decision is evidence that a significant part of the population of Massachusetts has internalized "moral autonomy" as a fundamental value. Although a relative newcomer to the constellation of constitutional values, moral autonomy, whether understood as a right to privacy or a broadly construed liberty interest, shows signs of becoming established both in the Court's opinions and in the public mind.

It is evident to anyone familiar with the heated disputes over abortion, homosexuality, teen sexuality, and the like in the United States, however, that this debate is far from resolved. Like debates over the meaning of religious freedom, debates over whether liberty ought to include a right to privacy or moral autonomy and, if so, what those rights mean in practice are likely to continue into the indefinite future. But this only further indicates the vitality of the constitutional tradition because, as MacIntyre teaches us, conflict over the meaning of fundamental agreements is the lifeblood of a living tradition.

Consent

There is an old adage that the Supreme Court is not final because it is right; it is right because it is final. That is clever, but misleading. The Court is not a moral tutor in the classical republican sense, and the Court has never relied exclusively on raw power to exercise its influence on the American constitutional tradition. Although it is not constitutionally required to do so, the Court explains its decisions in written opinions that are designed not only to instruct lower courts and lawmakers on matters of law but also, especially in cases involving contentious public moral issues, to persuade the public that its decisions are just and fair. While the process of constitutional adjudication plays a key role in the development of America's constitutional tradition, the tradition is not the sole province of the courts and legal professionals.

Generally speaking, the public moral debates that we have been discussing—about the meaning of equality and the meaning of liberty or fundamental rights—take place in an institutional complex composed of civil society (that realm of discourse protected by the First Amendment in which people are free to air beliefs and opinions free from the coercive powers of the state), politics (where elected representatives bring their constituents' beliefs and opinions to bear on questions of general interest), and law (where particular disputes between adversaries are decided through a process of adjudication). Although one or another of these institutional realms may be more prominent on a given dispute and their relative influence may shift over time, all three are involved in the development of the American constitutional tradition. A more thorough treatment of the constitutional tradition than we are able to offer here would analyze the evolution of constitutional meanings in popular discourse, political discourse, and legal discourse and attempt to unpack how developments in one have influenced developments in the others.

It is important to recognize, in fact, that one of the most critical debates in the constitutional tradition, both historically and at present, concerns precisely the relative weight to be given to each of these institutional realms in the development of the tradition. These are, simply put, debates about the nature of authority in a tradition whose third foundational commitment is the proposition that the legitimacy of government derives from the consent of the governed. In a government whose constitutional structure is based on the concept of separation of powers, who has the authority to say what the Constitution means? Surprisingly, on this crucial matter, the Constitution itself is virtually silent.

Early in our history, the silence was broken when Chief Justice Marshall established that the Supreme Court had the power of judicial review in *Marbury v. Madison* (1803). Marshall boldly asserted that "[i]t is emphatically the province and duty of the judicial department to say what the law is." Subsequently, the Supreme Court came to be regarded by most Americans as the principal and authoritative interpreter of constitutional meaning. Constitutional scholars refer to this approach to constitutional interpretation as "judicial supremacy," which sees the Constitution fundamentally as a legal document—a formal, written contract—and thus the province of legal specialists—lawyers, law professors, and judges.

The notion of judicial supremacy, which implies an expansive concept of judicial review, has always been subject to criticism, especially during periods when there is intense disagreement about decisions rendered by the Court. When considering various approaches to constitutional interpretation, however, it is important to distinguish between more general discussions about which branch of government is best suited to interpret the Constitution from debates about the worthiness of different approaches to jurisprudence that particular Supreme Court justices adopt.[8]

Most critics of "judicial activism," in fact, assume judicial supremacy. Chief Justice Rehnquist, for instance, one of the most vocal critics of an activist judiciary has also been one of the most jealous defenders of constitutional adjudication against attempts by the legislature to force the hand of the Court on controversial issues.

---

8 Interpretive questions dealing with jurisprudence often concern the relative merits of the "textualist" approach, which is favored by Justice Scalia as against a "living Constitution" approach, which was favored by Justice Brennan.

Justice Scalia, by contrast, adopts a more "majoritarian" view of constitutional authority. In Scalia's sometimes vitriolic attacks on the direction the Court has taken in the latter half of the twentieth century, he complains that the Court has read commitments into the social contract—the Constitution—that aren't explicitly stated there. One element of Scalia's complaint addresses his commitment to a "textualist" jurisprudence, which requires that insofar as possible judges should rely upon the plain meaning of the text of the Constitution, informed by the immediate historical context in which the words were written. They should avoid "discovering" new rights not explicitly enumerated. This in turn requires that judges defer to the wishes of democratically elected legislatures on controversial matters of moral concern (Scalia 1997).

Thus, in a speech to the Woodrow Wilson International Center for Scholars (2005), Scalia remarked that the Court's 2003 decision overturning Texas' anti-sodomy law must have been based on "I don't know. The Sexual Preference Clause of the Bill of Rights, presumably." From this perspective, when, for example, the Court recognizes "privacy" or "moral autonomy" as fundamental rights and applies them to disputes over the justice of laws restricting abortion and homosexuality, the Court is violating the will of the majorities who voted to restrict those rights and imposing new contractual obligations that the parties to the contract—the people—have not voluntarily agreed to; the Courts are engaged in "judicial tyranny." Real authority over constitutional meaning lies with voting majorities.

The alternative that Scalia proposes gives further evidence of his majoritarianism: "You want a right to abortion: create it the way most rights are created in a democratic society. Persuade your fellow citizens it's a good idea, and enact [a constitutional amendment]. You want the opposite, persuade them the other way" (2005). In other words, according to Scalia, the proper way to recognize rights that do not appear in the text of the Constitution is to have democratic majorities vote them into existence.

What this view fails to take into account is the fact that one of the principal purposes of the Bill of Rights was to place certain inalienable rights *beyond* majoritarian control. Majorities, simply because they are able to produce the necessary votes to achieve their objectives, can use the amendment process to deprive minorities of their rights. One has simply exchanged "judicial tyranny" for "tyranny of the majority."

Justice Kennedy, writing the majority opinion for the Supreme Court in *Romer v. Evans* (1996), tackled this problem head on, concluding that a Colorado state constitutional amendment denying homosexuals the constitutional guarantees against discrimination enjoyed by all other citizens of the state violated a cherished principle of constitutional adjudication: that no group of citizens can be deprived of equal protection of the laws because of the animosity the majority feels towards them. Scalia's invitation for democratically elected majorities to express their will through the amendment process does nothing to protect the rights of unpopular minorities. Surely, the Colorado amendment that stripped protection from homosexuals violates a foundational constitutional value: that majority rule never extends to the extinction of minority rights.

A third approach to answering the question of who should interpret the Constitution focuses on the fact that the Constitution itself does not speak directly to the question. Indeed it is this silence that, according to George Thomas, provides the crucial clue to the problem of authority in the constitutional tradition. Quoting John Agresto to make the point, Thomas argues that the answer lies not in "what the Constitution is—law—but [in] what it establishes—a constitutional democracy of separated powers, checked and balanced" (2004, 240). In this "departmentalist" view, "the design of government, rather than any enumerated right, was meant to constitute the main protection for individual and minority rights" (Glendon 1991, 24–25). By dividing power between state and national government and between the various branches of government, the Constitution sought to prevent the government or any particular branch of government from becoming powerful enough to intrude on the rights of citizens.

It is important to recognize that loyalty to any of these positions shifts with the political winds. That is to say, that participants in the debate about authority tend to prefer positions that appear, at that particular moment, to be most favorable to achieving a particular outcome. As Barry Friedman has noted of constitutional theorizing about judicial review,

> Over the last century or more there have been two general positions taken about judicial review: that it is a blight in a democratic system that must be curtailed, and that it is a valued part of U.S. government essential to the protection of constitutional liberty. One is a critique, the other a justification. Progressives and conservatives have advanced both positions (in various permutations) at different times, depending upon which position seemed most apt to present circumstances, given their political views. (Friedman 2004, 149–150)

For our purposes, it is sufficient to point out that the debate about authority is itself constituted by and constitutive of an ever-evolving constitutional tradition.

Constitutionalism Living and Dead

It is entirely mistaken to think of equality, rights, and consent as sums fixed by the Constitution—that is, to think of American constitutionalism as a tradition in the Burkean sense, in which meanings are passed down unchanged from one generation to the next. Such a tradition, MacIntyre reminds us is either dead or dying. A "dead" constitutionalism might suffice, as it clearly does for Antonin Scalia, if the Constitution is seen merely as a legal document or even as a morally neutral plan for distributing and limiting the power of government. But if, as we have argued here, the Constitution is seen as a foundational text that evokes what the American people believe to be ultimate principles of justice and creates a forum for ongoing debate about the practical meaning of those commitments, then constitutionalism emerges in its full glory as a living tradition of moral enquiry.

Recognizing constitutionalism as a tradition of moral enquiry leads to some noteworthy conclusions.

The first, emphasized by McGraw, is that the primary role of the government, especially the courts, is to preserve what she describes as a "two-tiered public forum" for debate and action, a system in which people are free, indeed obligated, to search their conscience about private and public moral issues in the context of dissenting views freely expressed (2003). Although arguing for a departmentalist view of the Constitution, Thomas captures the spirit of what we have argued here. He writes: "the Constitution calls forth continual debate about constitutional meaning. The 'settlement' of constitutional issues is not an essential feature of our constitutional system and, thus, constitutional politics with overlapping views, discontinuities, and essentially unsettled meanings are inherent features" (Thomas 2004, 233).

A second conclusion follows, which is that the system depends not on citizens' compliance with external authorities invested with the power to enforce the written law, but rather on citizens who internalize constitutional values. It is in this sense that the Founders expressed their conviction that American democracy was suited only for a virtuous people. Just as Locke, who so profoundly influenced the Founders' thinking about religion and religious freedom, believed that piety consisted not in an outward show of compliance with religious authorities and the profession of orthodox beliefs but in individual conviction, so too the Founders thought about virtue. Virtue lies not in mere obedience to fixed moral rules, but in an inner orientation to and pursuit of the good in a context where people are free to make difficult choices about alternative courses of action. In the American constitutional tradition there is no more virtue in the citizen who complies with authorities simply because they enjoy political or legal power than there is piety in the Christian who mindlessly recites a creed without contemplating or understanding its meaning.

Since the 1960s the Court has come to play the dominant role in defining the terms of public moral debate, but this does not make the Court a moral tutor in the classic republican sense. Litigants turn to the Court because it has come to be regarded as the most consistent and reliable guarantor of individual rights, and of minority rights in particular. When it does its job effectively, the Court explains its decisions in terms that the public can accept and internalize as just and fair. *Brown v. Board of Education*, the 1954 decision that ended school segregation stands out as a good example. Whatever qualms Americans have about the "activism" of the Court in *Brown*, most Americans today find segregation morally abhorrent and intuitively recognize that it is inconsistent with the highest ideals of the American constitutional tradition.

Finally, seeing the Constitution as establishing a framework for moral debate leads to the remarkable conclusion that it is possible to pass an unconstitutional amendment to the Constitution. Consider Amar and Brownstein's (2005) objection the proposed Federal Marriage Amendment:

> The Constitution ought *not* be amended to forestall acceptance of legal developments that are beginning to receive serious attention and consideration for the first time, and are starting to gain democratic traction in the polity... Enacted at moments of high politics, federal constitutional amendments embed into our Supreme law principles that are intended to endure... An amendment that cuts off debate precisely at the time when people's views are evolving stands a high chance of looking anachronistic and embarrassing, just as the Eighteenth Amendment's prohibition of alcohol feels so dated and out of touch today...
>
> Proper amendments should ordinarily seek to codify the resolution of an issue that already has been sufficiently vetted both by debate and experience. When long-term closure on a particular question has been reached—closure that would likely exist, more or less, even without the formalized act of an amendment—an amendment is appropriate, to memorialize and entrench the resolution that has been achieved, and to provide courts a means of enforcing it.

An amendment, such as the one they are discussing, intended to "short-circuit ongoing democratic deliberation" about the practical application of constitutional agreements to particular issues just as those disputes are ripening in legal, political, and popular discourse undermines the institutional framework for public moral debate that the Constitution establishes. In this case, change to the Constitutional ceases to be the product of a tradition of moral enquiry and becomes, instead, an exercise in raw majoritarian power decidedly at odds with the moral agreements that constitute the foundation of the tradition.

Failure to understand constitutionalism as a tradition of moral enquiry, moreover, has unfortunate results. Consider Mary Ann Glendon's complaint about "rights talk" in contemporary American public discourse (1991). She gives the example of the lively public discussion that followed the Supreme Court's 1989 ruling that burning the American flag is constitutionally protected free speech. On the *Today* show, Jane Pauley asked a member of the American legion to explain his opposition to the ruling. His initial reply was "The flag is the symbol of our country, the land of the free and the home of the brave." But Pauley pressed him further on what he meant. Glendon recounts:

> The legionnaire seemed exasperated in the way people sometimes get when they feel there are certain things that should not have to be explained. The answer he came up with was, "It stands for the fact that this is a country where we have the right to do what we want." Of course he could not really have meant to espouse a principle that would have sanctioned the very act he despised. (1991, 8)

Whereas the legionnaire framed his opinion in terms of liberty, another individual interviewed later the same day on National Public Radio framed his opinion in terms of property rights. Glendon recounts his defense of flag-burning: "He said, 'The way I see it, I buy a flag. It's my property. So I have a right to do anything I want with it'" (1991, 8).

Glendon concludes her discussion of the episode with this analysis of the effect of rights talk on public discourse:

> To speak in this careless fashion is not without consequences; in fact, it sets us up to fail twice over—first, by cheapening or betraying our own meaning..., and second, by foreclosing further communication with those whose points of view differ from our own. For, in its simple American form, the language of rights is the language of no compromise. The winner takes all and the loser has to get out of town. The conversation is over. (1991, 9)

But the conversation is *not* over; in fact, it has just begun. By translating their subjective feelings about flag burning into the language of rights, the legionnaire and the NPR guest have moved from purely subjective feeling-response to the realm of public moral discourse. Once the claim is asserted in terms of fundamental agreements—that individuals are possessed of certain liberty or property rights—the conversation can begin about the practical meaning of those agreements—the proper extent and limits of the right, and whether and how it applies in this particular dispute.

Imagine, instead, that the legionnaire had simply retorted, "It's just wrong," and the NPR guest simply said "There's nothing wrong with it." The conversation *would* be over.

Or imagine a more common scenario, one with which Americans are intimately familiar from news talk shows, in which the speakers frame their opinion of public moral issues in terms of a particular religious tradition. In such a conversation, one speaker might say, "as a Christian, I believe that abortion is wrong." Another might reply, "but I'm not a Christian and I believe that abortion is not wrong." Yet another, "I'm a Christian and I believe that abortion is not wrong." And so on. Without reference to some points of fundamental agreement and a common language to carry on the debate, the discussion is over. Each is left with his own subjective opinion, and the debate over abortion laws devolves into a culture war of tradition against tradition.

Framing the debate within the constitutional tradition, by contrast, allows the participants to argue in terms that they all understand. As Wald notes, we may still disagree about who has the better argument, but it is still a "more productive and satisfying debate than rejecting the other person out of hand" (2003, 317).

What Glendon fails to appreciate, apparently, is that constitutionalism does not reject or privilege any particular viewpoints, but rather subsumes them into a larger, more complex moral debate. When we understand constitutionalism as a tradition of moral enquiry, we can see that the language of rights is not a "language of no compromise;" it is rather a language that makes it possible for people of conflicting viewpoints to engage in meaningful debate about the practical meaning of shared moral agreements.

The example of the legionnaire hints at the probable source of the objection. That is, framing the issue in terms of the constitutional tradition may lead to what some, from a parochial perspective, perceive as the "wrong" conclusion. Indeed, as the case of the legionnaire indicates, framing the issue in terms of the constitutional tradition might well lead people to revise their opinions. Might the legionnaire come to recognize that the values that the flag symbolizes and that make it worthy of respect lead to the practical conclusion that flag burning should be protected as free speech? That there is virtue in the Court's decision?

Does such an evolution of the Legionnaire's thinking about the issue "cheapen" his meaning? We think not. It rather brings him into a more meaningful and productive discourse with other participants in the debate, especially those who do not share his own viewpoint. Indeed, if the Legionnaire is quick, he might recognize that translating his views into terms of the constitutional tradition provides him with a compelling argument for not burning the flag, as it is a symbol of the very rights that the flag burner claims to be exercising. Might the flag burner come thus to recognize that there is virtue in *not* burning the flag and finding some other way to express his discontent?

Most Americans, in fact, have come to recognize the merits of conducting public moral discourse in terms of the American constitutional tradition. Thus, we found that in the debate over same-sex marriage, even religious leaders tended to frame their public arguments, for and against same-sex marriage, in constitutional-legal terms. Yamane (2000) found a similar pattern in a study of the testimony by representatives of faith-based organizations to legislative hearings about capital punishment and welfare reform in Wisconsin.

To give one example of how parochial perspectives are routinely translated into terms of the constitutional tradition for the purpose of public deliberation, the Catholic Church's complaint in *Catholic Charities of Sacramento v. The Superior Court of Sacramento County* about a California statute requiring employers who receive state funding to provide contraceptive coverage in their health insurance plans rests not on the proposition that contraception is immoral but rather on the proposition that the law requires the church to do something that the Church teaches is immoral and thus infringes on religious freedom.

The recognition that contemporary public moral discourse increasingly takes place in terms of the American constitutional tradition concerns some. Powell, for instance, argues:

> Christian theology and American constitutionalism are competing traditions. By offering as its goal and justification the achievement of social peace and community—in the actual language of the Constitution, 'domestic tranquility' and 'a more perfect Union'—constitutionalism

implicitly claims for the American constitutional order a justice and 'ordered unity in plurality, a genuine *res publica'* that Christianity recognizes only in community constituted by God. (1993, 46)

Christians, from his perspective, who internalize constitutionalism risk apostasy to the Christian tradition. He therefore concludes, "There is no Christian constitutionalism" (1993, 292).

We have no satisfactory answer to this dilemma. The risk would appear to be greatest among those, including some prominent evangelists, who confuse Christianity with constitutionalism, arguing that Christianity is the religion *of* the constitutional tradition. From Powell's perspective, that position would appear to be contrary to both Christianity *and* constitutionalism. Ultimately, however, this is a theological question about whether Christians can live faithfully in a society where constitutionalism is sovereign. We can only point out that Powell himself argues that they can and, in fact, should participate in public moral debate and learn to use the terms of constitutional argument to advance their positions. As we have shown, Christians historically have helped to shape the tradition in profound ways.

Constitutionalism, properly understood, extends the same invitation to Muslims, Buddhists, Jews, Jains, secularists, and others. Indeed, one of the most remarkable accomplishments of the constitutional tradition is its ability to enter into dialogue with these external traditions and defend itself in a way that satisfactorily answers their conflicts with the tradition most of the time.

References

Amar, Vikram, and Alan Brownstein. 2005. "President Bush's Proposed Same-Sex Marriage Amendment: Part One in a Series on Wise and Unwise Constitutional Amendments." *Findlaw's Legal Commentary* [on-line] (February 4, 2005). http://writ.findlaw.com/commentary/20050204_brownstein.html.

Bellah, Robert N. 1967. "Civil Religion in America." *Daedalus* 96 (Winter): 1–21.

———. 1975. *The Broken Covenant: American Civil Religion in Time of Trial.* New York: Seabury Press.

Choper, Jesse H., Richard H. Fallon, et al. 2001. *The American Constitution: Cases and Materials.* St. Paul, Minn.: West Group.

Foner, Eric. 1998. *The Story of American Freedom.* New York: WW Norton.

Friedman, Barry. 2004. "Cycles of Constitutional Theory." *Law and Contemporary Problems* 67: 149–174.

Glendon, Mary Ann. 1991. *Rights Talk: The Impoverishment of Political Discourse.* New York: Free Press.

Grimké, Angelina. 1988. "An Appeal to the Christian Women of the South." Page 297 in *The Feminist Papers: From Adams to de Beauvoir.* Edited by Alice Rossi. Boston: Northeastern University Press.

Grimké, Sarah. 1837. "Letters on the Equality of the Sexes." http://www.pinn.net/~sunshine/books-sum/grimke3.html. Retrieved March 24, 2005.

Hammond, Phillip E. 1998. *With Liberty for All: Freedom of Religion in the United States.* Louisville, Ky.: Westminster John Knox Press.

————, David W. Machacek, and Eric Michael Mazur. 2004. *Religion on Trial: How Supreme Court Trends Threaten Freedom of Conscience in America.* Walnut Creek, Calif.: AltaMira Press.

Jacoby, Susan. 2004. *Freethinkers: A History of American Secularism.* New York: Metropolitan.

Karst, Kenneth L. 1983. "Why Equality Matters." *Georgia Law Review* (Winter). http://web.lexis-nexis.com/universe/document?_m=63d9997510a99be01ea765eb2180bb45&_docnum=1&wchp=dGLbVzb-zSkVb&_md5=b5a426ad9028875ca69e5e7bfdb4bbeb. Retrieved, March 15, 2005.

Katz, Stanley N. 1988. "The Strange Birth and Unlikely History of Constitutional Equality." *Journal of American History* 75: 747–762.

Levinson, Sanford. 1988. *Constitutional Faith.* Princeton, N.J.: Princeton University Press.

Levy, Leonard. 1999. *Origins of the Bill of Rights.* New Haven, Conn.: Yale University Press.

Machacek, David W., and Adrienne Fulco. 2004. "The Courts and Public Discourse: The Case of Gay Marriage." *Journal of Church and State* 46: 767–785.

Machacek, David W., and Phillip E. Hammond. Forthcoming. "Unsecular Humanism: The Supreme Court and American Public Culture." In *Taking Religious Pluralism Seriously.* Edited by Barbara McGraw. Waco, Tex.: Baylor University Press.

MacIntyre, Alasdair. 1988. *Whose Justice? Which Rationality?* Notre Dame, Ind.: University of Notre Dame Press.

McGraw, Barbara A. 2003. *Rediscovering America's Sacred Ground: Public Religion and Pursuit of the Good in a Pluralistic America.* Albany: State University of New York Press.

Pole, Jack R. 1993. *The Pursuit of Equality in American History.* Berkeley: University of California Press. Revised edition. First edition 1978.

Powell, H. Jefferson. 1993. *The Moral Tradition of American Constitutionalism: A Theological Interpretation.* Durham, N.C.: Duke University Press.

Rakove, Jack N. 1998. *Declaring Rights: A Brief History with Documents.* Boston: Bedford Books.

Rodgers, Daniel T. 1987. *Contested Truths: Key Words in American Politics Since Independence.* New York: Basic Books.

Scalia, Antonin. 1997. *A Matter of Interpretation: Federal Courts and the Law.* Princeton, N.J.: Princeton University Press.

————. 2005. "Constitutional Interpretation." Unofficial transcript of a speech given at the Woodrow Wilson International Center for Scholars, March 14, 2005. Available at http://www.threebadfingers.com/?p=20.

Thomas, George. 2004. "Recovering the Political Constitution: The Madisonian Vision." *The Review of Politics* 66: 233–256.

Tocqueville, Alexis. 1969. *Democracy in America.* Translated by George Lawrence, edited by J. P. Mayer. New York: Harper & Row.

Wald, Kenneth D. 2003. *Religion and Politics in the United States.* Fourth edition. Lanham, Md.: Rowman & Littlefield Publishers, Inc.

Walker, Thomas G. 1992. "Suspect Classifications." Page 848 in *The Oxford Companion to the Supreme Court of the United States.* Edited by Kermit L. Hall. New York: Oxford University Press.

Wood, Gordon S. 2003. *The American Revolution: A History.* New York: Random House.

Yamane, David. 2000. "Naked Public Square or Crumbling Wall of Separation? Evidence from Legislative Hearings in Wisconsin." *Review of Religious Research* 2: 175–192.

(Re)Making Tradition in an International Tibetan Buddhist Movement: A Lesson from Lama Gangchen and Lama Michel[*]

Frank Usarski

Preliminary Remarks

The present article addresses one of the key-questions that motivate this volume—*how is tradition actively constructed rather than passively received?*—by analyzing the case of a Brazilian *tulku*, a reincarnated Tibetan lama. The *tulku* in question was identified by the Gelugpa-monk Lama Gangchen (Thinley Yarpel Lama Shresta), who was born in 1941 in West Tibet, went into exile in 1963, and finally became the founder of a Tibetan Buddhist international organization. The latter is currently composed of more than 70 local institutions, including the *Centro de Dharma da Paz Shi De Choe Tsog* in the city of São Paulo founded in 1988 as the movement's very first occidental institution. Until today, Isabel Villares Lenz Cesar and Daniel Calmanowitz, a former married couple, play an important role within this center. It was one of their two children, their now twenty-four year-old son Michel Lenz Calmanowitz, who, at the age of eight, was identified by Lama Gangchen as a *tulku*.

This example offers special insights into the ambiguous situation of Tibetan Buddhism as it attempts to establish itself in Western countries, where it faces "the corrosive and destructive effect of contact with modes of thinking that reject and undermine their basic postulates."[1] This case's heuristic potential is due to the presence of two tendencies that challenge the religious heritage of Tibetan Buddhism: first, Lama Gangchen can be characterized as a "modernist" Tibetan monk, whose disciples are exposed to an approach that in many respects is quite unconventional compared to a clearly conservative style of transmitting Tibetan Buddhism to a Western audience; second, Lama Michel's homeland, Brazil, is well known for a high degree of religious syncretism, with a population

* This article is based on a revision of a former essay published in two versions: "Seu caloroso coração brasileiro e a energia pura de Maitreya atuam muito bem juntos. Reflexões sobre Lama Michel," in Frank Usarski (ed.), *Budismo no Brasil*, São Paulo: Lorosae 2002, 287–317; "'Lama Michel' – ein westlicher tulku und seine Funktionen innerhalb der Lama Gangchen-Bewegung." *Zeitschrift für Religionswissenschaft* 12.1 (2004): 23–42.

1   Samuel 1995. I am grateful for the author's permission to quote from this draft.

that is quite flexible in terms of accepting, combining and innovating religious doctrines and practices of different origins (cf. Carpenter and Roof 1995, 48).

The article summarizes the circumstances of the identification and propagation of Lama Michel as a reincarnated lama and analyzes the benefits that arose for Lama Gangchen and his followers due to the existence of a *tulku* within their movement. Before entering into this discussion, it is necessary to sketch the underlying concepts as well as the general circumstances under which the case of Lama Michel occurs.

Reflections Upon the Notion of "Tradition"

Tradition can be defined as a continuum of communication along the line of generations (cf. Assmann 2000, 19) for the sake of maintaining the identity of a cultural system over time. While it is hard to imagine an objective criterion that could serve to unambiguously evaluate the historical authenticity of a religious tradition, system-theory suggests that the latter strives for "identity" by acts of self-reference. More simply, it is up to the believers, or at least their "opinion leaders," often in the sense of a higher hierarchic instance, to judge whether the present state of their tradition is "in tune" with a set of alleged "fundamentals" considered crucial for the authenticity of *their* system (cf. Seiwert 1986).

In routine times, the issue of identity can disappear from the top of the agenda of a religious community, but at certain points in the group's history the issue becomes crucial. As Misztal (2004, 74) puts is, "when individual and collective identities are taken for granted, the past is not an issue, yet, with the weakening of the theoretical and the practical importance of religious and national beliefs as stable sources of identity, memory assumes an enormous importance."

One of the factors that challenge a group's identity is a threat to the local boundaries that facilitate a community's experiencing itself as a distinct entity, a threat often linked to issues of territory (cf. Stark and Bainbridge 1996, 62–63). Exile is a striking example of this situation, "in which social and national identities do not [...] coincide" and "social relations are 'lifted out' from local contexts" (Hidle 2001, 2).

Needless to say, even within clearly defined geographical settings, the notion of "tradition" is misleading since, instead of the maintenance of a single, homogeneous and unambiguous heritage considered congruent with the standards of the past, collective memory is horizontally segmented and vertically stratified according to the emphases that different sub-groups and levels of society lay on certain aspects of what constitutes the symbolic totality within a given culture (cf. Edgerton 1942; Redfield 1956; Spiro 1982; Neves 2004). Under propitious circumstances, a number of relatively autonomous traditions can develop. Some may coexist in mutual harmony and others in conflict.

The Significance of the *tulku*-System for the Maintenance of Tibetan Buddhist Traditions

Seen from this angle, the internal structure of Tibetan Buddhism is not sufficiently described in terms of its foremost sub-divisions since "while it is customary to speak of the four main 'schools', 'orders', 'traditions' or even 'sects' of Tibetan Buddhism [...] these terms may imply a hierarchical structure and a degree of coherence and exclusivity which did not in fact exist" (Samuel 1995). What really counts for the identification of (or with) a particular Tibetan Buddhist spiritual heritage is the personal relationship between a teacher and his disciples embedded in the institutional framework of a local monastery that possesses a remarkable degree of economical and administrational autonomy (cf. Samuel 1995), a feature that, among other peculiarities (Rabgey 2005), is also true for Tibetan Buddhist communities in exile.

Since at least the fourteenth century, the system of reincarnated lamas (*tulkus*) has been an effective means of tradition-preservation within the overall framework of Tibetan Buddhism. Due to his *karmic* predisposition and the cultivation of his innate potential within the educational framework of the monastery to which he is associated, a *tulku* is considered a carrier of a collective memory that synchronically connects a particular religious institution to its past and contributes to the further transmission of its accumulated spiritual heritage.

The re-establishment of Tibetan Buddhism outside of Tibet, in reaction to the Chinese occupation of its traditional homeland, has proved that the *tulku*-system is primarily a *historic* phenomenon whose maintenance does not necessarily depend on specific *geographic* surroundings. In terms of criteria such as kinship, ethnicity and language, the currently several thousand lines (cf. Lopez 1999, 17) of reincarnated *lamas* still represent a "Tibetan" peculiarity. However, there are indications that at least some parts of Tibetan Buddhism are beginning to attribute a more "globalized" character to the *tulku*-system, allowing for the possibility that, besides the great number of reincarnated lamas born to "native" families, there are reincarnations which do not fulfill this "traditional" criterion (Mackenzie 1996a).

Perhaps the two most cited *tulkus* born to parents not "naturally" belonging to a Tibetan Buddhist community are Alice Zeol and Osel Hita Torres.[2] Alice Zeol, better known as Jetsunma Ahkön Lhamo, was the first Western woman formally recognized and enthroned as a *tulku* shortly after having been identified as the reincarnation of a lama by Penor Rinpoche, currently one of

---

2   Needless to say that the issue is predestined to be a subject of improvable claims including speculations on the *tulku* status of the action movie star Steven Segal (cf. Seager 1999, 118) or of even abstruse spiritual gossips such as the idea that Queen Victoria was a manifestation of the female *tulku* Palden Lhamo (cf. http://www.sociologyesoscience.com/asia/karmapa-3.html; 13 June 2005).

the main representatives of the Palyul Lineage within the Nyingma tradition (cf. Sherrill 2001). Where Jetsunma Ahkön Lhamo was identified at the age of thirty six, Osel Hita Torres, born in 1985 to Spanish parents and maybe the most famous of the Western *tulku*s (Rawlinson 2001, 129), became known as the "boy lama" after he had been declared the reincarnation of Lama Yeshe (1935–1984), founder of the Foundation for the Preservation of the Mahayana Tradition (cf. Mackenzie 1996b). The case of Lama Michel is in some respects similar to that of Lama Osel.

Tradition Recovered: How Michel Lenz Calmanowitz Became a *tulku*

Shortly after Lama Gangchen had settled in Italy, Monica Benvenuti, a Brazilian, met him in Milan. The spiritual relationship between Ms. Benvenuti and the monk deepened when she assisted him in Goa, India, during a Health Fair, where the Tibetan treated clients with traditional Himalayan methods. Ms. Benvenuti became fascinated with Lama Gangchen's holistic medicine and decided to invite the monk to São Paulo. It is said that, after returning to Brazil, Monica Benvenuti consulted an astrologist to discuss her plan. The astrologer recommended that she collaborate with one of his other clients who—according to astrological readings—had extraordinary organizing talents. This client was Isabel Villares Lenz Cesar, at that time married to Daniel Calmanowitz, and mother of two children, a boy, Michel, born in July 1981, and a younger girl, Fernanda. Ms. Benvenuti contacted Isabel, who knew nothing of Lama Gangchen, and finally managed to convince her to contribute to the realization of the monk's visit to Brazil. As Isabel Lenz Cesar herself reported, the plan to establish a local Center at São Paulo was spontaneously introduced to her by Lama Gangchen while meeting her for the first time in a São Paulo hotel room. He had addressed her with the words: "You will be the one who is going to establish my first center." Since that day Isabel has been committed to the monk: in 1988, she established the São Paulo Center of Dharma for Peace in the same house in which her own psychology practice is located and she has played a key role as a local transmitter of Lama Gangchen's teachings.

In December of 1995, Lama Gangchen looked back to this beginning: "I visited Brazil for the first time in 1987, when I found a special couple, Isabel and Daniel, with two children, Michel and Fernanda. Immediately we started a good friendly relationship and [...] I noticed that the children were special. I didn't get round to say anything, I just went over to observe the various facets of their qualities, energies and behaviors" (Lama Gangchen 1996, 15). At that time, Michel had been five years old.

The hypothesis that the boy was not only very special but even a *tulku* was reinforced by other Tibetan Lamas who visited São Paulo after the establishment of the center or who met Michel in Asia while he was traveling with Lama Gangchen and some of the Brazilian group members to holy Buddhist places.

In 1993, at the Borobudur-Temple, Lama Gangchen performed a special ceremony to confirm that he had recognized Michel as a *tulku*. In February of 1994, the boy-lama entered the Tibetan Buddhist monastic community of Sera Me, South-India. In a letter written shortly thereafter, Lama Gangchen laid out the details of Lama Michel's reincarnation.[3] Referring to several auspicious signs, messages, visions and dreams, the monk specified that, in the fifteenth century, Michel was Drubtchok Gualwa Samdrup, a High Lama of the monastery Gangchen Tchopel Ling. In those days, the *tulku*, who is now Michel, was the master of Lama Gangchen. He was considered a great Yogi trained in various traditional disciplines, including Buddhist philosophy, astrology and healing, and was capable of performing effective initiations. The master (today Lama Michel) died when his disciple (today Lama Gangchen) was thirteen years old. Since that time the deep spiritual relationship between these two *tulku*s had continued, and they had met in several subsequent lives. Finally, in July of 1994, Michel was officially enthroned in Sera Me as a *tulku*.

Although Michel Calmanowitz entered Sera Me monastery in early 1994, he did not lose contact with his family; rather it seems that he welcomes any opportunity for even short visits to São Paulo. Since the Centro de Dharma is an integral part of his parents' lives, it is only natural that, besides his family, the local followers of Lama Gangchen benefit from these short visits by Lama Michel. Particularly in the first years after Lama Michel had been declared a *tulku*, these semi-public meetings in the Center were of vital importance for consolidating the members' conviction that whenever the son of Isabel and Daniel returned to his former hometown, they were blessed by the presence of an outstanding, charismatic disciple and potential successor to Lama Gangchen. In addition, since the very beginning of Lama Michel's career, the idea of his special status was nourished by his mother's reports of auspicious signs during her son's early childhood, including an extraordinary mature understanding of Buddhist doctrines and a rudimentary innate knowledge of Tibetan Buddhist terms.[4]

The important role that Isabel Lenz Cesar played in the social construction of Michel's reputation as an incarnated lama can be exemplified by her behavior on the occasion of the commemoration of the 10th anniversary of the Centro de Dharma, held on the 3rd of December, 1998. On that day, the premises of the institution she founded were unusually crowded with followers and sym-

---

3   This information was published on the Internet; cf. http://www.promeiramão.com.br/dharma/dharm3.htm.

4   Cf. "Lama brasileiro chega a SP para série de palestras," *Estado de São Paulo*, 25/10/1999, section A9; Débora Crivellaro, "Aprendiz de Buda," in *Época*, 1 de novembro de 1999: 50–51.

pathizers of Lama Gangchen who were expectantly waiting for Lama Michel, invited as a special guest. As the rumor circulated that the latter was already on his way, dedicated members began to prepare the reception befitting a *tulku* by distributing flowers and long white silk scarves (*kata*s), which were to be offered at the moment of Michel's arrival. As soon as Michel had finally taken the elevated seat normally reserved for Lama Gangchen, the visitors witnessed Isabel Lenz Cesar prostrating herself thrice in front of her son, demonstrating her veneration to a human being with elevated religious standing.

Lama Michel's mother also acts as publicist, informing the Brazilian media, prior to the arrival of her son, of workshops, lectures, *puja*s and retreats to be held under his guidance. The increasingly public image of Lama Michel as *tulku* in recent years is illustrated by numerous articles in nationally-circulated newspapers like the *Folha de São Paulo* and in widely-read magazines like *Veja*, by TV programs, including features on *Globo*, the most important channel in Brazil, and by an invitation to "bless" the 2004 São Paulo Fashion Week and to give a short public speech.[5] The Brazilian press, in general kindly disposed towards religious phenomena, went so far as to declare him "the little Buddha of São Paulo"[6] and "the spiritual leader of the new Millennium."[7] This character-ization not only corresponds to the beliefs of the followers of Lama Gangchen but appears also to be shared by political representatives, such as the Municipal Chamber of the city of Florianopolis, capital of the Federal State of Santa Catarina, whose president once welcomed Lama Michel, as if it were the most natural thing in the world, as "the reincarnation of a Tibetan lama."[8]

The Propagation of Lama Michel's *tulku* Status as a Means of Relating the Presence to the Past

In accordance with the reflections above on the notion of "tradition," one can understand any moment of a given tradition either in terms of a commitment to the past or a projection into the future. Starting the discussion of the case of Lama Michel with a reflection from the perspective of the "backwards" func-tionality of a tradition, the Tibetan exile must be taken into consideration. For Tibetan fugitives who settled in certain countries, particularly in neighboring Himalaya-regions, the corrosive effects of their exile are lessened through the

---

5   Cf. "Lama visita SPFW e abençoa evento," *Folha de São Paulo*, 23/6/2004, caderno Ilustrado.
6   Cf. "Lama brasileiro chega a SP" (see above note 4).
7   Cf. Crivellaro (see above note 4), 50.
8   Estado de Santa Catarina, Câmara Municipal de Florianópolis, 1999, *Ata da 97ª Sessão Ordinária, do 6º Período Legislativo, da 13ª Legislatura, Realizada em 17 de Novembro de 1999.*

re-establishment of Tibetan Buddhist monasteries that facilitate the identification with and maintenance of the Tibetan culture. However, Lama Gangchen's activities lack the support of such an institutional framework, and he has conducted his activities under circumstances religiously and culturally foreign to those under which Tibetan Buddhism emerged and blossomed. In this situation, Lama Gangchen is personally challenged by at least two interrelated problems. The first is of social-psychological nature. The second one has to do with the necessity to gain credibility as an authority who stands for a "legitimate" version of Tibetan Buddhism. After having reflected upon these two challenges, a third, more general aspect emerging from the dynamics of "religious transplantation" will be discussed separately.

The *tulku* Michel as a Reminder of Lama Gangchen's Personal Identity and Present Status

Holding constantly to the idea of oneself as a Tibetan Buddhist master is not easy in a culture that does not share the same values and does not recognize this type of religious "carrier." In other words, the difficulty in question derives from the fact that Lama Gangchen's *individual identity*, here defined as a concept of an *ego* associated with a certain status and a set of pre-defined roles, is in tension with a social structure whose patterns are not supportive of his self-image (cf. Fitzenreiter 2004).

As Panglung Rinpoche puts it, it is therefore almost unavoidable that, to the extent that Tibetan monks have to rely on themselves in foreign parts of the Western world, they have to deal with alienation and culture shock in the face of unexpected peculiarities of their host cultures (cf. Rinpoche 1991). In such a situation, the identification of a Western *tulku* not only compensates the socio-psychological need of the identifier's *ego* for an identity-stabilizing significant *alter*, it also reinforces the religious plausibility necessary for holding ground against a predominant non-Buddhist world-view. This is even more true when the recognized *tulku* is believed to be a counterpart of a profound spiritual relationship that had deepened in the course of a series of previous lives, as it is said to be the case with Lama Gangchen and Lama Michel.

Besides its socio-psychological benefits, the above claim is also conducive to Lama Gangchen's efforts to present himself as a "recognized" representative of an age-old Tibetan Buddhist wisdom. The same tendency is already evident in his reference to one of his former incarnations as Truphul Lotsawa, a great twelfth-century translator and scholar who was far ahead of his time and whose religious writings were preserved in the memories of subsequent incarnations, including Lama Gangchen, ready to be finally revealed to the present generation (cf. Lama Gangchen 1998, 25–29). One can assume that followers who take this claim seriously also welcome Lama Gangchen's recognition of Michel Calma-nowitz as a proof for the extraordinary mental capacities of their master.

Seen from the standpoint of Lama Gangchen, both the identification of a former incarnation of himself and the recognition of Lama Michel as a close spiritual companion already known from the past are means of a retrospective legitimation of his religious status.

Lama Michel's Contribution to the Revaluation of Traditional Tibetan Religious Capital

There is no doubt that, at their core, Lama Gangchen's teachings are grounded in the Tibetan tradition. The methods of Self-Healing, for example, which Lama Gangchen emphasizes, are based upon Tibetan Buddhist principles, symbols and insights in the mind–body correlation (cf. Lama Gangchen 1991). However, while Lama Gangchen insists that his message for the occident is based on the teachings of the Buddha as they were laid out 2500 years ago, he also admits that he had to figure out "the most appropriate approach for the Western mind. There are so many different techniques [...] of Buddhist tradition that I was not sure, in the beginning, which method was the best to teach" (Lama Gangchen 1995, 19). Lama Michel has said of his master, "Lama Gangchen doesn't have a traditional way, because he left Tibet, applied himself to the West and adopted his teachings to the people here" (Lama Gangchen 1996, 30).

This readiness to combine "genuine" elements with techniques and approaches stemming from other backgrounds leads to a religiosity whose authenticity in terms of Tibetan Buddhism is not always evident. Such an attitude is advantageous in the "religious market," fostering the acceptance of Tibetan Buddhism in a Western setting. This is especially true for Brazil, a country known for its syncretism. However, as long as the question of the authenticity of Tibetan Buddhism is taken into account, Lama Gangchen's openness is not without problems. In other words, the present situation of Lama Gangchen's movement, at least in Brazil, is ambiguous.

This is clear in the light of Michael Pye's model of the transplantation of a religion. According to Pye (1969, 236) "the transplantation of a religion involves a complex [...] interplay between what is taken to be the content of the religion and the key factors in the situation which it is entering." That's why he subdivided the corresponding process into three phases: the phase of contact, the phase of ambiguity and the phase of recoupment.

Considering the phases as a chronological order, one can say that a trans-planted religion has to present itself within new surroundings by addressing potential new adherents on their own terms. Different degrees of this adapta-tion are conceivable. It may be regarded as sufficient to translate religious text into the language of the host culture. The changes are more severe if certain aspects of the transplanted religion are emphasized while others are pushed to the side. To make the transplanted religion even more attractive, new influences may be integrated or combined with traditional teachings and practices. In this case, representatives may suffer sentiments of ambiguity, feeling a tension between old and new elements and fearing loss of the religion's integrity. As a consequence, efforts may be made to revaluate the former heritage and to distinguish the religion more sharply from its environment. According to Pye, however, these endeavors do not simply restore the religion as it was prior to the transplantation. Rather, they will lead to a modified form, showing influences of the host culture.

In terms of these dynamics of transplantation, Lama Michel can be considered a mediator who is capable of reducing tensions between traditional and new elements, as we have noted with respect to the current situation of Lama Gangchen's movement. There are symmetrical differences between the religious trajectories or locations of Lama Gangchen and Michel Calmanowitz. The former is a monk from Tibet now proselytizing in the West. The latter was born in the West but now lives in a Tibetan Buddhist monastery in the East, being trained according to the old monastic tradition. The community of which he is part consists of four hundred Asian monks who are Buddhists by birth. Like all the others, Michel has to follow a strict monastic routine. His lessons include the Tibetan language, so that he is capable to devote himself to the classical disciplines of the Vajrayāna. For several hours a day, he memorizes sacred texts since he knows, "In Buddhism there is a greatest concern for memorizing, because the monks have the habit of reciting and of debating philosophy. And when someone is going to a debate, he has to know everything; he cannot take the text and read. He has to have everything in his mind" (Lama Gangchen 1996, 39). Furthermore he already has made the value of the purity of the Tibetan Buddhist teachings clear: "We have to take care not to confuse the ideas, since on this basis the road of wisdom will persist much longer" (Lama Gangchen 1996, 29).

Michel Calmanowitz has expressed, in his own words, his preparedness to stay some twenty years in the monastery (Lama Gangchen 1996, 48). This can be taken as a hint that one day he will leave the community of Sera Me in order to play a more active role within the international movement of his master. In this case, an impact on the current repertoire of Lama Gangchens teachings can be expected. A religious expert who, like the Brazilian Lama Michel, has been intensively educated in the old tradition, will be capable of contributing to the recoupment of Tibetan Buddhist spiritual heritage in compensation to one-sided concessions Lama Gangchen has made towards a Western audience. This doesn't mean that a "recuperated" Lama Gangchen movement will completely lose its Western touch. Rather, the occidental will continue while at the same time traditional Eastern elements will be re-enlivened.

The Propagation of the *tulku* Michel as a Possible Means
of Preparing the Future

According to Rodney Stark, the success of a new religious movement in its second generation depends on various elements, including a collectively recognized religious authority capable of compensating for the loss of a previous charismatic leader. As far as the movement of Lama Gangchen is concerned, Lama Michel seems poised to fulfill this role: Lama Gangchen has made clear that Lama Michel is his most auspicious disciple and will follow his footsteps as a master. This perspective is obviously shared by members of the movement, including Lama Michel's mother, who emphasizes in one of her books that she strongly feels "how much we are responsible for the continuity of our master's teachings" and that "Lama Gangchen Rinpoche trusts in Lama Michel as someone who will continue his work" (Cesar 2001, 71).

Presupposing that this will occur, it remains an open question in what direction Lama Michel will lead the movement in the future. However, the religious-transplantation model suggests certain general tendencies likely to occur in the course of the further development of the Lama Gangchen movement.

The process of recoupment is limited by the legitimate interest of any religious movement to guarantee at least its future existence as an increasingly integrated element of the new host-culture. To put it in terms of rational-choice-theory, in order to continue to grow, the desire of a religious movement to increase the value of its "supply" by re-strengthening its traditional roots has to be balanced against the "demands" on the side of potential future members. If a religious system is capable of managing this equilibrium, it enters the fourth stage of the transplantation process, that is, according to Baumann in direct reference to the model of Michael Pye, the period of "innovative self-development" (cf. Baumann 1994).

While it is still a mystery if Lama Michel will successfully mediate between tradition and innovation, it is very likely that he will soon intensify his activities in his homeland. This concentration on a South American country could be an indicator of a more general trend within Western Tibetan Buddhism as a whole. After many Tibetan Lamas have established numerous centers in Europe and the USA, Latin America could become a privileged field of future activities. If there is at least something to this prospect, not only Lama Michel, but also Lama Osel, the "boy-lama" from Spain mentioned above, could play an important role. While the Portuguese speaking Lama Michel will continue to dedicate himself to Brazil, Lama Osel would be in a position to teach Tibetan Buddhism to the Spanish-speaking population of the rest of the continent. This is speculative of course, but one must not forget that both Lama Michel and Lama Osel are ordained monks of the Sera Me monastery, South India, and are, at least in terms of their institutional backgrounds, already closely connected to each other.

Concluding Remarks

According to John Pettit, the Tibetan "diaspora has had to grapple with a unique set of concerns," a situation that has challenged Tibetans "to evolve an authentic set of responses to its role as recipient and preserver of Tibetan Buddhist values and practices." In this context, the propagation of "non-native" *tulkus* by Tibetan lamas engaged in the transmission of Vajrayāna-Buddhism to a Western audience is an especially intriguing manifestation of "the creative potential of Tibetan people [...] to adjust and survive in a changing world" (cf. Anand 2000, esp. 271).

It is obvious that further research is needed to deepen our understanding of the mechanisms and dynamics that characterizes this particular phenomenon of "tradition (re-)making." There is no lack of material: various Western *tulkus*, including at least two more in Brazil,[9] await investigation from the perspectives that constitute the academic study of religion. It is my hope that these reflections on Lama Michel might play some role in motivating further research into these issues.

References

Anand, Dibyesh. 2000. "(Re)imagining nationalism: identity and representation in the Tibetan diaspora of South Asia." *Contemporary South Asia* 9.3: 271–287.

Assmann, Jan. 2000. *Religion und kulturelles Gedächtnis. Zehn Studien.* München: Beck.

Baumann, Martin. 1994. "The Transplantation of Buddhism in Germany. Processive Modes and Strategies of Adaption." *Method & Theory in the Study of Religion* 6: 35–61.

Carpenter, Robert T., and Wade Clark Roof. 1995. "The Transplantation of Seicho-no-ie from Japan to Brazil: Moving Beyond the Ethnic Enclave." *Journal of Contemporary Religion* 10.1: 41–54.

Cesar, Bel. 2001 *Viagem Interior ao Tibete. Acompanhando os Mestres do Budismo Tibetano Lama Gangchen Rimpoche e Lama Michel Rimpoche.* São Paulo.

Edgerton, Franklin. 1942. "Dominant Ideas in the Formation of Indian Culture." *Journal of the American Oriental Society* 62: 151–156.

Fitzenreiter, Martin. 2004. "Genealogie – Fiktion und Realität sozialer Identität (Thesen)." *Genealogie – Fiktion und Realität sozialer Identität.* Workshop am 04. und 05. Juni 2004

---

9   The first one is Lama Segyu, a former Umbanda-medium, formally recognized as the *tulku* in 1997 (cf. http://www.pbnet.com.br/openline/mepcarv/port/lama.htm; access 30/4/2005). The second one is Lama Kalden identified in 2001 (http://www.djampelpawo.org/index.php?acx=biok; access 17/6/2005). Furthermore in 1994, the Brazilian press reported the arrival of the American boy-lama Wyatt Arnold to Brazil. It was said the young *tulku* had been identified as the reincarnation of the Tibetan monk Aka Nyima by Chagdud Tulku Rimpoche, a Nyingma-Master, who shortly before had moved the headquarters of his movement from California to the city of Três Coroas (Federal State of Rio Grande do Sul). Cf. *Lama tibetano traz pequeno Buda ao Brasil*, Folha de São Paulo, 04/09/1994, caderno Cotidiano.

in Berlin. *Internet-Beiträge zur Ägyptologie und Sudanarchäologie*, Vol. V (IBAES V). http://www2.rz.hu-berlin.de/nilus/net-publications/ibaes5/lay.html.

Hidle, Knut. 2001. "Place, Geography and the Concept of Diaspora – A Methodological Approach." Pages 1–16 in *Geografi Bergen*. Arbeider fra Institutt for geografi – Bergen, Nr. 244. Bergen.

Lama Gangchen. 1991. *Autocura. Proposta de um mestre tibetano*. Milano: Sherab.

———. 1995. *Zamling Shide Bang Chen Da Sel II – Clara Luz da Lua Mensageiro da Paz Mundial, Livro II*. Milano.

———. 1996. *Uma Jovem Idéia de Paz. Conversas com o Lama Michel Rimpoche*. São Paulo: Sarasvati.

———. 1998. *Ngelso – Autocura III*, Vol. 1: *O Guia para o Supermercado dos Bons Pensamentos*. São Paulo: Sarasvati.

Lopez, Donald S., Jr. 1999. *Prisoners of Shangri-La. Tibetan Buddhism and the West*. Chicago: University of Chicago Press.

Mackenzie, Vickie. 1996a. *Reborn in the West. The Reincarnation Masters*. New York: Marlowe.

———. 1996b. *Reincarnation – The Boy Lama*. Boston: Wisdom Publications.

Misztal, Barbara A. 2004. "The Sacralization of Memory." *European Journal of Social Theory* 7.1: 67–84.

Neves, Luis Felipe Baêta. 2004. "Migrant Memories and Temporality." *Diogenes* 201: 27–33.

Pettit, John W. "Tibetan Buddhism in Diaspora-Individuals, Communities and Sacred Space." http://www.damtsig.org/articles/diaspora.html (access 11/06/2005).

Pye, Michael. 1969. "The Transplantation of Religions." *Numen* 16: 234–239.

Rabgey, Losang C. "Rethinking Tibetan Identity." http://www.tibetanculture.org/articles/rabgey.htm (access 10/6/2005).

Rawlinson, Andrew. 2001. "Western Buddhists Teachers." *Journal of Global Buddhism* 2: 123–138.

Redfield, Robert. 1956. *Peasant Society and Culture: An Anthropological Approach to Civilization*. Chicago: University of Chicago Press.

Rinpoche, Panglung. 1991. "Die Situation des tibetischen Buddhismus in den modernen pluralistischen Gesellschaften des Westens." *Dialog der Religionen* 1.2: 187–196.

Samuel, Geoffrey. 1995. "Tibetan Buddhism as a World Religion: Global Networking and its Consequences." Revised version of a paper presented to a conference organized by the Department of Theology and Religious Studies, King's College, University of London, December 1995. Online: http://users.hunterlink.net.au/ ~mbbgbs/Geoffrey/global.html.

Seager, Richard Hughes. 1999. *Buddhism in America*. New York: Columbia University Press.

Seiwert, Hubert. 1986. "What Constitutes the Identity of a Religion?" Pages 1–7 in *Identity Issues and World Religions: Selected Proceedings of the Fifteenth Congress of the International Association for the History of Religions*. Edited by Victor C. Hayes. Bedford Park: Australian Association for the Study of Religions.

Sherrill, Martha. 2001. *The Buddha from Brooklyn*. New York: Vintage.

Spiro, Melford E. 1982. *Buddhism and Society. A Great Tradition and its Burmese Vicissitudes*. Berkeley: University of California Press.

Stark, Rodney, and William Sims Bainbridge. 1996. *A Theory of Religion*. New Brunswick: Routledge.

Afterward: Tradition's Legacy[1]

Steven Engler

Tradition's name—like that of religion, culture, and discourse—is "Legion." The trick with such terms—possessed of many spirits, haunting sites where the dead past is buried, and capable of throwing off all shackles—is to chase them out, if not into the open, at least into a herd of concepts and contexts more amenable to analysis. "Tradition," in other words, is best approached through its relations to other ideas and through the work it does in specific historical and social circumstances. Emphasizing several dimensions of this relationality, this final chapter highlights the theoretical insights offered by the contributors to this book. It also explores the parallel between tradition and the gift, in order to develop two themes that have remained largely implicit in this book: relations between tradition's indeterminacy and social boundaries; and the ideological function of the belief that the pure and unadulterated transmission of tradition is possible.

Etymologically, the English word "tradition" refers to the act of handing over. A diverging web of related meanings emerges primarily from Christian and, by extension, other religious conceptions of authority: "tradition" refers to beliefs passed down, above all orally, from generation to generation, including the Oral Torah (first known usage in 1380 CE); to oral instruction, including teaching the Creed to catechumens (1500); to transferring the possession of objects (1540); to the apostolically-legitimized teachings of the Roman Catholic Church (1551); to custom or normative usage more generally (1593); and to the *sunna* of the Prophet Muhammad (1781). Insofar as the content of tradition is seen as sacrosanct, questions of authenticity are shifted to the process of transmission. This is indicated by a second cluster of meanings, according to which tradition is an improper transfer of that which is valued: tradition is also betrayal, including delivery of oneself or others over to Satan (1482) and the surrender of Christian scriptures to persecuting authorities (1840).

The basic metaphor of "handing down something meaningful and valued" portrays "tradition" as the other of various forms of semantic rupture. Tradition roots continuity of meaning in externalities (e.g., creeds, texts, rituals, and institutions) that function as warrants of authenticity by virtue of their

---

1 Some elements of this chapter appear in the entry, "Tradition," in volume 4 of *The Brill Dictionary of Religion*, Kocku von Stuckrad, Ed. (Leiden: Brill, 2005).

perceived contiguity to the past: e.g., the authority of the *Hadiths* is a function of their accurate repetition of historical originals. Discontinuity can result from severing the link to externalities: e.g., the Radical Reformation was radical due to its innovative internalization of discipline, breaking the self-consciously historical and institutional relation between *restitutio* and *traditio*. Discontinuity can also result from severing perceived links to the past: e.g., the forces of colonialism, modernization, and globalization have created social, economic, and political ruptures, undermining the long-established identities of cultural groups around the world.

"Tradition" embodies the alleged continuity that legitimizes claims of authoritative transmission within religions and that justifies the types of analysis and comparison that form the core of the academic study of religion. However, the concept raises complex questions, as do all acts of transmission or translation. Does that which is transferred remain the same or is it changed, as it passes between different generations, social groups, languages, and cultures? To what extent is the continuity of tradition a "natural" effect of social and institutional structures, and to what extent is it a strategic construct of human (or superhuman) agents? What epistemological and ideological issues are implicit in attempts to characterize traditions as authentic or inauthentic, genuine or invented? Is it possible to evaluate these latter sorts of judgments beyond simply taking sides between, for example, orthodoxy and heterodoxy, insider and outsider, or colonized and colonizer? As these questions indicate, the issue of tradition quickly calls into play a host of others. This book, as a whole, makes a case that tradition must be studied in specific contexts; this "Afterward" attempts to note some of the theoretical issues that arise in doing so.

The initial impetus for this book and initial drafts of several of its chapters stem from a session held at the American Academy of Religion conference in Atlanta in 2003. During the question period following that session, Frank Reynolds asked the presenters, "What is the object of study in these papers?": Jake Carbine replied "tradition," Greg Johnson "rhetoric," and Rick Colby "innovation"; whereas Susanna Morrill suggested that her approach took all of these into account. This exchange illustrates a central theme of this book: talking "tradition" helps us talk of other things, e.g., power, agency, authority, rhetoric, ideology, community, temporality, memory, continuity, innovation, identity, modernity, and the construction of histories. The disparate objects, approaches and goals of the papers in that session—and of the chapters in this book— remind us that "tradition" shapes and is shaped by all these.

This book's approach is relational because "tradition" is part of a complex conceptual web, spun between past and future, between founders and followers, between communities inside and communities outside its ambit, and among variant traditions: "Claims of 'tradition' are made in mutual dependence upon one another, in constructing *alternatives* in a religiously 'productive' framework of pluralism" (von Stuckrad, infra, p. 223; original emphasis). In addition, webs of *religious* tradition show us something further: the prophetic dew that high-lights their perennial renovation reflects both worldly and otherworldly lights.

The papers in this book, with varying degrees of emphasis, take into account five sorts of relationality: *(1)* relations between "tradition" and other concepts; *(2)* internal relations between elements within traditions and among the processes that shape them; *(3)* external relations between distinct tradition(s) and between that which is "traditional" and that which is not; *(4)* relations between givers and receivers of tradition, between ideal origins and practical developments, between past, present and future; and *(5)* relations between academic traditions and the traditions that they study. The sections of this final chapter look at each of these in turn.

The Conceptual Polarity of Tradition

Tradition is generally defined with reference to one extreme of a set of opposed concepts. Just as "sacred" takes on determinate meaning in contrast to "profane" and "culture" in contrast to "nature," the meaning of "tradition(al)" is clearest in opposition. It is commonly held to be *(a) static, ancient, conservative, unitary, local, continuous, passive, received, and repetitive,* in contrast to that which is *(b) dynamic, modern, reforming, plural, global, discontinuous, active, invented, and inno-vative.* Analyzing "tradition" thus involves clarifying the relational tensions between these concepts. Much of the interesting theoretical work in this book frames cases where tradition ostensibly manifests the characteristics of list *(a)* while actually operating according to the logic of list *(b)*. Colby, for example, offers an Islamic example of reform masquerading as tradition (infra, pp. 33–50); Hughes shows how an invented tradition reflected and played a role in modern struggles over Jewish identity and values (infra, pp. 51–74).

"Tradition" gains its purchase where these conceptual tensions are read normatively: where old/new, static/dynamic, and received/innovated become aligned with good/bad, right/wrong, and acceptable/unacceptable. It is this superposition of normative and conceptual polarities that makes "tradition" such a broad and effective label, with great powers of legitimation due to its identification with previously established authority. As a result, holding or taking this high ground has great strategic value for both conservative and reactionary forces.

A key analytical use of "tradition" in the study of religion is the Weberian distinction between traditional, charismatic and rational-legal forms of author-ity, especially as embodied in the tension between priest and prophet (Weber 1978, 38, 54, 424, 439ff, 1158ff.; cf. Hjelm, infra, pp. 109–123). Here, "tradition" is defined in terms of its conservative function, and it is analyzed from the point of view of specific social and institutional structures. Pierre Bourdieu relativized

Weber's distinction, holding that the tension between priest and prophet, orthodoxy and heterodoxy, established and innovative authority, tradition and innovation, plays itself out in every "field" in which humans struggle for control over some form of "capital," whether economic, cultural, artistic, or religious (Bourdieu 1985, 1987, 1991). For Bourdieu, the priest's role is conservative, maintaining control of religious capital, where the prophet's is radical, trying to capture a share of that capital by marketing innovative religious goods. Prophets are "the *initial producers* of the principles of a (quasi-) systematic view of the world," and priests, churches and other recognized authorities are "the agencies of reproduction" of such worldviews: "[T]he struggle for the monopoly over the legitimate exercise of religious power over the laity and over the administration of the goods of salvation is necessarily organized around the opposition between *the church* and *the prophet*" (1991, 22); "The prophet stands opposed to the priestly body as the *discontinuous* to the *continuous*, the extraordinary to the ordinary, the non-routine to the routine and the banal..." (1987, 126–127). The church or priest's orthodoxy consists of conservation and maintenance of tradition, and the prophet's heterodoxy consists of strategies of succession and subversion.

In this light, "tradition" refers both to a position within social struggles — functioning in part as a status marker — and also to a conceptual tool used by those engaged in such struggles. It is a label whose descriptive and normative dimensions are inseparable, because any attempt to disentangle them presupposes a point of view (e.g., religious or academic) with its own presuppositions and value judgments. As such, tradition — whether invented from whole cloth or authenticated by divine authority — is both "traditional" and radical, depending on what sort of priest, prophet, or scholar is claiming or investing its mantle.

This sort of tension is particularly clear in Machacek and Fulco's contribution to this book. They argue for a prophetic and against a priestly view of American Constitutional tradition:

> It is entirely mistaken to think of equality, rights, and consent as sums fixed by the Constitution — that is, to think of American constitutionalism as a tradition in the Burkean sense, in which meanings are passed down unchanged from one generation to the next... [I]f, as we have argued here, the Constitution is seen as a foundational text that evokes what the American people believe to be ultimate principles of justice and creates a forum for ongoing debate about the practical meaning of those commitments, then constitutionalism emerges in its full glory as a living tradition of moral enquiry. (infra, pp. 338–339)

Machacek and Fulco argue for a non-traditional view of "tradition." That is, they try explicitly to shift the semantic allegiance of the concept away from list (*a*), above, toward list (*b*), suggesting that potential for innovation and openness to the future should be seen as key elements of this tradition. More to the

point, they argue—playing the Pharisees against Sadducean conservatives—
that this tradition consists of more than timeless principles; this tradition
consists of the ongoing interpretation and application of these principles.

"Tradition" implies continuity with the past, but the nature of that continuity, along with the nature of the past and its relation to the future, are subject
to debate. Michiaki Okuyama's discussion of Yasukuni Shrine instantiates this
clearly. Taking a stance regarding the "newly invented 'tradition' of Yasukuni
Shrine" requires that one first take a stance regarding a number of related
issues: the nature and status of Shinto and its relation to Japanese history and
culture; the Constitutional history of Japan, with its prominent American
intervention; as well as the religious and/or secular status of the country's
Imperial and democratic systems (Okuyama, infra, p. 107). One's view of this
tradition will be shaped by one's view of these and other issues.

"Tradition" tends to serve as a vague umbrella term for a host of disparate
concepts that stand in stark conceptual and normative tension with others, and,
as a result, the term is an object of intense partisan struggles and ideological
distortion. For these reasons, as most of this book's authors note, it makes little
sense to talk about tradition apart from determinate contexts. The term is largely
empty except as a place holder for a set of potential tensions between more
specific concepts and the evaluations attached to them: it tells us "from that
direction comes authority"; but we need to scope out each instance of this general sight line on its own ground. The magnetic pole of tradition shifts radically
depending on who holds the compass and where they stand: "Traditions are
continually negotiated, and shifting. They can never be fully grasped, because
individuals and groups are always adapting them to fit personal, historical,
and cultural circumstances" (Morrill, infra, p. 142).

Scholars of religion need to examine which specific conceptual polarities
are given which specific normative evaluations in relation to which specific
tensions between conservative and reactionary forces. A descriptive academic
approach to "tradition" must take into account the vested interests and value
judgments that shape its variously situated uses, including scholarly uses:
tradition is "a category that cannot be removed from the historical and
hermeneutic contexts in which it is being employed" (Hawley, infra, p. 317);
"the notion of 'tradition' should not be taken as an analytical category of
historiography. By contrast, scholars should apply it only with reference to its
emic meaning and function" (von Stuckrad, infra, p. 211).

The Internal Dynamics of Tradition

Whether static legacy or dynamic construct, tradition is not unitary. Complex
relations *within* a given tradition are also important. Susanna Morrill (infra,
pp. 127–143) highlights four dimensions of this complexity. *(1)* Religious tradi-

tions are formed by the interaction between various elements of religiosity (e.g., ritual, belief, scripture, and institutions). *(2)* They are dynamic and potentially discontinuous. *(3)* They are shaped by different social groups (e.g., popular and elite, female and male). *(4)* A given religious community can contain a variety of different, event conflicting, traditions. Once again, these points remind us of the need to analyze tradition in very specific contexts. As Carbine suggests, "tradition" is "as an interpretive category to refer to particular thoughts, practices, and people which have coalesced around particular visions of social, historical, and/or religious continuity and rupture" (infra, p. 146). Scholarship must explore these various dimensions of particularity in order to make sense of the complexity that manifests itself within "religious tradition(s)."

The tendency in the study of religion, however, has been to generalize "tradition," on the one hand, and to lose sight of general complex relations within religions by pursuing largely context-independent micro-studies, on the other. One of the most significant examples of this is the widespread appeal to anthropologist Robert Redfield's distinction between "great tradition" and "little tradition" (1956). According to Redfield, the former tends to be elite, urban, universal, textual, "religious," orthodox, scholarly, refined, central, and, above all, "consciously cultivated and handed down" (1956, 70); whereas the latter tends to be popular, peasant-based, local, oral, "superstitious," heterodox, folk, unrefined, peripheral, and unreflective. Redfield stressed the need to study mutual interactions between the two: "Great and little tradition can be thought of as two currents of thought and action, distinguishable, yet ever flowing into and out of each other" (1956, 72). In a related claim, McKim Marriott (1955) suggested that processes of "universalization" and "parochialization" were responsible for the slow two-way movement between village and more global levels. Foreshadowing Hobsbawm and Ranger (1983), Milton Singer (1972) emphasized the strategic use of public ritual to manage portrayals of India's great tradition, arguing, contra Redfield, that great/little does not correspond to modern/traditional, because much that is "modern" is old and many "traditions" are recent inventions.

The great/little distinction has been criticized as over-generalized, undertheorized, colonialist or orientalist (reflecting biased outsider discourses), and elitist or fundamentalist (reflecting biased insider discourses). Even granted some potential value, the distinction has suffered from two main problems: it hides normative assumptions behind a descriptive tool; and it has too often justified an exclusive focus on one or the other extreme (e.g., on village-level micro-analyses or global generalizations based on normative texts), ignoring mutual influences between these levels of analysis and the ideological dimensions of the distinction itself. Moreover, it has often been used to buttress the use of vague and problematic concepts like "Hinduism" or "the Hindu tradition," ignoring the need to pay attention to specific contexts, including the academic history of such terms (cf. Fitzgerald 1990; 2000). In general, the great/

little distinction and other such dichotomies are useful in drawing attention to the spectrum of complexities within traditions, but they are misleading if reified or over-generalized.

A more important spectrum of complexity—one central to this book—is that ranging from identity to invention, from real to illusory continuity with the past (cf. Henten and Houtepen 2001). Seeing tradition simply as "the given" ignores agency, i.e., the strategic value of claiming the high ground of tradition in struggles for power. Malinowski emphasized that myth is "a hard-working active force" (1992 [1926], 101); recent scholarship extends this insight in seeing "tradition" as a strategic device. As Hjelm concludes, "tradition is actively constructed and...its importance for any given group is situational: each social and cultural context generates different uses for tradition as a legitimation strategy" (infra, p. 121). This recognition prompts us to examine not the nature but the use of tradition: tradition "is not determined by the static purity of its 'ancientness,' but rather by how its 'ancientness' is imagined and used" (Grieve, infra, p. 280).

Inventing tradition is a tactic for claiming normative authority. This is commonly done in two steps: first, re-imagining the past in terms of present norms, and then claiming that the authority of this past legitimizes that set of norms over its competitors: the present is projected onto the past, creating perceived continuity. Hughes' analysis, for example, leads him to define tradition as "a modern construct, something that effectively allows a particular group to inscribe themselves and their values on an earlier time or space. This temporal or spatial period is subsequently upheld as the standard by which to live in the present" (infra, p. 54).

Appeals to tradition can exhibit various degrees of continuity, creatively appropriating aspects of the past in order to assert a less unitary view of the present. As Robinson notes, Joshua Rocker innovated within one aspect of Jewish tradition to raise the possibility of alternative conceptions of relations between tradition and modernity:

> Rocker...understood that the Jews who constituted his audience had detached themselves from an immediate connection with the Jewish tradition of yesteryear, but might yet be reached through innovative literature emanating from that tradition... Joshua Rocker attempted to use the power of the Hasidic tradition, not to oppose modernization as such, but to show his readers that there were different paths available to them as Jews other than a lockstep acculturation into an American "melting pot." (infra, pp. 292–293, 294)

The heuristic distinction between genuine and invented traditions, like that between great and little, tends to be overdrawn. It is important to recognize both the extent to which more "genuine" traditions can be used as strategic tools in social struggles, and the extent to which self-consciously "invented" ones can perform all the functions of tradition: narrating histories; maintaining perceived continuities in belief, practices and institutions; shaping personal and group identities and roles; structuring social boundaries and hierarchies; legitimizing normative standards; framing rich emotional experiences in the face of phenomena perceived as sacred; and linking these and other functions as a legacy for future generations.

The External Dynamics of Tradition

"Tradition(al)" is often a label applied from outside a given community or period, looking "in," and looking "back." As Despland notes, "The traditionalist does not know he lives in a tradition... It is the post-traditionalist who ordinarily (and somewhat triumphantly) sees others as enmeshed in the nets of tradition" (infra, p. 22). Tradition is conceptualized in terms of oppositions; hence, it emerges explicitly only in the face of phenomena seen as non-traditional. As a result, the conceptual boundaries marked by tradition often correspond to social boundaries. In addition, the temporality of tradition places it, above all, in tension with the perceived boundaries of modernity: colonialism, imperialism, orientalism, and globalization are very active fronts in battles of "tradition."

Hobsbawm suggested that the invention of tradition—and the "(re)-invention" of "extinct" traditions—has become more frequent in modernity, as "the old ways" of genuine traditions have become threatened by rapid social transformation (1983, 4–8). Terence Ranger, in the same book, argued that Western scholars and administrators invented African "tradition" as the other of modernity. Where African societies had, as a matter of historical fact, been characterized by "multiple identities" and "overlapping networks of association and exchange," this "pre-colonial movement of men and ideas was replaced by the colonial custom-bounded, microcosmic local society," whereas "there rarely existed in fact the closed corporate consensual system which came to be accepted as characteristic of 'traditional' Africa" (1983, 247–248, 254).

Of course, the agency of invention is not limited to the colonizers. Both insiders and outsiders are involved in tugs-of-war with the newly woven ropes of invented tradition. And the distinction between insiders and outsiders becomes blurred where systems of belief, practices, and institutions are transplanted from one cultural context to another, leading to processes of what Usarski calls "tradition (re-)making" (infra, p. 355). The (re)invention of tradition has been an important indigenous strategy in resisting or rejecting colonization, modernization, and globalization. In this light, the authenticity of tradition can be framed in terms of autonomy—not continuity—as characterized by a wider or narrower scope of agency: tradition can be read as "volitional temporal action," with its contrary being "not change but oppression" (Glassie 1995, 409, 396). Is, for example, the Melanesian re-invention of tradition through the invented discourse of *kastom* inauthentic because it self-consciously appropriates and inverts colonial discourse, or is it authentic because it is a product of indigenous agency (cf. Johnson, infra, p. 195; Babadzan 1988)? The latter alternative is closed to us if we insist that post-colonial traditions invented by indigenous communities are always and only oppositional and counter-hegemonic: i.e., that "the discourse of the dominant shapes and structures the discourse of the dominated" (Keesing 1994, 41). This is overly deterministic, however, denying indigenous agency because it is not "pure," as if the possibility existed of any action free of ideological and material constraints: "Just because what is done is culturally logical does not mean the logic determined that it be done.... [T]raditions are invented in the specific terms of the people who construct them..." (Sahlins 1999, 409).

When societies meet on contested ground, concepts like "tradition" or "culture" are not easily defined. They are inevitably complicated by tensions between continuity and rupture, subjugation and domination, structure and agency, colonialism and subalternity, purity and hybridization. These complications hold horizontally, among comparable social groups, vertically, among groups with different degrees of power, and diachronically. This becomes even more obvious in interstitial and inter-cultural situations. In the midst of this complexity, and where "scholarship" tends to be invested in western institutions, "tradition" varies according to a panoply of perspectives, among which none seems definitively objective, true, or ideology-free.

In an important sense, then, all tradition is genuine and all tradition is invented. Certainly a given religious text, image, gesture or role can remain "the same" over generations, but its historical, cultural, social, hermeneutic, and institutional context is more dynamic; in fact, the focus on the static nature of the one is an effective tactic for denying the dynamism of the other. The present is never identical to the past. If "genuine" tradition is that which is passed down absolutely pure—with no alteration in content, form, or context— then there is no genuine tradition; if "invented" tradition bears no relation to past practices and beliefs, then there is no invented tradition. Tradition is necessarily perceived as authoritative; its power, if only the potential to reign in innovation, is always on display. That is, if "genuine" tradition is received passively with no awareness of the strategic possibilities that attach to its authority, then none is genuine; if "invented" tradition is constructed with no aim other than strategic use, then none is invented. Studying "tradition," then, requires that the scholar bracket the insider's premise that tradition is an unaltered reproduction of a past original, in order to study the work of tradition as a work-in-progress: "traditions are sites of innovation. This is to say that traditions have histories" (Weiss, infra, p. 175).

"Genuine" and "invented" are extremes on a spectrum and, as always, the work of creating, legitimizing, maintaining, negotiating and altering social relations takes place in the contested middle ground. An overly sharp distinction between the passive reception of a tradition identical to that of the past and the active construction of strategically innovative tradition imposes a naïve conception of intentionality and action, ignoring the complex realities of hegemony and ideology, by which human activity both shapes and is shaped by structural constraints. All tradition is both genuine and (re)invented, if only because it is inseparably bound up with the identities of both transmitters and receivers. As Grieve and Weiss state, "Actors perpetuate, and allow themselves to be shaped by, traditions because they perceive them to be at least partially true. Tradition is not only something constructed by prior subjects, but also contributes to the construction of subjects, insofar as it is prior to them" (infra, p. 7). In this light, tradition is both the agent of its own invention and a means by which human beings (re)constitute themselves as historical agents in changing times.

The Give and Take of Tradition

Insofar as tradition implies handing on, relations between giver and receiver are central. Despland's paper, for example, emphasizes the agency of transmitters and receivers of tradition and their recourse to the medium of language (infra, p. 19–32); and Carbine suggests that lineage lies at the heart of a dynamic tension between continuity and rupture in Burmese Buddhism (infra, p. 145–174). The theme of time, of appeals to and continuity with the past, has been a prominent one in this book, but the extent of tradition's temporal indeterminacy and the relation between this indeterminacy and social boundaries, as well as the curious status of tradition's allegedly ideal mimesis have remained largely implicit. This section of this chapter explores parallels between tradition and the gift in order to clarify these issues.

Tradition is legacy. It is a gift given from one generation to another. As with all gifts, it presupposes, legitimizes, and maintains certain social and institutional relations, and it does this in and through time, in and through the implicit expectation of a counter-gift. Developing this parallel between tradition and the gift will clarify the status of tradition's relation to social continuity and to modernity.

Gifts promote and maintain social solidarity through four mechanisms. First, gifts evoke counter-gifts, in formalized exchanges or in the more general sense of "you scratch my back I'll scratch yours" or "next time, dinner's on me" (Mauss 1990; Malinowski 1961, 176ff.). Sociologist Alvin Gouldner argued that exchange behaviour is governed by "the norm of reciprocity" (1973a). He argued that reciprocal exchange gives solidity to social structures and that the desirability of this solidity leads people to act reciprocally from a perceived sense of duty or in deference to the opinions of their peers: reciprocity makes altruism possible through egoism (cf. Schumaker 1992, 31).

Second, the precise nature and/or amount of the counter-gift as well as the time of its being offered are indeterminate. Following Gouldner, Marshall Sahlins distinguished between "indefinite," "balanced," and "negative" reciprocity (1972).[2] In indefinite reciprocity, goods and assistance are given freely ostensibly without regard for any return. Reciprocation generally does occur, but potentially over a long period and in a manner not easily weighed against the original act of giving. (Who among us calculates and compares the precise cost of inviting friends to dinner after those same friends have played host? Who calculates the precise moment at which such a return visit must be paid?) In balanced reciprocity the value of the goods exchanged are reckoned closely and equivalent goods are exchanged with little delay; this category includes economic or market exchange. In negative reciprocity, on the one hand, each party attempts to get something for nothing (cf. Gouldner 1973b): examples of negative reciprocity range from haggling to theft.

The key contrast here is between market and gift, between balanced and indefinite reciprocity. Contracts specify times of return, terms of interest, and precise penalties for temporal default; mutual favours, informal gifts between friends, and *rendre service* demand a return whose quantity or time of return is not precisely calculated (Schumaker 1992, 21ff.). The social functions of informal understandings like "you scratch my back; I'll scratch yours" are premised on a state of affairs where neither the degree nor timing of needs is known in advance or calculated after the fact (cf. Derrida 1992, 41).

Third, gift relationships generally obtain more among those who are socially close, and more formalized (market or balanced reciprocal) relations occur between strangers and more distance associates (Bourdieu 1990, cf. Nelson 1969). In pre-modern, small-scale, and local (i.e., "traditional") societies, gift relations distinguish "us" from "them," keeping "us" together; whereas relations with "them" are characterized by, and shaped by, more calculable and quantifiable market-type relations. In modern societies, exchanges are more commonly mediated by formalized market-like exchanges.

Fourth, the social function of gifts often depends in part on two sorts of misrecognition, one on the part of participants within the cycle of reciprocity, and one on the part of outside observers (Bourdieu 1990, 98ff.). Observers, such as anthropologists, tend to see gifting in synchronic terms, as a "cycle" of gift and counter-gift. However, this externalized theoretical perspective under-emphasizes the element of time, of uncertainty, that defines the practice of gifting (cf. Taylor 1993, 56–57). This uncertainty allows actors "room for strategies that consist in playing with the time, or rather the tempo, of the action" (Bourdieu 1990, 106). However, these strategies can only work if the expectation

---

2   Given the importance of Lévi-Strauss' very different concept of 'generalized exchange' it is best to refer to Sahlins' concept of 'generalized reciprocity' by this alternative that he suggested: 'indefinite reciprocity.'

of a return is disguised. The practical perspective of participants necessarily fails to perceive the element of exchange, of calculated reciprocity, that is essential to the theoretical understanding of gifting: "Gift exchange is the paradigm of all the operations through which symbolic alchemy produces the reality-denying reality...[of] a collectively produced...misrecognition of the 'objective' truth" (1990, 110).

Time is the medium of this misrecognition on the part of actors with the cycle of gifting:

> The interval between gift and counter-gift is what allows a relation of exchange that is always liable to appear as irreversible, that is, both forced and self-interested, to be seen as reversible... [T]he lapse of time that separates the gift from the counter-gift is what allows the deliberate oversight, the collectively maintained and approved self-deception, without which the exchange could not function. Gift exchange is one of the social games that cannot be played unless the players refuse to acknowledge the objective truth of the game. (Bourdieu 1990, 105)

In other words, the element of uncertainty in the gift, especially its temporal indeterminacy, has for the sociologist an obvious function of promoting social cohesion and marking social difference. In this sense, the structure of the game forces one to return gifts for one's own sake. But, these functions presuppose that the participants in the cycle of exchange to some extent ignore this fact: their mutual "self-deception" is to see these forced gifts as free; and it is because they are seen as free that they are able to function as tokens in this social game. The anthropologist sees a synchronic system, missing the actors' temporal tactics. The actor sees a case of free agency on the part of the giver and pure receptivity on the part of the receiver, turning a blind eye to the systemic expectation, indeterminacy, and social functions of the cycle of gift/counter-gift.

That is, both outsiders (excepting perhaps this more recent scholarship) and insiders (excepting perhaps certain astute "players") oversimplify, occluding the extent to which individual freedom and social determinacy, agency and structure, ideology and hegemony are entwined in gift exchange: the outsider sees the system as a *fait accompli*; the insider sees giving as pure activity and receiving as pure passivity; whereas the cycle of reciprocity, with its two roles, is, like all social systems, both bound and free, constructing and constructed, eternally given and endlessly invented.

Tradition parallels each of these four dimensions of the gift. *(1)* Legitimacy is the counter-gift of tradition: to receive tradition is to grant it authority, to give respect to one's elders, to one's teachers, or to the tradition's founder(s). Tradition is a bequest of that which is considered to be meaningful and valued; to act upon tradition, to follow it, to embody it, to preserve it, to maintain it, and to pass it on, reflect and (re)constitute that meaning and value. To receive—tradition *qua* tradition—is to give. In general, gift exchange creates both affiliation and hierarchy:

> The act of giving seems to create simultaneously a twofold relationship
> between giver and receiver. A relationship of *solidarity* because the giver
> shares what he has, or what he is, with the receiver; and a relationship
> of *superiority* because the one who receives the gift and accepts it places
> himself in the debt of the one who has given it…at least for as long as
> he has not "given back" what he was given. (Godelier 1999, 12; original
> emphasis)

Tradition functions in the same way, with the debt of tradition being repaid
not only by respecting it but also by passing it on to the next generation.

(2) The precise weight of tradition, and which aspect(s) will be taken as
essential or fundamental, cannot be known in advance. This dimension of
indeterminacy closely parallels that of indeterminate reciprocity. On the one
hand, those who give fealty to tradition necessarily emphasize some sub-set of
the beliefs, practices, and institutions to which they are heirs. (The nature and
extent of their counter-gift of legitimation is indeterminate.) On the other hand,
the temporal dimension of this allegiance is triply indeterminate: emphasis on
the importance of allegiance to given aspect(s) of tradition waxes and wanes,
depending on a variety on historical circumstances; the extent to which the
origin of a given tradition is portrayed as rooted in either the distant or recent
past is subject to tactical variation; and tradition is received and implemented
within a variety of different temporalities, i.e., different relations between conceptions of agency, structure(s), past, present, and future (Asad 2003, 178–180).
(The time of tradition's counter-gift is indeterminate.) These various dimensions of indeterminacy are degrees of freedom in the invention of tradition.

(3) The bequest and receipt of tradition, like that of a gift, delimits a social
sphere of insiders, of "us" as opposed to "them": those who receive tradition
in trust and give it due respect vs. those who must weigh and pay for words of
wisdom in the treacherous market of ideas. The indeterminacy of the gift marks
out a sphere of close social relations in opposition to the calculations of the
market, which define more formalized relations. Benjamin Nelson, analyzing
Jewish and Christian views of usury, labeled these the spheres of "tribal brotherhood" and "universal otherhood" (1969).

Tradition manifests this tension between brother and other in several ways.
On the one hand, differences in belief and practice within a tradition can be
more acceptable, more open to negotiation, trivialization, and mutual interpretation, than the differences that mark the boundaries of tradition(s). This
greater degree of "give and take" marks the sphere of the insider, as is
especially clear in tensions between popular and elite religiosity. For example,
Catholics often genuflect before the altar, unaware that they "should" do so
before the tabernacle (which is not always situated behind the altar), but parish
priests are willing to "let this go" in order to focus on more important issues;
and Evangelical Christians often reject belief in the Trinity at the popular level
even where that belief forms part of the official "platform" of their denomi-

nation.[3] On the other hand, small markers of difference in belief or practice can invoke a rigid and dramatic boundary between "traditions." For example, despite general uniformity during *salat* among the men in the mosque on Fridays, there is a certain degree of variation in dress, in floor coverings, in the formality of the lines of worshippers, in the speed, timing, and scope of prostrations, in the positioning of hands, in the presence and comportment of male children, etc.; these same elements of variation are visible in both Sunni and Shi'a mosques. However, the placing of a small clay table on the floor where the forehead is to make contact is an absolute marker distinguishing Shi'a from Sunni prayer. Flexibility regarding tradition as received marks a sphere of insiders and points of rigidity mark the boundaries of that sphere.

Most significantly, (4) two sorts of misrecognition prevail with respect to tradition. Tradition's insiders tend to see the passing down of tradition as active and its reception as passive: something is given, and that same thing is received without alteration. From the perspective of participants within the give and take of tradition, pure tradition (genuinely identical to the past) is a pure gift, its origin distinct from the specific agency and interests of the previous generation—except where it is received from a founder, in which case the gift (like grace) is framed even more radically as pure, unfettered agency. The counter-gift is occluded: giving respect in return is not perceived as a contingent act with systemic social functions and several dimensions of indeterminacy but as a necessary and automatic recognition of true authority.

Tradition's insider, that is, sees a contingent and doubly interested exchange as if it involved a timeless moment of donation/reception. This misrecognition of contingency, indeterminacy, and the tactics of interest allows for the illusion that nothing is lost or altered in the act of transmission. Receiving any communication involves creative acts of historically and socially contextualized recognition, selection, interpretation, differential emphasis, and mimesis;[4] but these are hidden by a myth of instantaneous transmission, which emphasizes pure activity and pure passivity, as if the hammered stamp of revelation had once again left its mark in a single sharp stroke.

Tradition's outsiders, including scholars of religion, pay attention to the many social functions of the systems of social relations that fall under the heading of "tradition." But, until recently, scholars have underemphasized the many dimensions of indeterminacy that allow for subtle play and contingent tactics. A rhetoric of nostalgia has obscured the strategies and tactics of "tradition" (cf. McCutcheon 1997, 33). Even the relatively recent recognition

---

3   These examples and the following draw on my own ongoing observations of and conversations with believers in Montréal, Camrose, Edmonton and Calgary, Canada.

4   Religious Studies might do well to pay attention to theories of communication here, which emphasize not simply who sends what to whom, but also the historical, social, and ideological contexts that lead to selectivity in both transmission and reception (cf. Griffin 2000; Marris and Thornham 2000; Engler 2005).

that much tradition is invented commits this error, insofar as it accepts the pure gift of "genuine" tradition as a foil, ignoring the extent to which all tradition is always, to some extent, both genuine and invented. At the very least, it is important to consider the extent to which receiving tradition *as tradition* involves a series of active judgments: "it is up to the believers, or at least their 'opinion leaders'...to judge whether the present state of their tradition is 'in tune' with a set of alleged 'fundamentals' considered crucial for the authenticity of *their* system" (Usarski, infra, p. 346; original emphasis).

Comparing tradition and the gift, then, tells us four things. First, tradition is a social process of selective transmission and reception: the give and take of tradition invokes the agency of both givers and receivers in specific historical and social contexts. Second, this agency operates on several dimensions of indeterminacy, regarding which aspects of tradition are emphasized in which contexts and with what timing. Third, the social effects of tradition, above all its role in fostering social solidarity and perceived continuity, are a function of this reciprocity, this give-and-take. Fourth, the myth of the pure gift, of unadulterated tradition passively received, is integral to these social functions: tradition works because the extent to which it is invented remains obscured.

This latter point tells us something more specific about religious tradition(s) in particular. Passing on that which is perceived as sacred ups the ante in terms of both the benefits of that which is transmitted and the costs of failing to receive or pass it on accurately. "Genuine" religious tradition is re-revelation. It is an ideal repeated, echoed, reflected, and transferred. Hence, the purity of *religious* tradition is especially threatened by adulteration. This is the significance of the secondary nexus of meanings associated with the word "tradition": betrayal, treason, and profaning the sacred by handing it over to impure hands.

For these reasons, religious tradition is especially invested in the misrecognition that consecrates "authentic" or "genuine" tradition. Its "sacredness" is linked to this ideology that denies strategic alteration in reception and transmission, that acknowledges no selectivity, interpretation or contextualization of that which is passed down, and that subordinates the agency of tradition's recipients to that of its founder(s). In a manner strictly analogous to Peter Berger's analysis of religion (1967), tradition is an extremely effective means of legitimizing, authorizing, naturalizing, and reifying social norms and roles because it is perceived by insiders as fixed, necessary, and unalterable; and this is so despite the fact that (from the outsider/sociologist's point of view, at least) it is constructed anew by each generation. Tradition's canopy becomes even more effective when it is seen as sacred.

Comparing tradition and the gift raises a fifth and final point: the ideologies of the pure gift and unadulterated tradition are not universal; they reflect specific historical and social conditions, especially those of modernity. In this light, Despland's comment that "It is the post-traditionalist who ordinarily... sees others as enmeshed in the nets of tradition" is especially significant (infra,

p. 22). It is not a coincidence that, as several chapters in this book have noted, tradition often presents (in symptomatic terms) as the other of modernity. Clarifying this point requires a closer look at the status of the gift in modernity.

Many scholars have suggested that gift exchange is characteristic of pre-modern societies and the market of modern societies: "Among examples of evolution which societies furnish, perhaps none is more striking than this gradual advance from the giving and receiving of presents by savages, to the daily balancing of a nation's myriads of business transactions by a few clerks in Lombard Street" (Spencer 1900, 403). Karl Polanyi held that the emergence of the market came about as a result of gradual historical development, that the development of the self-regulating market is unique to the modern West, and that the moment of its mature development marked a radical discontinuity in economic and social relations: "Instead of economy being embedded in social relations, social relations are embedded in the economic system" (1957, 57). This alleged historical transition from gift to market also informs one of two accounts of modernization in the work of Pierre Bourdieu; however, by clarifying Bourdieu's account, we can see that this common claim is misleading (Engler 2003). Gift and market exchanges (indefinite and balanced reciprocity) are common in ancient, medieval, and modern societies; the key factor in historical periodization is not the presence or absence of market relations but the manner in which different forms of exchange are integrated with different forms of social affiliation.

It is not the market that is characteristic of modernity but the extent to which market relations are integrated with social and institutional differentiation. More importantly for present purposes is a corollary to this: a certain *relation* between gift and market characterizes highly differentiated, urbanized, societies (including modern globalized societies). The ideology of pure gift delimits a sphere of social relations that stand as the other of the market:

> The radical opposition which so many anthropologists have discovered between the principles on which gift and commodity exchange are founded derives in part, we believe, from the fact that *our* ideology of the gift has been constructed in antithesis to market exchange. The idea of the purely altruistic gift is the other side of the coin from the idea of the purely interested utilitarian exchange... (Parry and Bloch 1989, 9, emphasis in original; cf. Strathern 1988, 18)

Jonathan Parry suggests that the tendency to characterize the gift as disinterested, altruistic, moral and emotional—and the market as interested, profit-oriented, amoral (or immoral) and rational—tends to emerge at the same time as, and in conceptual opposition to, the market in certain sorts of societies:

> an elaborated ideology of the 'pure' gift is most likely to develop in state societies with an advanced division of labour and a significant commercial sector. But what is also in my view essential to its articulation is a specific type of belief system, as is suggested by the fact that in all of

the major world religions great stress is laid on the merit of gifts and alms, ideally given in secrecy and without expectation of any worldly return...a *universalistic* ethic of disinterested giving can surely only encourage the creation of a separate sphere which is immune from the requirements of such a demanding precept. The ideology of the pure gift may thus itself promote and entrench the ideological elaboration of a domain in which self-interest rules supreme. (1986, 467–469; emphasis in original)

As the other of the market, then, the pure gift defines and legitimises its social and normative boundaries. This closely parallels Timothy Fitzgerald's argument that the category of "'religion'...along with its partner 'the secular'" became more sharply distinguished in modernity, with religion serving as "the special repository of traditional values" thus clearing a space for "western liberal capitalist ideology" to function in a sphere free from these norms (2000, 4–6).

This further comparison of tradition and the gift highlights a final point, then: the sharper tensions between tradition and non-tradition in modernity are a sign of ideology at work. The functions of "tradition" in modernity include not only those of maintaining social cohesion and continuity within traditional spheres, but of colluding in the maintenance of non-traditional spheres. Tradition does this by sharpening a normative distinction (tradition vs. non-traditional values) and by aligning it with certain social boundaries. Insofar as "tradition" evokes the image of a distant past present here and now in an unadulterated form—handed down in its purity by generations of those who accepted and retransmitted it without alteration, re-interpretation, or selection— it necessarily operates according to a logic of difference, marking a contrast with those elements of the present seen as discontinuous with the ("rightly" valued) past. The pure gift marks a domain of pure values:

When idealized, the "uncalculating" gift operates in the imaginary as the last refuge of a solidarity, of an open-handedness which is supposed to have characterized other eras in the evolution of mankind. Gift-giving becomes the bearer of a utopia (a utopia which can be projected into the past as well as into the future). (Godelier 1999, 208)

Tradition also bears this utopian stamp, legitimizing certain norms both by projecting them into the past—from whence they return as "traditional"—and by sending them on into the future allegedly unaltered.

The act of re-transmission—the passing of an eternal torch to future generations—reduces past, present, and future to the same idealized and timeless state; it erases temporal difference and, thus, agency. Receiving and passing on tradition equates future and past, occluding the interpretive and creative activity of the present generation, and legitimising present social relations as an identical link in this chain. Insofar as it is held to be equivalent to its past and future manifestations, genuine tradition is like a virus, reproducing itself by diverting the agency of host cells toward its own replication, so that the activity of those cells becomes no more than an echo—a reproduction aimed at nothing beyond further reproduction—of the agency of the virus itself. Idealized tradition is always already "the given." The acts that constitute its reception and transmission invoke a pure agency that transparently reproduces the past in the present, ensuring its future reproduction "as is" (i.e., "as was," and "as will be"). Tradition is a catalyst, acting without being acted upon. It is not a medium that can be acted upon (as changing it is ruled out); rather, it informs its recipients, who receive it and pass it on. Conceived in this pure manner, tradition is like a wave, transmitted through the medium of human societies. This book asks two key questions regarding the wave of tradition: "What impurities in its medium, what sources of friction, and what independent processes in the medium itself, slow, alter, divert, and refract tradition as it passes through human societies?"; and "What are the social and ideological functions of ignoring the creativity and indeterminacy inherent in tradition?"

Academic Traditions and "Religious Traditions"

A distinct set of relations external to tradition(s) is that between scholars and their objects of study, i.e., between academic traditions and religious traditions. Given the concept's complexity, using "tradition" as a synonym for "religion" is problematic. To speak of "religions" at one point and "religious traditions" at another has the same minimal aesthetic value as referring to the present book as a "volume" on occasion: it offers some rhetorical variety. However, where "book" and "volume" are synonyms, "religion" and "tradition" are not. The concept of tradition, as this volume makes abundantly clear, carries with it a wide variety of context-specific assumptions. Any uncritical use of the term implicitly accepts certain of these. At the very least, it assumes that religious phenomena have some vague but essential link to the past. Thus, equating "religions" and "traditions" uncritically invokes the same faulty logic by which Christianity was labeled *superstitio* in ancient Rome whereas Judaism qualified as *religio*: the latter was old, a tradition. (The prevalence of this assumption goes some way toward explaining the curious neglect of the study of New Religious Movements when it comes to hiring decisions in the field.)

Arguably, Religious Studies has a vested interest in the implicit equation of "religion" and "tradition." Russell McCutcheon (1997), for example, argues that the academic study of religion uncritically accepts distorting assumptions in defining "religion" as a distinct phenomenon (thus legitimizing an autonomous academic field with distinct subject matter, methods, and theories). One important move in this game is to project the essence of religion into the past, emphasizing the distinction between tradition and modernity. On this view, authentic human life is rooted in traditional relations to "the sacred." For

McCutcheon, the link between religion and tradition has two main problems. First, it manifests a vague and untenable "politics of nostalgia," in which the modern is found lacking when measured on the scales of tradition, despite the fact that "the vague and subjective nature of such categories as 'traditional' and 'authentic mode of human existence'" result in the absence of "specific criteria to determine the status of these supposedly archaic values" (1997, 33). Second, it is ironically biased against those whose idealized "traditions" are studied: the "rhetoric and ideology of traditionalism effectively manufactures a stereotyped native who is distinct from, and less than, the modern rational and individualistic Western human being" (1997, 177). Issues of continuity and agency, like those of authority and legitimacy, are inseparable and must be examined with an eye to specific social and historical contexts.

In general, western academic traditions on "tradition" manifest a familiar spectrum of views, from realist through constructionist to relativist. The latter end of this spectrum suggests that the distinction between genuine and invented traditions—e.g., between actual historical situations and orientalist/colonialist constructions of them—presupposes the modernist distinction between real and represented (Friedman 1992, 849). No tradition can be judged genuine or not without clear criteria for evaluating the correspondence between present and past practices. Hobsbawm's influential distinction, after all, reduces primarily to that between truth and fiction: "insofar as there is...reference to a historic past, the peculiarity of "invented" traditions is that the continuity with it is largely fictitious. In short, they are responses to novel situations which take the form of reference to old situations, or which establish their own past by quasi-obligatory repetition..." (Hobsbawm and Ranger 1983, 1). In the light of epistemological questions over naïve correspondence views of truth and ideological questions over competing representations of self and other, the distinction between genuine and invented traditions appears neither obvious nor innocent.

This raises the possibility that any search for genuine religious tradition(s) reflects an invented aspect of Western political/academic traditions: "how do we defend the 'real past'...and 'genuine' traditions...if we accept that all cultural representations—even scholarly ones—are contingent and embedded in a particular social and political context?" (Linnekin 1992, 250). "Tradition" quickly unfolds into issues of truth, authenticity, authority, autonomy, and power; and distinct academic traditions inform varying answers to important questions in the field: e.g., can we make sense of the alleged unity of "Hinduism" as an ancient tradition founded on the Vedas without giving a central role to both (a) the Western academic tradition on this "tradition" and (b) the traditions invented by nineteenth-century Hindu Reform movements as they reacted to colonial portrayals of Indian history?[5] Richard King, for example, suggests that

---

5   On the dangers of assuming that 'Hinduism' refers to one unified religious tradition see Sontheimer and Kulke 1989 and cf. Brockington 1981. On the role of Religious

the secular and reductionist tendencies of the academic study of religion are rooted in a post-Enlightenment valuation of modernity vs. tradition, a constructed rupture often linked to that between progressive West vs. timeless East (1999, 46).

It is arguable that religious studies can never escape the situated and limited perspective of its own invented tradition(s) re "tradition(s)." The most obvious corrective, as this book tries to model, is to approach "tradition" not in an absolute sense—by trying to state the truth of tradition or the facts of the matter regarding genuine traditions—but relationally, by looking at connections and tensions between "tradition" and other concepts, and by examining the work of "tradition" in specific historical and social contexts.

References

Asad, Talal. 2003. *Formations of the Secular: Christianity, Islam, Modernity*. Stanford: Stanford University Press.

Babadzan, Alain. 1988. "Kastom and Nation-Building in the South Pacific." Pages 199–228 in *Ethnicities and Nations: Processes of Interethnic Relations in Latin America, Southeast Asia, and the Pacific*. Edited by Remo Guidieri, Francesco Pellizzi and Stanley J. Tambiah. Austin: University of Texas Press.

Berger, Peter L. 1967. *The Sacred Canopy: Elements of a Sociological Theory of Religion*. New York: Anchor Books.

Bourdieu, Pierre. 1985. "The Market of Symbolic Goods." Translated by Rupert Sawyer. *Poetics* 14: 13–44.

———. 1987. "Legitimation and Structured Interests in Weber's Sociology of Religion." Translated by Chris Turner. Pages 119–136 in *Max Weber, Rationality and Modernity*. Edited by Scott Lash and Sam Whimster. London: Allen and Unwin, 1987.

———. 1990 [1980]. *The Logic of Practice*. Translated by Richard Nice. Stanford: Stanford University Press.

———. 1991. "Genesis and Structure of the Religious Field." Translated by Jenny B. Burnside, Craig Calhoun, and Leah Florence. *Comparative Social Research* 13: 1–44.

Brockington, John L. 1981. *The Sacred Thread: Hinduism in Its Continuity and Diversity*. Edinburgh: Edinburgh University Press.

Derrida, Jacques. 1992 [1991]. *Given Time: I. Counterfeit Money*. Translated by Peggy Kamuf. Chicago: University of Chicago Press.

Engler, Steven. 2003. "Modern Times: Religion, Consecration, and the State in Bourdieu." *Cultural Studies* 17.3&4: 445–467.

———. 2005. "Discourse." In volume IV of *The Brill Dictionary of Religion*. Edited by Kocku von Stuckrad. Leiden: Brill.

Fitzgerald, Timothy. 1990. "Hinduism and the 'World Religion' Fallacy." *Religion* 20: 101–118.

———. 2000. *The Ideology of Religious Studies*. Oxford: Oxford University Press.

Studies in constructing the category of Hinduism see Fitzgerald 1990 and 2000. See also Hawley and Weiss, infra.

Friedman, Jonathan. 1992. "The Past in the Future: History and the Politics of Identity." *American Anthropologist* 94.4: 837–859.

Glassie, Henry. 1995. "Tradition." *Journal of American Folklore* 108: 395–412.

Godelier, Maurice. 1999 [1996]. *The Enigma of the Gift*. Translated by Nora Scott. Chicago: University of Chicago Press.

Gouldner, Alvin W. 1973a. "The Norm of Reciprocity." Pages 226–259 in *For Sociology: Renewal and Critique in Sociology Today*. New York: Basic Books.

———. 1973b. "The Importance of Something for Nothing." Pages 260–290 in *For Sociology: Renewal and Critique in Sociology Today*. New York: Basic Books.

Griffin, Emory M. 2000. *A First Look at Communication Theory*. 5th edition. New York: McGraw-Hill.

Henten, Jan Willem van, and Anton Houtepen (eds.). 2001. *Religious Identity and the Invention of Tradition*. Assen: Royal Van Gorcum.

Hobsbawm, Eric, and Terence Ranger (eds.). 1983. *The Invention of Tradition*. Cambridge: Cambridge University Press.

Keesing, Roger M. 1989. "Creating the Past: Custom and Identity in the Contemporary Pacific." *Contemporary Pacific* 1: 19–42.

King, Richard. 1999. *Orientalism and Religion*. London and New York: Routledge.

Linnekin, Jocelyn. 1992. "On the Theory and Politics of Cultural Construction in the Pacific." *Oceania* 62: 249–263.

Marriott, McKim (ed.). 1955. *Village India: Studies in the Little Community*. Chicago: University of Chicago Press.

Marris, Paul, and Sue Thornham. 2000. *Media Studies: A Reader*. 2nd edition. New York: New York University Press.

Malinowski, Bronislaw. 1961 [1922]. *Argonauts of the Western Pacific*. New York: E. P. Dutton.

———. 1992. *Magic, Science and Religion*. New York: Doubleday.

Mauss, Marcel. 1990 [1925]. *The Gift: The Form and Reason for Exchange in Archaic Societies*." Translated by W.D. Halls. London: Routledge.

McCutcheon, Russell. 1997. *Manufacturing Religion: The Discourse of Sui Generis Religion and the Politics of Nostalgia*. Oxford and New York: Oxford University Press.

Nelson, Benjamin. 1969. *The Idea of Usury: From Tribal Brotherhood to Universal Otherhood*. 2nd edition. Chicago: University of Chicago Press.

Parry, Jonathan. 1986. "*The Gift*, The Indian Gift and The 'Indian Gift.'" *Man* 21.3: 453–473.

———, and Maurice Bloch. 1989. "Introduction: Money and the Morality of Exchange." Pages 1–32 in *Money and the Morality of Exchange*. Edited by Jonathan Parry and Maurice Bloch. Cambridge: Cambridge University Press.

Polanyi, Karl. 1957 [1944]. *The Great Transformation: The Political and Economic Origins of Our Time*. Boston: Beacon Press.

Redfield, Robert. 1956. *Peasant Society and Culture*. Chicago: University of Chicago Press.

Sahlins, Marshall. 1972 [1965]. "On the Sociology of Primitive Exchange." Pages 185–230 in *Stone Age Economics*. Chicago: Aldine-Atherton.

———. 1999. "Two or Three Things That I Know about Culture." *Journal of the Royal Anthropological Institute* 5: 399–421.

Schumaker, Millard. 1992. *Sharing Without Reckoning: Imperfect Right and the Norms of Reciprocity*. Waterloo, Ont.: Editions SR.

Singer, Milton. 1972. *When a Great Tradition Modernizes*. New York: Praeger.

Sontheimer, Günther, and Hermann Kulke (eds.). 1989. *Hinduism Reconsidered*. New Delhi: Manohar.

Spencer, Herbert. 1900. *The Principles of Sociology*. 3 vols. Vol. 3. New York: D. Appleton and Co.

Strathern, Marilyn. 1988. *The Gender of the Gift: Problems with Women and Problems with Society in Melanesia*. Berkeley: University of California Press.

Taylor, Charles. 1993. "To Follow a Rule..." Pages 45–60 in *Bourdieu: Critical Perspectives*. Edited by Craig Calhoun, Edward LiPuma and Moishe Postone. Cambridge: Polity Press.

Weber, Max. 1978. *Economy and Society*. Edited by Guenther Roth and Claus Wittich. Berkeley: University of California Press [1968].

List of Participants

Editors

STEVEN ENGLER is an Instructor in the Humanities Department at Mount Royal College, Calgary, Canada and a Visiting Professor (2005–2006) in the Programa de Estudos Pós-Graduados em Ciências da Religião, Pontifícia Universidade Católica de São Paulo, Brazil (supported by the Fundação de Ampara à Pesquisa do Estado de São Paulo [FAPESP]). • Recent publications: "Constructionism vs. What?" *Religion* 34.4 (2004): 291–313; "Teoria da Religião Norte-americana: Alguns Debates Recentes," *Rever* 4/4 (2004): 27–42; and "'Science' vs. 'Religion' in Classical Ayurveda," *Numen* 50/4 (2003): 416–463.

GREGORY PRICE GRIEVE is an assistant professor in the Religious Studies Department of the University of North Carolina, Greensboro, U.S.A., where he is a specialist in South Asian and Himalayan religions. His work draws upon contemporary literary theory, cultural criticism as well as postcolonial and postmodern methods for the study of religion. • He has recently published articles in *Numen, Culture, Theory and Critique* as well as *Studies in Nepalese History and Society*. He is co-editor of the recently launched web-journal, *Megatherium.net* that carves out an emergent and transformative social space for the intersection between politics, art and critical theory.

Contributors

JASON A. CARBINE is visiting assistant professor (2005–2006) in the Department of Religion at Amherst College, Amherst, Mass., U.S.A., teaching various courses on Buddhism. • His publications include *The Life of Buddhism*, co-edited with Frank Reynolds (Berkeley and London: University of California Press, 2000), "Yaktovil: The Role of the Buddha and Dhamma," in *Life of Buddhism*; "Burmese, Buddhist Literature in," in *Encyclopedia of Buddhism*, editor-in-chief Robert Buswell (New York: Macmillan, 2003); "Sangha," in *Encyclopedia of Monasticism*, edited by William Johnston (Chicago: Fitzroy Dearborn Publishers, 2000). At present, he is preparing a book manuscript based on his Ph.D. dissertation. He is also working on a translation project under agreement with the Pali Text Society.

FREDERICK (RICK) COLBY is an Assistant Professor of Comparative Religion at Miami University in Oxford, Ohio, U.S.A. • His dissertation (Duke University, 2002) traced the construction of a popular strand of an Islamic ascension narrative and is being revised for publication. Dr. Colby recently completed an edition and translation of a compilation of sayings about Muhammad's ascension assembled by the early Sufi mystic al-Sulami (Fons Vitae, expected 2006).

MICHEL DESPLAND is professor in the Department of Religion at Concordia University, Montréal, Canada. • Recent publications: "The Indians of the Saint Lawrence Valley and Their Religion: An Essay on Four Centuries of Scholarship in French," *Studies in Religion/Sciences religieuses* 32.4 (2003): 461–484; "Two Ways of Articulating Outsider's Knowledge of Polynesian Culture and Religion: Melville's Typee and Mardi," *Method and Theory in the Study of Religion* 16 (2004): 105–121; and *Comparatisme et christianisme* (Paris: L'Harmattan, 2003).

MICHAEL HAWLEY is an instructor in Indian religions at Mount Royal College, Calgary, Canada. • He is the author of "The Making of a Mahatma: Radhakrishnan's Critique of Gandhi," *Studies in Religion/Sciences religieuses* 32 (2003): 135–148.

TITUS HJELM is a post-doctoral researcher in sociology of religion, especially the study of new and alternative religions, at the Department of Comparative Religion, University of Helsinki, Finland. • Recent publications include a book on the construction of Satanism in the Finnish media and an edited book on Wicca (both in Finnish). He has written articles on new religious movements and religion in Finland for journals, anthologies and encyclopedias, including *Journal of Contemporary Religion, Religious Innovation in a Global Age* (ed. George Lundskow), *The Brill Dictionary of Religion* (ed. Kocku von Stuckrad), and *Worldmark Encyclopedia of Religious Practices* (ed. Thomas Riggs).

AARON W. HUGHES is an assistant professor of Religious Studies and Jewish Studies at the University of Calgary, Canada. • Recent publications: *Texture of the Divine: Imagination in Medieval Islamic and Jewish Thought* (Indiana: Indiana University Press, 2004); and *Jewish Philosophy A–Z* (Edinburgh: Edinburgh University Press, 2005).

GREG JOHNSON is Assistant Professor in the Department of Religious Studies, University of Colorado at Boulder, U.S.A. • His recent publications include "Narrative Remains: Articulating Indian Identities in the Repatriation Context," *Comparative Studies in Society and History* 47.3 (2005): 480–506, and "Facing Down the Representation of an Impossibility: Indigenous Responses to a 'Universal' Problem in the Repatriation Context," *Culture and Religion* 6.1 (2005): 57–78.

FÉLIX ULOMBE KAPUTO is a professor at the University of Lubumbashi, Democratic Republic of Congo. • Recent publications: "Terror and Terrorism:

From Religious to Social Life," *CLV* 12 (2002); "Savannah Kingdoms and the Daily Oral Perpetuation in D.R. Congo," *Likundoli, série A: Enquête d'Histoire Congolaise*, Número special (2003): 90–108; "Globalisation: Gender, Religion, Poverty or Failure of Women's NGOs in Lumbashi," *Recherches Linguistiques et Littéraires* 9 (2004): 60–78.

DAVID W. MACHACEK is associate director of Humanity in Action, a New York based not-for-profit organization dedicated to engaging student leaders in the study and work of human rights. He teaches in the graduate program in public policy and law at Trinity College in Hartford, Conn., U.S.A. and serves on the Connecticut State Commission on National and Community Service. • Recent publications: *Sexuality and the World's Religions* (edited with Melissa M. Wilcox; Santa Barbara: ABC-CLIO, 2003); *Religion on Trial: How Supreme Court Trends Threaten the Freedom of Conscience in America* (with Phillip E. Hammond and Eric Michael Mazur; Walnut Creek, Calif.: AltaMira, 2004); "The Problem of Pluralism," *Sociology of Religion* (2003): 145–162; and (with Adrienne Fulco) "The Courts and Public Discourse: The Case of Gay Marriage," *Journal of Church and State* 46 (2004): 767–785.

SUSANNA MORRILL is an Assistant Professor in the Department of Religious Studies at Lewis & Clark College in Portland, Oregon, U.S.A. • Her dissertation, "White Roses on the Floor of Heaven: Nature and Flower Imagery in Latter-day Saint Women's Literature, 1880–1920," is being published by Routledge.

MICHIAKI OKUYAMA is Associate Professor at Nanzan University and Permanent Research Fellow at the Nanzan Institute for Religion and Culture, Nagoya, Japan. • His doctoral dissertation, published in Japanese as *Comparison, History, and Interpretation in Eliade's Study of Religion* (Tokyo, 2000), earned the 9th Nakamura Hajime Award in 2001. Other works include "Approaches East and West to the History of Religions," *Japanese Journal of Religious Studies* (Spring 2000); "Spiritual Quests in Contemporary Japanese Writers Before and After the Aum Affair: Ōe Kenzaburō and Murakami Haruki Around 1995," *Bulletin of the Nanzan Institute for Religion and Culture* 25 (2001); and "Religious Nationalism in the Modernization Process: State Shinto and Nichirenism in Meiji Japan," *Comparative Civilizations Review* 48 (spring 2003).

LEE D. RAINEY is an Associate Professor at Memorial University of Newfoundland, Canada, where she teaches Chinese philosophy, Chinese religious traditions, Chinese language, Buddhism, and Japanese studies. • She has most recently written a chapter, "Women in the Chinese Traditions," in Leona M. Anderson and Pamela Dickey Young (eds.), *Women and Religious Traditions* (New York: Oxford University Press, 2004). She is working in two areas of Confucianism: pre-Han and Han Confucian theories of music, and logical problems in the Han dynasty yin-yang theories.

IRA ROBINSON is professor of Judaic Studies in the Department of Religion, Concordia University, Montréal, Canada. • His last book, co-edited with Michael Brown and Daniel Elazar is *Not Written in Stone: Jews, Constitutions and Constitutionalism in Canada* (Ottawa: University of Ottawa Press). His next book, *Rabbis and Their Community: Studies in the Immigrant Orthodox Rabbinate of Montreal, 1896–1930* has been accepted for publication by University of Calgary Press.

FRANK USARSKI is, since 1998, Professor at the Catholic University of São Paulo, Brazil. He lectured between 1988 and 1992 on comparative religion at the German universities of Hannover, Oldenburg and Bremen. In 1992 he joined the Department of Philosophy at the College of Education, University of Erfurt, were he trained teachers of "ethics," a subject taught at public schools as an alternative to confessional religious classes. In the same period he lectured comparative religion at the Universities of Chemnitz and Leipzig.

KOCKU VON STUCKRAD is Assistant Professor of Religious Studies at the University of Amsterdam, Netherlands, subdepartment "History of Hermetic Philosophy and Related Currents." • He has published widely on methodological and historical aspects of European history of religion from antiquity to the present, with particular focus on esotericism, astrology, and philosophy of nature. His publications include a *History of Western Astrology: From Earliest Times to the Present* (London: Equinox, 2006), *Western Esotericism: A Brief History of Secret Knowledge* (London: Equinox, 2005), and *Schamanismus und Esoterik: Kultur- und wissenschaftsgeschichtliche Betrachtungen* (Leuven: Peeters, 2003).

EARLE H. WAUGH is Professor Emeritus of Religious Studies and Director of the M.V. Dimic Research Institute at the University of Alberta, Edmonton, Canada. • Recent publications: *Memory, Music, Religion: Morocco's Mystical Chanters* (Columbia, S.C.: University of South Carolina Press, 2005); *The Shaping of an American Islamic Discourse: A Memorial to Fazlur* Rahman (ed. with Frederick M. Denny; Atlanta: Scholar's Press, 1998); *Alberta Elder's Cree Dictionary* (ed. with Nancy LeClaire and George Cardinal; Alberta: University of Alberta Press, 1998); as well as a number of articles.

RICHARD WEISS is a lecturer of South Asian Religions at Victoria University in Wellington, New Zealand. His research to date has been on traditional medicine in South India. • Recent publications include "Divorcing Ayurveda: Siddha Medicine and the Quest for Uniqueness," in *Pluralism and Paradigms in Modern and Global Ayurveda*, edited by Frederick Smith and Dagmar Benner (State University of New York Press, forthcoming); and "The Social Power of Miracles," in *What is Religion For? Proceedings of the International Association for the History of Religions 2002 Conference*, edited by Joseph Bulbulia and Paul Morris (Wellington: Victoria University Press, 2004).

Index of Names

Index of Topics